In Praise of *The Art of Agile Practice*

"*The Art of Agile Practice* gives you choices rather than a prescription: a view of the ecosystem of agile processes and practices from which you can create your own agile approach … Composite Agile Method and Strategy (CAMS) synergizes three important agile concepts: Agility in projects; the balance of Agile principles and practices with the disciplines of a formal process; and incorporation of Agile values in the entire organization."

"Whether you are a business analyst, developer, project manager, executive, or playing any other role within your organization, I am sure you will enjoy reading this book and find it relevant to your work."

—Steve Blais (PMP, Solutions Architect, Sarasota, Florida), from the Foreword

"As head of a team of business process management consultants, I see this book of immense value in synergizing end-to-end processes that bring together a sensible combination of Agility with formal planning in projects."

—Murray Heke (New Zealand)

"Combining Agility with planning is the best way to proceed forward in the world of methods. This book outlines precisely that—a carefully thought practice of Agile."

—Brendan Trewartha (Australia)

"Adopting Agile at an organisational and individual project level has been picking up pace over the last decade. This book makes a significant contribution to the discussion on successfully adopting Agile principles in project delivery and business change."

—Channa Achilingam (Australia)

"As a consultant I find the material in this book directly applicable in practice. A must have on the practitioner's desk."

—Louis Taborda (Australia)

"Time to market with quality products that deliver outcomes is critical to our business. With a combination of development in-house complimented with outsourced resources, a CAMS based approach to an agile business with the more formal business management alongside faster product development is a key part of our success."

—Keith Sherringham (director of Valued Communities)

"I have been familiar with Dr. Unhelkar's thinking over the last few years, and find his ideas most relevant to any company interested in developing Agility as I define it: "a management approach that facilitates the rapid creation of business value by embracing change and learning from it". Taking advantage of value-adding elements of both Agile practices and traditional methods, Dr. Unhelkar proposes a superior model that transcends the software development and project boundaries to produce substantial, positive impact on the overall functioning of the organization."

—Adriana Beal (Sr. IT Business Consultant, Austin, Texas)

"This work elevates Agile as a value system across an organization—way beyond the practice of agile in software development projects. This is a business book as much as a software process related work."

—Norbert Raymond (Australia)

"We have run successful training courses in Agile project management based on the material in this book. This book is an ideal accompaniment to a 3 to 5 day Agile training course."

—Thomas Charles (Kuala Lumpur, Malaysia)

"At last a book that recognises that Agile is as much a mindset as it is an approach to developing software. For decades, organisations have grappled with the need for agility to remain competitive in global markets, only to be frustrated by long development cycles for vital IT innovation, and too often, disappointing outcomes. Agile approaches to software development were proposed to improve these outcomes. But interconnected fields such as business analysis and project management have for too long looked to standardised, command-and-control approaches and practices, derived from engineering perspectives of the world. In this book, Dr. Unhelkar, through his Composite Agile Method and Strategy (CAMS), proposes a composite method, and demonstrates how business analysis and project management can benefit from adopting elements of agile thinking. Dr Unhelkar makes a convincing argument as to why business analysis is required as an integral part of Agile projects."

—Judy McKay (Head, Information Systems)

"Dr. Unhelkar's global thought-leadership is amply visible in this book. CAMS is the way to capitalize on the value of Agile without losing the benefits of planning. Excellent work and worth having on every Agile (and Planned) desk."

—Haydn Thomas (Australia, USA)

"This books provides invaluable support to project coaching – especially in the Agile context."

—Karen Sleeman (Australia)

"The concepts of Composite Agile Method and Strategy (CAMS) have been in the making for over past five years. I have followed the progress of this research and enjoyed applying it in practice."

—Dinesh Arunatileka (Colombo, Sri Lanka)

"Dr. Unhelkar's latest book is an excellent blend of theory and practice. He brings together the formality of planned SDLC with Agile practices, and combines Agile in projects with Agile as an organizational value."

—Houman Younessi (RPI, Hartford, Connecticut)

"CAMS is a very practical viewpoint on how to use Agile. On its own, Agile may only remain at software development level. This book shows the path to its application across an entire organization."

—Karan Karandikar (Boston, Massachusetts)

"This book is written in an easy to read, lucid style. It is also organized neatly in chapters with key points and discussion questions. This book makes it easier for a higher degree student to learn the concepts of Agile quickly—and then start applying them in practice. An excellent option as a text book for Agile related courses."

—Vipul Kalamkar (MSU, India)

"The fundamentals of CAMS are based on more than three years of solid research combined with practice. CAMS in application software development and business analysis brings the benefit of Agile practices and techniques that improve process quality and increases the opportunities to deliver a project in time, within budget, and produce a high quality products. CAMS as demonstrated in this book, enables projects to capitalize on the advantages of Agile together with the practicality of varied project types. The value of creating and configuring an instance of CAMS and applying it in practice through the project development life cycle is the key message of this book."

—Mohammed Al-Maharmeh (Sydney, Australia)

"This book examines Agile concepts, which have proven so vital to the ability of software teams to create products that delight the customer, and extends them throughout the business. Dr. Unhelkar delves into the need to tailor the Agile approach to a group's unique circumstances and requirements—resulting in what he calls CAMS—Composite Agile Method & Strategy. The result is a book that will inform and inspire both teams and leaders throughout the organization."

—Karen Fine Coburn (Cutter Consortium)

"The research underpinning this work makes it all the more worthwhile in practice. Employing action research methods to investigate how Agile is used in organizations has resulted in this very practical material."

—Yi-Chen Lan (Sydney, Australia)

"Process for the sake of process takes away productivity and does not achieve anything. This is true of Agile processes as much as planned ones. Every step of the process should be justified from the value added by the process taking into account the friction added and facilitation value of the process."

"Bhuvan Unhelkar makes the practitioner think of methods to achieve the right balance and keep the delivery as the ultimate focus. If the project cannot survive the current or next phase it does not matter if while the methodology is scientifically correct or not. CAMS allows the practitioner to focus on the current phase of the project keeping an eye on the trophy (i.e., the project deliverable)."

"Combining Agile methods and planned process in CAMS is a unique contribution made by this book. The book uniquely extends the CAMS concept beyond software development and project management to business strategy and development. A must read for practitioners of Agile and business strategy."

—Moti Bhatia (New Jersey)

"Dr. Unhelkar presented to our members on the values of Agile and business analysis. His views on the importance of practicing Agility together with formal business analysis, as expressed in this book, were extremely well received."

—Clinton Towers (Chair of IT SIG,
The Institute of Chartered Accountants Australia)

"Agile can be applied at individual, project and organizational level. This book brings together the application of agile at these three levels together. A must have for practicing Agile coaches and mentors."

—Haydar Jawad (United Kingdom)

The Art of Agile Practice

A Composite Approach for Projects and Organizations

Advanced and Emerging Communications Technologies Series

Series Editor-in-Chief: Saba Zamir

ADSL: Standards, Implementation, and Architecture, Charles K. Summers

After the Y2K Fireworks: Business and Technology Strategies, Bhuvan Unhelkar

The Art of Agile Practice: A Composite Approach for Projects and Organizations, Bhuvan Unhelkar

Electronic Bill Presentment and Payment, Kornel Terplan

Fiber Optics Illustrated Dictionary, Julie K. Petersen

Green IT Strategies and Applications : Using Environmental Intelligence, Bhuvan Unhelkar

Handbook of Emerging Communications Technologies: The Next Decade, Rafael Osso

Intranet Performance Management, Kornel Terplan

Maximizing Benefits from IT Project Management: From Requirements to Value Delivery, José López Soriano

Mobile Enterprise Transition and Management, Bhuvan Unhelkar

Multi-Domain Communication Management Systems, Alex Galis

Protocols for Secure Electronic Commerce, Second Edition, Mostafa Hashem Sherif

The Telecommunications Illustrated Dictionary, Second Edition, Julie K. Petersen

Web-Based Systems and Network Management, Kornel Terplan

The Art of Agile Practice

A Composite Approach for Projects and Organizations

Bhuvan Unhelkar

CRC Press
Taylor & Francis Group
Boca Raton London New York

CRC Press is an imprint of the
Taylor & Francis Group, an **informa** business
AN AUERBACH BOOK

CRC Press
Taylor & Francis Group
6000 Broken Sound Parkway NW, Suite 300
Boca Raton, FL 33487-2742

International Standard Book Number: 978-1-4398-5118-0 (Hardback)

Library of Congress Cataloging-in-Publication Data

Unhelkar, Bhuvan.
The art of agile practice : a composite approach for projects and organizations / Bhuvan Unhelkar.
p. cm. -- (Advanced & emerging communications technologies)
Includes bibliographical references and index.
ISBN 978-1-4398-5118-0
1. Information technology--Management. 2. Agile software development. 3. Information technology projects--Management. I. Title.

T58.64.U54 2013
658.4'038011--dc23 2012021065

Visit the Taylor & Francis Web site at
http://www.taylorandfrancis.com

and the CRC Press Web site at
http://www.crcpress.com

Shalini

Contents

Foreword .... **xxiii**
Preface .... **xxv**
Author .... **xxxi**
Acknowledgments .... **xxxiii**
Agile Terms and Acronyms .... **xxxv**

PART I CONTEMPORARY AGILE AND ITS CHALLENGES IN PRACTICE

1 Introducing Agile in Practice **3**
Objectives 3
Introduction 3
Agile in Practice—A Business Issue 7
Budget and Agility 8
Time and Agility 9
Requirements and Agility 10
Quality and Agility 11
Understanding Enterprise Agility 11
Strategy, Method, and Practice of Agile 13
Conversational Model for Software Development 15
Agility—Art, Craft, and Engineering 16
Correlating Agility to Planned Processes 17
Agile Coverage in Organizations 19
Agile Organizational Methods Spaces 20
Business Methods Space 21
Planned Methods Space 21
Pure Agile (Solution) Methods Space 22
Governance Methods Space 22
Agile Manifesto, Principles, and Practices 23
Agile Methods 24
Composite Agile—Research Project 25
Conclusions 27
Agile in Practice: Road Map 1 27

Discussion Questions........ 28
References........ 28

2 **Landscape of Agile and Planned Methods........ 31**
Objectives........ 31
Introduction........ 31
Defining Agile........ 32
What Comprises Agile?........ 34
Agile Manifesto........ 35
Agile Values........ 35
Agile Principles........ 36
Agile Methods Landscape........ 40
Extreme Programming (XP)........ 44
Scrum........ 47
Roles........ 48
Artifacts........ 49
Scrum Meetings........ 49
Scrum Flow........ 49
Agile Unified Process (AUP)........ 49
Crystal........ 50
Lean........ 51
Kaizen........ 53
Adaptive Software Development/Agile Project Management........ 54
Feature-Driven Development (FDD)........ 55
Test-Driven Design (TDD)........ 55
Planned Process Life Cycles and Agile........ 56
The Waterfall-Based SDLC........ 56
The Spiral-Based SDLC........ 57
The Fountain-Based SDLC........ 58
The IIP—Iterative, Incremental, Parallel Development Process........ 58
A Practical Agile Manifesto........ 59
Individuals and Interactions Together with Processes and Tools........ 59
Working Software Together with Comprehensive Documentation........ 61
Customer Collaboration Together with Contract Negotiation........ 61
Responding to Change Together with Following a Plan........ 61
Agile Practices........ 62
Analytical Practices........ 63
Requirements Practices........ 63
Development Practices........ 64
Design Practices........ 65
Project Management Practices........ 65
Quality Assurance Practices........ 65
Operational Practices........ 66
Testing Practices........ 67
Conclusions........ 67
Agile in Practice: Road Map 2........ 67
Discussion Questions........ 68

References.. 68
Further Reading.. 69

3 **Agile Challenges in Practice..71**
Objectives.. 71
Introduction... 71
Agile Project Challenges...74
Agile Organizational Challenges in Practice... 78
Project-Specific Agile Challenges.. 79
Matrix of Agile Challenges... 79
Project Type and Agile Challenges.. 79
Project Size and Agile Challenges...81
Organizational Domain and Agile Challenges... 82
Business Type and Agile Challenges.. 83
Scalability and Agile... 84
Project Management and Agile... 84
People Management and Agile.. 86
Business Analysis and Agile.. 87
Testing and Agile.. 88
Metrics and Measurements in Agile.. 89
Enterprise Architecture and Agile... 89
Maintenance and Agile... 90
Documentation and Agile... 90
Legal and Compliance Issues and Agile..91
Expanding Agile Challenges at the Organizational Level..91
Strategic versus Tactical Agile... 93
Conclusions... 95
Agile in Practice: Road Map 3.. 95
Discussion Questions.. 95
References.. 96

PART II COMPOSITE AGILE METHOD AND STRATEGY AND ITS APPLICATION IN PRACTICE

4 **Composite Agile Method and Strategy (CAMS)...99**
Objectives.. 99
Introduction... 100
Composite Agile: Balance and Coverage... 100
Taxonomy of Organizational Methods and Their Agile Touch Points...................104
Software Agile (Development)..109
Business Analysis...109
Testing..109
Modeling and Architecture..110
Software Processes and Agile..112
Rational Unified Process (RUP)..112
Process Mentor..113
Object-Oriented Process, Environment, and Notation (OPEN)....................113

IT Governance and Agile ... 113
Control Objectives for Information and Related Technology (CoBIT) ... 114
Information Technology Infrastructure Library (ITIL) ... 114
Project Management and Agile ... 114
Business Management and Agile ... 115
Six Sigma ... 115
Kaizen ... 115
Kanban ... 116
Composite Agile Method and Strategy (CAMS) ... 116
Life Cycles as Basis for Composite ... 121
CAMS Architecture ... 123
Initial Iteration ... 126
Major Iteration ... 127
Final Iteration ... 127
The CAMS Repository of Agile Practices ... 128
CAMS in Practice: Configuration ... 131
Practicing CAMS—Role-Based Execution ... 135
Advantages and Limitations of CAMS ... 135
Advantages of Composite Agile ... 135
Limitations of Composite Agile ... 136
Conclusions ... 136
Agile in Practice: Road Map 4 ... 137
Discussion Questions ... 137
References ... 137

5 Composite Agile and IT: Enablement, Development, and Maintenance ... 139
Objectives ... 139
Introduction ... 140
Emergent Information Technologies: Agile Enablers ... 141
Cloud Computing ... 142
Mobile Technologies ... 142
Business Intelligence ... 143
Web Services and SOA ... 143
Applications Integration ... 144
Social Media ... 144
IT Areas of Work and Agile ... 144
Development and Agility ... 145
Configuration and Agility ... 145
Integration and Agility ... 146
Conversion and Agility ... 146
Deployment, Training, and Agility ... 146
Maintenance and Agility ... 147
Architecture, Design, and Quality ... 147
Requirements (Functional, Nonfunctional, and Interface) ... 148
Agile Practices and CAMS Process Maps ... 148
Enterprise Architecture Process Map ... 148
Roles in Enterprise Architecture ... 150

Deliverables 150
Activities and Tasks in Enterprise Architecture 152
System Architecture Process Map 152
Roles in System Architecture 152
Deliverables 154
Activities and Tasks in System Architecture 154
Nonfunctional (Operational) Requirements and Architecture (Enterprise and System) 159
System Design Process Map 164
Roles in System Design 164
Deliverables 166
Activities and Tasks in System Design 166
Implementation Process Map 166
Roles in Implementation 166
Deliverables 168
Activities and Tasks in Implementation 170
Agile Elements in Implementation 170
Deployment Process Map 176
Roles in Deployment 178
Deliverables 178
Activities and Tasks in Deployment 178
Conclusions 178
Agile in Practice: Road Map 5 180
Discussion Questions 180
References 181

6 Collaborative-Agile Business Management 183
Objectives 183
Introduction 184
Agile Business Management 184
Composite Agile Method and Strategy (CAMS) 185
Business Agility and CAMS 185
Six Sigma in Composite Agile 188
Kaizen in Composite Agile 188
Kanban in Composite Agile 189
Agility in Learning Organizations 191
Collaboration and Agility 192
Collaborative Business Processes and Agility 192
Collaborative Cluster Formation 193
Business Size and Collaboration 194
Characteristics of Collaborative-Agile Business 194
Customer Experience through Collaboration 196
Knowledge Management Collaborations and Agility 196
Evolution in Knowledge Management 197
Knowledge Synchronization for Agility 199
Documentation and Knowledge Management 201
Enterprise Risk Management (ERM) with Collaborative Agile 201

Market Expansion through Collaboration ... 202
Global Trade and Agility ... 202
Organizational Leanness and Restructuring ... 203
Outsourcing and Offshoring with Collaborative Agile ... 203
Legal Compliance and Tax Management with Collaborative Agile ... 204
Carbon Consciousness and Lean-Agile ... 204
Evolving Complexities in Collaborative-Agile Business ... 204
Types of Collaboration ... 205
Physical Collaboration ... 205
Electronic Collaboration ... 205
Mobile Collaboration ... 206
Reaching Collaborative Intelligence in Agile Business ... 206
Collaborative Data and Agility ... 206
Collaborative Information and Agility ... 206
Collaborative Process and Agility ... 207
Collaborative Knowledge and Agility ... 208
Collaborative Intelligence (CI) and Agility ... 208
Reaching Collaborative Business Process ... 208
Broadcasting Business Processes ... 208
Informative Business Processes ... 208
Transactive Business Processes ... 209
Operative Business Processes ... 209
Collaborative Business Processes ... 209
Business Evaluation Process Map ... 210
Roles in Business Evaluation ... 210
Deliverables ... 210
Activities and Tasks in Business Evaluation ... 212
SWOT Analysis ... 212
Strengths ... 212
Weaknesses ... 214
Opportunities ... 214
Threats ... 214
PESTLE Analysis ... 214
Cost–Benefit Analysis ... 215
Change Management in Agile Business ... 216
External Changes ... 217
Internal Changes ... 217
Risks and Challenges in Collaborative-Agile Business ... 218
Conclusions ... 218
Agile in Practice: Road Map 6 ... 219
Discussion Questions ... 220
References ... 220

7 Business Analysis and Composite Agile ... 223
Objectives ... 223
Introduction ... 223
What Is Business Analysis? ... 225

Business Analysis and Agility 228
Handling Agile Challenges in the Context of Business Analysis 228
Scalability 228
Outsourcing 228
Technology 228
Compliance 229
Business Rules 229
Change 229
BA and Agile Practices in CAMS 231
Business Analysis Frameworks and Agility 236
SFIA, IIBA (BABOK®), AIBA Frameworks 238
SFIA and Agile BA 238
BA-SFIA Levels 1–4 245
BA-SFIA Levels 4–6 246
BA-SFIA Levels 6–7 246
Comparing SFIA and IIBA with Agile 247
Business Process Management and Agility 248
Business Process Reengineering (BPR) 250
Processes: Individual, Organizational, and Collaborative 252
Customer-Driven Analysis and Agility 254
Requirements Modeling Process Map 255
Roles in Requirements Modeling 258
Deliverables 258
Activities and Tasks in Requirements Modeling 262
Conclusions 262
Agile in Practice: Road Map 7 266
Discussion Questions 266
References 267

8 CAMS Project Management and ICT Governance 269
Objectives 269
Introduction 270
Planning and Agility in CAMS 270
Declaration of Interdependence and Agile Project Management 273
Organizing Composite Agile Projects 275
Project Management Process Map 280
Roles in Project Management Process Map 280
Deliverables in the Project Management Process Map 282
Activities and Tasks in the Project Management Process Map 282
Leadership and People Management in Agile Projects 293
Soft Issues and Subjective Skills 294
Agile Team Formation 296
IT Governance and Business Agility 304
The IT Governance Frameworks 305
Control Objectives for Information and Related Technology (CoBIT) 306
Information Technology Infrastructure Library (ITIL) 306
Conclusions 307

Agile in Practice: Road Map 8 ... 309
Discussion Questions ... 310
References ... 311
Further Reading ... 312

9 Composite Agile: Quality, Testing, and Metrics ... 315
Objectives ... 315
Introduction ... 316
Quality Context: Management, Assurance, and Control ... 317
Quality Management Process Map ... 322
Roles in Quality Management ... 322
Deliverables ... 322
Activities and Tasks in Quality Planning ... 323
Quality Assurance Process Map ... 327
Roles in Quality Assurance ... 327
Deliverables ... 327
Activities and Tasks in Quality Assurance ... 329
Quality Techniques and Agile Practices ... 329
Quality Control Process Map ... 336
Roles in Quality Control ... 337
Deliverables ... 337
Activities and Tasks in Quality Control ... 337
Organizing Testing ... 337
Test Data ... 345
Analyzing Risks in Testing Risks: Analyzing ... 346
Composite Agile Metrics and Measurements ... 348
Challenges of Agile Projects Metrics ... 349
Fundamentals of CAMS Estimation ... 351
CAMS Metrics in Practice ... 353
Planning Metrics ... 354
Requirements Metrics ... 354
Development Metrics ... 356
Testing and Release Metrics ... 356
Role-Based CAMS Metrics ... 357
Applying Estimation and Metrics in CAMS ... 357
Conclusions ... 362
Agile in Practice: Road Map 9 ... 362
Discussion Questions ... 362
References ... 363
Further Reading ... 364

10 Agile Adoption in Organizations ... 365
Objectives ... 365
Introduction ... 366
Organizational Adoption of Agility and Business Transformation ... 366
Adopting of CAMS: Reasons and Value ... 369
CAMS Organizational Adoption—High-Level Road Map ... 370

Agile Business Transformation—Internal and External Factors....373
External Influencing Factors....374
Customer Relationship....374
Business Partners....374
Government Regulatory Factors....375
Sociocultural Environment....375
Internal Factors and Responses....375
Business Structure....375
Business Innovation....376
Business Compliance....376
Technology Management....376
People Management....377
Product Management....377
Organizational Focus Areas in Agile Business Transformation....378
Business Transformation Process and Organizational Focus Areas....378
Diagnose....379
Plan....379
Enact....380
Measure and Review....380
Work Areas for ABT....381
Business Model....381
Product and Service Portfolio....383
Customers and Partners....384
ICT Systems, Applications, and Databases....385
Operational/Organizational....386
Business Processes....387
Networks and Infrastructure....388
Regulatory....388
Varying Influence of ABT....389
CAMS and Center of Excellence....390
Configuring, Training, and Upskilling in Agile Business Transformation....393
Money....394
Technology....395
Process....396
People....396
CAMS and Process Maturity—The CMM Standards in an Agile Environment....398
Conclusions....401
Agile in Practice: Road Map 10....402
Discussion Questions....402
References....403

PART III CASE STUDIES IN CAMS

11 Case Study: Outsourced Project....407
Objectives....407
Introduction....407
Outline of the Case Study "MITS"—An Outsourced Project....408

Composite Agile Road Map for an Outsourced Project 409
Understanding the Project 409
Extent of Agility in Configuring CAMS 411
CAMS Process-Map-Based Activities in an Outsourced Project 415
Creating CAMS-Based Project Iterations 418
Use of CAMS Metrics in Outsourced Projects 419
Overcoming the Challenges of Outsourced Projects with CAMS 422
Uncertainty in the Scope of Work 422
Leadership and Direction 424
Payment Contracts Based on Delivery 425
Determining Correct Iterations and Releases to Deliver the Product 425
Service Level Agreements after Delivery 426
Formal Requirements Modeling 426
Iterative and Incremental Implementation of Solution Design 427
Quality Control and User Acceptance Testing 427
Ongoing Maintenance of the Solution 427
Conclusions and Lessons Learned 428
Discussion Questions 428
References 428

12 Case Study: Organizational CAMS in an Insurance Business 431
Objectives 431
Introduction 431
Hartford Insurance Company (HIC) Case Study Outline 432
Goals of Agile Business Transformation 434
Composite Agile Road Map 437
Diagnose (0–3 Months) 442
Plan (4–6 Months) 443
Enact (7–12/15 Months) 443
Review and Manage (15–18 Months) 443
Configuring Composite Agile 444
HIC and Collaborative-Agile Business 446
Balancing HIC's ABT Enactment 450
Conclusions and Lessons Learned 453
Discussion Questions 454
References 454

Appendix I: Agile Interview Summaries 455
Business Analysis and CAMS 457
Project Management and CAMS 458
Development with CAMS 459
Testing and CAMS 460
Architecture and CAMS 460
Metrics and Estimates in CAMS 461
References 461

Appendix II: Business-Analysis-Related Associations and Standards 463

Appendix III: Role-Based CAMS Metrics 467
Project Manager 467
CAMS Task: Planning—Requirement Prioritization 467
The Number of Packages (Subsystems/Components) in the System 467
The Number of Dependencies between Subsystems/Components/Packages in the System 468
Project Schedule and Rhythm 468
Total Budget and Investment 468
User Load (Peak and Off-Peak) 469
CAMS Activity: Monitoring Team Members 469
The Speed of Implementation of a User Story 469
Efficiency of Response to Changes 470
CAMS Activity: Risk Management—Collaborative 470
Metric: The Potential Impact of Risks 470
Average Risks per User Story 471
Business Analyst 471
CAMS Activity: Requirement—Collaborative 471
Total User Stories 471
User Story Dependencies 472
CAMS Activity: Change Management—Negotiable Requirement 472
Iteration Changes 472
Architect 473
CAMS Activity: Design—User Feedback 473
Tolerance to Change 473
Programmer 473
CAMS Activity: Coding/Implementation—Pair Programming 473
System Layers 474
Standards Compliance 474
The Number of Owners/Contributors 474
Tester 475
CAMS Activity: Testing—Continuous 475
Defects per Iteration 475
Performance Comparison with Previous Iterations 475

Appendix IV: Telecom User Stories 477

Index 485

Foreword

The Art of Agile Practice: A Composite Approach for Projects and Organizations brings a practical and pragmatic approach to the application of the benefits of Agile to software development *and* business. This book makes me reflect on the past four decades of IT and its strivings under two sets of values: One is based on *what* we produce and the other is on *how* we go about producing. These values are interdependent. A project that performs well by producing high quality, in time and within budget, *will* add value to an organization.

Unfortunately, over the years, the *how* aspect of development took significant precedence over *what* was being produced. Increasingly *heavier* processes with severe management controls resulted in minimal value to business. Time delays and budget overruns became common. Projects that delivered on time and within budget had defects that required years of repairs and adjustments. Projects that delivered the perfect product were delivered past their use by dates and resulted in a negative return on investment. There was a major erosion of faith in IT and its value to business.

In time, the experienced developers were joined by a new breed of software developers. These developers started coding in grammar school, hacking in high school, and sought careers in business software development instead of engineering or computer science. Understandably, these new programmers rebelled against the overemphasis on the "proper execution of projects" that did not increase the value to the organization. The experienced developers concurred.

The need for Agile evolved out of this chaos. The focus of Agile is on using the available technology to speed up the delivery of the product and employ the talents and skills of the development team to make it happen. Agile is a move away from the management-centric processes of command and control.

The Agile focus, however, appears to be ignoring the successes of IT using formal, planned project management and development processes. For example, many systems that we all accept as part of our everyday existence were developed following planned, structured approaches: airline reservation systems, banking demand deposit systems, most of the payroll systems, ATM machine systems, the Internet, and most point of sale systems, to mention a few. A sensible combination of the two was required—and *The Art of Agile Practice* delivers precisely that.

Agile value is not magical. Contrary to the claims of a few "anti-Agilists," Agile processes and practices also require significant discipline, organization, and rigor. The team does not produce working software without an internal project process to follow and the technology to support it. When there is only one month (or less) to produce something of value to the organization, the risks of mistakes and missteps are higher than ever. The business and development teams need the discipline to explore the requirements, examine alternatives, and a rigorous method for arriving at the solution. CAMS expands the Agile choices and embeds them within the framework of formal, planned processes. The importance of following a prescribed route to reduce risks and enhance traceability is duly recognized in this book.

The Art of Agile Practice starts with selecting the appropriate approach and practices to use. The selection is not done by a committee for all projects; the configuration and instantiation of CAMS is done with every new Agile project and can be modified with each iteration. This is as much an art as it is a science. How much overhead do we need? How much documentation? Who will be doing what? It all depends on the product we are producing and the ultimate value of that product. In other words, practitioners do not restrict work to a single method. *The Art of Agile Practice* gives you choices rather than a prescription: a view of the ecosystem of agile processes and practices from which you can create your own agile approach, one that fits with the specific, unique situation you are in, and one that changes as circumstances dictate. The key to the whole composite approach is the delivery of value to the organization.

Agile values and principles have applicability way beyond software development. Agile methods are not a replacement for existing methods. Instead, agility has a role to play together with the existing methods and frameworks in the organization. While agile software development can bring about positive change in the development of new products, its real value is in the transformation of an organization to an agile one. This theme has been appropriately discussed in this book under Composite Agile Method and Strategy.

CAMS synergizes three important Agile concepts: Agility in projects; the balance of Agile principles and practices with the disciplines of a formal process; and incorporation of Agile values in the entire organization. Starting with the configuration of the project based on the CAMS approach and following the process maps and appropriate practices, the organization can shift its focus from a single Agile approach to a combination of relevant activities, tasks, deliverables, roles, and practices that suit each corporate initiative.

Bhuvan rightfully does not provide a silver bullet in this book because there is none. Rather, he uses Agile together with proven business practices to provide a best of breed approach. With something for the pure Agilist, the business person looking for outcomes, and those involved in activities needing rigor, the book gives a balanced view of Agile in the practical world.

Whether you are a business analyst, developer, project manager, executive, or playing any other role within your organization, I am sure you will enjoy reading this book and find it relevant to your work.

Steve Blais, PMP

Solutions Architect
Sarasota, Florida

Preface

Who would not want to be *agile*? The elite athlete, the army general, the opera singer, the belly dancer, the professional golfer, the heavyweight boxer, the high seas sailor, the commercial pilot, the top-end banker, and even the federal politician—they all desperately strive for agility. Why? Very simple—agility facilitates rapid adaption to changes. Nature and business are replete with tales of survival, prosperity, and growth that are directly attributed to the enviable characteristic of nimbleness or simply agility. It is this agility that enables a springbok to outrun a lion or an ant to carry a load more than 20 times its size. Agility makes possible a small "startup" in southern California to pitch itself against the might of large, well-established brick-and-mortar organizations.

On the other hand, history also abounds with examples of utterly static, nonmovable, nonagile recordings and documentations that are invaluable in their own right. For these nonagile relics bring to us, today, the knowledge of bygone eras. Consider the temples of Khajuraho in central India that bring to us today the human knowledge and experiences from a thousand years ago through elaborate statues and wall carvings. Also, those roughly etched Aboriginal whale and kangaroo engravings recorded permanently on ironstone at Muogamarra Nature Reserve on the outskirts of Sydney, Australia, encapsulate knowledge from two to five millennia ago. Similar example of non-agility is depicted in the U.S. Plymouth Rock in Massachusetts that preserves the 1620 disembarkation of the English colonists, who later became known as the Pilgrims. All of this "data" records, encapsulates, and, later, conveys the initial observations, analyses, conclusions, and insights from aeons. These are the examples of what would be considered pretty "nonagile" in the context of contemporary or pure interpretation of the agility as you and I are used to.

This book, *The Art of Agile Practice,* discusses an all-encompassing agile approach to business that acknowledges and respects the relevance and impact of Agility in software development. Subsequently, this book quickly transcends software boundary and moves into holistic business Agility. As indicated by the subtitle, *A Composite Approach for Projects and Organizations*, this book responds to the dire need to consider "methods" holistically and to integrate them with business strategies that can be applied not only to projects but also across the entire organization. While methods still remain vital for organizational success, the era of singular methods (or methodologies) for specific purposes within the organization leading to "methods friction" has to be overhauled. A composite method, which is also integrated in the business strategy of the organization, is envisaged here.

Needless to say, the starting point for this line of thinking is heavily intertwined with the contemporary Agile software development methods such as Scrum and Extreme Programming (XP). Hence, these methods and the underlying Agile Manifesto, is the starting point of this discussion.

It is to be mentioned here that despite the popularity of these Agile methods as a *new* approach, it is worth noting that Agility in software development is not as new as it may appear to be. Agile approach encompasses the natural way to write code—conversational, visible, and responsive—that has been around since the inception of software development.

As an "old time" COBOL programmer, I wrote my first code in 1982 for a payroll application. This Tata organization I worked for in Pune, India, used to manufacture trucks and had a 14,000 strong payroll. As a beginner in the domain of software engineering, I vividly recollect sitting next to the user who dictated to me his requirements in a conversation or two. The code was cut directly from what the user had described, the output was shown to the user instantaneously, and further changes were made to the code on the spot. There was some documentation on the back of a used cigarette case (passive smoking was ages away from being recognized as harmful and yellow sticky tags were yet to be invented). Pretty Agile! It certainly worked then. And there is no reason why Agile as an approach to software development would not work now.

The foundation of this book is to make Agility the ultimate goal of any business and the desired outcome of software Agility. Practicing Agile methods on their own or limiting them to software development and maintenance is not enough to provide what the business is looking for. Therefore, there is a need to bring business and software agility together, and in fact, to merge business and software agility through the methodological aspect of an organization. This will eventually lead to an Agile organizational culture and provide immense value to business.

This book strives to treat Agility as a strategic approach to leading, managing, and operating business organizations in a holistic manner. The book starts with an overview of the Agile approach that is tilted toward the "art" form of development, thereafter followed by the current Agile landscape in the industry. A discussion of the challenges faced by practitioners of Agile methods in practice ensues. The Composite Agile Method and Strategy (CAMS) is then presented in detail to show how it handles the challenges of pure Agile practices in real organizations and projects. This discussion, in Chapter 4, is the core of this book wherein the composition (or amalgamation) of Agile and non-Agile approaches is discussed and demonstrated. The underlying research basis for CAMS is also alluded to in this discussion. Subsequent chapters in this book discuss and demonstrate the validity and applicability of CAMS in various organizational and project-based initiatives such as governance, business analysis, enterprise architecture, quality assurance, and testing. Chapter 10, the final informative chapter in this book, discusses the all-important approach to organizational adoption for CAMS. Such an organizational adoption model provides the road map for transforming existing methods and processes under the CAMS umbrella. Finally, there are a couple of case study chapters to demonstrate the CAMS approach in practice.

Readers

You would be interested in reading *The Art of Agile Practice* if you are playing one (or more) of the following roles:

1. Decision makers: Strategic decision makers in the industry would like to understand the popularity of Agile methods and, eventually would like to oversee the application of Agility as a strategic approach to business rather than only software. Approach to transforming to an Agile organization is a part of this discussion. The relevant chapters are Chapters 1, 4, 6, and 10.

2. Developers, designers, and architects: They are keen to understand how their Agile work relates to organizational agility. Process maps depicting enterprise architecture, system architecture, system design, implementation, and deployment will be of immense value to these readers. Chapters 2, 4, 5, and 9 will be extremely relevant to developers.
3. Project managers: They deal with both IT and non-IT projects. These managers will find the discussions in this book very relevant, particularly Chapters 1, 4, and 8 (containing process map for project management).
4. Quality managers, testers: Discussions in Chapter 9 (containing process map for quality management, quality assurance, and quality control) are specifically aimed at these readers. The outline of the quality management function, testing, and metrics within CAMS is highly relevant. Chapters 1, 4, and 9 are thus of immediate interest.
5. Trainers and teachers: This book is organized in such a way that it will be highly conducive to industrial training and to higher degree courses. The discussion points, action points, and case studies will be relevant in this regard. The discussion topics can be used for interactive discussions within a classroom environment.
6. Academics and researchers: This book is relevant for researchers and academicians who are keen to investigate methods further. This book is based on research conducted at both masters and doctoral levels. Further research activities can be based on the material herein.

Mapping to a Workshop

The manner in which this book is organized lends itself to a two–three day training course or workshop that can be delivered in public or as an in-house customized training. Alternatively, this book can be used over a 13-week education course for higher degree students that includes process discussions and consideration of Agile values at both software and business levels. The chapters are organized to correspond roughly to such lectures with an option to choose from the case study chapters.

The sessions and topics for the two-to-three-day workshop would be as follows:

Day	*Session*	*Presentation and Discussion Workshop Topic*	*Relevant Chapters*	*Comments*
1	8:30–10:00	What is Agile? Review of Agile methods; challenges in using Agile	1, 2, 3	Going beyond software and into the business realm. Brief study of XP, Scrum, Lean-Kaizen
	10:30–12:00	Composite Agile Method and Strategy (CAMS)	4	Fundamentals of balance; planned + Agile; taxonomy of processes (Six Sigma, Kaizen, ITIL, IIBA, Scrum, TOGAF, Prince2, CMM). An IIP life cycle for CAMS

continued

Day	*Session*	*Presentation and Discussion Workshop Topic*	*Relevant Chapters*	*Comments*
	1:30–3:00	Composite Agile in software development, maintenance, and design	5	Extending known Agile approaches to a composite approach; process-components for development and design
	3:30–5:00	A case study	11 (or 12)	Outsourced Mobile Applications Development (or Hartford Insurance Company)
2	8:30–10:00	Composite Agile in business management; business analysis	6, 7	Six Sigma, Kaizen, and their usage in Agile organizations; exploration of business needs through Agile practices
	10:30–12:00	Organizational adoption of composite Agile	10	Challenges in adopting composite Agility; adoption process; Centers of Excellence for Agility
	1:30–3:00	Project management, testing and metrics with composite Agile	8, 9	Extending Prince2 with Agility; ISTQB and Agility; metrics for estimations in composite Agile
	3:30–5:00	Second case study	11 (or 12) (any one)	Outsourced mobile development project (or Hartford Insurance Company)

Contents and Chapter Summaries

This book has 12 chapters. The book is divided into three parts. Part I is made up of the first three chapters that describe Agility and its challenges. Part II presents the Composite Agile Method and Strategy, and its application to development, business management, business analysis, project management, and quality. Part III comprises two supporting case studies in the practice of Agile. The chapter layout reflects ease of learning—consisting of Objectives, Introduction, body of chapter, Conclusions, Agile in Practice, Discussion Questions, and References—interspersed with sidebars and concluding with action points that provide step-by-step guidance on implementing the discussions. The book has a comprehensive index, a table of terms and acronyms, and appendices that are invaluable for practitioners. The following table provides a brief overview of each chapter.

Chapter	*Description*
Part I: Contemporary Agile and Its Challenges in Practice	
Chapter 1	Describes Agile as an all-encompassing business concept and value
Chapter 2	Describes the Agile landscape, Agile Manifesto, and Agile values. Outlines the popular Agile methods—and revisits the Agile Manifesto in practice
Chapter 3	Highlights the Agile challenges in practice
Part II: Composite Agile Method and Strategy and Its Application in Practice	
Chapter 4	Presents the core study of this book—Composite Agile Method and Strategy (CAMS)
Chapter 5	Shows how CAMS can be applicable to development, design, and architecture of software systems
Chapter 6	Discusses business management (e.g., Six Sigma, Kaizen) and composite Agile
Chapter 7	Presents business analysis (business needs exploration) and composite Agile
Chapter 8	Project management, IT governance, and composite Agile
Chapter 9	Quality management, testing, metrics, and composite Agile
Chapter 10	Organizational adoption of composite Agile
Part III: Case Studies in CAMS	
Chapter 11	Case study in applying CAMS to an outsourced/offshored project
Chapter 12	Case study in applying CAMS to an insurance product development project

The following appendices provide supporting information:

Appendix	*Description*
Appendix I	CAMS research project—Summaries of interviews on use of Agile in business
Appendix II	Business analysis related associations and standards
Appendix III	Role-based CAMS metrics
Appendix IV	User stories that reveal functional requirements of a telecom company

Language

All my publications use gender-neutral language as far as possible. However, in order to maintain the simplicity of reading, *she* and *he* are used interchangeably. Terms like *user* and *developers* represent roles and not people. We usually play more than one role at a given time—such as *consultant, academic,* and *analyst.* As a result, the semantics behind the theory and examples may change depending on the role you are playing, and this needs to be kept in mind as you read this book. "We" throughout the text, primarily refers to the reader and the author—you and me. Occasionally, *we* refers to the general business or the ICT community depending on the context.

Critiques

Critiques of this work are welcome. The author will be grateful to you for your comments, feedback, and criticisms, as they will surely add to the overall knowledge available on mobility and mobile transitions. Here is a big *thank you* to all readers and critics in advance.

Bhuvan Unhelkar

Author

Bhuvan Unhelkar (BE, MDBA, MSc, PhD; FACS) has spent close to three decades in the information and communication technologies (ICT) industry as a strategist as well as a hands-on professional. As the founder of *MethodScience.com*, he has demonstrated consulting and training expertise in business analysis, software engineering, Agile processes, mobile business, and green IT (environment) in banking, financial, insurance, government, and telecom verticals. He is an adjunct associate professor with the University of Western Sydney, Australia (where he had formed the Mobile Internet Research and Applications Group—MIRAG) and a visiting faculty at the University of Technology, Sydney, MS University, Baroda, India, and Rensselaer Polytechnic Institute (Hartford Graduate Campus), CT, USA. He has authored 17 books and several executive reports (Cutter, Boston, USA), supervised numerous PhD students, and has extensively presented and published papers and case studies. Dr. Unhelkar is a Fellow of the Australian Computer Society, life member of the Computer Society of India, president of the Rotary Club in St. Ives, Sydney (and a Paul Harris Fellow), a Discovery volunteer at NSW Parks and Wildlife, and a previous TiE mentor.

Dr. Unhelkar obtained the PhD degree in the area of "object orientation" from the University of Technology, Sydney, in 1997. Subsequently, he has designed and delivered course units such as *Global Information Systems, Object Oriented Analysis and Design, Business Process Reengineering,* and *IT Project Management* to the industry as well as across universities in Australia, China, and India.

Other CRC Press books by the same author:

- *Mobile Enterprise Transition and Management,* 2009
- *After the Y2K Fireworks,* 1999
- *Green IT Strategies & Applications,* 2011

Other notable publications in the area of Agile:

- Agile Business Analysis, *Cutter Executive Report*, April, 2012
- Agile Project Management, 3 day course (delivered globally)

Acknowledgments

Abbass Ghanbary
Adriana Beal
Akshai Aggrawal
Amit Lingarchani
Amit Pradhan
Amit Tiwary
B. Ramesh
Bharat Bhambaney
Bhargav Bhatt
Bharti Trivedi
Brendan Trewartha
Channa Achilingam
Christopher Payne
Dale Nott
Ekata Mehul
Houman Younessi
Javed Matin
Julian Day
Keith Sherringham
Louis Taborda
Mohammed Maharmeh
Moti Bhatia
Nawaz Sharif
Norbert Raymond
Prashant Risbud
S.D. Pradhan
Saba Zamir
San Murugesan
Sanjay Vij
Siddharth Bhargav
Simran Aujla
Steve Blais
Sumit Ahuja
Terry Versace
Thomas Charles
Toral Bhatt
Vipul Kalamkar
Warren Adkins
Yi-chen Lan
Yogesh Deshpande
Zahra Saeed

Specifically, students and friends at the University of Technology Sydney, University of Western Sydney, and the M.S. University of Baroda also merit my heartfelt gratitude for their valuable inputs, criticisms, and the work done on various research projects.

Finally, thanks to my family: Sonki and Keshav, Asha and extended family, Chinar and Girish, and Amit. This book is dedicated to my aunt, a lady par excellence who never gave up in life: she remained true to a young man who died within an year of her marriage, she educated herself and became the principal of a school, remained ferociously independent, and maintained her sharp brain until her last breath. She was the epitome of Agility and stability combined.

Note 1: Some people participated in various research projects supervised by me, notably Dr. Mohammed Maharmeh, Zahra Saeed, and Sumit Ahuja.

Note 2: All figures in this book are from the author's consulting and training work at http://MethodScience.com and are used here with permission.

Agile Terms and Acronyms

Acronym	*Description*
APM	Agile project management
AUP	Agile Unified Process
BABOK	Business Analysis Body of Knowledge
BPMN	Business Process Modeling Notation
CAMS	Composite Agile Method and Strategy
CMM	Capability Maturity Model
CMMI	Capability Maturity Model Integration
CoBIT	Control Objectives for Information and related Technology
COBOL	COmmon Business-Oriented Language
DSDM	Dynamic Systems Development. An iterative and incremental approach with heavy emphasis on continual user involvement
FDD	Feature-driven development Feature (agile dev.) Small piece of business function
IIP	Iterative, incremental, and parallel
ITIL	Information Technology Infrastructure Library—a best practice framework describing an end-to-end service management environment
JIT	Just in time (a production strategy)
ProcessMentor	An OO SDLC method
OMG	Object Management Group
OPEN	Object-Oriented Process, Environment, and Notation is an SDLC framework with the elements: a metamodel, a repository of reusable method components/fragments, and construction/usage guidelines

continued

Acronym	*Description*
PERT	The Program (or Project) Evaluation and Review Technique is a model for project management designed to analyze and represent the tasks involved in completing a given project
PM	Project management
PMBOK	Project Management Body of Knowledge
Prince2	Projects in Controlled Environments. "Prince2" refers to the second major version and is owned by the UK Office of Government Commerce (OGC)
RAD	Rapid application development
RUP	Rational Unified Process
SDLC	Software development life cycle
Six Sigma	A business management strategy to improve the quality of process outputs by identifying and removing the causes of defects (errors) and minimizing variability in manufacturing and business processes
SME	Subject matter expert (also occasionally small and medium enterprise)
SOX	Sarbanes–Oxley Act mandating full disclosure
Story (agile development)	A unit of requirement (usually functional)
TDD	Test-driven development
UML	Unified Modeling Language is a standardized modeling language for software engineering
XP	Extreme programming

I

CONTEMPORARY AGILE AND ITS CHALLENGES IN PRACTICE

Chapter 1

Introducing Agile in Practice

It is not the strongest of the species that survives, nor the most intelligent that survives. It is the one that is the most adaptable to change.

–Charles Darwin

Objectives

- Initiate a discussion on the importance of Agility
- Outline the fundamentals of Agility and their relevance to both software and business
- Illustrate the significance of "Art of practicing Agile" in craft and engineering
- Distinguish Agile business from Agile methods and outline the relationship and areas of synergy between the two
- Explore the scope and benefits of an integrated and holistic method for an Agile organization and make that a part of the overall strategy
- List some currently popular Agile methods as the origin for the overall Agile movement
- Highlight the importance and value of using a composite approach to Agile methods in business practice
- Allude to a research project underpinning what has come to be known as CAMS or Composite Agile Method and Strategy

Introduction

The Art of Agile Practice is a discussion on a consistent, integrated, and strategic approach to "Agility" in business. Transcending Agile as a software development method, this discussion encompasses the entire gamut of methods in an organization, including business processes, governance standards, project management, quality management, and business analysis. This holistic approach enhances the ability of an organization to adapt and respond quickly to changing internal and external business circumstances (see Figure 1.1) as well as reduce "methods friction." This

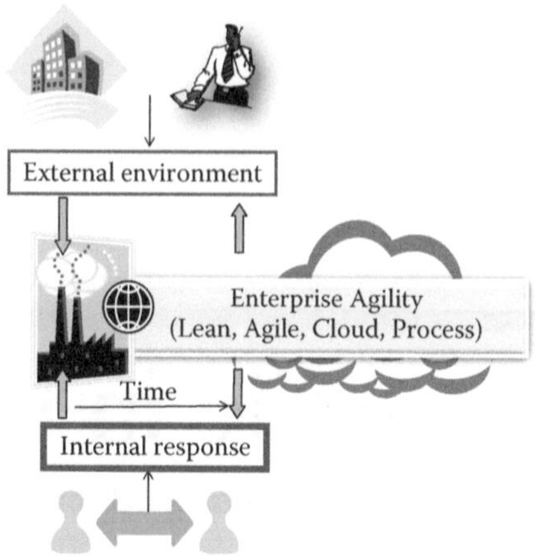

Figure 1.1 Agility reflects an organization's ability to respond to both external and internal changes.

ability to respond to change can be a factor that determines the success or failure of a dynamic business in today's environment.

Agility has a vital, strategic role to play across all dimensions of business. However, the close intertwining of almost all business functions with corresponding underlying software systems implies that an Agile business will necessarily require corresponding Agile software systems. Therefore, the methods and practices associated with contemporary Agility (e.g., Scrum; Extreme programming, XP) are encouraged as an integral part of the overall Agile approach to business. These Agile methods, however, are only a part of the overall comprehensive Agile approach required by any business. Such a comprehensive Agile approach in business encompasses wide-ranging considerations of people–process–technology–money within and outside business, rendering overall Agile value to business.

Business agility has to accommodate the many nuances of organizations, such as their clientele, markets, type, and size, as well as geographical considerations. For example, smaller-sized organizations may have the potential to be inherently Agile owing to their Lean structure. Alternatively, large and well-established organizations, although moving slowly, would have the resource base to further exploit new opportunities. Similarly, small and medium enterprises (SMEs) can exploit electronic and communications technologies in order to connect and collaborate with one other—and thereby remain Agile. Large business organizations, on the other hand, can possibly create decentralized business structures or outsource noncore business processes to create and maintain their agility. The art of Agile in practice explores and capitalizes on the possibilities offered by information management, mobile technologies, business intelligence, knowledge management, and service orientation to create an Agile ecosystem in and around the business. The ensuing balance between the core and noncore business processes renders the entire organization collaborative, Lean, and Agile.

Despite these virtues of agility in business, whenever a discussion on Agile methods is broached, attention usually is directed toward Agile *software* development methods such as Scrum, XP, test-driven development (TDD), and Crystal—to name but a few. The popularity of Agile methods in software development can be attributed to their promise to accommodate change and deliver rapidly to the expectations of business references (Unhelkar, 2010). Alan Radding, back in 2002, described "these new programming methodologies" as "*adaptive*—because they react to changing user input, *Agile*—for their frequent iterations and continual testing, and *lightweight*—because they emphasize small teams and downplay documentation." Such characteristics of a software development team, in fact, any team, are viewed as beneficial because of the promise of adding immediate value to business by enabling and accommodating change.

In the context of software development, Agile is viewed as a method (methodology) within the solution space. Prior to the advent of the Agile method(s), software development was characterized by planned methods. An important focus of these planned methods was to get all of the requirements up front. Furthermore, there were fervid attempts to get the requirements correct and complete before proceeding to the next stage of development. The unreal assumption that correct and complete requirements will remain static through the development of the solution turned out to be the bane of planned software development methods. It was impossible to get the requirements completed up front, as the business reality kept changing and, equally important, because people often just did not know what the requirements were. As it turned out, this exercise was not even necessary, because some features were seldom used. The business environment continued to be increasingly dynamic and requirements aged quickly and became redundant. The lack of engagement between business and information and communications technology (ICT) seen in planned methods and the use of documents as a tool to blame one another for nonperformance also occurred.

The dynamic needs of the business and lack of progress and engagement within software development led to a recognition that software development has a paradigm different from, say, construction or manufacturing. Fuzziness in system requirements is not an exception and needs to be accommodated within it. The new paradigm of software, as Beck correctly described in his keynote, "Fred Taylor, making software, and conversation" (Beck, 2000), is *conversation.* While formal, planned approaches to software development had their justifications, the rapidity of changes engulfing businesses demanded equally rapid changes in software development practices. "Conversations" between business and software became the cornerstone of quality and efficiency in developing software applications and products; it is the basis of an Agile method.

This new "conversational" paradigm, forming the basis of Agility, assumes significance for both software *and* business owing to the inseparable mesh of business and its processes with software systems, related applications, software packages, and the underlying architecture. A bank, an insurance company, an airline, or a hospital simply cannot function without integral support from ICT systems and processes. Agile methods promise to provide that crucial ability for businesses to change, as these methods enable corresponding software systems to change rapidly. This integral nature of software systems with business also nudges the business to make forays into areas that had not been envisaged a decade ago. For example, the phenomenal impact of mobile technologies on banking, or the influence of social media on air travel, has led to many different products and processes that these businesses had not anticipated a decade ago. Therefore, it is only prudent to explore Agility in the context of business. The reach of Agility, when considered at an organization level, is breathtaking. We appear to stand at the crossroads of a business paradigm that is way beyond what once was considered as only a software development paradigm.

An Agile approach brings the key activities and deliverables of a project out in the open (and on the wall, literally) on Day 1. Furthermore, an Agile approach encourages and supports the team in a way that enables collaboration and flexibility. By its very nature, Agility delves into the realms of psychology, sociology, and culture, requiring proper understanding and applicability of these erstwhile "soft" domains to ICT, projects, and business.

Investigation of contemporary Agile methods in practice will uncover their myriad touch points in the organization. These Agile touch points in an organization include technologies, systems, architectures, management, processes, and people (including the human resource [HR] departments themselves). Therefore, Agility, as understood and discussed in this book, is not restricted to software development. Instead, it is a core philosophy of business that results in the formulation of Agile strategies with applicability across an entire organization—albeit in close association with software development and maintenance.

Having acknowledged the popularity of contemporary Agile methods as a *new* approach, it is worth noting that agility in software development itself is not new. The Agile approach encompasses the natural way to write code—conversational, visible, and responsive. Software development efforts at the outset of the information technology (IT) industry decades ago were, in fact, quite open to these Agile principles and practices. However, as software development moved from "handwritten," hardwired pieces of code to large-scale procedural systems (typically based on COBOL and C—as in most banking and financial institutions) and later with object-oriented (OO) and component-based development (typically using C++ and Java with underlying, large-scale relational databases), it started producing humongous systems and applications with minimal documentation. A well-known result of this lack of processes documentation and balancing of risks was a unique global IT project, Y2K, that incidentally got completed on time (Unhelkar, 1999), although the need to create and follow plans, the need to create and validate requirements (Glass, 1997), and the need to formally test software were felt much before Y2K. Software development life cycles (SDLCs) such as the waterfall and spiral life cycles came into being because of lacunae in relevant planning, modeling, documentation, and sequencing in software development. Formal SDLCs brought a rigor into planning and requirements gathering. The epitome of planned processes and their universally accepted grading was the Capability Maturity Model (CMM) that measured the maturity of software development processes.

As mentioned earlier, planned approaches sought requirements and modeled them until they could be reasonably identified as necessary, correct, and complete. For a dynamic business, this overall SDLC was taking too long. Increasingly SDLC became an excuse to avoid that crucial conversation between the users and the developers. Commercial contracts, requirements documents, and outsourcing became instruments of scope creep, delayed delivery, and irrelevant solutions. While planned SDLC did mean to have an element of communication and agility in it, it also became the bearer of blame for failed software projects.

Agile provided a way to break the nexus. Some element of planning, requirements, and testing were always envisaged within Agile. The popularity of Agile, however, seems to be its challenge as well. This is because Agile started to be used sans the formal elements of planning, requirements, and testing. These formal elements not only play an important part in new development but they are also quite crucial to maintenance. Also, practitioners of pure Agile come across challenging situations wherein reliance entirely on the principles and practices of Agility does not seem to hold. Some of these interesting challenges, described later in this book, include scalability, offshoring, package development, traceability and, as mentioned, maintenance. What seems to be successful in one situation (such as new software development) does not seem to carry the same value in another situation (such as maintenance of legacy code or large infrastructure builds).

Agile is not an alibi for detailed thinking, planning, and modeling. Neither is Agile, as propounded in software development arena, an excuse (particularly in large and complex transformation programs) for strong stakeholder management. Documentation, modeling, planning, and contracts are required to ensure alignment of all the disparate activities. The manner and extent to which these artifacts are created is a fine balancing act.

The need to merge planning with Agility, the need to bring together business and software agility, and the need to provide a unified approach to methods in an organization could not have been higher. The need for methods, more as a business–technology strategy, provides the foundation for a composite Agile approach to business in practice.

The discussion in this chapter (and in fact, for most part, in this book) focuses on this need for and the synergy between business and software agility. The nature of software that lends itself to such synergy and the alignment of software agility with other methods (relating to project management and ICT governance) so as to avoid "method friction" is also discussed. Accordingly, this discussion shifts the focus of Agility from software development to all activities across an entire organization. Agility in this way is considered in the various levels of processes within the organization such as those of project management, ICT management, and business management. Eventually, this discussion leads to an argument for the formation of a composite Agile approach to be used in software development, maintenance, and business management.

Agile in Practice—A Business Issue

For Agile to be successful in practice, it has to be considered as an amalgamation of a method (or a process) together with a suite of principles and practices based on the Agile Manifesto. This amalgamated approach, termed *composite Agile*, is a comprehensive organizational framework that provides the basis for a business–technology synergy. Such Agile approach embraces methods at various levels depending on their relevance, principles, and practices. In bringing together planned and Agile behaviors, and in bringing business, technology, and operational views of an organization together in a method cum strategy, composite Agile relies on the cornerstone of "balance." In fact, Agility is all about balance.

Thus, in addition to synergizing the varying process-related views and behaviors within and across an organization, Agility in practice also aspires to keep them in balance. No matter how well a strategy is produced, a lack of balance in its execution will lead to greater complexity, uncertainty, and potential failure. The fundamental argument for what is called Composite Agile Method and Strategy (CAMS) is that methods and processes within an organization should be congruent to each other. CAMS starts by setting the right mix of planning and Agility in any organizational initiative. What is even more important in CAMS is the maintenance of balance as the initiative progresses, changing the mix of planned and Agile elements, similar to the continuously balancing flagpole of a tightrope walker.

As mentioned earlier, Agility aspires to deliver immediate value to business and is thus endearing to both business and software developers. Figure 1.2 provides an overall view of how software projects relate to businesses and the correlation between software agility and business agility. The left side in Figure 1.2 depicts the known aspects of an IT project. These variables are made up of four dimensions—time, budget, functionality, and quality (Unhelkar, 2003; this is discussed in further detail in Chapter 8). Business users, developers, and managers continuously vie for a greater share of these project variables. This may be attributed to the fact that each role within the IT project has a different perspective on what it wants from the project output.

On the right Figure 1.2 depicts a business with its stakeholders. These business stakeholders are rightfully keen (even desperate) on business agility. In a creative discussion on Agile methods in practice, the crucial need of business agility has to be continuously kept in mind as also the fact that software Agility is only a means to an end and not an end in itself. Such a discussion has to therefore welcome the otherwise intangible factors such as political and sociocultural behavioral dimensions in projects and organizations. The success of Agility depends on how it correlates the business (user) demands with the corresponding ICT systems. Such a correlation is therefore an important ingredient for a composite Agile strategy. The following discussion highlights the crucial interrelationship between the aforementioned four standard project management variables and Agility.

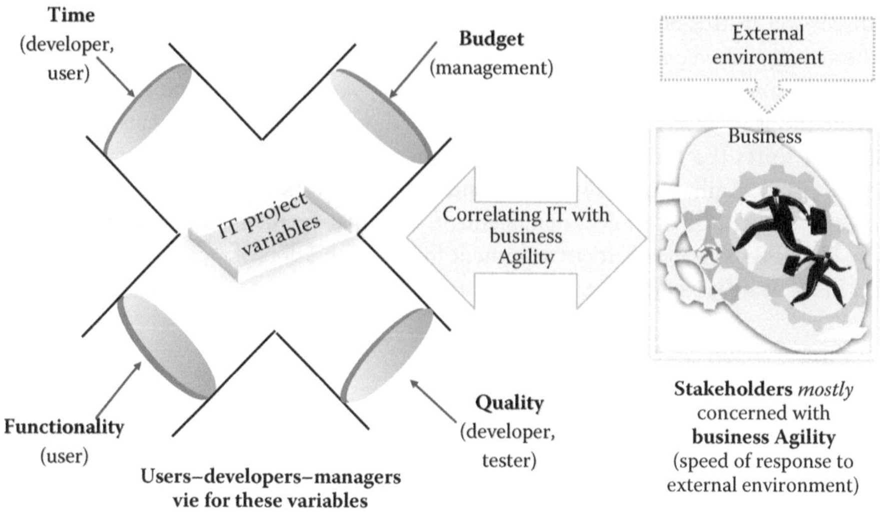

Figure 1.2 Business is interested in business Agility that should be correlated with IT Agility.

Budget and Agility

The budget (financial outlay) for any project, particularly a software project, is of immense interest to the business stakeholder who is sponsoring the project. A suitable cost–benefit analysis provides an understanding of the financial boundaries of the project. Software projects can be of different sizes and types, and can have varying degrees of formalities. Depending on the level of formality, the budget is explicitly spelled out or implied internally. Most budgets are based or allocated on the functionality desired and the quality acceptable. However, there are times when a project kickoff occurs before the budget has been finalized. This is a scenario wherein the sponsor has a rough idea, based on business experience, of what the project will cost, and also has the ability to influence, if not control, the major steps within the project execution. The skills of a sponsor in "guesstimating" is invaluable in Agile as also his understanding of the requirements.

Project completion within a stipulated budget is considered to be an important criterion for its success. Budgets and associated costs are therefore crucial control mechanisms. Among all project variables, they are easy to measure, and can be expressed in numbers that are commonly understood. These budgets and costs numbers are the first thing that a project manager focuses on—even if they are in the form of a simple spreadsheet.

An interesting aspect of project costs is that their focus is usually on development costs rather than on maintenance. Even though the real value of the project output comes only during its operational phase, the focus remains on the development. This is perhaps because the success of a project manager is usually measured on the delivery of the project, and maintainability of the system is far out in time. The situation changes, however, when the project is part of a program delivering a packaged software solution. In that case, the quality of the system and its maintenance costs start coming into play at the very outset. The cost of maintenance of software over its lifetime is usually more than its development costs. Since the life of a software system and its quality are difficult to measure, maintenance costs are not easy to compute. The up-front costs that can be associated with the quality of a software product can provide an interesting justification for Agile practices. This is so because Agile practices focus on developing and immediately demonstrating the output to the user. This "conversational" approach to software development increases not only quality but also the perception of quality in the minds of the user. The conversational paradigm, however, also results in difficulty in quantifying the budget for the overall project. Costing and budgeting for projects using Agile practices can benefit by considering the following factors:

- Giving credence to guessing + estimating, a vital ingredient in Agile project management
- Bringing in experience and expertise from both business and technology domains
- Considering budgets in terms of Agile practices and their iterations and not only in terms of deliverables
- Making provision for variations of budgets based on earlier deliverables
- Demonstrating "quick business benefits," especially in Agile projects, through a commonly agreed return on investment (ROI) figure

Time and Agility

Usually, in practical software projects, the developer and the user could be vying with each other for more versus less time. This can also happen in other nonsoftware projects, wherein those generating the artifacts need more time to do so, but those responsible for their application and use want them to be produced as quickly as possible. Therefore, management has to continuously focus its attention on time. Time is more difficult to estimate, as compared with budgets, and difficult to *track as well*. This is because time appears to be *nonlinear*, especially in software projects.

The "art" of managing time requires substantial skills in anticipating nonroutine situations that a project is likely to encounter. The ability to understand the implications of a missed checkpoint "beyond that checkpoint" is a combination of art and engineering. The "context" in which a deadline is missed is far more important than the actual linear time traversal. Modern-day software projects are interconnected to many aspects of the business, which, in turn, are connected with other businesses and the industry. Some timelines are internal and aspirational and may easily vary in an Agile project. Other timelines and their checkpoints have many dependencies from both technical and marketing perspectives. A missed deadline can have a snowballing effect that may not always be easy to estimate and anticipate. Agility aims to think through some of these time aspects and manage the risk surrounding the project. These risks can only be considered in an integrated manner (as against piecemeal risks) corresponding to the business outcomes.

Estimating the time required for a task can itself become a long-drawn task. Agile practices need to keep in mind the task at hand and ensure that only the bare necessary "time" is spent in estimating time. The following are some important considerations in Agile practices in terms of time and its estimation in projects:

- Time is nonlinear—therefore one day at work (especially in a software project) is not necessarily the same as another day (or hour).
- Time is nonlinear—therefore a day at the start of a project is not the same as a day in the middle or toward the end of a project.
- Time changes depending on the context (e.g., Y2K project), and therefore time estimations on effort required can change depending on the context.
- Time reflects the importance of and the risks associated with a project (or any other activity within the organization).

- Time (similar to a budget) can influence the decision to "buy or build." To build takes far more time than to "buy," but it provides greater flexibility for a longer time.
- Experience in estimating time is an important element of close-to-correct time estimates.

Requirements and Agility

Functionality or requirements represent the expected behavior of the system from a user's viewpoint. The sheer importance of specifying these functional requirements has resulted in the profession of "requirements modeling" (Chapter 7). The functional requirements of a system are specified through many different techniques such as user stories, use cases, and simple requirements statements. No matter how well an "Agile project" runs, it still needs proper and formal functional requirements up front. There is no alternative to spending (and even, occasionally wasting) time and effort in producing functional (and nonfunctional) requirements of a system (or project) up front.

Requirements are notorious for what is known as the *creep* factor. For example, users discover new requirements the moment they start discussing the requirements they already know with the developers. At times, an additional functionality can change the overall value a user derives from the system. Therefore, a good methodological approach to software development needs to account for this common possibility of "just this one small extra" right from the outset. This is where Agility plays an excellent role in incorporating additional requirement as well as making the users responsible for the effect of that additional requirement on the project. While well-meaning users believe that the extra requirement they are asking for is worth the development effort, the small requirement from the user's viewpoint can result in a fairly complex operation with a suite of changes required to the application, graphical user interface (GUI), database, and security. These additional requirements tend to "creep" on to the software developers resulting in substantial increase in the overall scope of the system. Additional requirements may not be easily subject to simple cost–benefit or time–benefit analysis, resulting in their incorrect prioritization. Sometimes, they are allowed to "creep in" to please a project sponsor or a key business stakeholder. Vested interests and related political issues* have the potential to pull the project goals "sideways" to unrelated or ulterior goals, which has a potential for negative impact on quality.

The following are some important considerations from the requirements viewpoint in an Agile project:

- Requirements still need to be described and modeled up front, as a part of the overall development life cycle;
- Additional requirements are expected, but they need to be managed as part of subsequent iterations;
- Responsibilities of functional creep are jointly shared by all stakeholders;
- Requirements need to be prototyped to be fully understood;
- Operational (nonfunctional) requirements are embedded within the overall requirements up front to ensure that their impact on the project is understood;
- Interface and usability requirements are likely to impact project time and budget lines;
- Variation in requirements are best understood when they are formally modeled.

* Also discussed in greater detail in Chapter 2, particularly Section 2.4 on project sociology and Section 2.5 on transactional analysis and games.

Quality and Agility

Quality relies heavily on the perception and expectation (Unhelkar, 2003) of the users and key stakeholders of the business. Agile plays a significant role in the user's positive perception of the software output. Software developers often find themselves dealing with customers that are business users. These users are looking for "quality" ways of using software that would satisfy their needs of providing the necessary products and services to satisfy the end customers. It is to be noted here that quality is a subjective element. Agility can play a substantial role in enhancing quality.

SIDEBAR

The nature of software development is such that its quality can be improved immensely through Agility. The inner urge of a developer to push the product out, the inner urge of a user to see the output before it is fully "cooked," and the ever-increasing concerns of management and stakeholders of relating visible deliverables with time and budgets, all come together synergistically in a composite Agile approach. Quality, however, is not restricted to a particular piece of code or data. Quality is also subjective—it depends on user perception. It is applied to a variety of levels within the organization to ensure it benefits through Agility. (A further detailed discussion on quality can be found in Chapter 9.)

Understanding Enterprise Agility

Agile values and practices have their roots in software agility. However, an enterprise (organization) can capitalize on the many positive aspects of Agile values and behaviors that emanate from software agility. This is because the nexus between business agility and software agility is strong. Application of such Agile values enables an enterprise to climb out of its cellars of formalities and excessive planning. At the same time, applying pure Agile approach without due credence to the formal needs of a business can often lead to projects with insufficient planning and documentation. This is a challenge to both software and enterprise-wide agility.

Enterprise agility has to be derived from applying Agile methods in practice. For example, enterprise-wide planning has to make provision for the much reduced formal requirements, scoping, and estimating that would occur in an Agile-driven project. These aforementioned activities turn out to be spot-on when developers are themselves managing the project. For large-scale enterprise agility, though, formal, exploratory, and model-based activities cannot be sidestepped. There is much reduced up-front business analysis (especially requirements modeling, for example) in an Agile approach although its significance cannot be overestimated. An Agile enterprise has to further make provision for time and effort for business analysis activities that feed into its software projects and systems.

Agile approaches depend heavily on the individual. People, their skills and motivation, and their intra- and intergroup communications remain fundamental to their success. Cockburn and Highsmith (2001) stress amicability, talent, skill, and communication as critical factors for the success of Agile. This application of Agility across the enterprise demands an overall understanding of the "soft" factor including sociocultural and psychological factors. Enterprise agility will need appropriate training and mentoring in its "people" areas for success. For example, training and coaching of the decision makers of the organization ensures strategy alignment, risk management, change management, and behavioral practices that can add significant agility to the overall enterprise.

Agile methods are made up of practices. For example, practices such as pair programming, TDD, and continuous integration are heavily used in projects following the Agile approach.

With increasing integration between method, process, standard, and frameworks within an organization, and even within a project, there is great scope for these practices to be abstracted from their software development base and widely applied in various enterprises.

In contrast to the above scenario, formal methodologies start with an underlying need to separate the individual from the product itself. Planned processes in software projects (particularly large-scale software projects) engender this separation and ensure that the development does *not* depend on an individual's subjective elements (e.g., motivation). However, an attempt to reduce the dependency on individuals leads to overwhelming procedural control and mammoth documentation. Thus, while the formal, planned approaches have much less dependency on the "soft" factors than the Agile ones, there is still a need to incorporate the "subjectivity" in them that comes from the Agile principles.

So what do we mean when we say "an enterprise is Agile" as compared with an "Agile method"? Figure 1.3 highlights what we mean by this business agility and the importance and value of Agile approaches in business. Business agility can be understood as a time measure of changes to the operating environment of the business and the time it takes for an organization to respond to that change (Ginige, 2003). An Agile organization will be able to quickly respond to a change in the environment; however, as the rate of environmental change increases, there may be increasing challenges to the rate of change (agility). All methods and frameworks employed within the organization have a responsibility to bridge the gap between a software project's agility and the overall agility of the organization.

An interesting aspect of enterprise agility is the correlation it has with a Lean organization. Being Lean is a precursor to becoming Agile—in fact, Leanness and Agility are intricately tied together. Changing business requirements are inevitable—and an Agile–Lean business will have corresponding Agile–Lean IT systems. Agile principles add direct value to business as they enable IT to cope with the changing business requirements (Unhelkar, 2010). This Lean–Agile tie-up is discussed in detail in Chapter 6.

Despite the popularity of Agile in the software development arena, enough care needs to be exercised when Agility is applied across an enterprise. An enterprise-wide Agile approach will dissuade the practitioner from approaching Agile as a unidimensional method that is focused only on software development. Instead, a holistic, comprehensive enterprise-wide approach will bring together the methods/processes/standards/frameworks across multiple tiers of an organization,

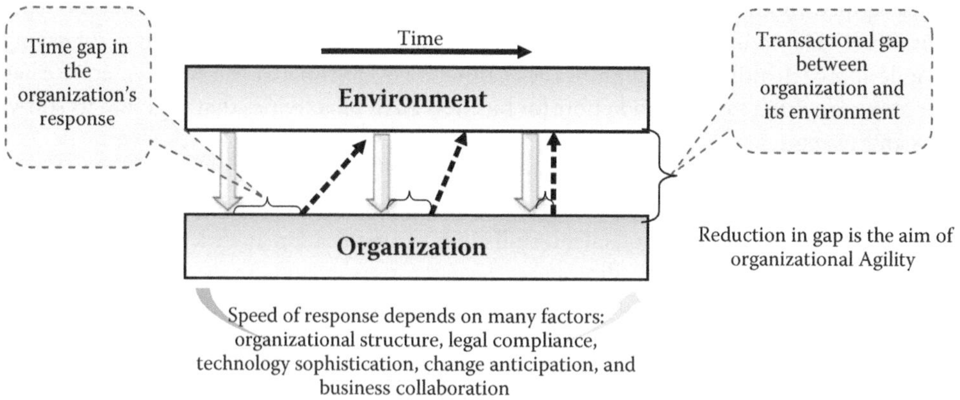

Figure 1.3 Business Agility closes the organization–external environment gap.

resulting in what is called a *composite approach*. Such an approach will not only focus on the practices of Agile that are commonly understood today but also bring the best practices, phases, and deliverables from the planned family of methods (methodologies). Enterprise agility stands to benefit by understanding and applying an Agile culture value system across all organizational functions.

For example, enterprise-wide agility will imply small teams involving customers and producers (developers) in short development iterations. However, once the tasks are complete, the team members are dissipated back to a common pool of resources. A composite approach to Agile makes full use of a community of practices and centers of excellences within the organization (discussed in detail in Chapter 10). While self-organizing, small teams implement features rapidly in short iterations, the larger pool of talent gets nurtured and developed through up-skilling and socializing team members. Overall, a composite approach to business agility is to add value by enhancing customer satisfaction and responsiveness to changing business environments.

Strategy, Method, and Practice of Agile

Figure 1.4 shows three major areas of performance of a business: the strategic or visionary aspect that requires nonroutine leadership; the operational or routine, business-as-usual decision making; and the projects- or task-based execution of a program of work. For an organization to be Agile, all three areas of performances of an organization need to be Agile. Therefore, a composite methodological approach across the organization will also have to consider these areas of performances. For example, while the visionary aspect of a business may be revolutionary in its approach to decision making, it has to consider the business-as-usual (operational) aspect wherein current customers, systems, and processes exist. Similarly, existing programs of work and the methods used to deliver through these programs need to be considered in enterprise-wide agility. Agile business, as shown in the intersecting center of Figure 1.4, is the one that synergizes between these areas of work.

While organizations require flexibility that enables them to respond to change, they also need solid structures that will enable them to weather the effect of change. There is a constant need

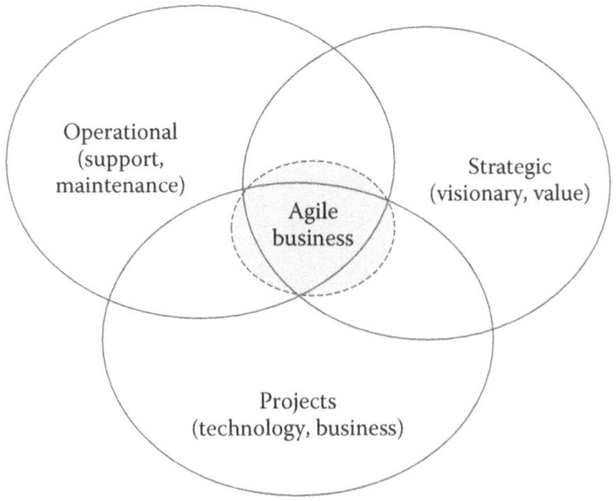

Figure 1.4 Agile business is the intersection of strategic, operational, and project performances.

to balance flexibility and structure. Any one method or approach to working will, therefore, not be suitable. The new era of methodologies will require the creation of repositories of all relevant methods, processes, frameworks, and standards that the organization might need and then dynamically picking elements from them to provide strategies and guidance to the functioning of the organization (Unhelkar, 2010).

Figure 1.5 shows the range of coverage of strategies and methods, and the positioning of projects where practices play a major role. The organization, overall, is not time bound. Also, neither is a part of the program. However, as shown in Figure 1.5, programs are made up of multiple projects and they can benefit by the practices of Agile. Linking the practices with methods and strategies provides an overall methodological framework for a program of work within the organization.

Agile practices provide success to a business organization when combined with many other methods that operate at software, governance, project, and business levels. The practices of Agile require substantial support from the entire organization. The following are the important considerations in practicing Agile, especially in medium- to large-sized organizations:

- Identification of key players and their socialization
- Identification of independent tasks whose practice can be handled using Agile principles
- Continuous and active sponsorship of the project by stakeholders
- Identification of formal "points of control," typically based on waterfall SDLC and their corresponding measures
- Dynamic leadership that goes beyond formal control
- Identification of Agile practices that will apply across the organization
- Creation of formal projects and their budget–time parameters
- Creation and application of governance and controls at program and organization levels
- Promotion of simplicity and trust across the entire organization, rather than a project within a program

The above points indicate the manner in which Agility can be made to benefit an entire organization. However, as mentioned earlier, the popularity of Agile has come about from software development. Therefore, let us also discuss the basis for derivation of the Agile model for software development and its crossover into business agility.

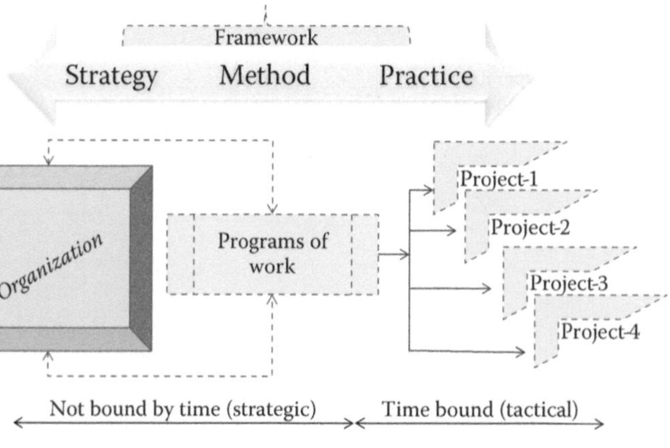

Figure 1.5 Strategy and method operate at different levels—yet they are closely interrelated.

Conversational Model for Software Development

Knowledge usually expands and builds on previous knowledge. The knowledge that we had in terms of engineering good-quality homes and cars was the one we decided to use for software engineering as well. The nature of software, however, is such that it is not always amenable to construction-type engineering (wherein the ground floor is constructed before the first floor) or manufacturing-type engineering (wherein the components are put together on an assembly line). Instead, the software development environment and the business whose needs it is catering to is fuzzy, rapidly changing, and cannot be easily standardized. While end-to-end software solution provides value to business, the software itself can be developed in bits and pieces with one area of development completed and other areas being developed later. Thus, the development, testing, deployment, usage, and maintenance of software is inherently different from construction and manufacturing.

Agile methods or, specifically, their practices bring about nimbleness to software development. These Agile methods are a different breed of methodologies that are primarily developer-centric and, in essence, radically different from the erstwhile application of the processes of construction and manufacturing to software development.

Agile methods, as understood today, start with the developer writing a part of the code. Demonstration of this code is then used in engaging the user in a "conversation" that will further explain the requirements. Coding and testing can benefit only by carefully "listening" to what the user is trying to say. To complement this listening by the developer, the user should be able to "speak" as clearly as possible. The listening and speaking is interspersed with bare minimum design. This approach is based on the basic discipline of software development, expounded by Beck (2000). This is as shown in Figure 1.6, which also indicates how the area of responsibilities are divided among the developer, the designer (a senior developer), and the customer/user. This is akin to the concept of "good enough software" described by Yourdon in *Rise and Resurrection of the American Programmer* (Yourdon, 1997). This model, together with the Agile Manifesto (discussed later), forms the basis for most Agile methods.

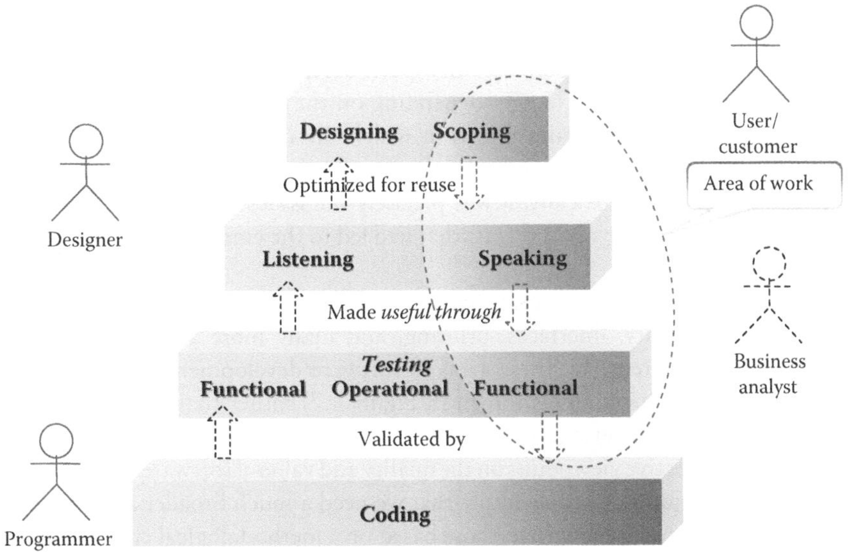

Figure 1.6 A "conversational" model of basic software development (leading to Agile).

Agility—Art, Craft, and Engineering

Primal software development in the 1960s and 1970s was very much a craftsmanship. Then came the term "software engineering." The software community hoped for every element of software to be standardized into components with interfaces that can be simply "plugged" into the myriad other software components, resulting in an enterprise-wide bank of systems. Far from reaching those expectations, software engineering processes, methods, and their corresponding maturity models bogged down software development that stunted programming creativity. Programmers could not relate to the massive documentation required in projects and, with twiddling fingers itching to code, wondered when the "real project" would start. Furthermore, programmers almost universally believed that the business does not know what it wants. Not that the documentation did not exist—but it was not standardized, was usually too late for the development effort, and did not have the visuals of use cases, activity graphs, and business domain class diagrams. The Agile Manifesto came right on cue.

Agile methods embrace high rates of change within the development cycle, primarily through high visibility of the development activities that are loosely dependent on each other. The developer directly incorporates within the code the change requests from the users. Needless to say, Agile, lightweight approaches require excellence and synergy among high-caliber individuals. These individuals operate with minimal contact, are highly synergetic, and are highly skilled. Constantine calls such a group a *utopian team**. Such teams of developers, literally out of the world (utopian), depend not only on their own skills but also on their ability to be part of the team (discussed in detail in Chapter 8 on project management). Like-minded, highly motivated, and equally skilled professionals align themselves to the commonly accepted goals of delivery to produce the end results. Also, in the context of this discussion, their work borders between art and craft, as shown in Figure 1.7: art because the work is so highly creative and unrestrained, craft because a team working in an aligned manner presents the feel of a handicraft industry.

Imposing a planned, heavyweight approach on such teams is likely to hinder project progress. The rigors of engineering need to take a step back when users, developers, business analysts, and managers appear together under an Agile project.

This consideration of the "human factor" in computing goes up by a few notches in a discussion on Agile because people permeate all aspects of Agile software development, usage, and maintenance. A piece of software changes depending on the demands of a user, which, in turn, may change depending on the circumstances in which the user operates. Occasionally ad hoc, direct, people-to-people interactions are most effective in bringing about immediate responses to changing circumstances. Paradoxically, it was precisely the issues associated with such free-form development bordering between art and craft that had led to the emergence of the formal software development methodologies.

Within the software itself, data, information, design, messaging, application, analysis, performance, reliability, security, interfaces, printing, and many more areas change continuously and demand continuous attention. These areas of software development need to be understood as a subjective form of engineering (as shown in Figure 1.7) rather than as the objective type of mechanical or electrical engineering.

This also implies subjective viewpoints on the quality and value of software to the user. Subjective needs of such a diverse group of people imply that we need a much broader and contextual study to understand software development than those based on a methodological checklist. This leads to

* Larry Constantine writes in *Constantine on Peopleware.*

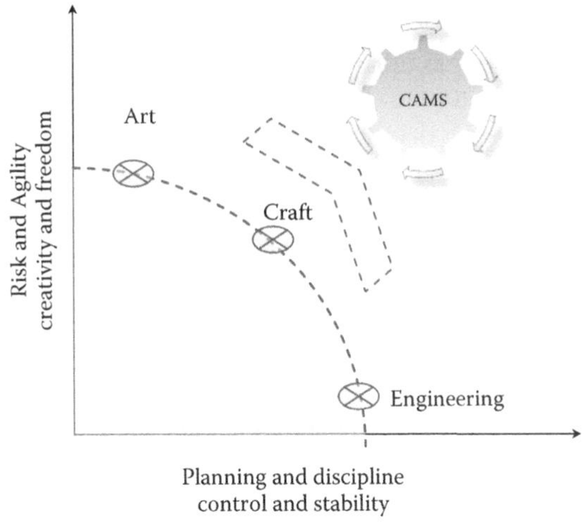

Figure 1.7 Art, craft, and engineering.

a need for Agility, similar to quality, to incorporate studies and experiences from other interesting domains such as psychology, sociology, and social sciences. Successful Agile projects will thus be a combination of planned project management factors and soft, human-related factors. Agility thus starts becoming balanced—using the rigors of engineering and the creativity of art.

SIDEBAR

One of the *key* elements for successful adoption of software *craftsmanship* is to come up with agreeable, accurate, and regular metrics and measures for the artifacts produced. This is one of the biggest challenges posed by Agile approaches—the ability of the project manager to estimate the cost, time, and scope up front and also to ascertain their effect on quality. (While project management is discussed in Chapter 8, Agile metrics are discussed in Chapter 9.) Agile, by its very nature, *evolves* the requirements as the project progresses. This leads straightaway to a potential dichotomy of needs—develop software as a craft but measure it as an engineering entity!

However, for Agile approaches to flourish and provide value to business (as they promise to and are capable of), there is a vital need to consider many aspects of *formal* or *planned* methods in software projects.

Correlating Agility to Planned Processes

As mentioned earlier, the ICT community did move away from what was intrinsically Agile, to an era of "formal," "heavyweight," "planned," or non-Agile methodologies. Medicine is considered a far more mature industry* not only in comparison with the number of years it has been around but also because it first asks what the problem is and then provides a solution. Until the advent of well-researched methodologies, which are also supported by industrial strength, computer-aided software engineering (CASE) tools, the software developers "prescribed" solutions for a problem

* It is only fair to accept that medical profession has more experience than the IT profession. After all, they have been handling viruses for millenniums on end whereas IT viruses are far too young.

that had not been properly understood and documented. Conversely, pure Agile practices also present challenges. For example, project managers and business stakeholders are left to wonder how to budget for software development that does not have detailed and up-front analysis phases and how to budget for a software system that may not subscribe to up-front documented requirements but, rather, promises to produce value *as the development proceeds*; and, even more importantly, why this reversion from the elaborate SDLCs, detailed planning phases, and up-front requirements capturing exercises to—once again—more "informal," "lightweight," Agile approaches.

SIDEBAR

Waterfall as a software development life cycle (SDLC) still has immense value as a philosophy behind software development. In addition to providing the sequential aspect of software development that is executed through phases and controlled through "gates," waterfall also signifies a vital characteristic—that of "least resistance." Water flows from a higher level to a lower level, always taking the path of least resistance. Therefore, a software development characterized by a waterfall SDLC can be easily directed to take the path of least resistance. This is an important characteristic of any software development. (A more detailed discussion can be found in Chapter 4.)

The earlier shift to formal requirements gathering, project planning, modeling, and documentation was driven by the fact that "specifications" on the back of an envelope were not good enough for significant, large-scale, and highly complex software development to succeed. The software community realized the *need* for planning, architecting, and designing a solution before it could commence coding and testing. An understanding of the sequential nature of software development emerged and was cast into the well-known waterfall SDLC (Royce, 1970). Software development, in this approach, followed the logical sequence of phases: analysis, design, code, and test. Maturity in terms of following this formalism was graded by mechanisms such as the CMM.*

However, the challenges in sequential development quickly came to the fore, as users started making requests for changes right in the middle of the development project. The response, in terms of the life cycle, was the introduction of iterations. Early attempts to incorporate iterations in life cycle are seen in Boehm's (1987) formulation of the spiral life cycle.

Then dawned the era of OO software development, and a raft of methodologies emerged, including Booch, Object Modelling Technique (OMT), Objectory, and others. At one point, the Object Management Group (OMG)† had ratified 63 different methods for OO software development. Proprietary methods such as the Rational Unified Process (RUP), Catalysis, and Process Mentor found their way into mainstream software development. By 1997, the OMG "stamped" a unified set of notations for visual modeling in the software life cycle, resulting in the Unified Modeling Language (UML).‡ Notwithstanding their OO nature, these were high-ceremony "formal" approaches with onerous documentation, checks, and audits of every step within the development process and a long life cycle before the user could see the output. Beck (2000) talked about XP as the new paradigm and suggested a set of practices that would turn software development into a dynamic conversation between business and technology.

The "Agilists," through their enriching experiences, have empowered these "new" methodologies. They have formulated these approaches, which are based directly on the lessons learned during coding, semiformalized them as practices, and thereby made a valuable contribution in the area

* www.sei.cmu.edu (Software Engineering Institute, Carnegie Mellon University).

† Object Management Group, www.omg.org.

‡ See Note †.

of software engineering. Some of these well-known Agile approaches to software development, also understood as lightweight methods, include Scrum, Crystal, adaptive programming, and XP.

It seems the software community has turned a full circle in its approach to development. The move is back to where we originally were, sitting next to the user, engaging him or her in a conversation, producing code in small and demonstrable chunks, incorporating the feedback from the user directly into the code, and keeping the documentation to the bare minimum or just sufficient to fit the purpose of development.

There appears to be very little in this approach that is *new*! Agile is similar to what the ICT community started with—albeit without the advantages and challenges of more than a quarter century's worth of additional experience emanating from many a software failure (Glass, 1997), use and misuse of methodologies, and incorporation of current and emerging technologies (such as Web Services, SOA, Web 2.0, Cloud, SaaS, and Mobility) in development.

Agile Coverage in Organizations

Agile is not one word. It comprises multiple areas of work within an entire organization. (As this gets written, a Webinar titled Big Agile is about to occur [Gat and Smits].) Agile influences both the internal and the external structure and dynamics of an organization. The following are the various dimensions of Agility that start from data and go through to business:

- *Data warehouse and Agility* deals with changes to the data, its storage, identification of its redundancies as well as handling the need for security through mirroring and off-site storages. The contents themselves and the speed of their access need to be considered for data agility. Ease of storage and retrieval of data and its accuracy are vital ingredients of agility.
- *Software code and Agility* is the popular software development approach that makes use of the Agile principles and practices. This aspect of agility has already succeeded within development projects. There is a certain positive correlation between software development and its business value.
- *Software model and Agility* considers the ease of change of software models, and the value they provide to development efforts. Software models facilitate agility by enabling discussions on development before the code is written. (More details on UML and agility can be found in Chapter 4.)
- *Maintenance and Agility* forms the most challenging part of agility as contemporary Agile methods do not seem to have given enough precedence to how a piece of software (system) is maintained post development. Pure Agile approaches lack traceability when solutions are in operation.
- *Business architecture and Agility* handles the overall organization of the business itself including its various departments, divisions, processes, and business functions. This model of the business changes to Agile.
- *Enterprise architecture and Agility* deals with the suite of software systems, databases, networks, and related architectural aspects of the enterprise. Enterprise Architecture provides stability and opportunity to balance risks.
- *Security architecture and Agility* requires the security setup of the organization to change corresponding to changing security demands. Security remains a nonfunctional requirement that is not amenable to user stories.

- *Process maps and Agility* can be used to provide the basis for modeling business processes (as well as indicating parts of processes to follow during development and maintenance). These process maps provide opportunities to formalize processes.
- *Business intelligence and Agility* deals with the ease of correlation between various data, information, and process areas of a business. Agility enables rapid correlations between changing data to arrive at collaborative business intelligence.
- *Business analysis and Agility* requires the incorporation of formal business analytical work within Agile projects. This work explores business needs and formalizes requirement models.
- *Management and Agility* brings together the organizational and control aspects of projects and Agility.
- *Leadership and Agility* encourages the application of creativity, innovation, and flexibility to Agile projects. Leadership within Agile projects focuses on facilitation rather than management.
- *Quality assurance, testing, and Agility* deals with creation of test cases and their execution at both technical and business levels. Testing also occasionally drives development.
- *Collaborative business and Agility* correlates with Lean–Agile business and basic Agility as a precursor for collaborative business and vice versa.

Each of the aforementioned areas of work in an organization requires attention when agility is introduced as a value system across the organization. Careful examination of these areas of work within an organization also leads to an understanding that this work can be divided among various organizational spaces. These organizational methods spaces are discussed next.

Agile Organizational Methods Spaces

The organization functions as a whole. Yet in order to understand its functioning, it can be divided into various architectural and methods spaces. This division makes the methods spaces more comprehensible by providing various "views" of the organization, which are sufficiently cohesive to provide a complete view. Creation of these views of the same organizational model is the mechanism for effectively understanding methods spaces. These separate methods spaces provide the opportunity to understand the way in which each type of method can secure the objectives of the project. For instance, a project that deals with implementing a third-party customer relationship management (CRM) package has greater need to specify the functional requirements. In such a project where the solution is provided by the CRM package, there is thus minimal opportunity to apply Agile development practices.

Figure 1.8 shows these four separate, yet related, methods spaces within an organization. The architectures corresponding to these spaces are also shown. These methods spaces are as follows:

- Business methods space: This area of work relates entirely to business. Methods such as Six Sigma, Lean, Kaizen, and Kanban play a role here.
- Planned methods space: This is where formal planning is undertaken and requirements are modeled. RUP and Object-Oriented Process, Environment, and Notation (OPEN) are examples of methods that can be used here.
- Agile methods space: This is the only solution space where the principles and practices of Agile can be applied directly.

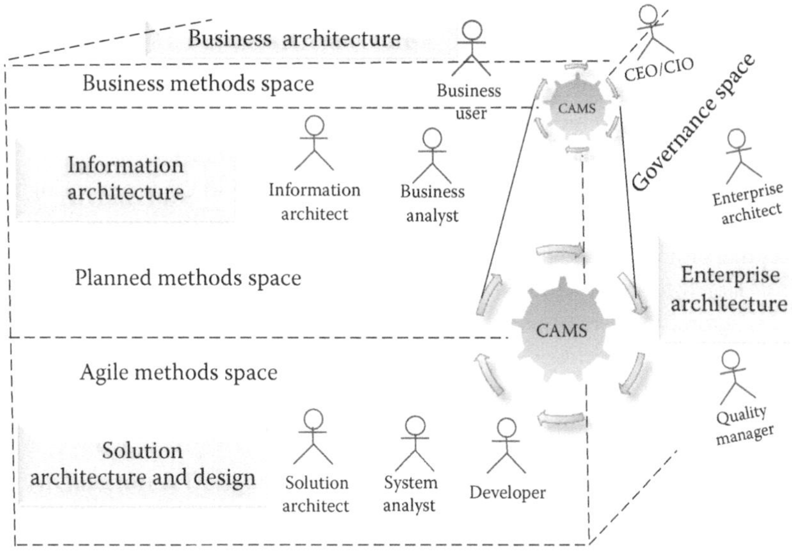

Figure 1.8 CAMS and various organizational spaces.

- Governance space: This deals with controls and reporting standards within the organization. Control Objectives for Information and related Technology (CoBIT) and Information Technology Infrastructure Library (ITIL) are examples of standards applicable within this space.

Appreciation of these methods spaces provides the necessary background to understand and apply values derived from Agile methods across the organization. However, it is also important to remember that these spaces are not watertight compartments. They are interdependent. The following discussion further highlights the significance of these four methods spaces.

Business Methods Space

This is the methods space in which business challenges are identified, root causes are investigated, and critical thinking applied. Therefore, formal methods such as Six Sigma, Lean, Kaizen, and Kanban play a major role in this space. The program of work can be generated through these methods and the scope of a project can be defined on the basis of the needs of the business. The methods in this space enable an organization to model and understand its value streams, the end goal of the business in undertaking an initiative, and the way in which it interacts with its customers and business partners.

Examples of activities in this method space include high-level business analysis, SWOT (strength–weakness–opportunities–threat) analysis, mind mapping, and root-cause analysis.

Planned Methods Space

Planned methods space uses formal approaches to the understanding and modeling of the problem. Primarily, this would be the problem that the business or the user of a system is facing. Less often, it could also be a technical problem. In the planned methods space, work goes into understanding, analyzing, and modeling the problem whose solution is to be developed. In some situations, the problem, requiring planned investigation and formal business analysis work, may be a combination of business and technology issues.

For example, in the case of projects dealing with existing legacy applications, there will be a need for the creation of a formal model of what exists, followed by a model of what is needed. This modeling will be guided by formal process maps in defining the problem.

Major activities that would take place in the problem space would be documenting and understanding the requirements, analyzing requirements, investigating the problem in detail, optionally creating a conceptual prototype, and understanding the flow of the process within the business. Thus, this method space largely focuses on the business or the user. Process mapping, requirements modeling with use case, user stories, and use of Business Process Modeling Notation (BPMN) would occur here. Planned methods use UML modeling constructs such as the use case diagram and activity diagrams, followed by high-level use of class and sequence diagrams, and, optionally, state chart diagrams.

Executable UML and MDA (Model Driven Architecture) border between planned and Agile methods space.

Pure Agile (Solution) Methods Space

Solution space deals with modeling and designing solutions. Eventually, these solutions are developed, tested, and deployed. Models in this space would use the information about the problem that is made available in the planned methods space. This is done to create and provide a solution that relates to and satisfies the needs of the user. Therefore, this is a technical space and is the one where most Agile practices are effective.

Activities in this space need detailed understanding of the programming languages, development of programming environments, understanding of databases, middleware, web application solutions, and a number of other related technical details. Good understanding of technology is therefore imperative to work well in the solution space. This should be coupled with a good understanding of how models in this space relate to the underlying technologies. Agile practices such as pair programming, continuous testing and integration, and integrative development can be freely employed here. These Agile practices can be coupled with modeling constructs such as design-level class diagrams, sequence diagrams together with their messages and protocols, state chart diagrams, and component diagrams (which represent the final executable chunks of code or libraries—in the Windows environment, these will be the ".exe" and the ".dll").

Governance Methods Space

Governance methods space deals with control as well as constraints within programs of work for the organization. Examples of methods or frameworks in this space include ITIL and CoBIT.

This method space includes planning and controlling the project, and handling the sourcing of project hardware, software, and people, as well as tracking both—the projects and the operational business—through checkpoints and reporting.

Architectural work that specifies constraints and limitations (based on a large amount of technical background work) may also be considered as a part of this background (governance) model space. System architecture can use considerable amount of material in the UML domain that deals with analysis patterns (Fowler, 1997) such as the work by Martin Fowler, design patterns by the Gang of Four (Gamma et al., 1995), cognitive patterns (Gardner et al., 1998), and anti patterns (Brown et al., 1998).

Furthermore, important strategic aspects of IT such as service agreements, reuse, outsourcing contracts, and reporting become part of this space. These aspects need organizational as well as industrial knowledge that influences ensuing decisions. Governance also influences the all-important "make versus buy" decision that is heavily influenced by the work in this space—the way abstract, yet precise and explicit models of software or components greatly influence the decision to buy (or not to buy) them.

The discussion thus far in this section was on viewing the organization and the projects through the four methods spaces. Agile, as was mentioned, operates in the solution space. We take a brief look at the basis of Agile methods in the solution space.

Agile Manifesto, Principles, and Practices

Agile methods base themselves on the popular Agile Manifesto (Agile Manifesto (Beck, 2001; Fowler and Highsmith, 2001)). This manifesto characterizes Agile as "a value statement not a concrete plan or process" (Coffin and Lane, 2007), thereby laying the foundation for the Agile values, priorities, and principles. These values aspire for minimal formal policies, processes, and procedures. Adhering to these values occurs more easily in the solution space where software development takes place starting with the inputs from the planned method space as compared with the traditional SDLCs. These Agile methods do not subscribe to formal planning, standardized templates for documentation, or step-by-step description of activities and tasks seen in planned space.

The four core statements of the Agile Manifesto are as follows:

1. Individuals and interactions over processes and tools
2. Working software over comprehensive documentation
3. Customer collaboration over contract negotiation
4. Response to changeover following a plan

The Agile Manifesto caters to the fact that traditional SDLC is too rigid to successfully deliver appropriate software. As business goals change, innovative projects require frequent experimentation. Thus, flexibility in actions takes precedence over up-front planning (Highsmith, 2004; Stober and Hansmann, 2009, p. 28).

The Agile Manifesto provides the basis for software development iteratively and incrementally. There are a number of Agile methods published for software development, such as XP, Scrum, Crystal, and adaptive software development (Abrahamsson et al., 2002). Agile projects can efficiently adapt to change and produce working products rather than be tied down to requirements engineering and planning (based on Fowler and Highsmith (2001)). These Agile methods are outlined in the next section.

Agile methods are characterized by Agile principles and practices. The characteristics of Agile principles as typically applied to projects are iterative, incremental, self-organized, adaptive, informal, communicative, courageous, and trustworthy. Corresponding Agile practices dictate the work that is carried out within Agile projects. Agile practices are discussed in great detail in Chapter 2. These Agile practices, based on the Agile Manifesto, can be categorized as analytical, requirements, development, design, project management, quality assurance, operations, and testing practices.

Agile Methods

Methods (also called *methodologies*, although, strictly speaking they are not the same) play a crucial role in software projects. This is particularly so in large projects that include myriad variables such as people, technologies, risks, changing requirements, and fluctuating stakeholders. These variables are far too many to be handled by a single person in the role of a project manager. When the project requires a group of developers to work together, then coordinating and managing their tasks, expectations, and understanding, together with the demands of the customer, becomes highly complex.

Figure 1.2 illustrates the variables of time, budget, functionality, and quality. Balancing these four variables together with the interests of various stakeholders is a complex need that keeps changing from project to project. Methods are an attempt to learn from previous attempts at software development, and then abstract and enshrine these lessons in a discipline. Chapman (2007) describes a software development methodology as a documented set of policies, processes, and procedures employed in the development of an information system. Methods help to abstract, generalize, formalize, unify, and standardize the approaches to software development and maintenance.

Planned methods, in particular, isolate (or at least minimize) the impact of the product quality from the caliber of the individuals. As a result of these, methods equip the management to estimate the time, budget, and resources required in a project at an early stage of the project.

Agile methods, however, are a different brand of methods that subscribe to the Agile Manifesto. Instead of isolating the individual, these Agile methods encourage and respect the subjectivity of an individual and align it in a team effort. Some of these Agile methods have been quite popular and well accepted by the developers. Customers (users), who see the advantages of visible development, are also highly supportive of these approaches. The following is a list of methods belonging to the Agile family:

- Extreme programming (XP) by Beck (2000): Perhaps this is the very first Agile method that is based on simple programming principles and focuses on individuals.
- Scrum (Schwaber, 1995; Schwaber and Beedle, 2001): This is the most popular of all Agile methods; it focuses on business value through demonstration and prioritization. The daily and 2- to 4-week cycles work well in practice.
- Crystal (Cockburn, 2004): This is a family of methods that is applicable to varying development scenarios depending on size and criticality of the projects. However, the range of applicability varies, depending on essential money, discretionary money, and comfort.
- Feature-driven development (FDD) (Palmer and Felsing, 2002): This is based around selection and integration of various development techniques to deliver prioritized features.
- Adaptive software development (Highsmith, 2000): This method continuously adapts/modifies the process to cater to the rapidly changing development situation and is based on the speculate–collaborate–learn phases.
- Dynamic systems development method (Stapleton, 1997): This is an iterative and incremental approach with heavy emphasis on continuous user involvement.
- Test-driven development (Beck, 2002): This method is based on the philosophy of writing the test cases first, before writing the code that is supposed to pass the test cases. It enables focus on quality and purpose of the code. Once the tests are passed, development can include refactoring of the code for future reuse.

A study of these methods and abstraction of their commonalities (described in detail in Chapter 2) forms the basis for the creation of a "composite" approach. Such composite Agile approach can be applied across an organization or to a program of work. This composite Agile approach to projects as well as organizations is envisaged as a very practical means of the use of methods. It forms the basis of most of the discussions in this book.

Composite Agile—Research Project

Practices in Agile software development over the last decade indicate that organizations currently tend to mix and match Agile practices and principles within planned approaches. This mixing is undertaken in order to maintain control and management as well as the ability to respond quickly to changes in the business ecosystem. There are two major considerations in this mixing of methods.

First is the need to integrate Agile into existing traditional SDLC so that it goes beyond the single level of software development. In attempting this, organizations still are confronted with an incompatibility between the Agile practices and principles and many of the other processes in the organization.

Second, the focus of the aforementioned attempts at integration of processes has remained at the software level only. However, there are many processes that are independent of all other methods and frameworks in the organization and that need to be considered together with software methods in order to achieve effective integration.

Experience shows that in practice, successful "Agilists" anyway tend to bring together a number of activities, tasks, and deliverables that are beyond the boundaries of "pure Agile." On the other hand, successful project managers and business leaders routinely apply Agile values and principles in their practice. This mixing and matching of process elements from Agile and non-Agile (formal) approaches that also include nonsoftware processes is a much more practical way of using methods in practice.

SIDEBAR: Agility Is Balance

Boehm (2002) noted that "Although many of their advocates consider the Agile and plan-driven software development methods polar opposites, synthesizing the two can provide developers with a comprehensive spectrum of tools and options." A similar viewpoint is expressed by Colin Bird in his blog: "I know many teams that do not subscribe to any particular flavour but are nonetheless both Agile and very successful. This fact makes Agile almost infinitely flexible such that it can and has been applied to many different organisations, cultures, technologies (including non IT projects), team size, team skill and team distribution." Perhaps the picture on the cover page of the special issue of *Information Age* on Agility* appropriately depicts what agility implies in practice: "a tightrope walker wearing ice skates and holding a balancing pole." Composite Agile is a balancing act not only in terms of methods but also as an overall organizational strategy.

This balanced approach to software development maintenance and also to business development and its operation is what is being advocated here. There is a need to recognize that planned processes have a significant role to play in software development. Also, the popularity of Agile practices needs to be recognized for the phenomenal role they play in bringing software development from the boiler room out into the open sun.

---

* *Information Age*, special issue on Agility—Programming on the straight and narrow, June/July 2002, publication of the Australian Computer Society.

This planned and Agile synthesis that Boehm refers to and the wide-ranging opportunities for Agile application alluded to by Bird have to be further elevated to the entire organization's functioning. Agility is perhaps best approached as a composite of multiple process elements from various levels within the organization—a composite Agile approach. This viewpoint lead to the creation of an industrial research project that culminated in a successful PhD and the formulation of industrial training courses. The aim of these industrial research activities was twofold:

1. To explore the validity of a composite Agile approach through a series of exploratory interviews with practitioners in various roles within the industry
2. To validate as well as update the initial model of composite Agile through action research

While the core output of these research activities remains with the researchers, the original model is extended, updated, and customized to suit industrial needs. Nevertheless, some aspects of these research activities are worth mentioning in the context of their application to industry. The research aspect of this discussion on composite Agile provides the necessary robustness and validity to the approach—as against documenting the approach entirely on the basis of a practitioner's viewpoint and observations.

A part of this research includes exploration of the viewpoints of 10 individual participants with the help of a researcher (this was a complementary masters-level research project). These viewpoints were explored through planned interviews, which included the study of various roles from developers and architects to project managers and testers. Both consulting and permanent positions were included in these interview-based case studies (see Appendix I for discussion and a spread of participants involved in these case studies).

The output of these formal exploratory interviews was analyzed and combined together with the author's experience to result in the CAMS. CAMS has been published by Unhelkar (2010), in order to comprehensively compose Agile principles to bridge the gap between Agile development and other management processes. It is an innovative approach to identify the conjunctions of Agile practices and existing management processes at different levels of an organization (Unhelkar, 2010).

Outputs from the initial interviews, discussions, and corresponding literature reviews continued to reveal that Agility has an instant charm that is way beyond software development. Entire organizations have shown keenness to implement the principles of Agility in their business strategies and methods, use of standards and practices, project management methods, and enterprise architecture and design standards. As these thought processes started getting revealed from the initial interviewees, the scope of the interviews was immediately extended with questions related to many other processes in an organization. This resulted in the examination and incorporation of "Agility" in processes related to business management (e.g., Six Sigma, Kaizen), project management (e.g., Prince2), IT governance standards (e.g., ITIL, CoBIT), and formal software processes (e.g., RUP, Mentor, OPEN—discussed in greater detail in Chapter 4).

The resulting analysis and discussion forms an important part in the justification of CAMS and its application in practice. This is so because composite Agile imbibes the practical value that comes not only from a combination of the formal (or planned, or heavy) and Agile approaches together, but also from a symbiosis of Agility across all of the organizational layers. The CAMS approach is thus not only a method and its combination but also a strategy. In CAMS, organizations can follow a sequence of steps to create their own instances of process, which require metrics and measurements to estimate, monitor, and evaluate from the perspective of product and process (Unhelkar, 2010).

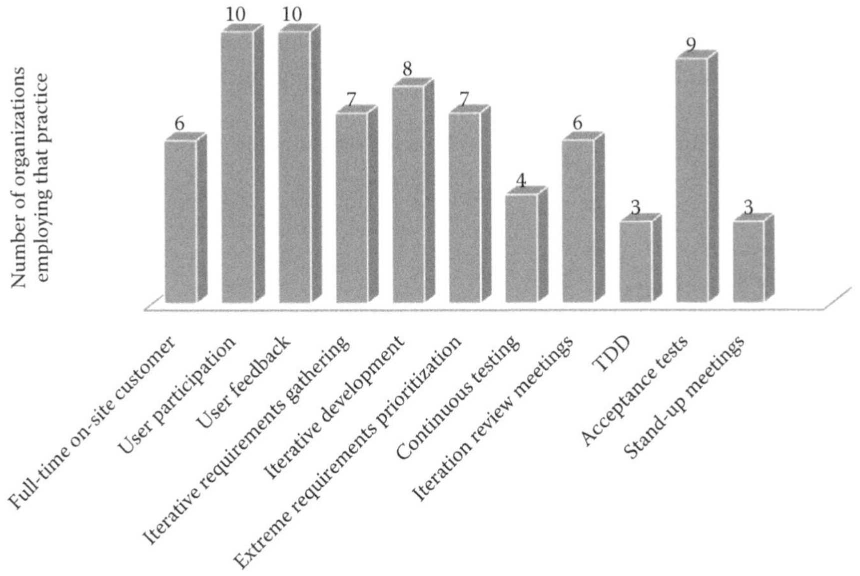

Figure 1.9 Agile practices in studied organizations.

Figure 1.9 highlights the Agile practices in the organizations studied through the interview process. The number of organizations employing a specific Agile practice, discovered through the interview process, are shown in the bar chart. For example, only six out of the ten organizations "interviewed" have a full-time customer (or end user) on-site, although all 10 organizations subscribed to user participation and user feedback.

These aforementioned research attempts led to the development of CAMS, which extends and builds on top of the existing principles and practice of Agile. (A detailed exposition of CAMS can be found in Chapter 4.) The Agile principles and practices based on the Agile Manifesto, together with the understanding derived from practice (in terms of how real-life projects use methods), provided an excellent basis for CAMS. Very soon, it was also discovered that the comprehensive Agile approach goes beyond software development and is applicable in operational optimization, business management, governance, customer care, and people management (HR). Agility has become an organizational value and culture rather than just a method.

Conclusions

This chapter broadly outlined the methods in an organization. Agile was discussed as an entire value system and culture in addition to being a development approach at the software level. Chapter 2 develops the understanding of Agile as a suite of methods.

Agile in Practice: Road Map 1

- Identify the current suite of methods and processes in your organization.
- List the challenges of time, budget, functionality, and quality within an important project in your organization.

- What are the crucial "methods friction" elements within your project (and organization)? These can be identified by listing the areas of work where one method (e.g., an IT governance framework) demands formal and in-depth documentation, whereas another method (e.g., XP) permits minimal documentation.
- Discuss and document the opportunities to introduce a composite approach within your organization.

Discussion Questions

- What is the difference between business agility and software agility? (Discuss with examples from your own work environment.)
- What are the limitations of a formal SDLC in practice?
- What are the potential challenges of a pure Agile approach in practice?
- How would you separate Agile methods and practices into art, craft, and engineering?
- What are the various modeling spaces within organizations? (These modeling spaces may not be easily delineated, yet they exist and it is worth identifying them.)
- Why do you think a Composite Agile Method should also be a strategy?
- How can a method framework empower delivery of software?
- How can a timely delivery of software enhance business agility?
- What is an Agile Manifesto?
- What are Agile principles and how are they used in creating Agile practices?
- Does identification of risks within a project also relate to risks associated with business outcomes? How do the two differ?
- Are your projects monetized to business outcomes or monetized by cost estimates of delivery? What is the difference between the two from an ROI calculation viewpoint? What tools and techniques have you come across to align soft skills within software delivery?

References

Abrahamsson, P., O. Salo, J. Ronkainen, and J. Warsta, *Agile Software Development Methods. Review and Analysis*, Vol. 478, VTT Publications, Espoo, 2002.

Beck, K., Fred Taylor, making software, and conversation. *CSE'00 Software Productivity in a Changing World, and JAOO Conference*, Aarhus, Denmark, September 2000.

Beck, K., *Extreme Programming Explained: Embrace Change*, Addison-Wesley, Reading, MA, 2000.

Beck, K., *Test Driven Development: By Example,* Addison-Wesley Longman, 2002.

Bird, C., Scaling Agile—Part 1, EMC consulting Blogs—Colin Bird's blog, viewed May 2012, http://consultingblogs.emc.com/colinbird/.

Boehm, B., A spiral model of software development and enhancement, *Software Engineering Project Management*, 128–142, 1987.

Boehm, B., Get ready for Agile methods, with care, *IEEE Computer*, 64–69, 2002.

Brown, W., R. Malveau, S. McCormick, III, and T. Mowbray, *Anti Patterns: Refactoring Software, Architectures, and Projects in Crisis*, John Wiley & Sons, Inc., 1998.

Chapman, J.R., Software development methodology, 2007, viewed 3 September 2009, http://www.hyperthot.com/pm_sdm.htm.

Cockburn, A., 2004, *Crystal Clear: A Human-Powered Methodology for Small Teams*, Addison-Wesley.

Cockburn, A. and J. Highsmith, Agile software development: The people factor, *Computer*, 131–133, November, 2001.

Coffin, R. and D. Lane, *A Practical Guide to Seven Agile Methodologies, Part 1*, Jupitermedia Corporation, 2007, viewed 29 September 2009, http://www.devx.com/architect/Article/32761/1954.

Fowler, M., *Analysis Patterns: Reusable Object Models*, Addison-Wesley Longman, Reading, MA, 1997.

Fowler, M. and J. Highsmith, The Agile manifesto, Tech Web, 2001, viewed 9 March 2009, http://www.ddj.com/architect/184414755.

Gamma, E., R. Helm, R. Johnson, and J. Vlissides, *Design Patterns: Elements of Reusable Object-Oriented Software*, Addison-Wesley Longman Professional, Reading, MA, 1995.

Gardner, K., A. Rush, M. Crist, R. Konitzer, and B. Teegarden, *Cognitive Patterns: Problem-Solving Frameworks for Object Technology*, Cambridge University Press, 1998.

Gat, I. and H. Smits, Cutter webinar entitled Big Agile is more than just a software method, http://theagileexecutive.com/2012/01/22/big-agile/.

Ginige, A., Re engineering software development process for e-business application development, *5th International Conference on Software Engineering and Knowledge Engineering*, San Francisco, CA, 2003. Work is in progress with Ginige at the University of Western Sydney.

Glass, R., *Software Runaways: Lessons Learned from Massive Software Project Failures*, Prentice-Hall, 1997. *Software Runaways* remains as a classic reminder of major software disasters, with and without methodologies.

Highsmith, J.A., *Adaptive Software Development: A Collaborative Approach to Managing Complex Systems*, Dorset House, New York, 2000, 392pp.

Manifesto for Agile software development, 2001, viewed 9 March 2009, http://www.agilemanifesto.org/.

Palmer, S.R. and J.M. Felsing, *A Practical Guide to Feature-Driven Development*, Prentice Hall, Upper Saddle River, NJ, 2002.

Royce, W.W., Managing the development of large software systems, *Tutorial: Software Engineering Project Management*, IEEE Computer Society, Washington, DC, pp. 118–127, 1970.

Schwaber, K. and M. Beedle. *Agile Software Development with Scrum*, Prentice Hall, Upper Saddle River, NJ, 2001.

Stapleton, J., *DSDM, Dynamic Systems Development Method: The Method in Practice*, Addison-Wesley, Reading, MA, 1997.

Stober, T. and U. Hansmann, *Agile Software Development: Best Practices for Large Software Development Projects*, Springer, Berlin; London, 2009.

Unhelkar, B., *After the Y2K Fireworks*, CRC Press, Boca Raton, FL, 1999.

Unhelkar, B., *Process Quality Assurance for UML-Based Projects*, Pearson Education (Addison-Wesley), Boston, 2003.

Unhelkar, B., Agile in practice: A composite approach, *Cutter Executive Report*, 11 (1), 2010.

Yourdon, E., *Rise and Resurrection of the American Programmer*, Yourdon Press, 1997.

Chapter 2

Landscape of Agile and Planned Methods

Objectives

- Discuss the "stability–agility" dichotomy of methods in the context of business and software
- Provide an overview of prevalent Agile methods used in software development, including their comparison and impact on delivery
- Understand the commonalities among prevalent Agile methods to enable abstraction of common practices that can be used by both business and software initiatives within the organization
- Relate the Agile methods to the Agile Manifesto in order to understand the foundation of these Agile methods
- Present an overview of the life cycles of planned methods (waterfall, spiral) to understand their foundation
- Outline a metamodel that would form the basis of a process (in this case, eventually, of a composite process)
- Consider a practical Agile manifesto that would replace the keyword "over" by "together with"

Introduction

This chapter begins with a discussion on the conceptual background to Agile methods, which provides an understanding of the reasons for the phenomenal popularity of these methods. An overview of Agile methods presented in this chapter provides completeness to the discussion on Agility and how it is currently being used in practice. The discussion on contemporary Agile methods also paves the path for understanding its challenges (as discussed in Chapter 3) and the formation of a composite Agile approach (part of the discussion in Chapter 4). The Agile Manifesto, the cornerstone of all Agile methods, is also discussed here. A pragmatic approach to Agile methods indicates that the manifesto can be fine-tuned to reflect what is experienced by many practitioners of Agile in real life. This chapter focuses on expanding, refining, and building on our current understanding of Agility from a very practical viewpoint.

The phrase "Agile method" often tends to be used as a proper noun—a specific method. In reality, Agile is a generic name that represents a family or suite of methods that subscribe to the Agile Manifesto. Thus, there is a necessity to understand the generic nature of Agile methods based on the manifesto and exhibiting the principles and values of Agile. There is also a need to summarize some of the well-known Agile methods in software and nonsoftware enterprises. Starting with a summary of the contemporary Agile methods, this chapter undertakes a comparison of these methods. The idea behind the comparison is to understand the differences among these methods as well as to abstract the commonalities among them. Such comparison will provide the basis for delving into the advantages and challenges of Agile in practice—which is undertaken in Chapter 3.

The discussion in this chapter is also complemented by a discussion on the life cycles of planned methods. Thus, there is a discussion of the waterfall, spiral, and fountain models of software development, followed by a discussion on process maps as components of processes and the elements that make up such process maps. A brief metamodel for a process is presented here to substantiate the discussion.

This chapter emphasizes the balance between the theoretical backdrop of Agility and the corresponding practical viewpoint. This, in turn, leads to a balanced investigation of the value provided by both the Agile approach and the planned approach. Underlying these discussions is also the fact that business, overall, is interested in business agility and that software agility is only a means to an end and not an end in itself.

Defining Agile

Agile can be considered as an umbrella term representing a suite of software development methodologies (or *processes*, as they are occasionally called). These software development methodologies are lightweight in terms of their rigor, less focused on planning, relatively thin on documentation, and primarily reliant on people and their interactions. Cottmeyer and Stevens (2009) describe these Agile processes as being made up of a steady input of a suite of prioritized requirements that are fed to the software development team. The team accordingly responds to these requirements by delivering the software at the end of the time interval agreed upon. There is considerable amount of subjectivity in Agile methods, since some of their discriminatory characteristics include trust, collaboration, and courage. The nimbleness accorded to both software development and business processes from the use of such Agile methods arises from their overbearing focus on outcomes and values. The "value" persuasion characterizes an Agile project right from the outset.

Agile approaches encourage people to bring forth whatever is in their minds for display on a "wall," literally "pasting" their models or thought processes using "sticky notes" or "3 in. × 5 in. cards." The "conversational" paradigm (discussed in Chapter 1—see Figure 1.6) comes alive in an Agile approach. This dynamic approach to projects eschews the large amount of documentation produced in formal or planned approaches. It is largely evident that such an approach to projects finds value not only in development of software but also in many other nonsoftware projects.

Figure 2.1 represents the dichotomy between stability and agility as applicable to business and software. While the formal methods and processes provide the necessary stability to both business and software development, Agile approaches enable rapid changes in both these areas of work. As shown in Figure 2.1, business agility is different from software agility. Also, it is business agility

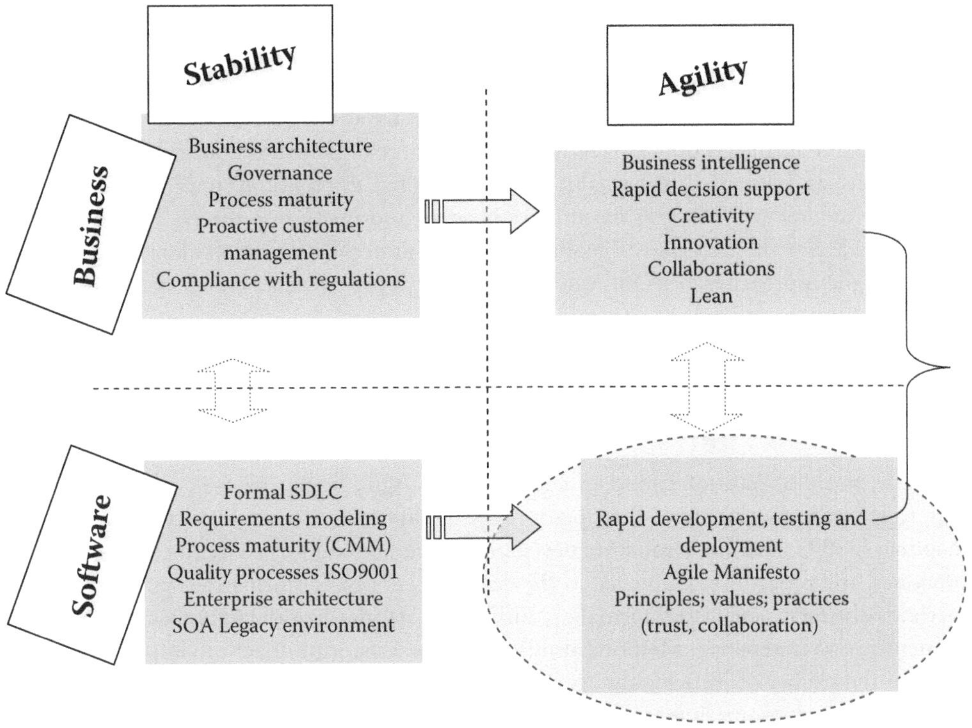

Figure 2.1 Relating Agility to business stability.

that is of great importance to key stakeholders in any software or nonsoftware project. Business finds stability through architecture, business process maturity, and compliance with regulations. Business agility is derived through business intelligence, collaborations, creativity, and innovations. Software stability is achieved through formality of SDLC and quality standard; whereas software Agility subscribes to the Agile Manifesto.

SIDEBAR

Software stability can be attributed to formal software development life cycles (SDLCs), software process maturity (through CMMI), and ISO9001 quality standards. Software agility, as discussed for the most part in this chapter, is based on the concepts of rapid development and deployment with bare minimal design and documentation. Given the comparative "informality" of Agile approaches, there is an understandable skepticism among methodologists and project managers that such an approach may not work in many projects that are large, that is, made up of many roles and people particularly if they are physically dispersed. The informality of the Agile approach provides significant positive value when it is used by a group of well-aligned, self-motivated individuals. However, not all projects are privy to such individuals. It is therefore necessary to apply pure Agile with considerable care and consideration, with due respect to the formal or planned elements of a project.

By its very definition, Agility is based on trust, interactions, and collaborations with the end users and customers. Geographically dispersed projects are bound to encounter challenges that, for example, "trust" can present, as team members may not have enough time and opportunity to build trust. Organizing teams on a formal basis, forming iterations, and undertaking development based on prioritization of stories provides a sound starting point for the application of Agility to larger and more complex, dispersed projects. Nonetheless, the sheer importance of agility in business and software domains is such that, irrespective of the size and type of projects, one cannot do away with it. As Highsmith (2009) correctly says, "Can large organizations afford to be inflexible and unresponsive and does delivering value to customers fail to be important?" Application and value of agility in large projects is as essential as in small and medium projects. The question, of course, is "How?" For the best part, the answer appears to lie in striking a balance between the planned and Agile approaches. This indicates a composite approach that is the best fit not only for software projects but also for the organizations as a whole.

What Comprises Agile?

What exactly is Agile? As understood in contemporary Agile literature, it is a methodological approach to software development. But does it really qualify as a full and detailed method?

Chapman (2007) describes a software development methodology as a documented set of policies, processes, and procedures employed in the development of an information system. We know that methods abstract, generalize, formalize, unify, and standardize the approaches to software development and maintenance. Methods also isolate (or at least minimize) the impact of product quality from the caliber of individuals. As a result, methods equip the management to estimate the time, budget, and resources required for a project at an early stage of the project. This detailed description of what a method is does not seem to be fulfilled by pure Agile methods. Agile, as a suite of methods, is largely governed by a few fundamentals. A discussion on these fundamentals, or basics, is helpful in understanding Agility and how it adds significant value to practical work. An understanding of Agility is also helpful in discerning what is Agile and what is not.

The four concepts on which Agility is based are presented in Table 2.1.

Any method or approach that claims to be Agile needs to consider the basics outlined in Table 2.1. This means an Agile method should subscribe to the Agile Manifesto, be based on Agile values, should adhere to the Agile principles, and contains a suite of Agile practices that can be carried out by various roles within the project. It should be noted, though, that when applied in practice, these basics of Agility are not separable entities; rather, they all appear together when used in practice and are called an *Agile method.* The basics of Agility are discussed in detail in the following sections.

Table 2.1 The Concepts That Comprise an Agile Method

Concept	*Description*
The Agile Manifesto	Provides the fundamentals of Agile methods
The Agile values	Explain how the manifesto can be implemented through a culture and value system
The Agile principles	Provide role-based guidance to applying the Agile Manifesto and values in real projects
The Agile practices	Involve execution of actions that subscribe to the Agile principles and are carried out by specific project roles

Agile Manifesto

The Agile methods base themselves on the popular Agile Manifesto (Agile Manifesto, 2001; Fowler and Highsmith, 2001). This manifesto characterizes Agile as "a value statement and not a concrete plan or process" (Coffin and Lane, 2007) and thereby lays the foundation for the Agile values, priorities, and principles. The Agile Manifesto provides four value statements:

1. Individuals and interactions over processes and tools
2. Working software over comprehensive documentation
3. Customer collaboration over contract negotiation
4. Response to change over following a plan

In each of the four value statements, the manifesto emphasizes precedence of the first part of the statement over the second part. At the software development level, such methods do not subscribe to the detailed and standardized templates for documentation. Nor do they provide the step-by-step description of activities and tasks seen in planned development approaches. These Agile Manifesto statements attempt to counterbalance the earlier formal methodology-based emphasis on documentation, process steps, detailed plans, and contractually obligated development artifacts.

The latter half of the statements within the manifesto represents the erstwhile focus of traditional software development life cycle (SDLC) or waterfall-based methods. Many of these characteristics of the formal SDLC are largely ingrained in the object-oriented (OO) approaches to software development resulting in substantial documentation and modeling. Eventually, the maturity of these planned processes also became important, leading to its being measured on a five-part scale called Capability Maturity Model (CMM), discussed in detail in Chapter 9. The manifesto attempts to *bring* this overemphasis on documentation, tools, negotiation, and planning into balance by suggesting a trade-off between the four pairs of items.

Therefore, undoubtedly, the Agile Manifesto plays a crucial role in providing the basis for all Agile methods. The manifesto, put together by highly experienced methodologists, many of whom have hands-on development experience, frees up development efforts from the mandates of formal phases (e.g., analysis, design, code, and test) and deliverables (e.g., project plans, functional requirements, and test plans). Not that there is no formality in Agile methods, but the manifesto indicates the areas of a project that need greater importance than was given before.

Agile Values

The Agile values aspire for the minimal but necessary formal policies, processes, and procedures required for delivery of a product. Adhering to these values provides possibilities of faster reaction to change by the organization as compared with the traditional approaches and life cycles. Agile values enable the spreading and dissipation of Agility across an entire organization. Such dissipation results in an Agile culture for the organization rather than agility being restricted to a project.

As such, these Agile values form the basis for human resources (HR) activities such as recruitment of new personnel, development and up-skilling of existing staff, and an overall basis for the understanding and enhancement of Agility across the organization. As Agility moves toward a value system for the organization, these Agile values get applied holistically to almost all areas of an organization including information technology (IT), HR, accounts, payroll, marketing, sales, inventory, and so on. Furthermore, since these Agile values are closely intertwined with one another, uplifting one or two Agile values in an organization starts positively impacting other values as well. Changes in values result in an overall change to the "value system" of the organization and subsequently to projects. Similarly, if one or two specific individuals start exhibiting these values, it usually has a "flow-on" effect on other members of the team and eventually to the organization.

Agile Principles

The Agile Manifesto and values discussed so far provide a basis for the development and application of the principles of Agile. Agile methods tend to be developer-centric, starting with the developer writing part of the code and demonstrating it to users in an effort to engage them in a conversation. This interaction through the code further clarifies and illustrates the built-in requirements incorporated in the code. The Agile principles reflect this conversational paradigm in software development, which has potential way beyond software itself.

SIDEBAR

Agile as an iterative and incremental approach to software development is performed in a highly collaborative manner to produce high-quality software that meets the changing needs of its stakeholders (Ambler, 2006). Badr (2006) underscores the importance of the Agile approach to software development as a means to rapidly creating a product that will add immediate value to its end users (also discussed by Ghanbary [2010]).

A detailed description of these Agile principles follows. These principles align themselves to the Agile Manifesto. Following their description, these principles are categorized into four understandable groups.

1. Customer satisfaction: Project members give highest importance to providing customer satisfaction through early and continuous delivery of valuable software. This customer satisfaction is achieved by engaging the customer in regular, ongoing conversations. The time spell between requirements elicitation and demonstration of the output is shortened, thereby leading to rapid customer feedback. This principle shifts the focus of the project team from planning to one that incorporates rapid changes into development. When applied at an organizational level, this principle encourages every member of the organization to query their own actions and outputs to see whether they add value to the customer or end user. Any activity that does not add value to the customer needs to be scrutinized and corrected, or replaced.
2. Acceptance of changes: This Agile principle embraces change irrespective of when such change appears in the development process. While planned methods refused to accommodate changes especially when they occurred late in development, the Agile approach makes provision for that inevitable change and welcomes it when it occurs. In addition to accepting the changes that the customer (user) will ask for, this Agile principle encourages the teams following Agile approaches to harness the change for the customer's competitive advantage. There is a shift in the development paradigm through this principle. This is because the focus also shifts from contractual delivery of software to the one that works for the customer.
3. Frequent delivery: This principle promotes frequent delivery of working software that will start adding immediate value to the customer's goals. The frequency of delivery can range from weekly to a couple of months. The shorter timescale of delivery enables visibility,

absorption, and feedback by the customer. As the interval between planning and delivery reduces, the customer gets the opportunity to view and understand the product and suggest changes before the development is completed. There is also significant opportunity to improve the efficacy of the development work due to early feedback.

4. Collaboration between business and developer: Developers, users, and business stakeholders work together closely according to this principle. Such close collaboration results in a common understanding between the business problem and the corresponding solution that is meant to help the business. Such direct collaboration is far more valuable than written, contracted documents because it helps the individuals understand the implied meanings behind requirements. Furthermore, the all-important *context* in which those requirements are being stated becomes clearer through this collaboration.
5. Self-motivation of individuals: This principle suggests that projects should be based around people who are motivated and self-directed and who can be entrusted with getting the "job done." These individuals need to be provided with the right environment and support to deliver the solution. Thus, Agile projects give credence to the skills and enthusiasm of the individuals and leverage them to produce visible outcomes. Such self-motivation eliminates the need for minute planning of tasks and their tracking by project managers.
6. Face-to-face conversation: The principle of face-to-face conversations among various stakeholders creates a common understanding of the problem as well as the goal of the project. In particular, an on-site face-to-face conversation between the users and the developers is the most efficient and effective method of conveying information within the project. These conversations reduce misunderstandings and subjective interpretations and thereby reduce the eventual errors within the deliverables. Through face-to-face conversations, clarifications, and follow-up, questions are answered on the spot, thereby significantly enhancing communication and reducing rework. (See communication among team members in DeMarco and Lister, 1987.)
7. Working software: The working software (or product) is maintained in its executable form right from the start of an Agile project. So, when the final delivery of the product occurs, that delivery is only an increment over what was already a working piece of software. When an Agile project commences, the concentration of the team members is on the actual delivery of the working product that is also tested. Therefore, this Agile principle eschews extensive planning and managing individuals and, instead, ensures that a working product is available throughout. The principle shifts the focus from an individualistic style of working (which may change from individual to individual and may require detailed monitoring) to a contributory working style based on sharing of tasks and responsibilities.
8. Sustainable development: Agile aspires for ease in development resulting from collaboration and communication among the sponsors, developers, and users. This opens up opportunities for long-term sustainable, even-paced development. According to this principle, software (or any product, for that matter) should be produced through a work–life balance rather than excessive hours every week. Owing to less friction and reduction in wastage of energy, such a balanced approach to development invariably leads to a development and maintenance effort that can be continued over a long time period. The *Unhurried* value alluded to in Table 2.2 is the one that can be said to form the basis for this principle.
9. Technical excellence: This principle promotes regular and ongoing attention to technical details that would result in excellence in design and development. This principle brings together the motivation of the individuals and their technical know-how to bring to fruition the product resulting from an Agile project. Technical excellence encourages individuals

Table 2.2 Core Agile Values and Behaviors (as Expected within an Agile Organization)

Values	*Description*
Trustworthiness	Ability to generate trust through consistency, reliability, and quality of work. Having respect for and valuing each member of the team, thereby creating working relationships that are less dependent on formal "role descriptions" and more reliant on each other through trust
Value focus	Ability to determine values and outcomes within projects, especially focusing on customer values by continuously asking the question, "How does my work add value to the key stakeholders?" Team members in Agile projects are thus engaged in productive work that can be traced as value to the end user or customer
Collaboration	Ability to work in a collaborative manner with various roles and at different levels within the organization to achieve the common goals of a project. The collaborative value of Agility extends beyond projects and throughout the organization leading to collaboration among different departments and, eventually, also among organizations
Facilitation	Ability to encourage multiple stakeholders to provide their inputs in order to achieve an outcome. Sensitivity to project dynamics and ability to overcome challenges through conversations, explanations, clarifications, and astute questioning is a hallmark of this value as exhibited by Agile project team members. Facilitation also includes negotiation among team members for improved output
Transparency	Ability to articulate thoughts, ideas, and values in a clear, unambiguous, and direct manner. Ability to share information, knowledge, and skills through various communication mechanisms and ensuring minimal hidden agendas. Thus transparency complements trust and vice versa
Courage	Ability to question status quos and "accepted norms" within projects and organizations, particularly in their "business as usual" state. Courage is valuable in enabling individuals and teams to accept mistakes, step out of their comfort zone, and, most importantly, to be ready to start afresh
Self-organization	Ability to manage own tasks with minimal (or no) supervision. This is a vital value in Agile projects as it enables facilitation and leadership to emerge as against the mundane "task management" as undertaken in formal projects. Self-organization implies team members are well synchronized with each other, with the project, and with organizational goals
Learning ability	Ability to be continually curious, inquisitive, and in a learning frame of mind. This ability is an important Agile value that enables team members to be responsible for learning and growing through personal involvement and commitment to the project. This value enables not only individual members to learn the techniques and technologies, but also the Agile coaches (and facilitators) to come up with improved metrics and estimates

Table 2.2 (*Continued*)

Values	*Description*
Unhurriedness	This is not a published Agile value thus far. However, the author's experience is that when a project is driven by values and not by tasks, the entire gestalt of the project changes for the better. Work is shared and carried out for the value it adds and not as a task to be completed. This also results in an unhurried work environment (akin to slow food as against fast food, resulting in significant enhancement of good-quality output). "Go slow in order to Go fast" summarizes this value for the author in practice

to take up the opportunity and the challenge of excelling in technologies. This individual technical brilliance is encouraged in terms of exploring and applying new technologies to the solution, ongoing improvement of code and design, regular testing, and incorporation of feedback from the customer within the solution.

10. Simplicity in design: This Agile principle, relating to the design of a system, has been based on an understanding that complex systems are never designed or developed as complex systems from the outset. Even the most complex system needs to start off as a simple, basic system with basic constructs. While complexity is inevitable, the principle dictates a simple start to it. Furthermore, complexity is hidden from end users and customers who are themselves not interested in the intricacies of design but, rather, on the actual solution.
11. Self-organized teams: This Agile principle encourages the formation of the "Utopian" teams that Constantine talked about in *Peopleware* (discussed in detail in Chapter 8 on managing Agile projects). These are the teams that require minimal supervision as the team members align themselves to a common goal and produce excellent outputs. The effort required in managing a team is better utilized in easing the team's function, and reduced supervision inculcates a higher degree of trust. The team strives to live up to the trust placed on it by the business as well as the manager.
12. Reflection: This is an important Agile principle that encourages teams to review and reflect on their output at regular intervals. As a result of this, teams are able to adjust their activities and fine-tune their output. Such teams plan dynamically and collaboratively to improve the way the resources, namely, people, processes, and technologies, are being used. Reflection also encourages team members to consider the many architectural, design, operational, and functional constructs resulting from previous projects that can easily feed into the current project and help improve the quality of the output.

A practical way to remember these principles is to group them on the basis of their context. Each principle can be understood in the context in which it operates. The groupings provide the context. This context makes it easier to remember the principles and, at the same time, convert them into Agile practices. Agile practices, based on the principles and their context, can also be made to fit on a 3 in. × 5 in. card and used as a cue by the user. Such grouping of Agile principles is shown in Figure 2.2. These groups of Agile principles can be summarized as follows:

- Customer-centric: These principles are focused on the external aspect of a project and they encourage provisioning of value to the end user.

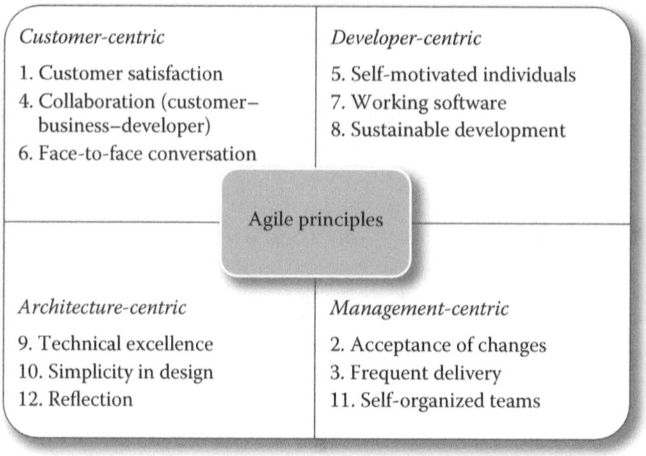

Figure 2.2 Contextual groups for Agile principles.

- Developer-centric: These principles are focused internally on a project and they enable the team members to function effectively and efficiently.
- Architecture-centric: These principles provide the basis for work that provides stability and ongoing improvement in the product as well as working style of the team.
- Management-centric: These principles enable the team to focus on organizing itself to reduce administrative overheads of time and effort, and at the same time enhance their working style.

SIDEBAR

While these principles are espoused here under the "Agile" banner, in fact, these principles benefit all practical work that happens in an organization. Agile approaches to software development have popularized these principles, but they have been important in projects and organizations much before Agile appeared as a method. Agile practices are based on these Agile principles. Transitioning to and applying the Agile principles across an organization and developing relevant Agile practices around them is the most beneficial way of using them.

These principles of Agile, in practice, influence not only Agile projects but the rest of the organization as well. Many of these principles influence the planned activities going on in a project or organization. Table 2.3 summarizes these Agile principles together with their Agile- and planned-method interpretations.

Agile Methods Landscape

Methodologies (or methods—although, strictly speaking they are not the same) play a crucial role in a large project. There are myriad variables in a large project including people, technologies, risks, changing requirements, and fluctuating stakeholders, to name a few. These variables are far too many to be handled by a single person in the role of a project manager. Also, if the project requires a group of developers to work together, then coordinating and managing their tasks together with the demands of the customer becomes a highly complex job.

Table 2.3 Interpreting Agile Principles in the Context of Both Agile and Planned Methods

Agile Principles	*Agile-Method Interpretation*	*Planned-Method Interpretation*
Customer satisfaction	Focused on satisfying customers through close collaboration and making value judgments on customer expectations through early and continuous delivery of valuable software	Customers do not know their expectations; formal descriptions of what they know and what they expect have to be carried out before development of the product can begin. Variance in expectation needs to be tightly controlled
Adaptive processes	Welcome changing requirements, even late in development and also change/adapt the process and practices to accommodate those changes. Harnessing of processes to provide customer with competitive advantage	Extension and frequency of change can derail a large project wherein requirements and development are separate phases through necessity
Rapid delivery	Deliver working software frequently, from a couple of weeks to a couple of months, with a preference to the shorter timescale	Rapid delivery may not have considered the cross impact of that delivery on subsequent deliveries of modules
Collaboration	Business people and developers must work together daily throughout the project	Collaboration during development is not the same as during maintenance, where the challenge is to understand what has been developed and deployed
Motivated individuals	Build projects around motivated individuals. Give them the environment and support they need, and trust them to get the job done	It is not always easy to get a group of self-motivated individuals. Also, how are team members to be rewarded for their effort?
Face-to-face communication	The most efficient and effective method of conveying information to and within a development team is through face-to-face conversation	In the era of globally dispersed projects, this principle may not be easy to uphold. Formal documentation and contracts can reduce the need for face-to-face physical communication
Working software	Working software is the primary measure of progress—as against documentation and modeling	Working software is the result of considerable modeling and design. Walk-through of these nonworking artifacts is an important contributor to quality

continued

Table 2.3 (*Continued*)

Agile Principles	*Agile-Method Interpretation*	*Planned-Method Interpretation*
Paced and sustainable development	Agile processes promote sustainable development. The sponsors, developers, and users should be able to maintain a constant pace indefinitely	Sustainable and unhurried development is relatively easily implemented for "in-house" projects. For external, contracted projects such pacing is difficult to implement
Technical excellence	Continuous attention to technical excellence and good design enhances agility	Large, third-party projects cannot always rely on individual technical excellence. Average talents also need to be used in these projects
Simplicity in design	Simplicity—the art of minimizing the amount of work done—is essential	While every design should start simplistically, almost all practical projects quickly become complex. Make provision for complexity through documentation, modeling, and detailed architecture
Self-organized team	The best architectures, requirements, and designs emerge from self-organized teams. Team members here depend not only on their own skills but also on their ability to be part of the team. Like-minded, highly motivated, and equally skilled professionals align themselves willingly to the commonly accepted goals of delivery, to produce the end results	Self-organization is not easily available. In fact, lack of self-organization was one of the root causes the software world moved to planned, heavyweight processes and their maturity indexes in the first place
Reflective development	At regular intervals, the team reflects on how to become more effective, then tunes and adjusts its behavior accordingly	Reflection needs to be documented to enable it to be of use to team members beyond those that are reflecting

In Chapter 1, the following variables were discussed and shown as usually vying against one another in a project: time, budget, functionality, and quality. Balancing these four variables together with the interests of various stakeholders is a complex process within any project. Furthermore, these project variables continue to occur in subsequent projects as well. Therefore, there is a pressing need to learn from previous attempts at software development, then abstract and enshrine these lessons in a discipline. This is where methods come into play. Methods are formed out of abstraction of experience, its generalization, and eventually its formalization through documentation. Agile methods, as mentioned earlier, do not subscribe to the entire discipline of formal software methods.

Besides, sponsors of software projects are the key business stakeholders who are more interested in agility at an organizational level rather than an Agile software development approach. Business agility at an organizational level was described in Chapter 1 as a time measure of changes to the operating environment of the business and the time it takes for an organization to respond to that change (Chapman, 2007). An Agile organization will be able to quickly respond to a change in the environment. With an increasing rate of change in the environment in which the business exists, there can be a corresponding reduction in the agility of the organization as it may not be able to keep up with the changes. Methods have a responsibility to bridge the gap between a software project's agility and the overall agility of the organization.

SIDEBAR

Agile methods, in particular, bring about nimbleness in software development whose ultimate goal should be to accord the much needed agility to a business organization. Agile methods, as understood today, are primarily developer-centric approaches to software development. They embrace high rates of change within the development cycle primarily through high visibility of the development activities and keeping those activities loosely dependent on each other. Change requests from the users are directly incorporated by the developer within the code.

Iterating the activities in order to incrementally produce the deliverable is at the heart of the Agile approach to software development. Figure 2.3 shows the basis of these iterations, which are integral to Agile.

A project is started by planning a suite of releases. Each release is made up of one or more iterations with the developer writing a part of the code. Demonstration of this code is then used in engaging the user in a "conversation" that will further explain the requirements. This conversation is the new paradigm of software development based on the basic discipline of software development, expounded by Beck (discussed in Chapter 1). Agile iteration—a short burst of time—undertakes a small piece of development, tests its efficacy, reflects on the results, and adapts the behavior appropriately. This positively impacts both the customer's expectation and the product's technical quality. In a rapidly changing business environment, the value of each iteration is derived from its continuous integration with all previous iterations and releases, as well as from other products and systems that the current development is required to interface with. Agile principles such as self-organizing teams and self-motivated individuals come into play in iterative development as they enable iterations to be crafted and carried out with minimal administrative (management) overheads. Thus, Agile, lightweight approaches require excellence and synergy among high-caliber individuals.

Many Agile methods subscribing to the Agile Manifesto have emerged recently. Some of these have been quite popular and well accepted by the developers. Customers (users), who see the advantages of visible development, are also highly supportive of these approaches. Table 2.4 lists

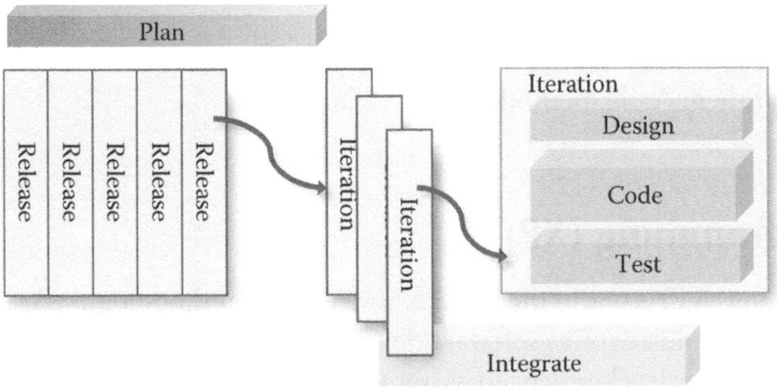

Figure 2.3 Iterative development at the core of Agile.

Table 2.4 Summary of Popular Agile Methods

Agile Method	*Comment and Characteristic*
Extreme programming (XP) by Beck (1999)	The first Agile method. Based on simple programming principles. Entirely focused on individuals
Scrum (Schwaber, 1995; Schwaber and Beedle, 2002)	More sophisticated and elaborate than other Agile methods. Focuses on providing business value through demonstration and prioritization. The daily and 2- to 4-week cycles work well in practice
Crystal (Cockburn, 2004)	A family of methods applicable to varying development scenarios depending on size and criticality. Claims relevance from 6 to 200 developers. The range varies, depending on Essential Money, Discretionary Money, and Comfort in Crystal.
Feature-driven development (FDD) (Palmer and Felsing, 2002)	Lends itself to combination with other methods. Based around selection and integration of various development techniques to deliver features
Adaptive software development (Highsmith, 2000)	Continuously adopts/modifies the process to cater to the rapidly changing development situation. Revolves around the Speculate–Collaborate–Learn phases
Dynamic systems development method (Stapleton, 1997)	An iterative and incremental approach with heavy emphasis on continuous user involvement
Test-driven development (Beck, 2002)	Test-driven development requires developers to create the tests that the code is supposed to satisfy. Passing the tests confirms that development and refactoring can follow
Lean software development*	Focused on gathering the "right" requirements and measured on the basis of their impact on the business. Lean is mainly based on the "root-cause"-oriented approach
Agile Unified Process (AUP)*	AUP is the Agile adaptation of the UP and stresses on high-risk elements being prioritized early in development. Summarized as "serial in the large, iterative in the small, [and] delivering instrumental releases over time"

these Agile methods and their corresponding unique characteristics. This is followed by a brief discussion of each of these Agile methods.

Extreme Programming (XP)*

Extreme programming (XP) is one of the better known Agile methodologies. As its name suggests it is a lightweight, flexible, and adaptive software development (ASD) method that claims to take the "best practices of software development to extreme levels" (Beck, 2000). Being developer-centric,

* http://www.ambysoft.com/unifiedprocess/agileUP.html. Site owned by Scott Ambler.

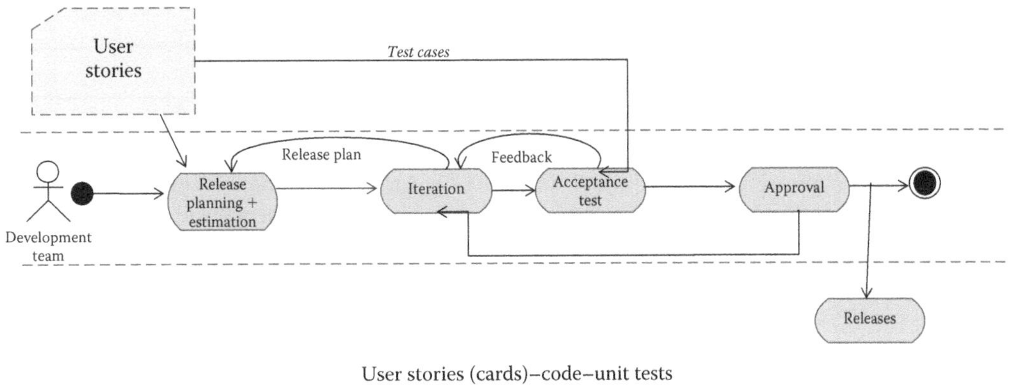

Figure 2.4 Extreme programming (XP) in practice.

XP emphasizes technical practices to promote skillful development through frequent delivery of working software. The relationship between customers and developers is encouraged within XP. Figure 2.4 shows the overall process followed in projects using XP. The requirements within XP are derived from user stories that are usually documented using 3 in. × 5 in. cards or post-it notes. Iterations of development are carried out, closely followed by corresponding acceptance tests. As also shown in Figure 2.4, user stories form the basis for user acceptance test cases.

XP welcomes change by enabling customers to provide ongoing inputs and establishing harmonious work environments (Beck and Fowler, 2001; esic-solutions.com; also see Extreme programming workshop http://www.cutter.com.ezproxy.lib.uts.edu.au/workshops/32.html).

One of the characteristic distinctions between XP and other methodologies is its cycle time and level of ceremony. XP recommends very short iterations between 1 and 4 weeks. XP is also a very low ceremony methodology. The minimal artifacts in an XP project include story cards, code, and unit tests.*

XP is also characterized by the Agile values discussed earlier. These XP values are communication, simplicity, feedback, and courage. These four values together determine the style of development (Beck and Fowler, 2001) and are strictly adhered to in XP projects.

1. Communication: Communication encourages the right type and mechanism for exchange of ideas. Practices such as unit testing, pair programming, and task estimation are based on good communication between the team members (Beck and Fowler, 2001).
2. Simplicity: XP claims that developing a simple task and changing it as required in the future is a better practice than putting in the effort of developing a complex task right at the beginning (Beck, 2000). As early as in 1992, Booch (1992) had stated that complex systems cannot be developed from scratch. Only simple systems can be planned and developed, and these would evolve into complex systems.
3. Feedback: Feedback on progress gives the team information on the time needed to complete a task, release, or system. Feedback on estimation and work provides information for improvement (Jeffries et al., 2000). Effective feedback is part of effective communication.
4. Courage: Courage is the ability to accept personal and team limitations. Examples of courage, as a value, includes discarding code that does not work or working to an 8-hour time box rather than for indefinite hours. Courage, however, needs to be tempered by project realities.

* Schwaber, K. and M. Beedle, http://www.methodsandtools.com/archive/scrum1.gif.

Table 2.5 Major XP Practices and Corresponding Practical Issues

Practice	*Description*	*Practical Issues*
The planning game	Determine the scope of the next release by considering business priorities and technical estimations. Update the plan when it changes	Difficult to determine the scope because of lack of formal planning. Similarly, estimations become a challenge, especially in outsourced projects
Small release	Develop a very small system simply and quickly and then expand the system in a direction that provides most business value—this is akin to the prototype-based approach, except that the prototype itself evolves into the system	Can become challenging especially in outsourced projects where the development is happening away from where the customer is
Metaphor	Direct all development simply on the whole system functionality	Creating a single metaphor for the whole project is difficult. People from different backgrounds will need different metaphors
Simple design	Make the design of the system as simple as possible to start with. It is the "whiteboard prototype" of the design itself that clarifies the context for the code	Leads to minimal requirements specification and architectural mistakes
Testing	Write unit test cases prior to coding as they clarify the purpose of the code to the developer	Creating tests for old code or outsourced code is time consuming
Refactoring	Restructure the system with no modification in its behavior	Refactoring may cause change in the schedule. Making changes to existing code interfaces might affect quality
Pair programming	This is best understood in practice as having one programmer focus on the functional aspect and another on the technical (code) aspect of the development. The roles can be swapped almost on a daily basis	Finding suitable balance of experience to satisfy both programmers is challenging for managers. It is an expensive practice that might reduce productivity
Collective ownership	Code and development is a shared task; therefore there is no time limit on any team member changing the code	Requires phenomenal trust and also stability of roles. Team members cannot move in shared tasks, but that is precisely what happens in reality

Table 2.5 (*Continued*)

Practice	*Description*	*Practical Issues*
Continuous integration	Continuous integration and testing of the system throughout the development requiring the developer to keep the code in working order throughout the development	Project manager must ensure that there are sufficient resources always available to allow integration by all programmers
40-hour week	Work only for 40 hours per week	When the team has schedule pressure this practice is almost impossible
On-site customer	Involve a customer representative full time in the project	Programmers and customer must learn to interact. Customers must learn to formulate and write acceptance tests
Coding standards	Write code in accordance with rules emphasizing communication through the code	Programmers must learn to work with other people's codes and follow the rules

Finally, XP is also characterized by a number of practices that are themselves based on the aforementioned values. These XP practices and their corresponding challenges are listed in Table 2.5.

Scrum

Scrum is a lightweight process that employs iterative and incremental practices (Schwaber and Beedle, 2001; also see footnote[†]). Highly popular in the Agile space, Scrum aims to provide immediate value to the customer, which then becomes a value stream through the incremental development cycle. The Scrum life cycle is shown as a process flow in Figure 2.5. The typical monthly cycle starts by getting the whole team together to set a shared and achievable goal. The team is then expected to *sprint* toward this goal, ensuring that its product increment matches up to the stated goal at the end of the period. Scrum projects are characterized by daily stand-up meetings that resynchronize the team with the sprint goal.[*]

Scrum is results oriented rather than effort driven. Throughout its sprint, the team maintains visible charts that make its progress visible to everyone so anyone can instantly see how it is doing, thus adhering to openness as one of its key principles, in practice.

Scrum may also be considered as a project management framework for managing the system development process of Agile projects. However, Scrum does not provide any particular development techniques for the implementation phase. Instead, Scrum focuses on the "facilitation" of the project team to produce flexible systems that provide the highest business value. That is the reason Scrum is used in many non-IT projects as well. Scrum is made up of roles, artifacts, meetings, and flow—as shown in Figure 2.5 and as briefly described next.

[*] http://www.devx.com/architect/Article/32836.

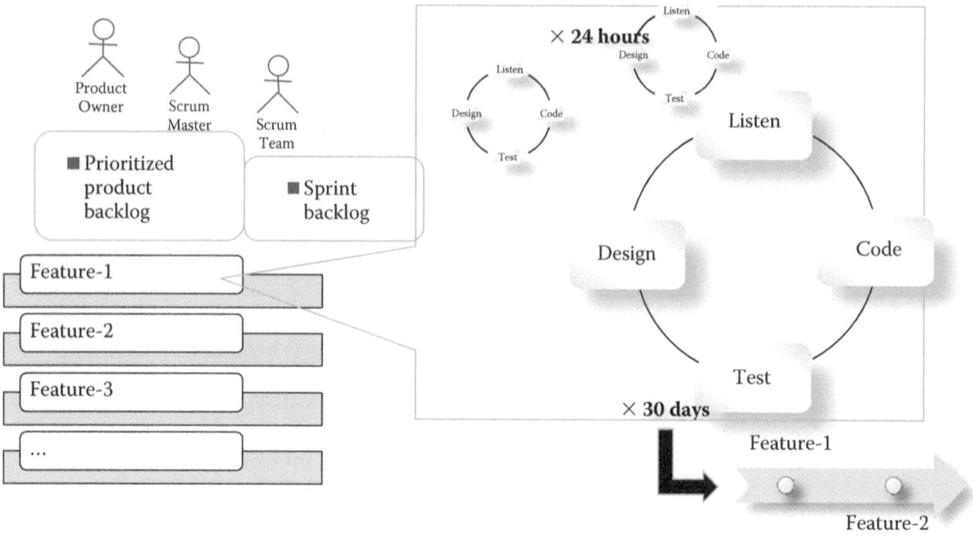

Figure 2.5 Scrum life cycle in practice. (Based on Schwaber K. and Beedle M., *Agile Software Development with Scrum*, Prentice Hall, Upper Saddle River, http://www.methodsandtools.com/archive/scrum1.gif, 2001.)

Roles

There are three different roles in Scrum. These roles include Scrum Master, Product Owner, and Scrum Team.

A *Scrum Master* is responsible for ensuring that the team follows the Scrum rules. She facilitates the removal of obstacles and interruptions from the team so that the Scrum Team can do its job without distractions. The role of a Scrum Master can be played typically by an experienced software engineer who is an interface between the management and the Scrum Team and manages the processes (Schwaber and Beedle, 2001). The Scrum Master is focused on facilitation rather than management—as against a project manager who is involved in detailed planning, resourcing, and budgeting of the team.

A *Product Owner* represents the business to the team and manages the return on investment by prioritizing the work. He is the stakeholders' representative who approves the changes to the product backlog. The Product Owner is in charge of getting the requirements and planning the releases (Cho, 2008). The equivalent of this role in a formal high-ceremony approach is the user representative. While the user representative provides the input into requirements, unlike in an Agile approach such as Scrum, the user representative is not always on board with the development.

A *Scrum Team* usually consists of a cross-functional group of 5–10 people who work on the principle of self-organization. A Scrum Team is thus egalitarian with the focus of the team being a commitment to getting the work done. The Scrum Team is thus responsible for planning its own work, tracking it, and taking full responsibility for the outcomes. As a result, should there be a project manager in such a team, his focus will be outward to the team. He would take responsibility for fostering cooperation with other teams in the organization, managing external expectations, and also, as and when required, maintaining project budgets and accounts.

Artifacts

Scrum also encompasses three artifacts. These artifacts include the product backlog, the sprint backlog, and the sprint burn down chart.

The *product backlog* is a high-level document that contains list of all the required features and a good-to-have features. Furthermore, the product backlog includes features that are prioritized by business value. The product backlog may also contain technology features (e.g., nonfunctional requirements) that may be prioritized by a combination of business and technology needs.

The *sprint backlog* is derived from the overall product backlog. This document, put together by team members, contains information about the features and how to implement them in the current sprint. A sprint can be considered as a time-boxed iteration focusing on a list of goals. Team members also estimate the required time for completing each feature in the sprint backlog. A sprint lasts for about 2–4 weeks. Sprints get updated as the tasks are completed or as new tasks emerge.

The *sprint burn down chart* is a chart showing the remaining work in the sprint backlog. It is updated every day (Lewis and Neher, 2007). This graphical document enables tracking of the remaining features on the vertical axis and the time on the horizontal axis (Cho, 2008). Each team member must have access to this chart.

Scrum Meetings

Scrum includes a number of meetings including the Daily Scrum meeting, the Sprint Review meeting, the Sprint Planning meeting, the Sprint Retrospective meeting, and the Scrum of Scrum meeting. The Daily Scrum meeting is a stand-up meeting for about 15 minutes that concentrates on what was achieved, what is going to be achieved, and the potential roadblocks to achieving it. The Sprint Review meeting is typically a half-day meeting that provides status update to management and the stakeholders. The Planning meeting can last a day, in which the sprint team and the Product Owner decide on the outcomes to be achieved within that sprint—resulting in the product and the sprint backlogs. The Sprint Retrospective meeting discusses what went right and what the areas for correction in the next Sprint are; finally there is opportunity for a Scrum of Scrum meeting that brings together Scrum teams working on separate but related Sprints, ensuring coordination and minimal overlaps among the various scrums.

Scrum Flow

Figure 2.5 depicts a Scrum Flow, with a typical project starting with the Product Owner creating a product backlog. The Sprint Planning meeting breaks down the product backlog into smaller features that become part of the sprint backlog. Each Sprint can last up to multiples of 30 days (as shown in Figure 2.5) and results in the delivery of a major feature from the sprint backlog.

Agile Unified Process (AUP)

The Agile Unified Process (AUP) is an Agile adaptation of the Unified Process (UP, Jacboson) formalized by Scott Ambler[*,‡] and also discussed by Craig Larman. Ambler succinctly summarizes AUP as "serial in the large, iterative in the small, [and] delivering incremental releases over time."

The "serial in the large" aspect of AUP brings about the four major phases of a UP project—inception, elaboration, construction, and transition. These phases, while sequential, do overlap one another.

1. *Inception* is an exploratory phase that develops a shared understanding of the scope of the new system and defines candidate architecture.
2. *Elaboration* expands the team's understanding of the system requirements by elaborating on the earlier needs; such elaboration also validates the prospective system architecture.
3. *Construction* is the development or implementation phase of the project and this is where the actual code is written (or deliverable of the project is produced). Most Agile practices are used in this phase.
4. *Transition* ensures completion of system testing and its deployment in production. Thus quality assurance and testing-related activities play a major part in this phase.

The "iterative in the small" aspect of AUP comes from the fact that each of the above-mentioned phases is divided into one or more iterations. The AUP disciplines can then be used within each of these iterations. These AUP disciplines include model, implementation, test, deployment, configuration management, project management, and environment. While these disciplines occur within each iteration, some of them span multiple iterations (i.e., apply to the entire project).

Crystal

Cockburn has put together a suite of methods following Agile principles that derive their name from geological crystals, representing a project's size and criticality. Clear, Yellow, Orange, Red, and Maroon are the spectrum of methods within the Crystal umbrella. Criticality is defined as the potential for the system to cause damage and is made up of Comfort, Discretionary Money, Essential Money, and Life (Figure 2.6). Size is defined as the number of people involved in a project; as the team size grows, Crystal changes to add more formality to the structure, artifacts, and management of the project. As shown in Figure 2.6, as project criticality increases the rigidity of the project needs to increase as well to ensure that the demands of quality and output are met with. Crystal has the following seven key principles:

1. Frequent delivery: This is characterized by a short development cycle as the deliverables are produced every couple of months. Customers are thus able to view the output and pass feedback. This frequent delivery becomes vital on critical projects wherein the feedback becomes a crucial part of the overall development process.
2. Continual feedback: The project team meets regularly to receive, discuss, and incorporate feedback. The meeting also includes stakeholders who are asked for their feedback on the project. This feedback not only ensures that the project is on track but also enables communication of new discoveries that may impact the project.
3. Constant communication: As facilitated by co-location of teams, this constant communication enables an ongoing dialogue with the person defining the requirements and within the project for all team members.
4. Safety: This is a unique principle of Crystal that comes in two forms. One is the safe zone that team members must have to be effective and to communicate truth during the project without fear of reprisal; this is true of most Agile methodologies. The other form of safety

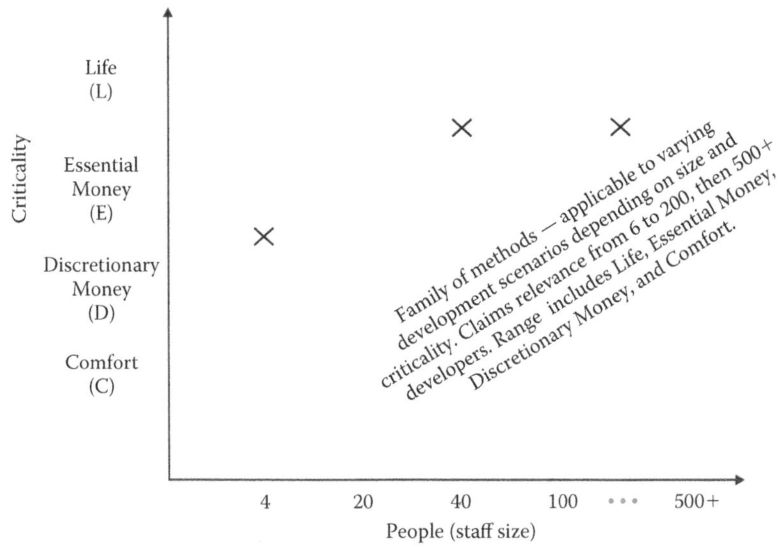

Figure 2.6 Crystal provides a range of Agility based on criticality of projects.

that only Crystal recognizes is that the purpose of each software project is not the same. Projects need to consider the safety of their end users and fine-tune the process to that end. For example, a product supporting open heart surgery requires a higher safety factor than a recipe organizer.

5. Focus: Team members are expected to know a couple of the most crucial priority items they are working on—and each team member should be working on—and should be given time to complete them without interruption.
6. Access to users: As with most Agile methods, Crystal expects that the project team will have access to one or more users of the system being built.
7. Automated tests and integration: Crystal has various capacities for verification of project functionality. Controls must be put in place to support versioning, automated testing, and frequent integration of system components.

Lean

Lean development is the Agile approach that has come out of the manufacturing sector. Lean, also known as Lean manufacturing, Lean production, and Lean business process, is a business improvement methodology that focuses on maximizing customer value while minimizing waste (Lean, 2009). The main goal of Lean is to provide the customer with more value while using fewer resources by reducing the slack between activities. Lean principles and practices are very similar to those of Kaizen.

Figure 2.7 shows the Lean development approach together with Kaizen principles in the center of the figure. The Lean approach is characterized by the following:

- The project pipeline is driven by business. This project pipeline is accompanied by scenario-driven development.

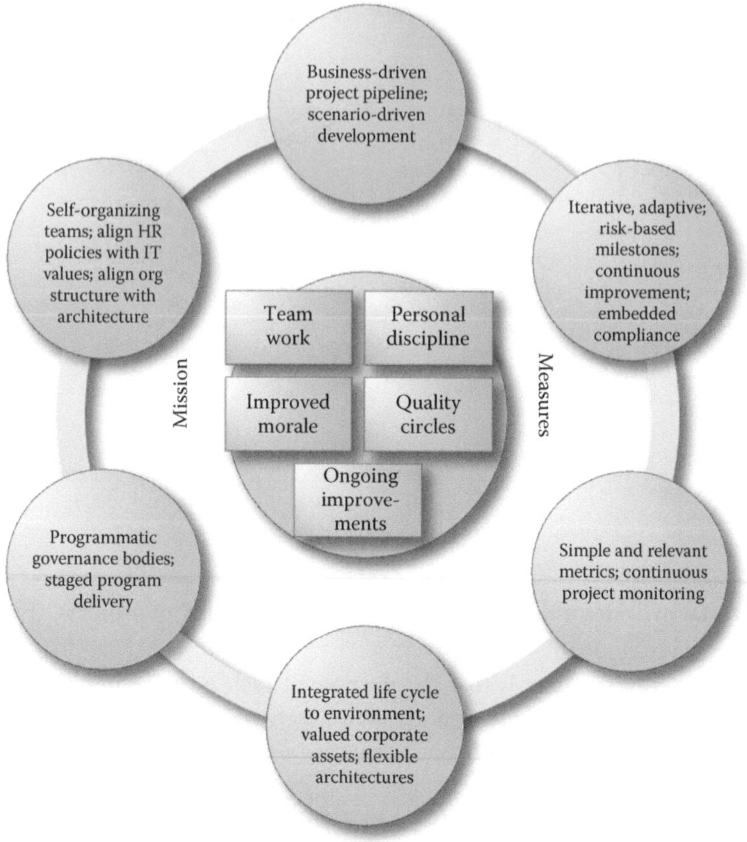

Figure 2.7 Lean development approach together with Kaizen principles.

- All work is iterative, adaptive, and keeps risks in mind. Milestones are also based on risks. The process is focused on continuous improvement and embedded compliance.
- The project is based on simple and relevant metrics and is continuously monitored.
- The project life cycle is integrated with the rest of the environment or business ecosystem, valued corporate assets, and flexible architectures.
- Programmatic governance bodies ensure control and compliance; program delivery is carefully staged.
- Teams are self-organizing; organization focuses on aligning HR policies with IT values and there is also alignment of the organizational structure with enterprise architecture.

Lean development brings together a strong team of people with technology, business, and even finance backgrounds. The reason for this mixture is to enable a collaborative decision-making process that can help management determine an action with due consideration to corresponding impacts on other parts of the organization. The Lean development approach prefers the building of working models as much as possible to off-the-shelf purchased software or templates.

Kaizen

Kaizen can be considered as a business strategy that is based around continuous improvement in areas of work within an organization that contribute to the goals and results of the organization. Therefore, Kaizen includes aspects of technology, leadership, quality, costs, productivity, employee satisfaction, security, and company culture. Kaizen is an approach that includes all staff in the organization to participate in the process of continuous and ongoing improvement. There are five founding elements in Kaizen that are shown in the middle of Figure 2.7.

1. Team work
2. Personal discipline
3. Improved morale
4. Quality circles
5. Ongoing improvement

Kaizen includes defining standards and then improving those standards on an ongoing basis (Kotelnikov, 2009). Furthermore, it provides employees with the required training, materials, and supervision to meet the standards (Hudgik, 2009). Agility at a business level finds significant mapping with Kaizen's founding elements. Therefore, together with Lean, Kaizen provides an excellent framework for business agility, transcending its focus beyond software agility as with other Agile methods discussed here.

Kaizen encompasses a cycle of activities to achieve continuous improvement. This life cycle can be understood as follows:

- Standardize a process to achieve a goal.
- Measure the standardized process through its multiple elements.
- Test the measurements of the process in the context of its requirements or goals.
- Innovate to achieve requirements and raise productivity.
- Standardize the new and improved processes.

Kaizen also has a number of principles that correlate to the Agile principles discussed earlier in this chapter. Following are the Kaizen principles together with a note on how they relate to Agility.

- *Manage operations and processes* instead of people.
  How they do things is more important than what they do. This principle is very similar to the Agile concept of trusting and empowering team members.
- *Utilize techniques* to accomplish ongoing improvement.
  Agile emphasizes development and improvement on an ongoing bases.
- *Customer satisfaction* is the key for performance measurement.
  Agile methods emphasize customer involvement and satisfaction.
- *Think of suppliers and customers as partners.*
  This concept is also the same in Agile methods. They consider the customer as part of the team to be able to deliver the right requirements.
- *Stop to solve* the problems as they occur.
  This leads to early achievement of the required quality. This principle is similar to the principle of reflection and, at the same time, the concept of continuous testing and test-driven

coding in Agile methods. Agile methods handle problems in a just-in-time (JIT) manner (Cottmeyer and Henson, 2008).

- *Utilize visual control* to avoid hidden problems.
  This is a practice that can be used in business analysis work for visual modeling to enable maintenance of consistency between design, architecture, and implementation.
- *Utilize reliable and tested technology.*
  This practice does not have a counterpart in Agile methods.

Adaptive Software Development/Agile Project Management

Highsmith's (2009) work in the area of Agility has been applied to adaptive software development (ASD), as in Figure 2.8, where a high-level view of ASD is shown. Similar to other Agile methods and approaches, ASD focuses on fewer projects where teams can work collaboratively. Figure 2.8 shows the essentials of ASD—collaboration, learning, and speculation. While speculation builds on experience and enables estimation of an iteration of work and deliverables, collaboration brings varied team members together. Learning is emphasized in this approach as a continuous element of the project itself. The continuous adaption, planning, and building of products (software) that results in iterative releases is wrapped by the three key principles of ASD.

Agile project management (APM) is another of Highsmith's works that provides a project management framework for Agile projects, facilitating dynamicity in project outcomes and the ability to adapt to changing circumstances. The concept of continuous improvement, small increments, and learning are all supported in APM. The output from the project is measured for every iteration, and the learning from such output is immediately fed into the process itself. Reflection

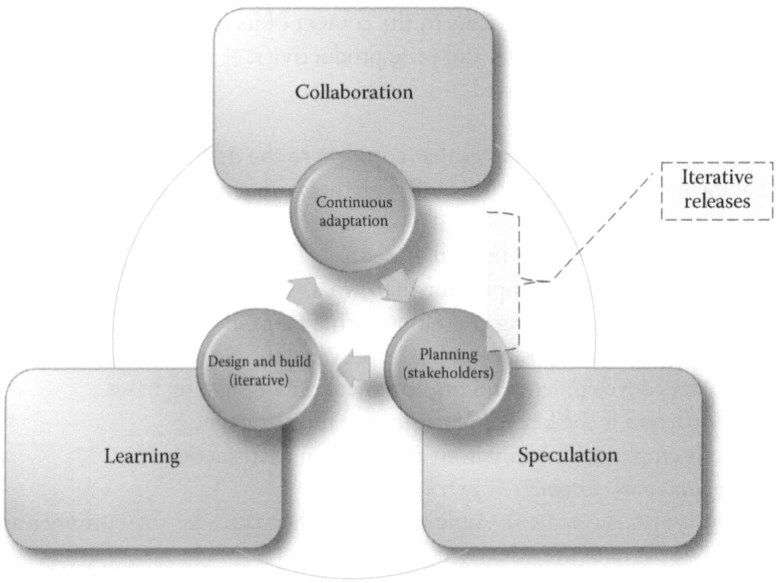

Figure 2.8 Adaptive software development to Agile project management. (From Fowler, M. and Highsmith, J., The Agile manifesto, Tech Web, viewed 9 March 2009, http://www.ddj.com/architect/184414755, 2001.)

on the part of team members is encouraged and APM results in a continuous and predictable value stream for the business.

Feature-Driven Development (FDD)

Feature-driven development (FDD), originally proposed by Coad et al., is based on creating a simple object model (or a domain model) from the initial user requirements (or feature). As shown in Figure 2.9 (based on original FDD by Coad et al.), this initial domain model provides a list of features that are prioritized and embedded in a plan. During the build phase, the initial feature is converted into a working program as quickly as possible. This building of features is a highly iterative process as shown in Figure 2.9.

As compared with traditional OO methodologies, FDD concentrates on people and on enabling them to deliver the features. "Good domain experts, good developers, good chief programmers. No process makes up for a lack of talent and skill" (Chapman, 2007).

In FDD, as with XP, the key seems to be assembling high-quality, self-organizing teams. Viewed from the outside, although FDD uses OO techniques, it is in fact a "light" OO methodology. For FDD, the feature list drives the requirements process. This approach does not prescribe a formal requirements-gathering phase. However, to arrive at the domain model, business analysis is inevitable although not explicitly stated.

Test-Driven Design (TDD)

Test-driven design (TDD) (Beck, 2003; Astels, 2003), is an evolutionary approach to development that starts by the writing of a test case corresponding to the feature required in the system (Figure 2.10). The writing of the test case is an indication of the overall understanding required by the developer of the specifications of the required feature. These specifications can be derived from user stories or use cases.

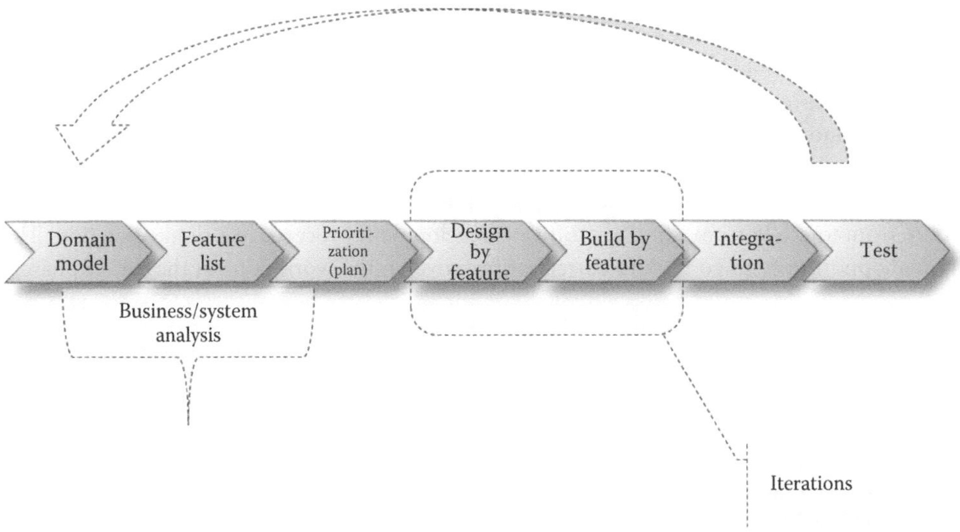

Figure 2.9 Feature-driven development (originally proposed by Coad et al.).

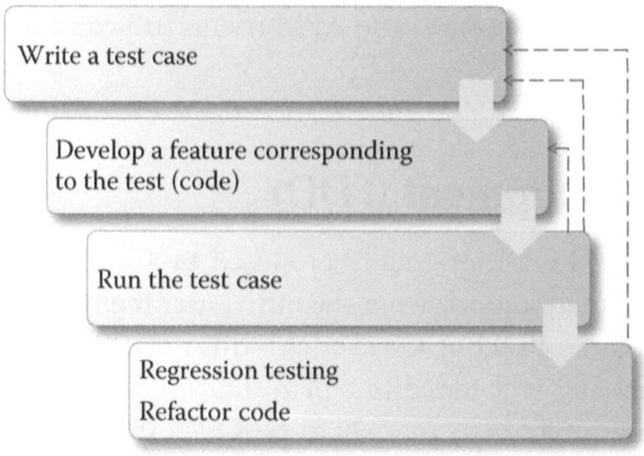

Figure 2.10 Test-driven design (and development).

The test cases written in TDD are with an intent to write the specifications more than validation (based on Martin et al., 2003). This approach forces the developer to think through the code in a way that will ensure it will pass the tests. Thus, TDD can be an important Agile requirement as well as a design technique. Furthermore, TDD is also a coding approach that focuses on writing a clean code that works (Ron Jeffries*).

Planned Process Life Cycles and Agile

Figure 2.11 provides an overview of the prevalent project life cycles and how they relate to Agility as a suite of practices. The following is a brief discussion of these life cycles.

The Waterfall-Based SDLC

The traditional, waterfall life cycle is a linear, phased approach to software development (Sommerville, 1989). While contemporary Agile approach may seem to be diametrically opposed to this traditional development life cycle, there are some important elements in this life cycle (such as controlling and reporting) that have a positive contribution to make in a composite Agile approach (discussed in Chapter 4). In a waterfall-based life cycle, deliverables such as the analysis model, designs, code, and tests are sequentially dependent on the previous deliverable in this approach. Thus, system design, in such an approach, will not proceed until the analysis model is signed off, and coding will proceed only after the design is signed off. Just as a waterfall travels in only one direction, from top to bottom, similarly software development proceeds in a single direction. There is minimal opportunity to go back to correct or improve on the work done in the earlier phase.

SIDEBAR

A process based on such sequential approach, and using the Unified Modeling Language (UML), would create all use cases up front followed by all the activity diagrams, and then the class diagrams, and others. Drawing of the class diagrams in a waterfall life cycle will not proceed until all the use cases have been signed off. Such a process would support the production of one deliverable at a time, and would not be able to facilitate user feedback and changes to the completed deliverables.

---

* http://www.agiledata.org/essays/tdd.html.

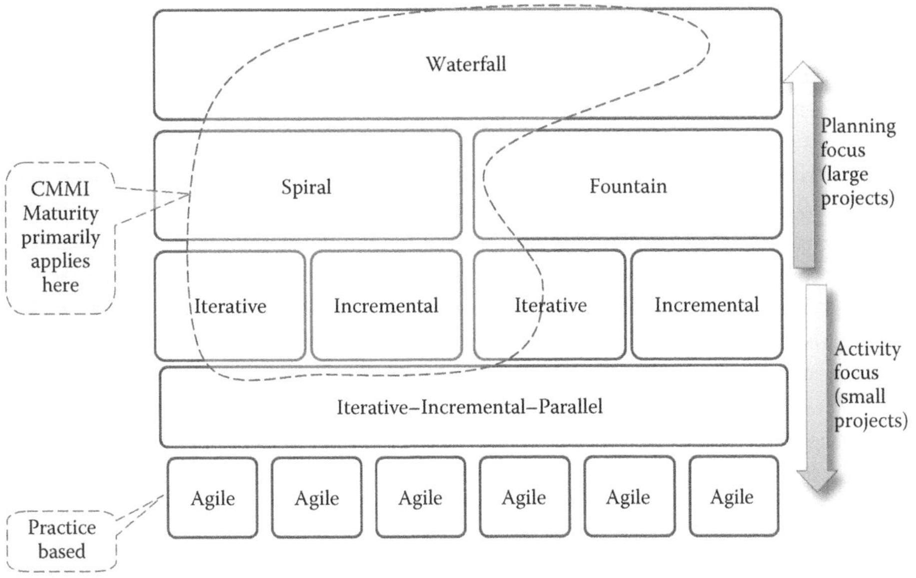

Figure 2.11 Overview of project life cycles.

When quality assurance techniques are applied to these deliverables produced at the end of each phase, the challenge is not just the accuracy of the output being tested but also its appropriateness to the purpose for which the users want the system. Since user expectations (and needs) would have invariably changed over the lifetime of a project, this often leads to the output (product) not fulfilling the requirements of the users. Despite its limitations, the waterfall-based SDLC is the overarching life cycle that seems to have formed the basis for all other life cycles. Hence, it is shown at the top in Figure 2.11.

The Spiral-Based SDLC

Barry Boehm's view of software development was that it proceeds in ever-expanding spirals (Boehm, 1986). He divided the software development into four quadrants:

1. Determine objectives, alternatives, and constraints.
2. Evaluate alternatives, and identify and resolve risks.
3. Develop and verify.
4. Plan the next phase.

Software development would start with activities in one quadrant, and would follow in a spiral fashion, passing through other quadrants in expanding spirals. These spirals can provide the basis for subsequent iterations in Agile approaches. Within the spiral model, though, deliverables are produced at the end of each quadrant of activities. These quadrants within the spiral model provide the basis for repetition. However, the approach focuses more on how systems will be implemented, rather than providing a full iterative support in dealing with the needs of the users. Nevertheless, the spiral is the starting point for iterative work within software development and has eventually found a place in Agile development.

The Fountain-Based SDLC

An iterative and incremental approach is depicted much better in terms of software development by the fountain model (Henderson-Sellers and Edwards, 1993). Just as water in a fountain goes up and then comes down again, similarly, software development proceeds in an iterative fashion—reaching a certain height in terms of requirements, design, implementation, and testing, and then falling back into the development pool.

A software process that provides feedback to the users and, in fact, to all other players in the project throughout the development, and across all deliverables would reflect the fountain model—incorporating the concepts of iterations and increments. Development in such an iterative and incremental process produces all deliverables iteratively. Thus, formal sign-offs at the end of each software phase will have to be readjusted when a fountain-based iterative and incremental approach to software development is adopted. Such processes mitigate the risks in a project by ensuring that the development in the solution space is in accordance with the needs expressed in the problem space (Unhelkar, 2003). Furthermore, the initial work in the solution space is used to influence the thinking in the problem space. This is made possible by demonstrating a small part of the solution to the modelers and the users in the problem space (by either actually developing that small solution, or by creating a prototype, or both) and getting their feedback. Similar to the spiral model, this fountain model of SDLC provides the basis for iterations in a composite Agile approach.

The IIP—Iterative, Incremental, Parallel Development Process

Figure 2.11 shows that the theories of the various SDLCs have eventually led to the creation of a formal iterative, incremental, and parallel (IIP) development approach. Besides the creation of IIP as a basis for software development processes, Figure 2.11 also shows, on the left, the growing importance of "maturity" of the processes based on these life cycles. The Capability Maturity Model (CMMI) provides the basis for maturity measures in software development. This section discusses the IIP followed in the creation of a process metamodel.

Figure 2.12 shows the life cycles discussed earlier as providing the basis for the creation of a software engineering process (SEP). An SEP is then made up of iterations and increments. Each SEP is architecturally made up of many components (or maps) of a process. Understanding an SEP can be most helpful in understanding the areas of a formal process within a software project. This understanding, in turn, provides opportunities to embed Agile practices within the elements of the formal process. The building block of an SEP, as shown in Figure 2.12, is a process map.

Each process map is made up of three key categories of elements—roles, deliverables, and activities. Each activity, in turn, is made up of tasks, and those tasks can be carried out by using one or more practices.

The activities and tasks within the process maps are performed in a collaborative fashion, with the relevant activities, tasks, and deliverables feeding off each other. As discussed in the earlier section on the fountain model, these iterations provide a feedback mechanism to the user and modelers in the problem space, enabling them to provide a complete and consistent model of what the system should do. The tasks themselves can make use of Agile practices, as part of a composite approach discussed in Chapter 4.

Typically, a software product can be developed in three iterations and each of these iterations will derive their activities and tasks from the process maps (these process maps are described later in this book). Each increment can be determined on the basis of a suite of functionalities (or features) required of the system. Additional chunks of the required functionalities provide the basis

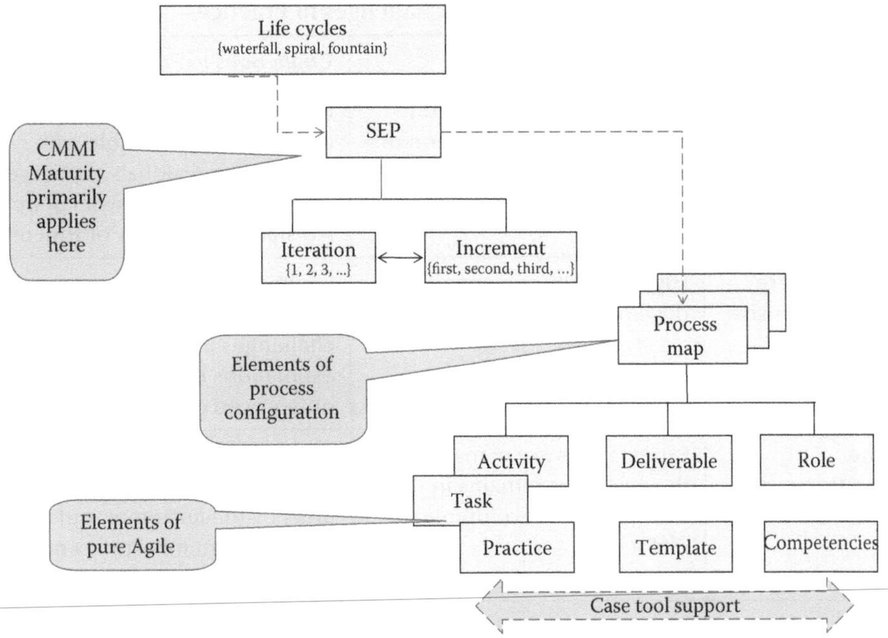

Figure 2.12 A process metamodel.

for additional increments of the system, resulting in an executable deliverable of direct benefit to the business users. Typically, each increment would also have a release number, and will be placed under change control mechanisms within the project. The iterations and the increments, in practice, tend to merge with each other, and are not as clearly separated as shown in Figure 2.12.

Usually, there are three iterations in delivering an increment, although more are possible. These iterations can be called the *initial*, *major*, and *final* iterations. A small project may encompass all iterations in one, and may not be delivered incrementally. A large project, where the software life cycle is based on the "waterfall life cycle," will also not have these increments and iterations—all activities and tasks will be completed in one attempt. However, for large and complex development following a high-ceremony process, all three iterations will be formally needed.

A Practical Agile Manifesto

While the popularity of the Agile Manifesto is understood and accepted, challenges arise in practice when principles and practices based on the Agile Manifesto are applied. Table 2.6 lists the four value statements of the Agile Manifesto, their major advantages, and the challenges arising from these value statements.

The four value statements of the Agile Manifesto start making more sense in practice if they can be slightly reworded as shown in Table 2.7 and discussed next.

Individuals and Interactions Together with Processes and Tools

Agile promotes individual interaction, whereas the waterfall software development promotes well-defined processes to manage all activities and tasks. These processes are organized around

Table 2.6 Agile Manifesto, Advantages, and Challenges in Practice

Agile Manifesto	*Advantages in Practice*	*Challenges in Practice*
Individuals and interactions over processes and tools	Flexibility and freedom for developers. Full utilization of an individual's skill and motivation	Excessive emphasis on the individual. Unworkable with "average" individuals and large projects. Unable to swap people. No standard process or tool used
Working software over comprehensive documentation	High visibility and speed of development	Limited traceability of requirements and designs. This also leads to challenges in contracts and estimations in third-party/outsourced development
Customer collaboration over contract negotiation	Expectations are managed as the customer remains in the center of the development effort	Misunderstanding and/or underestimation of development tasks by the customer; outsourced development milestones not easily discernable
Responding to change over following a plan	Changing external business environment has to be handled and required changes incorporated in the development as it progresses	Estimations and measurements provide the biggest challenge due to lack of planning and completion of requirements against which delivery can be made

Table 2.7 A Practical, Revised View of the Agile Manifesto

- Individuals and interactions *together with* processes and tools
- Working software *together with* comprehensive documentation
- Customer collaboration *together with* contract negotiation
- Responding to change *together with* following a plan

the process metamodel shown in Figure 2.12 and comply with standards such as ISO9000 and CMMI. However, software development can vary from project to project depending on the type and size of the projects. A detailed and formal process for a complex software system will be expensive when applied to other relatively simple software products. Agility lays due emphasis on the individual and her initiative to produce results. The need to remove the emphasis on the individual was precisely at the heart of the planned software movement and process maturity models. While Agile teams are empowered to self-manage and take decisions, the quality of that self-management and the decision-making process are highly subjective.

The Agile approach further argues that dialogue cannot simply be replaced by tools; instead, tools are only used to facilitate communication. In a complex requirement, a user may not be experienced enough to fully understand the terminology in documents and the modeling diagram. Tools can provide a pragmatic mechanism to collaborate among various stakeholders, enabling them to exchange ideas and solve problems. Therefore, in practice, it makes sense to provide balanced importance to both individuals and tools: *individuals and interactions together with processes and tools.*

Working Software Together with Comprehensive Documentation

An SEP based on linear, planned approaches is focused on documentation as a basis for discussions, agreement, and eventual development of software that complies with the specifications within the documentation. Thus, in a plan-driven approach, documentation is significant in describing all the requirements and design as a blueprint for further work. Without proper documentation, the working software becomes an artifact that is dependent on an individual and her/his personal knowledge of the product. Even with formal documentation, there are multiple interpretations of the same document by different stakeholders. The insufficiency of documentation needs to be counterbalanced by the otherwise huge volume of fine-grained documents that have to be written and verified by various stakeholders. The quality and maintenance of the documents can jeopardize the project if not properly managed. Thus, while the case of a user's direct contact with a working piece of software is justified, the need to create an appropriate level of documentation is also very strong. Developing a workable solution supported by documents is an effective way of working—in software and also outside of the software domain. This leads to an understanding that we need: *working software together with comprehensive documentation.*

Customer Collaboration Together with Contract Negotiation

While Agile values revolve around "Customer involvement," a practical question arises as to whether contracts can be accorded even slightly lesser importance than collaborating with the customer. The participation of users is invaluable throughout the development life cycle. Such involvement provides continuous and valuable inputs to requirement elicitation, negotiation, and prioritization (Coram and Bohner, 2005). As compared with this direct customer/user collaboration, in practice, most software development projects require a contract to be signed off. Such a contract is mandatory when it comes of outsourced (offshored) development and maintenance, with the contract containing details of each phase of delivery, payments against delivery, quality of delivery, and quality of service to be provided after the product has been delivered. Agile teams break a contract into several "staged" contracts based on each critical progress step in large projects (Karlstrom and Runeson, 2005). Thus, business changes are rapidly reflected by the revision of contracts for each stage. Customers are always involved in revisions of contracts as they are also the ones who sign off on stages and phases of delivery. Practical experience suggests that there is a need for *customer collaboration together with contract negotiation.*

Responding to Change Together with Following a Plan

Change is understood only in the context of a plan. Therefore, any response to change needs to understand the original plan. Thus, while change itself is unavoidable and unpredictable, planning has a significant role to play in such changes. However, planning can become an endgame in itself and then it becomes deleterious to the project. As Tudor and Walter (2006) mention, a tailor who delivers a suit six months after the measures were taken will most likely find that the person for whom the suit was made has changed. Thus, Agile tends to focus its effort on "change" rather than plan because conditions change often and this "happens faster than the plan can be modified" (Coram and Bohner, 2005).

Planning in a waterfall-based formal life cycle requires due consideration of multiple factors within the project. Such planning incorporates thoughts from multiple stakeholders and previous experiences. Up-front approval provides the benchmark for the project, and subsequent (inevitable) changes can be made against that benchmark. While revisiting the plan can be a costly exercise, lack of emphasis on planning up front in a project can be equally costly—especially if the individuals on whom the project is relying are not available for one or more reasons. Thus, a more pragmatic viewpoint on this aspect of the manifesto would be *responding to change together with following a plan.*

Agile Practices

A revised and practical Agile Manifesto creates opportunities for embedding the precious principles and values of Agile within aspects of a planned process. The best way to go about this amalgamation is to consider the Agile values as the basis for a suite of Agile practices. Then, depending on the needs of the process map, these Agile practices can be embedded in the process map. The execution of the Agile practices is the purview of the practitioners within those projects.

Thus, based on the revised Agile Manifesto, Agile values, and the 12 Agile principles discussed, we end up with a suite of Agile practices that also lend themselves to logical groupings. Table 2.8 lists the headings under which Agile practices can be grouped. While some of these Agile practices

Table 2.8 Groups of Agile Practices

Group	*Practice*
Analytical practices	Focus on exploration of the business needs and high-level strategic objectives
Requirements practices	Provide the basis for carrying out formal requirements gathering and modeling for functional, nonfunctional, and interface aspects of the system
Development practices	Are the well-known coding practices that are primarily derived from pure Agile methods
Design practices	Deal with reflection, refactoring, and creation of robust architectures and designs
Project management practices	Provide the basis for planning, tracking, and reporting of projects even when they are based on Agile methods
Quality assurance practices	Form the basis of quality strategy including quality assurance standards and maturity
Operational practices	Deal with the practices within an organization that deal with its daily operational aspects and that are specific to the domain of the organization
Testing practices	Expand on the quality assurance practices and, at the same time, have their own suite of practices derived from test-specific processes such as TDD

appear to be specific to software projects, in reality, all of them are applicable across an organization and in both software and nonsoftware projects.

Analytical Practices

Analysis can be considered as the competency of breaking down a problem into its constituent parts that enables its understanding. Once a problem is divided into its constituent parts, it is easier to understand and model the problem and, eventually, a solution for it can be designed. Analytical practices come into play at the highest level of business needs wherein the exercises of business analysis (discussed in detail in Chapter 7) lead to an understanding of the business, its directions, its risks, and its opportunities. Analytical practices, together with the process map that guides and supports analysis, helps in understanding the business needs and problems and enables the analyst to participate in identifying solution options.

Table 2.9 lists some of the analytical practices that can add value to an Agile project.

Requirements Practices

Requirements for a project follow from the results of formal business analysis. Requirements can be functional, nonfunctional, and interface requirements for a project. These requirements are best produced in a collaborative manner with input and participation from all stakeholders. Regular discussions, workshops, and negotiations lead to excellent requirements that also reflect priorities of all parties concerned.

Table 2.9 Analytical Practices

Practice	*Description*
Questioning and listening	Focuses on the crucial skills of asking the right questions and listening carefully to the answers. This forms the basis of "conversation" in Agile projects
Root cause investigation	Does the investigation go beyond the symptoms and reach the real cause of a business problem? This practice can make use of data analytical tools to identify correlations between factors causing a problem
Mind mapping	A simple practice of creating a map of the situation within an organization or a project; this practice enables visualization of the problem and, therefore, its understanding and solution
PESTLE–SWOT Analysis	Popular techniques that can be used as analytical practices. Strengths–weaknesses–opportunities–threats of an organization can provide immense value in terms of analyzing the business problems. Political–economic–social–technical–legal–environmental analysis provides added context and understanding in analyzing business problems
Risk balancing	A practice that enables continuous comparison of the various risks in making organizational-level decisions. Decisions are influenced, through this practice, based on the extent of their impact on business

Table 2.10 Requirements Practices

Practice	*Description*
Collaborative requirements	Produced together by users, developers, and all other stakeholders
Negotiable requirements	Users and developers negotiate which project factors to sacrifice in order to produce requirements with highest value to business
Requirement prioritization	Requirements are prioritized based on negotiations of all parties throughout the project (and not just at the start of the project)
Implementation of the most business valued features	Developers implement and demonstrate the features that will provide immediate value to business. These features will change dynamically throughout the project
Customer feedback	Users provide immediate feedback in terms of the relevance and accuracy of the requirement that is implemented

Formal requirements models enable easier and appropriate implementation of features that add the maximum business value. Feedback on requirements is a crucial aspect of good requirements modeling. Table 2.10 lists some of the requirements practices that can add value to an Agile project.

Development Practices

Development practices, such as pair programming, are highly popular within software projects and are all derived from the pure Agile approaches. These development practices focus on rapid

Table 2.11 Development Practices

Practice	*Description*
Pair programming	Enhances quality, but increases costs
Frequent delivery of working software	Provides high visibility to the user and enables frequent changes
Full time on-site customer	Enables dynamic requirements gathering as well as demonstration of components for their relevance and priority
Continuous testing	Provides validation during the development stage rather than at the end of the project
Continuous system integration	Enables newly developed code to be in sync with the existing technical environment. This cannot be done with the production environment; hence, a separate production-like test environment is required

and frequent delivery of working software by ensuring close collaboration with the customer. Furthermore, almost all development practices are closely complimented by testing practices—as testing is as important as development in an Agile project, if not more. Table 2.11 lists some of the development practices that can add value to an Agile project.

Design Practices

Design is considered complementary to development, and "just sufficient design" to enable development appears to be the theme for Agile projects. Simplicity in design is encouraged even if the end result is expected to be complex. Table 2.12 lists a few design practices that can be handy in an Agile project.

Project Management Practices

Project management goes way beyond managing people within Agile projects. Thus, some aspects of project management are dispersed within an Agile project. Project management deals with motivation and morale, empowering of individual team members to enable them to take the right decisions, and ensuring that there are no obstacles to the progress of the team. Table 2.13 lists some of the project management practices that can be handy in composite Agile development

Table 2.12 Design Practices

Practice	*Description*
Simple design	Enables sufficient visualization of the component and how it relates to other components and existing systems
Code refactoring	Facilitates reuse of a code and the functionality associated with the code
User interface refactoring	Facilitates reuse of user interfaces, their designs, and their navigation maps
Database refactoring	Facilitates use of data models and repositories

Table 2.13 Project Management Practices

Practice	*Description*
Responsible individual team members	Responsibility of managing the project is delegated to the individuals in the project
Empowered team members	Team members are allowed to make decisions and carry out tasks through empowerment rather than direction
Joint team ownership	Enables each team member to feel part of the contributing team
Stand-up meetings	Reduces administrative overheads and possible time wastage

projects. Some of these practices can also fit in with the development practices, but they are listed here as part of a development project.

Quality Assurance Practices

Quality assurance in Agile projects can provide the background for carrying out quality-specific activities in these projects. For example, walk-throughs and inspections can be carried out at appropriate times within an Agile project—such as when the design is created or the code is produced. Quality practices facilitate carrying out of quality initiatives such as design refactoring and requirements prioritization. Table 2.14 lists some of the quality assurance practices that are valuable in an Agile project.

Operational Practices

Operational practices enable an organization to carry out its day-to-day operations with ease. Therefore, these operational practices become important not only in software development and maintenance but also in the overall running of an organization. These practices are, therefore, specific to the business domain of the organization as well as to the background constraints placed on the operation of the organization. Table 2.15 lists some of the operational practices that can be applied in a composite project.

Table 2.14 Quality Assurance Practices

Practice	*Description*
Walk-throughs and inspections	Brief code walk-throughs and possible inspections by partner coder; also ensures quality initiatives such as design refactoring and requirements prioritization
Audits and reviews	Enables formal validation of the development approach as well as the output. Crucial for accounting systems that deal with compliance
Operational dependencies	Validation and verification of newly implemented features in terms of their dependencies on existing features

Table 2.15 Operational Practices

Practice	*Description*
Maintain "business as usual" processes	This practice deals with the maintenance of the existing business processes in the most optimized manner (e.g., through modeling, walk-throughs, and simulations)
Enable continuous learning	Ensures the organization is in an ongoing learning mode by embedding learning systems throughout the organizational processes (for various roles including managers, users, and even customers)
Ongoing measures and reporting for improvement	This is the practice of measuring data on process performance by creation and implementation of metrics

Table 2.16 Testing Practices

Practice	*Description*
Test case writing (before development)	This is based on the TDD approach (discussed earlier in this chapter); the test cases form an important part of describing what the requirements are
Test planning	This separates different categories of tests: unit, integration, system, nonfunctional, and acceptance testing
Prioritize test cases	Prioritization is based on risks associated with the product being tested, as well as the risks in testing
Execute tests	There is a continuous execution of tests—especially with integration—to ensure a correct working product throughout development
Facilitate and coordinate	Facilitation and coordination take place between various roles involved in development and specifying requirements (stories)

Testing Practices

Table 2.16 lists some of the testing practices relevant to a composite Agile project. These practices are primarily derived from TDD. However as discussed in detail in Chapter 9 on testing, these practices can be significantly embellished through other source such as the ISTQB.

Conclusions

This chapter summarized the contemporary Agile methods, their values, and practices. The Agile Manifesto was revisited from a more practical and balanced perspective. A comparison was made between the planned (traditional) SDLCs and Agile methods. A metamodel of a process was provided. This chapter indicates the many challenges faced by practitioners of Agile. Chapter 3 highlights and discusses these practical Agile challenges.

Agile in Practice: Road Map 2

- List the existing life cycle being followed in your organization (this may not be a formal life cycle, but the chances are it is a sequential, phased approach to development).
- Discuss the Agile Manifesto in the context of your organization (this discussion should include the revised Agile Manifesto). Not all four items will immediately appeal. Start with the one that is the easiest to apply.
- Have you considered/used any of the Agile methods discussed here in your organization? In either case, list the most appropriate Agile method for your projects. Then discuss its potential advantages and limitations in the context of your organization and the projects going on therein.
- Does your organization have a matured process for software related activities? Is its maturity measured on a CMM scale?
- List the most relevant Agile practice group to your organization. Set up a workshop with key stakeholders on the value and challenges of that practice group.

Discussion Questions

- This chapter discussed a range of Agile methods and approaches that exist. Consider any one of the Agile methods and discuss the need to take the best practices from it that can be applied by you in your organization.
- Discuss the challenges you would face in implementing Agile values across your organization.
- Discuss the need to create an overall methods framework that meets business needs.
- Which parts of an Agile method provide flexibility to business? How do they differ from flexibility in software development? (*Hint:* Agile values provide direct flexibility to business if implemented across the organization.)
- How do methodological requirements change depending on type of project, maturity of the business, and the product being developed?
- Discuss the impact of Agile values on financial management, risk management, project management, and stakeholder management of business.

References

Beck, K., *Extreme Programming Explained: Embrace Change*, Addison-Wesley, Reading, MA, 2000.

Beck, K., Manifesto for Agile software development, 2001, viewed 9 March 2009, http://www.agilemanifesto.org/.

Beck, K., *Test Driven Development: By Example*, Addison-Wesley Longman, Boston, MA, 2002.

Boehm, B.W., A spiral model of software development and enhancement, *ACS Software Engineering Notes*, 11 (4), 14–24, 1986.

Chapman, J.R., Software development methodology, 2007, viewed 3 September 2009, http://www.hyperthot.com/pm_sdm.htm.

Cho, J., *Issues and Challenges of Agile Software Development with Scrum*, Vol. IX (2), Colorado State University, Pueblo, 2008.

Cockburn, A., *Crystal Clear: A Human-Powered Methodology for Small Teams*, Addison-Wesley, 2004.

Coffin, R. and D. Lane, *A Practical Guide to Seven Agile Methodologies, Part 1*, Jupitermedia Corporation, 2007, viewed 29 September 2009, http://www.devx.com/architect/Article/32761/1954.

Cottmeyer, M. and V.L. Henson, *The Agile Business Analyst*, VersionOne Inc., 2008, viewed 12 March 2009, http://www.versionone.com/whitepapers.asp.

Cottmeyer, M. and D. Stevens, Rethinking the Agile enterprise, *Cutter Executive Report*, 10 (7), 2009.

DeMarco, T. and T. Lister, *Peopleware: Productive Projects and Teams*, Yourdon Press, NJ, 1987.

Fowler, M. and J. Highsmith, The Agile manifesto, 2001, Tech Web, viewed 9 March 2009, http://www.ddj.com/architect/184414755.

Henderson-Sellers, B. and J.M. Edwards, The fountain model for object-oriented systems development, *Object Magazine*, 3 (2), pp. 71–79, 1993.

Highsmith, J., Scaling Agile: People and organization, 9 April 2009.

Hudgik, S., Kaizen, graphic products, 2009, viewed 23 August 2009, http://www.graphicproducts.com/tutorials/kaizen/kaizen-getting-started.php.

Kotelnikov, V., Kaizen: The Japanese strategy of continuous improvement, 2009, viewed 23 August 2009, http://www.1000ventures.com/business_guide/mgmt_kaizen_main.html.

Lewis, J. and K. Neher, *Over the Waterfall in a Barrel—MSIT Adventures in Scrum*, IEEE Computer Society, Washington, DC, 2007.

Palmer, S.R. and J.M. Felsing, *A Practical Guide to Feature-Driven Development*, Prentice Hall, Upper Saddle River, NJ, 2002.

Schwaber, K. and M. Beedle, *Agile Software Development with Scrum*, Prentice Hall, Upper Saddle River, NJ, 2001.

Sommerville, I., *Software Engineering*, Addison-Wesley, Reading, MA, 1989.
Unhelkar, B., *Process Quality Assurance for UML-Based Projects*, Addison-Wesley, Reading, MA, 2003.

Further Reading

Abrahamsson, P., et al., *Agile Software Development Methods: Review and Analysis*, VTT Electronics, Oulu University, Oulu, 2002.
Ambler, S.W., A manager's introduction to the Rational Unified Process (RUP), 2005.
Ambler, S.W., Disciplined Agile software development: Definition, 2009, viewed 4 August 2009, http://www.agilemodeling.com/essays/agileSoftwareDevelopment.htm.
Beck, K. and M. Fowler, *Planning Extreme Programming*, Addison-Wesley, Boston, MA, 2001.
Bellis, P., Project methodologies: An introduction to Prince2 methodology, JISC Infonet, 2003.
Callahan, G.A., Suitability of extreme programming and RUP software development methodologies for SOA applications, *Seminar on Enterprise Information Systems: Service Oriented Architecture and Software Engineering*, Helsinki University of Technology SoberIT, Helsinki, Finland, 2007.
Carnegie Mellon University *Method Engineering Using OPFRO*, Software Engineering Institute, 2006, viewed 15 September 2009, http://www.sei.cmu.edu/library/abstracts/presentations/methodengopfro.cfm.
Cohen, D., M. Lindvall, and P. Costa, An introduction to Agile methods, *Advances in Computers*, 62, 1–66, 2004.
Clear, T., The waterfall is dead... long live the waterfall!! *ACM SIGCSE Bulletin*, 35 (4), 13–14, 2003.
Dyba, T. and T. Dingsoyr, Empirical studies of Agile software development: A systematic review, *Information and Software Technology*, 50 (9–10), 833–859, 2008.
Firesmith, D. and B. Henderson-Sellers, *The OPEN Process Framework: An Introduction*, Addison-Wesley, London, US, 2001.
Firesmith, F., B. Henderson-Sellers, and D. Zowghi, *Using the OPEN Process Framework to Produce a Situation-Specific Requirements Engineering Method*, Software Engineering Institute, 2005, viewed 15 September 2009, http://www.sei.cmu.edu/library/abstracts/whitepapers/openprocesssep2005.cfm.
Henderson-Sellers, B., Object-oriented methods and processes, *International Conference on Software Methods and Tools*, Wollongong, NSW, Australia, pp. 7–12, 2000.
Holweg, M., The genealogy of Lean production, *Journal of Operations Management*, 25 (2), 420–437, 2007.
Hugos, M.H., How Agile analysts get things done, *Computerworld*, July 14, 42 (28), p. 25, 2008.
Jeffries, R., A. Anderson, and C. Hendrickson, *Extreme Programming Installed*, Addison-Wesley, Reading, MA, 2000.
Imai, M., *Kaizen = (Ky'zen): The Key to Japanese Competitive Success*, Random House Business Division, New York, 1986.
Keller, P.A. and T. Pyzdek, *Six Sigma Demystified*, McGraw-Hill, New York, NY, p. 497, 2005.
Kruchten, P., *The Rational Unified Process: An Introduction*, 3rd ed, Addison-Wesley, Reading, MA, p. 336, 2003.
Liker, J.K., The Toyota way: 14 management principles from the world's greatest manufacturer, 2004.
Melnik, G. and F. Maurer, *Comparative Analysis of Job Satisfaction in Agile and Non-Agile Software Development Teams*, Springer, Berlin, Heidelberg, 2006.
Minnesh, K., Agile project management: How to succeed in the face of changing project requirements, *Cost Engineering*, 47 (10), 29, 2005.
Paetsch, F., A. Eberlein, and F. Maurer, Requirements engineering and Agile software development, *WETICE, Twelfth International Workshop on Enabling Technologies: Infrastructure for Collaborative Enterprises*, Linz, Austria, p. 308, 2003.
Rajlich, V., Changing the paradigm of software engineering, *Communications of the ACM*, 49 (8), 67–70, 2006.
Royce, W.W., Managing the development of large software systems, *Tutorial: Software Engineering Project Management*, IEEE Computer Society, Washington, DC, pp. 118–127, 1970.

Stamatis, D.H., *Six Sigma Fundamentals: A Complete Guide to the System, Methods, and Tools*, Productivity Press, New York, NY, p. 1, 2004.

Tan, C. and H. Teo, Training future software developers to acquire Agile development skills, *Communications of the ACM*, 50 (12), 97–98, 2007.

Turk, D., R. France, and B. Rumpe, *Limitations of Agile Software Processes*, Colorado State University, Fort Collins, CO, 2002.

Chapter 3

Agile Challenges in Practice

Life is really simple, but we insist on making it complicated.

–Confucius

Objectives

- Identify the challenges faced by organizations as they attempt to practice Agile methods
- Summarize Agile challenges into four categories: technologies, people, processes, and money
- Separate the challenges in Agile at a tactical level (in projects) versus challenges faced in strategic adoption of Agile across an entire organization
- Separate the challenges in using Agile in software projects versus Agile in nonsoftware projects
- Describe role-based challenges in the use of Agile—as various roles within a project have their specific responsibilities and, therefore, unique challenges
- Describe the challenges associated with the use of Agile in different project types (e.g., package implementation versus new development; software development versus product manufacturing; in-house versus outsourced) and sizes (e.g., small versus large) of projects
- Outline the need for an organization-level adoption model to ease the transitioning to Agile (the model itself is discussed in detail in Chapter 10)
- Understand the influence of business domain and product type on organizational adoption of Agile
- Discuss the starting point for business transformation with Agility—based on business-operational issues that lead to business-strategic discussions

Introduction

Agile is a commonly used term that seems to represent the strivings of many organizations and of programs of work within those organizations. The challenges of Agility in practice need to be considered in the backdrop of these organizations and projects. This chapter highlights various aspects of Agility with respect to the challenges it poses in practice. Agile values, principles, and practices pose challenges at different levels within an organization. The aim of understanding and discussing these challenges is to overcome them through a balanced, composite approach to managing projects and organizations.

The following aspects of Agile challenges are worth considering in greater detail:

- Projects versus organization: For example, Agility at the project level is primarily focused on software development, whereas the challenges of adopting Agile values, such as trust and collaboration, span an entire organization and the way its business functions.
- Individual versus team: An individual can interpret and apply Agile principles and values as she may deem fit; when it comes to interpreting the same values in the context of an entire project team, the "human" elements and subjectivity come into play.
- Software versus nonsoftware projects: Software projects aimed at producing software solutions to business problems can benefit (and have benefited) by using pure Agile approaches; but when an organization adopts Agility across all its working dimensions, nonsoftware projects (such as the human resources [HR] department's reorganization of the hierarchy, or procurement of a new warehouse, or even a carbon-reduction initiative) also come into play.
- Types and sizes of projects: A small software development project versus a data warehouse integration project versus a service-oriented architecture (SOA)-based exposition of existing legacy applications code—all vary. The type and size of each project poses its own unique challenge in terms of using Agile approaches within them.
- Business domain of the organization: For example, a hospital would use Agility at both projects and organization levels as compared with, say, an airline; in the case of the former, the emphasis will be on patient care and medications, whereas in an airline it will be on passenger safety and enjoyable experience.
- Service versus infrastructure business type: For example, a hospital business that is focused on providing services and care to patients versus a manufacturing company producing cars or televisions versus a large infrastructure project (say, dealing with erection of mobile transmission towers in a telecom company)—each will use Agility differently and with varying emphasis on its values and principles.

Figure 3.1 provides a high-level summary of these challenges in adopting and using Agile approaches at the individual, project, organization, and collaborative levels. For example, an individual newly participating in an Agile project would wonder about his career prospects in an environment where all tasks are shared. Another example at the project level would be where the organization has committed to the Agile approach across the board but is faced with projects that are not software development projects. Challenges in applying Agile practices in these kinds of projects are different from those in specific software development projects.

SIDEBAR

Agility can pose challenges from both theoretical and practical perspectives in organizations and projects. For example, Agile methods lack the mathematical rigor that was the basis of some of the planned methods (methodologies). Perhaps the lack of a comprehensive metamodel to provide the foundation for Agile methods is also lacking. A question worth asking in this regard is, "Was Agile used to develop Agile?" Certainly, a substantial amount of background thinking, planning, discussing, and modeling was used in the development of planned methods and their corresponding models (e.g., metamodels for the Unified Modeling Language [UML] and earlier models in entity-relationship [ER] diagrams). Was a similar amount of modeling and documentation used in Agile methods development?

An important separation, in this chapter, is between Agile as practiced in software development projects and Agile as an all-encompassing value system for an entire organization. For example, Brenner (2009), in his discussion on practical aspects of Agile, states "the success rates of adopting Agile methods on a large scale have been disappointing." Good progress has been made at the project level, but when it comes to programs of work, success with Agility has been elusive. This lack of success exists even after the resistance, delays, politics, and bureaucracy have been handled to a certain extent.

For example, consider Agility at the software project level. At this level, it is primarily a suite of practices that are used by the development team and facilitated by the Agile coach. This facilitation and practicing works well in highly motivated teams with controlled project conditions. The jump in productivity and output quality of Agile teams leads to its popularity and subsequently the desire to apply it across the enterprise.

However, this in turn has led to challenges within challenges; for example, the challenges of scaling up Agile practices (mentioned in Chapter 2) such as "pair programming," "on-site customer," and "dynamic scoping" can be interesting not only within software projects but also in the realm of how (and which of) these practices are promoted and applied within an entire organization.

Differences exist between how an organization operates and how the Agile approaches work at project levels. For example, transforming to an Agile organization may not be through an Agile process. Rather, a very formal, planned approach to adopting Agile that includes all the principles of systems thinking, change management, and business transformation may be required. Applying Agile practices to an organization is thus an important and major challenge in Agile usage.

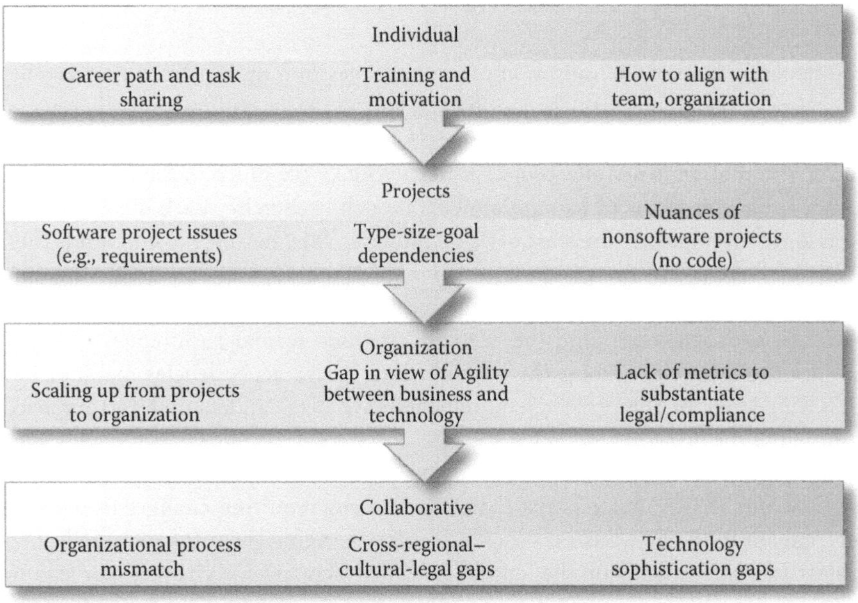

Figure 3.1 Agile challenges at various levels within and across organizations.

Agile Project Challenges

At the software project level, numerous challenges emerge in the use of Agile. For example, project managers in charge of software development and maintenance projects are interested in formal requirements documentation, scoping, and estimation of the work required in the projects. Agile methods, based on the Agile Manifesto, give far less importance to these project factors. An up-front and detailed business analysis is also eschewed in an Agile approach although its significance cannot be overestimated. Outsourced projects find it difficult to get a user on board the project as expected in an Agile approach. Component and third-party services developers face similar challenges when it comes to Agile projects.

An important aspect of an Agile approach is the phenomenal importance it gives to an individual. Therefore, people, their skills, motivation, and communication are crucial ingredients of a successful Agile project. Cockburn and Highsmith (2001) stress amicability, talent, skill, and communication as critical factors for Agile success. How to implant these attributes within a Agile project team? This requires greater understanding of the sociocultural aspect of a project than its technical aspects. Facilitation, leadership, and personal contacts assume far greater significance in a pure Agile approach than in a planned approach to a project. In contrast, formal methodologies in software projects (particularly large-scale software projects) separate an individual's subjective elements (e.g., motivation) from the actual process. Formal or planned methods typically create a work breakdown structure and assign resources to the tasks within the project.

The issues specific to the use of Agile methods mentioned at the start of this chapter need to be considered in the context of the already known issues and challenges that are faced in software development. These issues have been discussed by a range of practitioners as they are encountered right from the start of the project. (See Dooley [2009b] and the interesting discussions on information technology [IT]-related issues in *Agile Software Development in Large Organizations* [Brenner; Lindvall et al., 2004].)

Some of these specific issues and challenges in IT projects are as follows:

- Requirements: One of the most common challenges in a project from the very beginning of software development is the lack of formal and sufficient requirements. Bennatan (2009) highlights the most common requirements problem as insufficient information at the beginning of the project. An Agile project officially kicks off much earlier than a traditional, planned project in terms of its requirements modeling exercise. Lack of sufficient information is quite acceptable at the start of Agile projects. This, however, compounds the original challenge of lack of information and formal requirements in any IT project. The importance of early requirements capture, modeling, and analysis cannot be discounted in a software project. In addition to scoping the needs of the user, formal requirements modeling also identifies dependencies among the requirements. These dependencies may not be evident unless a majority of the project requirements have been understood and modeled at the beginning of the project.
- Changing purpose of software: Software systems are developed for a specific business purpose; however, that purpose keeps changing, thereby requiring changes to the software to make it adapt to the new business requirements. Changing the software to reflect continual business adaption is a major challenge. Continual demand for changes can lead to errors, poor service, and business resentment. As the number of users increases, the difficulty of adapting to change also increases. In a pure Agile approach, the purpose of the software also evolves as the development progresses. The complexity of a system in operation (such as the

number of users, performance, and scalability) requires to be understood in development through a formal, planned methodology.

- Rework: Most software products undergo rework after the project is completed. The business needs identified at the start of a project usually change by the time it is completed. Agile projects are quite comfortable with these changing requirements. These requirements, however, are encapsulated in story cards pasted on visible charts and walls. Changing the requirements later in the life of the system, reworking the code written by someone else, and tracing the changes from requirements to code lead to major challenges in software projects. The question of how these story cards can be used when the system moves into maintenance needs to be explored in much greater detail than has been done thus far.
- Budget and resource relationship: While the budgets and costs appear as precise figures, the resources (typically human resources) are very difficult to quantify. Therefore, a loose relationship emerges between costs and resources for a project. Managing budgets without tight correlation to resources can skew the entire project.
- Scope creep: This is a challenge even after formal requirements have been captured and documented. Slowly increasing scope, or changing scope, can easily derail a project—mainly because the effect of scope creep is not linear. A small increase in the required functionality can result in affect the plans for its data conversion, integration, and testing. This, in turn, results in time and budget overruns. While the well-intentioned demand for a new functionality has to be accommodated (and is done so quite well in an Agile approach), extreme care is required in modeling, discussing, and agreeing on the changes and the corresponding effect till the end of the development life cycle.
- Technology creep: This can be an interesting and challenging factor that emanates from the availability of newer technologies than the ones used at the start of the project. While the scope creep appears from the business user's side, the technology creep can appear from the developer's side in a project. As the original technology with which project estimates were made is superseded, this creep factor can throw the entire project estimate off balance. The time, resources, and deliverables based on a new development environment, test tools, and deployment can be dramatically different. The need to incorporate the newer technology or its newer version may be justified; but it is important to model or prototype the change as well as reevaluate the project plans and cost benefits in the context of the new technologies.
- Soft issues: These are the people issues that invariably exist in a software project. Morale and motivation, and leadership and facilitation—these issues provide a major challenge to a software project mainly because they are very difficult to quantify. For example, interactions among team members, personal motivation and goals, and changing personal circumstances—all of these impact a project, but most of them remain hidden underneath the facade of a person. Project managers are not trained in handling these soft issues and yet their impact is substantial. The role of a developer and a project manager is quite blurred in an Agile approach. The two roles are distinct in practice. This leads to a mismatch between the expectations of a product owner and the development team. Developers may not necessarily be managers, and vice versa—leading to further challenges in terms of soft factors.
- Inaccurate estimates: A vital challenge in software projects is the need to make estimates for the project to be sanctioned. And these estimates are to be made at an early stage, with minimal information about the project. Use of previous projects data (metrics) and experience in the domain can help alleviate part of this challenge.
- Tracking slippages: While time slippage is an inevitable part of a software project (due to some of the issues above), a crucial aspect of project management is to incorporate those

slippages back into the project plans as soon as possible. This "feedback" of slippages and missed deliverables requires a detailed project plan to start with, and the ability of project managers to incorporate the changes quickly. Similar to the scope and technology creep factors, the slippages in time, budgets, and deliverables are also not linear; every delay in the delivery of a module can have multiple ramifications on other deliverables, people, and user expectations of the rest of the project.

- Version control and release: There is a significant amount of unpredictability in terms of version releases, especially in large and complex systems made up of multiple packages. Lack of sophistication of version control during development, testing, and operation can all add to the challenges in software projects.

SIDEBAR

A methodological approach that subscribes to the Agile Manifesto (discussed in Chapter 2) attempts to overcome the shortcomings of "standard" project management. The Agile Manifesto facilitates close collaboration between developers and domain experts, between managers and developers, between testers and users, and also among these various roles within a project. On-site communication, self-organization, rapid and frequent delivery of products, demonstrated value to business, and welcoming of changing requirements are the hallmarks of Agile methods. The difficulty, in practice, is an "oversubscription" to the Agile Manifesto. There is nothing, per se, that is out of place in the manifesto. Not too dissimilar to formal development methodologies, it is the application of Agile in practice that can be out of balance. Restoring that balance also implies balancing formal planning with the flexibility and informality of Agile.

In addition to the general challenges in typical software projects, there are some specific issues that appear in Agile approaches in those projects. While Agile projects subscribe to the Agile Manifesto and have some excellent principles and practices to guide them, these pure Agile approaches also have corresponding challenges. Some Agile-specific issues and challenges are as follows:

- The priority is to satisfy the customer. While this can be achieved through early and continuous delivery of valuable software, there are many practical situations that prevent early delivery of a working code. For example, there may be requirement dependencies that cannot be easily elicited through user stories; without due consideration to these dependencies, a working code may not be easily delivered to the customer's satisfaction.
- Capitalize on changes to the customer's advantage. This is achieved by welcoming late, changing requirements. Yet such changes impact the budget and business operations. Third-party software development may only occur when requirements are fixed and any change needs to be subjected to stringent change-control requests. Handling of multiple parties involved in a project requires legal contracts and controlled changes that are not easy to implement in Agile projects.
- The need to demonstrate and deliver working software every couple of weeks to a month has always been the desire of developers from the beginning of computing. Prototypes and mock-ups have been used in the past; and even today, these are standard tools for customer engagement, requirements gathering, and expectation management. Agile approaches thrive on developing and extending prototypes to full-scale products. Yet, at times, a continuously working software may not be feasible because of factors such as technical dependencies or changing requirements.

- Developers and business stakeholders must work together in a collaborative style on a daily basis throughout an Agile project. This collaborative working style exposes business experts to the product development cycle (Thomsett, 2009). This may not always be convenient or logistically possible as the key business stakeholders are also focusing their attention on running the business. Agile development scenarios in which the whole team is co-located is inevitably more efficient in its communication than the other extreme, in which team members are distributed all around the globe (Dooley, 2009a). The logistics of getting the team together not only across geographical boundaries but also across those of cultures, language, time zones, and value systems heavily impact Agile project communications. Motivated and self-aligned individuals are the key to a project's success, irrespective of the methodology being used. Should it then be really a privilege of Agile only? The nonavailability of such individuals was one of the root causes for large and complex projects to follow formal, planned, and mature software development life cycles (SDLCs) in the first place.
- Practicality of face-to-face conversation needs to be considered. While a face-to-face conversation is indeed the most effective method of conveying information, its practicality is always a question. For example, in some instances, such as while dealing with offshore projects or third-party services development, this conversation is not possible. In other situations, even if such conversation is made possible, it is not binding. For example, a verbal agreement between the user and a developer in terms of a field positioning is quite acceptable in an Agile project; but if that field position has compliance requirements associated with it, then it has to be documented formally.
- A working software may not always be the primary measure of progress. There are numerous and vital activities that need to take place in real-life projects that do not necessarily produce a working software, for example, work on modeling requirements with use cases. Another example is the creation of detailed architectural diagrams that do not directly produce a working software. Yet, these (and similar) activities are vital for the project. Focus on sustainable development is important but indexing it to a working software can be a challenge in itself.
- Team commitment, especially as part of Agile planning, can be highly subjective. Extracting a team commitment to developing a certain number of stories can defeat the basis of the Agile Manifesto. Yet, without some indication of the development effort, the rest of the planning within and around the project can suffer.
- Self-organized teams cannot always be "designed." Good self-organized teams have to "happen" on the basis of establishment of working relationships, trust, and common understanding. Such "happening" of a self-organized team is an absolutely crucial element to the success of an Agile project. Large and complex projects do not have the privilege (in terms of time as well as quality of personnel) to enable the "happening" of a self-organized team.
- According to the Agile Manifesto, "Responding to change over following a plan," is important. Therefore, locking a development effort to a plan is against the Agile value. Yet, how many projects in real life can progress without a firm baseline that is indeed lockedin? In practice, even pure Agile projects need a certain amount of commitment and planning before the development begins—albeit it is not fully documented as done in planned projects.
- Setting a goal in a sprint (specific to the Scrum method) is an important aspect of that sprint. Yet, this goal can be based on a subjective understanding of the team in terms of what the user wants. There is usually a need for explicitly stating the goals as is done in planned methods. For example, the stories within a sprint are geared toward a goal. However, during the actual sprint, new ideas and values may be discovered that would change the goal. Does the team have the liberty to change these goals? In practice, the team may not have the

privilege to change the goals—especially if the project is an outsourced development where contracts for delivery of software have been signed.

- Planning in Agile projects (especially Scrum) can be based on project velocity. This project velocity is the number of stories a team can actually deliver ("done") per sprint with normal speed. There is no commitment in ascertaining the project velocity and, therefore, there is a constant struggle between the Agile and planned elements within a large project.

Agile Organizational Challenges in Practice

Figure 3.2 shows typical challenges faced by organizations as they attempt to use the Agile approach to their development projects as well as their business operations. These challenges include scalability in projects, applying some Agile practices in outsourced projects, handling legacy applications within the organization, using Agile practices within formal project management, undertaking business analysis and requirements modeling work within Agile projects, user acceptance testing, planning and execution, configuring and customizing software packages (typically procured off-the-shelf), and creating documentation and models for legal compliance as and when required. These challenges have been around even before Agile approaches became popular;

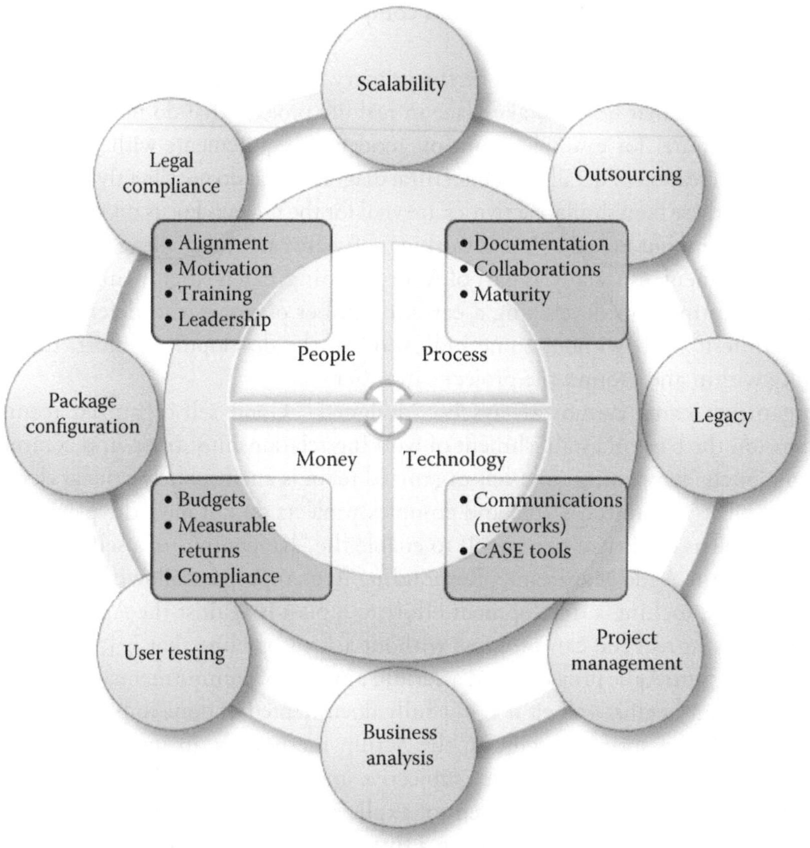

Figure 3.2 Agile organizational challenges in practice.

however, with the growing relevance of agility at the organizational level, these challenges become even more important. They are discussed in greater detail later in this chapter after project-specific challenges have been discussed.

Project-Specific Agile Challenges

Matrix of Agile Challenges

Figure 3.3 summarizes the challenge of adopting Agile at the project level. These challenges can be grouped into four categories—project type, project size, the domain or industry sector, and the type of business. These challenges are discussed now.

Project Type and Agile Challenges

SIDEBAR

Booch, in *Best of Booch* edited by Eykholt (1996), says, "While it is unfair to apply stereotypes to any specific projects we make some broad generalizations." Booch then proceeds to highlight the differences between sizes of projects based on factors such as the language of implementation. For example, C++ projects tend to have a large number of developers compared to, say, the Smalltalk development projects. Smaller sized projects, based on technologies that are conducive to such small, distributed working styles, have an immediate appeal for Agile method usage. It is worth correlating the technologies for development with the project size and then ascertaining the extent to which Agility can be practiced in such projects.

There are different types of IT projects that serve different purposes within the organization. For example, software development projects focus on producing new functionalities, whereas integration projects are primarily focused on bringing disparate systems together and making them talk with each other. Besides, there are outsourced projects, data-warehousing projects, and even many non-IT projects. Each project type would use the Agile approach differently. Most Agile approaches fit in well with new development, but with some project types (such as outsourced and integration projects) pure Agile approaches do not work well. Furthermore, ongoing maintenance

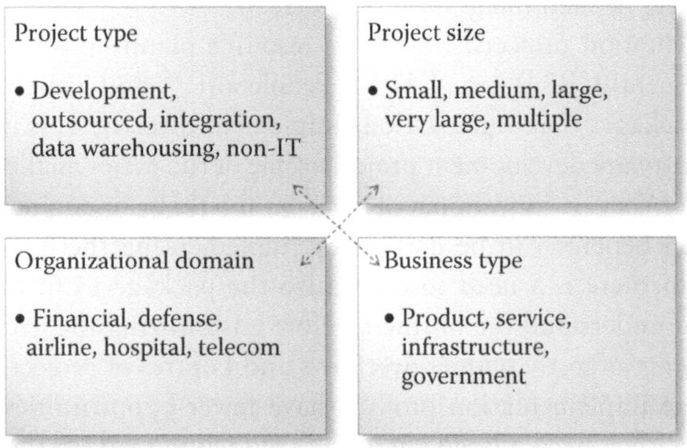

Figure 3.3 Agile project challenges form a complex matrix.

and services also may not benefit by Agile practices as the latter are predominantly development centric. Following is a discussion on different project types and how Agility can be used in them. Needless to say, these are not watertight compartments, and in each of these project types, there is some influence and some effect of other project types as well.

- Development projects: We consider here the typical "greenfield" development project. Agile approaches to software development are most conducive in these projects wherein coding is at the center of activities surrounded by Agile best practices. Writing large e-commerce applications from scratch would fall into this category of projects. Greenfield development projects have significant freedom in terms of creating new software but, at the same time, the highest amount of risk. While these projects have the best opportunity to apply Agile in practice, they can also suffer because of reduced emphasis on modeling and design.
- Integration projects: Well-established, large organizations have very few opportunities for developing new, stand-alone applications. Instead, these organizations have "integration projects" that can include new development interfacing with existing applications. For example, an integration project can focus on creating a suite of eXtensible Markup Language (XML) or Web Services messages to send or retrieve information from a large existing legacy database or a Common Business-Oriented Language (COBOL) legacy application. These are businesses that have substantial investment in legacy procedural code. Integration projects help in retrieving legacy information and data and presenting it to the Internet-savvy users. This requires retrieving data, massaging it, and presenting it to the Web user with integrity and security. Integration among applications, between various types of user devices (e.g., computers versus mobile gadgets), and between process workflows can all be an important and substantial exercise. An integration project may not have much opportunity for the use of user stories. Agile principles (e.g., customer collaboration) may also not be required as a large part of integration may be technical—occurring in the background and not facing the customer. Integration projects have far less freedom than new development projects, in terms of creating models and choosing languages and databases for implementation. The concepts of refactoring, discussed by Fowler, can be applied in these projects. Refactoring involves recasting the existing applications to improve their performance. In an integration project, refactoring may happen but is not mandatory. Modeling in such projects will have to focus on the interface to the existing system rather than the new development. This further reduces the opportunity to apply pure Agile practices in such integration projects.
- Package implementation projects: Enterprise resource planning (ERP) and customer relationship management (CRM) (e.g., SAP™, PeopleSoft™, and Siebel™) projects are popular third-party packages that organizations implement directly. This is in contrast with the major in-house software development projects. One of the major challenges of these package implementation projects is "how much of business should be re-engineered and reorganized, so that maximum benefits can be derived by implementing the package?". The reverse is also true, wherein there is a need to customize the package to fit the needs of the business. The need to understand the business before customizing the package seems to be less understood, leading to costly budget overflows and failures of projects implementing these packages. Package implementation projects have fewer opportunities to apply pure Agile practices, whereas they need a large amount of modeling work in the problem space to be performed by business analysts.

- Outsourcing projects: A growing number of organizations use outsourcing as a means of keeping the costs down. Increasingly, outsourcing can be a strategic move to free up resources that can be directed toward the core business. In these outsourced projects, the ground is fertile for miscommunications and misunderstandings. Agile projects, in particular, have to make extra effort to minimize these misunderstandings and improve communications between the parties involved in outsourced (and especially offshore) projects. Formal modeling and documentation is most helpful in such projects to scope and control the deliverables. For example, some large projects have used the Unified Modeling Language (UML) in their terms of contracts, wherein payments were tied in with the delivery of software modules that would satisfy a complete use case or a suite of use cases within a diagram. Unless the Agile values and principles are embedded within the development of these deliverables, they present significant challenges in such outsourced projects.
- Data-warehousing and data-conversion projects: Data-warehousing and data-conversion projects focus on contents, their integrity, and security. The kind of activities in these projects, such as the entity-relationship (ER) modeling approach, may not always lend themselves to Agility. A wide spectrum of modeling techniques, together with Agile practices can be used in data-warehousing and data-conversion projects (e.g., class diagrams). The ability of classes to represent tables can be used to create and refine schemas, as well as to provide the ability to manipulate the data through the class behavior. Conversion of data would obviously benefit by its representation through class diagrams as well as package diagrams, as these diagrams ideally represent the relational tables.

Project Size and Agile Challenges

Project size—small, medium, large, very large, and multiple projects—can be considered as providing an indication of the complexity of projects. Agile approaches need to be tempered to suit the size of the projects. Typically, small-sized projects with cohesive team members benefit highly with pure Agile approaches. However, as team sizes grow, there is greater demand for the overheads of coordination and administration. As soon as formality is introduced in project planning and execution, the advantage of pure Agile tends to reduce.

- Typically, a small project comprising five programmers and lasting for a period of about 6 months would be ideally placed to make extensive use of Agile principles and practices. An "experimental" or pilot project in the "small" category is also likely to benefit with Agility. Such a project can be used to experiment with Agile itself, or may be a part of a new, major development. Pilot projects can have high visibility, and their results can be used in taking further decisions related to, say, deploying Agility across the organization. The focus of small projects is limited and very specific; the team composition will necessarily comprise an experienced "mentor." This is because there is a fair bit of learning expected of the team members, as well as of the organization, in these small projects.
- A medium (or intermediate)-sized project would involve between 15 and 50 people and would last for around a year or more in terms of time. Budgets for such medium-sized projects would range from $1 million to $10 million. Typically, these projects can also make use of most Agile principles and practices. There will be a need for greater formality in these projects than in the small projects—and therefore lesser opportunity to apply all of the Agile practices.

- A project with more than 100 person-years worth of effort and with a budget of more than $10 million could be categorized as a large project. To start with, no large project should be attempted without sufficient knowledge and some experience of Agility as well as formal methods and techniques. A large project will have to be broken down into many small projects for effective agility. Furthermore, a large project has to identify and modify its Agile practices to suit the development effort that may be happening in small pockets. Large projects need greater modeling and documentation to facilitate communication and quality and, therefore, need a mix of agility and formality. Large-project artifacts include code, ER models, data flow diagrams, flowcharts, plain English documentation, talks with the users, architectural descriptions, or any such concepts that exist in the pool of knowledge of the existing environment. An important criterion in large projects is the level of formal documentation required. If modeling and documentation are not undertaken to a sensible level, not only is there potential for duplication of effort, cost blow out, and even lack of delivery, but there is also every chance that the delivered product may not be easily maintainable when it is in operation. Agility promotes collaboration, discussion, face-to-face interaction, and so on—which are excellent practices when a product is in development. However, these practices do not help much when a product is in maintenance and change requests need to be traced back to the original requirements and models. While the hope is that a project that is planned, organized, and modeled correctly will have less problems of "creep factor," there will be formal needs for projects to be scaled up depending on the business opportunities, changing focus or, although unlikely, availability of more resources. Formal project planning, scoping, and controlling are invariably required to avoid scope creep and to maintain the project on track. Therefore, Agile practices that are based on collaboration over documentation will not easily apply to this project.
- Very large projects are multidimensional, multiparty projects that could be a program of work. Therefore, Agility as a value system has to be carefully considered before being applied to these very large projects. There will also be a need to create metamodels and metaprocesses that can be deployed in handling these very large projects. The need for integration with existing legacy systems, databases, and networks is a big challenge in these projects. Extensive modeling of architecture, solution design, and integration are expected in these projects. Models of problem space and solution space, and architectural models in the background space will be produced following a high-ceremony quality process and will be subject to elaborate quality assurance techniques and rigorous quality control.

Organizational Domain and Agile Challenges

Organizations operate in various industries (also called *domains*). Examples of organizational domains include finance, defense, airlines, hospital, and telecom, to name but a few. Each of these domains or industrial sectors has its uniqueness in terms of projects. For example, a financial domain project will be intensive in terms of data and processing, whereas a telecom project will be more intense on networks and communications. Therefore, the financial project will have higher functional requirements that are amenable to storyboarding and development design by features. The telecom project will have greater infrastructure needs and requirements that cannot be put up on a story card. Defense will have a high need for security-related infrastructure, whereas a hospital will be focused on patient flow and care. How do the Agile principles and practices apply to each of these domains? Being aware of the nuances of these organizational domains is vital in applying Agility.

Business Type and Agile Challenges

Examples of business type can be product, service, infrastructure, and government. Each type of business has its own type of projects and, therefore, unique ways of applying Agility. For example, development of a product (e.g., a car or computer) is different from development and offering of a service (e.g., airline flight or patient care). Product development can benefit from Agile practices such as customer collaboration, on-site customer, and stand-up meetings. However, the service industry may not find all of the development-centric Agile principles relevant. Similarly, infrastructure projects also need a different approach to using Agile. Prototypes, for example, can be immensely beneficial for these types of projects but the opportunity to iterate and also having a working "code" (infrastructure) may not always be possible.

Figure 3.4 compares major characteristics of Agile and traditional or planned software methods. The differences in the characteristics of these methods include the ease of development, estimation (quantification), personality traits, collaboration, tools usage, and type of development. This comparison also indicates the gap representing the challenges that projects face when they use Agile in practice. These challenges, also depicted separately in Figure 3.5, need to be examined keeping in mind the potential synergy between the two approaches. These challenges may apply to any type of project. Figure 3.5 also provides keywords that highlight an example of the challenges associated with an Agile project.

When these Agile challenges are studied in greater detail, they lead to an understanding that Agility needs to combine the best of multiple process worlds. Table 3.1 summarizes these software

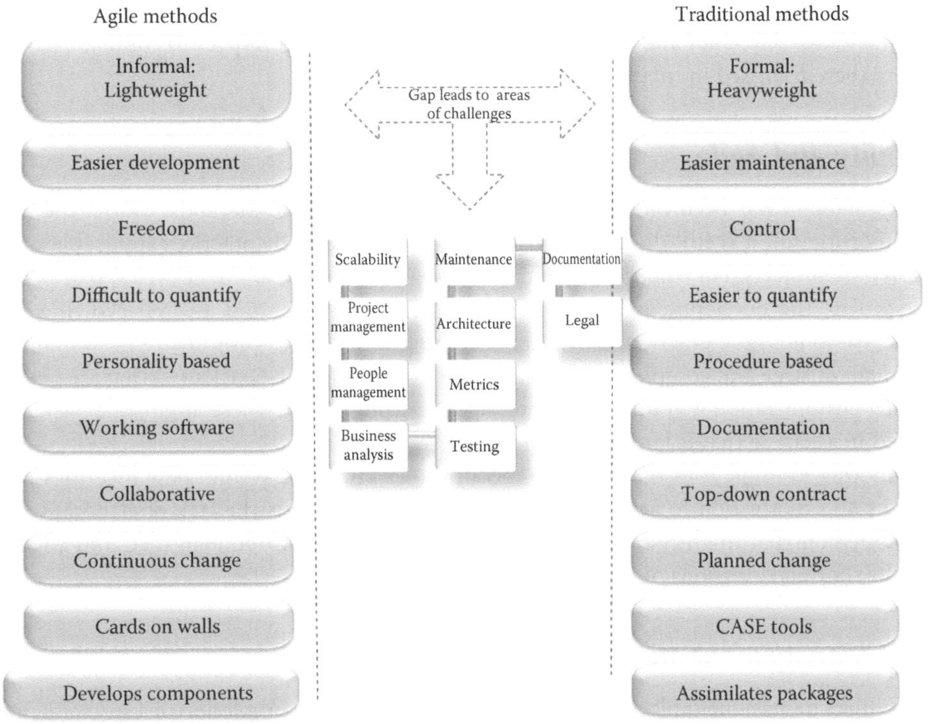

Figure 3.4 Differences between Agile and traditional software projects leading to an understanding of project-level challenges in using Agile.

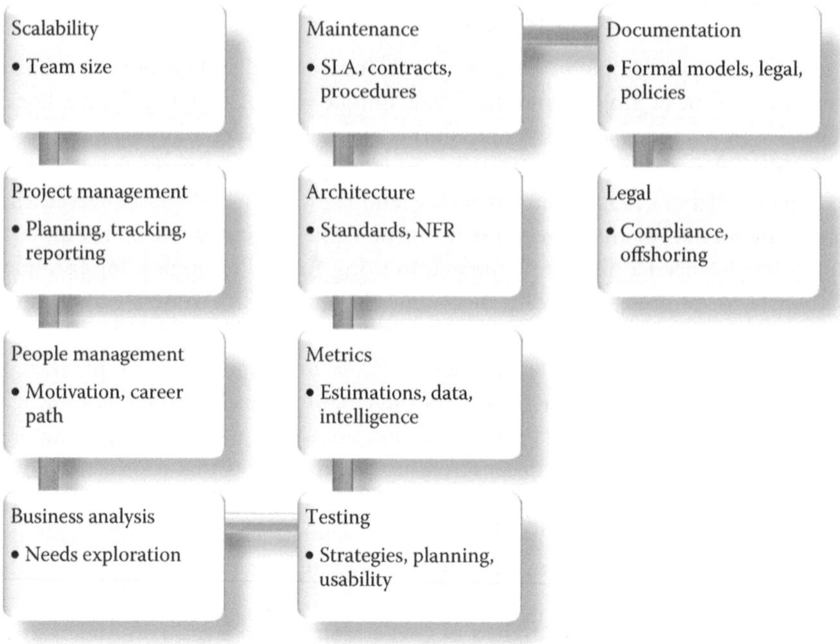

Figure 3.5 Expanding Agile challenges in a project.

development characteristics and the corresponding challenge with respect to Agility. These challenges are then discussed in further detail.

Scalability and Agile

Lack of scalability has been one of the earliest criticisms of Agile methods. While the Agilists refute this criticism, it is still difficult to visualize some of the Agile practices applicable to large-scale software projects. For example, frequent releases in short development cycles, pair programming, starting the development before completing requirements, and an ever-evolving project direction are some Agile practices that start becoming unwieldy as project size grows. Similarly, development of large and complex software packages (typically, ERP packages) that are developed for further customization will find it challenging to use pure Agile. These large-scale packages are developed in a setting that is far removed from the actual users.

Yet another example is of the stand-up meetings (15 minutes). While these meetings provide high focus and motivation to arrive at agreements, the downside is the lack of elaborate and in-depth discussion that might be required for issues too complex to be identified and sorted out within the shortened versions of the meetings.

Project Management and Agile

Formal project management plays an important role in successful completion of a software project. Project management requires careful planning, estimation, coordination, tracking, and control. These project management activities are not formally carried out in an Agile approach. Agile disrupts the task-based management approach.

Table 3.1 Summary of Software Development Project Needs and Corresponding Challenges Faced in Agile Development

Software Development Characteristics	*Challenges with Respect to Agile Methods*
Scalability	Raising the applicability of Agile principles and practices to large-scale projects with interchangeability among people as well as roles
Project management	A formal, up-front, yet iterative and incremental project plan that would also accommodate ongoing changes is difficult to create in a pure Agile approach
People management	Self-aligned and self-motivated individuals is a subjective element and is difficult to achieve. Makes successful Agile implementation difficult
Business analysis	Formal and solution-independent, up-front requirements engineering that is not directly used by pure Agile practitioners
Testing	Integration, user acceptance, and nonfunctional testing is not seen as important as functional development within Agile
Estimation and metrics	Absence of formal planning makes estimation extremely difficult—especially in outsourced and package implementation projects
Scalability	Raising the applicability of Agile principles and practices to large-scale projects with interchangeable people and roles is difficult within Agile
Architecture (constraints)	Development of new components and applications requires adherence to existing architectures for which authoritative documentation and knowledge are required (contrary to the Agile approach)
Maintenance	Maintenance without the initial developers being a part of the team becomes very difficult because of lack of documentation and modeling
Documentation	Lack of formal documentation prevents capture of process knowledge and therefore also its refinement
Legal/compliance	Contract-bound projects such as outsourced-offshore projects have legal need for formal models on which payments can be made

However, in the interviews conducted as a part of the Agile research project (see Appendix I), many participants felt that project management processes, such as Projects in Controlled Environment (Prince2) and Project Management Body of Knowledge (PMBOK), have an important role to play even in Agile projects. For example, project management practitioners believe that even early project management techniques such as the Gantt and Program Evaluation Review Technique (PERT) charts can coexist with the practices of Agile. Scott Ambler (2005–2009) as an

Agilist, continues to highlight the importance of project initiation and planning, project execution and control, and project closure phases within an Agile project. Jim Highsmith's entire approach to Agility is the subject of a book called *Agile Project Management*, which highlights the importance of project management in Agility.

Planning of Agile projects (in comparison with waterfall-based, sequential, large projects) has the challenge of incorporating the iterative and incremental practices of Agile. For example, Scrum focuses on iterations and increments from the outset (Schwaber and Beedle, 2001). Devoid of specific development techniques, Scrum itself becomes a project management framework made up of roles, artifacts, meetings, and flow (Coffin and Lane, 2007). Thus, the creation of a correlation between traditional project management artifacts and Agile ones continues to happen regularly in practice.

Project execution undergoes changes with a project being often broken down into subprojects and tasks and sprints being applied within those tasks. Formal project management needs to understand and incorporate these sprints within the sequential phases of a project.

SIDEBAR

Agility in software project management can start with the questions "Which is the Agile method to use?", "and why?" The Agile landscape is vast (Chapter 2), and it can be a daunting task to pick a method. Project team members may not agree and the key stakeholders may know much about these methods. There is no internationally agreed common standard (like a metamodel) for Agile methods. This leads to considerable confusion even before a project starts. Additional consideration, in terms of Agile, is the transitioning of a development team to an Agile approach. Owing to the differences in approach, this transitioning can, in itself, become a project that needs to be managed formally. Recruitment, training, locating, and getting a properly functioning Agile team can be a challenging exercise in itself. This challenge is further exacerbated by the expectation that it complete the transition quickly. (See Chapter 10 on Agile adoption.)

Formal project management starts with formal requirements that need to be signed before design and development can proceed, whereas Agile thrives on the opportunity to explore and produce ever-improving solutions based on learning during development. Furthermore, Agile builds on individuals and their skills and motivation. Organizations usually have multiple projects going on simultaneously. This requires people movement on a regular basis—something Agility cannot cope with easily. This is mainly because projects with higher priorities continuously "pinch" people from lower priority projects. This people movement disturbs the vital team integrity in Agile projects.

People Management and Agile

Agility can and does create uncertainty in the minds of individuals, especially those that are used to formal, well-defined, contract-based working. A person in an Agile project finds everything from requirements to testing occurring in a collaborative, informal manner. This can result in problematic situations involving people who are used to the formality of project management methods such as Prince2.

Agile approaches also require additional training and investment on people, leading to a shortage of people on current projects. There is also a dearth of people with Agile experience. Thus, even the HR departments responsible for hiring require to be updated on the new Agile requirements. Setting up a center of excellence (discussed in Chapter 10) and dispersing Agile competencies across the organization through Agile mentors, trainers, and coaches is an important aspect of changing to an Agile approach.

Agile approaches emphasize cross-functional teams of developers, testers, subject matter experts, and architects. However, businesses are not organized in that manner. Businesses organize themselves through key business functions. Dealing with Agile teams and roles, while the rest of the business is hierarchical, is a challenge. Furthermore, there is an underlying assumption in organizational HR that all processes must be optimized for individual performance. As discussed by Cottmeyer and Stevens (2009) a matrix of team members across multiple projects is to be created by HR. This results in substantial dependencies between projects and uncertainty in the minds of individuals.

SIDEBAR

Agile projects cannot guarantee that every team member will be Agile. Different people have different working styles, preferences, and personalities—not all of which are suited to Agile. However, when a project scales up, such project members are also required. Agile teams may end up with people who are geared for a formal work style. Face-to-face collaboration, relative lack of documentation, daily stand-up meetings, ongoing conversations, and stakeholder interaction are practices that are not suited to every person's working style.

Sociology and psychology are important factors in an Agile project. Not every project manager is trained in these areas. Yet, subjectivity of individuals is given high credence in Agile. Chapter 8 discusses in detail the leadership aspect of Agile project management.

Going beyond projects, and into organizations, Agility requires training across departments and processes that go beyond the software project. This produces a demand for both external and internal training that projects and organizations may not be geared up for.

Business Analysis and Agile

According to the Standish group,* three major reasons for project success are user involvement, executive management support, and a clear statement of requirements. Formal business analysis provides crucial clarity and completeness in terms of requirements. This is the activity of capturing, modeling, and managing requirements. Clarity in requirements comes about through collaboration with the user. The role of a business analyst, however, has expanded to encompass needs analysis, high-end business modeling, and risk management. The business analyst can undertake basic technical data analysis through to analyzing and documenting business requirements, needs, and strategies (more details can be found in Chapter 7).

Agile approaches are not conducive to undertaking formal business analysis. For example, the detailed use cases, function points, text-based descriptions, and even spreadsheets that are used in documenting requirements are not usually employed in Agile projects. Instead, requirements in Agile projects are primarily derived from user stories that are short statements written by the customer in a post-it note format (see the sidebar).

SIDEBAR

User stories are a popular mechanism to document user requirements for a system. User stories are written in the format "As a (role) I want (something) so that (benefit)." Written on small, 3 in. × 5 in. post-it notes, user stories provide an excellent mechanism for the user to write short, sharp features that depict the functionality she expects from the system. User stories clarify the "what and why" of the requirements. Once written, these stories are put up on a wall or on a big, visible

* The Standish Group Report, CHAOS Manifesto, 2012. © The Standish Group 1995, http://www.standishgroup.com/.

chart for everyone to observe and follow. In Scrum, these stories are put together in a product backlog—a document containing a list of all necessary and good-to-have features. The developers, with input from the users, prioritize the stories on the basis of their immediate business value. An estimate is made of the time required to complete a bunch of stories. This results in an iteration plan which, in turn, delivers a working module. A caveat—user stories do not cover all functionalities required of the system. For example, the nonfunctional requirements of the system are not easily documented on a story card. User stories are described in detail in Chapter 5.

While user stories are quite popular in document requirements, they are not the only technique used by a business analyst. Business analysis goes much deeper into the various aspects of requirements including functional, nonfunctional, and user interface requirements. These requirements are explored, modeled, captured, and managed as a part of business analysis. Agile projects with minimal up-front business analysis run into difficulty when the system moves into production. Changes resulting from user requests are difficult to trace on the story cards, provided the cards are available! (Chapter 7 contains a detailed discussion on business analysis in composite Agile.) The need for separate, formal, business analysis work requires precedence over user stories in practice.

Testing and Agile

In Agile approaches, the focus of evaluation is on code testing, integration testing, and functionality testing through user feedback. This is an ongoing process and, admittedly, improves the quality of the code. Some Agile approaches, such as test-driven development, write the unit tests before coding; the purpose of the code would thus be clarified to the developer.

Agile methods demand a high level of continuous testing that many projects may not be geared up for. For example, in many projects the testing function and associated facilities may be provided separately. At times, the effort to create repeated 'integration testing' for the project iterations can exceed the project capacity. Infrastructure and equipment to support integrated Agile testing may also not be readily available. These factors add significantly to the challenges of testing in an Agile project.

Agile testing also has the specific challenge of nonfunctional (operational) testing. The need to plan the number of times the code should be integrated is an activity of formal methods rather than of Agile. Use of testing tools is also a challenge as Agile methods are focused on the testing of the code directly by the developer. Most organizations carry out manual testing in order to qualify a product. This involves more effort and time as well as cost. Hence, there is a need for an automation testing system or tool in which quality objectives can be defined and are followed against a benchmark. The need for a separate and dedicated test for operational functions and the need for the customer to carry out a formal acceptance test are highlighted in Agile methods.

Furthermore, software testing is carried out by different people and at different times. The need for a common repository where all bugs are reported in a standard format cannot be overemphasized. Organizations face the challenge of not having standards and tools for recording, collating, and reporting on the errors discovered, resulting in overall loss of quality. This may result in possible inadequate testing because of potentially inadequate or less thorough testing of the product.

The advantages of planned and formal regression testing may not be fully derived in a pure Agile approach. This is so because an Agile life cycle is focused on continuous testing and does not need a separate regression-testing phase. In practice, however, there is a need for a dedicated testing phase that can also handle regression tests. A dedicated testing phase also provides for testing of cross-dependencies as well as retesting of all functionalities. This kind of test planning is the purview of planned methods. Formal test plans require creation of a sufficient number and type of test cases that would not only test all functionalities of a system but would also make provision for retesting of the system after fixes have been effectuated.

Metrics and Measurements in Agile

One of the biggest challenges that Agile approaches pose is to the ability of the manager to estimate the project variables that were discussed in Chapter 1. The cost, time, and scope need to be estimated correctly in order to ascertain their effect on quality. A reliable metric for estimation purposes is required. And estimations are possible only when the product is visible—not only in the present but also in the past. Past experience plays a crucial role in metrics and measurements.

Agile, by its very nature, *evolves* the requirements as the project progresses. Therefore, complete documentation and modeling of requirements at the beginning of the project is not mandatory in Agile.

With proper understanding, experience, commonality of goals, and small teams, this lack of up-front requirements is not a major issue. However, when it comes to large projects or where projects span geographical and working boundaries (such as outsourced projects), accurate estimations through established metrics is vital. Agile attempts at this estimation in some ways. For example, the team velocity in Scrum* provides a metric that deals with the number of story points that can be delivered by the team in a specific iteration. Other product metrics can provide the amount of work completed.

This would result in a metric value for percentage of project completed as, perhaps, inaccurate. Therefore, and for similar reasons, these estimates are created for the most likely, optimistic, and pessimistic scenarios. Intuition and experience play a crucial role in Agile estimations, but that relates to specific, individual characteristics rather than a generic role-based expectation (e.g., all project managers cannot come up with an accurate estimate). See Chapter 9 for a detailed discussion on composite Agile metrics and estimations.

Enterprise Architecture and Agile

SIDEBAR

The industrial research project referred to in Chapter 1 (and also described in Appendix I) investigated an important question relating to Agility and complexity. For example, one of the interview respondents mentioned that starting with a simple design is a "no brainer." What the respondent meant was that even most complex systems can and should start with a simple design. The concern, however, was whether simplicity of design applies to a solution or to the overall enterprise. One viewpoint that was consistently expressed was that detailed enterprise-level architecture formulation is vital for the myriad correlations and interdependencies that exist among systems. The importance of an enterprise architecture (EA) became apparent when the complexity of systems and their interrelationships were discussed. Agility can only benefit by a detailed EA as it enables the study of these interrelationships and dependencies between systems, databases, security, networks, and business functions.

An enterprise architecture (EA) can highlight the many limitations that may exist for a system (and eventually an organization) to become Agile. EA correlates dependencies, abstracts common behaviors, and provides constraints on what a system can or cannot do.

---

* Interesting discussion on http://www.onemoreagileblog.com/2009/07/common-agile-metrics.html.

As already described in the discussion on type and size of projects, increase in size and complexity of product and project demands increases architectural and design work. This is true irrespective of the user of Agile methods in a project. An important question to ask is the level and intensity of up-front architectural work required before the Agile iterations start.

Most large-scale solutions also have a "throw away prototype" that is developed to eke out uncertainties in both requirements and the technical solution. Such prototype development is an elaborate exercise that does not itself lead to the solution but provides invaluable insights into the architecture of the solution. A prototype can also help understand the nonfunctional requirements of the system such as scalability and performance. Developers are usually aware of this IT infrastructure in the background. In addition, EA makes the limitations of an IT infrastructure explicit for the developers. Thus, even if the developers focus only on the solution space (as they do in an Agile project), they are benefited by having an EA. In the absence of an EA, large projects can suffer from lack of architectural attention.

Maintenance and Agile

Agile methods focus on new developments in the solution space. (For discussion on problem, solution, and background spaces, see Unhelkar [2003].) There is an equally important need for methods to help, support, and guide maintenance activities. When planned methods are used in practice, they provide the models and documentation, and they also provide the step-by-step guidance in development activities. The recording of these steps within a method also provides the basis for its maintenance. As planned methods matured, their maturity was also measured on the scale provided by the Capability Maturity Model (CMMI, discussed in Chapter 10 on organizational adoption). A CMM-based maturity scale provides opportunities not only for new development but also for ongoing maintenance including metrics (CMM Level 4) and optimization (CMM, Level 5). This maintenance aspect of systems (especially those that are built into the legacy procedural code) does not appear to be addressed very well in pure Agile methods.

Documentation and Agile

Documentation (using word descriptions, UML-based models, architectural models, and even Excel spreadsheets) captures thought processes of one person or team for use by another. Documentation can be valuable to the authors of the documents usually at a later point in time after the system is released to production. Documentation within software development has often revolved around clearly identified requirements, the capturing of sufficient information for effective and efficient development, and the ability of team members to create, maintain, and use the documents.

Agile, based on the Agile Manifesto, has a minimalist approach to documentation. This approach can become a major challenge when compliance and audit requirements dictate extensive documentation. Effort is required to decide the extent of documentation, its relevance, and the tools and technologies to be used in creating and managing that documentation. Quality documentation is one that is fit for a purpose and that is regularly "used." There is a need for a more substantial and formal documentation than is envisaged within Agile projects, especially for large projects in practice that require development effort by multiple parties. For example, where one party has defined a database, another defined the business logic, and yet another the interface functionality, there would be a need for not only documentation of their respective models and designs but also additional documents to tie database fields to interfaces and processing logic.

Ongoing change and reworking is welcomed by methods subscribing to the Agile Manifesto. Such change, however, is not restricted to software development. Changes can come from business, from the ecosystem in which business exists, from legal and audit needs, customer demands, and, of course, technology-based changes. Many of these changes have a significant impact and there is a need to document them, especially when traceability of changes is important. In addition to the developers passing on their knowledge through documentation, there will be a need to document changes to business policies and procedures.

Legal and Compliance Issues and Agile

Legal and compliance issues influence the effectiveness of Agility within business. These legal issues require consideration of the following:

- Contracts: The difficulty of defining and costing of contracts when the scope of work is not agreed upon and tightly defined.
- Compliance: The area of compliance, and proving compliance, is difficult to achieve using current Agile practices. The approach of ongoing change to production systems (often significant when new features require major architectural changes) leads to ongoing compliance issues and expenses.
- Audit: Changes to systems need to be recorded and be auditable in case of disputes within the business and between businesses. Current Agile practices often underestimate the business impacts and cost associated with audit.
- Milestone payments: Payments for contract-based work done is often on milestones delivered. Beyond differences in expectation of what a milestone actually constitutes and what is in and out of scope, use of the pure Agile approach can pose management challenges, especially if reworking occurs and it impacts an agreed or delivered milestone.
- Legal issues: Businesses have to take care with Agile, as the more open-ended nature and less defined aspects inherent to Agile create legal issues whether in good faith or induced to take advantage of an opportunity. Lack of substantial documentation (discussed earlier) can pose a challenge downstream from a development project as it moves into maintenance and if there is a need for certification or audits to ensure compliance with internal policies or external legislations.
- Supplier cost: Changing requirements and reworking make it harder for suppliers to accurately quote and tender for work. Unless the business takes on the risk and provisions for it within budgets (Sherringham), the approach is for suppliers to increase the price to manage the risk. Beyond cost impacts, this also causes legal disputes between parties.
- Facilities access: Policies regarding access to real and virtual facilities create problems for external stakeholders who collaborate with developers. Beyond experiencing long lead times for approval, access policies are not all owned by the legal department, and multiple approvals are required for the same individual.

Expanding Agile Challenges at the Organizational Level

Agile challenges have been discussed primarily at project levels. This section expands on Agile challenges from an organizational viewpoint. Agility at an organizational level operates in multiple dimensions. For example, organizational Agility would include not only handling of large and complex projects but also creation of policies and procedures based on Agile principles for operational business (or business-as-usual). Organizational Agility also broadens the scope of Agility as applied to large, infrastructure projects and to business decision making. The challenges in this section are expanded further in Chapter 10 together with strategies for overcoming them.

The broader application of Agility at the organizational level poses challenges that are different from the Agile software development challenges. A traditional organization, based on formal policies and procedures, has to handle the challenge of redoing its policies that would reflect Agile values and principles. This is then followed by the challenge of changing its culture, its people, politics, and processes and retraining the personnel to use Agility. These organizational issues can be classified, as shown in Figure 3.6 into factors of people, process, technology, and money. Challenges in each of these factors can be correlated to the project factors discussed earlier.

People at the organizational level can subjectively apply or digress from Agile principles and may, at times, actively subvert Agility owing to a feeling of insecurity. Leadership in Agile organizations needs to be on top of their game. Delays and doubts in Agile policy decision making can percolate down to Agile projects and confuse the teams. A vital people-related challenge in adopting agility across the organization is the fuzziness in recognizing contributions to collaborative effort. This is so because the Agile approach encourages shared tasks and contributions, thereby making it difficult to identify contributors. This, in turn, poses a challenge in terms of performance evaluations of employees, their promotions and rewards, and career positions.

Financial resources, or lack thereof, can also impact the practice of Agility at the organizational level. For example, if the entire organization moves toward face-to-face collaboration instead of document-based interactions, funds will be required to enable that collaboration. Alternatively, teleconferencing may be employed, but it may not produce the same level of collaboration as face-to-face interaction would.

The process challenges at the organizational level can also be interesting, especially as Agility uses nonconventional methods for visibility of activities and tracking of progress. For example, with the applicability of transparency and visibility in an organization, the practice of placing project artifacts on the "Wall" comes into play. The "Walls" have become a significant paraphernalia in Agile approaches, which are then adorned with visible charts and post-it notes, and associated with stand-up meetings. Can an entire organization operate in this fashion and not have corresponding detailed documentation of its activities? This question arises when we strive for organization-wide agility as against only for a project.

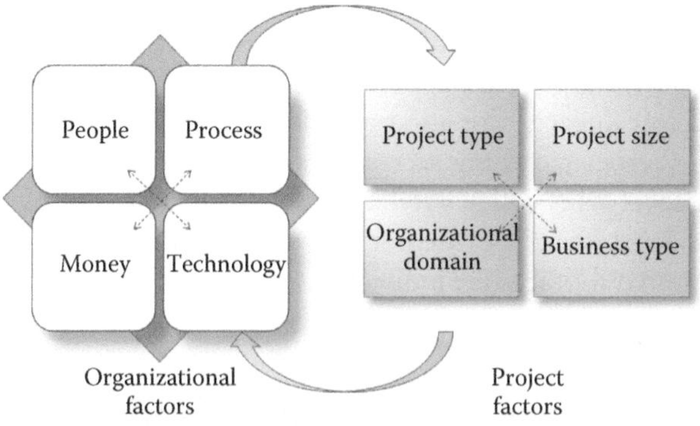

Figure 3.6 Expanding on the organizational-level challenges in adopting Agility.

Challenges associated with money revolve around the lack of rigor in defining and finalizing the scope of activities when Agile is used across the organization. As also mentioned in the discussion on the challenges at the project level, Agile works on trust and collaboration—something that does not work very well at the business level, especially when businesses are increasingly moving toward service-based electronic and mobile businesses. (This is discussed in Chapter 6.)

SIDEBAR:

The following are some of the interesting needs that lead to challenges, based on roles that use Agility not only in projects but also across the organizations:

- The developer's needs for on-site user participation. The need to strike an ongoing rapport with the user can be new to developers especially if they are used to the planned processes with detailed documentation and modeling.
- The project manager's need for scope and control. This is always challenged in an Agile environment that thrives on exploring the scope as the project progresses. Tracking and reporting the progress of a project is another crucial challenge of a project manager.
- The quality manager's need for applying quality techniques including walk-throughs, inspections, and audits. Quality is also closely related to metrics and measurement that are derived from previous project experiences; this may be lacking in Agile projects.
- The tester's need for test planning and test execution. As most Agile methods profess ongoing, continuous testing, the formal tester may come across issues especially with nonfunctional (operational) testing.
- The user's challenge in participation. This is similar to the developer's challenge. Users need to learn to participate in Agile projects, and that may be a new thing for them.
- The business sponsor's challenge. This lies in exhibiting trust and confidence in a project whose results cannot be guaranteed. Through formal processes and their associated documentation, business sponsors would "lock" the project in. This is not possible with Agile approaches.
- The auditors challenge. This lies in validating organizational expenses as well as project costs and progress. Since trust, honesty, and courage provide a major basis for Agile projects, formal activities of audits and inspections become difficult; this is particularly so when the system (or product) has moved from development into production where it is supporting the business.

Strategic versus Tactical Agile

Organizational challenges in adopting Agility go beyond the specific challenges discovered within projects. Organizational adoption thus forms a major topic of discussion (as undertaken in Chapter 10). However, in terms of the challenges faced in the use of Agile, it is worth mentioning here the extent of challenges faced when Agility is considered at an organizational level. As shown in Figure 3.7, the culture and values of an organization are at the top—they are the most challenging to change and implement, yet that is precisely the focus of a composite Agile approach (discussed in detail in Chapter 4). At an organizational level, there is a need to consider Agile as a strategy rather than as only a method. Thus, Agile adoption will have to be considered in the context of the vision and mission of the organization. Contemporary Agile methods focus only on the project—which is a tactical aspect of the use of Agility in organizations—and there it is popular as it seems to succeed quite well. The challenges of Agility in terms of deliverables, templates, measures, and metrics come into play when the principles and practices of Agile have to be

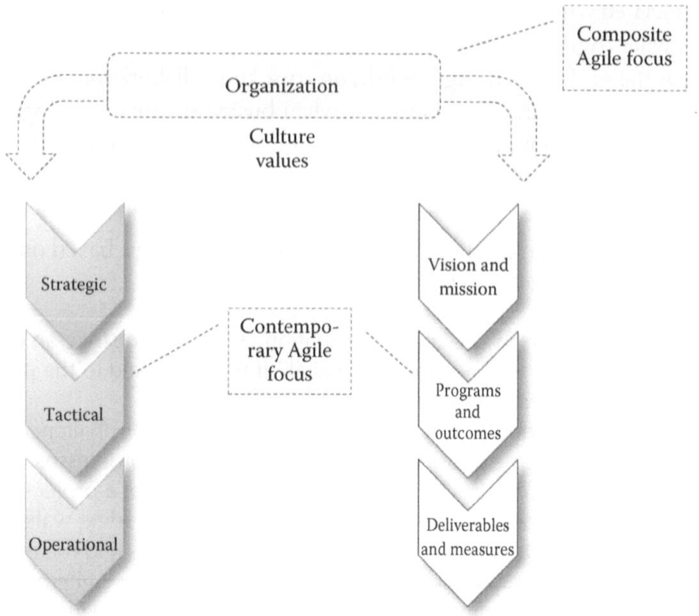

Figure 3.7 Organizational agility goes beyond program/project focus at a tactical level.

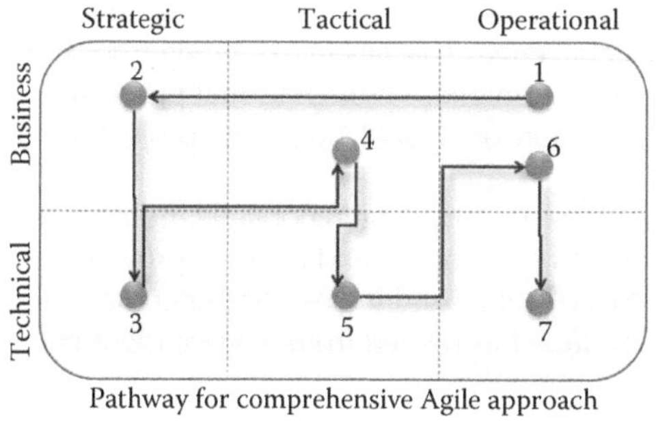

Figure 3.8 Pathway for a comprehensive Agile approach: operational business challenges should be the impetus for a comprehensive, composite approach to Agile.

applied at project and operational levels. Thus, the challenges of Agility become wide and varied when it is applied at a strategic level in the organization.

The importance of the operational level of business in creating projects and programs for transformation is depicted in Figure 3.8. Projects associated with change in organizations usually start with a business problem being faced by the organization in its operation. For example, a business may find it is losing customers to its competitors, or customer complaints for billing errors are on the rise. These are operational-business problems that are shown as (1) in Figure 3.8. These problems need to be investigated and analyzed at a strategic business level (2). This is where business-level Agility plays a positive role in enabling this investigation in a trustful, honest, and collaborative manner. The output of analysis, at a strategic-business level results in a discussion of strategic-technical options (3) that would fit the solution. In the example at hand, an upgrade of the software system or implementing a new callcenter can be considered as a strategic-technical dimension of the potential solution. Here, technical agility providing, say, practices for prototyping or enabling key business stakeholders onboard in terms of providing input in technical decision making can come in handy. This potential solution needs to be considered from the tactical-business viewpoint (4) followed by tactical-technical implementation of the solution (5). This solution is then deployed—making it an operational-business (6) solution. A composite Agile approach that concurs with both formal planning and using Agile practices provides excellent opportunity for the end users to have a good idea of what the solution is before it is formally deployed. Finally, at the operational-technical level (7), there is a need to provide for operational support such as browsers and operating systems.

Conclusions

This chapter discussed the challenges encountered by projects and organizations as they embrace Agile values and principles. These Agile challenges were discussed in the context of project types and sizes and the way in which Agility is used by different roles in practice. These challenges were discussed in the backdrop of the discussion in Chapter 2, which summarizes the contemporary Agile methods and explains the Agile values, principles, and practices that are based on the Agile manifesto. With this understanding, in Chapter 4, we discuss what would be a composite approach to the use of Agile in practice. Such a composite Agile approach is not just a method, but also a strategy for the organization overall. Hence it is called Composite Agile Method and Strategy (CAMS).

Agile in Practice: Road Map 3

- Organize a workshop to discuss the challenges your organization faces currently in terms of methods and strategies. Include the key business and technology decision makers in your workshop.
- List the output of this workshop in terms of challenges, but divide them into organizational challenges versus project challenges.
- Discuss the importance and need of adopting Agile values and principles at the organizational level with the stakeholders. Can the organization afford not to worry about agility at the organizational level, and be comfortable by using the Agile values and principles at the project level?
- Agile values and principles have a lot to offer to software development and business operations. Discuss with the key stakeholders about NOT selecting and customizing "a" methodology; instead, discuss the possibility of a strategic approach to methods that will not be limited to software projects but apply across all aspects of business.
- What are the risks associated with the use of a pure Agile approach in your organization? Separate the risks of Agile at the organizational project levels.
- Involve your HR department to gather their views on which areas of the organizational hierarchy can be moved to Agile and which other bits simply have to remain part of formal, planned policies and procedures.

Discussion Questions

- How are the challenges associated with the use of Agile values and principles different at individual, project, and organizational levels?

- Discuss, with examples, a few organizational-level challenges associated with the use of Agile.
- Why does the type and size of a project affect the way in which Agile is used in practice? Discuss with examples from your own experience of projects.
- Where do you see the importance of documentation far outweighing the needs of an organization to apply Agility?
- What are the advantages of a formal, planned approach when it comes to testing? Why do you think a pure Agile approach will not be enough to assure and control the quality of a software product?
- Agile approaches do not give importance to documentation. Describe areas of work in an organization where documentation is as important as face-to-face communication.
- What is the difference between the use of Agility as an organizational strategy versus its use at a tactical, project level? What should be the starting point for the creation of a program of work (projects) in an operating organization?

References

Bennatan, E.M., A fresh look at software requirements: Part I-III, *Cutter/UBS AG*, 10 September 2009.

Brenner, R., A systems view of Agile methodology adoption: Part I—The issues, *Cutter*, 10 (7), 2009.

Cockburn, A. and J. Highsmith, Agile software development: The people factor, *Computer*, 34 (11), 131–133, 2001.

Coffin, R. and D. Lane, A practical guide to seven agile methodologies, part 1, Jupitermedia Corporation, 2007, viewed 29 September 2009, http://www.devx.com/architect/Article/32761/1954.

Cottmeyer, M. and D. Stevens, Rethinking the Agile enterprise, *Cutter*, July 2009.

Dooley, B.J., Cutter report on virtual teams and the Agile development environment, 25 July 2009a.

Dooley, B.J., Implementing organizational change for Agile development, *Cutter Report* quoted in UBS AG, November 2009b.

Eykholt, E., ed, *Best of Booch*, SIGS Books & Multimedia, New York, NY, 1996.

Fowler, M., *Refactoring: Improving the Design of Existing Code*, Addison-Wesley, June 1999.

Highsmith, J., *Agile Project Management: Creating Innovative Products*, Pearson Education/Addison-Wesley, 2nd Ed., 2009.

Lindvall, M., D. Muthig, A. Dagnino, C. Wallin, M. Stupperich, D. Kiefer, J. May, and T. Kähkönen, Agile software development in large organizations, *IEEE Computer*, 37 (12), 26–34, 2004.

Schwaber, K. and M. Beedle, *Agile Software Development with Scrum*, Prentice Hall, Upper Saddle River, NJ, 2001.

Sherringham, K. and B. Unhelkar, Achieving business benefits by implementing enterprise risk management, *Cutter Executive Report*, 7 (3), 2010.

Thomsett, R., Agile sponsorship: The next element in the Agile evolution, *Cutter Executive Report*, 1 April 2009.

Unhelkar, B., Process QA for UML projects, 2003.

II

COMPOSITE AGILE METHOD AND STRATEGY AND ITS APPLICATION IN PRACTICE

Chapter 4

Composite Agile Method and Strategy (CAMS)

Be aware of wonder. Live a balanced life—learn some and think some and draw and paint and sing and dance and play and work every day some.

–Robert Fulghum

From All I Really Need to Know I Learned in Kindergarten

Objectives

- Describe the fundamentals of the Composite Agile Method and Strategy (CAMS) based on a balanced mix of planned and Agile approaches
- Elevate Agility as a value system that operates at the organizational level as against operating only at the level of software projects
- Present a taxonomy of organizational methods that cover software development, business analysis, testing, architecture, business management, governance, and project management that will provide an understanding of varied methods usage across an organization
- Create awareness of the vital issue of "methods friction" that exists among the multitudes of methods used at various levels in an organization
- Describe software development life cycles (SDLCs) in the context of Agile methods to provide the starting point for a composite Agile approach
- Create a mapping between the various roles in an organization and their corresponding methods of interest
- Define an Agile practice together with what constitutes such an Agile practice (skills, attitude, experience, influence)
- Demonstrate the way in which Agile practices can be embedded in the formal and planned process maps in order to create the composite approach to project-based work
- Outline how process maps can be configured within the formal iterations carried out in the planned methods used in software projects

- Describe and explain what constitutes the CAMS architecture in practice—bringing together iterations, increments, process maps, and Agile practices
- Discuss the basis for creation of a CAMS instance that can be used in practice for the development as well as operational activities of an organization
- Reference a research project that has been used as a basis for CAMS

Introduction

This chapter describes and explains the Composite Agile Method and Strategy (CAMS). As its name suggests, CAMS is more than a "methodology." CAMS can be considered as a holistic, strategic approach to methods and processes in an organization. Such an approach is not independent of the business. Rather, it is embedded in the overall business-technology dimensions of the organization. Thus, CAMS is made up of not only Agile values and principles but also formal, planned process maps. The resultant *composite* process maps (described later in detail) are invaluable in software development projects. These process maps also provide support through their documentation and modeling formalities as the system moves into the operational phase. CAMS, however, is not restricted to software. CAMS is also an umbrella term that includes methods, standards, and frameworks from the realms of business, governance, architecture, and quality. As a strategy in itself, CAMS enables synergies between the various methodological approaches and frameworks within the organization. CAMS considers agility as part of an overall organizational culture and an enabler of responsiveness to change. CAMS has the effect of changing the external and internal structure and dynamics on an organization. Therefore, efforts at implementing CAMS closely resemble a business transformation program requiring excellence in change management.

As argued throughout this book, the nimbleness in business requires much more than software Agility. Business Agility is an organizational culture that results from the adoption and the application of Agile values across all tiers of the organization. CAMS can be used as a framework that facilitates adoption of such Agile values by business and its transformation to a Lean, Agile, and collaborative organization. Extending the strengths of contemporary Agile methods, CAMS becomes an all-encompassing approach to the projects as well as operations of an organization. By viewing all the organizational methods simultaneously and by applying them across all tiers of an organization, CAMS helps in understanding and reducing the "methods friction" that inevitably exists in an organization. CAMS smoothens the use of methods. CAMS also relates methods to the business strategy of an organization. Thus, many nonsoftware functions of an organization, such as accounting, legal, human resource (HR), and leadership functions assume importance in CAMS. This chapter discusses these aforementioned issues and the way in which CAMS promises to be a strategic and practical approach to handling them.

Composite Agile: Balance and Coverage

SIDEBAR: Methods Friction

Agile methods have an impact on the organization that goes way beyond the realms of software development. In most medium to large businesses, information technology (IT) and business not only strive to align themselves, but IT *is* the business. All banking, finance, insurance, and related organizations discover that IT is integral to their core business. Therefore, what happens with Agile in development has the potential to influence everything else happening in the organization—particularly in the context of processes and standards used in the organization. For example, IT governance standards (such as Control Objectives for Information and related Technology [CoBIT] and Information Technology Infrastructure Library [ITIL]); project management standards (Projects in Controlled Environments, Prince2); methods, such as Rational Unified Process (RUP) and Object-Oriented Process, Environment, and Notation (OPEN); and business management processes (such as Six Sigma, Kaizen, and Kanban) are all intertwined with Agility in IT development. The need to understand all these methods together could not have been higher. Without a comprehensive and strategic approach to methods, these methods continue to operate, compete, and conflict with each other at different tiers of the organization. This is known as *methods friction*. CAMS takes a strategic approach to methods and processes in an organization aimed at overriding methods friction.

Figure 4.1 presents the fundamental philosophy of the CAMS. This philosophy is portrayed as a balance between planned methods and Agile methods—primarily coming out of software development. This balanced approach to methods promises to benefit business significantly. This is based on the fact that business is keen on and interested in business Agility and not necessarily in software Agility. Software Agility on its own, without the backdrop of planning and associated formalisms, may not be able to provide business with the agility it wants. Instead, such pure software Agility can actually create the many challenges in practice, as discussed in Chapter 3. These challenges can be obviated only through a balanced composition of planning and control on one hand and the versatility of Agility on the other. This balance is depicted in Figure 4.1. Planned methods (mainly associated with software and based on the waterfall life cycle) provide the control that business wants, and Agile methods (iterative) provide the flexibility that business wants.

As Boehm, in the context of Agile methods, mentions, "Although many of their advocates consider the Agile and plan-driven software development methods polar opposites, synthesizing the two can provide developers with a comprehensive spectrum of tools and options." Composite

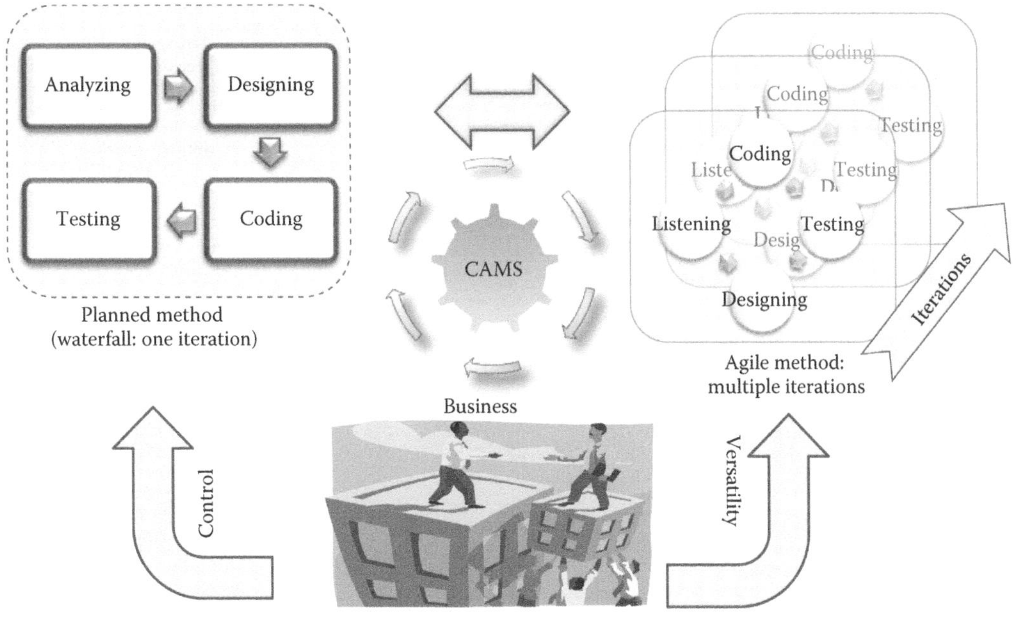

Figure 4.1 Fundamental of composite Agile: balance between planned control and versatility of the Agile approach.

Agile is this attempt to bring the two approaches to software development together and in balance. Furthermore, CAMS does not just restrict this balancing act to software development. The balance between planning and flexibility needs to be extended to the way in which an entire organization functions. Thus the rigors and controls of information technology (IT) governance have to be matched by Agile values of collaborations, and the phases of formal project management need iterations and daily stand-ups. These Agile values in practice are seen across many departments and divisions such as inventory, sales, and HR that may have nothing to do with software development.

All methods and frameworks (such as those used in the business management, IT governance, project management, software development, architecture, and testing spaces) have to be revisited and considered simultaneously and synergistically in the way the organization functions. These methods in practice have to be dynamically mixed and matched depending on the types of projects, organizational goals, and associated risks. This balance of methods, their simultaneous usage, and their elevation to the organizational level is what is propounded by CAMS.

The need for and value of CAMS becomes apparent when many different and increasingly complex organizational methods and processes are considered together. Figure 4.2 shows these increasingly complex tiers of work in an organization and the relevant importance of methods and frameworks in those tiers (shown on the right). This figure underscores the basis for CAMS—that is, Agility is no longer restricted to software development but expands to play a positive role in multiple organizational tiers and domains. These organizational tiers and corresponding processes used within an organization (shown in Figure 4.2) are as follows:

- IT development processes (discussed in greater detail in Chapter 5) deal with software models (e.g., the Unified Modeling Language, UML), coding standards, and testing. IT development is where the entire Agile movement started in the first place. Hence, this is an area of work that is extremely conducive to Agile practices.

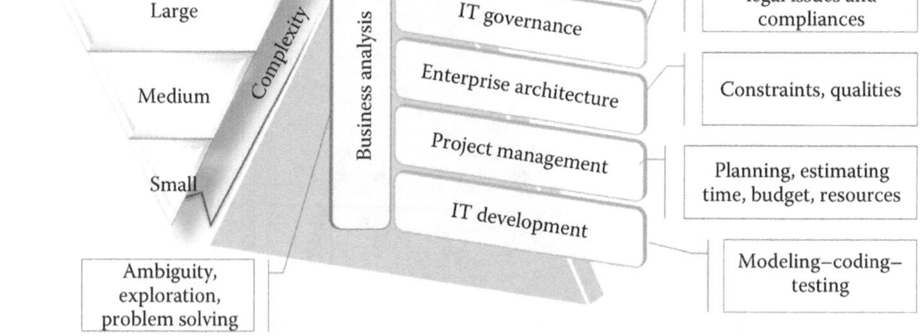

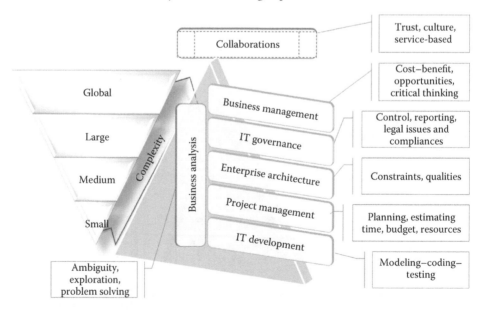

Figure 4.2 Agility transcends software projects and moves into many increasingly complex organizational processes.

- Project management (discussed in greater detail in Chapter 8) is made up of its own processes that deal with planning, estimating, budgeting, and resourcing. These activities are planned out in detail and carried out with formality. They provide the requisite control and reporting structure that is of immense use to project managers.
- Enterprise architecture (EA) covers a broad area of work that enables the balancing of risks and arriving at technical decisions that apply at both system and enterprise levels. EA also deals with constraints (or limitations) of a solution and the qualities expected of it (typically a software system). EA is discussed in greater detail in Chapter 5.
- IT governance deals with control, reporting, and compliance aspects of the organizational function. These governance processes provide the decision makers with precise information on the state of their business as well as management of their service-level contracts. These governance processes are increasingly also legal requirements for the directors.
- Business management (discussed in greater detail in Chapter 6) processes can be understood as a management framework used to manage existing business and explore new business opportunities. Business management understands business needs, weighs them against the costs and risks associated with satisfying those needs, and arrives at programs of work that will generate value streams. Techniques such as cost–benefit analysis, strengths–weaknesses–opportunities–threats (SWOT) analysis, identification of risks, and critical thinking are a part of the repertoire of the business evaluation process map.
- Business analysis processes (discussed in greater detail in Chapter 7) enable exploration of business needs, modeling of business requirements, and collaborative problem solving. Business analysis primarily deals with ambiguity in business by undertaking root cause analysis through questioning, observing, modeling, and correlating. Eventually, business problems are translated into functional, nonfunctional, and interface requirements that are implemented in software systems.
- Collaborative processes (discussed in greater detail in Chapter 6) are the ones that transcend organizational boundaries and enable multiple organizations to get together to satisfy a customer need. Enabled through the technologies of communications (e.g., Web services and mobile telephony), a collaborative process needs to handle issues of trust and culture as through services.

Figure 4.2 also shows the increasing complexity of the various methods for small, medium, large, and global organizations. Small organizations need fewer rigors of methods. These organizations are inherently Agile because of their simplistic structures, centralized decision making, and relatively few software systems. In comparison, medium-sized organizations experience increasing complexity of processes—although they also have ample opportunities to embed Agile practices within their processes. For example, increasing control and reporting will be required through governance processes for a medium-sized organization—yet the decision makers in these organizations can easily employ Agile values such as face-to-face communications and collaborations at the organizational level. Large organizations have many departments and divisions and comprise of a multitude of layers (e.g., all the layers shown in Figure 4.2). These layers of work also require increasingly rigorous planning and control. Global organizations are large organizations that are also spread geographically across many regions. Therefore, these large and global organizations have to also bring in legal issues, regional customer preferences, and sophistication in communications in using processes and frameworks. Composite Agile effectively becomes an umbrella of methods that brings together methods corresponding to the layers of an organization shown in Figure 4.2. In order to achieve that synergy of methods, it is important to understand these methods, the level at which they operate, the value they add, and the practical challenges in using them. This understanding starts with an investigation of the taxonomy of organizational methods.

Taxonomy of Organizational Methods and Their Agile Touch Points

SIDEBAR

The value proposition of Agile as a software development method is to enhance the ability of a business to change and to respond. *Agile* is thus a term that represents business Agility. Business Agility is closely tied with software Agility. Initially, however, there may be a need to separately study and understand both business and software. Eventually, the two (and all other) agilities of the organization need to merge. Composite Agile is the merging of software and business agilities from the many methods resulting in CAMS. CAMS in practice will comprise all methods and processes in an organization. CAMS will also be more than methods—it will be a strategic approach to business Agility.

The taxonomy of various processes (inventory of processes) within the organization at varying levels is depicted in Figure 4.3. These processes, also listed in Table 4.1, need to be studied and understood in order to facilitate a smooth interplay among them. The interfaces between the elements of these organizational processes and the practices of Agile are dubbed *touch points*. Some touch points, as listed in Table 4.1, are areas of work where Agile practices can be embedded in organizational processes. This merging of Agile practices in formal process maps (discussed later) results in real addition of value in a composite approach. This embedding of Agile practices in the organizational processes forms the basis for subsequent discussion of CAMS, its configuration, and usage.

CAMS bases itself on increased understanding of all organizational processes and the way they impact the functions of that organization. Figure 4.3 shows a classification or groups of these processes. Figure 4.3 also shows examples of processes within the taxonomy as also an approximate relationship between these processes. While some processes are technical in nature, others are more orientated toward business. A brief description of these processes follows.

- Software Agile (IT development): The impact of Agile methods (e.g., Extreme programming, XP; Scrum) is the maximum when used in software development projects. Coding and testing are the major activities related to Agile. Planned activities such as formal requirements modeling are kept minimal in software Agile processes when they are used in software development.
- Business analysis: These processes (e.g., International Institute of Business Analysts' [IIBA] Business Analysis Body of Knowledge [BABOK], Skills Framework for Information Age [SFIA], and Australian Institute of Business Analysis [AIBA] among others) enable and support the exploration of business needs to enable decision making. Business analysis also includes modeling of business requirements (functional, nonfunctional, and interface). These requirements (or features) can be modeled in detail with use cases and activity diagrams. Alternatively (or additionally), user stories can also be used in this modeling.
- Testing: Processes can include test-driven development (TDD), such as ISTQB® and its variants. These processes or frameworks provide significant focus on testing and test cases as a means of driving the development work. Writing of test cases before coding is a mechanism to enable user acceptance of the development work. In fact, test cases can also be used as the

Table 4.1 Organizational Processes and Examples of Their Agile Touch Points

	Software Development Life Cycles	*Software Processes*	*Project Management Processes*	*IT Governance Standards*	*Business Management Processes*	*Business Analysis*	*Testing*	*Modeling, Architecture*
Planned processes	Waterfall Spiral RAD/JAD	RUP OPEN	PMBOK Prince2	CoBIT ITIL	Six Sigma Kaizen, Kanban, Lean	IIBA SFIA AIBA	ISTQB	UML, BPMN TOGAF Zachmann
Agile touch points	Iteration formation, repetition	Process config-uration	Planning, facilitating, compliance	Control, reporting, estimation	Collaboration beyond organization, negotiation risks	Modeling requirements (user stories), value-driven, operations	Test-driven development, prototyping	Just enough design, cross-check constraints, integration

RAD, Rapid Application Development

JAD, Joint Application Design

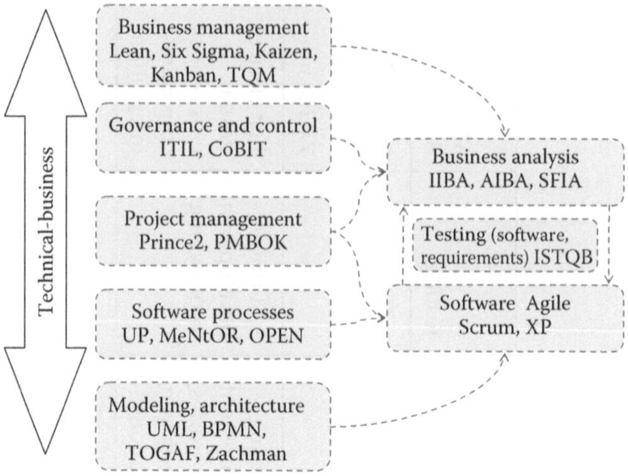

Figure 4.3 A taxonomy of processes and standards across technical and business levels in the organization.

basis for development. Test standardization boards, such as ISTQB, provide a uniform basis for testers to ascertain their competency levels and apply them in practice.

- Modeling, architecture (UML; The Open Group Architecture Framework, TOGAF): They provide a wide-ranging suite of notations and diagrams that, together with corresponding computer-aided software engineering (CASE) tools, form the basis for large-scale systems modeling, design, and development. While the two areas of work—modeling and architecture—are separate, they are outlined here as mechanisms to understanding constraints and limitations, balance risks, and enhance quality.
- Software formal processes: These are the planned development processes (e.g., Rational Unified Process [RUP] and Object-Oriented Process, Environment, and Notation [OPEN]) that are based on formal software development life cycles (SDLCs) (e.g., waterfall). These formal software development processes came into prominence in the mid-1990s when the object-oriented approach became popular and the Object Management Group (OMG) became globally known. The process maps with CAMS (discussed later) can be considered part of the formal software processes and have been used to plan and direct projects.
- IT governance/management: This includes the overall management function that can be further extended to governance. Standards such as Information Technology Infrastructure Library (ITIL) and Control Objectives for Information and related Technology (CoBIT) play a major role in providing service-level standards. These IT control and governance processes also enable maintenance of software assets (such as models and architectures—beyond the code), traceability of requirements, and their deployment after development.
- Project management (e.g., using Projects in Controlled Environments [Prince2] or Project Management Book of Knowledge [PMBOK]): Project management provides mechanisms for planning, controlling, and reporting of projects through the formally defined activities and deliverables. Planned projects are governed by the four factors of time, budget, resources, and quality. These four factors have to be in balance to execute successful projects. Astute project management also undertakes up-front business analysis (particularly requirements

modeling) that can aid in scoping the project, making sensible estimation of time and effort, and also undertaking revision of those estimates.

- Business management: Processes here guide the exploration of business needs, risks, and capabilities. Business management undertakes modeling of the aforementioned factors (and many more) to ascertain the risks and benefits of a program of work. Agility provides the business with the opportunity to change its direction in response to external risks and also to ensure flexibility of the IT systems to support that change. Lean, Six Sigma, Kaizen, and Kanban are examples of business management processes that enable continuous optimization of work in business. These business processes need to relate to the software development and maintenance activities that are undertaken at the project level.

The tiers of an organization (shown in Figure 4.2) and the processes and frameworks employed in those tiers (shown in Figure 4.3) are owned, in practice, by one or more roles. Thus, in considering the impact of one process on another, it is important to keep in mind the role that is using that particular process. Figure 4.4 shows the complex reality of the organizational processes discussed thus far. An understanding of the interdependence between these processes is a crucial step in avoiding methods friction. Since each of these processes is based on (or owned by) a role, Figure 4.4 shows the primary roles that are involved in the use of these organizational processes. As can be seen, each role has to not only understand and apply their own processes and standards, but also be aware of (and even apply to an extent) the processes used by other roles in the organization. Typical organizational roles and their use of processes can be described as follows:

- The business analyst (e.g., using IIBA) is interested in exploring business needs and modeling business requirements. The business analyst needs to be aware of the phases, activities, and deliverables of project management, development, and testing processes in order to avoid method friction.
- The project manager (e.g., using Prince 2) needs to be aware of development processes as well as business analysis and governance processes. Understanding the deliverables of project

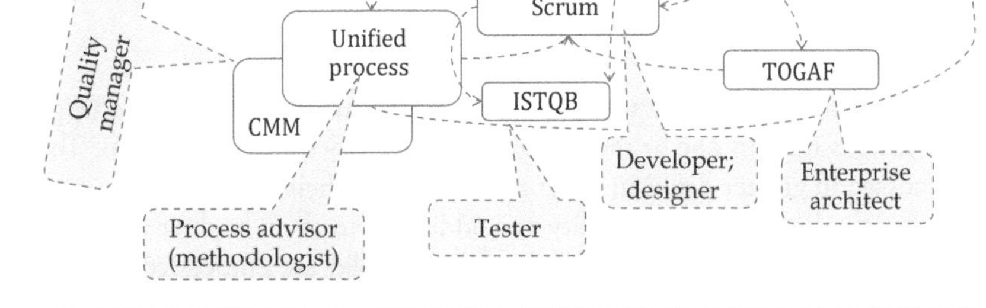

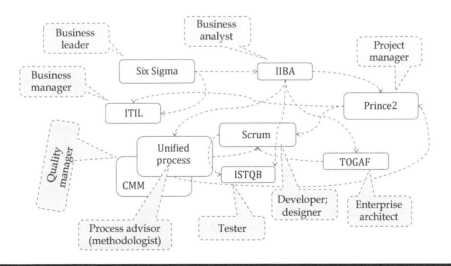

Figure 4.4 Complex interrelationships between processes and frameworks—a role-based organizational view.

management (such as the formality of a project plan and its tracking) in the context of business analysis (and its deliverable, such as the functional model) can help the project manager understand the interdependencies between the two deliverables. This is a means to avoid methods friction in CAMS.

- The business leader (e.g., using Six Sigma) continues to optimize and improve business processes. The business leader is also interested in the output of business analysis work (especially at the needs exploration level) and IT governance processes that help him with the legal requirements.
- The quality manager (e.g., using Capability Maturity Model, CMM) is interested in the SDLC and its maturity. Quality processes also interact with project management processes and the quality manager needs to be aware of the constraints provided by the business and EAs.
- The process advisor (methodologist, e.g., using UP) is interested in the configuration of the software development methods as well as the interaction of these with other methods. This understanding of the interplay of methods is crucial in understanding and avoiding methods friction. A process advisor, through this understanding, can configure a composite iteration that has minimum methods friction. This can be done by ensuring that the activities between various methods do not conflict with each other, deliverables are not duplicated or missed, and output is subject to quality assurance (QA) techniques.
- The enterprise architect (e.g., using TOGAF) is interested in how the developer will use the constraints and qualities of the architecture, together with the business needs specified by the business analyst. This role provides an understanding of the risks associated with technical decisions and thereby prevents the project work from going down the wrong path.
- The developer/designer (e.g., using Scrum) is primarily interested in undertaking solution-level design and development work using an Agile approach. However, this role needs to be aware of the various development life cycles, architectural constraints, and the project management method being used in the project.
- The tester (e.g., using ISTQB), apart from testing, is interested in the Agile method used in development and the output of the business analyst (to design acceptance tests). This awareness of the tester ensures that she is able to participate in the development activity by correctly timing the tests and providing feedback of the results to the developers for their action.
- The business manager (e.g., using ITIL) is interested in controlling and managing the business. Therefore, IT governance processes become important to this role. A governance framework such as ITIL provides an understanding of the service-level maturity for the business. Such governance framework is influenced by project management methods such as Prince2 because of its control and reporting features.

The discussion thus far outlines the taxonomy of organizational processes (Figure 4.3) and the interest of various roles in one or more organizational processes (Figure 4.4). These processes need to be discussed in greater detail in order to understand their Agile touch points. The discussion of various methods and the way Agility can add value to them at their corresponding touch points paves the way for CAMS. Agile values and principles are embedded in these aforementioned methods. Agile practices are particularly made to fit in with the process maps for software development. The following is a discussion of these processes with an intent of moving toward a composite Agile process framework.

Software Agile (Development)

Agile software development, as a method, subscribes to the Agile Manifesto. The focus of these methods is on producing a working code (or its equivalent). Individuals have substantial freedom in following these methods and, yet, they are considered an integral part of the team. Contemporary Agile, understood as a method, provides key guidance at the software project level. For example, through Agile principles, the users are made part of the development team. Such collaboration bridges the gap between specifications and the end product. Agile, through its short and sharp iterations, also ensures that the product reaches the users as soon as practicable. These Agile methods have been presented in Chapter 2 and their limitations highlighted in Chapter 3. Since the methods are themselves Agile, the only Agile touch points of interest to these methods are the nonsoftware areas of work in the organization. For example, Agile principles such as simplicity, transparency, and courage become extremely interesting when they are applied in business functions such as accounting and HR. CAMS is interested in elevating and using the Agile values and principles across an entire organization and not just software projects. Thus, in CAMS, Agility also gets used in business analysis, testing, modeling, and architecture.

Business Analysis

Business analysis deals with elicitation of requirements, planning, and managing the requirements documentation, analyzing requirements, understanding and communicating business needs to all stakeholders continuously, and providing input into the solution. The practice of business analysis uses a wide array of techniques. For example, high-level business needs are explored using mind mapping, root cause analysis, and SWOT analysis. Detailed requirements modeling is undertaken with use case modeling, activity graphs, and Business Process Modeling Notation (BPMN) diagrams.

Understanding and modeling of the problem enables balancing the various factors (and risks) associated with a problem. This, in turn, enables a business analyst to arrive at an appropriate recommendation for the solution. Business analysis recommendations consider the fact that IT-based solutions may not be the only way to solve business problems. Business analysis processes aid decision making at the organizational level. For example, business analysis considers business needs and weighs it against the risks (e.g., through a SWOT analysis). The output of this analysis can assist business in taking the correct decisions. Agile values of collaboration and trust can be brought into this decision making. Business analysis is also undertaken in software projects at a requirements modeling level. Thus, business analysts model functional, nonfunctional, and interface requirements. Features can also be written as user stories written on story cards. The Agile touch points with business analysis are explored further in CAMS (Chapter 7).

Testing

Testing represents a wide array of activities that occur in both software and business processes as well as in projects, and across the organization. For example, testing can occur in an Agile project almost on a daily basis (continuously) whereas, in the same project, the user acceptance test may occur right at the end of a release. Testing may occur for the process of recording a customer complaint in a call center environment, or it may test the carbon emission of a process during business as usual (BAU). Testing needs its processes and frameworks that will help and guide the testing process. Depending on the project demographics as well as organizational situations, testing frameworks have to change to reflect those specific needs. Testing also has to relate to the QA activities being undertaken in a project as the QA activities are aimed at preventing errors (as against testing, which is focused on detecting errors). While standards such as the ISO9001 have been popular in the overall QA area, there are specific testing standards and frameworks for testing that are of interest to composite Agile. For example, the testing framework as assessed by the ISTQB has a positive role to play in providing formal testing activities and tasks that can be carried out in composite Agile. The ISTQB is working on a Testing Body of Knowledge (TBOK) 2 that provides a suite of principles for testing that can be embedded with the Agile principles and practices. For example, the formal activity of "test planning" can make use of the Agile principle of collaboration; and the "testing" activity itself can use the Agile practice of continuous testing as the code is being developed. Chapter 9 discusses testing in CAMS in further detail.

Modeling and Architecture

Modeling and architecture are primarily derived from the planned approaches to software development. They can also be applied in other nonsoftware projects where modeling is a mechanism of creating a blueprint of a problem or solution without actually developing the full solution. Therefore, modeling can significantly enhance the quality of a product—as it enables discussions, clarifications, and management of expectations. Architecture, which is also based on the creation of models, is aimed at specifying the constraints applicable in understanding a problem and putting together a solution. Thus, both modeling and architecture rely heavily on visual diagramming techniques aimed at enhancing problem solving. These techniques are discussed next with a view to understanding their standards and frameworks so that they can operate together with Agile principles and practices.

Modeling

Within the software domain, the earliest modeling effort was through flowcharts and programming sheets. This effort was quickly followed by entity-relationship (ER) and data-flow diagram (DFD) techniques, made popular during the relational database (RDB) era. Later, in the mid-1990s, the Unified Modeling Language (UML, current version 2.0) of the OMG (www.omg.org) became the de facto modeling standard for analysis and design. Modeling, through the UML, can be carried out in understanding the problem, casting the solution, and understanding the background constraints and limitations. Thus, the modeling effort in UML occurs in problem, solution, and background spaces (Unhelkar). The UML came about as a combination of the three most popular methodologies of that time: Booch (1994), Object Modeling Technique (OMT) (Rumbaugh et al.), and Objectory (Jacobson et al., 1993). Later several other methodologies merged into it, resulting in the current, formal UML version 2.0. This has resulted in 13 official diagrams in the UML—some of which offer excellent opportunity to boost Agility in practice. The rigors of the UML metamodel and the opportunities through model-driven architecture (MDA) can provide the robustness, and the Agile principles and practices provide the flexibility in a composite Agile project. Combining the collaborative and customer-centric principles of Agility with the formality of UML diagrams provides excellent value and quality in practice.

Consider, for example, the four different ways in which UML is meant to add value in software projects. These four ways of UML usage can benefit the use of Agile principles and practices as briefly discussed.

1. Visualizing: This is the primary purpose of the UML; its notations and diagrams provide an excellent industry standard mechanism to represent pictorially the requirements or business processes, solution, and architecture. Placing UML models on large, visible charts within software projects can be a useful way of applying Agile practice. Use case diagrams and activity diagrams also provide excellent means to present the requirements of a user. Combining these formal visual techniques with the story cards of Agile provides both control (traceability) and flexibility of a project.
2. Specifying: Together with visual representations, UML also facilitates specification of some of the artifacts. This includes specifications for actors, use cases, classes, attributes, operations, and so on. Specifications can provide the details of a model and thereby open up opportunities for applying quality techniques. Although pure Agile approaches are not too keen on in-depth specifications, Agile principles such as simplicity in design and acceptance of changes can be carried out in a much easier manner through detailed and formal specifications. For example, specifications of a feature on a user story can be inserted in the specifications of a use case and, thereby, formalized and controlled in a project.
3. Constructing: UML can also be used for software construction as it is possible to generate the basic code (C++, Java, VB, Smalltalk) from UML visual representations, depending on the CASE tool being used. The current literature on Executable UML also suggests that UML can and will be increasingly used in construction of software. This "construction" usage of UML comes closest to what the Agile methods talk about. Agility can play an important role in promoting the construction of software using UML—as it is much easier and faster to use Executable UML as against an executable code.
4. Documenting: With the help of UML, additional and detailed documentation such as requirements, architecture, design, project plans, tests, and prototypes can be provided to enhance specifications and visual representations. Agile, as understood in software domain, is not focused on creating substantial documentation. However, the composite Agile approach pays' significant attention to documentation. This documentation appears within the process-maps, as discussed later in this chapter.

Chapter 5 presents a list of UML diagrams and the way they can add value in an Agile project. This understanding is a part of the overall move of an organization toward composite Agile.

Architecture

The architecture provides the basis for structural stability that can apply to both BAU operations of an organization and the new initiatives and projects. Architecture can be understood as an abstraction of the systems and processes in an organization. Specific architectural frameworks, such as TOGAF and the Zachmann framework, also include people, in addition to processes and mechanism, to change/transform an organization.

Agile methods recommend just enough architecture and design. There is no detailed and long-drawn art architectural exercise in Agile projects. This may well work for straightforward development projects. However, creation and adherence to architecture is important in any kind of project. Typically, an EA provides a bird's-eye view of all of the IT assets of the organization. An EA can be an all-encompassing model of an organization's technical (IT) architecture, systems, contents (databases), interfaces, applications, networks, and solutions. Such a view enables understanding and balancing of risks in taking technical and business decisions. EA can also enable alignment of these aforementioned elements with the business strategic objectives and vision

(McGovern et al., 2004). Thus, architectures enable consideration of the enterprise-wide effect of technical decision making. Architectures are made up of a suite of guidelines, patterns, and corresponding frameworks. These frameworks standardize the application of architectures within an organization and also help their understanding across an industry. While this is discussed in detail in Chapter 5, here is a brief mention of TOGAF primarily from its Agile touch points. TOGAF is based on the following four layers of architecture.

1. Business architecture defines business strategy, governance, organization, and key business processes; Agile principles can be used in order to collaborate with key business stakeholders to arrive at the business architecture. The governance and organizational structure of the business can also benefit by the application of Agile principles and practices that enable change.
2. Data architecture defines the structure of an organization's logical and physical data assets and associated data management resources; prototypes and UML's class models can be used together to create models (schema) of data architecture.
3. Application architecture specifies individual application systems and their deployment—which can be supported by Agile's iterative and incremental releases and flexible requirements capturing; UML's package and component diagrams can be used to create a distributed application architecture.
4. Technology architecture specifies the software infrastructure intended to support the deployment of core, mission-critical applications. UML's state diagrams can be used for real-time modeling and deployment diagrams for modeling the overall technology architecture.

Creating and using visual models of the above architectures provides the basis for discussions of constraints and limitations on how the user stories or features are developed. These architectural considerations enable an understanding of the dependencies that stories have on each other. Furthermore, EAs are not created specifically for an Agile project; instead, they are organizational-level models that provide the basis and input for Agile projects.

Software Processes and Agile

Formalizing these SDLCs leads to planned software processes. The core building blocks of these software processes are their roles, deliverables (with templates), activities, and tasks (Unhelkar). These building blocks are supported by guidelines for configuration into usable "components," "chunks," or "fragments." Within the composite Agile approach described here, they are called *process maps* (described in greater detail in Figure 4.11). Eventually these process maps, as building blocks of a process, can be embedded in CASE tools. Three software processes (listed in Table 4.1), the RUP, Mentor, and OPEN, are described below in the context of Agile.

Rational Unified Process (RUP)

The focus of RUP is mostly on UML-based visual models rather than on text-based documentation. RUP enables all team members regardless of their role in the project to "share a common language, process and view of software development" (Rational Software, 2001). Notice how Agile methods focus only on sharing of code rather than on sharing of visual models. Furthermore, pure Agile methods also depend for such sharing on the specific motivation and skill of a team member. However, workers in RUP have roles in a project that are more elaborate and more formally defined than in an Agile process. Activities are assigned to a worker who formally owns and completes them. There is minimal formality in the assignment of tasks in Agile—and minimal individual ownership (as it is joint ownership). Artifacts, which are project deliverables, are primarily comprised of a code in Agile projects. Workflows in RUP provide higher levels of granularity for activities as they enable sequencing of a group of activities.

RUP claims to be incremental and iterative. According to Kruchten (2003), the iterations in RUP enable a more efficient use of resources and a high level of code reuse. This is in line with the Agile practices of iterations and refactoring. However, according to Chatterjee (2006), RUP is not able to manage enterprise-level issues and organizational issues too well. Agile on its own is also not able to manage organizational issues. RUP is a formal process that needs to be initiated and customized according to the "organizational assessment and the production of a development case" (Ambler, 2005). There is no such need for up-front work in configuring and using a process in Agile. Agile and RUP can work together only when Agile practices are embedded within the activities and tasks of RUP.

Process Mentor

Process Mentor is a platform for creating and modifying process architectures that cover the entire SDLC. This includes process support for concept exploration, alternative evaluation, business investigation, requirements analysis, system modeling, design, development, implementation, and testing (Process Mentor, 2009). The stages within Process Mentor include business investigation, requirements, modeling, design, development and testing, and project management. These stages are supported by road maps, process units, and roles. The development and implementation modules of Process Mentor are the ones that lend themselves to the use of Agile principles and practices. Thus, once again, the importance of Agility in this planned process comes from the way in which the activities and tasks of development are carried out, rather than their sequencing, tracking, and reporting.

Object-Oriented Process, Environment, and Notation (OPEN)

Object-Oriented Process, Environment, and Notation (OPEN) is a software development process framework. The OPEN process framework is made up of three main elements (Firesmith et al., 2005). These three elements are a metamodel, a repository of reusable method components (or method fragments), and construction and usage guidelines (OPFRO, 2009). OPEN is a flexible and tailored process framework that covers business, quality, modeling, and reuse issues within the SDLC (Henderson-Sellers and Unhelkar, 2002). A number of opportunities exist to embed Agility within the OPEN framework. For example, the "Build" method fragment can easily make use of most practices of Agile. Similarly, opportunities for inserting Agile principles and practices within the development and testing method fragments exist within OPEN. OPEN also bases itself on the fountain model of software development (see the sidebar). Hence, OPEN is inherently iterative and incremental.

IT Governance and Agile

Standards for IT governance have emerged with the increasing need for control and compliance by businesses. Two popular IT governance standards that are worth exploring in the context of Agility are the CoBIT and ITIL standards. The impact of Agile on a governance process can be significant because the Agile Manifesto gives precedence to individuals and interactions over documentation. Consider however, the Sarbanes–Oxley (SOX) style compliance requirements, which state that there should be evidence of certain requirements and the sign-offs at the end of every stage of the project for audit. The need for auditable and formal documentation needs to be acknowledged and acted upon in practice—irrespective of the use of Agility in development. For example, formally documented requirements provide the basis for secure contracts. Specifications and documentations can also provide traceability of requirements, their testing, and their acceptance by the user. Thus, there is a need to merge the use of governance frameworks together with Agile principles. Such a merger improves the understanding among the business, developers, and even auditors.

The two common governance standards of CoBIT and ITIL are briefly mentioned in the context of Agile in the following (for a detailed discussion in composite Agile see Chapter 8).

Control Objectives for Information and Related Technology (CoBIT)

CoBIT (latest v 5.0) creates the opportunity for corporate governance to understand IT operations and vice versa. Agility has the responsibility and the opportunity to influence corporate governance. Organizations employing CoBIT usually customize it according to their IT infrastructure, business values, and risk profile (Moeller, 2008). Agility can be combined with controls and documentation of CoBIT to improve collaboration and understanding as well as providing documentation and control of organizational level activities. Considering the CoBIT activities in the context of Agility also encourages greater alignment of IT development with business goals. Business can specify their governance and control requirements, and developers can prioritize them together with business (the balancing act is as shown in Figure 4.1).

In projects, specifications and prioritization relate to the development of the functionality of the system. They do not play a role in the strategic decision-making process such as whether to buy an enterprise resource planning (ERP) solution. This is where business analysis and project management competencies play a part. Therefore, CoBIT has to be used to combine IT governance together with business analysis and Agility. A synergy between the methods that support the analytical methods and governance is required in implementing CoBIT.

Information Technology Infrastructure Library (ITIL)

Since ITIL focuses on the mapping of IT strategies with business strategies, it has substantial relevance to the discussion of Agile in practice. ITIL is a set of operational guidelines that evolved from a British Government initiative. The importance of ITIL is the help it provides to IT departments in improving their quality of service (QoS). ITIL (2009) has five core publications or disciplines made up of services delivery and support; planning and implementing service management; security management; managing IT infrastructure and applications; and managing overall software assets of the organization. These disciplines have initially focused only on IT operations. This, in turn, enables IT operations to increasing their QoS through uptime, rapid problem resolution, and improved security.

Project Management and Agile

Project management, especially in software projects, can be considered as a profession in its own right. Despite the uniqueness of software projects, the phases, roles, and deliverables of project management have gone a long way in streamlining software development activities. Software projects are served by project management processes such as Prince2 and PMBOK. Highsmith* states that Agile teams are asked to be Agile, flexible, and adaptive, but are then told to conform to planned scope, schedule, and cost goals. They are asked to adapt, but inside a very small box. That small box is the development task within a project. The way to expand that box is to consider the activities and tasks within these branded project management methods from an Agile perspective. This combination of Agility within project management results in a composite process. (Chapter 8 discusses in detail how this is achieved.) A composite project approach explores the opportunities of using Agile together with a planned project management method. For example, projects employing Prince2 have a controlled and structured beginning, middle, and ending (Bellis, 2003). These projects have the rigor of Prince2 combined with the flexibility of Agile practices—but only when embedded within the activities and tasks of Prince2.

Business Management and Agile

Processes that manage and optimize businesses are removed from the nitty-gritty of software development. However, these pure business-level processes operating in the business methods space also stand to benefit by Agile principles and practices. Processes at business levels and Agility have many complementary elements in them. This view of business and Agile was also ratified during the interviews undertaken in the associated composite Agile research project (see Appendix I). Furthermore, software Agility also complements business Agility. For example, while the processes of Kaizen eliminate waste, they need corresponding modifications and upgradation of the supporting software. Agile practices can be used in undertaking software modifications. This section discusses three processes briefly (Six Sigma, Kaizen, and Kanban) in the context of Agile.

Six Sigma

Six Sigma is a data-driven business management strategy that provides tools to reduce defects in any process (product or service) and bring about improvement in the performance and quality of a process (Yang, 2005). The fundamental idea of Six Sigma is the possibility of measuring the defects in a process that can eventually lead to systematic discovery of eliminating a process defect (Keller and Pyzdek, 2005). Six Sigma mandates give the stages Define, Measure, Analyze, Improve, and Control. These stages bring about a certain rigor and control to the business processes of the organization.

While Six Sigma provides a framework that is rigid for good reasons, Agility enables flexibility at the software development and maintenance levels. Agile values and principles can be embedded in businesses using Six Sigma. For example, the rigors of Six Sigma's stages can be upheld but the time shortened with the help of the Agile values of iteration and visibility. Six Sigma and Agility can complement each other as the two are focused on two different aspects of an organization—the pure business aspect and the software support aspect. Collaboration and coordination between the business stakeholders and the software developers who maintain the code is necessary in a complementary approach.

Kaizen

Kaizen is a business strategy that focuses on continuous improvement in a number of aspects of a company's results (Imai, 1986), such as quality, productivity, cost, staff satisfaction,

* Highsmith, J., www.cutter.com.

security, company culture, leadership, and technology. The idea of continuous improvement at the company level ties in with Agile values at the organizational level. Kaizen aims to involve every employee in the organization from the chief executive officer (CEO) to the workers (Liker, 2004) in the attempt to enhance quality. Kaizen includes defining and improving the defined standards (Kotelnikov, 2009) on an ongoing basis. Furthermore, it provides employees with the required training, materials, and supervision to meet the standards (Hudgik, 2009). The five founding elements of Kaizen, teamwork, personal discipline, improved morale, quality circles, and suggestions for improvement, seem to have surprising similarity with Agile approaches. The Agile development approach maps to Kaizen at the business level. Kaizen also has a number of principles that relate to Agile (described in detail in Chapter 6).

Kanban

Kanban as a method can provide support for managing the BAU as well as product portfolio management. This is because Kanban is based on "visibility" of everything that goes on in a business or its projects. Kanban is thus a mechanism to provide ongoing work within the organization without overloading teams and projects. The dependencies of various roles on one or more methods within an organization were shown earlier in Figure 4.4. The sequencing of activities and tasks within those methods can all add up to delays and overloads if not properly monitored. This is also a challenge of methods friction, and this is where Kanban can help when used in a composite approach.

Kanban attempts to make the "overloading" of projects and teams visible to the decision makers of the organization. Kanban then attempts to "de-stress" the teams by not putting strict timelines (deadlines) on the delivery of work products. When teams are free from the stress of delivery, they are able to be more productive and can sustain their development for a very long term—precisely what the Agilists have been advocating through Agile values and principles.

Visibility of work is the key to Kanban. This visibility and an understanding that "timeboxing does not necessarily lead to reduction in time" has organization-wide applicability. In fact, Kanban will provide value only when it is applied across organizations and it balances intra- as well as interteam overloadings. In a composite strategy for all organizational methods, Kanban has applicability in project management and business analysis, and even in specific testing projects.

A composite approach, as developed next, uses Kanban to de-stress the entire organization (as against just a project) by examining the impact of one method (e.g., ITIL at the service level) on another (e.g., Agile using TDD).

Composite Agile Method and Strategy (CAMS)

The processes discussed thus far apply to the software, project, and business tiers of an organization. Agile values and practices promise to play a significant role in all of these organizational level processes. In order to realize that promise, however, the commonality of many features of the planned approaches together with the Agile practices need to be extracted and summarized. Furthermore, as the preceding discussion on the various methods used in an organization indicates, Agile practices need to be elevated and applied across an organization. This forms the basis for CAMS.

CAMS need not be considered as a specific method but, rather, an overall umbrella of methods that covers planned and Agile development, business needs exploration, business analysis, project management, QA, and governance processes. Thus, CAMS has a much broader focus than what is called the *hybrid Agile* (McGevna, 2012), which aims to synergize aspects of planned and Agile software methods only for software development projects. CAMS investigates the use of Agile principles and practices at *all* levels of the organization. This merger and balancing indicates that Agile need not be so much an independent methodology that would replace the existing process being used by the organization, but rather a suite of practices that need to be carried out within and across those existing processes. The result is an Agile culture that becomes embedded within the formalities of planned processes for development and operations of the organization as a whole.

As a part of the research project investigating CAMS, interview-based discussions were undertaken (see Appendix I for details of this research project and the interviews). On the basis of the responses from the participants, a mapping of organizational activities and processes that are primarily important in those activities was created. This mapping is shown in Table 4.2. The ticks in the table indicate that a process is actively used in carrying out a specific organizational activity. (This affirmation of the role of a process in an organizational activity was based on responses from interview participants described in Appendix I.)

The many processes shown in Table 4.2 are used at various levels in an organization. The ticks in the table indicate the predominant area of contribution of a process when a particular activity is carried out in an organization. For example, the organizational activity of change management will require processes dealing with project management, business management, and business analysis. The absence of a tick in a process activity box, however, does not mean the process is not used at all. A process such as Prince2 in project management or Scrum in pure Agile development will have some influence or other across the entire organization. Table 4.2 highlights the extreme importance of some processes for the corresponding organizational activities.

The processes listed in Table 4.2 are also not exclusive to one another. These processes have many commonalities. Abstracting the common areas within these processes provides the basis for their composite use. At the same time, there are areas of activities within a process that can tend to compete against one another. This vying of processes for similar organizational activities forms the basis for "methods friction." Advances in Agile approaches, in particular, have a large bearing on methods friction. Reducing methods friction is a key ingredient of the composite Agile approach across the organization.

Consider the many distinct methods that are in use in an organization. Figure 4.5 shows the business, projects, and software development methods to start with. Instances of these methods in the business area include Six Sigma and Lean, whereas those in projects area are Prince2 and PMBOK. RUP and OPEN are examples of formal methods in software development. Figure 4.5 also shows that the governance frameworks (e.g., ITIL, CoBIT) can play a role between business and projects. SFIA and IIBA are examples of business analysis frameworks that support analytical work between projects and development. This figure shows the increasing impact of Agile methods on these various frameworks and standards. In addition to understanding the growing impact of Agile on these methods, it is also important to understand that these methods have different priorities within an organization. For example, Prince2 is focused on major, well-defined phases to execute a project. ITIL is focused on activities to optimize service levels. SFIA and IIBA can be used to enhance the business analysis area of work in an organization.

A process can be considered as a description of the way in which work is carried out in a project. Each process is made up of elements as shown on the left in Figure 4.6. These elements include roles, activities, tasks, techniques, practices, and deliverables. A process distributes its elements in workable "chunks" called *process maps.* (Figure 4.11 shows an example of how these elements are organized in the form of a process map.) The elements of a process are described next.

The *role* provides a description of the profile of a person or persons who will be involved in executing the process. In a planned process, this role is defined and documented in detail. The person

Table 4.2 Summary of Formal/Planned Organizational Processes and Their Relevance to Organizational Activities

	Processes Used across Organizations							
Organizational Activities	*Modeling and Architecture*	*Software Processes*	*Project Management*	*Governance and Control*	*Business Management*	*Business Analysis*	*Testing*	*Software Agile*
Explorations and needs analysis					√	√		
Requirements management	√	√	√		√	√	√	
Solution/system design	√	√	√				√	
Development (coding/implementation)	√	√	√				√	√
Testing (system, user acceptance)		√	√			√	√	√
Modeling and architecture	√					√	√	√
Iterative and incremental approach		√	√					√
Quality assurance	√	√					√	
Change management			√		√	√		
Value-stream mapping					√	√	√	√
Planning for projects and programs			√	√	√	√		√
Monitoring and control				√	√	√		
Metrics and measurement			√			√	√	√
Risk management				√		√	√	√
Communication (organizational)					√	√	√	√
Deployment and training of products	√	√	√	√	√	√		
Strategic alignment (of technologies with business)				√	√	√	√	
Maintenance and operational support	√	√		√		√		

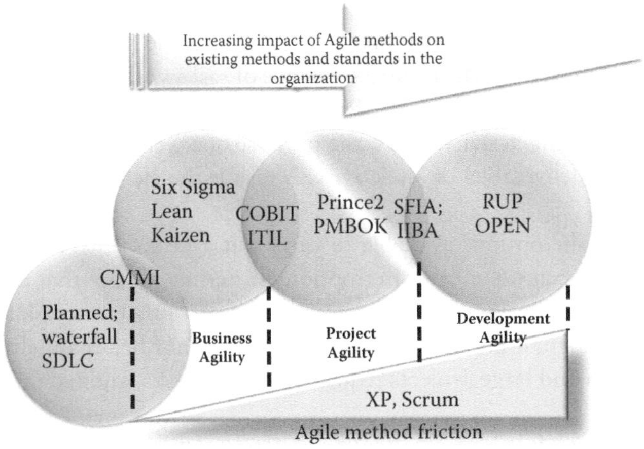

Figure 4.5 Methods friction potential due to increasing impact of Agile methods on the existing IT, project management, and business processes within the organization.

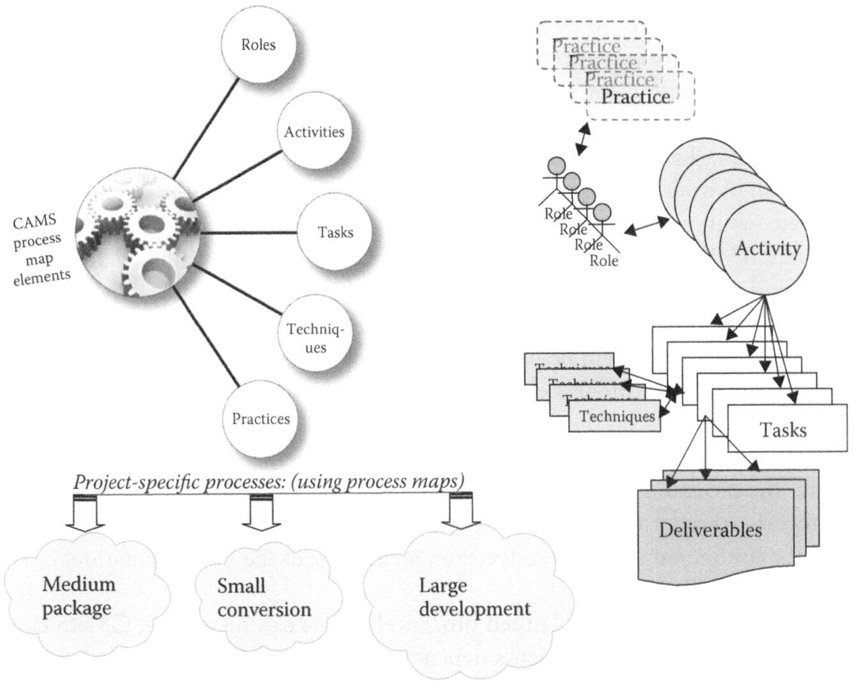

Figure 4.6 Planned and Agile elements of a process: basis for process configuration.

playing the given role can also be the recipient of the process output. Agile methods also describe roles such as product owner and Agile coach. But the rigor applied to each team member's role is much less in Agile than in planned methods.

The *activity* is a granular description of the work to be carried out by the role. Activities have a sequence or dependencies. Some activities can also be performed in parallel by more than one role.

The activity element in a process is the controlling element for a set of tasks within the process. Therefore, the activity element on its own does not have the same concrete existence as the tasks. Roles carry out the activities by performing a sequence of tasks within the activities.

The *task* is the basic element of work carried out in a process. A task is carried out under the umbrella of the encompassing activity. Thus, the purpose of a well-defined task is to help the role achieve the outcome (or deliverable) of an activity. A task is the element that appears in a project plan in a formal method.

The *technique* offers the options available to carry out a task. Thus, a task specifies the step to be carried out, and a technique can offer options in terms of how that step is to be carried out. Techniques can be descriptions of alternative ways of carrying out a task (Henderson-Sellers and Unhelkar, 2000). In small projects, the techniques may not be separately spelled out to the tasks. However, medium and large projects require activities, tasks, and techniques to be precisely described and tiered.

Agile *practice* represents the physical execution of actions within projects—guided by the principles and values of Agile. All Agile practices are based on the Agile Manifesto. Agile practices are directly carried out by roles in a project. These Agile practices are in some ways similar to the techniques of a planned method. Agile practices (shown in greater detail in Figures 4.12 and 4.13), carried out by individuals, support the activities and tasks to be performed within a process. These practices have the opportunity to be embedded in a wide area of work: analytical, requirements, development, design, project management, QA, operations, and testing.

A *deliverable* is the output (or result) produced by a process. These deliverables are produced by the roles responsible for various activities. The activities themselves are carried out by executing a set of well-defined tasks. Techniques and practices are employed within the tasks. Since deliverables are the result of work carried out by the roles, they are also called *work products*. Deliverables can be concrete, as in a set of documents, or they can be abstract, as in a "motivated team." Deliverables in CAMS are usually produced iteratively. That means, even if a deliverable is shown as being produced as a result of activities, only some of the tasks within the activities will result in a partial completion of the deliverables. Eventually, more activities, tasks, techniques, and Agile practices within the activities, will be performed to complete the deliverable.

The various categories of process elements described thus far are created and stored within a repository. Process elements can then be sourced from this repository in order to create a workable instance of a process. These elements are further grouped together in workable "chunks" to form process maps. The process maps (described in Figure 4.11) can be repeated across multiple iterations of a process—thereby forming the basis for an instance of a process. For example, process instances can be configured for small conversion, medium package implementation, or large-scale development projects (Figure 4.6).

The extent to which Agile and planned process elements can be used in CAMS can change. This dynamic mixing of process elements depends on the type of project, risks, and leadership decisions. Figure 4.7 shows the way in which the project leadership can decide to bring together these Agile and planned elements. Figure 4.7a shows the variation that a project leader can bring about between the rigidity (or rigor) of the planned method and the flexibility of the Agile method. The two approaches in Figure 4.7a are not exclusive to each other. Formal creation and the use of process maps can increase the planned elements in a process, whereas the use of Agile practices without fully producing the deliverables can increase the Agile elements in a process. Figure 4.7b shows the extent of these methods: Agile methods have a smaller reach within the organization, planned project methods are wider, and business and governance methods extend across the organization. Project leadership has to combine with organizational leadership in order

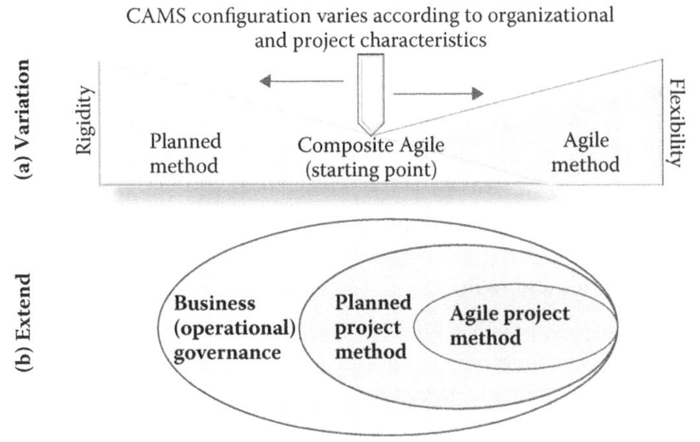

Figure 4.7 Variation of planned and Agile elements in a composite method configuration depending on organizational and project characteristics.

to decide the extent of Agility across the organization. Finally, the process expert putting these elements together needs to keep in mind the changing nature of this configuration. For example, an initial setting of a composite process may have more Agile and less planned elements; but as the project progresses, there may be a need to increase the formality in the project owing to increased risks or rigorous contracts.

Life Cycles as Basis for Composite

Waterfall as a linear model divides the project into sequential phases that prevent iterations. Since each stage employs the output of the previous phase, completion of the previous phase is obligatory. This staged approach provides rigorous control and discipline. Typically, the phases in a waterfall process are requirements and analysis, design, implementation or coding, testing, and maintenance. The project is tightly controlled through these phases with considerable documentation and formal reviews at the end of each phase. This results in a much better accuracy in estimations and improved measurements of deliverables. The waterfall approach is most suitable for projects that have clear and stable requirements or where the development team is relatively inexperienced.

Pure Agile methods with their flexibility are in total contrast to the waterfall method. Boehm's (1987) spiral model combines linear and iterative models in response to the demand for changes in the middle of a development project. Spiral life cycle enables the project to traverse four quadrants: objective determination and requirements gathering, design and risk identification and correction, development and verification, and planning for the next iteration. Each iteration starts with identification of stakeholders and their business goals and stops with "review and commitment." These quadrants (iterations) provide the first inkling of Agility (as understood today) within the planned approaches to software development.

Occasionally, the fountain model, signifying increasing iterations, has also been used. This line of thinking is based on the development of some requirements to form a software pool with the outputs falling back into the pool as water from a fountain does. This line of thinking came about during the object-oriented software development methods and it reflects the Agile principles of iterative development.

Finally, rapid application development (RAD) provides an excellent formal life cycle that embraces iterations in requirements planning, user/functional design, construction or development, and implementation and testing. The time-boxed prototyping of RAD is similar to the 40-hour week of a programmer in XP. However, the scalability challenge starts appearing early on in RAD, and that is also reflected in the challenges of Agile approaches.

SIDEBAR: Software Life Cycles and Agile

A software development life cycle (SDLC) is a background conceptual model that we use to guide a software project sequentially. Two of these popular SDLCs are the waterfall (Royce, 1970) and the spiral (Boehm, 1987). Occasionally, Rapid Application Development (RAD) (Maner, 1997) and later, in the object-oriented era, even the fountain mode (Henderson-Sellers) got classified as SDLCs. Each life cycle represents a line of thinking for software development with its own characteristics, strengths, and weaknesses. Understanding these life cycles can assist in the adoption of Agility within them.

One of the important practices used in Agile is the formation of iterations. Figure 4.8 shows a classic "wall" in an Agile project. This wall has large visible charts on it that display the artifacts. Figure 4.8 shows examples of stories. Typically, this iteration is divided into three visible parts—"To do," "Doing," and "Done." The user stories written on the cards are initially placed in the "To do" chart. Later, as the daily stand-up meetings are conducted and progress is achieved, the story cards start moving right to the "Doing" chart. Eventually, as stories are tested and accepted they are placed on the "Done" chart. These short, sharp Agile iterations have an important role to play in the configuration of major, planned iterations as part of CAMS. The CAMS iterations control not only a project but the overall business transformation in an organization as well. The Agile iterations are limited to within a project. They can become part of the SDLCs when used in a software project. The strategy for composite methods uses a combination of the rigors of formal SDLCs and the tremendous flexibility of Agile practices within software projects. This is the basis for a CAMS process architecture.

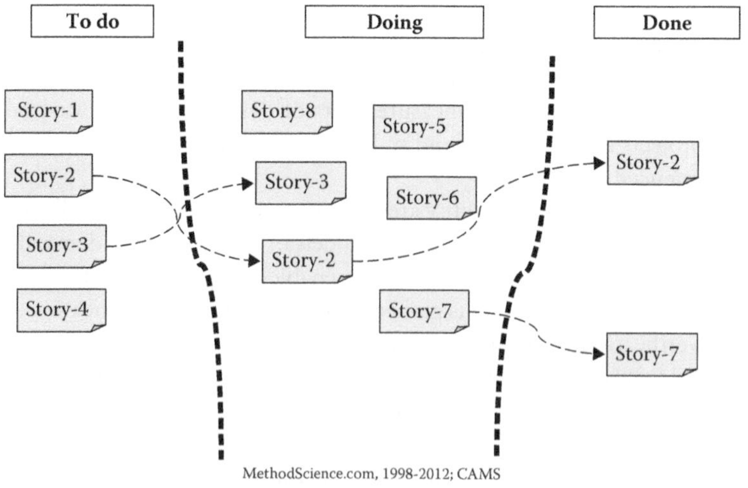

Figure 4.8 Three simple parts of an Agile iteration.

CAMS Architecture

The CAMS process architecture is made up of the following:

- CAMS repository: This holds all the principles and practices that are sourced from business, formal (planned), and at Agile levels. The repository is maintained and updated independent of the actual project work. Elements from the repository can be prefabricated as a process map. Such a repository is ideally owned by the center of excellence for CAMS.
- Configuration of CAMS: This is the drawing of relevant elements from the CAMS architecture and repository into an *instance* of a process. The process maps of CAMS are embedded in the iterations and increments of the overall CAMS life cycle. Apart from project-level usage, such CAMS configuration is of importance in a large transformation program. This is so because large-scale transformations become an integral part of the organization's business strategies that go beyond a project or two.
- Enactment of CAMS: This is the application of the method and strategy in practice. This enactment is dynamic, and continuously updates the configuration of the method. An organization adopts CAMS, configures it, and then undertakes its enactment in real-life transformation.
- Measurement with CAMS: This refers to the metrics and measurements during and after enactment. Analysis of the measures provides information on project velocities, defect rates, and rework. Thus, measurement and the data resulting from post-project reviews become an excellent source of information for the center of excellence for CAMS. Insights gained during a project (or an iteration) are enhanced and supported by metrics and measurements in CAMS.

Figure 4.9 shows the architecture of CAMS from a configuration perspective. This configuration, with its life cycle, iterations, increments, and Agile practices, can be applied to a business transformation program within an organization. The top layer of this CAMS architecture shows the waterfall or sequential aspect of the program. This layer is derived from the waterfall SDLC thinking (see the sidebar). The sequencing of phases will be affected by the type and size of an organization and the nature of its projects. For example, a third-party-driven (consulting) business transformation will have far more rigor, planning, and quality checking before the transformation moves from one phase to another. The sequencing of phases provides the necessary accounting control and reporting required in large transformation programs.

The tier below the sequential life cycle for an entire program (Figure 4.9) is the one that deals with project management. A program is made up of multiple projects. Each project can have (typically) three iterations—initial, major, and final. This iterative approach derives its thinking from the spiral SDLC (see the sidebar). Within these major iterations, a product can be developed incrementally through Increment-1, -2, and -3 as shown in Figure 4.9. Each increment can represent the development of a subsystem or a package. Within that development, though, there is opportunity for more lower level iterations. It is at this level that the basic Agile iteration described in Figure 4.8 fits in. The Agile iteration can source the many Agile practices that are made available through the organizational CAMS repository. Accompanying the business transformation of the program are the change management practices. Business transformation and change management are shown on either side of the project work in Figure 4.9 to indicate their applicability across the entire organization.

The iterative and incremental aspects of CAMS apply at the project as well as transformation program levels. Figure 4.10 goes deeper into the configuration of the initial, major, and final

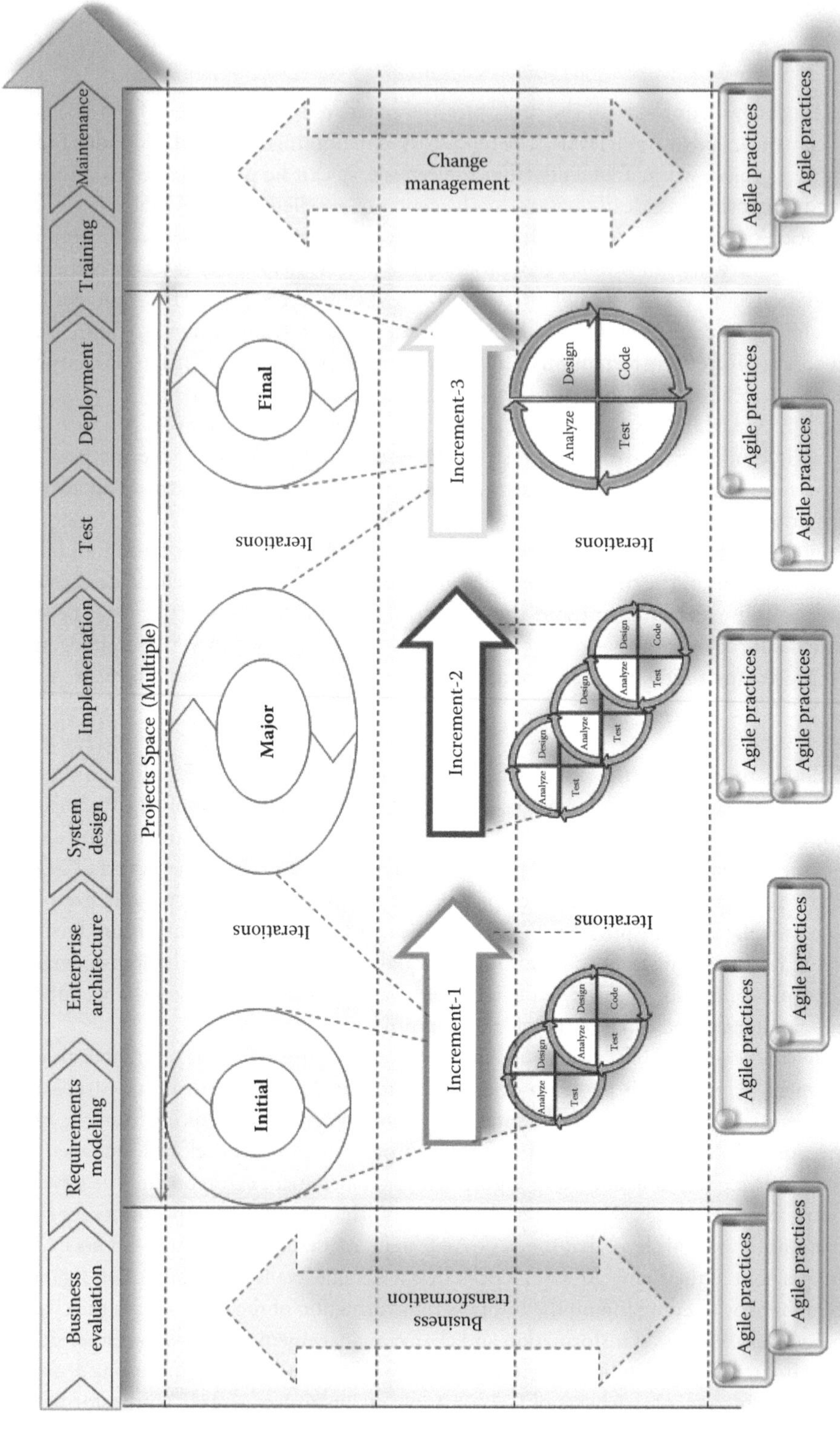

Figure 4.9 The core CAMS architecture that embeds Agile practices in iterations and increments, which are part of the overall business life cycle.

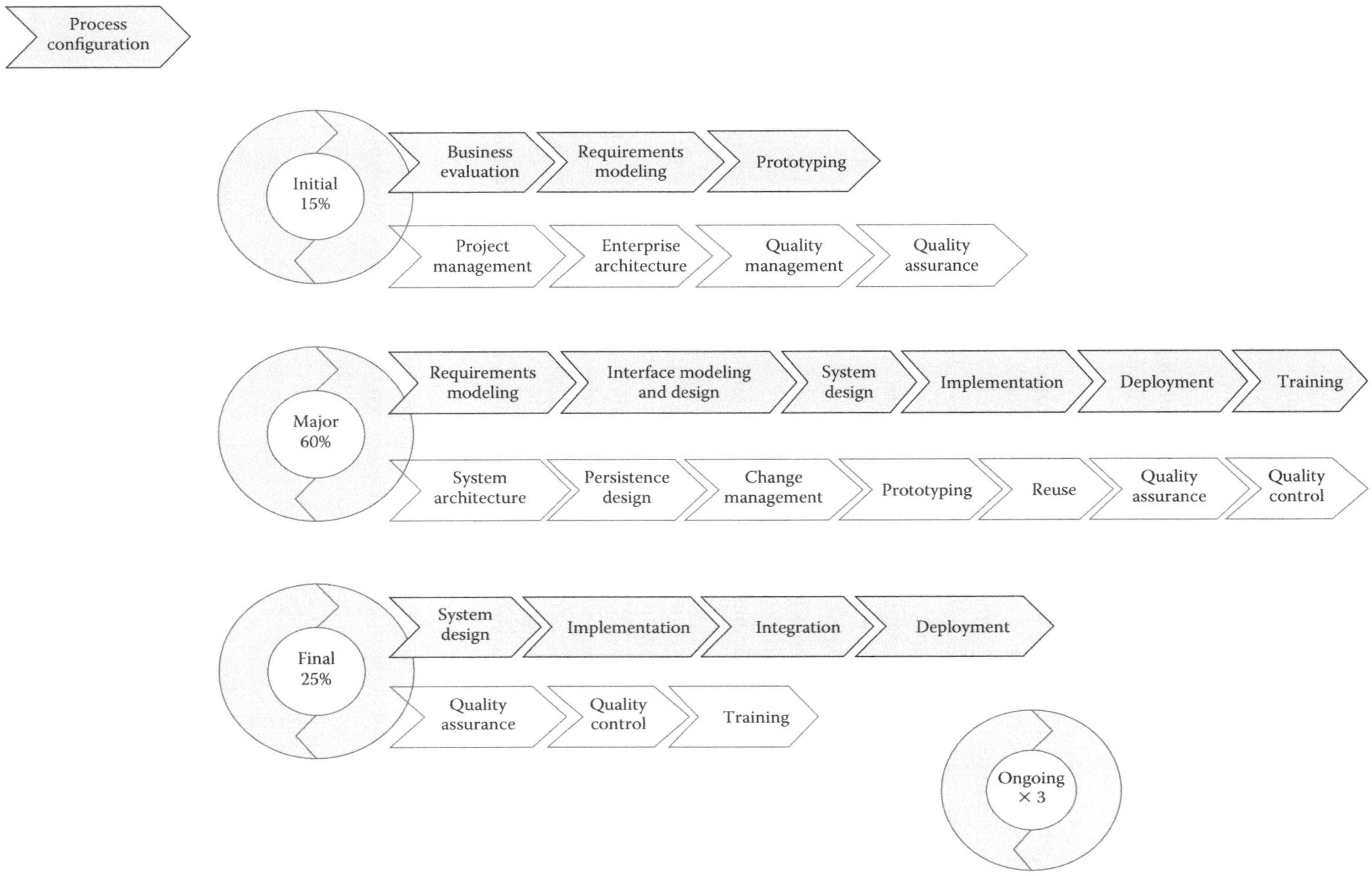

Figure 4.10 Configuring process maps from planned methods for iterations in practice.

iterations. These iterations, as shown in the figure, are configured for a project within the program of work. For this example configuration, the relative effort in these three iterations is shown as 15%, 60%, and 25%, respectively (Unhelkar, 2003). The three iterations and the corresponding process maps in those iterations are further explained in the following:

Initial Iteration

Initial iteration would usually involve 15% of the overall effort (time and budget) in the project. During the initial iteration, the following should be reasonably achieved:

- Revisiting and evaluating the business goals of the project
- Opportunity to continue or stop a particular initiative (a collaborative decision-making process used by the steering committee of the project)
- Detailed understanding of the scope of the project by all stakeholders
- Organizing project teams with a flattened structure (Chapter 8 discusses in detail the leadership and management aspects of a composite Agile team together with its structures)
- Fine-tuning the process maps to be used in this, first, and subsequent iterations
- Creation of requirements model for the project using, for example, context diagrams, use case diagrams, and activity diagrams
- Deriving initial user stories (e.g., the stories in the "To do" section in Figure 4.8) to the formal use cases and activity diagrams
- Creating business domain models (using class diagrams of the UML), state chart diagrams, and sequence diagrams
- Documenting the nonfunctional requirements (NFR) (also called *operational requirements*) of the system; positioning the NFRs within the context of the EA
- Creating prototypes of the NFRs to provide a detailed understanding of these requirements, their limitations based on the EA and, eventually, the test strategy for these requirements
- Identifying the graphical user interface (GUI) requirements of the project together with the application of the principles of usability
- Completing the organization of the quality management infrastructure (Chapter 9)

While some activities in this iteration are the core activities that are performed by the main process maps, others are supporting or background activities. The process maps for the core activities and tasks are shown in the first row for the initial iteration in Figure 4.10, whereas the second row of chevrons represents the supporting/background process maps. The core process maps for the initial iteration in a project are as follows:

- Business evaluation
- Requirements modeling
- Prototyping

The process maps that will be performed in the background are as follows:

- Project management
- Enterprise architecture
- Quality management
- Quality assurance

Major Iteration

Major iteration follows on from the initial iteration and comprises the major part of an initiative. At the end of this major iteration, close to three-quarters of the project, or 75% (including the 15% in the initial iteration), will have been completed. This also indicates that three-quarters of the overall effort needed for the project will have been expended. The effort figures are based on the experiences of past projects; hence they are "in retrospect," based on measures derived from showcases of iterations completed in previous projects. These figures can vary depending on the type and size of the project and domain of the organization. Chapter 9 provides a detailed discussion on estimation.

At the end of the major iteration, the following should have been reasonably achieved:

- Modeling of problem space must be completed. (This implies completion of use cases and activity diagrams.)
- Most of the design-level classes should be complete and mapped to user stories.
- Implementation of most user stories written thus far should be complete. (In Figure 4.8, more than half the user stories will be in "Done" but with provision for some more in "To do".)
- Design and layout of most user interfaces must be completed.
- Creation of system architecture based on the EA should be completed.
- Designs should be refactored and reused at the code level.
- First attempts should have been made to deploy a part of the system. (This will not only make a functional piece of software available to the user but will also test out the process of deploying the system when it is fully developed, reducing the risks of last-minute surprises.)
- Releases of the system, based on discussions with user, must be organized.
- Classes must be mapped to the database design to ensure integration with the database.
- Test beds must be populated for upcoming full user acceptance testing.

The processes that will be performed with high intensity in this iteration are as follows:

- Requirements modeling
- Interface modeling and design
- System design
- Implementation
- Deployment

The following are the process maps in the background:

- System architecture
- Persistence design
- Change management
- Prototyping
- Reuse

Final Iteration

During the final iteration in a development process, all of the remaining activities and tasks related to a development project are completed. This implies that all "necessary" elements of a process map have been completed and have been "sufficiently" covered to provide a robust system (or increment of a system). The following will have been achieved at the end of this iteration:

- Problem, solution, and background space models have been completed.
- All models will have been subjected to quality checks.
- All user stories and corresponding classes will be completely designed, implemented, and tested by users.
- Packages have been integrated, and users have tested them.
- The system has been released in planned increments to the users.
- User training on the product has started.
- Help desk or other relevant support has been organized.
- Data conversion, if relevant, is complete, and the database is populated with relevant data for business usage.

The process maps that will be performed with high intensity in this iteration are as follows:

- System design
- Implementation
- Integration
- Deployment

Process maps that remain in the background but continue to be performed with high intensity in this iteration are the following:

- Quality assurance
- Quality control
- Training

The CAMS Repository of Agile Practices

Figure 4.11 shows a *process map*, which is a collection of a subset of the activities, tasks, roles, and deliverables in a process. Within CAMS, a process map also shows Agile practices that are relevant to a particular activity or task. Practices, like techniques, are different ways of achieving a task. These elements that make up a process map are shown in Figure 4.6. Thus, a process map indicates a logical collection of process elements including Agile practices that are put together to accomplish a sizable chunk of the process. The term *process map* is meant to signify that a suite of process elements are treated as a unit, having a common set of roles working on a logically cohesive set of activities and tasks, resulting in a significant deliverable within that area of the process.

Figure 4.11 shows how a process map is organized. The roles are shown on the left with the activities on the right. Agile practices are shown embedded with (next to) the activities. Eventually, a deliverable is produced. While Figure 4.11 is a template for a process map, the ones shown as part of iterations in Figure 4.10 include real process maps such as business evaluation, requirements modeling, system architecture, and quality control.

In CAMS, an Agile practice forms an important part of each process map.

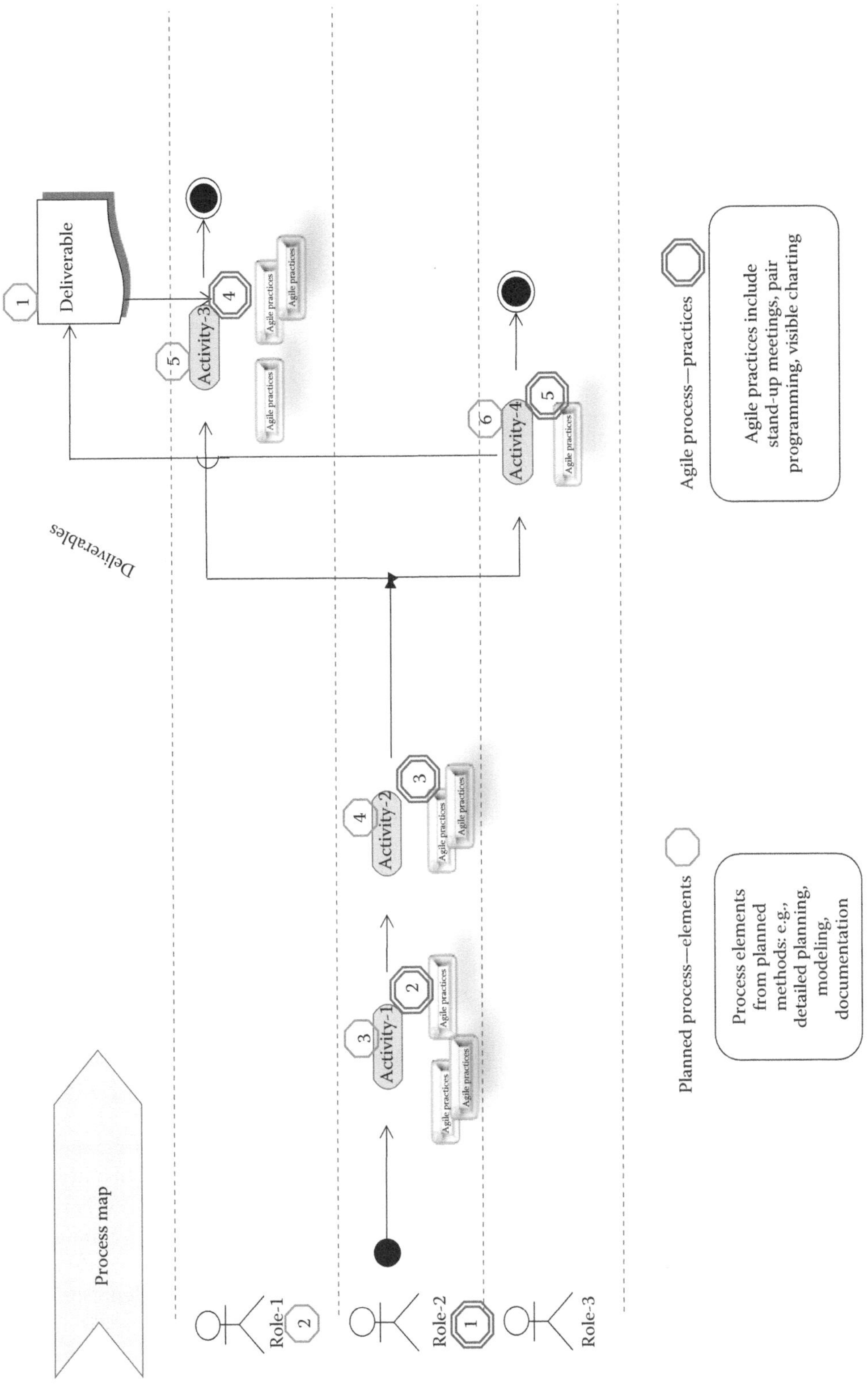

Figure 4.11 Embedding Agile practices within activities of planned process maps.

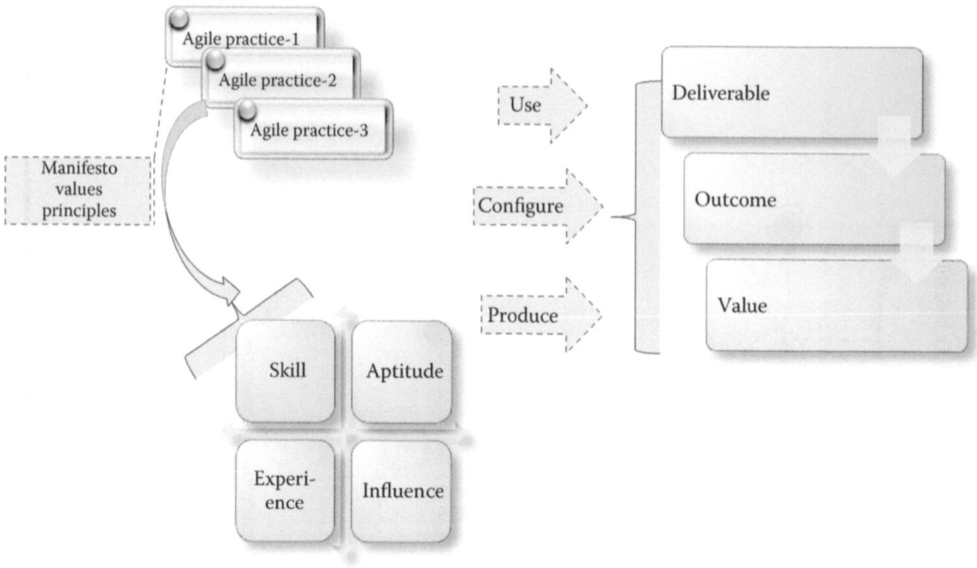

Figure 4.12 Each Agile practice is made up of skill–aptitude–experience–influence; it uses and produces deliverables–outcomes–values.

Figure 4.12 shows an Agile practice in greater detail. Each Agile practice (such as a "stand-up meeting" or "writing user stories") can be seen as being made up of four parts:

1. Skills are the basic knowledge of how to undertake a particular practice (e.g., how to write a story card).
2. Aptitude is the interest and desire of a particular person to use the skill (always keeping in mind that Agile is a subjective methodological approach that gives importance to soft factors such as aptitude).
3. Experience involves undertaking an Agile practice (e.g., how many story cards a person has written and how well they have been written).
4. Influence is the extent of the reach of a particular person's Agile practice (e.g., the influence of the stories written by a developer; is that influence across the entire project or restricted to a small module within a sub-system?).

An Agile practice can be used by many activities within multiple process maps. Understanding an Agile practice through the quartet of skills–aptitude–experience–influence is crucial in their use in process maps as well as the up-skilling of staff with transformation programs.

Figure 4.13 shows 10 groups of Agile practices. These Agile practices are derived from multiple Agile methods. Therefore, in practice, you may use the suggested Agile practice, or modify it to suit your project/organization or, eventually, you may even create your own practices. For each practice, however, you will have to be aware of the need for skill–aptitude–experience–influence discussed in Figure 4.12.

What is more, at present, companies tend to not only integrate software development with Agile practices, but also develop a composite Agile at different levels of management within the organizations. To implement this concept, CAMS suggests the coherent incorporation of Agile practices into the existing architecture of business process and organization management.

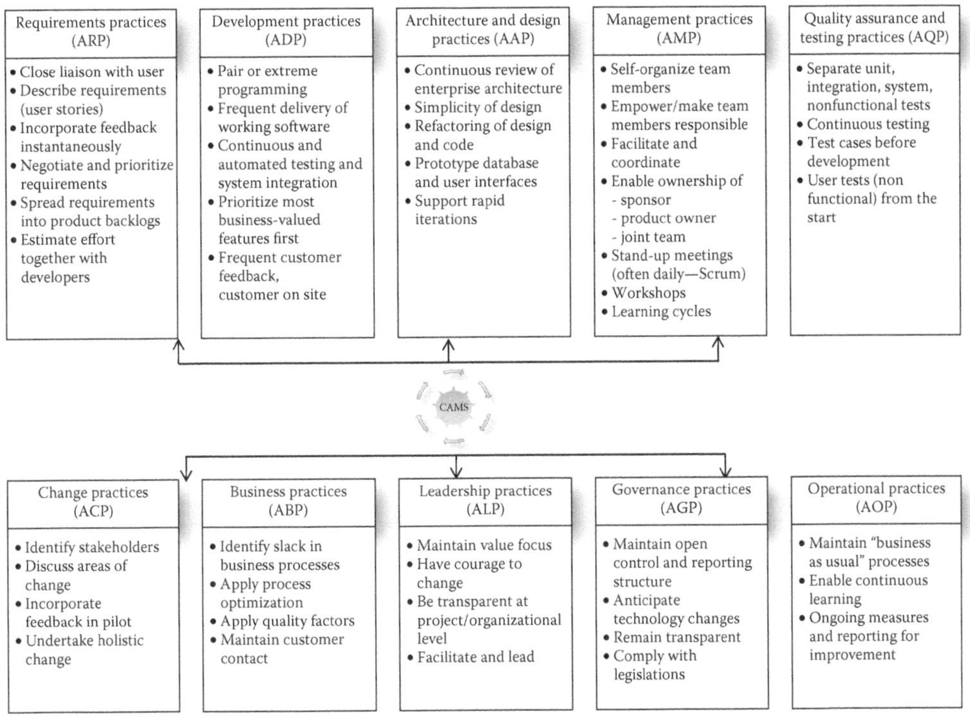

Figure 4.13 Groups of Agile practices that can be embedded in CAMS.

The CAMS repository of Agile and formal processes is further refined through a matrix of these features, as shown in Table 4.3. Many Agile features directly relate to the IT, project management, and business processes, whereas others are relatively on their own, yet applicable at the organizational level. This relationship is gleaned from responses to the interview questions and discussions undertaken in the research project mentioned in Appendix I.

CAMS in Practice: Configuration

Having established the basis for CAMS in business transformation as well as software projects (Figure 4.9), its iterative approach (Figure 4.10), and the description of Agile practices (Figures 4.12 and 4.13), how does one go about using CAMS?

Figure 4.14 suggests the major steps in configuring and using CAMS in practice. Each of these steps will receive inputs from both planned and Agile methods available to the organization:

- Diagnose project requirements (project type, size, industry sector): This involves investigating the various projects types and sizes within the organization. A study of past projects together with the project on hand can help decide on the best approaches and techniques to incorporate into CAMS for these projects.
- Select from a repository of process elements/Agile practices: This involves selecting the right elements from the CAMS repository that are suited to the nature of the project. The repository can be made up of both Agile and planned elements, and this selection provides a starting point for the use of a method instance.

Table 4.3 Agile Features in IT, Project Management, and Business Processes

IT, Project Management, Business Process Features / *Agile Features→*	*Incremental*	*Iterative*	*Collaborative Manner*	*Collaborative Requirements*	*Negotiable Requirements*	*Requirement Prioritization*	*Developer-Centric Requirement (Stories)*	*Continuous Development*	*Pair Programming*	*User Participation/On-site User*	*Continuous Testing*	*Continuous Integration*	*Rapid Delivery/Small Releases*	*Empowered Team Members*	*Communication*	*User Feedback by Demonstration*
Requirements					√	√				√					•	
Design	√	√														
Coding/implementation	√	√				√							•	•		•
Testing										√	√	√				•
Business modeling																
Iterative and incremental development	√	√														
Quality assurance										√	√	√				•
Change management																
Value delivery	√	√				√				√			•		•	
Planning	√	√				√				√			•			
Monitoring change																
Performance measurement										√						•
Risk management										√						
Communication										√					•	
Deployment/delivery	√	√				√							•			
Maintenance/support																

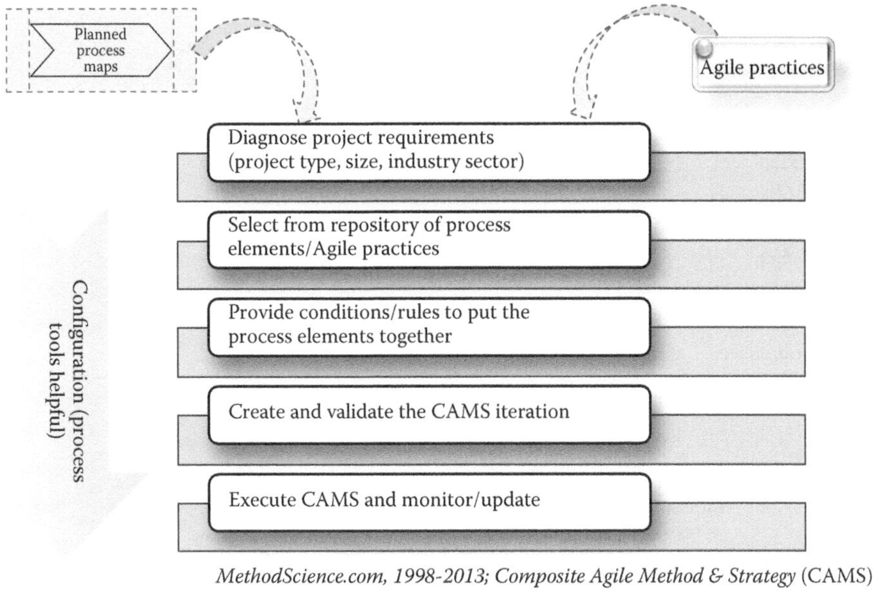

Figure 4.14 CAMS configuration and execution in practice.

- Provide conditions/rules to put the process elements together: This involves defining and providing rules and guidelines on how to integrate the CAMS process elements together and applying them in practice. The variation and extent of planned versus Agile (Figure 4.7) are a part of these conditions required to put together a process map based on the relevant process elements.
- Create and validate the CAMS iteration: This involves measuring how well the company performs when applying the CAMS process during the project iterations. The validation of a CAMS instance can occur through a pilot project.
- Execute CAMS and monitor/update: This involves application of CAMS in practice and continuous monitoring and review of how well the company applied instances of CAMS in practice. The balance between planned and Agile elements continues here on an ongoing basis. Metrics and measurements provide the necessary feedback to the project leadership enabling fine-tuning of the process elements.

SIDEBAR

CAMS for an organization can be presented in many different formats. It can be a formal document made available on the organization's Web site, or articulated as a wiki within the project. The material presented in this chapter can be extended and modified to reflect the methods used in the organization and the way in which their elements will be used in practice. Creation of a repository of elements from the many organizational processes can be put in a database that can be made available to projects using CAMS. PowerPoints and video posts can be used in documenting and promoting the CAMS approach within the organization. In all practical uses of CAMS, it is important that it is primarily promoted as a strategy—as much as a composite method—that bridges the business strategy and the technology–product strategies. Thus, CAMS will never be a one-off method to be used in a project; instead, it is an ongoing strategic approach that enables transformation to an Agile and collaborative style of working in an entire organization with minimal methods friction.

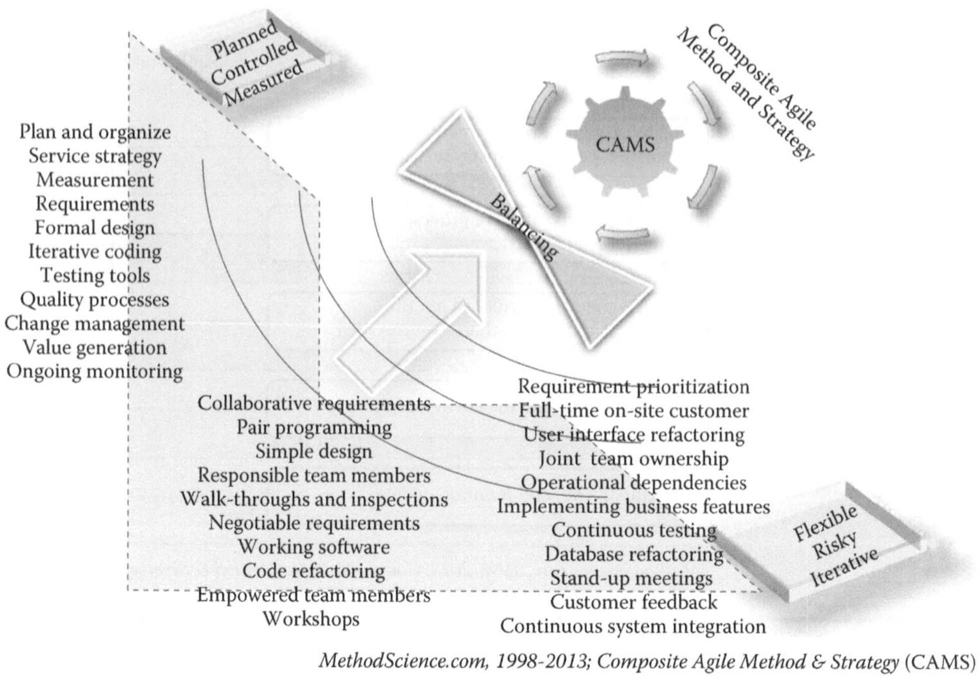

Figure 4.15 Using the CAMS repository in practice.

The CAMS repository is a collection of all elements from all processes being used at every level within the organization. An abridged example of this repository corresponding to various activity groups is shown in Figure 4.15. This repository covers a wide spectrum of process elements that are derived from the Agile, IT, project, and business levels of the organization. Depending on the type and size of the organization, and the specific methods that it is using, this repository can change.

However, the process elements can stretch the spectrum of elements that are leaning toward the planned/controlled/measured scale, and the ones that are toward the flexible/risky/iterative scale. These elements need not be newly derived, but are available from the existing planned processes (project management, business management, and software development) and the Agile processes. There are a number of variables that need to be considered when it comes to configuring a CAMS instance. For example, people-specific factors such as personalities, formation of cross-functional teams, and characteristics of the project (such as outsourced project), are considered in CAMS.

Agile principles and practices can be made to relate to the planned processes within the organization. Eventually, this results in configuring a CAMS iteration (discussed in detail in Chapter 10). It is worth mentioning that CAMS provides process guidance to all tiers in an organization. Thus, in practice, a method can be selected from each of the levels of business and the IT project and embedded with relevant Agile elements to produce an approach that works across the organization. For example, Agility can help in identifying and refining the vision and goal of the organization. The presence of an on-site customer easily relates to the business processes that have a need to provide input to the development activities in order to understand the potential of the software to the business. The practice of continuous testing can be applied within a formal process by ensuring that each individual piece of requirement is tested as soon as it is developed (this could be based on individual use cases or user stories, but within the phase of a formal process). The iterative and incremental approach that is so popular within Agile can be inserted in the project plans created within, say, Prince2.

Note that keeping the *instance* of CAMS flexible to incorporate changes in time is vital. Therefore, a CAMS instance is a combination of a project plan as well as practices and guidelines that go along with the plan. Flexibility of methods is required at two levels—first, the flexibility of configuring the method in different ways and, second, the flexibility accorded by the method in the middle of development/maintenance. CAMS subscribes to both levels of flexibility by ensuring that the project plan remains a dynamic document that is changeable.

Practicing CAMS—Role-Based Execution

The practice of CAMS varies depending on the role in the organization using CAMS. CAMS itself is a result of many investigations into the specific needs of a role in an organization in terms of methods usage. Appendix I (Agile Interview Summaries) provides an abridged version of the detailed interviews that were carried out by the researchers in the composite Agile research project. These interviews are a good indication of the way in which the participants eventually would use CAMS. These participants represented real roles in real organizations where processes were used. The roles of the participants included business analysis, project management, developers, testers, architects, and quality roles.

SIDEBAR

A composite approach across the organization appears practical. However, there is a need to explore the validity of such an approach with research and investigation. The need to explore the validity of such a composite Agile approach in practice resulted in a research project. As a part of this research, the viewpoints of 10 different participants were explored. The roles of these participants ranged from developers and architects to business analysts, project managers, and testers, and included consultants as well as permanent roles. The interviewees came mainly from the financial sector (typically insurance, banking, and mortgage). While this was also a limitation of the study, still these were precisely the type of medium- to large-sized organizations that were keen to express the needs to come up with an approach to development and management that would combine Agility with existing methods. The sentiments and viewpoints expressed during the interviews endorsed a *composite* approach to the use of Agility in organizations. While acknowledging the relevance and impact of Agility in development, the overwhelming majority of interviewees stressed that Agility must transcend software development and assume importance across the entire organization. The result is the setting out of CAMS as an all-encompassing approach to the use of Agile principles and practices across various process elements within the organization. This study eventually resulted in a successful PhD and a master's degree.

Advantages and Limitations of CAMS

Advantages of Composite Agile

- Draws attention to the entire spectrum of organizational processes with the aim of ensuring the best utilization of Agile in the context of these existing processes
- Provides a balance between pure Agile practices and the process elements of a formal, planned method

- Encourages the use of CASE tools for modeling and processes in both problem and solution spaces, as compared with the relatively low importance given to tools in pure Agile
- Enables the control of activities, tasks, and deliverables within the project and, at the same time, enables sufficient flexibility for the developers
- Facilitates the management of staff turnover—instead of developers carrying the project knowledge entirely in their heads, some of it is also documented using visual modeling techniques
- Enables metrics and estimations of various activities and deliverables within the project at appropriate stages
- Utilizes the experience within the organization that is derived from business, governance, and project management, as well as development
- Creates opportunities to have maturity levels (similar to CMM) that can be used to compare processes within and across various organizations
- Provides the freedom to express individual skills and motivation within the boundaries of formal processes being used by the business
- Creates opportunities for up-front and complete requirements that can be made legally binding
- Measures deliverables that can be used for payments for outsourced/offshored projects

Limitations of Composite Agile

- While there is support for the concept of CAMS, significantly more research and experimentation is required in order to make it readily usable in all types and sizes of projects.
- CASE tools need to be upgraded to enable modeling, measurements, project tracking, and reporting.
- Consideration of wider cultural nuances is required within the CAMS projects, that is, not just the nuances between different roles within the project but also across geopolitical regions.
- The importance of soft issues needs to be accepted across the entire organization—CAMS on its own cannot promote sociocultural issues without support from organizational leadership.
- CAMS does not have a metamodel; eventually a metamodel that represents *all* organizational processes should be developed to overcome the uncertainty of which organizational processes to include in (or exclude from) CAMS.

Conclusions

This chapter presented the fundamentals of CAMS. The core argument for CAMS and the way in which it incorporates the many organizational-level processes were presented. For each organizational process, a discussion on where and how Agile can play a role in those processes was also provided. Most importantly, the wide-ranging process considerations of CAMS were discussed in the context of methods friction. A description of CAMS architecture and the way in which it can be configured in practice was provided. This chapter provided the details of CAMS—setting the path for discussion on how CAMS can be used in development (Chapter 5), business management (Chapter 6), business analysis (Chapter 7), project management (Chapter 8), and testing, quality, and metrics (Chapter 9). These topics are expanded in the subsequent chapters.

Agile in Practice: Road Map 4

- Create a detailed list of all methods and processes in your organization (refer to Figure 4.3)
- Identify the roles primarily responsible for each of these methods (and locate the people who are playing these roles).
- Create a suite of questions that deal with the two major aspects of usage of these methods in the organization and address them to the corresponding roles: (a) the what/why/how of the current method and (b) the potential areas of methods friction.
- CAMS will be an umbrella document that outlines the activities and tasks, roles, and deliverables associated with each of the methods. You can start the creation of a CAMS repository in a simple database or spreadsheet. Later, this repository can be moved to a sophisticated CASE tool for processes.
- The area of CAMS instance dealing with software development and maintenance will be made up of process maps and Agile practices. Agile practices will be embedded within the process map. Create a pilot process map for a part of your development/maintenance work (detailed process maps are discussed in subsequent chapters).
- Embed two selected Agile practices within your pilot process map. Undertake a walk-through of the process map to check if the process map and the corresponding Agile practices will work in your environment (in the initial stages, this will require some fine-tuning).
- Ensure the process map is displayed in a big visible chart.
- Outline the strategies to up-skill people (roles) corresponding to the selected Agile practices that they will use (skills–aptitude–experience–influence).

Discussion Questions

- Compare the needs for versatility versus control within your organizational context. Specifically, list a few areas of work within your organization that demand control and others that demand flexibility.
- What are the specific methods being used in your organization that relate to each of the areas described in Figure 4.2? Discuss them in the context of the size of your organization.
- What is "methods friction?" How does methods friction affect your organization?
- How can "methods friction" be avoided or reduced in your organization? (*Hint:* identify the touch points between methods and discuss whether they are supportive of or conflicting with each other. Then work out the elements of the methods that need to be kept and those that need to be dropped.)
- What is a process map? What are the elements that make up a process map?
- What makes up an Agile practice? Discuss, with examples, a couple of Agile practices and also show how they add value by providing input into deliverables and outcomes.
- How would you create an Agile iteration that will fit in with a formal process map?
- Discuss the creation of a CAMS instance using a CAMS repository.

References

Ambler, S.W., A manager's introduction to the Rational Unified Process (RUP), 2005.

Bellis, P., Project methodologies: An introduction to Prince2 methodology, JISC Infonet, 2003.

Boehm, B., Get ready for Agile methods, with care, *IEEE Computer,* 35 (1), 64–69, 2002.

Boehm, B., A spiral model of software development and enhancement, *Software Engineering Project Management, Computer*, 21 (5), 61–72, 1988.

Chatterjee, S., *Examining the Enterprise Unified Process: Seeing beyond the Rational Unified Process*, ITtoolbox Project Management, 2006, viewed 13 September 2009, http://projectmanagement.ittoolbox.com/documents/examining-enterprise-unified-process-13288.

Firesmith, F., B. Henderson-Sellers, and D. Zowghi, *Using the OPEN Process Framework to Produce a Situation-Specific Requirements Engineering Method*, Software Engineering Institute, 2005, viewed 15 September 2009, http://www.sei.cmu.edu/library/abstracts/whitepapers/openprocesssep2005.cfm.

Henderson-Sellers, B. and B. Unhelkar, *OPEN Modelling with UML*, Addison-Wesley, Harlow, 2002.

Hudgik, S., Kaizen, graphic products, 2009, viewed 23 August 2009, http://www.graphicproducts.com/tutorials/kaizen/kaizen-getting-started.php.

Imai, M., *Kaizen = (Ky'zen): The Key to Japanese Competitive Success*, Random House Business Division, New York, NY, 1986.

ITIL What is ITIL? APM Group Ltd., 2009, viewed 16 July 2009, http://www.itil-officialsite.com/AboutITIL/WhatisITIL.asp.

Keller, P.A. and T. Pyzdek, *Six Sigma Demystified*, McGraw-Hill, New York, NY, p. 497, 2005.

Kotelnikov, V., Kaizen: The Japanese strategy of continuous improvement, 2009, viewed 23 August 2009, http://www.1000ventures.com/business_guide/mgmt_kaizen_main.html.

Kruchten, P., *The Rational Unified Process: An Introduction*, 3rd ed, Addison-Wesley Professional, p. 336, 2003.

Liker, J.K., The Toyota way: 14 management principles from the world's greatest manufacturer, 2004.

Maner, W., Rapid application development, 1997, viewed 3 September 2009, http://www.cs.bgsu.edu/maner/domains/RAD.htm.

McGevna, V., Consider hybrid agile, 2012, viewed April 2012, http://www.projectsatwork.com.

McGovern, J., S. Ambler, M. Stevens, and V. Sharan, *A Practical Guide to Enterprise Architecture*, Pearson Education, Inc., 2004.

Moeller, R., *Sarbanes-Oxley Internal Controls: Effective Auditing with AS5, CobiT, and ITIL*, John Wiley & Sons, New York, NY, p. 384, 2008.

OPEN Process Framework Repository Organization (OPFRO) 2009, viewed 12 August 2009, http://www.opfro.org/index.html?Sources/OPEN1.html~Contents.

Process Mentor Process mentor, 2009, viewed 17 July 2009, http://www.processmentor.com/index.html.

Rational Software Rational Unified Process, Best Practices for Software Development Teams, 2001, viewed 16 August 2009, http://www.ibm.com/developerworks/rational/library/content/03July/1000/1251/1251_bestpractices_TP026B.pdf.

Royce, W.W., Managing the development of large software systems, *Tutorial: Software Engineering Project Management*, IEEE Computer Society, Washington, DC, pp. 118–127, 1970.

Unhelkar, B., Process QA for UML-based projects.

Unhelkar, B., Demystifying the UML, demystifying the UML 2.0 in Information Age.

Yang, K., *Design for Six Sigma for Service*, McGraw-Hill, New York, NY, p. 466, 2005, http://istqb.org/pages/viewpage.action?pageId=5767286.

Chapter 5

Composite Agile and IT: Enablement, Development, and Maintenance

Any fool can write code that a computer can understand. Good programmers write code that humans can understand.

–Martin Fowler

Objectives

- Revisit the popular role of Agility in the context of software development
- Discuss emergent information and communications technologies (ICT) as enablers of business Agility
- Position Agile practices in the architecture, design, implementation, and deployment of a software system
- Describe the enterprise architecture process map in Composite Agile Method and Strategy (CAMS) together with its Agile practices
- Describe the system architecture process map in CAMS together with its Agile practices
- Discuss the importance of organizational Web portals in presenting agility to an end user (customer)
- Discuss the importance of nonfunctional requirements specifications (NFRS) in projects and their influence on business Agility
- Describe the system design process map in CAMS together with its Agile practices
- Describe the implementation process map in CAMS together with its Agile practices
- Describe the pure Agile elements (roles, artifacts, ceremonies) within the implementation process map in practice
- Revisit user stories within the implementation process map
- Describe the deployment process map in CAMS together with Agile practices

Introduction

This chapter discusses Composite Agile Method and Strategy (CAMS) in the context of software development and maintenance. The discussion herein is software centric, as compared with the ensuing chapters that deal with business and project management aspects of an organization and CAMS. This development-centric aspect of Agility is the one that made it quite popular. Agility in software development, highlighted in Chapter 2, is revisited in this chapter. The Agile practices, however, are placed within the process maps of CAMS. This provides for the formal, planned aspect of the development process. Developers, designers, and architects should find these CAMS process maps helpful as they provide process guidance corresponding to the respective roles. Embedding Agile practices within these process maps will substantially enhance the quality as well as throughput of the respective deliverables.

SIDEBAR

"A Long Long Time Ago, Software Development Was Indeed Agile"

The relative informality of Agile methods and their overwhelming focus on "working code" is not new to software development. At the start of the computing era, projects were informal and, indeed, working code was seen as a predominant criterion of successful delivery. Programmers and users sat side by side and conversed during development. In the absence of 3 in. 5 in. cards and sticky notes, user stories were scribbled on the back of an envelope. However, that original Agile-like approach of the 1970s and early 1980s that apparently "lacked processes and standards" appeared to be the cause of many software project failures. The software community, together with the project management community, moved toward formal, planned approaches to developing and maintaining software. The formal software development life cycles (SDLCs) expanded into detailed, formal processes (Unified Process; Object-Oriented Process, Environment, and Notation (OPEN); and others). In fact, it was the lack of standardized modeling notations that resulted in the Unified Modeling Language (UML). In addition to expanding the SDLCs into processes, there was a substantial emphasis on measuring the maturity of those development processes resulting in the Software Engineering Institute's Capability Maturity Model (CMM) and international standards such as ISO9001. The current fascination with Agile in software development needs to reconnect with what once happened when software development became an industry of its own.

Agile methods have primarily come out of the software development arena. Therefore, it is inevitable that any discussion on Agility involves a discussion on the way in which Agile methods can be used successfully in software development and maintenance. The discussions on composite Agile, as presented in Chapter 4, are shown in practice here. The CAMS process maps of architecture, design, implementation, and deployment show how Agile practices can be embedded and used.

The balancing aspect of CAMS in practical software development is important. This balance is achieved by embedding Agile practices in the software-related process maps. CAMS also emphasizes the importance of the crucial maintenance aspect of software systems. A large part of organizational resources and effort go into maintaining software systems—at times even more than the effort required in developing them. CAMS emphasizes formal modeling and documentation within the process maps to ensure ease of maintenance when a software system is in operation.

This chapter also expands on the capabilities of emergent information and communications technologies (ICT or simply information technology, IT) as the key enablers of Agility. IT (its systems, processes, and infrastructure) influences changes in the way an organization operates; IT is also influenced and undergoes change when the business changes to an Agile business.

For example, as IT progresses beyond processing of "information" and enters the arena of knowledge management (KM), business intelligence (BI), and service-oriented architecture (SOA), it rapidly enhances the organization's capabilities to become Lean and Agile. CAMS further expands the methods focus beyond software development and applies IT to the entire organization. Thus, CAMS encourages a careful study of the aforementioned technologies and their application in practice to significantly enhance an organization's capacity to respond quickly and effectively. These information technologies are discussed next from the point of view of their business impact on organizational Agility.

SIDEBAR

Exploring the commonalities in software development approaches before the popularity of formal methods and standards, and the Agile values and practices of today will provide architects, designers, and developers with an excellent understanding of how to use Agile in practice. Very few of the actual practices of current pure Agile approaches are "new"; most appeared in some shape or form in the original approach to software development. Similarly, the Agile values, outlined earlier in Chapter 2, are not new. Management literature has espoused these values for decades. Yet, the way the Agile movement highlights these Agile values and practices is excellent. For example, Agile values of simplicity in design and courage in accepting errors are immediately welcome in software projects. Composite Agile Method and Strategy (CAMS) takes up and promotes these Agile values in software development and maintenance. Furthermore, the extension and merger of software processes and the excellence of Agile practices is also applied by CAMS at the business level.

Emergent Information Technologies: Agile Enablers

The Internet and its variants (Intranet, ExtraNet, Web 2.0, Internet Multimedia Services (IMS), and Web Services) (Murugesan, 2010) are all continuously put to use in enabling collaborations in business. In addition to organizational collaborations, even at a personal level, collaboration is facilitated by numerous Internet-based communications tools and technologies that include mobile gadgets, digital assistants and pods, instant messaging, and social media networks. "Customers want high-quality products at low prices, and they want them now" (Gates, 1999, from his discussion in *Business @ The Speed of Thought*). ICT has become a major contributor in enabling business to expand their offerings, reduce their overheads, and provide faster turnaround and higher quality.

Figure 5.1 highlights (on the left) a suite of emergent ICT that can play a role in enabling business Agility. The effect of ICT in making a business "collaborative Agile" is discussed in greater detail in Chapter 6. The discussion here explores the characteristics of these technologies in the way they enable business Agility. Starting with the ever so important cloud computing, the technologies enabling collaborative-Agile business include the applications themselves, mobile technologies (MT), middleware/IMS, Web services/SOA, groupware/social media, BI, and data warehouse/content management system (CMS).

These technologies can be used to enable organizations to shift their noncore activities to their collaborating partners—who have specific expertise in them. This ICT application frees up an organization to concentrate on its core competency. As a result, collaborating organizations become efficient, Lean, and Agile. Collaborations through the application of emergent ICT also widens the scope of offerings of a business, adding to its effectiveness.

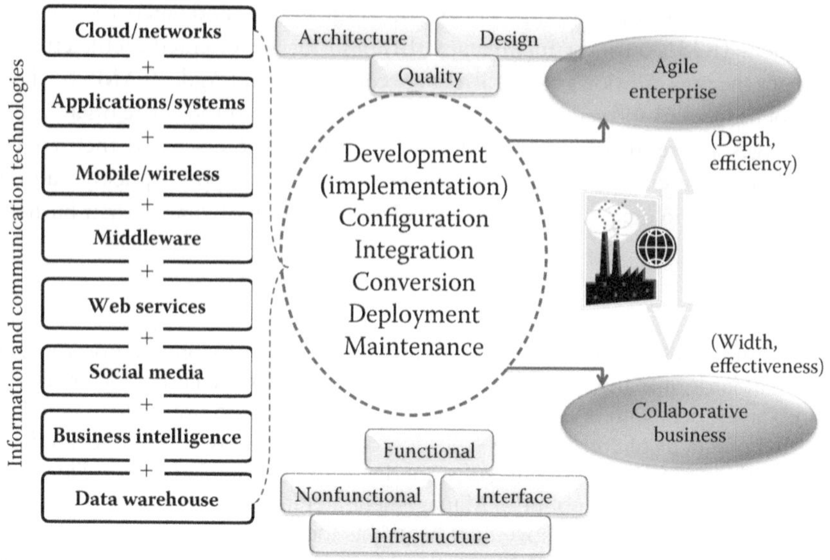

Figure 5.1 Software development technologies and areas of work leading to collaborative-Agile business.

Work in an IT project (or a program of work) makes use of the emergent IT to produce business value. IT work includes configuration (e.g., of packages), implementation (software application), integration (with other applications and systems), conversion (of data), deployment (especially of services), and maintenance. As shown in Figure 5.1, a CAMS-based project commences with formal requirements gathering. As also shown in Figure 5.1, these requirements are grouped as functional, nonfunctional, interface, and infrastructure. The stability of the systems and solutions is achieved by due consideration to architecture, design, and quality. Following is a discussion on the emerging IT and their role in rendering a business Agile.

Cloud Computing

Cloud computing expands on the erstwhile provision of IT services over the Internet, having advantages in terms of Agile business. The cloud enables pooling of resources—hardware, software, and networks. This results in the shifting of these noncore and infrastructure-related activities outside the organization, thereby freeing up resources. The providers of services on the cloud have similar advantages. They can focus on the IT services in which they have expertise. They can offer these services to multiple vendors. Sharing of resources and services is a key offering of the cloud that enables organizations to become Lean and Agile.

Mobile Technologies

Mobile technologies (MT) are an important enabler of electronic collaborative businesses. MT enable location and time independence. The overall impact of mobility has been summarized by Unhelkar (2008, 2009). Mobility has had a significant impact on the quality of life for individuals. This impact is on the working and social lives of individuals. For example, location independence enables employees to strike an improved work–life balance. Mobile devices also change the way customers interact with business. For example, most banking and airline-ticketing activities can be easily carried out without standing in a queue. When it comes to Agile practices, mobile connectivity extends the ability of team members in ongoing participation in daily stand-up meetings and showcases (something they would have otherwise missed). While location-aware mobile connectivity has dramatically increased the ability of individuals to communicate, it is important to handle the challenges in terms of privacy and new social protocols.

Business Intelligence

BI is an important enabler of collaboration between systems and across an organization. Therefore, BI tools such as SAS, Informatica, Cognos, SAP, and Oracle BI can be used by not just one organization but a collaborating suite of organizations to share data–information–knowledge. With such increasing electronic collaborations and subsequent sharing, organizations are able to "shed" their extra "weight" around their noncore processes. Such shedding, in turn, creates opportunities for businesses to use each other's services in a collaborative manner, resulting in collaborative intelligence (CI).

CI would also enable a much better utilization of the BI tools mentioned earlier. For example, collaborations among businesses using the aforementioned BI tools will enable much better growth forecasts and accurate current states of the organization. The ability to tap into participating collaborators is the best way to ascertain reliable forecasting of growth figures. For example, the growth numbers of an organization will be tempered by the strategies of a collaborating partner. Similarly, the BI tool vendor's promises of executive dashboards can be extended to collaborative dashboards that take into account performances and growth of collaborating organizations.

Web Services and SOA

The technology of Web Services (WS) together with the concept of service-oriented architecture (SOA) enables the ability of organizations to offer and consume services. This leads to a collaborative approach in business. Owing to the use of available services from external service providers, there is significant opportunity for the organization to "trim down," be Lean, and hence Agile. Services can be understood as self-contained (and usually object-oriented) software components that have well-defined interfaces. SOA provides the architecture for information systems to offer and publish, as well as locate and consume services.

Agility and SOA are increasingly being discussed together (see Dooley, 2011 as also Allen). Agile organizations use collaborative information systems to assimilate software contents and corresponding software components from many different sources including internal and external contributors such as employees, customers, and users as well as the various regulatory governmental bodies. The ability of executable services being made available across different communication channels enhances an organization's ability to "source" rather than "build" its noncore services. This services-based approach also results in overall less software code, lower cost of developing and deploying software solutions, and increased standardization (Hazra, 2010).

Web Services have had a further significant impact on enabling the organization to function in a Lean and efficient manner. This is based on the ease of sharing and exposure of information with well-defined message formats to exchange data. The interaction and exchange of data and information of the business applications through the eXtensible Markup Language (XML) and further extending it through MT create significant opportunities for businesses to remove all their noncore processes from their mainstream. This also results in changes to the internal organizational structure as the need to carry out mundane, face-to-face supervision wanes, rendering that particular management activity and, eventually even that hierarchy, redundant. This is an essential ingredient of Agile enterprises.

Applications Integration

The Web Services technology adopted by Web 2.0 opens up doors for integrating applications. According to Murugesan (2007, 2010), Web 2.0 is a collection of technologies, business strategies, and social trends, more dynamic and interactive than its predecessor Web 1.0 technology. This results in the integration of business processes, internally as well as externally. Applications integration is further facilitated by the fact that Web 2.0 provides a platform for applications that can be accessed directly by users through their browser. Thus, this second generation of Web technology contributes to easy collaboration and integration of applications on the Internet. This integration provides an organization with the ability to streamline its processes and thereby become Lean and Agile.

Social Media

Social media networks started out as a means for individuals to collaborate in a social way (e.g., Facebook, LinkedIn, Twitter). The technologies of social media are now much more prominent in the creation and promotion of business. In fact, a business almost has its twin personality on the electronic media (e.g., see http://site.mycybertwin.com/). As a business tool gaining rapid prominence, social media have a significant role to play in enabling business Agility. Social media networks facilitate business Agility through collaborative content creation and its modification, dynamically relating to partnering businesses and individuals, and providing support to a cross section of customers and society that may itself not be Internet savvy. For example, see the discussions on application of social media networks beyond their top-end business applications and creation of social groups in "Social Media Networks for the Middle of the Pyramid" (www.sln4mop.org).

IT Areas of Work and Agile

Each of the aforementioned ICT is affected by the way in which work is carried out in the organization. These areas of work, as shown in Figure 5.2, include development, configuration, integration, conversion, deployment and training, and maintenance. As also depicted in Figure 5.2, each of these IT areas of work makes use of architecture, design, and quality disciplines. Each area of work also benefits from functional, nonfunctional, and interface requirements. Occasionally, infrastructure requirements also influence the areas of work. Agile values, principles, and practices need to be discussed in the context of these areas of work. As seen, development is an important, yet small part of IT work in an organization. This is the only area of IT work that has been the focus of contemporary Agile methods. The remaining areas of work, encircled in Figure 5.2, do not seem to be given sufficient importance in pure Agile. CAMS focuses on these areas of work as well and considers how Agile values can be applied to these remaining areas of work. This widening of Agility beyond development in an organization is discussed next.

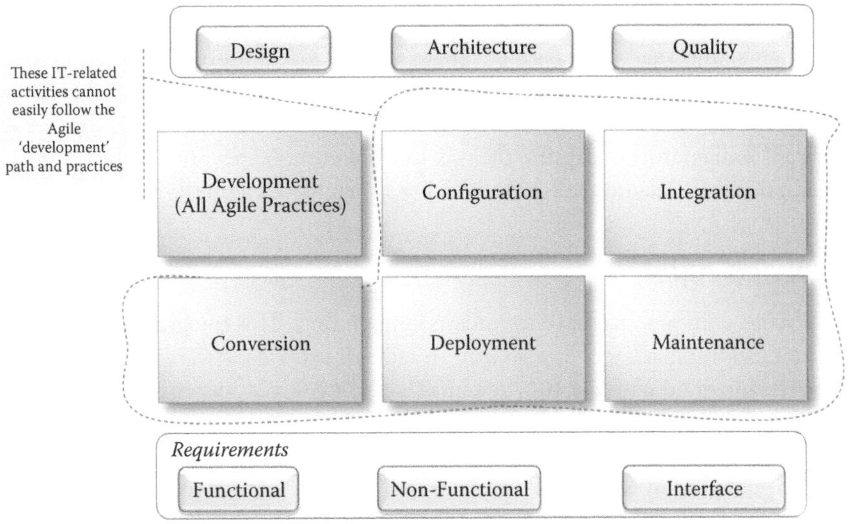

Figure 5.2 IT areas of work and Agile.

Development and Agility

Various contemporary Agile methods were highlighted in Chapter 2. A quick look at all these methods is sufficient to indicate that they are all focused on software development. Understanding and documenting user stories, collaborating with multiple stakeholders, and producing a working code—these are some of the major activities happening in Agile methods. Scrum, Extreme programming (XP), and other methods have their own variations, but they are all focused on developing a new piece of code. This kind of work is also called "*greenfield*" development—a kind of development with no "baggage" from the past. Agility opens up an opportunity for the working code to be continuously shown to the user and, thereby, getting the feedback on the spot. An Agile approach provides excellent means to manage expectations as the user sees the product as it is being developed. The class and sequence models of the Unified Modeling Language (UML) can accompany the functional stories within development. Nonfunctional requirements (NFR), however, do not get the same importance as functional ones; they can be modeled through prototypes and can be limited by the enterprise and system architectures.

Configuration and Agility

This is an area of work within an organization that deals with configuring a software package for use. This type of work is different from new development, as very limited amount of coding takes place here. Instead, the effort of the project team is to configure the system by setting up its various parameters. For example, when a ready-made software package is implemented, a significant amount of work is required to create user access levels, user IDs, configuration of business rules, embedding of organizational logos, and so on. Agile values enhance collaboration and communication in this kind of work. As it is not new development, there is much less opportunity to create user stories for requirements and following them up with development and testing. The type of testing required in configuring a system is also different from the testing needs in development.

For example, the focus on testing in configuring a system will be on the parameter fields, their permitted contents, and the business rules. There is very little opportunity to apply Agile development practices (e.g., pair programming) in such a situation. Instead, CAMS recommends the use of formal requirements modeling techniques (such as use cases or Business Process Modeling Notation (BPMN) diagrams) to capture the way in which users expect to use the system. A formal requirements model can dictate the way in which a system is configured.

Integration and Agility

All major IT projects in practice have to undergo integration. This integration is not only among the various modules and packages of a system. In fact, almost all software products, when used in practice, need to integrate with existing systems (including legacy systems), databases, networks, and security modules. Thus, integration is a major activity in a software project that requires modeling of interfaces, running of pilot tests, and application of architectural constraints. With the exception of integration within the modules of a project, the rest of the integration activities do not need to use the Agile principles and practices required in development. For example, integrating a system with a back-end legacy system would not require user stories and may not follow the Agile estimation approaches. The user has very little "functional" requirements for such a back-end integration exercise.

Conversion and Agility

Most business transformation programs focus on changing the way a business operates. While this change involves changes to software systems, and at times, complete replacement of the systems, still the data stored in the back-end databases does not change to that extent. Existing accounts, customer details, and transaction history are usually required to be preserved. In most cases, these data need to be converted to a new database to enable their use in the new system. Thus, a significant part of the IT area of work involves conversion and cleansing of data. The pure Agile methods, with their dynamic requirements gathering and focus on working code, do not provide much information or guidance in terms of data conversion. Neither is there an Agile principle or practice that provides guidance in terms of timings for data conversion (especially if the existing system is still live and operational), data integrity, and security.

CAMS considers a combination of formal models and processes to undertake data conversion, together with prototyping and discussion with users in terms of nonfunctional requirements specifications (NFRS). The NFR aspect of a system can provide major input into data conversion. The converted data has to comply with these NFR, especially relating to performance, volume, and security.

Deployment, Training, and Agility

Deployment of a system requires a significant amount of work that goes beyond the technical releases of a system. For example, releasing a system to the user would require corresponding user training, documentation, and technical support. These are areas of work that have very little to do with "Agile development." However, the Agile focus on providing value to a user is important in working out the details of deployment and training. CAMS gives equal value to documentation as to development; therefore, the documents and models created during development are modified and kept up to date as part of the training and deployment of a system.

Maintenance and Agility

Maintenance of a system is a part of its ongoing life cycle. A system in use will require changes that are different in nature to the changes required by users while the system is developed. For example, changes to a functionality when the system is deployed requires additional considerations such as criticality of the system, affordable downtimes, and cross-functional dependencies.

Legacy applications and systems are often mission critical and actively support complex business processes. Furthermore, these systems are often heavily integrated with other applications and databases and provide critical information feeds to many other applications and business areas. Maintaining these systems is a big challenge, and replacing them is an even bigger challenge. The challenge in handling legacy is primarily due to the interdependencies of these systems. When large-scale COBOL (COmmon Business- Oriented Language) and Pascal applications were developed, the concepts of object-orientation, encapsulation, and components did not exist. Therefore, legacy applications have multiple integration points with existing systems and databases. Users stories, as units of functionality or features, are simply insufficient to enable in-depth modeling of these systems. Pure Agile mechanisms are also insufficient to maintain new and integrated systems as they move into production. Legacy software in maintenance and its replacement software require much more than current Agile in terms of principles and practices.

CAMS creates models and documentation that provide traceability and maintainability. CAMS does not limit the focus of work to new development. In creating models, CAMS gives importance to the inevitable needs of data conversion, integration, and maintenance. Thus, CAMS encourages the creation of formal documentation and models in new development as well as the use of existing models when dealing with the aforementioned areas of IT work.

Architecture, Design, and Quality

Figure 5.2 shows architecture, design, and quality factors that influence all areas of IT work. These factors or background characteristics are important in providing stability to the systems being developed and the organization as a whole. These factors require due consideration irrespective of whether there is development work being undertaken or whether the system is in maintenance. For example, a large part of the architectural work (that also influences the infrastructure requirements for a project, mentioned next) is not necessarily a part of a software development phase. Agile methods, with their focus on new development, recommend "just enough architecture and design." Although a solution design for a system can follow this precept of "just enough design," that is not true with the architectural aspect of a system. This is mainly because the architecture of a system is a part of the overall enterprise architecture (EA) of the organization. CAMS explores architecture for a system in the context of the overall EA with a view to providing structural stability to the solution. Therefore, as mentioned in Chapter 4, CAMS balances a new solution with business-as-usual operations as well as other initiatives and projects in the organization. Creating a new system design with due credence to existing EA also enhances reuse and quality. This is so because the study of existing architecture reveals existing, stable, and operating areas of the organization that can provide a robust basis for creation of new system designs. Existing designs from previous projects as well as architectural models can be reused in new projects. Architectural frameworks, such as Zachmann and The Open Group Architecture Framework (TOGAF), are used in CAMS to go beyond a specific software solution and provide control and guidance at the enterprise levels. The use of such frameworks provides a much broader understanding of the enterprise and the context for a project. This, in turn, results in quality at a macro level for the organization as it improves both technical and business decision making.

Requirements (Functional, Nonfunctional, and Interface)

Figure 5.2 shows three major categories of requirements. These are the functional, nonfunctional, and interface requirements. Occasionally, infrastructure requirements also influence the areas of IT work. Usually, however, project work does not create major infrastructure requirements; instead, projects are required to adhere to these requirements. (Hence, *infrastructure* is shown in italics in Figure 5.2.)

Functional requirements are of specific use in new development projects. These requirements dictate the way in which a user wants to use the system. Documenting functional requirements helps not only in development but also during the maintenance phase of a system, as the requirements can be traced and used to weigh the changes demanded by users. NFR have a greater influence when systems are being integrated and when data is being converted. The NFR usually encompass the entire system (as against a specific functionality of the system). Therefore, they can be used to ensure the quality of data conversion and cross-system integration. Interface requirements can include user interfaces, system interfaces, and printer interfaces. With the increasing use of mobile gadgets, the user interface requirements need in-depth investigation and modeling that will have to cater to the dynamicity of user devices, location, and personalization needs.

The aforementioned two groups of factors (architecture, design, and quality; and the 3 + 1 types of requirements) can make use of modeling standards and architectural frameworks. For example, the use of UML (under the CAMS umbrella) is one of the most practical ways of applying these factors to the IT areas of work shown in Figure 5.2. For example, Ambler (2004) has succinctly discussed the application of all 13 UML 2 diagrams to the development of Agile models. Combining the pure Agile principles and practices together with the modeling standards of the UML and architectural frameworks (e.g., Zachmann and TOGAF) promises to enhance both quality and traceability in practice. Table 5.1 provides a list of UML diagrams and the corresponding comments that provide a quick understanding of what value these diagrams can add to an Agile project.

Agile Practices and CAMS Process Maps

The discussion thus far highlighted the many emergent ICT and their relationship with Agility. The various areas of work in ICT and the way in which Agile influences them have also been noted owing to their close interdependency. Furthermore, the importance of formal modeling with the UML was also highlighted in practice. This discussion forms the basis of combining Agile practices with the formal process maps of CAMS. Five such process maps—enterprise architecture, system architecture, system design, implementation, and deployment—together with their embedded Agile practices are discussed in the following sections.

Enterprise Architecture Process Map

CAMS brings together the process elements involved in the development and maintenance of EA. The process map for EA shows the relevant Agile practices embedded in it. Practical EA is an

Table 5.1 List of UML Diagrams and Potential Usefulness in Agile Projects

UML Diagrams	*Brief Description and Importance in Agile*
Use case	Documents the functionality or business processes from the user's viewpoint; user stories from Agile projects can be embedded in use cases to provide greater details and, later, traceability of requirements
Activity	Models the flow within a use case or the system. This is a detailed visual representation of a business function. Dependencies between user stories are easily ascertained by these diagrams (e.g., modeling epics)
Class	Represents the Classes, entities and attributes, business domain objects and, database tables; Agile development can benefit by identifying and modeling classes after the stories have been identified. Many business rules that cannot be easily recorded on story cards can be reflected in these diagrams
Sequence	Represents the interactions between objects and their timelines; again, sequence modeling can benefit the "working code" in Agile projects, as it provides an excellent basis for walk-throughs and inspections
Interaction overview	These relate to general high-level interactions that show dependencies between components. May be used early on in an Agile project
Communication	This relates to interactions between objects and their sequencing alternative to sequence diagrams and is used similarly in an Agile project
Object	Objects and their links, primarily being whiteboard techniques, can directly add value to discussions in Agile projects
State	The run-time life cycle of an object can be used together with class and sequence diagrams to understand code behavior. Can assist in refactoring. Also provides documentation and traceability in Agile code
Composite structure	Component or object behavior at run-time. This diagram was introduced later in UML in order to show run-time collaboration amongst multiple objects belonging to a component
Component	Models the executables, linkable libraries, etc. Can assist code compilation and redistribution in Agile projects of greater interest to architects than developers
Deployment	Visualizes the hardware nodes and processors in a deployed system; can be used as architectural diagram (although mainly at system architecture level) in an Agile project to ascertain load distribution, security needs, etc.
Package	Models subsystems, organizational units; can contribute to creation of iterations and increments in Agile projects
Timing	Presents the time concept during object interactions; enables comparison of states of multiple objects at run time, hence can be an invaluable white board discussion technique in Agile projects

ongoing artifact that need not be developed for every project. Instead, in practice, the EA is referred to during a project and updated as a result of the project.

Figure 5.3 illustrates the EA process map. This process map is made up of roles, activities and Agile practices, and deliverables that relate to EA. As a part of a project, the EA process map focuses on the creation of an architecture that will provide the qualities and constraints for the product being developed.

Roles in Enterprise Architecture

The following are the roles in an enterprise architecture process map.

Quality manager: The quality manager is responsible for the quality of the documentation of the EA. This is an ongoing responsibility that applies quality techniques to the model of the EA.

Enterprise architect: This is a key role in the EA process map. The enterprise architect is a main source of knowledge for the EA. This person uses her knowledge of the business domain as well as the technical knowledge to create and update the EA. The domain knowledge, technical knowledge, and experience of the organization are used by this role to provide ongoing continuity to the EA; hence, an enterprise architect needs to be fully aware of all these areas. An interesting crossover managed by this role is that between business architecture and EA. While the enterprise architects mostly come with a technical background, there are times when they have a substantial influence on the business architecture.

Development team: The development team participates in the EA creation and update process by providing input into the capabilities and limitations of the technical environment. This is a project-based role for the team or the lead developer; however, the effect of the work by this role goes beyond the project and into the enterprise.

Deliverables

The following are the deliverables in enterprise architecture process map.

Enterprise architecture: This is a model or a document that records the overall architecture of an entire enterprise. The EA can be a combination of models, descriptions, prototypes, and policies. This is a relatively stable document (as compared with the system architecture, SA) as it embodies multiple systems, their dependencies, data warehouses, networks, and security. The EA can be based on standards such as TOGAF and Zachmann. The enabling information technologies shown in Figure 5.1 appear in an EA from a technical angle. There are other nontechnical aspects of EA such as people and processes that also appear in the EA model.

System architecture: The initial documentation (sketch) of the SA can be produced when this process map is executed. It is later enhanced in the SA process map.

Reuse strategy: This strategy assists in implementing reusable designs and architecture. This strategy is also valuable in refactoring designs. This strategy deliverable provides both inputs to the design decisions and output from the designs that can be stored for use in future projects.

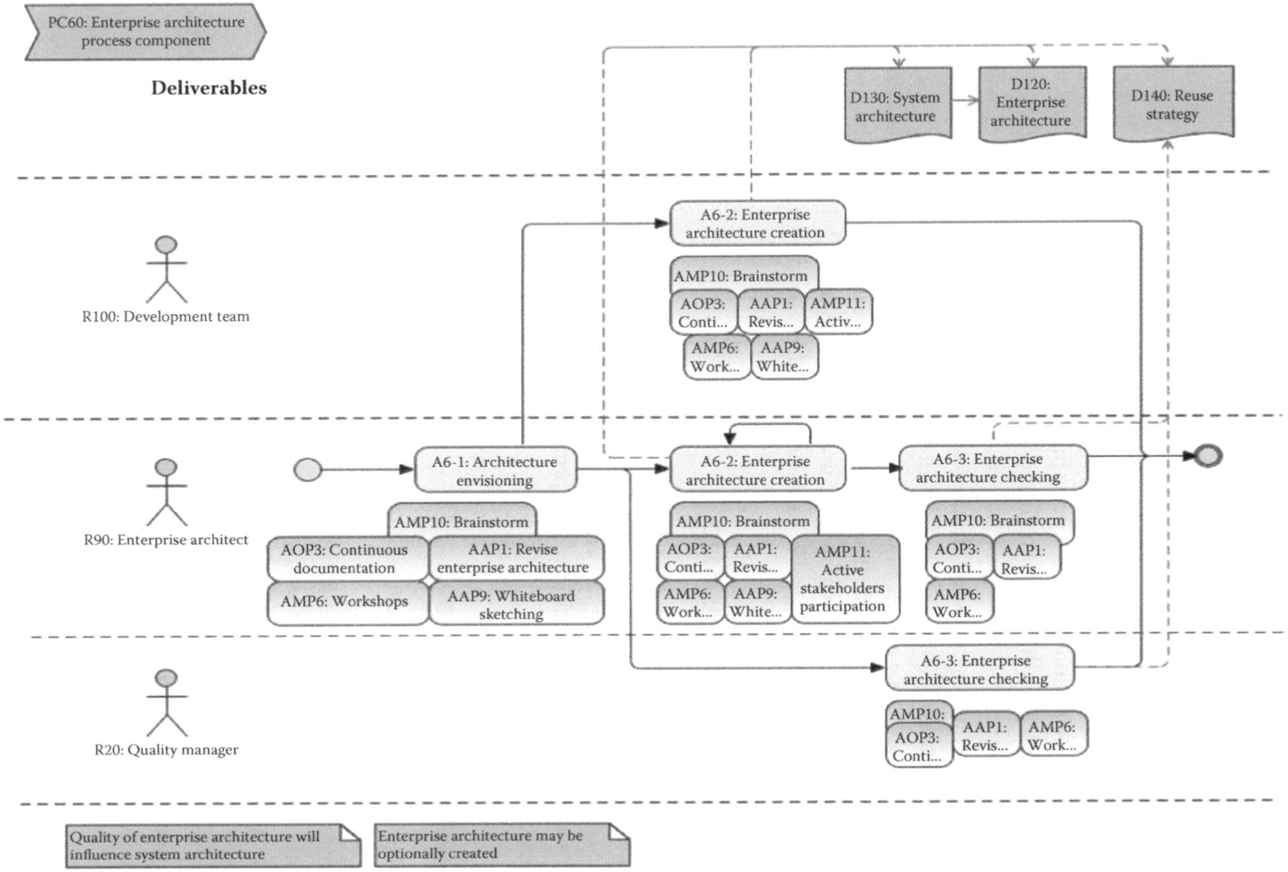

Figure 5.3 Enterprise architecture process map in CAMS.

Activities and Tasks in Enterprise Architecture

Table 5.2 demonstrates the activities and tasks with related deliverables and roles for the EA process map. Moreover, the Agile practices that would be used during the process map execution are also shown in this table.

Figure 5.4 shows an EA as an umbrella architecture that covers SA. This, in turn, influences system design and implementation. Figure 5.4 shows that standards such as TOGAF and Information Technology Infrastructure Library (ITIL) have an impact on EA. UML also has an influence in terms of facilitating creation of visual models for EA, SA, and system design. The enabling information technologies, shown earlier in Figure 5.1, are a part of EA and are considered in decision making.

CAMS encourages the use of detailed documentation for creation and maintenance of EA. Relevant Agile practices, as shown in the process map, can be used to add quality and value to the EA. Figure 5.4 acknowledges this importance of using Agile practices in the creation and maintenance of EA. For example, "stakeholder participation" in an Agile manner provides major input to the EA that lasts beyond a single project. Brainstorming, in an Agile manner, is another example of using Agile practices in the creation and maintenance of EA. Stability of EA is an important factor in providing support for quality in development projects. As Highsmith mentions, "getting up-front architecture wrong in serial development usually means poor long-term adaptability because no one can stomach changing architecture late in a project" (Highsmith, 2009). This is true of all types of development approaches that make use of EA for the creation of SA and design.

System Architecture Process Map

As shown in Figure 5.4, a good starting point for the development of an SA is the boundaries of the overall EA. Figure 5.5 further details the system architecture process map comprising activities such as architecture envisioning, SA creation, incorporation of reusable architecture patterns, and operational requirements validation. This process map with its embedded Agile practices is described next.

Roles in System Architecture

The following are the roles in a system architecture process map.

- Quality manager: Similar to the role in the EA process map, the quality manager here is responsible for the quality of the SA. However, this is a specific responsibility relating to the system (product) in development. In small- and medium-sized projects, the same person plays the role of quality manager in EA and SA process maps.
- Project manager: He is responsible for the management of the project and, as such, for the management of SA creation and its validation through the quality manager.
- Enterprise architect: This is the person responsible for the creation of the SA that is based on the EA. In large and global projects, the role of a system architect can be separated from an enterprise architect. In most projects, though, the two roles are carried out by the same person. Functioning at a system level, this role is responsible for the creation of a good and unambiguous SA.
- System designer: He is responsible for creating a solution design. This role is an important technical role that has to interact with the enterprise architects, developers, as well as the business analysts in order to clarify the meanings of the user requirements. The system design is closest to the code.

Table 5.2 Details of the Enterprise Architecture Process Map: Activities, Tasks, Deliverables, and Roles

Activities	*Tasks*	*Deliverables*	*Roles*
A6-1: Architecture envisioning	Understand current enterprise architecture Understand current operational requirement Agile practices: AOP3: Continuous documentation AMP10: Brainstorming AAP1: Review and revise enterprise architecture AAP9: Whiteboard sketching AMP6: Workshops	D120: Enterprise architecture	R90: Enterprise architect
A6-2: Enterprise architecture creation	Create information architecture with reuse Update reuse strategy Create and update security architecture Model key business processes/functions Identify key business processes Agile practices: AMP11: Active stakeholders participation AOP3: Continuous documentation AMP10: Brainstorming AAP1: Review and walk-throughs (EA specific) AAP9: Whiteboard sketching AMP6: Workshops	D130: System architecture D120: Enterprise architecture	R90: Enterprise architect R100: Development team
A6-3: Enterprise architecture checking	Validate vendor (supplier) architectures against existing EA Check the model of problem space (MOPS) against enterprise architecture Check the model of background space (MOBS) against enterprise architecture Check the model of solution space (MOSS) against enterprise architecture Agile practices: AOP3: Continuous documentation AMP10: Brainstorming AAP1: Revise enterprise architecture AMP6: Workshops	D140: Reuse strategy	R90: Enterprise architect R20: Quality manager

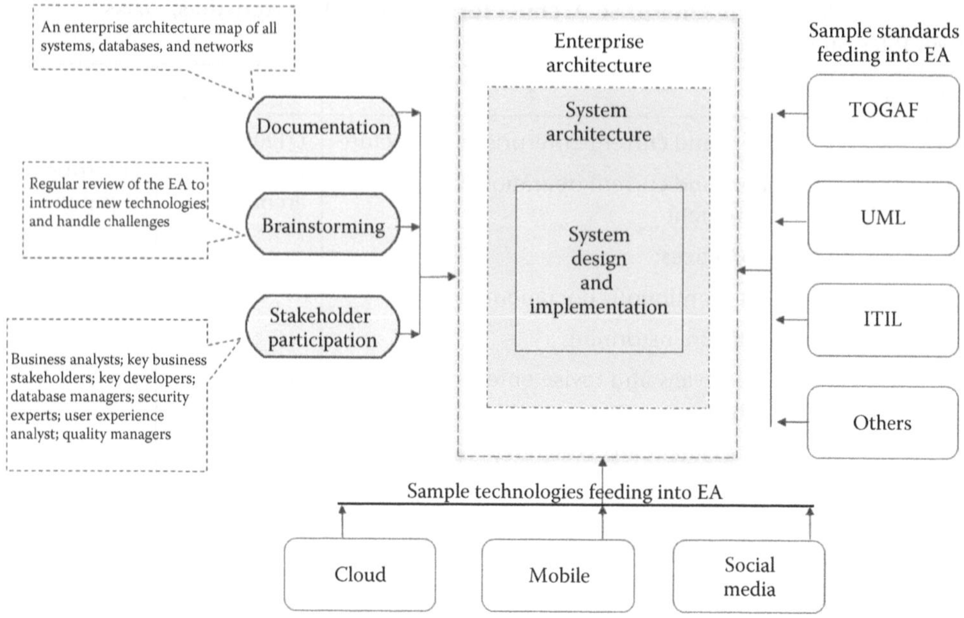

Figure 5.4 Enterprise architecture and Agile practices.

Deliverables

The following are the deliverables in a system architecture process map.

System architecture: This is the main deliverable of the SA process map. As mentioned, the initial documentation of the SA is produced within the boundaries of EA and is enhanced in the system architecture process map.

Reuse strategy: This assists in implementing reusable designs and architecture. This is an important contributor to the SA as it focuses on reusing existing designs, patterns, and lessons learned from previous architectures.

Activities and Tasks in System Architecture

Table 5.3 summarizes the activities and tasks with related deliverables and roles for the SA process map. Moreover, the Agile practices that would be used during the process map execution are included.

Figure 5.6 highlights the various factors that an enterprise architect has to consider at the application development level. These factors are relatively stable, a "given" at the enterprise level. They change, however, in the context of an application (system) being developed. Thus, an SA will have to consider the following important dependencies:

- These are business processes that influence the SA. For example, collaborative and interoperable business processes have to be factored in while creating a system-level architectural model. Process models using BPMN/UML provide necessary visual artifacts (especially in CAMS-based projects) for considerations in creating the SA.

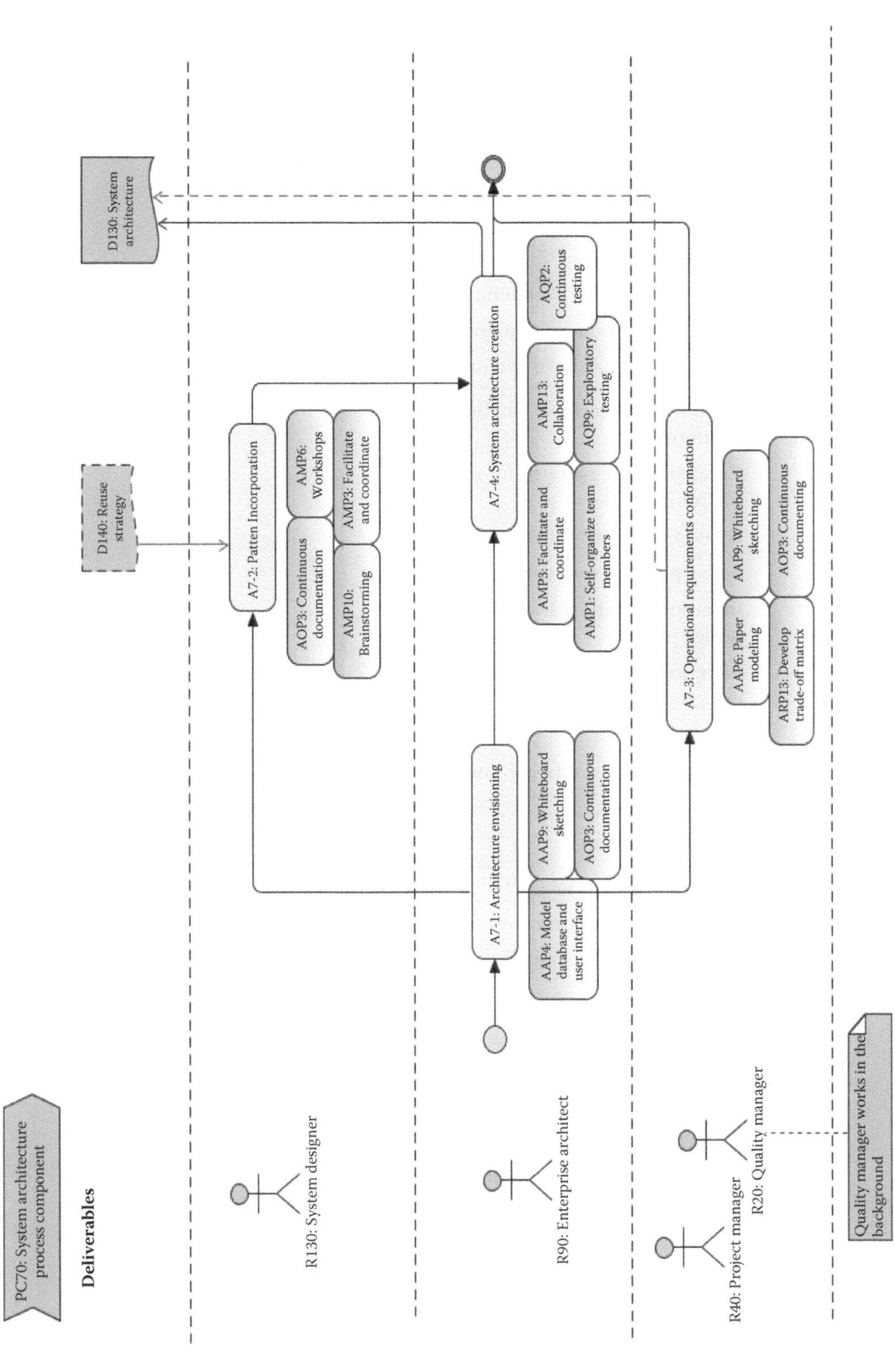

Figure 5.5 System architecture process map.

Table 5.3 System Architecture Process Map

Activities	*Tasks*	*Deliverables*	*Roles*
A7-1: Architecture envisioning	Understand current system architecture needs Understand current operational requirement Relate to enterprise architecture Agile practices: AAP9: Whiteboard sketching AOP3: Continuous documentation AAP4: Model database and user interface		R90: Enterprise architect
A7-2: Pattern incorporation	Identify situations that can be put in "patterns" Create suitable patterns for use within the project Experiment with and validate patterns Select patterns for use within the project Incorporate patterns within system design Incorporate patterns within system design Agile practices: AMP3: Facilitate and coordinate AMP10: Brainstorming AMP6: Workshops AOP3: Continuous documentation		R130: System designer
A7-3: Operational requirements confirmation	Performance requirements Scalability requirements Security requirements Volume requirements Agile practices: AAP9: Whiteboard sketching AAP6: Paper modeling ARP13: Develop trade-off matrix AOP3: Document continuously	D130: System architecture	R40: Project manager R20: Quality manager

Table 5.3 (*Continued*)

Activities	*Tasks*	*Deliverables*	*Roles*
A7-4: System architecture creation	Create information architecture Execute architecture prototyping Create network architecture Create database architecture Agile practices: AMP3: Facilitate and coordinate AMP1: Self-organize team members AMP13: Collaboration AQP2: Continuous testing AQP9: Exploratory testing	D130: System architecture	R90: Enterprise architect

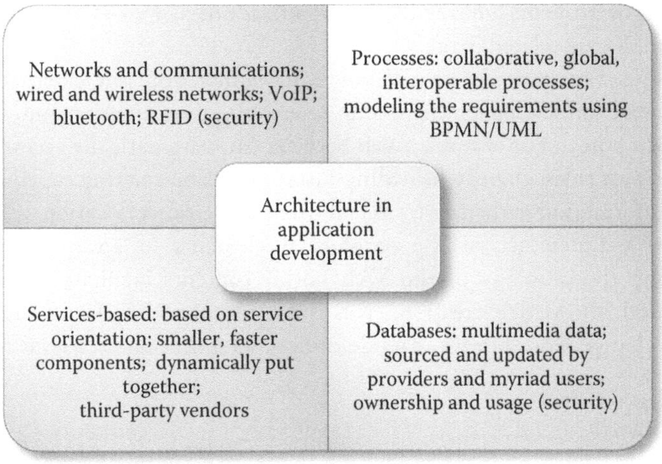

Figure 5.6 System architecture and application development.

- Availability of networks and communications specified in the EA provide the constraints and limitations in the creation of network specifications for an SA. For example, the extent to which an organization provides for wired and wireless communication networks can dictate whether a system can make use of them in its own solution. Voice-over-Internet Protocol (VoIP), Bluetooth, Radio Frequency IDentification (RFID), and associated securities are examples of these network considerations in an SA.
- Technologies of service-based and service-oriented architectures provide the basis for the architectural constraints and qualities of an SA. For example, SOA-based systems will be able to use smaller, faster, remote services that can be dynamically put together to create business workflows.
- Databases and their constraints derived from the EA dictate the SA considerations. For example, if the organization has existing, multimedia databases, then the SA will be constrained by these databases. Sourcing of contents and their updates (e.g., through social

media networks) by myriad users requires system-level decisions including permissions for updates, security of updates, and validity of contents.

Discussion on EA and SA invariably lead to a detailed consideration of the organization's Web portal. A Web portal is, effectively, the electronic front end or face of a system and the business itself! Therefore, in CAMS-based projects, the Web portal is given significant importance. The issues impacting the electronic portal of an organization, in turn, affect the implementation and deployment of a software solution. Figure 5.7 (based on Unhelkar and Deshpande (2004), further developed in Deshpande and Unhelkar) shows the factors affecting Web portals in the context of Agility. Earlier, in this chapter, enabling technologies of Web Services, SOA, and application integration were discussed. These IT enablers are used in developing these Agile Web portals.

- External agencies: The agility of a portal depends on the external sources accessing and updating its contents. Who are these external agencies, partners, and collaborators? Categories of organizations accessing these contents include business partners, industry bodies, and consortiums, governments and regulatory organizations as well as research centers (when it comes to compliance-related data).
- What are the *technologies used in gathering information* from the external agencies? These technologies ease (or challenge) the process of gathering information and, therefore, impact the Agility of a portal. For example, Web Services can automatically access and update data based on business rules, thereby providing instant decision-making capabilities to business. MT enable information gathering from end users at their own location.
- Analysis and maintenance of the ontological elements of an organization's contents: Understanding the ontology of the Web portal contents facilitates their analysis, cross tabulation, and knowledge creation. This, in turn, provides the organization with the flexibility to change. For example, data definition, its source and retrieval details, associated

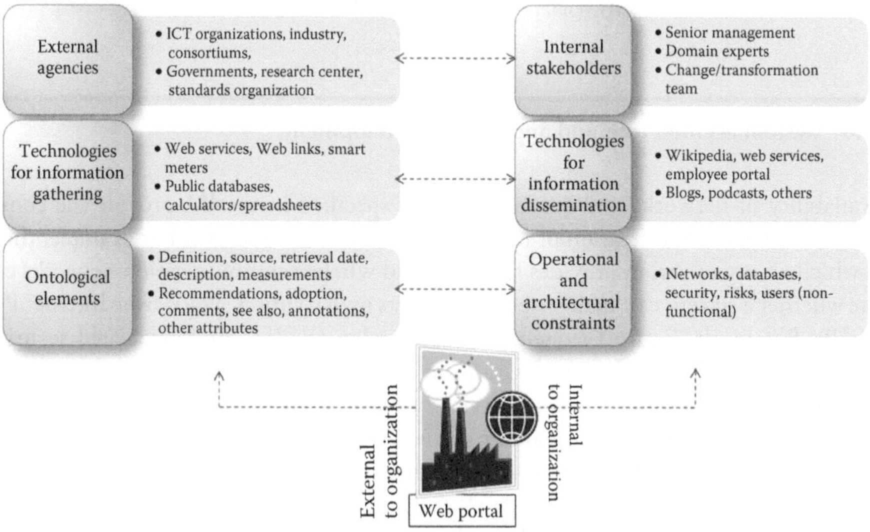

Figure 5.7 Embedding Agility in an organization's Web portals.

measurements and related annotations—all add up to provide insights on the new products to be developed and change the existing business processes—resulting in improved Agility.

- Internal stakeholders: Agile values encourage collaboration among all internal stakeholders—especially when it comes to presenting the electronic front end of the organization. Thus, input from senior decision makers, domain experts, and people involved in transformation exercises are included in the workshops to formulate the organization's Web portals. These stakeholders can also properly assess and report on the risks associated with collaboration with external parties.
- Technologies for dissemination of information: This can become as important as the technologies for gathering information. Some technological channels, such as the Internet and mobile broadband, can be also used in providing information. Social media (and increasingly social life) networks are employed, as a part of the Web portal (internally and externally), to disseminate information. For example, an employee portal and blog, associated video and audio podcasts, and internal Wikis provide a strategic medium for information provision to the organization. This timely provision of information enhances the speed and accuracy of decision making for an Agile organization.
- Operational and architectural constraints: Analyzing the ontological elements externally also leads to an understanding of the internal constraints in the organization. Most operational constraints for a system and also for the organization are internally imposed. The limitations of the organization (e.g., available bandwidth) and architectural constraints from the background space (e.g., use of a specific CMS) can influence the way in which a Web portal gets created and presented to the electronic world. Operational constraints, in particular, are very closely tied to Agility.

Nonfunctional (Operational) Requirements and Architecture (Enterprise and System)

Nonfunctional requirements (NFR) describe the many requirements of a function, project, or system that is not directly related to its functionality or behavior. These NFR come into play when the function or system is in operation. Therefore, these requirements are also called *operational requirements* of a system. In addition to a function or system, NFR also apply at the organizational level.

Architectural and operational constraints have a significant influence on the electronic front end (Web portal) of an organization. The EA limits the type and size of the contents, their analysis and knowledge creation, and the interaction of the user with the organization. The operational constraints, described in the NFRS, also limit the extent to which a system can operate within the technological boundaries of the organization. The NFRs, shown earlier in Figure 5.1 and revisited in Figure 5.7, have not had sufficient discussion in the pure Agile literature thus far. For example, there is hardly any advice on whether an NFR can be put in a user story or not. Besides, the format of a user story is not conducive to NFR, anyway. So, the NFRs tend to be kept in the background while functional requirements are developed. CAMS redresses this situation by paying due attention to NFRs through its SA and system design process maps. The NFRs are also made to relate to the organizational portal, thereby ensuring consistency between the operation of a system and the rest of the organization.

NFR can be understood broadly as the various "qualities" or attributes of the system in operation and the corresponding "constraints" on the system.

Agile as a method was discussed in Chapter 2. Agile approaches throw a challenge to both functional and NFR because of the time and opportunity available to document both categories of requirements in Agile projects. Creation of a prototype for the NFRS becomes vital at the start of the project. Business analysis collaborates with both technical and business specialists to create prototypes and ensure that the NFR will be eventually met when the system is fully developed and integrated. There is no point, for example, in discovering that 128-bit encryption will not work for a specific application once the application has been fully developed. NFRS should be tested as early as possible in a project by creating technical prototypes. In Agile projects, not only can functionalities implemented be tested on a daily basis but also the NFR.

Figure 5.8 shows the two major categories of NFR.

The constraints are usually derived from the EA, whereas the qualities tend to be specified at the SA level.

- Constraints: These are the limitations on the SA and system design. Adhering to the constraints during SA and system design ensures proper functioning of the deployed system within those organizational parameters. Examples of such constraints at various levels include the following:
  - Organizational (e.g., 100 mbps bandwidth)
  - Project (e.g., $350,000 budget)
  - Time frame (e.g., must be live by a due date)
- Qualities: (e.g., 1 defect per million; or 23 hours 58 minutes uptime per day)
  - Organizational (e.g., 3 second response time)
  - Project (e.g., every requirement subject to walk-through)

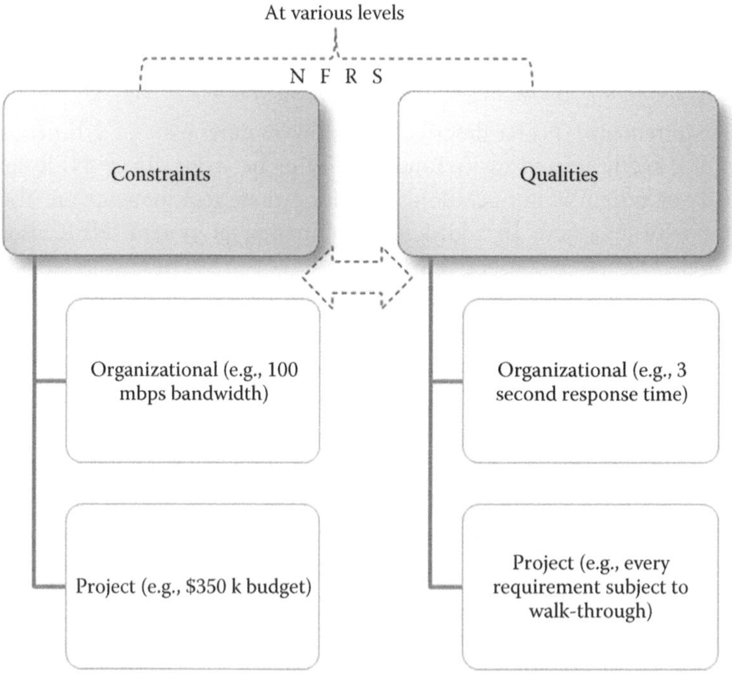

Figure 5.8 NFRS and Agility.

The business analysts, together with the key business users and architects, are in an excellent position to investigate and specify these NFRS. Furthermore, business analysts can also outline the acceptance criteria (tests) for these NFRS. The *qualities* (also referred to as "ilities") of the system are specified in collaboration with the users and domain experts; the *constraints* are usually dictated by the architects. It is important that these NFRS are not ignored (as occasionally happens, as they can be less glamorous than the functional requirements) and, instead focused on right at the start of the project. Interactions with the key business stakeholders and domain experts is necessary but never sufficient when it comes to NFRS because the experts themselves are making educated estimates (guesstimates) to arrive at NFRS. For example, the number of accounts expected to be opened in the first year of a banking application (100,000) can be "anybody's guess." Having said that, there is no choice but to make those estimations right at the beginning of the project to ensure that the architecture of the system caters to those requirements. Owing to the guess work involved in NFRS, it is also a good idea to pair these requirements with the corresponding *assumptions.* Again, for example, with 100,000 accounts expected to be opened in the first year, the assumptions can be excellence in on-line marking and correlation with the bank's social media. As can be seen, these requirements are crucial in satisfying the needs and "experience" of the users of the system when in operation and also in its eventual acceptance.

Business stakeholders and domain experts participate in workshops usually organized by the business analysts to ascertain these otherwise unfamiliar and unclear requirements. Lack of standardized modeling constructs (especially in a pure Agile approach) for NFRs also means they are not visually modeled. Furthermore, the business stakeholders themselves may not know the fully nonfunctional requirements up front. For example, the uptime required of a system or the resources required to achieve that uptime may remain uncertain and unmodeled at the start of a project.

To help improve the estimations and assumptions, CAMS recommends formal involvement of business analysts early in a project. The architects and solutions designers together with the business analysts undertake early prototyping (and/or proof of concept) of the "solution." The close operation of business analysts with business stakeholders, architects, and solution designers, especially when it comes to NFRS, is an important part of CAMS in practice.

For example, if the business is demanding a 3-second response time for any query on its new solution (a performance-related *quality* expected of the system), then the enterprise architect can say, "no, that will not be possible as we only have a certain bandwidth available, 100 mbps." Once this is discussed (although not necessarily sorted out or resolved) up front, it opens up the doors for the business stakeholders to either increase their budgets to achieve the quality they are expecting of the solution or, alternatively, tone down their expectations. If these NFRS are left untouched or not discussed till later stages of the solution, then the expectations and the offerings of the solutions do not match.

SIDEBAR

There is no one-to-one relationship between functional and nonfunctional requirements. However, a careful inspection of the functional requirements can always throw light on the NFR. Many nonfunctional requirements specifications (NFRS) apply at the project and organizational levels rather than at an individual functional level. This could be another reason why NFRS usually lag behind the functional requirements. Testing of NFRs can also lag behind, "since we do not have a system, there is not much we can do in terms of checking it out for its performance."

Creation of an early prototype of the system where the NFRs can be tested out is encouraged in CAMS. Instead of only focusing on the implementation of functional requirements, the enterprise architect and the solutions designer can work together to load the databases and run the prototypes against these test databases. This is how the NFRS (including performance, scalability, and security) and their incorporation in the solution are carried out in CAMS.

As NFRS apply across the organization, business stakeholders may not fully understand the level at which these requirements will apply to a software system. The business analyst highlights an NFR and its relationship with cost and time. The qualities the business stakeholders expect of a system need to have associated costs and time, both of which will go up as the expectations of the business increase. Note that these are not new functionalities expected, nor are these associated with the higher quality of those functionalities (requiring higher rigor in testing). These qualities in NFRS are the characteristics of the system when it will be in operation. Higher demand of NFRs from the system have corresponding costs and time that need to be factored in.

For example, stakeholders will agree to the highest possible security, 24 7 uptime, and mirroring of data to improve global performance. Unless business analysts show a direct relationship between each of these NFRS and corresponding costs and times required in achieving them, these NFRS will continue to appear (and increase) as the project progresses.

Figure 5.9 shows examples of the most common NFR of a system. These NFR are not isolated—instead, they are applied together on the basis of the constraints of the EA. Pure Agile has very minimal suggestions, in terms of its practices, to identify and model NFR. CAMS encourages detailed discussion, modeling, and prototyping of the solution to enable handling of these NFR. Following are examples of these NFR, as highlighted in Figure 5.9:

- Performance (Bandwidth): This is usually specified in terms of the speed of response expected from a system. This performance requirement for an Internet-based deployment depends on the available bandwidth.
- Scalability (time): This is the expected growth and use of the system over time. Scalability includes system parameters such as data storage and performance related to the system as the number of users grows.
- Security (levels): This requirement can vary widely, going from a specific function or use case in a system through to the organizational policies in terms of access to its web portals. Examples of security requirements include encryption (e.g., 128 bit), policies on passwords, and browser requirements.
- Availability, maintainability (QoS): Examples of these requirements include permissible downtime for maintenance, number of times a system is allowed to be off-line, and expected quality of service (QoS) for differing categories of system failures.

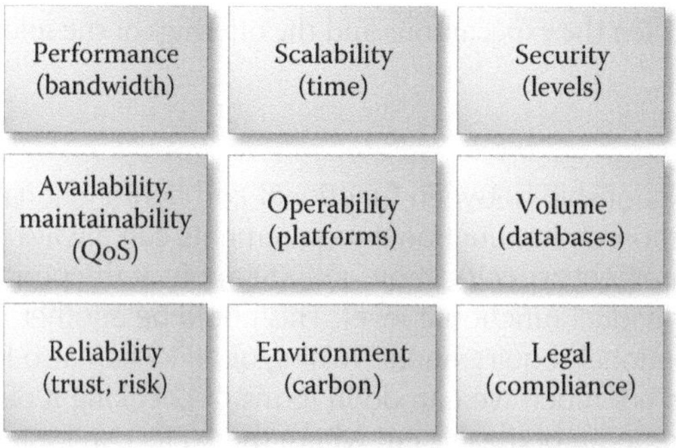

Figure 5.9 Types of NFR.

- Operability (platforms): Almost all systems in operation today require a back-end operating system and a front-end browser technology. This requirement specifies the type of operating platform and the browsers used for the system. Owing to the dynamically changing devices and locations (in case of mobile interfaces) the specifications of browsers becomes very important.
- Volume (databases): This requirement covers the volume requirements of the system. This is typically the size of the database that is expected when the system is in operation. The size of data is not only the one required in current usage of the system but also the volume required for mirroring and backup storage of system data.
- Reliability (trust, risk): This NFR is based on the criticality of the system. For example, an aircraft navigation system can have a reliability specification that is closer to Twelve Sigma (as against Six Sigma)—implying a one-in-billion, rather than a one-in-million defect.
- Environment (carbon): The increasing importance of environmental consciousness in business (Unhelkar, 2011) implies that most new systems in development will have a requirement that specifies its carbon content. While some business systems may not be directly contributing to carbon emissions, their effect on the back-end data servers will increasingly come into calculations for overall carbon emissions of the organization. Alternatively, carbon emission management systems (CEMS) will have a more detailed specification for its carbon capacity, which will be specified as nonfunctional as well as functional requirements.
- Legal requirements (compliance): Financial systems invariably have requirements for tracking and auditing. While some of these requirements are functional in nature (e.g., logging the details of the auditor), others that deal with the creation of audit trail and backups may not directly be functional. Instead, the legal requirements are specified as nonfunctional and require careful walk-throughs and inspections for their verification in the system.

The NFRs are not limited to a system only; instead, they can apply at various levels within an organization. The level of NFR applicability is helpful in deciding whether the requirements should be part of the overall EA, or apply at a specific system level, or even go down to a single unit of functionality. Contemporary Agile does not go into the details of NFRs, neither does it delve into the levels of these requirements. CAMS, however, is keen to identify the levels of NFRs and use them for EA, SA, and the corresponding verification and validation of these architectures. Figure 5.10 shows the various levels at which NFRs apply:

- Organization-level NFRs include policies relating to electronic access, available bandwidth and data warehouse resources, and human resources (HR) requirements relating to users.

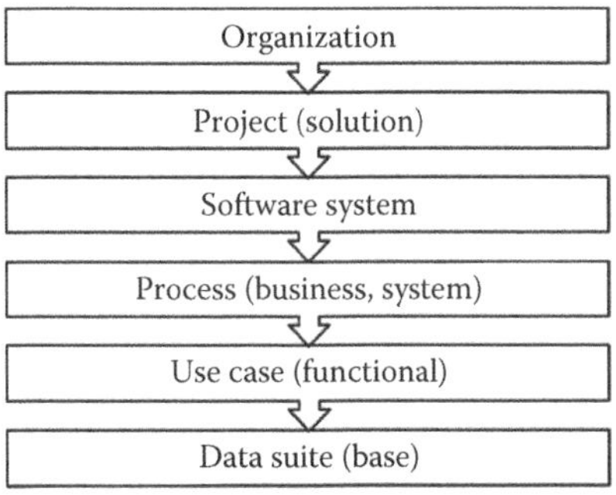

Figure 5.10 NFRS apply at various levels.

- Project (solution)-level NFRs relate to the solution being provided through the initiative. This solution can be much more than the actual software system. For example, operational procedures and rules associated with the solution can be specified as NFR at this level (note that these are the rules associated with the operation of the solution and not the business rules embedded within its functionality).
- Software system level NFRs relate to its development, deployment, and operation. For example, an operating system or a browser requirement can relate to the operation of a software system but not necessarily to the entire organization.
- Process (business, system)-level NFRs can become part of the business process management. Examples of these requirements include detailed business rules specification as well as system-level rules. Rules do not have interfaces and are not directly visible to users. However, they need to be specified and also configured for operation as is done through NFRs.
- Use case (functional) level can also have an NFR. For example, a use case dealing with placing an order for goods may have a much more stringent security requirement as compared with the access of the portal for information or quotation for goods.
- Data suite (base) requirements are directly related to a piece of data, a table, or a database in which the data are being stored. These NFRs are based on the performance, volume, and scalability needs of the system. As against the requirements applicable to a process or a functional unit, these requirements are applied only to the data at the database level.

System Design Process Map

Composite Agile undertakes formal system design interspersed with Agile practices. System design can be considered as an ongoing activity throughout the development of a system. It is carried out with respect to SA and EA. System design is closely intertwined with implementation of the process map. While pure Agile approaches finer details in terms of system design (e.g., XP), in CAMS, this design is carried out under the auspices of a process map. Such process-map-based system design can identify reusable classes and components from the architecture, re-factor existing classes, and suggest a disciplined approach to ongoing improvement of code. System design can be carried out top-down or bottom-up depending on the needs of a project. For example, a software solution that is based on a large number of available components will have a bottom-up design; a solution that is starting from scratch will have a top-down approach to design. In either case, however, the practices of Agile can be embedded in the formal activities of system design. For example, the daily stand-up meeting of Agile can be used to carry out dedicated design decisions (Bossavit, 2009).

Figure 5.11 depicts the system design process map, which comprises of such activities as advanced business class analysis, advanced instance design, coding, project tracking, and quality assuring model of solution space (MOSS). Thus, system design is exclusively undertaken in the solution space.

Roles in System Design

The following are the key roles in the system design process map:

- System designer: This is the main role in this process map. The system designer is required to focus on the design of the solution that is closely dependent on the implementation language and the technical environment for implementation. The quality aspect of the system design process component comes from the background knowledge of technological facets.

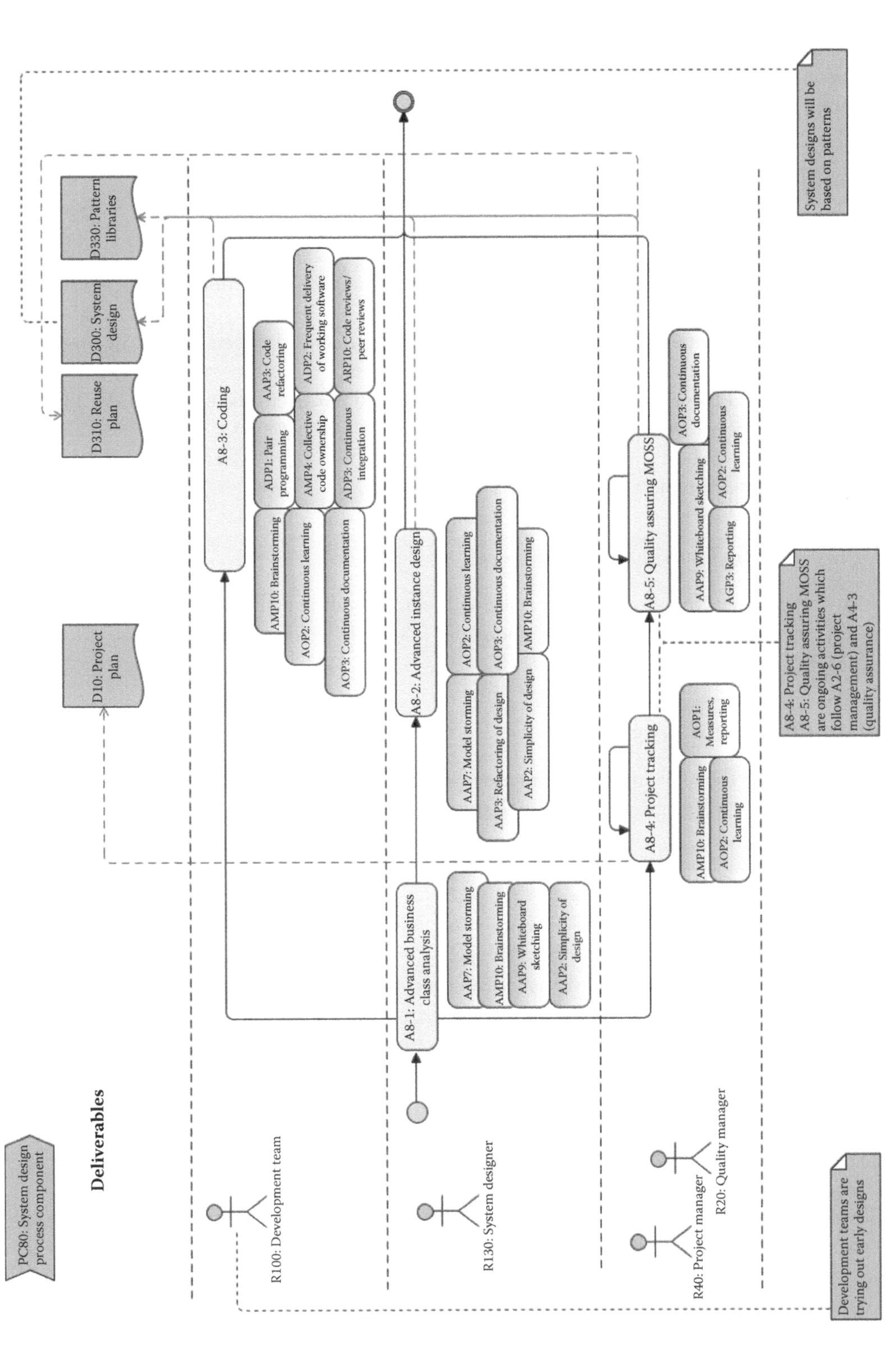

Figure 5.11 System design process map.

- Quality/project manager: In this role, the quality and project managers keep track of the project progress as well as assure the quality of the system design.
- Development team: In this role, the development team provides continuous support to the system designer in checking the feasibility of the design and testing it with the code.

Deliverables

The following are the deliverables in the system design process map:

System design: This contains the details of the system layout and the technical design that form part of MOSS.

Reuse plan: This contains the background support for reusing the plan created during the iteration, allowing the process component to reuse them.

Pattern libraries: This contains all the design and pattern libraries created or modified for local and organizational-level patterns.

Project plan: This contains the organizational project plan, which provides the detailed description of the type of project and category.

Activities and Tasks in System Design

Table 5.4 demonstrates the activities and tasks with corresponding deliverables and roles for the system design process map. In addition, the Agile practices, which would be utilized during the process map execution, are included.

Implementation Process Map

Figure 5.12 presents the implementation process map. This process map provides process guidance in terms of coding/implementing the software system.

Roles in Implementation

The following are the roles in the implementation process map.

- Development team: This is made up of multiple developers responsible for implementing the product. These developers iteratively implement the designs created in the system design process map. There is regular communication among the team members and with other roles using Agile practices, such as the system designer and the business analyst (e.g., daily stand-up meetings). The team also participates in the activities of sprint planning and sprint review.
- System designer: The system designer supports the development team by explaining the designs that are created as part of the model of the solution space.
- Business analyst: The business analyst ensures that the development team clearly understands the requirements that are documented through user stories and use cases. The business analyst provides input on the functional, nonfunctional, and interface requirements to the development team.
- User, Product Owner, Scrum Master: The primary purpose of these roles is in planning the iterations and then the sprints. Occasionally, for large-scale developments, the role of an

Table 5.4 System Design Process Map

Activities	*Tasks*	*Deliverable*	*Roles*
A8-1: Advanced business class analysis	Business class diagrams Instance models in MOPS Agile practices: AAP7: Model storming AAP2: Simplicity of design AMP10: Brainstorming AAP9: Whiteboard sketching	D300: System design	R130: System designer
A8-2: Advanced instance design	Create advanced sequence diagrams Create advance state chart diagrams Agile practices: AAP7: Model storming AAP3: Refactoring of design AAP2: Simplicity of design MP10: Brainstorming AOP2: Continuous learning AOP3: Continuous documentation	D300: System design D330: Pattern libraries	R130: System designer
A8-3: Coding	General (standard) coding Inclusion of reusable libraries Agile practices: ADP1: Pair programming AAP3: Code refactoring AMP4: Collective code ownership ADP2: Frequent delivery of working software ARP10: Code reviews/peer reviews ADP3: Continuous integration MP10: Brainstorming AOP2: Continuous learning AOP3: Continuous documentation	D300: System design D330: Pattern libraries	R100: Development team

continued

Table 5.4 (*Continued*)

Activities	*Tasks*	*Deliverable*	*Roles*
A8-4: Project tracking	Measure progress through metrics Report on progress Refine estimates based on progress Agile practices: MP10: Brainstorming AOP2: Continuous learning AOP1: Measures, reporting	D10: Project plan	R20: Quality manager R40: Project manager
A8-5: Quality-assuring MOSS	Identify the models for QA checks Select relevant quality techniques Apply quality checks to models Mark and report on errors (syntax, semantics, aesthetics) Recheck the quality after fixes Agile practices: AAP9: Whiteboard sketching AGP3: Direct reporting (stakeholders) AOP2: Continuous learning AOP3: Continuous documentation	D300: System design (refine) D310: Reuse plan D330: Pattern libraries (refine)	R20: Quality manager R40: Project manager

iteration manager is created separately. The Scrum Master, together with the development team, plans the sprints based on the input from the previous sprint with metrics. The Product Owner and the user play supporting roles in iteration and sprint planning. The Product Owner provides feedback on the deliverables during the reviews.

Deliverables

The following are the deliverables in the implementation process map.

- Code: This is the key deliverable for the implementation process map. Code, however, is not a single deliverable. A substantial amount of integration is required for the code produced with other systems, databases, and validation processes.
- Test cases: This contains units of testing focused on the implementation. Writing good test cases before development is a popular Agile approach to development.
- Requirements specification: This is a model of the requirements—primarily functional requirements. The business analyst in the role of a requirements modeler takes charge of this

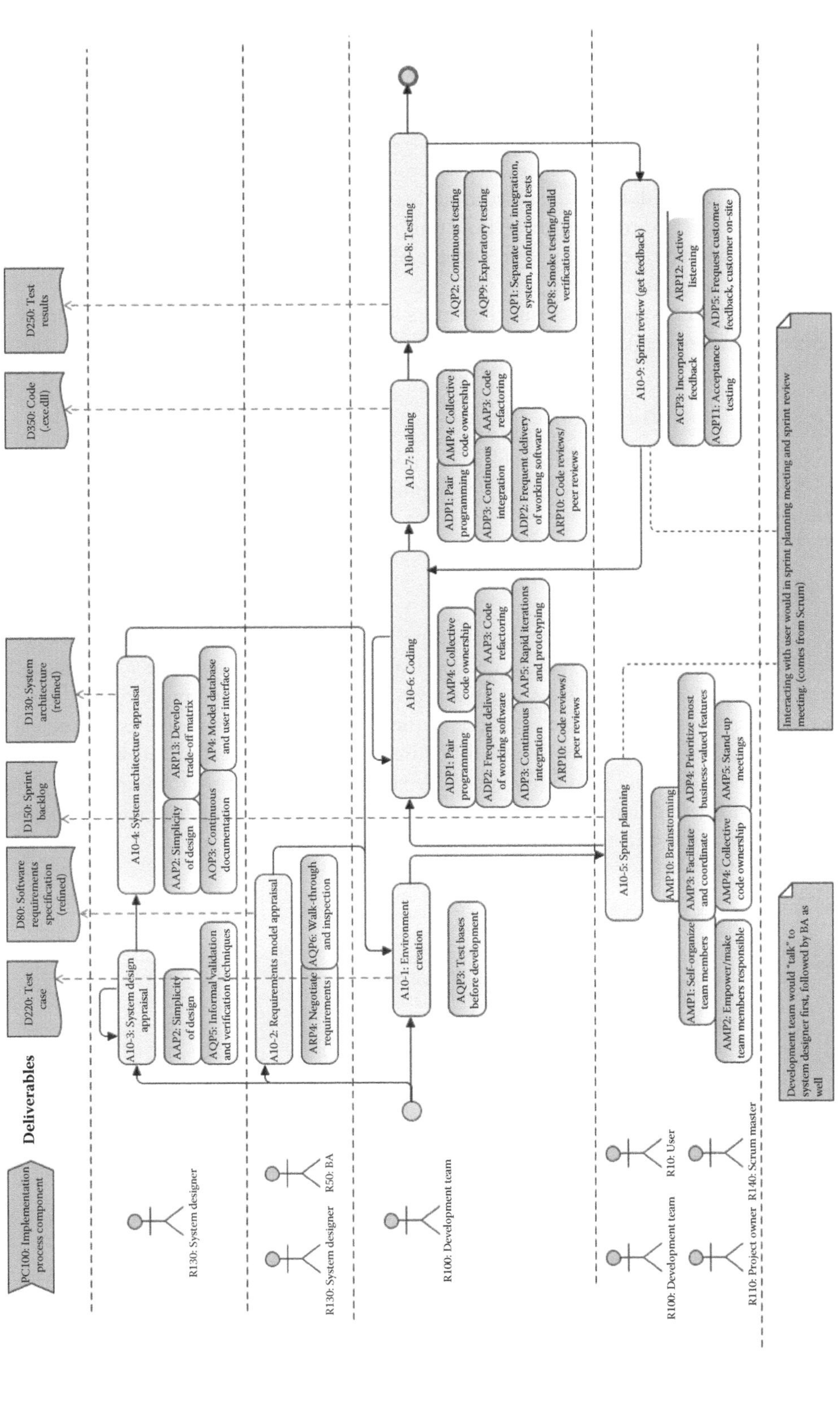

Figure 5.12 Implementation process map in Table 5.5.

deliverable. This requirement, produced earlier through the requirements modeling process map, is refined and used here. The development team understands and uses the requirements to produce the code.

- System architecture: This is also a deliverable produced earlier but refined by the system designer during development. This deliverable is refined not only for current use but also for future system development.
- Sprint backlog: This document derived from Scrum is effectively a list of items to be completed and delivered during a sprint. The sprint-planning activity determines the number of items/tasks that have been completed and the outstanding tasks (some of which would be shifted to the next sprint).
- Test result: This deliverable contains the results from the testing of the code (in this implementation process map).

Activities and Tasks in Implementation

Table 5.5 lists the activities, tasks, deliverables, and roles for the implementation process map. In addition, the example Agile practices that can be combined with the planned process elements are also listed in the table.

Agile Elements in Implementation

The implementation process map, as summarized in Table 5.4, has examples of Agile practices embedded in it. These Agile practices are derived from the contemporary Agile methods used in software development projects. Thus, some aspects of Agile methods correlate to a subset of the formal process maps. For example, an Agile method (typically Scrum) describes its elements as roles, and ceremonies are artifacts (shown in Figure 5.13). These Agile elements are primarily used in software development. Therefore, these Agile elements also appear in the implementation process map. A brief description of these three categories of Agile elements (roles, ceremonies, and artifacts) and the way they are used in the implementation process map follows.

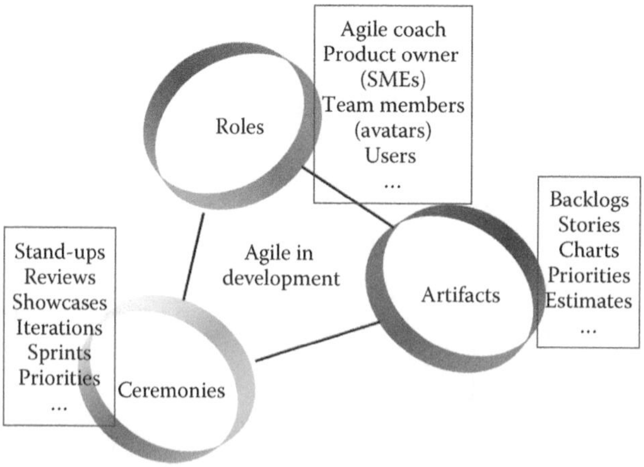

Figure 5.13 The three categories of Agile elements.

Table 5.5 Implementation Process Map

Activities	*Tasks*	*Deliverable*	*Roles*
A10-1: Environment creation	Install coding language environment (e.g., editor) Create test cases for the classes (code) Prepare to code classes Agile practices: AQP3: Test-driven development (write test cases before coding)	D220: Test cases	R100: Development team
A10-2: Requirements model appraisal	Participate in system (package) reviews Further explain use cases/user stories Agile practices: AQP6: Walk-through and inspection ARP4: Negotiate requirements AOP3: Continuous documentation	D80: Software requirements specification (refined)	R50: Business analyst R130: System designer
A10-3: System design appraisal	Support the coding Language of choice Modify design Agile practices: AAP2: Simplicity of design AQP5: Informal validation and verification techniques		R130: System designer
A10-4: System architecture appraisal	Provide operational input Finetune architecture Agile practices: AAP2: Simplicity of design AOP3: Document continuously AAP4: Model database and user interface ARP13: Develop trade-off matrix	D130: System architecture (refine)	R130: System designer

continued

Table 5.5 (*Continued*)

Activities	*Tasks*	*Deliverable*	*Roles*
A10-5: Sprint planning	Select high-level requirement from the product backlog Plan sprint based on project metrics Agile practices: AMP5: Stand-up meetings ADP4: Prioritize most business-valued features AMP1: Self-organize team members AMP3: Facilitate and coordinate AMP4: Collective code ownership AMP2: Empower/make team members responsible AMP10: Brainstorming	D150: Sprint backlog	R140: Scrum Master R110: Product Owner R100: Development team R10: User
A10-6: Coding	Write test harness Update reusable component libraries Unit test Code classes Agile practices: AAP5: Rapid iterations and prototype ADP1: Pair programming AAP3: Code refactoring AMP4: Collective code ownership ADP2: Frequent delivery of working software ADP3: Continuous integration ARP10: Code reviews/peer reviews	D350: Code	R100: Development team

Table 5.5 (*Continued*)

Activities	*Tasks*	*Deliverable*	*Roles*
A10-7: Build	Build the system Link the interface with other systems Incorporate reusable component libraries Execute the system Agile practices: ADP1: Pair programming AAP3: Code refactoring AMP4: Collective code ownership ADP2: Frequent delivery of working software ADP3: Continuous integration ARP10: Code reviews/peer reviews	D350: Code	R100: Development team
A10-8: Testing	Component test System test (incremental) Integration test (incremental) Agile practices: AQP2: Continuous testing AQP1: Separate unit, integration, system, nonfunctional tests AQP8: Smoke testing/build verification testing AQP9: Exploratory testing	D250: Test results	R100: Development team
A10-9: Sprint review	Present working increment Get customer feedback Get other stakeholder feedback Introduce changes according to feedbacks Agile practices: AQP11: Acceptance testing ACP3: Incorporate feedback ADP5: Frequent customer feedback, customer on site ARP12: Active listening		R100: Development team R140: Scrum Master R10: User R110: Product Owner

Roles

Agile methods have limited project roles. This is mainly due to their focus on development. These typical Agile roles are as follows:

- Agile coach: This role is focused on enabling the team to reach its goals. This is a facilitator who encourages the team internally and protects the team from external influences. A good Agile coach is as much a team member as a coach. She would work toward removing the blockages and show stoppers. There is very little "task management" undertaken by this role.
- Product owner: This is the key business person for whose benefit the product is being developed. This person can also provide subject matter expertise (as an SME), although in large projects the two roles (product owner and SME) are different. In CAMS, certainly the key stakeholder and the SME are separately identified, with the latter on the advisory side of the project. Users are also separately identified in CAMS and they provide valuable input not only during development but also in testing and deployment of the system.
- Team members: These are the developers, coders, and also testers. These are technical experts who assume the responsibility of developing the product in close cooperation with the product owners and users. Occasionally, team members take on "Avatars" to enable easier allocation of tasks across multiple or parallel iterations.

Ceremonies

Agile practices are described as part of Agile methods. A ceremony is the carrying out of an Agile practice (practices were discussed in Chapter 2 and later, as a part of CAMS in Chapter 4). Stand-up meetings, iteration planning and estimation, iteration review, writing user stories, prioritization of features, showcase for a release, testing, and the short, sharp sprints—these are all part of Agile project ceremonies. These ceremonies are embedded within the activities and tasks of the implementation process map. CAMS also embeds these ceremonies in many other process maps as relevant.

Artifacts

Owing to their focus on working code rather than on documentation, Agile methods define minimalistic artifacts as deliverables. CAMS has a more detailed description and templates for its deliverables. Following is a discussion of Agile artifacts (stories, features, backlogs, and charts) that can be part of the implementation process map.

Stories—User stories are a popular means of documenting the functional requirements of a system. They document a unit of functionality described by the user. Stories form an important artifact embedded in the implementation process map. User stories can be written at both informal (high-level) and detailed levels. Figure 5.14 shows examples of stories. Figure 5.14a and b also indicates how priorities can be put up on the story card. (See the sidebar for user stories and features. Also see Appendix IV for samples of user stories involving the different roles found in a telecom company.)

Features—Features are a list of requirements from a product. While the functional requirements can be documented with user stories, many of the NFRs cannot be written in that format. Lower level, detailed features may occasionally be written on the story cards, but not in a user story format (see Figure 5.14). Cottmeyer and Stevens (2009) describe features as "functional threads of

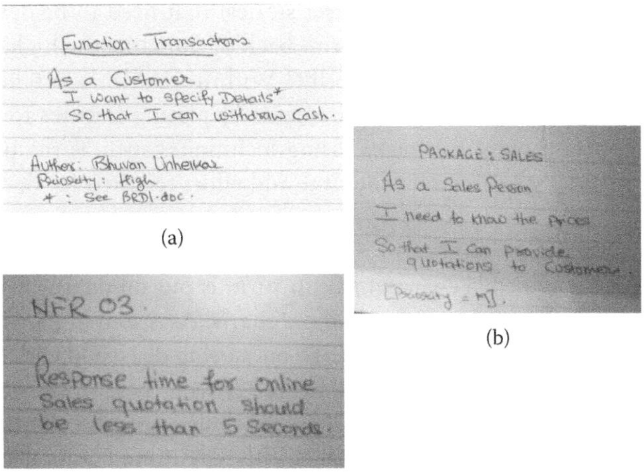

(a) (b) (c)

Figure 5.14 User story as a unit of functionality.

working software that are independent of each other and can be scheduled and prioritized independently." Features, as high-level descriptions of functionality, can be scheduled independently; however, detailed features and NFRs may have many dependencies.

SIDEBAR "User Stories"

A user story documents a conversation with the user (Ambler, 2012). Thus, stories are short high-level requirement artifacts. Mike Cohn discusses a more formal approach in his popular book *User Stories Applied*. This formal approach has the following format:

As a (role) I want (something) so that (benefit).

In CAMS, user stories can be based on detailed use cases—with the use case providing the basis for a collection of user stories. In turn, a user story can be an inspiration for a detailed use case documenting the interaction between the user and the system. Stories are documented on a small 3 in. 5 in. card and placed as part of the product backlog on the wall.

User stories depict functionality. Story cards themselves can be used to depict a unit of requirement that may not necessarily be functional. Thus, story cards can be easily used to put up NFR of the system. Similarly, provisioning of services with the system can be put up as features on a story card. These stories will then not be stories, but statements of requirements that are not from a specific user's viewpoint. Once again, while the focus on agility remains on adding value to the end user, there appear to be many requirements of a system (or overall at an organizational level) that do not seem to have an obvious user. These are specifically the NFRs discussed earlier in this chapter. There can also be interface-related requirements, quality and usability specifications, and legal requirements that may not fall within a user story format. However, for the sake of visibility in an Agile project, it is worth placing those requirements in a story card format and putting them up on the visible charts. Examples of such features that are used within the implementation process map and put up on story cards are the expected peak customer numbers—3000 on-line customers per hour; browsers for on-line customers to include IE 7.0 and latest version of Safari for mobile; and total customer records = 10 million (volume).

Product Backlog—The product backlog artifact in Agile mainly comprises of the prioritized functionalities (e.g., a list of user stories) that are scheduled for development. Product backlog also contains all other features (in addition to the user stories) that need to be developed. A product backlog is a superset of the sprint backlog; a sprint backlog contains the highest priority features that are to be developed in that particular sprint. Within CAMS, a product backlog can be expanded into a combination of detailed requirements (depicting features to be developed) and a corresponding project task plan. Estimates (using techniques such as the planning poker) are applied to the features usually to ascertain the time and effort required for development.

Charts—Agile methods stress visibility in a project. Therefore, all requirements (features) are placed visibly on a large and visible chart which, in turn, is put up on a wall. Figure 5.15 shows such use of visible charts and the stories pasted on the charts. As is seen in Fig 5.15, some stories are on the "product backlog chart." These stories are the ones being discussed with the user. Therefore, they can be considered in the "requirements" stage. In CAMS, these stories are handled by business analysts. Other stories have moved to analysis and design (handled by the system designer) and they are typically a part of the sprint backlog. The remaining charts depict stories that are coded, tested, and accepted by the user. Charts can be organized in different ways. Figure 5.15 shows an example of the progress of the stories in a project. However, charts can also be created separately for iterations, and stories on the charts can be annotated with priorities and estimates.

Deployment Process Map

Implementation (coding) of a system is usually followed by its deployment. Software packages that are not developed internally by a business may not get deployed immediately after development. For example, typical enterprise resource planning (ERP) packages developed by a specialist organization may be sold to multiple other businesses. Once these packages are sold, they need to be configured and deployed in an organization. Figure 5.16 represents the deployment process

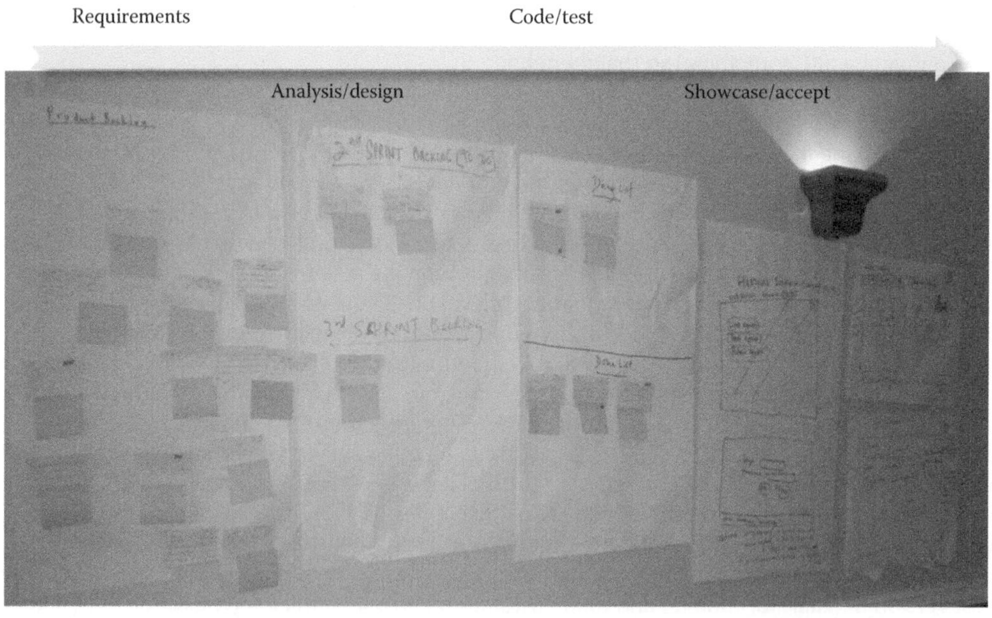

Figure 5.15 Visible charts depicting product/sprint backlogs in an implementation process map in practice.

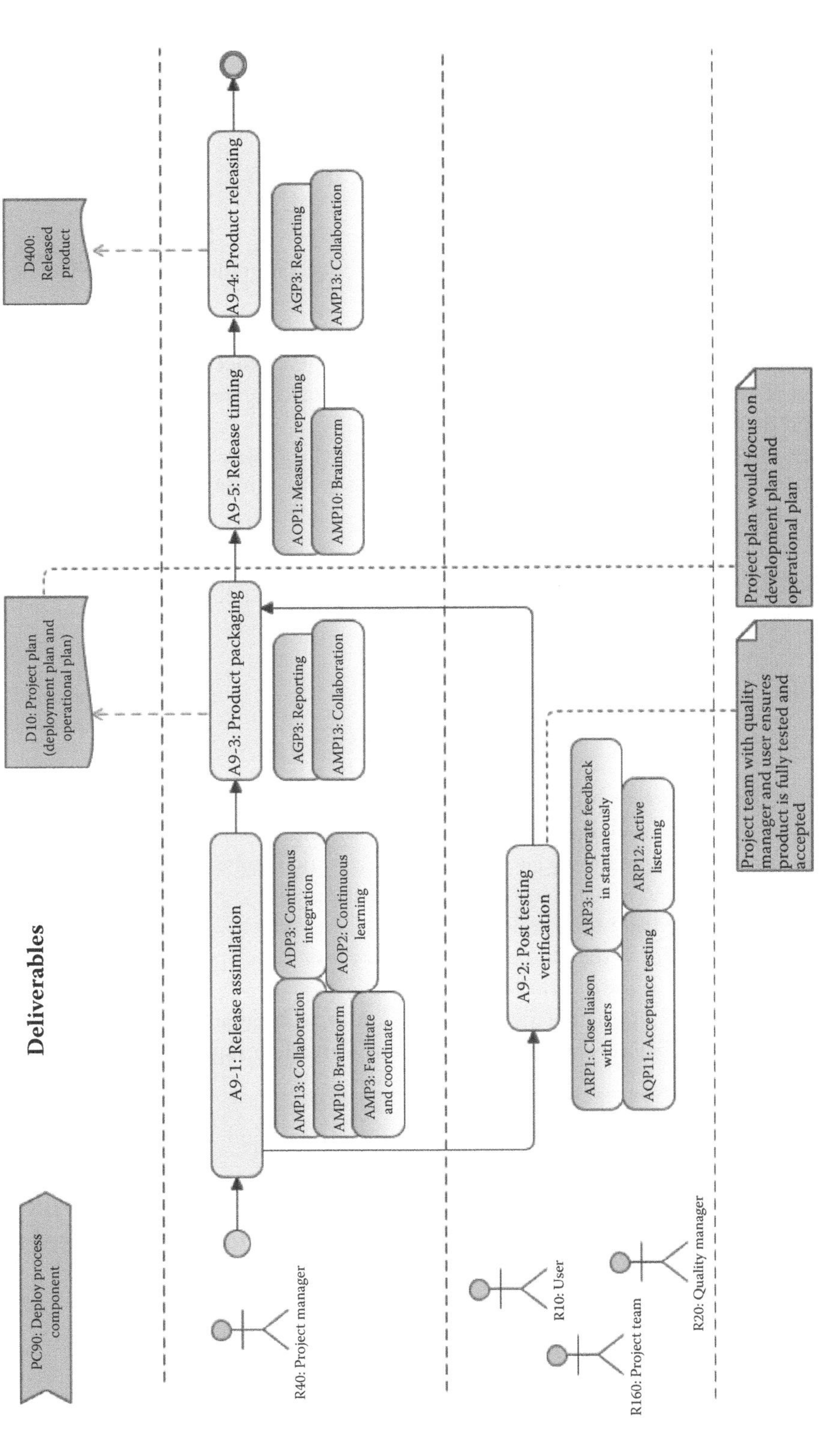

Figure 5.16 Deployment process map.

map in CAMS. This process map shows the roles, deliverables, and activities involved in deploying a system. Example Agile practices relevant to the activities and tasks are also shown in the process map and listed in the table that follows.

Roles in Deployment

The following are the roles in a deployment process map.

- Project manager: This role in involved in planning the configuration and deployment of the system.
- Project team: This team takes the technical responsibility for the deployment of the system. While there is hardly any "coding" during the deployment process map, still a substantial amount of technical knowledge is required to set the correct parameters for the configuration and then to deploy the system.
- Quality manager: The quality manager, along with the project manager, participates in organizing the deployment. This role, in particular, is responsible for the verification and validation of the system before it is deployed.
- User: The user would participate in the deployment by ensuring that the system is configured correctly. Users specify the requirements for a system or a package; therefore they are in the best position to ensure its validation and deployment.

Deliverables

The following are the deliverables in a deployment process map.

- Project plan: The project plan in deployment is a subset of the overall project plan but focused on deployment and operation of the system. The deployment plan focuses on the tasks required to send the product across to the organization and end users in the real world. The deployment aspect of a system also includes setting up and monitoring its operational parameters—as specified in the project plan.
- Released product: This is the final product that has been developed, tested, and deployed. The released product is the one that is given to the users.
- System architecture: During deployment, the SA may be referenced and cross-checked by the system designer before its deployment. Lessons learned during deployment can be used in updating the SA.

Activities and Tasks in Deployment

Table 5.6 presents the activities and tasks with the corresponding deliverables and roles for the deployment process map. Relevant Agile practices are also shown together with the planned activities and tasks.

Conclusions

This chapter discussed the application of Agile methods in architecture, design, development, and deployment. The value of this discussion, as compared with a straight discussion on Agile

Table 5.6 Deployment Process Map

Deployment activities	*Tasks*	*Deliverable*	*Roles*
A9-1: Release assimilation	Assimilate software system (its components) for deployment Assimilate hardware and operating components for deployment Agile practices: AMP13: Collaboration AMP3: Facilitate and coordinate ADP3: Continuous integration AOP2: Continuous learning AMP10: Brainstorming		R40: Project manager
A9-2: Post testing verification	Complete the acceptance test Ensure user's readiness to accept system Agile practices: AQP11: Acceptance testing ARP1: Collaboration with users ARP12: Active listening ARP3: Incorporate feedback instantaneously		R160: Project team R20: Quality manager R10: User
A9-3: Product packaging	Package the final product (e.g., get downloads ready) Package the user guide for deployment Package registration information Agile practices: AGP3: Reporting AMP13: Collaboration	D10: Project plan (deployment Plan and operational plan)	R40: Project manager
A9-4: Product releasing	Release and deploy the final physical product Enable downloads and installs Open up e-mails/Internet communications associated with deployment Agile practices: AGP3: Reporting AMP13: Collaboration	D400: Released product	R40: Project manager

continued

Table 5.6 (*Continued*)

Deployment activities	*Tasks*	*Deliverable*	*Roles*
A9-5: Release Timing	Ensure correct release dates Ensure correct release time Agile practices: AOP1: Measures, reporting AMP10: Brainstorming	D400: Released product	R40: Project manager

methods, is the opportunity to embed Agile practices within the formal process maps. Existing use of Agile methods in an organization will be augmented through the use of composite Agile process maps. CAMS, however, promises a lot more to the overall organization. Chapter 6 discusses the business management aspect of CAMS followed by Chapter 7 on business analysis, and Chapter 8 on project management.

Agile in Practice: Road Map 5

- Organize a workshop to discuss the current processes used in your organization for EA, SA, and system design, implementation, and deployment.
- List the major advantage and key challenge in each of the above process maps in the context of your organization.
- Explore how Agile practices can be used to overcome the challenges identified in the current organizational practices related to the aforementioned five process maps.
- Investigate the use of UML within your organization. If there is no usage of the UML, investigate any other modeling techniques in use. This investigation will also lead to the discovery of any associated computer-aided software engineering (CASE) tools in use for modeling.
- Conduct a walk-through of the CAMS process maps. Identify areas of the process maps that need to be modified to show where formal techniques and the use of UML can be embedded with Agile practices. Start initially with a small project and then proceed with the organization.
- Which emergent technologies discussed at the beginning of this chapter are in use in your organization? Explore the use of each of these technologies from two separate angles: their technical suitability and their impact on your business' agility.
- Investigate the existing electronic front end of your organization (your Web portal). List the current factors influencing your portal. Consider the factors discussed in this chapter and whether they can be used in improving your portal presence.

Discussion Questions

- Discuss how, in your opinion, cloud computing can assist business agility. (Extend your discussion in terms of comparing software-as-a-service (SaaS) and cloud architectures.)
- Explain how MT enable Agile business processes. (*Hint:* This explanation should include the location and time independence provided by MT. Also, security-related challenges can be included in the discussion.)

- What are the key technical process maps discussed in this chapter? Discuss them in the context of the corresponding Agile practices used within these process maps.
- Why do you think an enterprise architect needs to be both technically knowledgeable and business savvy?
- How can Agile practices be used in gathering and modeling NFR?
- Discuss, with examples, how you would use Agile practices in SA and system design.
- Why is a Web portal important in the discussion of an Agile business? What role can a Web portal play in making an organization Agile?
- Give an example of an Agile role, artifact, and ceremony. Explain how these Agile elements fit into the implementation process map of CAMS.
- List two advantages and two challenges in modeling requirements with user stories in a CAMS-based project. (*Hint:* include challenges that go beyond the development of the system and when it moves into production.)

References

Allen, P., Agile SOA governance-illusion or reality, *Cutter Executive Update*, 11 (22), 2008.

Ambler, S., *The Object Primer: Agile Model Driven Development with UML 2*, 3rd ed, Cambridge University Press, New York, 2004.

Ambler, S., Introduction to user stories, viewed 21 Aug 2012, http://www.agilemodeling.com/artifacts/userStory.htm.

Bossavit, L., Making sense of Agile design practices, *Cutter Executive Report*, 2009.

Cottmeyer, M. and D. Stevens, Rethinking the Agile enterprise, *Cutter Executive Report,* 2009.

Deshpande, Y. and B. Unhelkar, Information systems for a green organisation, *Handbook of Research in Green ICT: Technical, Business and Social Perspectives*, ed. B. Unhelkar, IGI Global, Hershey, PA, p. 116, 2010.

Dooley, B., Agile SOA, *Cutter Executive Report,* 13 (6), 2011.

Gates, B., *Business @ The Speed of Thought*, Chapter 9, Viking, Warner Books, New York, p. 141, 1999.

Hazra, T., SOA: Understanding the practice 2010—Creating business-driven services, 2010.

Highsmith, J., *Agile Project Management—Creating Innovative Products*, Addison-Wesley, Redwood City, CA, 2009.

Murugesan, S., Understanding web 2.0, *IT Professional,* 9 (4), 34–41, 2007.

Murugesan, S., *Handbook of Research on Web 2.0, 3.0, and X.0: Technologies, Business, and Social Applications*, IGI Global, Hershey, PA, 2010.

Unhelkar, B., Mobile enterprise architecture, *Cutter Executive Report,* 11 (3), 2008.

Unhelkar, B., *Mobile Enterprise Transition and Management*, Auerbach, New York, 393 p., 2009.

Unhelkar, B., *Green ICT Strategies & Applications: Using Environmental Intelligence*, Auerbach, New York, 2011.

Unhelkar, B. and Y. Deshpande, Evolving from web engineering to web services: A comparative study in the context of business utilization of the internet, *Proceedings of ADCOM 2004, 12th International Conference on Advanced Computing and Communications, 15–18 December, 2004*, Ahmedabad, India, 2004.

Chapter 6

Collaborative-Agile Business Management

What we need to do is learn to work in the system, by which I mean that everybody, every team, every platform, every division, every component is there not for individual competitive profit or recognition, but for contribution to the system as a whole on a win-win basis.

–W. Edwards Deming (1900–1993), ***American Statistician and Author (With Permission)***

Objectives

- Outline Agile business management with the required business policies, with an understanding of the business ecosystem and risks, and of leadership and the role of metrics
- Relate collaborative business and its processes with enterprise Agility
- Show the competitive advantage of collaboration (more than competition) in modern businesses environment
- Illustrate the importance of the role of business intelligence and knowledge management (KM) within collaboration in an Agile business
- Discuss the management aspect of Agility that is based on collaborative business strategies
- Address aspects of business transformation and change management with respect to an Agile business
- Discuss the way in which policies, practices, and metrics can be used as enablers of change for business Agility
- Correlate "systems thinking" to business Agility in learning organizations
- Discuss the importance of knowledge synchronization in a learning organization and its importance to business Agility
- Present a business evaluation process map using the Composite Agile Method and Strategy (CAMS) to provide formal process control together with embedded Agile practices
- Show the place for strengths–weaknesses–opportunities–threats (SWOT), PESTLE, and cost–benefit analysis in undertaking "business evaluation"

Introduction

The popularity of the word "Agile" is a reflection of the ever-increasing demand of businesses to remain Lean and responsive to changing external and internal circumstances. Agility is far more influential when applied to the overall enterprise rather than only to its software development environment. The Composite Agile Method and Strategy (CAMS) provides a framework for giving business the nimbleness it needs while ensuring the required integrity and robustness. This chapter discusses the way in which CAMS adds value to "Agile business management." CAMS brings together an organization's capacities and capabilities (people–process–technology–money) in a creative and optimum way to enable it to become Lean, collaborative, and Agile. An important enabler of such enterprise-wide Agility is collaborative information technologies (IT). Chapter 5 discussed these enabling IT and the opportunities they accord for business to collaborate rather than compete. Together with communications, the information and communications technologies (ICT) play a crucial role as an enabler of business collaborations in a ubiquitous global market. This, in turn, has resulted in a major paradigm shift in the business world. The long-held Darwinian theory of the "survival of the fittest" has itself changed to indicate that species grow because of the mutual support and help they provide to each other in a collaborative group. Business thinking is also shifting to realize that supporting, aligning, and collaborating with each other has greater potential for survival and growth—especially as electronic and mobile communications dramatically change the concept of distance. For example, mobile service providers can easily collaborate with corresponding content providers—sourcing contents from businesses that specialize in mobile contents and themselves concentrating only on providing the services and infrastructure. Similarly, technologies of cloud computing, Web Services (WS), and service-oriented architecture (SOA) create opportunities for businesses to shift their noncore processes outside of the organization (see Chapter 5, Figure 5.1). This collaborative approach creates opportunities for the business to focus on its own core strength while allowing the partnering business to do the same. These business collaborations are closely intertwined with Lean and Agile business and, together, form part of a collaborative-Agile business strategy. CAMS encourages a business to revisit its structure and dynamics to optimize its value stream. Such optimization will capitalize on the offerings of ICT to change the way in which the business is organized and operated. Accompanying this reorganization of business is the engineering of business processes through modeling, reviewing, and efficiently implementing the processes. Agility in business creates opportunities for collaborative global transactions (Unhelkar et al., 2010).

This chapter expands on the collaborative potential of ICT in the creation and management of an Agile business. As such, this chapter discusses "business evaluation" as a process map within CAMS that provides formal guidance to an organization in evaluating business-level alternatives and risks. Popular techniques of strengths–weaknesses–opportunities–threats (SWOT), Political, Economic, Social, Technological, Legal and Environmental (PESTLE), and cost–benefit analysis are alluded to only to underscore the role they can play in Agile business decision making. This chapter discusses practical ways in which businesses can apply the ICT on the basis of the Lean-Agile discussions of Chapter 5.

Agile Business Management

To remain competitive, businesses continuously strive to become *Lean* and *Agile.* This reflects a fundamental change in the business thinking of "bigger is better" (characterized by the centralized, industrial era) to that of "collaboration and sharing" (characterized by the ICT-based knowledge era) where a distributive business operating environment is becoming the norm. This change in fundamental business thinking perforates the once well-defined boundaries of a business organization.

A typical global, multinational organization is increasingly becoming a fuzzy entity with myriad physical and electronic links and Web-based transactions that regularly transgress its organizational boundaries. In addition, the business structure itself is fluid; it is made up of myriad virtual business units, outsourced and offshored processes, cloud-based data centers, service-based architectures, dynamic decision making, customer support through third-party call centers, and supply chains. These elements and processes of a business come together electronically and, then, also disperse with equal alacrity.

The ever-increasing sophistication of the Internet renders an amorphous structure to businesses. No discussion on business strategies is complete without due consideration of collaboration and Agility. Collaboration in the context of this discussion implies a business approach that shifts the emphasis from directly competing with each other to supporting each other. This support is based on the rapid and large volume of exchange of data, information, and knowledge. The endgame of this shift is to provide enhanced customer experience and, thereby, business growth.

An implication of these aforementioned changes to business is the flattening of the business structure (Unhelkar, 2010). "Agility" and "collaboration" are two keywords that complement each other to enable businesses to flourish and grow by capitalizing on the ICT enablers.

Composite Agile Method and Strategy (CAMS)

Business Agility and CAMS

SIDEBAR

Agile business management is the capitalization of information and communications technologies (ICT) to support organizational decision making and knowledge management (KM), which regularly transcends geographical boundaries and extends supply chains. The end result is an optimized value stream of the entire business ecosystem, which, in turn, empowers the customer in a self-sustaining cycle. This cycle of ICT enablers and customer empowerment begetting each other places a premium on both. Business Agility strives for the appropriate customer response. ICT strives for organizational Leanness. Agile principles ensure full visibility of the work across the entire value stream. The CAMS supports business Agility by describing formal working policies and procedures that encourage team-based Agile protocols. These Agile protocols, which are based on Agile principles, can include, say, time-boxed activities, continuous improvement, and visibility. CAMS extends Agile in terms of provisioning of work, reviewing the state of work, ascertaining feedback from key stakeholders through demonstration, and ensuring high the high quality quality of the final deliverable.

Business Agility is less of an activity or a method and more of a comprehensive and holistic business strategy. An Agile business has an agile culture and value system around it. CAMS plays an important role in the creation of such business Agility. It encompasses all methods and frameworks within the organization. This includes business methods, governance frameworks, and project management approaches.

Understanding the Agile touch points within these methods helps the organization reduce "method friction" (described in Chapter 4). Incrementally, changes are made to the areas of these methods where the formality of control vies with the flexibility of Agility. For example, a formal contract (deliverable) mandated by the governance framework is produced through negotiations, but the Agile value of customer collaboration and face-to-face communication is also carried out. Similarly, other elements of a method or framework, such as its roles, tasks, techniques, and practices are examined and adjusted to overcome the method friction points.

People issues are considered paramount in the way in which business Agility is brought about through this transition. Not only are individual workers affected when an organization shifts to overall Agility but so also are the senior managers and decision makers whose style of working is affected by the changes to the business methods and processes. Above all, CAMS addresses the culture of an organization.

The rate of transition of a business to Agility also needs to be continuously adjusted to ensure a high comfort level for people. Dynamicity in terms of skills, attitude, and knowledge of individuals has to be factored in as the organization adopts a composite Agile approach. Formal policies and key performance indicators (KPIs) need to be tied in with risks and leadership to achieve a balanced business Agility.

Figure 6.1 summarizes the areas of consideration for a business as it embarks on its transformation to Agile. Agile business management is the use of these business functions in an attempt to bring about fundamental changes to the business. These changes are as described in the following.

- Business policies: This is the formation of new business policies and updating existing ones to incorporate Agile values within them. These business policies elevate the focus of Agility from project-based to organizational, strategic Agile.
- Business ecosystem: This considers the change brought about not only in the business that is shifting to Agility but also to the many partnering organizations and their relationships.

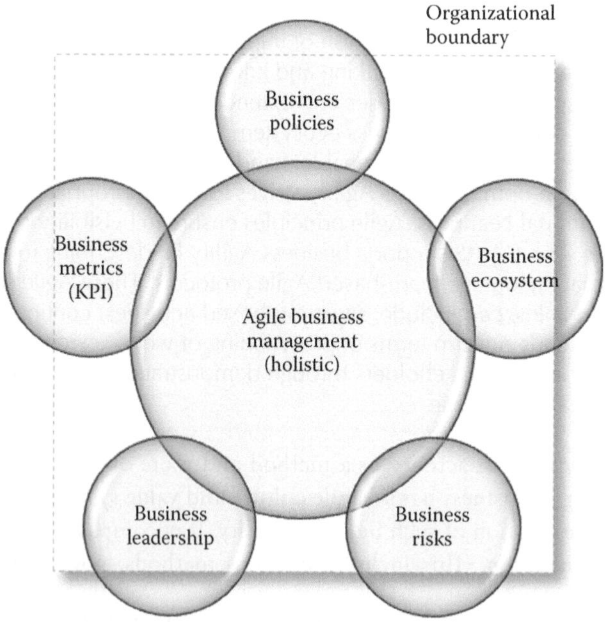

Figure 6.1 Business Agility with CAMS.

Techniques such as PESTLE analysis are helpful in ascertaining the impact of collaborations and Agility on the business ecosystem and vice versa.

- Business risks: These are the risks associated with changes in the internal management structure as Agility is embraced, as also the changes to external relationships. These risks start emerging as soon as an organization makes attempts to inculcate Agile values and behaviors (discussed earlier in Chapter 2, Table 2.2) in its interactions—as compared with the original contract-based interactions and relationships.
- Business leadership: This is affected and, in turn, affects the Agile changes. Visionary Agile leadership changes the way in which an organization is structured, its culture, and the way in which it operates. Agile, as a value system relies, more on leadership and less on management. This, in turn, requires changes to the way in which management functions in an organization. Relinquishing control, facilitating sharing of tasks, and accepting informality in reporting are important changes brought about by leadership rather than management.
- Business metrics: These comprise the measures and indicators in terms of what constitutes success in terms of an Agile business. The KPIs change their focus—as a business transforms to Agile—from being purely objective measures to include a certain amount of subjectivity in them. For example, an Agile business will not index employee reward structures to merely an objective measure of customer satisfaction; instead, the business metrics for customer satisfaction will include subjective discussions and insights gained from interacting directly with the customer.

Initially, CAMS gives due credence to the existing organizational processes, standards, and frameworks at the business level. Examples of these processes at the business level include Lean, Six Sigma, Total Quality Management (TQM), and Kaizen. Kanban is also gaining increasing popularity at both business and technical levels. Figure 6.2 shows these processes associated with business management together with the IT governance and project management processes. Avoiding the "method friction" among these three crucial levels of processes is important for a Lean-Agile business.

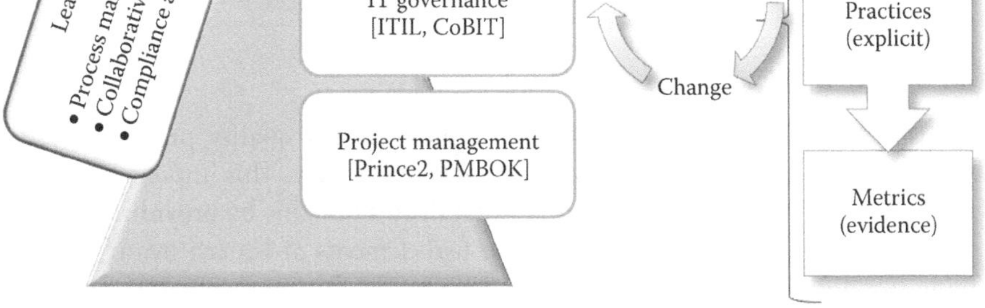

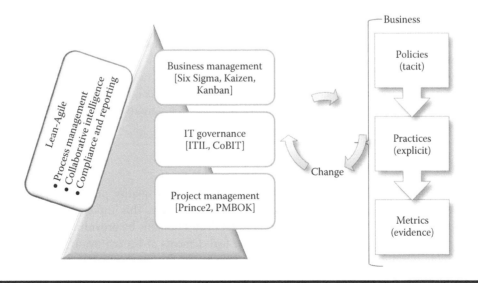

Figure 6.2 Organizational impact of CAMS—changes to policies, practices, and metrics.

A Lean-Agile business is best served through relevant process management, use of collaborative intelligence (CI), and also formality in compliance and reporting requirements. Figure 6.2 also shows that the policies, practices, and metrics can provide crucial help in transitioning a business to Agile:

- Policies (tacit): These are the business policies that start nudging the organization toward Agile. While they are presented, published, and promoted throughout the organization in a formal way, these Agile business policies also promulgate through the organization in a tacit manner. People involved at all levels within the organization need to be aware of the reasoning behind the changes to the methods and processes, and the way in which Agility is adding value to the organizational performance.
- Practices (explicit): These involve the explicit use of Agility; while they are derived from the policies relating to Agility, practices of Agility require training, coaching, and mentoring. Awareness of Agility across the organization makes it easier for people to practice the changes resulting from Agility.
- Metrics (evidence): These are the measures (KPI) referred to in Figure 6.1. Metrics are more important in a composite Agile approach than in a pure Agile one, as they provide crucial evidence of the success of an initiative; metrics can also be used to ascertain the value derived by customers from Agility (discussed in greater detail in Chapter 9).

SIDEBAR

Enterprise Agility has been defined as "a time measure between two significant changes in the environment and time it takes for an organization to respond to that change" (Unhelkar and Ginige, 2010). An Agile enterprise is capable of responding quickly and effectively to a change in the environment. These changes can be imposed on the enterprise externally (e.g., demands of customers and partnering organizations), as well as internally (e.g., through changes to human resource (HR) structures and processes).

Six Sigma in Composite Agile

This leads to the application of knowledge management (KM), discussed later in this chapter.

Six Sigma, as a business management strategy, is focused on improving performance and quality of processes. Six Sigma can use tools and techniques (e.g., knowledge management systems, KMSs) to optimize processes and reduce defects. In the context of Agility, five stages of Six Sigma—Define, Measure, Analyze, Improve, and Control—are used. These are summarized in Table 6.1.

Kaizen in Composite Agile

Kaizen is a business strategy based on continuous improvement of quality, productivity, cost, staff satisfaction, security, company culture, leadership, and technology. This improvement is achieved by involving every person within the organization and, additionally, by providing them with the required training, materials, and supervision. The five elements of Kaizen (team work, personal discipline, improved morale, quality circles, and suggestions for improvement) are quite close to Agile values and principles. For example, team work in Kaizen is the same as task sharing in Agile. Personal discipline and improvement in morale are subjective topics that are also similar to the

Table 6.1 Six Sigma in Composite Agile

Activities	*Description*
Define	This stage deals with defining and understanding a problem. It enables determination of the scope of an iteration in CAMS based on business priorities. This formal definition of a problem in Six Sigma is most helpful to business when it is carried out together with the Agile principles of collaboration and face-to-face conversation
Measure	This is the activity of measuring the output of a process or the process itself through a suite of predefined metrics. This phase of Six Sigma becomes more relevant in composite Agile as there is a need to formalize measures within the composite approach (as discussed in Figure 6.1). While pure Agile approaches measure project progress and quality through working software and user feedback, composite Agile raises the measures across the organization, especially in indicating the performance of the business
Analyze	This is the phase that helps in developing better understanding of a business problem; analysis also enables relating the effects to the root causes of the problem. This phase of Six Sigma can make use of the "working prototype" of Agile to ensure a detailed analysis of the business problem and an instantaneous feedback from the key stakeholders
Improve	This stage deals with optimizing the solution and considering alternative solutions. This phase of Six Sigma can benefit highly from some Agile practices, such as refactoring and continuous improvement. Refactoring can be valuable when restructuring, and improvement of a system takes place without necessarily modifying the external behavior of the system. Continuous improvement, on the other hand, involves ongoing changes to the system from the user's perspective
Control	This stage deals with the activity of monitoring a project and evaluating the results at the end. This phase of Six Sigma benefits from the Agile practices of evaluating the results of the project at the end of each release. The equivalent of a working software of Agile is the "working prototype" of a business process or initiative. Control deals with ongoing monitoring, measuring, and optimizing of a business process. Customer feedback is also incorporated at the end of each integrated release of the product

focus on individual initiatives and their alignment with the team in Agile. Furthermore, Kaizen expands on its founding elements in terms of some principles that are also closely associated with Agile. Table 6.2 shows the relevance of Kaizen in terms of composite Agile at organizational level.

Kanban in Composite Agile

Kanban is based on delivering business value incrementally. Therefore, Kanban can easily provide value in a CAMS approach across an organization. As discussed by Shalloway (2011) in *Demystifying Kanban*, not only does Kanban aid software development but it also plays a role in the business as a whole. For example, the Agile principle of cross-functional teams gets easily employed by Kanban at the business level wherein the business is treated as a single cross-functional team containing

Table 6.2 Kaizen in Composite Agile

Activities	*Description*
Manage operations and processes instead of people	The manner in which people do things is even more important than what they do. This principle is very similar to the Agile concept of trusting and empowering team members. The formality in terms of process management and measurement provides CAMS with the necessary control even while Agile concepts are played out
Utilize techniques to accomplish ongoing improvement	Agile, through its practices, emphasizes ongoing improvement of developers and users through training, coaching, and mentoring. The use of techniques draws attention to up-skilling an organization (and its teams) through training and education, pilot programs, publishing of practices, etc.
Customer satisfaction is the key basis for measuring the performance of an initiative	While Agile methods emphasize customer involvement in developing a product, in a composite approach, customer satisfaction is considered integral even in ongoing operations, maintenance, and strategies for upgrades of systems and processes. Besides, CAMS would require the customer to jointly define the success criteria before the project commences along with the developers of the systems or processes, and then to measure the output along those predetermined measures
Think of suppliers and customers as partners	This principle is exactly what Agile advocates, albeit at the development level. At the business level, however, suppliers and customers can be closely aligned with businesses through the emerging ICT such as Web Services and mobile technologies (discussed in detail in Chapter 5). Partnering is not only in terms of sharing of information but also in collaborating to offer new products and services across multiple geographical regions
Stop to solve problems as they occur	This is an important principle that leads to early achievement of the required quality. Agile is, of course, focused on continuous testing and test-driven coding. This principle in CAMS implies stopping any activity that is going on in order to fix the errors discovered. Agile methods handle problems in a just-in-time (JIT) manner (Cottmeyer and Henson, 2008). CAMS approaches the fixing of errors as a combination of formal "stop and inspect" and informal "test and fix as we go along"
Utilize visual control to avoid hidden problems	This principle has the opportunity for further expansion in the Agile arena, especially when it comes to capturing and modeling requirements. While Agile aims to evolve the requirements, utilization of visual models and controls can help in identifying errors of misunderstanding as well as in managing expectations. UML- and BPMN-based visual models enable the maintenance of consistency between design, architecture, and implementation
Utilize reliable and tested technology	This practice can be used in development environments, databases, mobile technologies, and service-oriented architecture (SOA). While an Agile approach may take risks in exploring an untried technology for implementation, CAMS would restrict that experimentation by focusing attention on the value stream

UML, Unified Modeling Language; BPMN, Business Process Modeling Notation.

members from the various business functions. Kanban can also help with prioritization of work, enabling its completion without interruption, and provisioning of timely feedback.

An important value that Kanban can add to a composite Agile project is the exposition of the team and its work to management. Instead of isolating and protecting teams, Kanban makes the team visible. This demonstrates the impact of overloading teams at both the individual and process-stream levels.

Agility in Learning Organizations

An Agile organization has to be a learning organization (Senge, 1990) because only through continuous learning and improvement can the organization manage to remain Lean and Agile. Learning is not an activity to be carried out at the end of a transition or change. Such learning and management of that learning (knowledge) is an ongoing activity that has to find place even in the routine, business-as-usual operation of the organization.

The concept of a "learning organization," as presented by Senge (1990), has direct applicability to an organization transitioning to a collaborative-Agile business. Technologies and processes of the organization are transitioned in such a way as to provide ongoing, real-time feedback to the agents of change in the organization. Such change not only enables embedding of Agility in the organizational processes but also keeps them current and responsive to changing circumstances. Figure 6.3 shows the relationship between the five disciplines of Senge and the corresponding Agile keywords. The five disciplines can help a collaborative-Agile business become a learning organization (or undergo a learning transformation).

The importance of these disciplines in the context of business Agility is discussed in the following.

- *Systems thinking* is made up of a long-term, systems view of the organization (or project). An important part of this view is that it accepts delays in action. An Agile value discussed in Chapter 2 is slowness of decision making. This slowness is to enable the all-important feedback loops. Systems thinking also encourages long-term industrial research, contemplation, and feedback.
- *Personal mastery* is the discipline of continually clarifying and deepening our personal vision, of focusing our energies, of developing patience, and of seeing reality clearly and

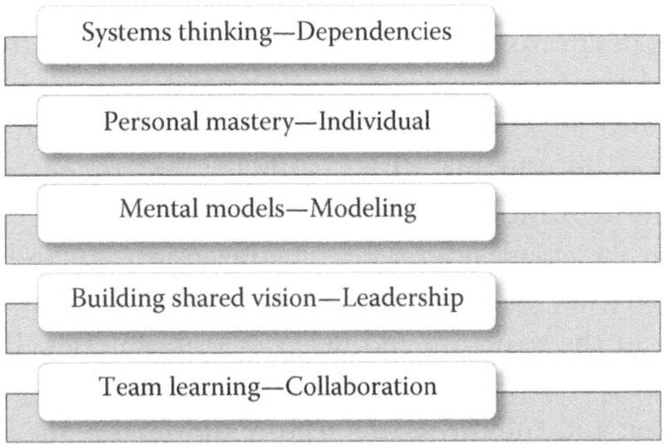

Figure 6.3 Embedding Agility in learning organizations and projects.

objectively. Personal mastery closely relates to the subjective emphasis on individuals in the Agile paradigm.

- *Mental models* are "deeply ingrained assumptions, generalizations, or even pictures and images that influence how we understand the world and how we take action." Agility disturbs the sociocultural models of a business organization. But business Agility can also capitalize on model building.
- *Building shared vision* is achieved by sharing the future state of the organization, as envisioned by the leadership. This sharing has to occur with every member of the organization, and is quite complementary to Agile organization values.
- *Team learning* is the process of aligning and developing the capacities of a team for a common goal. An important ingredient of such team alignment is the process of conversation or dialogue. The Agile paradigm is heavily focused on task sharing, collaboration, and ongoing learning. Such learning is supported by communication technologies and KM.

Collaboration and Agility

Collaborative Business Processes and Agility

A sustainable organization can be understood as a perpetually existent organization. A Lean-Agile business that is collaborating with other businesses in its ecosystem has a tremendous opportunity to sustain itself over a very long period of time.

SIDEBAR

The process flows across the entire organization provide an understanding of the work that gives an overall value to one or more end users. Thus, a value stream becomes more important in a composite Agile approach than in handling singular processes. Furthermore, such a business-driven approach focuses on the right balance (loading) of work across the entire value stream. Balance in work cannot be achieved by focusing on singular processes.

Such a collaborative business ecosystem is an ongoing, dynamic suite of businesses that do not come together as a static, one-off event. Dynamicity in collaborations is a constantly flowing and ebbing tide of Agile organizations that come together to provide a product or service to a customer, and, once that purpose or goal is achieved, they recede within their so-called original boundaries. As identified by Ginige (2006), collaborating and building strong business relationships is becoming an effective way of surviving and growing in the market.

Cloud computing and the formation of service-oriented business clusters further enables a business to strategically shed all its extra weight. This occurs as cloud-based architecture frees up organizational resources by sourcing all its needs for underlying technologies and systems in the form of utilities through the cloud. All noncore activities and competencies of an organization can be shifted to the cloud, leaving the organization *Lean* and *Agile*. This focus of the business on its core competency and shifting the rest of the business activities into the cloud bring significant changes to the structure and behavior of businesses. Process maps that enable development and deployment of Web Services (from a collaborative perspective), cloud computing (from an Agile perspective), and enterprise architecture (to provide stability to the organization) provide the formality required in terms of change management in a collaborative-Agile business.

Due consideration to the aforementioned technologies enables overcoming of risks and challenges in the formation of a collaborative-Agile business.

Collaborative Cluster Formation

Collaborative business, as discussed by Ghanbary (2007) and Ghanbary and Unhelkar (2007), revolves around the collaborative portal for businesses that links individuals and systems, enables information sharing, improves real-time interactive communication, and facilitates seamless collaboration. Electronic or E-collaborations, powered by Web-enabled applications, are not merely popular within and between organizations but are a cause for and a rapid facilitator of the grouping of organizations (Unhelkar, 2003). Agile businesses need to tap into this capability to form groups, link organizations together, and create "virtual" teams that lead to the formation of business clusters at a global level. Such groupings readily change market dynamics and the end result is a global village, also called an *Advait* enterprise (Unhelkar, 2003) that is built on the communications capabilities of the Internet. These communications capabilities are used in forming clusters (and cluster of clusters) to serve the customer. The demand in terms of the type, volume, and location of the product and/or service can change rapidly and a collaborative business is capable of handling that demand through partnering and collaborative alliances.

Thus, the higher an organization's ability to collaborate, the greater are its chances to remain Lean and Agile. Clusters of collaborative businesses can be formed in many different ways. Formation of clusters further leads to the formation of clusters of clusters (multiple clusters). Clusters of businesses can also be formed around a common horizontal theme or a vertical market. It would then be wise to extrapolate this trend and expect the clusters to collaborate with each other. For example, a cluster formed around travel, which includes numerous airlines (e.g., the OneWorld cluster for airlines), would start interacting heavily with a cluster formed around hotels, which would then perhaps interact with a car rental cluster. As the cluster-to-cluster interactions continue to be on the rise, the result can be one single business thread running through all clusters, as they are all connected with each other in some way or the other.

The horizontal and vertical markets (or axes) along which collaborative clusters are formed can be summarized as follows (Unhelkar, 2003):

- Horizontal clusters: When businesses that do not have direct dependencies on each other come together to provide products and services to each other, and to each other's clients, one can say they are horizontally clustered. These may be businesses belonging to the same industry (such as multiple airlines) or businesses that are complete in their own right, yet collaborating with each other (such as a cluster made up of hotels, airlines, and car rental companies). This is to state that an airline does not directly depend on a hotel for its business input, and neither does a car rental company on an airline. Such horizontal clusters facilitate "sideways" business transactions that open up opportunities to serve a customer that would otherwise be lost because of limited offerings. Horizontal clusters are more customer-centric than organizational-centric as they focus on the effectiveness of customer services. Therefore, an organization that is part of a horizontal cluster will appear more agile to its customers than internally, say, to its employees.
- Vertical clusters: These clusters of businesses are the ones wherein the output of one business is an input into another business. There is a certain amount of dependency in this chain of businesses clustered vertically as against the horizontal clusters that do not have direct dependencies. An example of a vertical chain would be a grocery store that provides input

into a restaurant, which in turn is embedded into a hotel. Vertical clusters are valuable to both the businesses and the customers. The businesses benefit by being able to tap into a "mega" supply chain that can stretch into numerous primary and secondary producers that continue to "value add." This results in the organization providing direct value to the end user or end customer. The end user is benefited by being able to realize cost advantages and getting value for a much reduced cycle time, especially where a service-based business is concerned. Vertical clusters enable organizational efficiency internally, thereby rendering the organization structurally Lean.

Business Size and Collaboration

Agility plays a varying role in facilitating collaborative business processes depending on the size of the organization. For example, the way a large business reorganizes itself to become Agile can itself be a complex transformation exercise as compared with a small business. The internal organizational and human resource (HR) structure of a large business is significantly disturbed as a result of Agility and collaboration. For a small business, there may not be any perceptible difference in the internal structure but a significant change in its business model can be perceived by the customers.

Thus, collaborative relationships include collaborating organizations of different sizes, having different company cultures, and complementary (noncompeting) core competencies (Morris, 2002).

SIDEBAR

Collaboration and enterprise agility is not a "one-size-fits-all" approach; rather, organizations must take into account their customers and the ability of internal structures and environment to respond. The considerable barriers such as costs of establishing data-sharing systems, and the compatibility of the many collaborative partners are significant factors impacting the ability of a business to be Agile and collaborative.

Table 6.3 lists the way in which the organizational setup and infrastructure are affected by an Agile business transformation based on business size.

Characteristics of Collaborative-Agile Business

Characteristics of collaboration and Agility support and promote each other iteratively in a business. Collaboration makes it easier for businesses to shift their noncore processes to their collaborating partners. In turn, this shifting of processes makes the organization Lean and Agile. Agility further facilitates the identification and shifting of noncore processes beyond the organizational boundary. This reorganization of businesses capitalizes on the Internet-based communications technologies and SOAs. These aforementioned technologies create a level playing field for businesses.

In addition to the size invariance, physical distance has also lost its impact on some business operations. This loss of impact is not just limited to shifting of "routine" work outside the organization. Many organizational processes are themselves changing owing to electronic and mobile business collaborations. For example, the cost advantage of an offshored project has started fading as a key advantage; instead, the opportunity to tap into a global pool of knowledge*, sharing

* See freelance.com for expanding "knowledge" outsourcing.

Table 6.3 Effect of Collaborations and Agility on the Organizational, Technical, and Third-Party Infrastructures of Large, Medium, and Small Businesses

Business Size and Organizational Setup	*Large*	*Medium*	*Small*
Internal organizational setup	Flattened organizational hierarchy; reengineered processes Promote, train, coach and mentor staff in Agile values across the organization; leadership crucial across all tiers of the organization	Needs to realign its processes with business partners. Management needs to move to leadership Collaborative-Agile opportunities due to medium size	Usually owner managed; already Agile in many ways as decision making is rapid, documentation is minimum, and risks are known to the individuals Subjective organizational setup, which remains so in Agile
Internal technical setup	Shift technical infrastructure to cloud; may create shared services (internal cloud) Part of strategic technological changes in an Agile business transformation	Able to tap into publicly available cloud and other technical infrastructure Easy data and information sharing due to medium size; needs to process-reengineer for Agility	Users of third-party technical services; do not aim to own technologies except very basic access technologies; strategy is to pay per usage Leadership/ management are exposed to value of collaboration
Facilitating infrastructure (third party)	Ability to make use of third-party infrastructure through cloud-based architecture; can become facilitators themselves; can drive collaborative Agile across their business ecosystem due to large-size advantage	Usually consortium-based facilitation; medium size enables easy sharing of infrastructure	Seeks help to form collaborations; unable to initiate or facilitate clusters of collaborations—can only participate in existing collaborations

of innovation and creativity, and availability of services round the clock are emerging as major advantages of outsourced/offshored projects.

Therefore, collaborative-Agile businesses will not be based on their size and location but on the way in which they serve their customers through astute KM, rapidity of responses, and global reach. Internally too, collaborative-Agile businesses will exhibit a Lean structure and rapidity of response.

Specific characteristics of collaborative-Agile businesses include enhanced customer experience, KM, enterprise risk management (ERM), market expansion, global trade, organizational Leanness, outsourcing and offshoring, legal and tax management, and carbon consciousness. These characteristics are discussed in greater detail next.

Customer Experience through Collaboration

Collaborative-Agile businesses are overwhelmingly customer-centric. Collaborative technologies are used not only to conduct a sale across borders but also to provide timely service to the same customer across boundaries. In many global post-sale scenarios, customer care is uneven. Global markets increase the risk of customer dissatisfaction. Electronic collaborations can be used to ameliorate these risks and help satisfy customer needs. Collaborative-Agile businesses provide a single unified face to the customer and also satisfy personalized and even peculiar needs of customers by the local know-how, expertise, and physical presence of alliance partners. This not only results in wider customer base but also in higher volume growth from the same customers.

Knowledge Management Collaborations and Agility

Collaborative-Agile organizations implement processes to manage and share their knowledge (within the organization and with partners). This KM is further extended to the dynamic synchronization of tacit and explicit knowledge within an organization (Unhelkar, 2010) and collaborative knowledge synchronization beyond its organizational boundary. The following are the advantages of KM in collaborative-Agile organizations:

- Supporting decision making: Assisting decision makers through correlations and insights that would otherwise not be possible for an individual. KM enables recording of decisions by leaders and makes it available to all tiers of the organization. This results in speeding up of decision-making capabilities down the hierarchy.
- Recording objective knowledge: Codifying and storing individual experiences enables their use in future; this recording abates the potential loss of that knowledge once the individuals leave the organization through change of jobs, retirement, or replacement.
- Creating awareness of knowledge: An Agile organization aims to equip every individual to take quick and accurate decisions that will benefit the customer and the organization. Employees and other users of the organization's systems need to be made aware of a body of knowledge created from certain previously solved problems and situations. Repeated creation and storage of knowledge can be avoided through this awareness, which adds to the collaborative and Agile capacities of the organization.
- Avoiding knowledge repetition: Building on the previous factor, staff and customers may seek the same body of knowledge informally (by talking with each other) and formally (by accessing and searching systems and databases). Agility encourages informal and tacit exchange of knowledge, whereas KMS—through its objective repository of knowledge—prevents repetition of knowledge discovery exercises and efforts.
- Encouraging innovativeness: Agility promotes continuous innovativeness as much as it makes use of such innovative ways of working. Innovative approaches to business processes and technical solutions are aided by making available the knowledge to build upon. Creativity and innovation of products and services in an organization need not start from scratch, and astute KM is a means of providing that launching pad for creativity. This, in turn, enables

the organization to remain agile and responsive to the changes in circumstances, including external demands from customers and internal needs of staff.

- Corporate knowledge sharing: Collaborating organizations bring their core knowledge and know-how together. For example, a bank collaborating with an IT service provider need not worry about the IT trends. Issues associated with IT trends will be handled by the collaborating IT partner. This will free up the bank resources, which the bank can then use to focus on its own core banking expertise. Thus, knowledge sharing through collaboration enhances organizational Agility.
- Individual knowledge sharing: Collaborations between people belonging to the partnering organizations, reinforced by KMSs, also result in tacit knowledge sharing by individuals. Collaborations enhance the overall pool of expertise in the organization without "reinventing the wheel." Agile values of trust, honesty, and collaboration are translated here at the tacit level, and knowledge sharing is facilitated. This, in turn, leads to benefits such as faster innovation of products, reduced duplication of efforts, savings in research and development costs, and enhanced employee satisfaction.

SIDEBAR

Knowledge management (KM) is all about encoding data and information in a form that transcends time and place. It has been a major human endeavor for eons. Engravings on rocks, statues and paintings, time capsules, storytelling, and, today, data warehouses and content management are all attempts to codify and preserve knowledge for future use. This future use can be in the next minute, hour, or century; the gap between creation, codification, and use of knowledge can vary substantially. For example, the knowledge gap for a currency options trader in the financial market may be a few seconds, but for an environmental scientist, it may be a few years. Other practical examples of collaborative knowledge sharing include those used in medical systems (wherein the expertise or breakthroughs from one group of medical professionals can be immediately used by others) or in fighting crime or preventing terrorist activities (through rapid sharing of information and knowledge in real time).

Collaborative-Agile organizations put together processes and systems for KM, especially knowledge sharing. Business Agility cannot be achieved without knowledge sharing.

Evolution in Knowledge Management

Agile business management makes use of knowledge technologies and processes to achieve the necessary Leanness. Figure 6.4 shows the five steps in the evolution, expression, and use of knowledge in organizations. These are observations, data, information, knowledge itself, and intelligence. Of these, observation and intelligence remain subjective (tacit), whereas data, information, and codified knowledge are objective (explicit). Each of these layers within and around an organization plays a part in business Agility. These five layers, including knowledge, and their relevance to business Agility are discussed below.

1. Observations: Observations are attempts at recognizing facts as seen by an observer. By their very nature, observations are subjective because they are usually influenced by the perceptions of the observer. Agile organizations encourage subjective observations but then encourage the observer to document and share those observations. Noting and recording of a business transaction, a customer interaction, or issues associated with a piece of equipment are all attempts to record observations. Observations of the same fact can be different depending on the context—the time, place, situation, and number of people involved in making

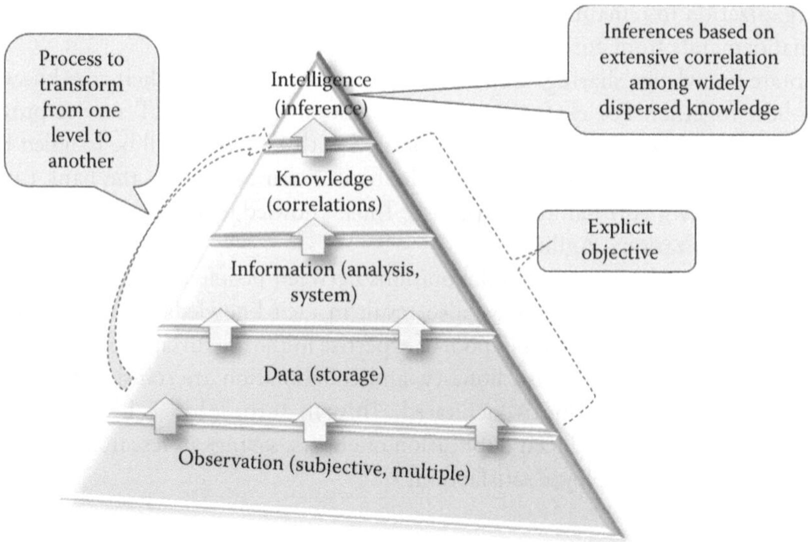

Figure 6.4 Knowledge management and Agility.

those observations. For instance, a customer complaint (fact) takes on a different meaning depending on the time factor involved (e.g., if it is urgent, as in the case of a complaint about a leaking toilet in a hotel room), the place (airport security vs airport rest rooms), and the number of people (a group petition vs a single, disgruntled customer). Observations are laced by the belief and value system of the observer. Therefore, there need to be multiple observations of the same reality over time, place, and people in order to ascertain its accuracy.

2. Data: Once an observation becomes regular and is trustworthy, it is converted to data. Data can be understood as a suite of observations consolidated and organized in an objective manner. Data can vary vastly, from the neatly organized rows and columns of a relational database through to the complex, multimedia data warehouses containing audio, video, photos, and charts. Data are objective, storable, and shareable and may be subject to varied analysis. Agile organizations value data because of the varied analytics that can be performed on it. There are two major categories of data, quantitative and qualitative. Each kind of data has a role to play in organizational Agility. For example, a passenger buying a ticket on an airline portal is generating both quantitative (e.g., ticket number, payment, receipt) as well as qualitative (e.g., satisfaction level, complaints) data. Agile business processes would facilitate recording of this data and making that recording available at various access points within the organization. Conversion between quantitative (recorded numbers and text) and qualitative (audio, call center conversation) data is a technical exercise but this exercise provides that important data synchronization, which can later be used in knowledge synchronization. Codification and storing of qualitative data can be different from that of quantitative data, and the ease and accuracy of conversion also has a bearing on business Agility.
3. Information: Analysis of data, in a systematic way, creates information. Data, on their own, are not always actionable, whereas information, based on the data, provides an opportunity for the stakeholders to act. Information provides meaning to the data. The process of converting data into information involves classification of the data, selective recall of the

data, application of algorithms to the data, and summarization of the results. For most practical purposes, information is also objective. This objective information can be stored and shared for effective decision making in an Agile organization.

4. Knowledge: Knowledge can be understood as rationalization and correlation of information through reflection, learning, and logical reasoning. When software systems attempt to mimic these primarily human characteristics, they are said to be using artificial intelligence. Information lies in silos, mainly dictated by the original classification of the data upon which it is based. Converting this information to knowledge is based on an objective view of knowledge. Such knowledge can be a well-documented process or the output of a multilayered analysis. In either case, this knowledge is more insightful for business Agility than information. Knowledge can also be understood as correlations between otherwise separate islands of information within and outside an organization. Both subjective and objective aspects of knowledge are based on correlations, either in the minds of the people involved in creating, managing, and using knowledge or the systems that reflect these same characteristics. The subjective aspects of KM, however, find immense support through the Agile values provided they are promoted across the organization.
5. Intelligence: Intelligence is made up of inferences based on extensive correlations among widely dispersed information and knowledge. Thus, while data, information, and (to a large extent) knowledge can be considered as objective, intelligence is almost exclusively a human trait and is therefore highly subjective. As such, business agility is boosted significantly through awareness and use of intelligence by decision makers. Intelligence as a specific human trait is based on numerous factors—obvious and hidden—such as personal experience, value system, time and location of decision making, sociocultural environment, and ability to make estimates and take risks. Unlike observations, however, intelligence provides the basis for action. Intelligence can make clever use of systems support but, in itself, is not entirely dependent on the systems. Intelligence, in turn, supports business agility as it assists an individual in distinguishing decisions based on their importance, relevance, context, and organizational principles. Intelligence cannot be organized and placed in databases and readily transferred through basic training. A combination of training, experience, and sharing of knowledge is required for the successful transfer of intelligence.

Knowledge Synchronization for Agility

Knowledge can be tacit or explicit. Business Agility is enhanced significantly if strategies are put in place to ensure synchronization between tacit and explicit knowledge.

Figure 6.5 shows knowledge synchronization between users and systems. The subjective aspect of knowledge is created and updated through observation, reflection, sharing, and imparting of that knowledge by individuals. Improving this subjective knowledge creation helps the "tacit" promotion of business Agility. This tacit knowledge life cycle is shown in the center of Figure 6.5. Examples of systems that support the explicit knowledge include HR, customer relationship management (CRM), supply-chain management (SCM), and carbon emission management system (CEMS).

The KM systems interaction is made up of artificial intelligence, semantic network, service orientation, content management, and search engines. These are shown in Figure 6.5 on the outside and form part of the explicit knowledge technology support cycle. These tacit and explicit traits are synchronized to achieve business Agility. Knowledge synchronization starts with the identification of the gap between what exists in an organization and the various knowledge types.

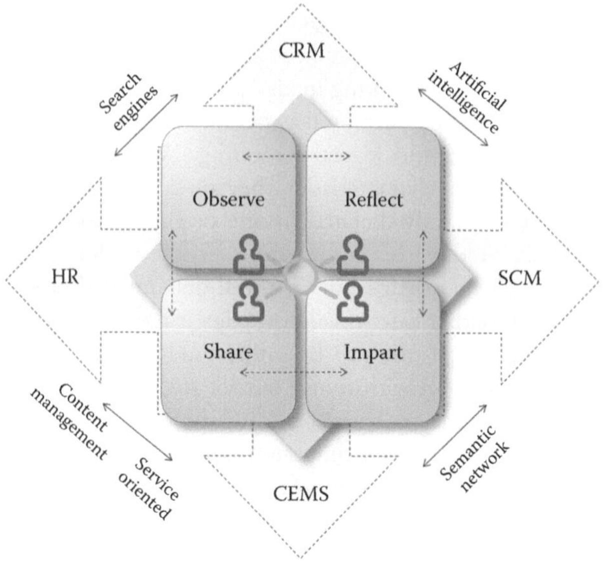

Figure 6.5 Dynamic knowledge synchronization provides agility between users and systems.

A list of the elements that make up this gap is then created. Synchronizing this gap is an important aspect of composite Agile, which aims to achieve zero latency in knowledge updates through systems and processes. Mobile messaging, event-driven mobile processes, and a combination of a publish–subscribe strategy for mobile content further facilitates business Agility through knowledge synchronization (Unhelkar, 2010).

The following are some of the examples that demonstrate the advantages of combining and synchronizing the knowledge in an organization in terms of business Agility:

- Ability to unify external business processes leading to a unified view of the organization to its customers. This view of the business to the customer can change smoothly, depending on the needs and location of the customer.
- Sophistication in search engines that enables CRM systems to provide customers with what they want and where they want it (i.e., location and time independence).
- Use of artificial intelligence algorithms in SCM to identify inventory levels with precision and place orders for materials to correspond with production schedules.
- Wireless semantic network that determines carbon emission levels with seamlessness and transparency and reports on those emissions levels within the organization and also to regulatory bodies.
- Use of mobile-enabled working environment (e.g., telecommuting) supported by HR-enabled workflows and processes.
- Service orientation in KM systems that enables a combination of processes from various existing systems and produces a higher abstraction of knowledge elements.
- Storing and sharing of various types of content across HR, CRM, SCM, CEMS, and other systems of the organization.
- Emphasis on system-based organization, communication and collaboration resulting in a learning organization.

SIDEBAR

What can be considered as a vital contribution of the Agile movement is the increasing focus of businesses to apply the discoveries of Agile values and principles to business. Through Agility, astute businesses manage risks through distribution of responsibilities and decision making, at the same time increasing knowledge capitalization. KM provides for business continuity and effective risk mitigation. This, in turn, enables businesses to implement Agile business strategies. For example, KM eases the effect of people movement. This is because KM models, documents, and shares knowledge by converting it from tacit to explicit, and back. The dynamicity in this synchronization opens up opportunities for easy people movement and, therefore, is closely related to business Agility.

Documentation and Knowledge Management

One of the key statement in the Agile Manifesto gives precedence to working code rather than documentation. Yet, a significant amount of organizational assets reside in documentation. Therefore, it is important for an Agile business to create a formal management strategy that uses KM, including fit-for-purpose documentation.

Some considerations with regard to business documentation include monetization of the value of documents, depreciation of document values, asset management of documents, peer review for assurance, assigning formal roles to document management, use of templates and patterns, deciding on the extent and intensity of documentation, and the costs associated with document management systems. Access, search, security, and backup of documents are also crucial in KM. Documentation of models and processes in various manual and electronic forms is an important element of a practical Agile business.

Within an organization, the quartet of people–process–technology–economics is continuously moving. The more agile an organization is, the greater is this movement. This, in turn, presents business and technical risks. An individual can carry knowledge of a particular process in his or her head. Such tacit knowledge is then locked in with that person. Therefore, even if tacit decision making is rapid (within a person), it can still prevent organization-wide agility. For example, if that person moves jobs or changes her career path, it impacts business Agility in a negative way.

Consider, for example, the systems shown in Figure 6.5. These systems are complex and require great expertise at a very technical level. Furthermore, there is also a steep learning curve associated with initial uses of these systems. Both technical knowledge of the systems and corresponding domain knowledge are required for KM. Yet, these systems are required to capture, store, and analyze the otherwise tactic knowledge carried by people subjectively. While the translation of tacit to explicit may require lead time and effort, it is still a required strategy in combining agility with formality and documentation.

Enterprise Risk Management (ERM) with Collaborative Agile

Collaborative businesses are able to reduce their risks by spreading them across the alliances. Enterprise risk management (ERM) has been discussed by Sherringham and Unhelkar (2010) from both internal and external perspectives. These risks, mainly associated with rapid and unexpected changes, can be handled in a better manner when organizations are able to collaborate with each other electronically. Similarly, risks associated with uncertain political climates can be spread through collaborations wherein the partnering organizations are themselves geographically dispersed.

Collaborations and Agility encourage companies to shift from a vertically organized, top-down type of organization to a more horizontally managed, interactive suite of organization. Horizontal and flexible structures enable employees to play crucial roles by interacting among themselves, and therefore, risks are spread across business areas resulting in a lower risk profile.

Collaborations also require trust. Trust and honesty have been important Agile values. Applying these Agile values at the collaborative business level is far more important than at the software development level. Mutual trust between collaborative businesses, their customers, and business partners is an integral part of building the collaborative business ecosystem.

Managing an Agile business would require continuous attention to time—as such business is geared toward change that is continuous. Collaborative-Agile businesses will most certainly impact the nature of capital investments as well as expenditures. CAMS considers the strategic relevance of methods and processes in the context of business Agility. Collaborative businesses are based on the premise of ubiquity, whereas the traditional competitive businesses work on the premise of scarcity. Thus, traditional economics is also changing in the new age of collaboration.

Market Expansion through Collaboration

Market expansion is a vital reason for formation of collaborative businesses. Business alliances between two or more organizations enable the partnering organizations to have access to each other's customers, suppliers, and the general markets where the organizations have been conducting business activities. Formation of such business alliances require use of a local know-how among all participating businesses. This usage enables the businesses to remain Lean and Agile. It is equally understandable that for some partnering businesses that are coming in for a different "geopolitical" climate, the social and cultural aspect of the local know-how may itself be too idiosyncratic to be relevant outside the particular local market.

For example, a computer chip manufacturer in Japan wanting to sell its products through alliance partners in Australia would want to understand the cultural and social nuances of the Australia–New Zealand region before embarking on the market expansion journey. Another common example is of a bank in Hong Kong wanting to expand its markets in the United States. It will have to adapt to the sociocultural value systems of the American market, which may be dramatically different from, say, the Gulf market, in terms of lending policies and value systems. Despite the challenges of differing cultures, however, businesses eventually find that through collaborations of alliances they are able to sell in a market that they had no access to earlier, without losing their agility.

Global Trade and Agility

Collaborative organizations are able to expand their trade globally. This expansion of opportunities for local organizations, otherwise restricted to certain geographical regions, is based on their ability to offer and consume services electronically. Instead of competing with an organization located in a specific geographical region, collaborative organizations try to leverage the strengths of each other across multiple regions and global markets. A restricted market may not necessarily be only a commercial or technological issue. The issues with limited business access can include legal, cultural, social, and behavioral issues. Each of these issues affects the trade of an organization. Agile values, such as trust, honesty, and courage, when promulgated across the entire organization, enable that organization to overcome the aforementioned issues and enable collaborations. Coupled with electronic communications, these Agile values provide significant impetus to global trade as they help transcend the many issues that limit business access.

SIDEBAR

Global trade is characterized by the opportunities and challenges associated with the global customer. While opportunities abound to sell products globally, a delay in shipping or nonuniformity of elements in a batch can spell the end of an order. Collaborative businesses can demonstrate extraordinary agility in responding to such global customer requirements because of the associated local presence. Such local presence allows these collaborative businesses to respond to customer needs across regions. Post-sale services and customer support are greatly enhanced in global businesses through electronic collaborations.

Organizational Leanness and Restructuring

Collaborations are an excellent enabler of Lean business. The principle of the *Lean* approach to business focuses entirely on value to the customer. A collaborative-Agile business is able to provide that value to the customer immediately without burdening itself with all possible services that the customer would require. Through collaborative effort, one organization is able to satisfy the varying needs of a customer. The number of products and services required by each organization to effectively serve its customers reduces in a collaborative effort. This, in turn, opens up opportunities for further efficiency and agility. Focused expertise in a product or service also enables reductions in wastage.

As a result, the organizational structure becomes Lean and focused. There is an inevitable "flattening" and "thinning" of the organizational structure. Although the customer is not particularly interested in how the business is organized internally, the "flattened" organizational structure serves the customer well. Flattened hierarchies of organizations result in a pruning of middle-management organizational structures. This in turn, encourages organizational Agility, as it enables faster decision making and reduced overheads.

SIDEBAR

Work by Hammer and Champy (2003) in the area of business process reengineering (BPR) represented initial attempts at enterprise Agility as it led to the creation of a flattened internal organizational hierarchy. This was so because, by using information technologies (IT), it was possible for an individual to carry out the required function without continuously referring to higher levels of management. For example, an account officer in a bank is able to open an account easily using the support of the bank's information systems without needing a manager. Reengineering of processes and their management is discussed in detail in Chapter 7 on business analysis.

Outsourcing and Offshoring with Collaborative Agile

Collaborative-Agile organizations strategize to outsource their noncore activities to another business organization that provides the service. This service is the core activity for the service provider. Offshoring further enables collaborating partners to capitalize on the unevenly distributed pools of skills and resources across the globe. For example, by outsourcing routine work, typically to another country or geographical region, there is potential for significant saving, as well as ability to provide service round the clock (by capitalizing on differences in time zones). This is invaluable, for example, in providing 24/7 call centers, which are made possible through the electronic and communication media. Offshoring of services including development, routine maintenance, and testing that comprise noncore organizational activities results in Agility; and such Agile organizations can further concentrate on their core activities, thereby enhancing customer experience.

Legal Compliance and Tax Management with Collaborative Agile

Global businesses are continuously treading through a maze of international rules and regulations. Neely and Unhelkar (2005) have highlighted the opportunities for legal and tax advantages through the collaborative approach to business. Collaborative, global arrangements enable businesses to research, produce, and sell across the globe and, at the same time, take advantage of the local rules and regulations of the governments of the environments in which they operate. For example, collaborations in the pharmaceutical domain can enable research to be carried out in certain geographical areas where it is permitted, but the benefit of the results can be shared by all customers. Other examples of collaborations that are quite popular are in the educational sector wherein services are sourced from education providers where they may otherwise not be physically available. Collaborative-Agile businesses are not hampered by legal limitations of a region and, as such, are able to remain flexible and responsive to international rules and taxation.

Carbon Consciousness and Lean-Agile

With the inevitable advent of the new carbon economy, the environmental responsibilities of businesses are assuming greater importance than ever before (Unhelkar, 2011; Business-IT Strategies Resource Centre, 2010). Collaborations and business Agility have a tremendous role to play in the carbon economy. A Lean and Agile business will inevitably be also a carbon-conscious business.

Collaborations create opportunities for removal of noncore processes out of the business vertical; this, in turn, also shifts the management of those processes out of the business (as mentioned earlier in outsourcing). The reduction in the total number of processes within the organization and the "sharing" of processes that occurs in collaborations is based on Agile values and principles.

When the pure Agile values that are promoted within a typical software development project are applied across and beyond the organization, they result in carbon savings. Examples of collaboration on carbon also include exchange of carbon data types, information, and knowledge using common message formats. That is the "new era" of operating even for large and global organization. Combined with the previously mentioned capriciousness in legal requirements for global organizations, the carbon benchmarks and permissible emission requirements add up to significant complexities. Collaborative Agile is the only practical way of handling these complexities and the associated challenges of the carbon economy.

Evolving Complexities in Collaborative-Agile Business

In order to understand the evolving complexities of processes, they can be categorized as individual (carried out by a user), organizational (carried out by multiple users), and collaborative (occurring across organizations). Technically, they can also be categorized as physical (occurring through face-to-face and paper-based interactions), electronic (occurring through the Internet-based communication medium), and mobile (occurring independent of location). This categorization of processes is based on original work on processes by Unhelkar (2003) and later by Unhelkar and Murugesan (2010), wherein a finer categorization is attempted. Figure 6.6 shows the evolving levels of complexities in a collaborative-Agile business. Figure 6.6 also shows the evolving complexity of Agile organizations from a business as well as technical viewpoint. The increasing levels of complexities from business process viewpoints (starting with "Broadcast" processes and going up to full "Collaborative" processes) are shown on the left. The right side of Figure 6.6 shows

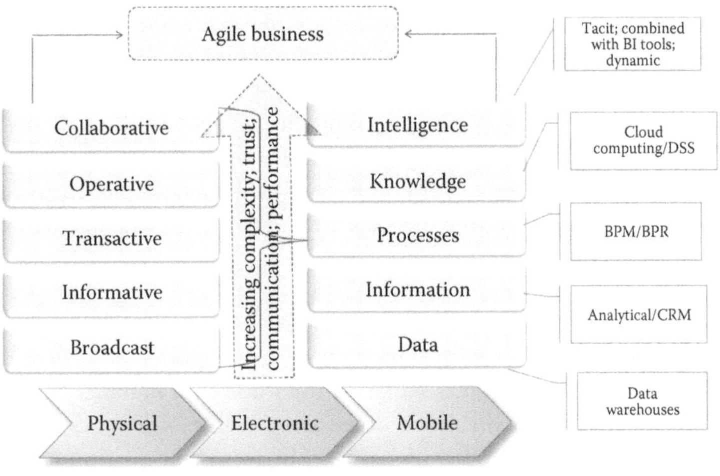

Figure 6.6 Evolving levels of complexities in collaborative-Agile business.

the evolving complexities of IT (starting with "Data" and going up to "Intelligence"). The types of collaboration and the evolving complexities of a collaborative-Agile business are discussed in greater detail next.

Types of Collaboration

Physical Collaboration

This is the traditional way in which businesses relate to each other. This is the people-to-people, face-to-face, manual process of collaborating with each other. Collaboration has been defined as "to work together, especially in a joint intellectual effort" (American Heritage Dictionary, 2000). Such collaborations can be long drawn and bureaucratic, and, in such cases, they provide limited opportunities for collaborations and Agility.

In physical collaborations there is a need to establish the partnering organizations, and then set up an alliance that would encompass both formal and informal agreements, followed by legal contracts, and eventual execution of the collaboration. This physical collaboration can be slow and time consuming, leading to a lost market opportunity. Whenever physical collaborations are formed, it is imperative that stakeholders and players in these partnering organizations quickly understand and establish working relationships. The sociocultural issues in physical collaborations are most crucial. Agility in such physical collaborations is limited as each organization is required to maintain full and independent operability. Yet, understanding the structure and dynamics of physical organizations provides the basis for their collaborations through electronic and mobile communications technologies.

Electronic Collaboration

An electronic collaboration uses Internet-based technologies to enable automated and continuous exchange of information between suppliers, customers, and intermediaries (Donnan, 2002). This collaboration is supported by tools that facilitate communication and information-sharing needs of collaborators either as individuals or in groups (Shuster, 2002). Electronic collaborations, although tool based, still face the challenges of mapping the trust between collaborating organizations during the establishment of collaborative work and life cycle. Web-service-based solution architectures provide opportunities for organizations to collaborate through their portals. The enhanced ability of information systems to connect and communicate with each other leads to a collaborative opportunity for Agile enterprises. Electronic collaborations open up agile opportunities as they also enable organizations to reuse their IT infrastructure and databases.

Mobile Collaboration

This is an extension of the electronic collaboration with the additional characteristic of being independent of location and time. This is based on the features of mobility that enable multiple parties to connect and collaborate with each other using mobile/wireless devices and networks. Mobility leads to dynamicity in collaborations, enabling real-time sharing of information and knowledge between the different parties that take part in the collaborative work (Unhelkar, 2009). This results in flexibility and support, and ad hoc relationships between multiple parties coming together to work for short-term, customer-focused goals. Agility in mobile collaborations is most enhanced as the infrastructure associated with physical and electronic organization is further reduced because of both location and time independence.

Reaching Collaborative Intelligence in Agile Business

Collaborative intelligence (CI) was discussed by Unhelkar and Tiwary (2010) where CI was shown to facilitate the sharing of intelligence across a group of collaborative organizations. CI is achieved through an incremental rise in technologies and complexities starting with data, then information, process, knowledge and intelligence, as discussed next. (KM, discussed earlier, plays a part in this evolving complexity. The subjective aspect of observation is implicit and not discussed separately here.)

Collaborative Data and Agility

Sharing of data (David, 2009) through well-connected, reliable, and trustworthy partners is the basic form of collaboration among organizations. This is the sharing of data across organizations that would otherwise be a repetition. For example, demographic data of a customer, such as her name and address, usually stored by another organization (e.g., a telephone company) need not be stored by the bank. Instead, these data are collaboratively available to the bank from the telephone company under "contracts." Such basic collaboration reduces the data storage overheads and contributes toward Agility.

Collaborative Information and Agility

This is the next level of sharing, that of information, in a generic way so that customer behavior is also personalized. For example, the bank now provides information on demographic behavior patterns such as spending styles, income groups, and geographical nuances (e.g., beach or hills or next to a large sporting arena) to the telephone company—once again, under contracts. Sharing of information creates opportunities for timely services and new products, thereby enhancing the agility of the organization.

Collaborative Process and Agility

Collaborative approaches aim to model and share business processes across multiple organizations. This collaboration of processes among businesses is the evolving step that follows the sharing of data and information. For example, there are opportunities to share the process of opening an account in a bank through a commonly created process model by a third party. Alternatively, the process of account opening from a bank can collaborate with the process of verifying the details of a person or reuse the basic "name, address, phone number" data and related information from yet another service provider. While the variation in each of these processes is accepted, many of the fundamental processes in modern businesses are streamlined. There is limited value in businesses trying to reinvent the processes that are now routinely known in the respective sectors, for example, in the banking, airline, and hospital sectors.

The collaborative advantage comes from reusing and sharing the processes across multiple organizations. Collaborative business processes are built on electronic and mobile communications and, as such, enable businesses to put together new customer-centric processes that they would not be able to do on their own. Creating process models for commonly known processes and making those processes available across organizations provide many advantages to those collaborating organizations, the most important one being their enhanced ability to respond to changes or, in other words, business Agility.

SIDEBAR

Ghanbary (2007) provides an example of collaboration in the medical domain. Through the collaborative-Agile approach, medical businesses are able to serve the patients relatively easily without the need for duplicated infrastructure, especially when the demand for services is high and one business has to rely on another to provide the required level of service. Various patient services can follow different paths through collaborative technologies and applications among these businesses. Three examples of collaborative medical processes discussed by Ghanbary that include interactions of the corresponding participating Agile organizations are described in the following.

Investigation of the disease: This is the first process that is carried across Hospital-1, Pathology Lab-1, and Pharmacy-1. The hospital, in this process, would provide information to the lab about the type of investigations required. The lab can correlate these investigations with any relevant previous knowledge on similar investigations. The pharmacy is kept informed of the investigation without any action at this stage. Data sharing can be significantly improved provided it is presented in a neutral format, independent of any platform or system; otherwise, it can be costly to convert large chunks of disparate information into a standardized format that can be used by multiple organizations.

Specification of medications: This is the second collaborative process activated by Pathology Lab-1 when it sends the results of the investigation to Hospital-1. At the same time, Pathology Lab-1 discovers (through a collaborative portal) that Pharmacy-1 is unable to handle the next steps in this process. Therefore, it shifts the request for specification of medication to Pharmacy-2. Pharmacy-2 provides the necessary medical specifications to Hospital-1 but, at the same time, keeps Pathology Lab-2 informed.

Treatment of disease: The third collaborative process includes Hospital-2, Pathology Lab-2, and Pharmacy-2. The response to the eventual treatment for the patient can come from Hospital-2, as that might be physically more convenient to the patient. Each of these businesses would be communicating and collaborating with each other to provide value to the customer, in this case, the patient. Similarly, doctors and other hospital staff can also collaborate internally. For example, should Hospital-2 be required to treat a large-scale emergency, the staff and expertise of Hospital-1 can be made immediately available through a collaborative portal.

Collaborative Knowledge and Agility

This level shares knowledge about an individual or a group of customers/users across multiple organizations. For example, location information about a mobile customer (person) can be correlated with other bits of information about that customer, such as buying history, to produce knowledge about that customer and, additionally, about that customer group. This knowledge can be invaluable in designing new products and services dynamically, rather than going through a full iteration of market research, prototyping, and customer feedback.

Collaborative Intelligence (CI) and Agility

This is a fully mature implementation of collaboration by a group of organizations within and across multiple industrial sectors with a common goal of enhancing customer experience. Conversely, a group of organizations at this level could also be the customers themselves, acting in a collaborative manner to achieve higher value. What is most important in a CI environment is that not only are the aforementioned data, information, process, and knowledge being shared but they are also made available at the right time and place for the participating organizations. Right from data hubs and warehouses through to operational processes and new product development, CI is a positive influence on business Agility. The real advantage of CI comes from having a strategy for multiple organizations to share these elements in a timely and succinct manner.

Reaching Collaborative Business Process

Collaborative business processes were discussed earlier as a part of evolving complexities of collaborative-Agile business processes. The entire process discussion itself is made up of five increasing levels of complexities, as shown in Figure 6.6, on the left. These are the broadcasting, information, transactive, operative, and collaborative processes that are employed by an Agile business. It should be noted that these business processes may themselves not be exclusive to each other, but may coexist within a business as it strives for Agility through collaboration. However, understanding each of these types of businesses can also help understand the approach to collaborative business.

Broadcasting Business Processes

This is the unidirectional aspect of the business that provides large-scale broadcasts of its products and services. Physical broadcasting is through print media, including newspapers and brochures. Electronic broadcast includes advertisements and related marketing material on professional and social Web sites. At a very basic level, it is scanning of the company's product brochures and putting them up on the Internet, resulting in what has been known as the *brochureware*. Mobile broadcasts are the messages appearing on an individual user's handset. Mobile broadcasts are the most convenient way to reach globally dispersed customers that may be on the move. The increasing importance of social media also has to be factored in.

Informative Business Processes

This informative aspect of the Internet (E-information) encompasses the provision of information to known or registered parties. Alternatively, information can be put up in the public domain for users/customers to pull that information as required (as against the aforementioned broadcast, which is "pushed"). For example, this aspect of business includes providing basic company contact details such as phone, fax, and physical address. As a result, the informative aspect of business has minimal maintenance and security requirements.

Transactive Business Processes

The transactive business is what is commonly referred to as *E-commerce* or *transactionware*. This is the beginning of collaboration. The earlier electronic data interchange (EDI) has now evolved into Internet-based financial transactions involving multiple parties. Transactive business on the Web involves ability to send and receive messages and thereby conduct business transactions, by communicating with multiple businesses behind the Web interface. Examples of these transactions include bookings and reservations, posting feedbacks, buying goods, and seeking services (the last two being paid for using another collaborative party, such as a credit card provider).

Operative Business Processes

This is the shifting of the operational aspect of the business on the Internet. Physically, this is used to involve detailed administration of the operations of the business. Electronically, this is the shifting of HR, timesheets, payroll, and personnel systems on the Web. Furthermore, internal production and inventory processes are also moved on the Web. Operative business results in close alignment of the business to its customers, suppliers, and internally to its employees. As a result, there is a large component of business-to-business (B2B) transactions in operative businesses.

Collaborative Business Processes

Collaborative business encompasses the previous four levels of business but further expands them for multiple organizations. Electronic communications facilitate data, information, process, knowledge, and intelligence to be shared across many organizations, as and when required. This sharing can result in broadcasting of marketing material, provision of information, ability to conduct multiparty financial transactions, and also share the operational aspects of each other's business. This is a truly collaborative business scenario—with the customer being the eventual beneficiary.

SIDEBAR "Collaborative Agile in Educational Domain" (Ghanbary and Unhelkar, 2007)

An example of the collaborative-Agile approach would be in the educational domain. The educational institute (e.g., a university or a training organization) initiates the collaboration. Among the many functions of an educational institution, three functions—marketing, course delivery platform, and student administration—can be sourced from partnering organizations. These would be, for example, organizations specializing in promotions, a service provider who has a platform for delivery of courses, and a third-party administration package operating in the cloud. Collaborative business process engineering (CBPE) (Ghanbary and Unhelkar, 2007) has been used for streamlining the activities, roles, and deliverables involved in the educational institution's transformation to a collaborative-Agile organization.

Enabling a collaborative-Agile educational institution will require sharing of data and information and cross-checking of the legitimacy of student administration (e.g., payment of fees, awarding of degrees). The risks associated with different interpretations and formats relating to the course contents (which is provided by the centrally position educational institution) as well as the need for handling different languages and expressions need to be handled up front by the collaborating organizations.

Business Evaluation Process Map

Figure 6.7 depicts the business evaluation process map of CAMS. This CAMS process map comprises activities such as business opportunity analysis, business proposal formation, steering committee approval, and project formation. The process map deals in detail with the exploration of business needs, and, in a way, investigates the prime reason for the existence of a project. Therefore, techniques such as SWOT, PESTLE, and cost–benefit analyses (all three discussed later within this process map) are put to good use while undertaking business evaluation. The collaborative-Agile concepts discussed earlier in this chapter also form part of the strategy of a business to decide to move in that direction. Therefore, the business evaluation process map becomes important in CAMS from an Agile business management viewpoint.

The process map also presents the very early approach to organizing a project. This is undertaken by the project sponsor, who starts with the activity of analysis of a business opportunity. This is followed by a business proposal formulation. The steering committee performs the activity of project approval in an iterative manner; the project manager handles the responsibilities of the project once the project is formed. This process component is important when undertaking a formal evaluation of the business reasons for a software project to proceed. Not only does this argument help those who are going to manage the project but it also helps to confirm the goals and objectives of the project in the minds of the project sponsor and the eventual end users. This process map deals with the initial understanding of the business problem, and the deliverables produced here—the *business case* and the *project brief*—form part of the model of the problem space (MOPS).

Roles in Business Evaluation

The following are the roles in the business evaluation process map.

- Business analyst: This is the main role in the requirements modeling process. In a project, this role is combined with the requirements engineer role. A business analyst is responsible for eliciting and documenting the requirements.
- Project manager: The project manager is an expert who is responsible for management of the project. This role's responsibilities are project planning, control, execution, and closing.
- Product owner: The product owner is the one who benefits or suffers losses as a result of project execution. The product owner has full authority in the project and is the one who needs to be satisfied with the quality of the final product.
- Steering committee: This is a group of people who are responsible for providing strategic leadership, controlling project scope, resolving project problems, offering support to the project when required, and performing a formal acceptance of deliverables. The members of the steering committee are the experts from different domains, such as finance, technology, human resources, and law.

Deliverables

The following are the deliverables in the business evaluation process map.

- Business case: This contains the reasoning for the project execution, scope of the project, risks, supposed business benefits, and time and cost estimates.

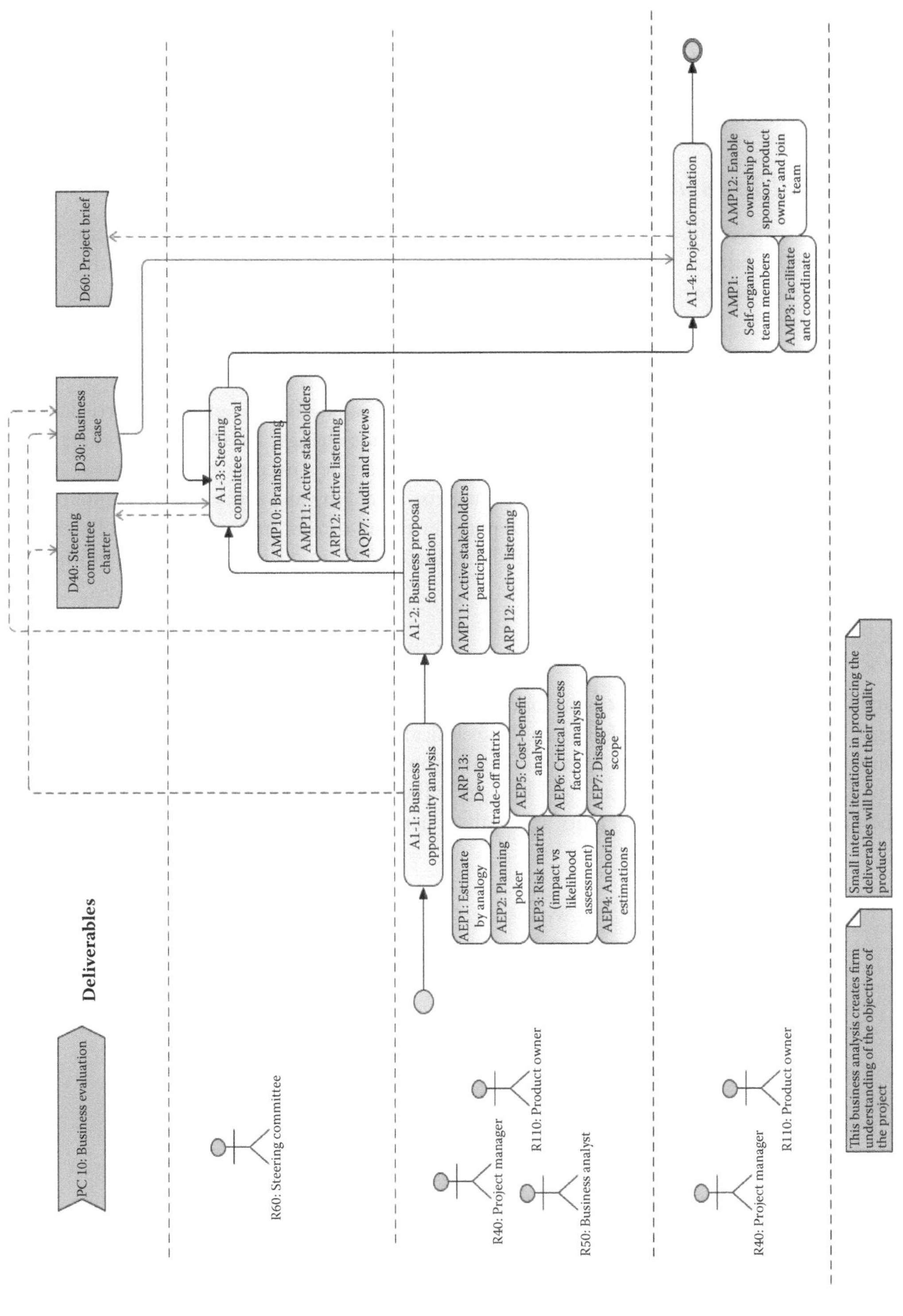

Figure 6.7 Business evaluation process map in CAMS.

- Steering committee charter: This is a document that explains the purpose and responsibility of the steering committee. Additionally, it provides the list of members of the steering committee with role descriptions. The meeting schedule and process are also documented in the steering committee charter.
- Project brief: This is a document with a short description of the project, the objectives, and project estimates.

Activities and Tasks in Business Evaluation

Table 6.4 demonstrates the activities and tasks with corresponding deliverables and roles for the business evaluation process map. Moreover, the Agile practices that would be utilized during the process map execution are included.

SWOT Analysis

Figure 6.8 shows a summarized version of the popular SWOT analysis. This analysis is carried out by a business during the evaluation of its options to undertake change. SWOT analysis can also be undertaken at a technical level within a project should there be a need to evaluate a particular technology. SWOT can be a two-dimensioned matrix. Strengths and weaknesses are internal, inherent characteristics of the organization. Opportunities and threats are external. The following is the description of a typical organization undertaking SWOT to decide on the Agile business transformation.

Strengths

Existing IT and systems provide the basis for communications in an Agile organization. Agility as a culture and value system can capitalize on the technical excellence of an organization.

Financial stability provides opportunities for an organization to experiment with Agility across the board. An organization with very tight budgets will not have the same freedom and strength to experiment, pilot, and dissipate agility across all its tiers.

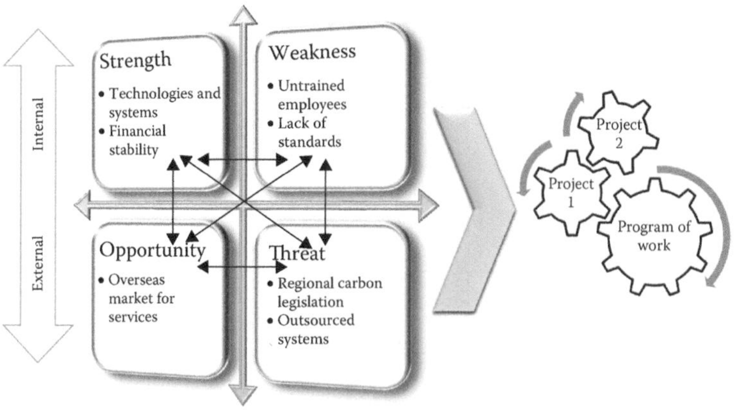

Figure 6.8 Use of SWOT analysis in business evaluation (an organizational example).

Table 6.4 Business Evaluation Process Map

Activities	*Tasks*	*Deliverables*	*Roles*
A1-1: Business opportunity analysis	Develop product vision Identify costs, benefits Identify business opportunity Understand the problem Define scope and constraints Identify risks Make estimates Agile practices: AEP3: Risk matrix (impact vs likelihood assessment) AEP5: Cost–benefit analysis AEP6: Critical success factors analysis ARP13: Develop trade-off matrix AEP2: Planning poker AEP1: Estimate by analogy AEP7: Disaggregate scope AEP4: Anchoring estimations	D30: Business case D40: Steering committee charter	R40: Project manager R50: Business analyst R110: Product owner
A1-2: Business proposal formulation	Document objectives Document risks, costs, benefits Propose to steering committee Suggest project management Document estimates Agile practices: AMP11: Active stakeholders participation ARP12: Active listening	D30: Business case	R110: Product owner R50: Business analyst R40: Project manager
A1-3: Steering committee approval	Study business case Take go/no go decision Approve project estimates Monitor project progress Agile practices: AMP10: Brainstorming AMP11: Active stakeholders participation ARP12: Active listening AQP7: Audit and reviews	D40: Steering committee charter (approved)	R60: Steering committee

continued

Table 6.4 (*Continued*)

Activities	*Tasks*	*Deliverables*	*Roles*
A1-4: Project formulation	Appoint project manager Appoint quality manager Appoint on-site customer/user Appoint members of team Determine other stakeholders Agile practices: AMP12: Enable ownership of sponsor, product owner, and join team AMP3: Facilitate and coordinate AMP1: Self-organize team members	D60: Project brief	R40: Project manager R110: Product owner

Weaknesses

Existing skills and motivation of employees can play an important role in Agile business transformation. Coaching and training in practicing Agile can only bear results with motivated employees. Lack of training and corresponding lack of motivation to be trained can be a major hindrance to Agile business.

Lack of existing standards and processes can create challenges in terms of understanding the value of processes in the first place. While existence of multiple standards can create "method friction," lack of standards can create the fundamental challenge of understanding the value of processes in the first place.

Opportunities

Agility together with collaboration is bound to open up multiple global opportunities. The transforming organization should have strategies to capitalize on these growing overseas market opportunities for products and services.

Threats

An Agile organization may encounter external threats such as demands to comply with regional legislations (e.g., carbon legislation). Lack of formal control over outsourced systems and processes can also present a threat to an Agile business.

PESTLE Analysis

PESTLE analysis sheds light on the many organizational factors that need to be considered in decision making. Supported by KM, ongoing PESTLE leads an Agile learning organization. Such a learning organization will capture and store the data and information associated with the following factors (also shown in Figure 6.9) and will continue to synchronize them with their associated tacit knowledge:

- Political: These include governmental policies, ease of import and export, and trade unions. Collaborative Agility will require exploration of the political climate to ensure it benefits through regional collaborations.
- Economic: These are made up of interest and exchange rates, stock markets, and size of the organization. These factors create or limit the extent to which an organization can become collaborative and Agile.
- Social: These include culture and values, health and population, demographics, workforce, and social media. These are primarily internal organizational factors affecting the manner in which the organization is structured. Externally, this factor influences the way in which customers (as again vendors) collaborate with each other.
- Technological: These include hardware, software applications, communications, and innovations. The primary influence of these factors in terms of collaborative Agile is the enhanced ability to communicate as Web Services as also the location independence provided by mobile Web Services.
- Legal: These include taxation, insurance, support for research and development, and compliance legislations. For example, legislations such as Sarbanes–Oxley will enforce a need for detailed governance and reporting, irrespective of the level of Agility desired by the business leadership.
- Environmental: These include climate, regional ecology, carbon emissions, and control. This factor is increasingly going to influence all types of businesses, irrespective of their Agility. However, with increasing collaboration and Agility, a business will become Lean and efficient—in turn having a positive impact on its carbon performance.

Cost–Benefit Analysis

Figure 6.10 shows, by way of an example, the many factors that businesses consider in terms of cost benefits in their decision making. This cost–benefit analysis is a part of the business evaluation process map discussed earlier. Cost–benefit analysis is regularly applied to decide on the

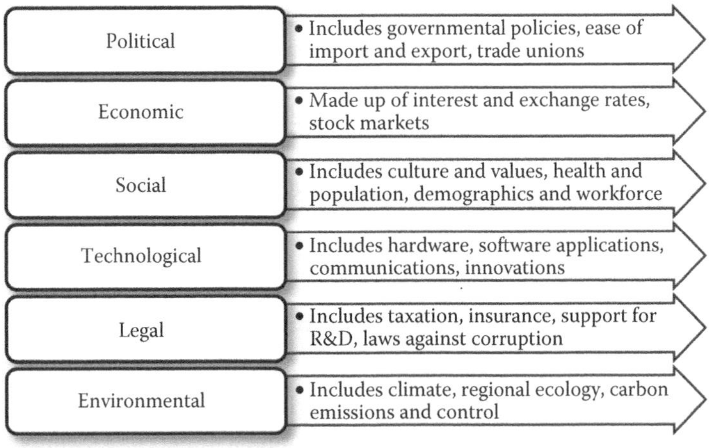

Figure 6.9 Use of PESTLE analysis in business evaluation—organizational factors in decision making.

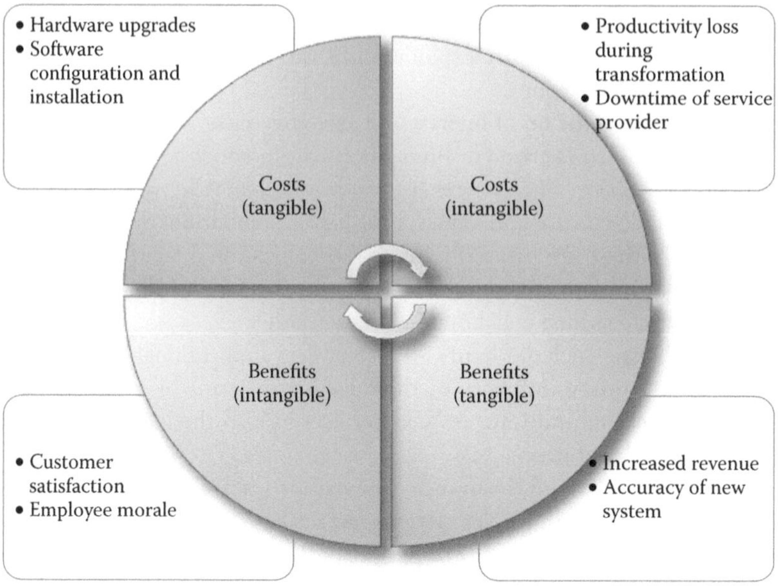

Figure 6.10 Use of cost–benefit analysis in business evaluation.

worth of a project or business initiative. An Agile business initiative can also be subjected to a cost–benefit analysis although that is only one use of this analysis.

- Costs (tangible): Examples of these tangible costs include hardware upgrades as well as software configuration and installation to provide support to Agility.
- Costs (intangible): These costs include productivity loss when a business transforms to an Agile business, for example, lack of service for a short time during transformation; or slow production due to employees learning new techniques downtime of the service provider.
- Benefits (tangible): These include increased revenue due to expanding reach of business and its ability to serve a wider suite of customers. For example, the ability to sell a product in a distant geographical region with the help of business partners who can provide post-sales service; accuracy and timeliness in new ways to doing things within the business.
- Benefits (intangible): Customer satisfaction in terms of appropriateness of product and service enhancement internally in terms of staff morale and motivation are examples of intangible benefits.

Change Management in Agile Business

As an organization shifts toward a collaborative-Agile approach to its business, it undergoes many changes. Awareness and anticipation of these changes is a part of the organization's business and technology strategies. A detailed discussion of these changes, as part of a comprehensive business transformation program is discussed in Chapter 10. Changes within a business due to a collaborative approach may be embraced, tolerated, or even resisted (Ghanbary, 2007). The results depend on the approach to collaboration by the leadership and management of the participating organizations. A certain amount of planning, anticipation, and envisioning on the part of the decision makers can immediately help an organization with its collaborative effort. If the leaders are unsure of what the change entails, as it moves toward collaboration, then the employees will not be able to undertake that change successfully.

These changes can occur at various levels in the organization depending on the size, complexity, and IT sophistication of the organization. These changes are grouped into two categories—external changes (with significant impact of web Services) and internal changes (primarily driven by cloud computing). They are briefly discussed next.

External Changes

- Marketing: This provides an interesting challenge in the collaborative eras wherein the organizational boundaries are difficult to define. Through electronic collaborations, an erstwhile competitor may now be a collaborator. Therefore, once marketing itself becomes a collaborative effort, the focus of an organization changes from competing with other organizations in the same horizontal market to combining their offerings to suit a wider range of customers. Electronic and mobile marketing take precedence over physical marketing due to the changing nature of offerings.
- Customers: Changes occur not only in the offerings but also in the expectations of the customers. As an organization becomes more collaborative in its offerings, customers start expecting greater and wider areas of service from the organization. As collaborative business facilitates offering services through partnering organizations, customers start expecting services from one portal rather than seeking out the services from other competing organizations. For example, a customer would routinely expect an airline to offer car and hotel rental services.
- Collaborators: These are the business partners that are coming together on an electronic portal to offer a wide variety of products and services. These could be the suppliers to the organization as also corporate customers who would be interested in collaborating for the products and services from a greater number of businesses. Through collaborative business processes, an organization is now able to offer variety as well as quantity to its customers, which it was unable to do in an earlier, noncollaborative era. An airline that was earlier competing with another airline is now able to quickly satisfy the needs of a customer organizing a large conference (for example) by providing the number of airline seats that it could not have provided prior to collaboration. There are also changes associated with the way in which a customer is dealt with—for example, if a product or service is not available where the customer wants it, collaborative business offers it from its partners that may be locally present where the customer is. This brings about changes to the manner in which businesses relate with each other.
- Regulators: These are the government or industry bodies that take the responsibility of ensuring compliance with the electronic contracts. Collaborations across geographical boundaries demand greater change in the way legislations are created and applied. Dynamic electronic contracts formed by collaborating organizations require corresponding electronic enforcement. Similarly, as cloud computing starts playing a strategic role in the business, regulations relating to privacy and security of data assume importance.

Internal Changes

- IT systems: These are the changes to the applications, databases, and networks of the organization. While the system changes affect both the internal and external parts of the organization, the changes themselves are brought about internally by the organization. Identification of databases and applications and shifting them onto the cloud is an important part of this exercise. Some large organizations may change in two stages—first, moving toward shared services (which is an internal or private cloud) and then to the public cloud.

- Business model: These are the changes that collaboration and Agility bring about to the way in which the business perceives its value. This changes the way in which products and services are created and used to provide value to the customer. The mission statement of the organization is likely to undergo change as it aspires to deliver a higher value to a dispersed suite of customers through its collaborative efforts.
- Management and HR: Agility, in particular, flattens the organizational hierarchy. Agile business processes do not require the earlier hierarchical structures as decision making is distributed. There will also be changes related to the number of people required to carry out a task, the way in which these people need to be managed and led, and the collaborative style needed in decision making. Such changes lead to a revision of management structure, redefinition of roles and responsibilities, and opportunities for different working style (e.g., freelancing contract work rather than full-time employment, or teleworking). Training plays a vital role in equipping the people involved in a change to carry out their newly defined activities, and is a part of the HR change.
- Business processes: These are the changes due to the ability of the organization to provide more services and products with optimized internal processes. Reengineering and management of processes is a part of this change, requiring excellence in process modeling and tools.

Whenever a change is introduced, there is a risk. A change management process creates an awareness of the inherent risks and implements the controls need to be put in place to mitigate those risks. A change management plan ensures that the changes are beneficial, determine how the change will occur, and manage the changes as they occur.

Risks and Challenges in Collaborative-Agile Business

Collaborative and Agile businesses are associated with certain risks and challenges that need to be identified and handled. These risks and challenges are both internal and external, and they revolve around the traits of these collaborative organizations. These risks and challenges primarily emanate from differences in the regional (geographical), technological, leadership, management, economic, political–legal, and sociocultural traits of the collaborating organizations. Despite the impact of technologies on collaborations and Agility, human factors still continue to provide a significant challenge to these collaborations. These risks and challenges revolve around organizational traits both internally and externally. Table 6.5 provides a summary of the traits, corresponding risks and challenges, and key approaches to ameliorating those risks.

Conclusions

This chapter highlighted the business management aspect of Agility. An important extension of the discussion on Agile, as elucidated in this chapter, is its close mapping with business collaborations. It was argued here that a business that builds on the ICT to shift its noncore processes outside its organizational boundaries will be Agile and collaborative. Various advantages and challenges of

Table 6.5 Collaborative-Agile Risks Corresponding to Organizational Traits

Organizational Traits	*Risks and Challenges*	*Key Amelioration Strategy*
Regional	Delivery and quality of product/ service at customer location	Continuous physical dialogue with collaborators; managing customer expectations
Technological	Interfaces; security	Extensive modeling, prototyping, and testing of Web Services and security features; walk-through of SOA
Leadership	Differing vision; vested interests	Exchange of mission statement; face-to-face discussion on business strategies
Management	Differing management styles; work safety; growth and training	Start with the commonalities in administration; use groupware; exchange HR plans; mutual training
Economic	Differing business models; Return On Investment (ROI) calculations	Keep returns, profits, and other economically sensitive data separate
Political–legal	Differences in laws, their interpretation and enforcement	Adoption of global copyright/IP laws; use of third parties/mediation
Sociocultural	Trust; privacy; incompatibility; communication gap	Create multiple communications channels; repeat communication; agree on codes of ethics

a collaborative-Agile business were discussed. Chapter 7 takes the discussion to greater depths of business analysis—an organizational function that goes beyond requirements modeling.

Agile in Practice: Road Map 6

- Revisit your current business policies in terms of use of processes and standards within the organization; investigate whether the current processes are helpful or restrictive. Interview the key users of the processes at various levels within the business. Their views should form the basis for process transition at business level.
- List the current processes used by your organization in order to manage and optimize the business. List also any IT governance and project management processes used in your business. Against this list of processes, identify the key advantages and challenges currently faced by your organization in their usage.
- Identify four different "touch points" where your business management, governance, and project management processes interact with each other. Describe, corresponding to the four touch points, the potential for "method friction." Provide an example for each touch point in order to clarify where the friction occurs.
- How is knowledge currently being managed in your organization? Is there a KMS in use? Investigate the system from a "learning organization" perspective (Senge, 1990).

- Study the business ecosystem in which your business exists. This study will include an understanding and modeling of the clusters of which your business may be a part. Model a collaborative business process that will serve a customer your business would otherwise not be able to serve had it not collaborated with other businesses.
- List a few noncore business processes that you would be comfortable in shifting outside of your organization, perhaps using a cloud-based architecture.
- Identify the metrics you would use to measure the impact of a noncore process on customer service. Further identify the risks associated with shifting the noncore process outside the organizational boundary.
- Discuss the opportunity for use of a composite process with your business stakeholders. Identify the key issues they might have in terms of use of a composite process. Discuss also the issues relating to transitioning the business activities of the organization to follow a composite process.

Discussion Questions

- Which processes are in use in your organization—at business, governance and project levels? Describe the formality imposed by these processes in the way your organization operates.
- How would you change and update your business policies to reflect the need for your business management process (e.g., Six Sigma) to reflect organizational Agility?
- Why is collaboration important for business Agility? And, similarly, how does an Agile business lends itself to collaboration?
- A learning organization needs to manage and synchronize its knowledge on an ongoing basis. Argue how this concept of a learning organization can be used to enhance business Agility.
- Provide an example of each of broadcast, informative, transactive, operative, and collaborative business processes in the context of your organization or an organization you are familiar with. Comment on how each of these processes can be made Agile with the use of ICT.
- Observe–reflect–share–impart form the tacit part of KM. Explain how they are synchronized in collaborative-Agile businesses to become explicit.
- Evaluate a business decision relating to shifting of noncore processes on the cloud. Use either/or SWOT, PESTLE, and cost–benefit analysis to arrive at the validity of the decision.

References

American Heritage Dictionary *The American Heritage Dictionary of the English Language*, Houghton Mifflin Company, 2000.

Unhelkar, B., Environmentally responsible business strategies for a green enterprise transformation, Business-IT Strategies Resource Centre, *Cutter Executive Report*, 13 (2), 2010.

Cottmeyer, M. and V.L. Henson, The agile business analyst, VersionOne Inc., 2008, viewed 12 December 2010, http://www.versionone.com/whitepapers.asp.

David, L., *Master Data Management*, Elsevier, Butterworth, Heinemann Press, pp. 1–28, 87–101, 177–199, 2009.

Donnan, D., CEO/Presidents' forum—Action plan for trading partner e-collaboration, GMA CEO/Presidents' Forum, p. 8, 2002.

Ghanbary, A., Collaborative Business Process Engineering (CBPE) Across Multiple Organisations, PhD thesis, University of Western Sydney, 2007 (Original model created).

Ghanbary, A. and B. Unhelkar, Collaborative business process engineering (CBPE) across multiple organisations in a cluster, *Proceedings of 2007 IRMA International Conference*. 19–23 May, Vancouver, Canada, 2007.

Ginige, A., From eTransformation to eCollaboration: Issues and solutions, *2nd International Conference on Information Management and Business (IMB 2006)*, eds. Yi-Chen, L. and B. Unhelkar, Sydney, Australia, pp. 15–23, 2006. www.aimb.org.

Hammer, M. and J. Champy, *Reengineering the Corporation: A Manifesto for Business Revolution*, Harper Collins, New York, NY, 2003.

Morris, A., The challenge of collaborative commerce, *IEEE Review*, 48 (6), 33–37, 2002.

Neely, M. and B. Unhelkar, The role of a collaborative commerce legal framework in IT-related litigation, *Cutter IT Journal*, 18 (11), 11–17, 2005.

Senge, P., *The Fifth Discipline: The Art and Practice of the Learning Organization*, Currency Doubleday, New York, NY, 1990, revised 2006.

Shalloway, A., Demystifying kanban, *Cutter IT Journal*, 24 (3), 2011.

Sherringham, K. and B. Unhelkar, Achieving business benefits by implementing enterprise risk management, *Cutter Executive Report*, 7 (3), 2010.

Shuster, K., Cross-industry standard key to ecollaboration success, in Ticona news release, Philadelphia, 2002.

Unhelkar, B., *Green ICT Strategies & Applications*, Auerbach, New York, 2011.

Unhelkar, B., Knowledge management in perspective: The dynamic knowledge synchronization model, *Cutter Executive Report*, 10 (8), 2010.

Unhelkar, B., *Mobile Enterprise Transition and Management*, Auerbach, 393 pp., 2009.

Unhelkar, B., Understanding collaborations and clusters in the e-business world, *Proceedings of 4th International We-B Conference, 2003, 24–25th November*, Edith Cowan University, Perth, Western Australia, 2003, viewed March 2012, www.we-bcentre.com/web2003/.

Unhelkar, B., Collaborative business and enterprise agility, *Cutter Executive Report*, 13 (9), 2010.

Unhelkar, B. and A. Ginige, A framework to derive holistic business transformation processes, *Proceedings of International Conference on E-Business (ICE-B)*, Paper 44, 2010, viewed March 2012, http://www.ice-b.icete.org/Abstracts/2010/ICE-B_2010_Abstracts.htm.

Unhelkar, B. and S. Murugesan, *The Enterprise Mobile Applications Development Framework*, Computer.org/ITpro, IEEE Computer Society Publication, pp. 33–39, 2010.

Unhelkar, B. and A. Tiwary, Collaborative intelligence, *Cutter IT Journal*, 23 (6), 2010.

Unhelkar, B., A. Ghanbary, and H. Younessi, *Collaborative Business Process Engineering and Global Organizations: Frameworks for Service Integration*, IGI Global, Hershey, PA, 323 pp., 2010.

Chapter 7

Business Analysis and Composite Agile

Objectives

- Understand the significance of business analysis (BA) in the organization in the context of composite Agile
- Outline the BA core areas of work (i.e., identify the business needs and capabilities and the corresponding functional and operational requirements) and the impact of Agile on them
- Highlight the value added by BA in exploring the business needs of the organization
- Discuss the various levels in the organization at which BA occurs and the way in which Agility impacts that work
- Describe the relationship of business analysts with multiple other roles in the business at both project and organizational levels
- Discuss business process management (BPM) and its relationship with Agility
- Review the leading BA frameworks (International Institute of Business Analysts, IIBA; Australian Institute of Business Analysis, AIBA; Skills Framework for Information Age, SFIA) and their importance in providing the basis for a composite Agile approach to business
- Present the requirements modeling process map that guides the activities of a business analyst within a project and position Agile practices within that process map
- Briefly review the use case, activity, class, and state diagrams of the Unified Modeling Language (UML) as used by business analysts to model requirements and show the relevance of these diagrams to Agile practices

Introduction

This chapter discusses business analysis (BA) in the context of the Composite Agile Method and Strategy (CAMS). BA can be considered as a profession in its own right similar to the leadership, management, accounting, and technology functions in an organization (Unhelkar, 2010b). The impact of BA in an organization is felt in its decision making, problem defining, critical thinking, requirements modeling, and quality assurance functions—to name but a few. This wide permeation of BA work demands its consideration along with Agile methods at both project and organizational levels.

BA and Agility need to work together to contribute toward the business goals (Unhelkar, 2010c). Incorporating BA skills in Agile-based approaches to software development and maintenance provides the necessary formality in investigating and exploring business needs. The formal descriptions of BA include models of how a business currently functions (as is) and how it should function (to be). Formal BA models also extract business knowledge that may otherwise be carried in its tacit form in people's heads. Explicit modeling of business needs and requirements helps in encapsulating business knowledge and improves user buy-in. This, in turn, enhances expectation management, management of risk, negotiations of outcomes, and agreements on testing. These are a critical part of delivery of products and services and form part of the overall CAMS life cycle.

CAMS is based on the premise that methods do not work well in isolation. Instead, the success of methods in organizations lies in a cohesive approach that includes methods and strategies for development, architecture, project management, BA, and governance. This chapter aims to gel the methods and frameworks of BA with the values, principles, and practices of Agile. While embracing the flexibility of pure Agile approaches, CAMS also seeks to leverage the benefits of business modeling, formalized requirements, and risk management in BA work. Therefore, CAMS defines formal activities, tasks, and deliverables of requirements modeling through a process map.

Business analysis includes a wide range of activities in an organization, occurring at various levels: from the strategic level of critical thinking and prioritization of business objectives through to the modeling of process flows and data elements. The skill set of a business analyst applies, among others, at technical, business, and quality levels. A business analyst can add value in almost all types of projects. Some Agile practices (especially writing of user stories and the creation of iterations and increments) provide a good starting point for combining Agility and BA. This is shown later in the requirements modeling process map, which plays a vital role in large and complex projects. Agile methods commence development of code without necessarily completing formal requirements modeling/engineering. CAMS expands on Agile practices within formal requirements modeling. For example, user participation and feedback from the key business stakeholders is encouraged but is embedded in formal requirements modeling deliverables. New requirements identified during user participation, and changes to existing ones, are formally documented in the requirements model. Formality in BA work enables incorporation of these changes in a smooth way within the development process. Formality of BA also augurs well for the operational aspects of the system and the business, as it provides for models, traceability, and ongoing risk consideration for the business-as-usual (BAU) scenario.

This chapter discusses these various aspects of BA and how it impacts (and is impacted by) projects and organizations that are transforming to Agile. CAMS also considers BA in the context of other organizational processes with the aim of reducing methods friction. Therefore, this chapter includes descriptions of the BA frameworks (International Institute of Business Analysts, IIBA; Australian Institute of Business Analysis, AIBA; and a subset of Skills Framework for Information Age, SFIA) that not only provide the BA standards but also help in positioning BA work in the context of other works in the organization. This chapter focuses on this synergy between BA and Agile values and principles from the point of view of how it can make a positive contribution under the CAMS umbrella.

What is Business Analysis?

Business analysis (BA) can be understood as a discipline that explores and identifies business needs, prioritizes them based on risks and business goals, and provides potential solutions that fulfill those needs (Unhelkar, 2010d). The SFIA defines BA as "The methodical investigation, analysis, review, and documentation of all or part of a business in terms of business functions and processes, the information used, and the data on which the information is based." These BA activities are carried out by business analysts in order to improve the processes and systems within and across organizations. BA activities employed in an organization include exploring the enterprise, justifying the costs and business benefits, creating visual models for requirement, and working together with the key stakeholders on the acceptance criteria.

While the traditional BA work occurred in the problem space, as Beal* outlines, BA work today occurs at varying levels within an organization ranging from high-level evaluation of business alternatives (irrespective of the underlying technical solutions) to documenting requirements from the point of view of a software system. BA helps in identifying the corporation's vision and strategy, aligning it with the business capabilities, creating use case models, writing user stories and features, undertaking modeling of business entities, and participating in acceptance testing. Therefore, BA plays a positive role in Agile projects (Unhelkar, 2010c), as it also influences enterprise architecture (Unhelkar, 2010b) and enables a synergy between business and information technology (IT) strategies (Unhelkar, 2010a).

CAMS formalizes these BA activities through its process map. BA activities in CAMS are made up of their roles description, practices, deliverables, metrics and measurements, tools and techniques, implementation, and maturity measures. BA in CAMS, especially in a large organization, is practiced through the combination of a BA framework, process maps, and Agile practices. Setting up of a "Center of Excellence for BA" (centers of excellence are discussed in Chapter 10), while embedding BA within all areas of business operations provides added impetus for BA work within Agile projects and organizations.

At project level, business analysts play a key role in requirements elicitation, their analysis, workshop facilitation, and running focus groups. Operating from a holistic as well as pragmatic operational perspective, business analysts go deeper into modeling functional requirements employing use cases or user stories, implementing process models, and utilizing data models that employ high-level class diagrams. A BA skill set also includes translation and clarification of requirements as expressed by the users and as understood by the developers. This work leads to what the Agile values are promulgating—an all important buy-in from key stakeholders that would ensure successful implementation.

Pure Agile approaches usually eschew the detailed work carried out by business analysts because the methods based on the Agile Manifesto focus heavily on the actual solution (typically, the software product). In contrast with the emphasis of earlier planned methods on modeling of requirements and associated documentation, there is a relative shift away from the need for detailed modeling, in-depth documentation, and extensive planning in an Agile project. Composite Agile, however, welcomes the substantial aspect of planning, modeling, and documentation that is carried out by business analysts, while emphasizing Agile values such as transparency and collaboration within the activities of BA.

Figure 7.1 shows the intersection of core areas of BA work with Agile values and practices. These areas of work include exploring and identifying business needs, prioritizing them, and providing

* In her interesting discussions on ModernAnalyst.com and in various other publications.

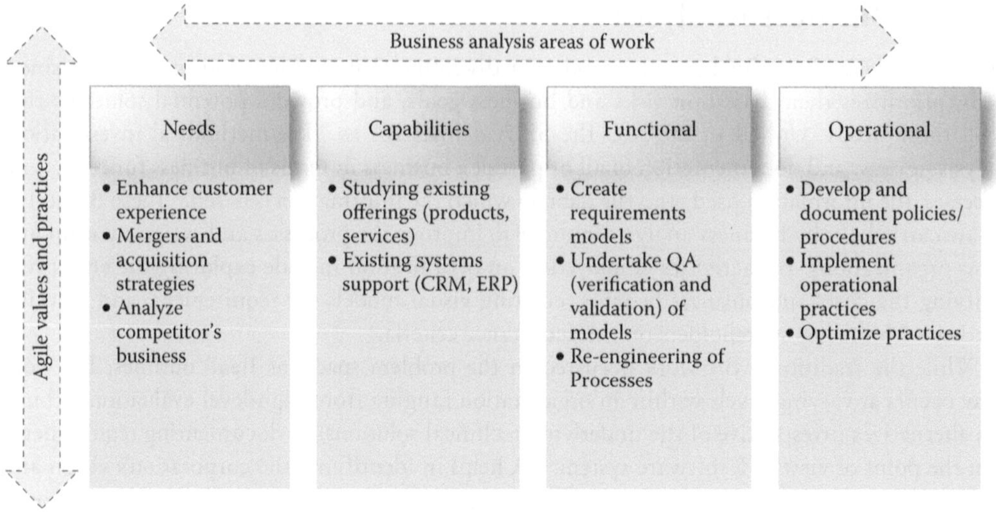

Figure 7.1 Core areas of business analysis work and Agile practices.

risk-based comparisons and solutions that can fulfill those needs. The work of a business analyst goes a long way in aligning any initiatives expressed by business with the corporation's vision and strategy, translating them into formal needs in the context of organizational capabilities, optimizing business processes, and supporting decision making.

Examples of skills and competencies used by business analysts include questioning, listening, documenting, modeling, negotiating, facilitating, translating, and presenting. These competencies are put to use by the business analyst in modeling functional and nonfunctional requirements of the systems, aligning the requirements with the business capabilities and goals of the organization, being aware of the technical solutions and systems, and carrying out basic data modeling and testing tasks. Understanding the structure of an organization together with its processes, the relationships of an organization with external parties, and the ongoing balancing of risks enables the business analyst to understand an organization's current and desired future state.* The core areas of work of a BA as shown in Figure 7.1 and practiced within CAMS are described further:

- Identifying the needs of the organization: This needs analysis requires abstraction and imagination skills coupled with knowledge of the business ecosystem. For example, here BA can handle decisions related to potential mergers and acquisitions, exploring strategies for business transformation, and identifying long-term goals of the organization. This area of BA work is primarily external facing from the organization. Risks associated with these BA activities are high and these activities cannot be clearly defined. Agile values and principles that embrace uncertainty and change provide excellent support in undertaking business needs analysis. The customer-centric Agile principles (see Figure 2.2 in Chapter 2) provide that Agile support to business analysts when they undertake "needs identification" with CAMS.
- Understanding the capabilities of the organization: The analysis here delves into the overall capabilities of the organization. These are the capabilities that can satisfy the business needs identified earlier—or provide a limitation on those needs. This area of BA work is internal

* Based on BA111—Core Competencies for the Business Analyst. Courses run by the Corporate Education Group, http://www.butrain.com/share/scedesc.asp?CID=15528&source=24581.

facing to the organization. Therefore, an in-depth internal understanding of the structure and dynamics of the organization is required in order to specify the capabilities. Analysis here includes modeling of existing systems and processes, ascertaining the gaps between current and future capabilities, and outlining the business options to fill those gaps. The architecture-centric Agile principles (Figure 2.2 in Chapter 2) are used in CAMS to carry out this BA work. These principles enable focus on organizational-level constraints and limitations.

- Modeling the functionality of the organization: Analysis in this area of work requires detailed understanding of business architecture, business processes, and behavioral flows. Changing (reengineering) business processes and their impact on the rest of the organization, including people and technologies, is studied and executed in this area of work. This is where the developer-centric Agile principles (Figure 2.2) come in handy and support the business analysts in CAMS.
- Modeling the operational requirements of the organization: Analysis here is the work required in understanding the requirements of BAU operations. This work explores and models the adherence to standards, use of metrics and measurements, dealing with service level agreements (SLAs) (including contract negotiations if the agreements are with third-party service providers), and ongoing maintenance and management of processes. Deployment of a system also requires an improved understanding of the nonfunctional requirements of the system. CAMS encourages business analysts to document and model the nonfunctional (operational) requirements by using the management-centric Agile principles (as shown in Figure 2.2) in carrying out this area of work.

SIDEBAR

Business analysis (BA) encompasses wide and varied activities that occur at various levels and in different ways in an organization. At the heart of these BA activities is the competency to deal with ambiguity and uncertainty. Business analysts are effective in performing a holistic investigation of the organization, including its internal structure and processes; its external relationships, technology, systems, and processes; and the corresponding environmental risks. These analyses and investigations are a means to understanding the current state of an organization and devising its future state. This can be extremely challenging as everything in the business world is dynamic, changing. The external customers, the legal and regulatory compliance, the internal organizational structure, the employees and their culture, the technologies for production, information systems and cross-organizational relationships—everything is in a state of flux. BA requires the courage to "jump in" to this melee of ambiguity and start making sense out of it.

The role and responsibilities of a business analyst include the modeling of reality, modeling of processes, and change management. However, not all the modeling performed by a business analyst is uniform. For example, functional requirements can be gathered and modeled in an iterative and incremental manner, while nonfunctional requirements are better described in one go (as they usually affect the entire system). In many organizations, funding for a project is based on the creation of a pilot project or delivery of the requirements scope. For example, getting the next round of financing might depend on an approved requirements document (Fischer, 2009). While Agile teams do not focus on producing these documents, a business analyst within a CAMS-based approach would recognize the need and work to produce these deliverables earlier in a project life cycle.

A holistic understanding of the business as well as the associated technologies is part of the business analyst's repertoire. Some BA work can be routine, requiring a basic ability to observe. In other cases, business analysts require excellence in detailed and in-depth modeling techniques. BA activities spread across many other areas of work in an organization. For example, BA activities intersect with enterprise architecture, quality assurance, and user-experience-related work. These BA activities need to be organized and standardized for practical use. A commonly accepted framework for BA can come in handy here.

Business Analysis and Agility

Handling Agile Challenges in the Context of Business Analysis

Challenges posed by Agile methods in projects and organizations were discussed in Chapter 3. CAMS suggests the use of a business analyst's skill set as a complement to the Agile values and practices and vice versa. This combination is a much better way of handling practical BA work, especially within the earlier parts of a project (Ambler). The Agile challenges discussed in Chapter 3 are further expanded and discussed here from a BA viewpoint.

Scalability

Business analysis activities should be able to scale up and handle a large number of processes. Agile practices used by business analysts also need to scale up. Managing large projects with large number of developers (typically, more than 50 developers, but the number can vary) requires breaking them down into smaller projects. These projects can then be assigned a package or subsystem for development. Business analysts in CAMS take advantage of Agile practices (e.g., visibility and collaboration) in undertaking requirements modeling. The organizational level and the scale of work become important in employing Agile practices. For example, beyond projects, and at the organizational level, BA has to scale up to handle macro decision making such as mergers and acquisitions and setting up of collaborations. Not all Agile practices are suitable for this kind of decision making.

Outsourcing

Outsourcing work, particularly that which is offshored, requires far more formality than is envisaged by the Agile Manifesto. Among the many needs of outsourced projects is the requirement of business analysts to model, in detail, the requirements for the project. These requirements are the ones that are outsourced for actual development. Ascertaining the quality of delivery of functionality against the requirements is also an important part of project work as the eventual payment is based on the successful testing of that documented functionality. Business analysts in CAMS are in an excellent position to create formal documentation using standardized notation and the corresponding tools. This output can be used in outsourced projects to index payments against delivery—something not easily possible while following a pure Agile method.

Technology

Business analysis interfaces with technology in ascertaining the capabilities of the organization and also in creating process models that will be supported by technologies. For example, networks and their bandwidths place technological limitations on the capabilities of a product. Business analysts undertake this investigation together with the enterprise architects to determine the availability of bandwidths required for a product to operate. Since this analysis is not a straightforward development activity, pure Agile practices may not be very helpful here.

Business analysts have to combine their analytical skills together with Agile practices in order to determine the technological capabilities for a project. Another example of challenge to Agile BA work can be the numerous legacy applications (in multinationals in particular) that require more effort in maintenance than in development. Here, the BA skill set reverts back to creative modeling of business processes that make good utilization of legacy data for online business. Furthermore, data-intense applications require modeling of myriad data formatted for multimedia that requires excellence in BA skills.

Compliance

Within an organization, there are many activities and artifacts, encompassing a myriad of rules and regulations that a business is required to comply with. Compliance with legislations that are external to the organization requires generation of artifacts including process models, documentation of business rules, SLAs, and contracts, among others. With the advent of Sarbanes–Oxley-type legislation, these artifacts become especially important in the IT department even when it is in operational mode. Formal needs for the documentation of business rules, models, and procedures require a BA skill set that may not concur with the values of the Agile Manifesto. CAMS encourages business analysts to start their work by identifying and listing the compliance needs of a project together with that of the product when it comes into operation. In doing so, not only does the business analyst ensure compliance with the legislations but also helps in protecting the intellectual property being generated during the project.

Another example of BA assisting with compliance is in the area of the environment. BA explores corporate environmental practices, sustainability policies, regulations, and contractual obligations of the organization and its suppliers to meet environmental standards. Such green BA (Unhelkar, 2011) brings together enterprise analysis, requirements elicitation and analysis, and solution assessment and validation in determining the green optimal solution that will fulfill the business needs. Green process areas dealing with procurement, operations, application design, and/or disposal of computing resources also make use of a BA skill set in defining the scope and requirements of the work to be carried out for carbon compliance purpose.

Business Rules

Business analysis has to specifically and separately deal with business rules. These rules are typically embedded electronically in the functional models of systems. Rules can also be paper based and followed manually within the organization. Business rules have a wide-ranging influence on the manual processes used by individuals within the organization as well as the software systems and applications with embedded business rules. Irrespective of the positioning of business rules, they have a bearing on the requirements. Therefore, there is a need to correlate rules to organizational policies and business requirements. Agile principles and practices may not easily enable modeling of rules. Rules are not the visible part of requirements; neither are they functional in nature. Therefore, a separate effort is required by business analysts to understand and document business rules within the overall project requirements.

Change

CAMS welcomes the pure Agile principle of encouraging and embracing change. What can be challenging in practice is the need to revisit, trace, understand, and compare the effect of change.

For example, when the requirement from a user changes (i.e., a user story changes), not only does that particular story change, but it may also require a previously "done" story to be "undone," worked upon, and then "redone."

Furthermore, as stories get developed, the insight caused by the addition of new stories invariably impacts completed stories. This change can be managed acceptably in a relatively small and bounded project. Large and complex projects discover that the impact of change of one story on others (especially "done" stories) can quickly escalate into confusion, rework, and even errors.

In fact, rework on stories can be the cause of complexity in some projects—especially as stories too tend to depend on each other. While developing stories fully does provide insights, not all of the new understanding and insights need to be gained by undertaking full development. A story is not fully "done" ("done-done") unless it is right. A story is "right" only in the context of other stories that may be in different stages of development.

Therefore, breaking the work down into small, achievable chunks (a story, or groups of related stories) still requires considerable amount of analysis that is focused on the "interrelationships" between the stories. There are many changes that can be easily picked up by good analysis work before developing a single story. Although many insights may be unforeseen, not all are unforeseeable. Besides, there is no guarantee that developing a story fully will necessarily provide the understanding that users need to bring about additional changes to the requirements.

Composite Agile focuses on substantial up-front requirements modeling that investigates and understands these interactions and dependencies. Formal BA work in modeling requirements reduces waste and rework. CAMS recommends numerous "if-then-else" scenarios up front in the analysis rather than during (or after) development of stories. Such analysis in modeling requirements expands the boundaries within which users "think."

SIDEBAR BA in Agile

Beal (2011) puts forward some excellent reasons why skilled business analysts are required even in an Agile work. For example, the "just-in-time requirements" of Agile, together with anticipated early user feedback may not always discover missing or inaccurate requirements. The argument here is that systems thinking, which considers in-depth impact of one activity or event on the rest of the system, may not always come naturally to many of us. The user involved in an Agile project may not always think the way a developer thinks. A business analyst, however, is trained to consider the impact of one decision on many other areas of the system. Critical thinking is a significant part of the BA repertoire. A business analyst starts with the premise that the behavior of a system is not just a sum of the behavior of its individual parts. Similarly, a software solution is much more than the sum total of all its stories. There is a lot more to a fully functioning system wherein stories have dependencies on each other and they interact with each other. This is a crucial area of work in projects that is well served by a business analyst.

This formal modeling of requirements in CAMS is also immensely helpful during acceptance testing. For example, when users are asked to explain or test their required features,* they tend to focus only on a particular feature they are testing. There may not be enough attention paid to its relationships with the rest of the system. As also put forward succinctly by Beal (2011), "unless you put sufficient effort into requirements discovery and analysis, requirements may not be completely known even *after* users have tested and approved pieces of functionality delivered sequentially." Further, note the nonuniformity in the changes to the requirements. In fact, different kinds of

* "To discover the details behind the requirement, the developer (or developers on project teams which take a pair programming approach), ask their stakeholder(s) to explain what they mean." Source: http://www.agilemodeling.com/essays/agileRequirements.htm. Scott Ambler's website.

requirements change at different rates (Brennan, 2010). For example, user interface requirements can change dynamically—and the greater the visuals provided to the user, the faster they change. However, operational requirements relating to a database or security may remain stable for a very long time. Understanding the subtle and gross variations in requirements is important in the judicious application of Agile principles and practices within BA.

BA and Agile Practices in CAMS

Agile values, principles, and practices have a role to play in BA work across projects and organizations. CAMS suggests embedding of these Agile practices within the BA activities in an organization. Figure 7.2 shows the opportunities for Agile practices by business analysts at various levels within the organization and projects. These are further described here:

- Business needs exploration: This is where business analysts bring in practices of questioning, brainstorming, and risk analysis in conjunction with senior business executives, subject matter experts (SMEs), and users. The business analyst works here, in exploring the "real" needs of the business through facilitation, negotiation, and problem-solving skills. The business analyst needs to understand the trends in the market and the opportunities that are likely to arise. For example, the need to comply in carbon emission trading creates market opportunities as well as the need to change existing offerings (Sherringham and Unhelkar).

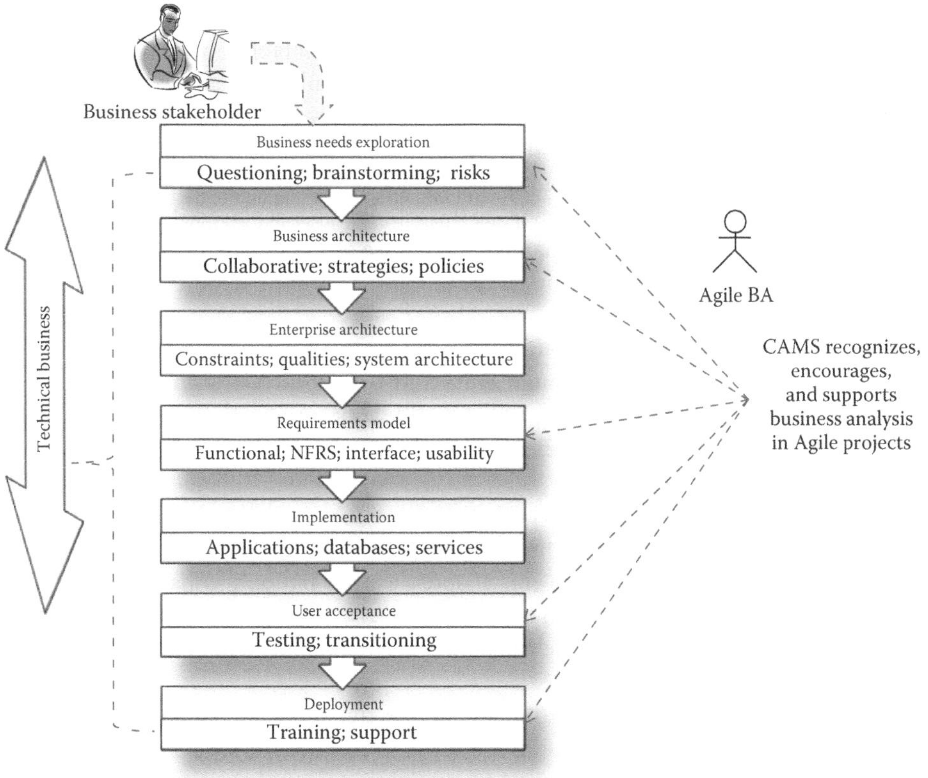

Figure 7.2 Levels of BA activities and opportunities for Agile practice.

- Business architecture: In dealing with *business architecture,* the analysts bring in their collaborative skills in understanding the myriad dependencies between various areas of a business. The formulation of strategies and policies is influenced by the understanding of the business architecture. The business analyst needs to understand the customers of a business and how the customers' business operates. This analysis includes what the customers need now as well as what their future needs are likely to include.
- Enterprise architecture: This is created and maintained at a more technical level than business architecture. BA deals with the constraints or limitations on the business needs and capabilities from a technical viewpoint, and the expected qualities of the system by the business stakeholders. Enterprise architecture influences the specific system architecture as the constraints and qualities at the organizational level, ascertained through BA, are applied to the system in development.
- Requirements model: This comprises the model of the functional, nonfunctional, interface, and usability requirements of the system. This has been the most popular BA activity and, although very important at a project level, is not the only major activity of a business analyst (as seen from the previously described activities here).
- Implementation: This is where the BA activities are carried out in close cooperation with the development and implementation activities relating to the actual software application, databases, and Web Services. While the business analyst does not directly produce these outputs, he is closely associated with this work by providing relevant inputs, explanations of the models, and pointing out to dependencies between requirements.
- User acceptance: User acceptance involves testing and transitioning the many business processes to the new processes based on the new implementation; these tests are all carried out in close association with business analysts. This is mainly so because the business analysts are responsible for defining the requirements and, so they are also in a position to test (and assist in testing) the newly developed solution.
- Deployment: This is where business analysts are involved in facilitating user training and providing the necessary system support as the solution gets deployed. Business analysts can also play a handy role during the maintenance phase of the system as they enable tracing of requirements and formally changing them.

Business analysis functions at various levels within an organization. At project level, BA competencies help improve quality through enhanced communication, process modeling, and analyzing risks. Figure 7.3 shows the value added by BA work specifically at the project level. This value of BA work in projects is further described next.

- *Communication* within a project, especially using visual modeling techniques (such as use cases, activity graphs, and business process models). CAMS encourages the use of these modeling techniques (discussed later in this chapter) as they not only enhance communication by providing the basis for discussion between the users, developers, and the business analysts but these same documented models also provide traceability later, when the system has moved into maintenance.
- *Management* of the project from a process perspective using the corresponding standards (and process maturities, e.g., Capability Maturity Model Integration [CMMI]). The requirements modeling process map, discussed later in this chapter, is a part of the composite approach to formalizing process engineering and requirements management. Process maps for project management, development, architecture, and quality assurance have to all relate

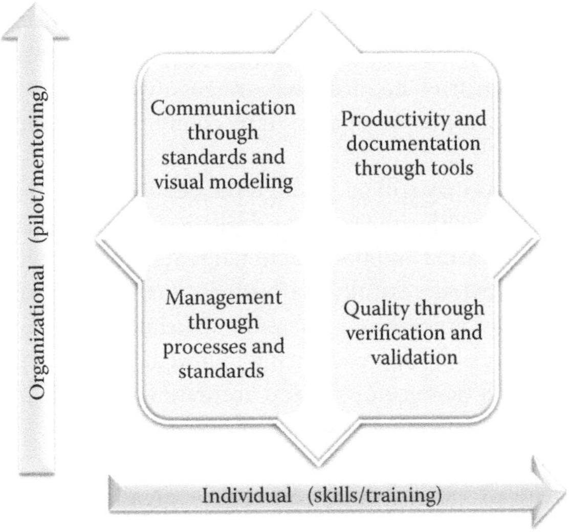

Figure 7.3 Business analysis—value in projects.

with the business evaluation and requirements modeling process map for the effective management of a project.

- *Documentation* with CASE tools (e.g., *Visual Paradigm, Enterprise Architect, Visio, Star* Unified Modeling Language [UML]) that facilitate sharing and maintenance of visual models. CAMS encourages the use of tools to enable sharing—especially if project members are dispersed physically—of requirements by business analysts with technical roles (architects and developers) and thereby enhance productivity and quality. Tools in the BA space also enable the important step of traceability of requirements when the system has moved into production.
- *Verification and validation* on an ongoing basis to handle quality. BA work adds immediate value to the quality of the product within a project because not only are requirements modeled formally but walk-throughs and inspections of the models themselves reduce errors and misunderstandings substantially before the actual coding has begun. The use of a quality standard (e.g., ISO9001) and a testing framework (e.g., International Software Testing Qualifications Board [ISTQB] discussed in Chapter 9) can also go a long way in enabling verification and validation activities of a business analyst as they provide a reference point to build on.

As also shown in Figure 7.3, the value addition by BA work occurs along two axes:

- Contributions made by individual business analysts and their associated up-skilling and training to make them effective at the project level.
- Strategic dissipation of BA skills and knowledge across the organization. Mentoring and coaching across the organization (as is facilitated through a Center of Excellence in CAMS) enhances this BA knowledge management that goes across from one project to another at an organizational level.

A practical view on BA is that it is a cost-saving and quality-enhancing activity when compared with undertaking actual, physical development without it. While making the initial development effort a part of the exploratory work involving prototyping is a good idea, undertaking actual development and using that as a means to capturing further requirements usually turns out to be more expensive. This cost is incurred because users are not always able to anticipate the effect of a functionality on the rest of a system. Composite Agile combines the Agile practices together with BA to realize cost saving.

While the business analysts may still go through the detailed rigor of capturing and modeling requirements, they collaborate with the users to prioritize the requirements as they get modeled and develop the detailed, functional and nonfunctional requirements only for the highest priority requirements. In order to do this successfully, the business analyst has to undertake a broad assessment of the situation (problem), understand where the stakeholders are coming from, and explain to them the analytical and modeling approach being followed. This will enable the stakeholders to express their requirements in a more complete and accurate way. Modeling of such requirements also has a major advantage in managing stakeholder expectations and, later, in undertaking the acceptance of the solution.

Business analysts relate to various other roles in an organization such as business leaders (business space), technical designer/developer (solution space), and enterprise architect and project manager (background space (Unhelkar, 2003). These interactions of business analysts with other roles occur as they undertake in-depth investigations of an organization's internal structure, its processes, its relationships with external parties, and its risks. Business analysts also delve into systems and technologies from an analytical viewpoint that helps the organization understand its current and desired future state. Occasionally, the role of a business analyst itself can take many forms including those as requirements modeler, data analyst, needs analyst, risk manager, and strategist. Figure 7.4 shows the relationship of business analysts to other roles within a project. The following is a description of this relationship of a business analyst with other roles in a CAMS-based project in which Agile values and principles are practiced together with formal roles and activities:

- Business stakeholders undertake high-level identification of business objectives, root-cause analysis, strength–weakness–opportunities–threat (SWOT) analysis, and cost–benefit analysis. They document business risks and achieve consensus among various stakeholders in terms of the objectives of a large initiative (e.g., a business transformation program). Business analysts create a common understanding between the many stakeholders and also the technical and architectural roles. Through translation, clarification, and communication, a solid understanding of what needs to be accomplished is provided to all stakeholders.
- Domain specialists (SMEs) identify key business needs that are specific to the business domain. Business objectives based on investigation and identification of root causes are carried out by domain specialists/SMEs together with business analysts. Their work includes in-depth discussion of the problem in the context of the business domain, exploration of previous solutions to business problems, and identification of patterns in problems, and their solution.
- The usability specialist identifies the usability needs and applies the principles of usability to interface design. This work is carried out by analyzing the business needs in terms of ease of use, security, and scalability needs of the electronic front end (Web portal), categories of users, and risks associated with the use of the system. Specifying the usability needs in the use cases and user stories and, later, after they are developed, ensuring that the usability requirements are met is a key activity of a business analyst together with the usability specialist.
- Business users/product owner are the roles that associate with a business analyst in terms of gathering of requirements, their documentation through detailed use cases, writing of features and requirements in user stories, identifying dependencies among stories, and putting

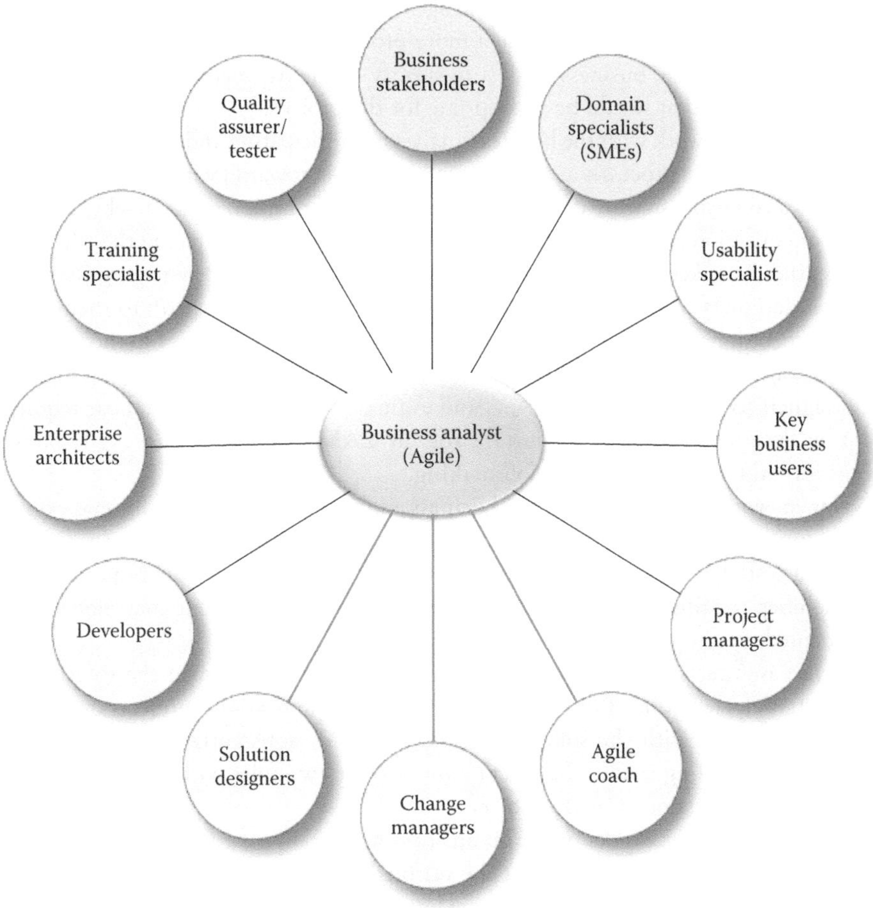

Figure 7.4 The business analyst and multiple organizational and project relationships.

together groups of use cases and stories based on common themes. Users and product owners also work with the business analyst in refining requirements on an ongoing basis and deciding together on their acceptance criteria. The business analyst, however, does not interfere with the business users/product owner's privilege to make decisions in terms of risks and priorities associated with functionalities.

- Project managers are responsible for managing time, budgets, and requirements. Business analysts work closely with project managers in updating the scope and priorities of requirements. Participating in the collaborative approach to managing projects enables the business analyst and the project manager to come up with appropriate schedules for design, development, and testing. Conflicts within projects can also be resolved through facilitation and negotiations on the part of these two important roles—the project manager and the business analyst. Eventually, the business analyst also assists the project team in terms of maintenance of the product by enabling traceability of requirements and undertaking ongoing testing of a product that is deployed.
- The Agile coach relates to the business analyst in undertaking Agile practices such as daily stand-up meetings, updating visible charts, and measuring project velocity. The business

analyst supports the coach in undertaking a comparative analysis and identification of dependencies among stories to enable a more productive and focused iteration. CAMS, in particular, requires the business analyst to specify to the Agile coach the extent and format of documentation that would be appropriate for the project.

- Change managers work with the business analysts in anticipating and planning for the change especially to business processes as the organization moves toward Lean-Agile business. Change managers also enable sharing of progress across the organization and, thereby, make it easier for the organization to change. Business analysts are geared to understand the effect of change and are, therefore, keen to associate with the person responsible for managing change.
- Solution designers work together with the business analyst and explain to them the impact of design decisions on business processes and vice versa. When it comes to the nonfunctional (operational) requirements of a system, the business analysts need to interact closely with the designers to experiment, prototype, and evaluate the correct level of those requirements. Solution designer's is a more important role in CAMS than in a pure Agile project as it brings formality in technical decision making.
- Developers work very closely with the business analysts in providing additional explanations of the stories, their dependencies, their usability requirements, and the way in which the users will test the stories. Business analysts regularly remind the developers of the hard-to-remember requirements, dependencies, and business rules (that may not all be easily documented on a story card).
- Enterprise architects work toward understanding the constraints on the solution from an organizational viewpoint and the qualities of the system at the project level. Enterprise architects together with the solution designers provide substantial technical input in the background modeling space. The interaction of these two roles with the business analyst is crucial to the success of a CAMS project.
- The training specialist works with the business analyst in putting together training plans for the solution and also working out the various modes of deploying that plan (electronic, paper, company intranet, etc.). During deployment, the business analyst helps in providing a range of examples (simple to complex) that will suit the training for various types of users.
- The quality assurer/tester, together with the business analyst, ensures that the solution meets the requirements. The business analyst can provide input into creating test strategy and test designs. The business analyst also helps in specifying the variety of suitable test data that will satisfy the needs of user acceptance testing.

Business Analysis Frameworks and Agility

Business analysis (BA) frameworks provide structural and behavioral basis for analytical work. CAMS formalizes BA work with the use of these frameworks. A BA framework describes the competencies, skills, mind-set, knowledge, and experience expected of the business analyst. This description is helpful not only in enhancing the quality of BA work but also in embedding Agile practices within the BA work. The knowledge and competencies required of a professional BA are standardized, ranked, and assessed within these frameworks. Once these competencies are standardized and ranked, it becomes easier to consider and use them in the context of Agile practices. BA frameworks also clarify the differences between BA and other areas of work in an organization. For example, a BA framework easily clarifies that requirements elicitation is an important yet only small part of BA. Enterprise architecture and IT governance are examples of other areas of work that are different from that of BA. A good BA framework will also indicate that software-related analysis is only a variation of the work undertaken by business analysts.

Requirements elicitation, their analysis, workshop facilitation, and running focus groups are examples of activities undertaken by business analysts. The intensity of Agile practices within these activities will change depending on the type, size, and complexity of the projects. BA uses the Agile practices of (say) on-site customer collaboration and negotiation to go deeper in modeling functional and nonfunctional requirements (using use cases or user stories), process models (using Business Process Modeling Notation, BPMN), and data models (using high-level class diagrams). A proficient business analyst in CAMS thus operates in a much more holistic way than any other role.

Business context is crucial for establishing, developing, and monitoring the right set of key BA competencies within CAMS. A company that specializes in software products for an international audience, for example, may need to emphasize competencies related to knowledge of ethnic-oriented issues and culturally appropriate communication techniques, whereas for a consulting company working with local businesses, the main focus may be on the ability to quickly understand the problem domain and present possible solutions to clients.

A BA framework also facilitates the application of a BA skill set across a wide range of industries. For example, aerospace and automotive, or engineering and financial services industries will apply BA in different ways. Some industries, such as the telecommunications industry, are heavy on infrastructure requirements, whereas financial services would have extensive functional requirements. Each industry has its nuances that require clarifications and explanations in the application of BA skills. A BA framework provides the basics of BA work that can be translated across these industries.

Competency models for BA have been developed by consortiums and associations (see Figure 7.5). These competency models need to be modified and fine-tuned to reflect the organization's concerns and goals. CAMS recommends starting off with an existing BA framework and then adapting it to suit the Agile style of working in an organization.

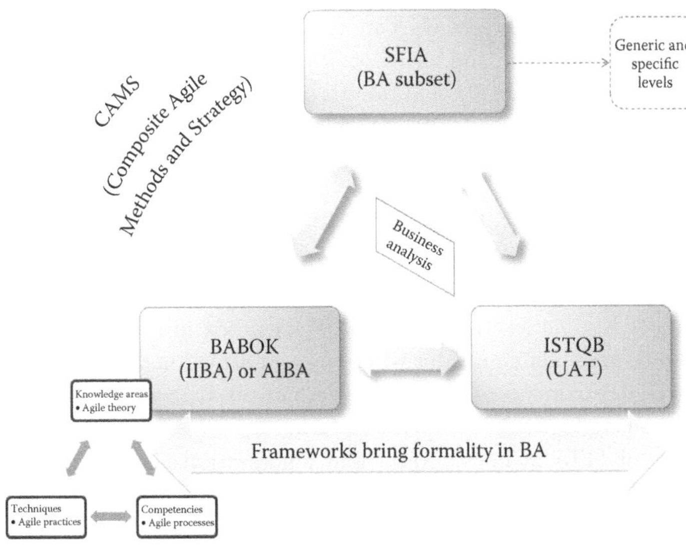

Figure 7.5 Agile business analysis and BA frameworks.

SFIA, IIBA (BABOK®), AIBA Frameworks

Figure 7.5 shows the popular BA frameworks of Business Analysis Body of Knowledge (BABOK), (IIBA), and the SFIA, which provide the basis for skills and competencies of BA. The AIBA* also offers an alternative competency model for BA. ISTQB is an increasingly popular testing framework that is also helpful in BA space (as it provides the basis for user acceptance testing activities, discussed in greater detail in Chapter 9).

Awareness of these frameworks and their constituting elements opens up the opportunity for incorporating BA work in Agile projects via CAMS.

The BABOK is by far the most popular among these frameworks. BABOK comprises three dimensions: knowledge areas, competencies, and techniques (shown on the bottom left in Figure 7.5). BABOK also provides a well-accepted description of a business analyst's responsibilities through six major activities: planning and monitoring, requirements elicitation, requirements analysis and documentation, requirements communication, enterprise analysis, and solution assessment and validation. IIBA, the owner of BABOK, runs certification exams for business analysts.

Table 7.1 lists the major activities within the BA space. These activities are primarily based on the BABOK. They are described here in the context of Agility. A mapping of these activities with SFIA (described next) is also provided in this description.

The SFIA† is a more comprehensive framework that covers all the skills required in the information age. CAMS considers a subset of the SFIA skill set that deals with BA and recommends the use of Agile practices within those BA skill sets. These SFIA-based skills for business analysts together with Agility are discussed next.

SFIA and Agile BA

The SFIA provides a common reference model for the identification of the skills needed in the information communications technologies (ICT) space. SFIA is expressed as a two-dimensional framework, one dimension containing the areas of work, and the second, the levels of responsibilities. The seven levels of responsibility in SFIA are further described through the four generic skills of autonomy, influence, complexity, and business. This framework lends itself to various mappings in IT-related domains. For example, in addition to being used by ICT practitioners (to position and label their skills), SFIA also assists human resources (HR) departments (to create a skills matrix and growth road map for employees), education and training providers (Lindley, 2010), and governments (e.g., the UK government).

Given the complexity of BA work spread over wide areas of an organization and through the many levels of responsibilities, the SFIA provides an excellent mechanism to create a reference framework for a BA. This BA framework can then be incorporated in the job descriptions, profiles of specific BA roles at various levels, corresponding expected mind-sets, and training requirements. This can also be of tremendous value when large, multinational organizations merge and/or are acquired. The HR departments of these organizations can base their recruitment, up-skilling, merging, and retention strategies on such a framework.

The applicability of SFIA at both project and organizational levels is of major interest to CAMS. Agile practices can be embedded in BA work through the well-defined SFIA skill sets.

* www.businessanalysis.com.au.
† www.sfia.org.uk.

Table 7.1 BA Activities and Agility

Activities	*Description*
Business analysis planning and monitoring	It deals with planning the analytical effort, especially up front even before a project has been defined. It starts with identification of stakeholders and is followed by selection of appropriate business analysis techniques, their sequencing, and approach to assessing the progress of the work. Iterations and increments, collaboration, and excellence in modeling can provide value in this activity (this activity maps to SFIA RLMT level 5).
Requirements elicitation	This activity is focused on eliciting requirements from key business stakeholders. These are high-level business needs, associated concerns and risks, and the discussion and documentation of the outlines of proposed solutions and transition requirements. UML-based models can provide the formal techniques for eliciting and tracing requirements. A working software as a prototype can clarify and prioritize requirements (this activity maps to SFIA REQM level 5).
Requirements management and communication	This activity deals with creating a shared understanding of the requirements across the project and the organization by ensuring all stakeholders are informed about the requirements. Management of requirements includes modeling them, documenting the models, and communicating them to a broad and diverse range of audience. Achieving consensus of requirements through collaboration and face-to-face communications is a key part of this activity (this activity maps to SFIA BUAN level 5).
Enterprise analysis	This is a broad-ranging domain analysis of the problem or business need. This analysis will identify a business need, and refine and clarify the definition of that need by placing it in the context of the enterprise; the end result is a problem definition that is created, keeping the entire enterprise-level context in mind. The ensuing enterprise architecture provides the balance between the various systems existing (and to be developed) in the enterprise (this activity maps to SFIA ARCH level 5).
Requirements analysis	This is the activity of elaborating and modeling key user requirements that can then be created into a solution that will meet the needs of the organization and stakeholders. Frequent changes can be accepted here and the simplicity of design influenced (this activity maps to SFIA CIPM level 5).
Solution assessment and validation	This deals with the verification and validation of the proposed solutions to determine the suitability of the best-fit solution, as well as identifying gaps and shortcomings in those solutions. Changing and fine-tuning the solutions is a part of this activity (this activity maps to SFIA BPRE level 6, BPTS level 5).

RLMT, Stakeholder relationship management; ARCH, Technical strategy and planning – Solution architecture; CIPM, Change implementation planning and management; BPTS, Business process testing.

The following are the SFIA skill sets used by business analysts operating at level 5 of SFIA (based on the author's experience*, this is the most common level applicable in practice to BA work):

- Stakeholder relationship management: The coordination of relationships with and between key stakeholders, during needs exploration, management, and implementation of business change. Business practices and leadership Agile practices benefit by the use of formal relationship management (these and subsequent references to Agile practices are from Chapter 4, Figure 4.13).
- Requirements definition and management: This covers the definition and management of business requirements and their scope. The specification of business requirements needs to be carried out to a level that enables their effective delivery. Agile practices including close liaison with users, writing of user stories, and estimation of efforts can be used in practicing this BA skill set.
- Solution architecture: This involves creation of structural frameworks (hardware, software, and other components) that meet the present and future requirements of an organization and understanding the interrelationships between these components. This work also includes participating in the design of solutions that automate business processes and resolve business issues in a particular business or functional area; providing direction and guidance on all technical aspects of the development of, and modifications to, information systems to ensure that they take account of relevant architectures, strategies, policies, standards, and practices; and ensuring that existing and planned systems and IT infrastructure remain compatible. Agile practices of simplicity of design, refactoring of design and code, and prototyping of database can be used in this BA work.
- Change implementation planning and management: This work involves the definition and management of the process for deploying and integrating IT capabilities into the business in a way that is sensitive to and fully compatible with business operations. Holistic approach to change, as shown in Figure 4.13, is a key part of this work.
- Business process improvement: This deals with the identification of new and alternative approaches to performing business activities and the analysis of business processes, including recognition of the potential for automation of the processes, assessment of the costs and potential benefits of the new approaches considered, and, where appropriate, management of change, and assistance with implementation.

Figure 7.6 shows an SFIA-based BA reference framework. This figure shows the two categories of SFIA skills, the specific and the generic. The seven levels at which these skills operate is also shown in this figure. CAMS considers this framework relevant in the BA space because of the relevant skills within its structure. The other important contribution SFIA makes is its generic category, which easily relates to the Agile values (described in Chapter 2) and Agile practices (described in Chapter 4). The four generic skills are described below.

1. Autonomy: This describes the level of freedom a person has in carrying out the tasks. The level of autonomy is determined by whether the person has the skills to follow instruction versus the skills and freedom to create instructions for others to follow. A business analyst working under the composite Agile umbrella will exhibit this generic skill set when she

* As an author of the Australian Computer Society's Business Analysis course and a distance education tutor for the same course.

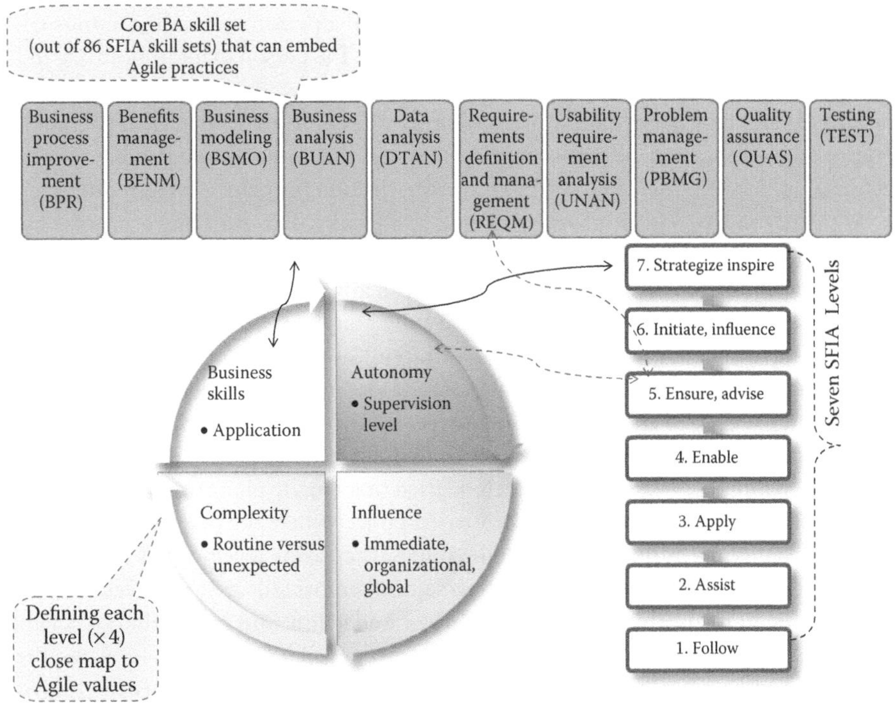

Figure 7.6 The SFIA-based business analysis framework.

works under broad direction but is fully accountable for her own technical work and/or project/supervisory responsibilities. Increasing levels of autonomy will imply the ability to establish her own milestones followed by those of the team. Assignments are received by an autonomous person in terms of key objectives. These objectives, together with an understanding of their value, result in creation of subsequent, detailed objectives and tasks, delegation of responsibilities, and provisioning of suitable autonomy to the team in terms of carrying out those objectives. An increasing level of autonomy indicates increasing skills and ability to initiate areas of work and set the key business objectives associated with that work.

2. Influence: This is indicative of the skill set of a person that brings about changes at various levels within the organization. Starting with influencing the work colleagues in the immediate vicinity, this skill leads to bringing about positive changes at the project, division and organization, and industry levels. In exhibiting this generic skill in a composite Agile project, the business analyst will influence peers, customers, suppliers, and the organization based on his specialism. Influence can be expanded based on the specialist skills together with undertaking significant responsibility for the work carried out by other members of the team. Planning and management of resources and allocation of tasks indicate an increasing level of influence. An Agile coach or project manager carries that influence through decisions that impact on the success of assigned projects, that is, results, deadlines, and budget. Increasing the range of influence depends on the creation of success stories, developing working relationships with colleagues and customers, and exhibiting excellence in BA-specific skills described separately.

3. Complexity: This skill is an indicator of the ability of a person to handle an unusual, highly interdependent, and rapidly changing suite of tasks. The person exhibiting this skill handles a range and variety of complex technical or professional work activities that are inherently multitiered and that depend on other activities to be completed. Increasingly complex work requires the application of skills in wide-ranging and often unpredictable contexts. The relationship between own specialism and wider customer/organizational requirements need to be clearly understood in order to handle complexity. For example, a process model for handling the cash withdrawal function in a bank needs to be weighted and compared for its risks versus its convenience in electronic, physical, and mobile user format.
4. Business skills: This skill enables a person to fully grasp and understand the way in which a business (typically a large and global organization) operates. A person exhibiting this skill advises the organization on the available standards, methods, tools, and applications that are relevant to his own specialism. This advice, in turn, is helpful to the decision makers in making correct choices from their available alternatives. The phases of "analysis, diagnosis, designing, planning, and execution" can be used in formally planning and evaluating work. Business skills are invaluable in a CAMS-based project where the project parameters of time, cost, and quality are as important as Agile values. Increasing levels of business skills include increasingly effective communication (formal and informal) at various levels (colleagues, subordinates, and customers), demonstration of leadership, and facilitation of collaboration between stakeholders who have diverse objectives. Analysis of high-level requirements, scopes, and risks are a part of this skill set. Business skills are also used in advising on the overall scope of major business initiatives and options for operational improvement. Generic business skills bring together creativity and innovation with the business knowledge and technologies to suggest holistic business solutions that will benefit the stakeholders (customer, user, business owners).

Figure 7.6, on the right, also shows the SFIA levels ranging from Level 1 through to Level 7. These levels, shown on the right in Figure 7.6, provide an indication of the overall competency of a business analyst in handling increasing levels of complexities and responsibilities in business. These seven levels of SFIA are (1) Follow, (2) Assist, (3) Apply, (4) Enable, (5) Ensure, Advise, (6) Initiate, Influence, and (7) Strategize, Inspire. In subsequent sections in this chapter, these SFIA levels are further expanded and mapped to BA activities in an Agile project.

In addition to showing the generic skill sets and levels in SFIA, Figure 7.6 also shows on top the core skill set of a business analyst. This skill set is derived from the original SFIA skill set comprising more than 80 skills. The skills selected for this BA framework are business process improvement (BPRE), benefits management (BENM), business modeling (BSMO), business analysis (BUAN), data analysis (DTNM), requirements definition and management (REQM), usability requirements analysis (UNAN), problem management (PBMG), quality assurance (QUAS), and testing (TEST). CAMS extends the original description and aims to place Agile values and practices within that skill set. This composition of Agile with BA skills can vary between organizations and their industrial sector. The sidebar provides one such description that can be used as a template for description of other BA skills. A more detailed description for each of the 10 skills from the SFIA skill set that apply to BA can be directly accessed through the SFIA Web site. When these core skills, the levels, and their definitions are taken together, a comprehensive BA framework emerges that provides a sound basis for describing BA work within and across organizations. Each component of the aforementioned skill set, belonging to the BA framework, is briefly described here:

SIDEBAR ***Business Modeling (BSMO)****

Category: Business change
Subcategory: Business change management

DESCRIPTION

The business analyst , using this *business modeling* skill, will be producing abstract representations (or models) of business situations. These models or representations are used by the business analyst to facilitate the communication and understanding of existing, conceptual, or proposed business scenarios. The mental and visual models are used to represent processes, data, organization, and time. Business modeling occurs at varying levels of detail and can be broken down to suit the situation. Agile values (mapping closely to the generic SFIA skills) together with the Agile principles and practices can be used by business analysts to carry out business modeling (BSMO):

(This skill is described from levels 2 through 6 in the SFIA and, accordingly, only those levels are described here in the context of the BA framework.)

LEVEL 2

Understands the purpose of creating requirements models and their benefits. Uses Agile techniques (e.g., user stories) together with established techniques (e.g., flow charts or activity graphs) as directed to model simple subject areas with clearly defined boundaries. Participates by assisting in more complex modeling activities. Develops models with input from subject matter experts (SMEs) and communicates the results back to them for review and confirmation. Uses the Agile practice of "incorporating feedback instantaneously" in the requirements model.

LEVEL 3

Conversant with various requirements modeling techniques (e.g., use cases, user stories) that cover the entire range of modeling situations. Creates "as is" and desired models. Able to select appropriate modeling techniques to meet the assigned objectives. Also able to decide which Agile practices will be relevant for use in the business modeling exercise. For example, uses negotiation and facilitation to gain agreement from SMEs on the models produced. Reviews resulting models with stakeholders and gains resolution of issues.

LEVEL 4

Conducts advanced BA (modeling) activities that are part of business change programs. Analysis at this level occurs across multiple business functions. Has an in-depth knowledge of organization-standard techniques. Able to plan and scope own modeling activities, select appropriate tools and techniques, and ascertain the right level of detail for meeting the assigned objectives. Contributes to discussions on the modeling approach together with the appropriateness and relevance of Agile practices. Obtains input from and communicates modeling results to senior managers for agreement.

LEVEL 5

The business analyst, at this level, is able to analyze situations holistically for the entire organization. The resultant models, including "what if" scenarios, are produced in support of business strategy. Has in-depth knowledge of a broad range of industry-wide modeling techniques. Advises on the choice of techniques and approach and influences customers accordingly. Is capable of developing models for unusual contexts. Fully aware of other methods,

* While the original name, code and description of this skill are produced by SFIA, I have extended and modified it here in the context of Business Analysis work. Similar modifications are required for the rest of the selected BA skill sets.

standards, and approaches used in the organization, and therefore, capable of understanding "methods friction" in the organization and taking initial steps to avoid it through Composite Agile Method and Strategy (CAMS). Takes the responsibility for planning and coordinating team modeling activities and for ensuring the quality of their work.

LEVEL 6

At this level, the business analyst is able to create modeling standards for use within the organization that are based on industry standards. Has continuing responsibility for the maintenance of models for a designated function. Initiates organization-wide modeling improvement activities and obtains customer buy-in to general changes. Understands "methods friction" and strategizes to avoid it through CAMS. Develops and spreads expertise in estimating efforts through metrics. May represent own organization as a modeling expert in industry initiatives.

- Business process improvement (business process reengineering, BPRE): This identifies new and alternative approaches to performing analysis of business processes. Recognizing the potential for automation and assessment of the costs and potential benefits of the new approaches within the analyzed processes is considered here. Where appropriate, management of change and assistance with implementation are provided. Examples of Agile principles relevant to BPRE include customer collaboration, acceptance of changes, and simplicity in design.
- Benefits management (BENM): This includes monitoring for the emergence of anticipated benefits (typically specified as part of the business case for a change program or project). Thus the program management team applies this skill set to ascertain and optimize the business benefits. Formal metrics and measurements throughout the project play an important part in BENM. Agile principles such as customer satisfaction and collaboration play an important part in managing expectations of the benefits (as perceived benefits can be as important as actual benefits from a customer's viewpoint).
- Business modeling (BSMO): This skill set focuses on the production of abstract representations (or models) of real-world situations to aid the communication and understanding of existing, conceptual, or proposed business scenarios. BSMO is predominantly focused around the representation of processes, data, organization, and time, thereby making use of the formal, planned elements in a project. Models may be decomposed to represent the business scenarios at varying levels of detail. Agile principles of simplicity in design, technical excellence, and face-to-face conversation can be applied in BSMO in particular. An example of how BSMO is used at various SFIA levels (2 through 6) is shown in the sidebar.
- Business analysis (BUAN): This skill is utilized in undertaking systematic investigation, analysis, review, and documentation of all or part of a business. BUAN carries out analysis in terms of business functions and processes, the information used within the processes, and also the relevant data. At the early levels of SFIA, BA focuses on requirements; but as the SFIA level increases to level 5 and above, BUAN skills are utilized in organizational-level (and abstract) decision making. BUAN benefits by some Agile principles. For example, BA is undertaken, keeping customer satisfaction in mind. Self-motivated individuals and self-organized teams assist in cross-functional BA.
- Data analysis (DTAN): It is a skill set used in the investigation, evaluation, interpretation, and classification of data. Such data analysis is undertaken in order to define and clarify data and information structures. These data and information structures represent relationships between real-world entities. Such data structures and schemas are the basis for modeling in composite Agile. These models enable linking of data with software systems, links between systems, and facilitate strategies for data storage, backup, and retrieval.

- Requirements definition and management (REQM): The definition and management of the business goals and scope of change initiatives is carried out by the use of this SFIA skill set. The specification of business requirements is detailed to a level that enables effective delivery of agreed changes. Requirements need to be defined in detail to improve processes and systems. While Agile methods focus on writing of user stories on story cards for requirements, formal methods document requirements through use cases, activity graphs, and BPMN. REQM can use the best of both formal and Agile approaches by creating viable specifications, subjecting them to quality assurance techniques, and setting the acceptance criteria for the solution.
- Usability requirements analysis (UNAN): The establishment, clarification, and communication of usability requirements (e.g., screen design/layout/consistency, response times, capacity) is undertaken here. Usability requirements can be considered as "nonfunctional requirements" in a project. The analysis of the characteristics of users and their tasks, the technical, organizational, and physical environment in which products or systems will operate, and the aesthetics of the solution can be provided through UNAN. Customer satisfaction and collaboration with the customer become vital in UNAN.
- Problem management (PBMG): The resolution of incidents and problems throughout a project life cycle (typically software life cycle), including classification, prioritization and initiation of action, documentation of root causes, and implementation of remedies is a part of PBMG. The Agile principle of self-organized teams that are anticipating changes and incorporating them in the solution is well equipped to handle problems.
- Quality assurance (QUAS): It is the SFIA skill set that is employed in ensuring adherence to the agreed quality standards within an organization. QUAS promulgates best practice throughout the organization and, thereby, supports sustainable development.
- Testing (TEST): This skill set focuses on using and maintaining *testware* (test cases, test scripts, test reports, test plans, etc.) that are used to measure and improve the quality of the software being tested. Testing embraces the planning, design, management, execution, and reporting of tests, using appropriate testing tools and techniques and conforming to agreed standards. Testing also makes provision for feedback on the tests carried out and planning and managing regression tests. Systems, configurations, packages, or services, together with their interfaces are tested in order to ensure that they perform according to specifications. This, in turn, requires specifications to be formally documented within projects as part of the composite approach.

Each of these levels of SFIA form a matrix with the generic SFIA skill set and the specific BA skill subset.

Figure 7.7 shows activities specific to the BA roles at various levels within an organization in the context of the SFIA skill set. These activities are divided into three layers or groups. BA contribution in an organization can be considered at each of these levels in the context of Agile projects. CAMS enables a business analyst to make a formal and substantial contribution to each of these layers or groups. At each of these layers of work, the business analyst enhances the accuracy of development, alignment of solutions, and improvement in quality.

BA-SFIA Levels 1–4

The first group, corresponding to SFIA levels 1–4, comprises operational or routine activities performed by a business analyst. These activities include data and requirements modeling, operational modeling, quality assurance and testing, and training the users for deployment. This is also the layer for maximum opportunity to employ Agile-related practices by business analysts.

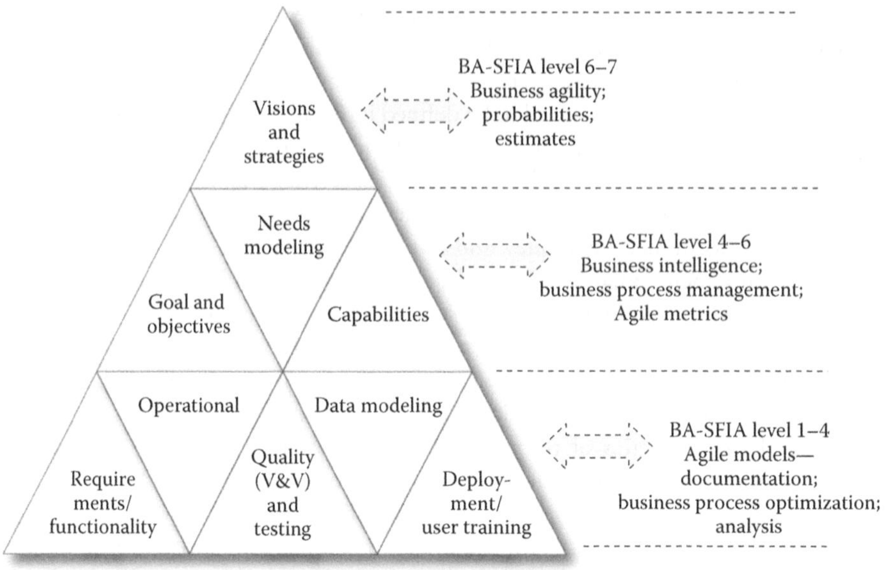

Figure 7.7 SFIA levels and BA-Agile (tools and techniques).

This is so because with the help of use case models, BPMN, and activity graphs, requirements modeling within projects is carried out here. Depending upon the depth of analysis required and the scope/area of influence, even operational requirements are created and prototyped, quality reviews undertaken, and acceptance tests organized. Participation in user training after systems are deployed also occurs at this layer. Use of Agile practices in order to create requirement models, design models, and carrying out of development occurs in this layer.

BA-SFIA Levels 4–6

The second group of BA activities, corresponding to SFIA levels 4–6, are more strategic than the previous level. Activities at this level include enhanced techniques for modeling business needs and capabilities. The level of work at this level includes strategizing to make use of business intelligence and business process modeling tools and technologies. Modeling at this level relates to the organizational processes within and outside the organization. Business analysts at this level carry out investigations to outline smart business strategies and set up programs for their implementation. BA skills at these levels include critical thinking, the ability to determine the needs and capabilities of a business, and the ability to prioritize business objectives. These BA skills capitalize on overall Agile values (especially at level 6) rather than on precise Agile practices, which are of greater value in the earlier levels. BA work at these SFIA levels enhances the maturity of the business through process maturity and the use of BA frameworks. This work may originate at the departmental level and eventually move to the organizational level.

BA-SFIA Levels 6–7

The organization, setting out in a new strategic direction, will required visionary analysis work that will be carried out by BA at levels 6 and 7. At these levels, the analysis deals with ascertaining the industry direction from a business perspective, organizing the people, processes, and technologies holistically, and setting long-term directions for the organization. The Agile values discussed in Chapter 2 form part of the work at this SFIA level. For example, skills and experience in applying Agile values can be used in ascertaining probabilities, estimates, and risks. The analysis work at this stage is a combination of abstract individual skills at the highest level and collaborative business intelligence and decision support systems.

Comparing SFIA and IIBA with Agile

Table 7.2 summarizes the mapping between SFIA and IIBA's BABOK competencies of business analysts and the corresponding impact on an Agile approach. As this gets written, the IIBA is inviting comments on its draft Agile extension to the BABOK guide (IIBA). The outline of this guide provides an excellent mapping between Agility and BA skills. In particular, the principles and practices of Agile related to BA, and the role of BA within Agile life cycles are neatly outlined in the draft (subject to further comments and improvements). The mapping between IIBA, SFIA, and Agile in Table 7.2 continues to underscore the theme of composite Agile—an amalgamation of Agile principles and practices with the known BA skill set that will result in value for the business.

Table 7.1 underscores the importance of BA and its frameworks in CAMS. The areas of work in BABOK and the skills subset of SFIA provide value to both project and business agility. Further

Table 7.2 SFIA–IIBA Business Analysis Competencies and Impact of Agility

IIBA's BABOK	*SFIA-BA*	*CAMS (Agile) Importance*
Planning and monitoring	Business modeling (BSMO)	Response to external changes is much better managed through models and plans created here
Requirements elicitation	Business process improvement (BPRE); data analysis (DTNM)	Individuals and their interactions can be further improved through processes and their documentation
Requirements analysis and documentation	Requirements definition and management (REQM); usability requirement analysis (UNAN)	Formal requirements documentation facilitate their analysis, review, and development of software
Requirements communication	Problem management (PBMG)	Customer communication (especially in outsourced projects) needs visual models, documentation, and tools
Enterprise analysis	Benefits management (BENM)	This is business agility and does not include software agility. Enterprise architecture frameworks and processes are integral
Solution assessment and validation	Quality assurance (QUAS) Testing (TEST)	Requires dedicated acceptance testing including for operational requirements that is *beyond* the tests to create working software

organization-specific work is required to amalgamate Agile principles and practices with the specific BA skill set required by the organization. For example, business analysts undertake stakeholder analysis, identification, and management of issues, risks, and requirements that are required in any project irrespective of its development approach. Agile principles within these activities will change depending on the business ecosystem and the business goals of the organization.

Business Process Management and Agility

SIDEBAR

Business process management (BPM) can be carried out in a number of ways, and using different tools and techniques. Innovation in business process reengineering is a synergy of business process thinking and corresponding tools and techniques. Orr (2007) has described the concepts and strategies involved in business process innovation including the major threads of business process thinking. This discussion also includes technical approaches, such as service-oriented architecture (SOA), that are closely intertwined with BPM. The relationship between SOA and BPM becomes more important in the green enterprise space as changes to processes to make them green cannot be brought about independent of the information and enterprise architecture. Michael K. Guttman and John H. Parodi have also outlined in their Cutter article the potential convergence of the BPM, SOA, and model-driven architecture (MDA) paradigms. This convergence leads to efficiency and effectiveness, and also business agility.

The CAMS umbrella provides business analysts with the opportunity to influence wider areas of the organization than developers working under pure Agile approaches. The focus of BA at an organization level includes not only modeling of requirements but also root-cause analysis, cost–benefit analysis, process modeling, value-stream mapping, and creation/use of metrics and measurements. This BA work overlaps the domain of business process management (BPM), which includes overall management of all internal and external processes of an organization.

BPM is a well-established industry practice encompassing process modeling, reengineering, and optimization of processes, and the measuring, merging, and elimination of business processes. Processes are one of the four core aspects of business organizations (among technology, people, processes, and money aspects of the organization). BA gets involved in BPM to enable changes to *the way* in which business is carried out. BPM facilitates the *Lean* approach to business optimization, which provides not only economic benefits to the organization but also advantages in terms of sustainability and environmental performance.

Processes are investigated by business analysts at an organizational level in order to undertake process transformation and management. A process can be understood as the "manner in which" things are carried out within and by an organization. Processes are thus the "how" aspect of an organization's functions. The manner of operating a machine, the manner of serving a customer, the manner of administering human relations, and the manner of sales and marketing activities by an organization are all examples of these processes. Other examples of the "how" of an organization include how a customer withdraws cash in a bank; how a passenger buys an airline ticket; and how a patient is admitted to a hospital. These are common examples of business processes that, in reality, are highly complex and intertwined with other processes as well as technologies and people.

Business analysis is involved in modeling and investigating these processes in detail in order to reveal invaluable opportunities to optimize them. Some processes are challenged for their necessity in the first place, others are optimized for efficiency, some others are made more effective and Agile, and all are measured in order to ascertain these characteristics. The exploration of processes in this manner leads to many opportunities to improve and optimize them. These business processes are analyzed based on the criteria of whether they are necessary, efficient, effective, Agile, and measurable in the context of an organization. These process characteristics are summarized in Table 7.3.

Business process management and optimization builds on the fact that significant advantages can be gained simply by changing the way things are being done in the organization. For example, in the cash withdrawal process by a customer, efficiency can be achieved by, say, not printing a physical receipt; or reducing the time in the queue for a physical cash withdrawal by applying the principles of operations research. While process reengineering and the corresponding process management have been a part of business strategies, here, we pay particular attention to processes from a Lean-Agile-collaboration perspective. Transforming the organization to one based on Lean-Agile processes is a part of business process reengineering (BPR).

Table 7.3 Process Characteristics and Lean-Agile Importance

Process Characteristic	*Description*	*Lean-Agile-Collaborative Importance*
Necessary	Challenges the need for the process in the first place. There is no point in making a process efficient and effective if it is not creating business value	Eliminating an unnecessary process (not involving in value creation) will also eliminate its associated wastage
Efficient	Models the process to study its various activities/tasks. Challenges, automates, and merges activities to ensure they are performed with the best tools, technologies, and people	Reduces wastage by optimizing and/or eliminating the activities/tasks within the process. Technology is embedded in the process
Effective	Ensures that the process is actually achieving the goals it is meant to achieve. A process that is otherwise efficient and Agile, but which does not achieve business goals is not considered as effective	Collaborative processes are more effective than individual ones as they operate using each other's strengths. Also, a process that is repeated more than once in order to produce the desired effect is an *inefficient* process
Agile	Deals with the ability of the process to change itself in response to (or in anticipation of) external and internal changes affecting the organization. Deals with the dynamicity of the process	An Agile process will change easily and effortlessly in response to a changing external situation. This flexibility is possible with Lean processes that are focused only on one specific business goal and are collaborating for the rest
Measurable	Enables monitoring, controlling, and ascertaining the success of its optimization. Ongoing management of process performance is also supported	Provides understanding of the Agile value in the process. Measurement helps in identifying the slack and optimizing it

SIDEBAR Business Process Management

Business process management (BPM) is an overall approach to modeling, optimizing, consolidating, and executing the business processes of an organization. Application of BPM results in improving the ways in which an organization (users and business areas within an organization) undertakes operations. BPM can be understood as a discipline of modeling, realizing, executing, monitoring, and optimizing business processes.* Each of these aspects of BPM can be applied to an organization within CAMS. Silver (2006) has described various flavors of BPM such as enterprise application integration (EAI), workflow, content management, and enterprise-wide human and system process automation. Composite Agile would undertake these BPM activities by embedding Agile practices within them. BPM approach in an organization can be considered as a set of management and technology disciplines focused primarily on workflow and process automation that drives the implementation of optimized and sustainable business processes.

Such optimization of processes covers many aspects of the performance. Processes can be optimized to ensure efficient utilization of resources. Alternatively, processes can be reengineered to creatively eliminate the use of some redundant or duplicate resources. For example, a home loan (mortgage) process that requires application by a broker, credit check validation, and risk assessment through three separate agencies can be electronically consolidated as one. Such reengineering of processes has been a hallmark of business efficiency over the past few decades.

Business Process Reengineering (BPR)

Reengineering has been described as the fundamental rethinking and radical redesign of business processes to achieve dramatic improvements in critical contemporary measures of performance such as cost, quality, service, and speed (Hammer and Champy, 1993). Davenport and Short (business process redesign, 1990) developed the ideas of reengineering further toward holistic redesign of the organization based on processes. BPR aims at a complete and radical change to the entire organization as against a piecemeal change per department. BPR includes fundamental changes to the processes and their ongoing management. BPR also creates organization-wide, holistic, and dynamic opportunities for optimizations that are not only limited to specific process changes but also changes on an ongoing basis. BPR can thus be considered as a vital aspect of CAMS as used by BA.

Process reengineering stands to gain from the concepts of "Lean" and "Lean IT." The popularity of these "Lean" approaches in business and IT can be attributed to their focus on reducing and/or eliminating wastages within the organization processes. The relevance of Lean specifically in CAMS was discussed in Chapter 6. Lean approaches are initially applied by large and global organizations in order to produce process optimizations because such large enterprises are ideally suited to apply and capitalize through Lean processes.

Large-scale processes and their corresponding value streams (such as those from mining, agriculture, and airlines sector) can be reengineered by their detailed modeling, application of metrics and measurements, and introduction of technologies (e.g., mobile technologies). This is mainly because of the potential for changes to the entire business practices, business models, and

* An ACS report "Carbon and Computers in Australia", 2010, cited by Graeme Philipson in HRG. http://www.aiia.com.au/docs/AIIA%20and%20the%20ICT%20Industry/Green/ACS%20Carbon%20and%20Computers%20Energy%20Consumption%20and%20Carbon%20Report%200510.pdf.

methods. Lean approaches have also been used toward greening an organization (Unhelkar, 2011), and studying their impacts on enterprises, government, and society.

Thus, it is not only the changes to the processes or "how" an organization operates that is important but also the underlying business models, technologies, and social aspects of that business. For example, business processes need not be only supported by technology resources, common infrastructure, or application platform but also through a transparent business methodology (see www.business-ecology.org) and business models. IT plays a substantial role in providing a utility or a service to the business that can then be used by the business in its models and methods, such as Lean, to become green.

BPM includes reengineering of business processes to optimize them. Reengineering of processes includes reevaluation of processes and also an understanding and modeling of their supporting hardware, software, and people. The BPR (Hammer and Champy, 1993) exercise depends heavily on undertaking a model-based, performance-driven approach that is applied to the entire organization.

Consider a manual distribution process, with steps leading from the manufacturer through to the warehouse, retailer, and the end user. A reengineering exercise will lead to the formulation of an electronically enabled process that will provide business efficiencies and effectiveness in terms of the distribution network. Such efficiencies are typically achieved by displaying the product on an organization's Web site and enabling the consumer to order it directly from the Web site. With such reengineering, the steps associated with the wholesaler and the retailer can both be avoided—although the intermediaries can be the technology service providers and content managers (Unhelkar and Ginige, 2010).

Further reengineering of a process is efficient and effective from a cost, time, and even carbon viewpoint. For example, the new process model will aim to completely eliminate the E-intermediaries. Customer-driven reengineering will optimize collaborative business processes to eliminate the steps that were required only because of lack of alternative technologies (Unhelkar et al., 2010) by using location-sensitive mobile technologies. The premise here is that if the same process goal is achieved with fewer steps, the process itself will be efficient and less prone to errors (due to reduced number of steps).

Metrics and measures help in understanding the effects of reengineering. For example, a reengineered process can be measured for the time, effort, cost, quality, and service involved in producing goods, undertaking customer searches, packaging and distributing goods, and administering the organization. The resultant quality and end-user experience due to BPR has spin-off benefits for the organization. As Nott (2010) mentions, increasing awareness of the environment among businesses has also opened up the opportunities for businesses to use the BPM approach to model, measure, analyze, and mitigate the carbon impact of business activities.

The BPR initiative leads to customer-focused processes whose end goal is to achieve customer satisfaction rather than create hierarchical reorganization. Serving a customer efficiently, providing an enhanced customer experience, and having an efficient and optimized supply chain reduces waste and increases value for the organization.

In addition to Lean and reengineering, it is also worth mentioning Total Quality Management (TQM) when discussing efficiency in business processes (more details in Chapter 8). TQM brought about significant changes to the way an organization operated—imposing discipline and quality consciousness to the organizational processes. The resulting improvement in quality leads to a reduction in rework. Such reduced rework occurs within a high-quality and efficient business process that achieves its goal in a single attempt for each process cycle. This in turn, reduces costs and increases user satisfaction.

Processes: Individual, Organizational, and Collaborative

CAMS aims for agility in all of the organizational processes. These processes within an organization can be categorized as individual, organizational, and collaborative processes that need to be considered in detail during process reengineering. Changes made to the processes can be either tactical (bearing immediate results) or strategic (long-term results). In general, individual processes tend to be tactical and tend to provide quick wins. Changes to collaborative processes tend to deliver longer term results, although modeling and optimization of the collaborative processes requires more time and effort and include more players and multiple systems.

SIDEBAR

Leanness and Agility of an organization can be achieved by understanding the differences between the core processes and peripheral activities of the organization. Modeling and optimizing of core processes have higher risks than the corresponding peripheral processes. For example, a hospital has its core competency of treating patients. A hospital is often associated with pharmacies for dispersal of medications and pathology laboratories for conducting a suite of tests on patients. These pharmacy and pathology processes closely support the core processes dealing with treatment of patients. The core and the peripheral or supporting processes need to be modeled, measured, and optimized. For example, a hospital should approach very carefully the modification of its patient-related core processes because there are corresponding increased risks to the patient. Therefore, each step within the process has to be studied before it is changed or eliminated.

Table 7.4 summarizes these types of processes and also lists the key factors that are important in handling these processes. Processes can vary widely depending on their importance, their

Table 7.4 Process Categories and Composite Agile

Process Categories	*Key Factors*	*Comments with Respect to Composite Agile*
Individual	Attitude, training	Personalized processes are influenced by attitude and training. Therefore, CAMS suggests additional attention in terms of motivation of the individual, his personal value system, and the corresponding personal reward and growth that the person would look for while practicing Agility
Organizational	Policies, rules, KPIs	Organization-wide processes can become Agile through their dynamic creation and management; this is particularly effective when applied to the underlying business rules that dictate the process. Metrics are crucial to demonstrate the ROI for the BPR exercise
Collaborative	Portals, forums, standards	Collaborative processes transcend organizational boundaries. These processes are put together through portals that generate knowledge based on multiple organizational inputs. Incorporating Agility in these processes is most challenging as these processes encompass processes, rules, and people from many organizations and across regions

KPIs, key performance indicators; ROI, return on investment

technology support, and the end goals they achieve for the organization. Ideally, processes need to be identified and modeled from end to end. In reality, especially for large businesses, there will be layers within processes leading to the idea of composite processes, that is, processes containing subprocesses and sub-processes containing activities. Furthermore, the business rules embedded within the business processes also need to be addressed in reengineering of processes. Consider, for example, the existing business rules associated with, say, a cash withdrawal process that requires two forms of identification that will have to be adhered to. The manner in which the rule is implemented (e.g., matching of signatures with stored electronic signatures, or validation of pin codes) can be optimized by modeling, studying, and changing the activities of the process.

During a BPR exercise, careful evaluation of all these business processes at individual, organizational, and collaborative levels within the organization needs to be undertaken. During this evaluation, these processes are listed, ranked (prioritized), modeled, optimized, and eventually, either retained or eliminated. Such evaluation of processes, independent of the technologies of implementation, is an important part of CAMS. This is mainly because CAMS isolates business processes and evaluates them for their merit to the end user who is not interested in the underlying technology. Therefore, a CAMS-based development effort follows the formal BPR while still using Agile practices as relevant. The business process evaluation steps, as applicable collectively to all processes in the organization, can be further described as follows:

- Listing of all processes within an organization: This is an initial list that is refined as the BPR exercise proceeds. This list can be created on the basis of the value creation of the organization and it can be categorized into primary, secondary, or supporting processes on the basis of the major functions of the organization such as production, inventory, supply chain, customer relations, finance, and HR. The end users are the customers for each group of processes. Therefore, collaboration with the end users is vital in identifying which processes actually exist and are carried out by users. Each group of processes can again have levels, such as end-to-end processes, subprocesses, activities, and tasks. Each process within the list can have a description of what it provides or which goal of the organization is served by the process.
- Ranking of the processes within the process list: This can be undertaken based on inputs from business stakeholders, SMEs, and enterprise architects. BPM exercises list the processes with the corresponding criteria such as their costs and effectiveness, and the ranking is meant to provide an understanding of which particular processes should be given the highest priority in terms of reengineering. The practices of prioritization within Agile approaches can be applied here to rank processes.
- Modeling process reengineering: This requires accurate modeling of those processes. If an organization has already undertaken a BPM exercise, process models for all major processes should be available. If not, the business transformation project can start by modeling the processes that are ranked high in the previous step. Process modeling can make use of the UML (particularly its use cases and activity graphs), user stories, BPMN and IDEF, as these are all well-known techniques for process modeling. Agile principles and practices can enhance modeling of processes by facilitation collaboration, maintaining simplicity in design of the processes, reflection to enhance quality, and acceptance of changes.
- Optimizing: This is the step of studying the processes that have been modeled from the point of view of optimizing them. Optimization depends on the various factors impacting the process, the opportunities provided by technologies (e.g., mobile technologies) to achieve the same process goals by eliminating steps, and applying the metrics to ascertain their success. In optimization, the process model can be studied to ascertain the resources consumed by the

activity. That activity can then be modified to cut the resources; alternatively, with the use of technologies and systems, some activities within a process can be totally eliminated if found to be unnecessary. The optimization of processes is a substantial part of the BPM exercise and has to be taken up with due consideration to all other dimensions of the organization (see the discussion on business transformation in Chapter 6). Metrics and measurements (discussed in Chapter 9) also play an important part in optimizing processes as they highlight and compare the benefits of optimization of processes.

- Retaining processes that are modeled and optimized: This will reduce their resource consumption and add value to the organization's end goal. These are the processes that can be retained and placed in a continuously optimized mode. These processes will also be the core business processes of the organization that have to be maintained in the best possible way. Therefore, processes that are ranking high on the priority list are most likely to be retained. Once retained, these processes need to be further optimized through iterations.
- Removing: This BPM exercise identifies processes that are either redundant/duplicated or are so excessively inefficient that they have to be replaced. These are the processes that will be removed from the suite of business processes. The impact of their removal has to be studied across all other business dimensions before the processes are removed. In practice, it is commonplace to discover some manual processes in organizations, which not many people were aware of. These processes are converted to systems-based automatic processes and the manual ones removed. The informal processes, however, are the most difficult to eliminate because they do not have proper process models and supporting technologies.

Customer-Driven Analysis and Agility

Reengineering of processes also leads to changes in existing organizational processes that demand a clear understanding of the potential disruptions resulting from those changes. These changes include the way the organization relates to the customers, the organization of the internal business, and the potential changes to the operating platforms. Most importantly, in undertaking BPR, customers should not be considered as "external parties." Instead, they should be invited to participate in the modeling, optimization, and management of processes. Some of the important considerations in customer-driven reengineering are as follows:

- Reengineering of processes also results in optimizing the internal organizational structure. This includes rearranging and repositioning people.
- Communications, together with IT, has led to the customers being able to effectively create their own products and services that are tailored to the specific needs; dynamic creation of products and services is the result of Internet-based communications.
- Knowledge management enables keeping track of customer preferences; now it can be used to manage the preferences of customers and the performance of the processes.
- Integration of processes is facilitated by the integration of the underlying applications and systems. Integrated processes offer tremendous opportunities for customers to fulfill their specific needs. At the same time, such integration also creates opportunities for overall collaboration and, therefore, Leanness.
- Knowledge about the customer, suppliers, and the manufacturing process can be used to strategically organize the manufacturing, call center support, and other assets of the organization in order to derive maximum value for the customer.

- Regular communications are set up with the customers in terms of their precise needs. Such identification of the needs of the customers up front enables their provision in an efficient and effective way, reducing the overheads associated with unplanned provisioning of customer requirements.
- Customer groups are created and kept engaged so that they can then participate in the strategic planning and policy formulation sessions. This can be done both face to face and electronically. An asynchronous discussion group resulting from an online collaboration can provide valuable inputs into the demands of current and future customers.
- Inputs from select customers can result in creation of training packages that facilitate ease of use of those processes by customers. Customer education and training can also result in effective use of business processes that makes use of technologies and positive attitudes in optimization of those business processes. This education and training can result in effective use of organizational processes.
- Measurement and feedback on customer service. Use of real-time metrics in terms of effort involved in business processes can result in an immediate impact on customer behavior.

Requirements Modeling Process Map

This section describes the requirements modeling process map in CAMS. This process map describes the formal process aspects of requirements modeling and also shows activities where Agile practices can be embedded. This requirements modeling can be considered as a subdiscipline of systems engineering that is concerned with the behavior, quality attributes, and also technical constraints. Requirements modeling is widely recognized as both a challenging aspect of software development and a crucial one because it lays the foundation for all the subsequent project work (Wiegers, 2006). Functional requirements of IT systems are modeled with use cases and activity graphs. Later, in CAMS, these use cases form the formal and controlling features for a number of related user stories.

Business analysis at the requirements modeling level includes gathering of business requirements, understanding and modeling processes, process analysis and optimization, and testing prior to deployment. The role of a business analyst owns and models the requirements of a system in a project. This is particularly so in a CAMS project wherein Agile practices are used by business analysts within the formality of the requirements modeling process map. Thus, the use cases described in this process map are understood and documented by the business analyst at the requirements modeling level. The business analyst is also responsible for working with the key business executives and users to determine the goal and expectation of the business process. These expectations are documented by the business analyst with reference to the technical capabilities of the IT solution. Business analysts also facilitate the diffusion of process knowledge within the organization. For example, social media tools can be used to share and promote Agility and Leanness within and across the organization.

Requirements modeling can be divided into three major parts: functional, nonfunctional (or operational), and interface. Occasionally, infrastructure requirements at an organizational level also appear as part of a system's requirement. These requirement categories are described next in the context of CAMS.

Functional requirements are the most well-known requirements as they describe the functionality or behavior of the system. They are associated with the required behaviors and operations of a system, defining its capabilities in terms of actions and responses. Functional requirements are frequently captured in the form of use cases (Unhelkar, 2006, P00A) and with the advent of Agility, through use stories. Functional requirements can arise as a consequence of new procedures or business rules emerging from corporate decisions, customer/user demands, and product usage. CAMS suggests the capturing of functional requirements through use cases and activity diagrams. Use cases can provide the subject area for a collection of user stories. However, without formal use case modeling, the functional requirements are not easy to specify in detail; neither are the business rules easily specified on user stories. A combination of formal use cases and activity graphs together with user stories is required to properly capture these requirements.

BA work is also involved in capturing functional requirements based on strategic business decisions. For example, consider a corporate guideline issued to help reduce paper reports by encouraging online reporting. While defining the requirements for a new application with reporting functionality, the business analyst must spend time investigating the capabilities needed in the system to convince users (system users and indirect users, such as managers and customers who do not work directly with the system, but need access to its outputs) to stop printing, and read from their computer screens instead. In order to achieve this objective, functional requirements may be added to the software specification to facilitate tasks related to reading and distributing online reports to their intended audiences.

There are requirements, however, that go beyond system behavior. These requirements describe the properties and attributes of the solution and are referred to as *nonfunctional requirements*. Examples of such requirements, as discussed earlier, include availability, performance, usability, portability, and robustness. The business analyst has to work together with the enterprise architect and the solution designer to put together the constraints for the product. Nonfunctional requirements need to be specified on the basis of experimental prototypes and not as iteratively as the functional requirements.

Interface requirements primarily revolve around the graphical user interface (GUI) or screens that provide information to the user and accept data from the user. These interface requirements can dictate the "look and feel" of the system, its color combinations, the navigability of its interfaces, and data entry features that prevent entry of erroneous figures (e.g., by using dropdown lists), and provide help and support to the user (e.g., tool tips). Interface requirements can also specify the interfaces between the system being developed and external systems. In situations where printing is required, these requirements deal with interfaces (e.g., layouts, exchange protocols) to the printing device.

Figure 7.8 depicts the requirements modeling process map that deals with the actual capture, engineering, and analysis of the requirements of the business in a project. This process map uses the primary mechanisms of use case modeling and activity diagramming to capture and document the problem that the business is trying to solve. In CAMS, it is absolutely crucial that those who ascertain the quality (domain experts in particular) are involved as extensively as possible in carrying out the activities and practices outlined in this process map.

The quality techniques of interviews and workshops are also very helpful in executing this process map. In addition to documenting the functional requirements in the problem space, this process map also encourages the user to provide the operational needs of the system. The user of the system or the business person who is involved in the project is ideally placed to provide the information on the expected volume, performance, and security needs of the system from the operational or nonfunctional viewpoint. This is all documented as a result of requirements modeling. Prototyping is also used in order to extract further requirements and refine the requirements already captured.

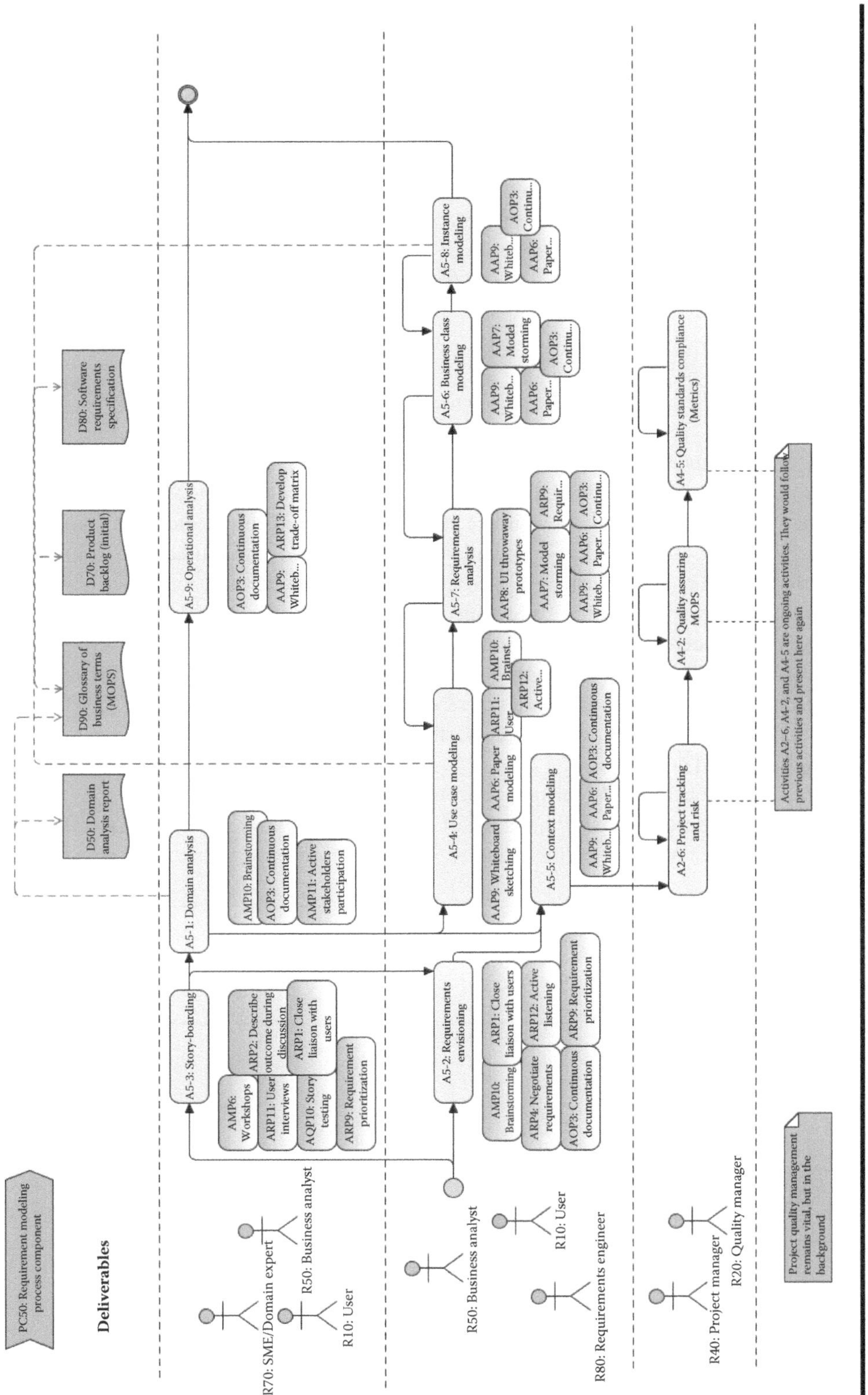

Figure 7.8 Requirements modeling process map in CAMS.

Roles in Requirements Modeling

The following are the roles in requirements modeling process map.

Business analyst (BA): This is the main role in the requirements modeling process. This role may either be combined with or (for small projects) be the same as the requirements engineer role. The business analyst is responsible for eliciting and documenting the requirements.

Subject matter expert (SME)/domain expert: An SME/domain expert is an expert with special knowledge and skills in the insurance area.

User: A user is an on-site representative of the customer.

Deliverables

The following are the deliverables in the requirements modeling process map.

Domain analysis report: The domain analysis report is a document that contains the results of the domain analysis conducted by the domain expert/SME, business analyst, and user. Figure 7.9 shows an example of a simple class diagram from the medical domain. Such a "static-structural" class model—also called a *domain model* when used at this high-level analysis—provides an excellent view of the key business entities and their relationships. In the example shown in Figure 7.9, the business analyst has identified key business entities such as hospital, department, doctor, surgical, consultation, dentistry, and operating theater. Optionally, this diagram also shows the relationships between classes. Figure 7.9 shows the association, aggregation, and inheritance relationships between classes.

Glossary of business terms: In this document, the ambiguous and essential terms for the project are explained and documented.

Requirements specification: The entire system behavior is described in this document. It includes functional specifications (MOPS, Model of Problem Space) and operational specifications (MOSS). The key business entities (Figure 7.9), user stories, use cases, and corresponding

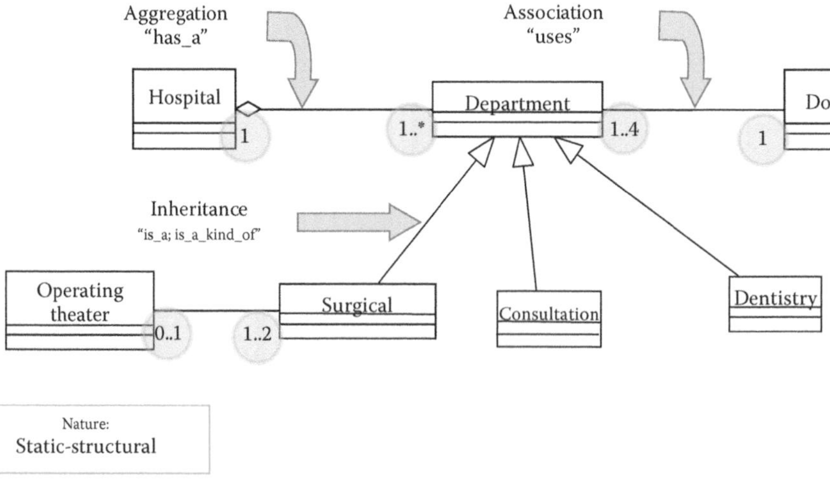

Figure 7.9 Business domain models (with class diagram).

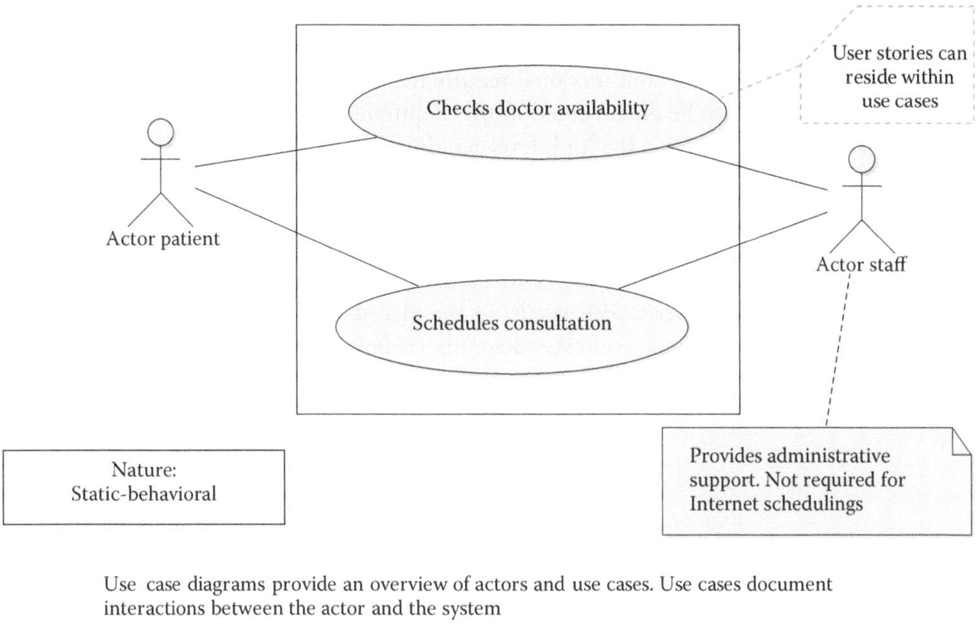

Figure 7.10 Use case diagram in requirements model.

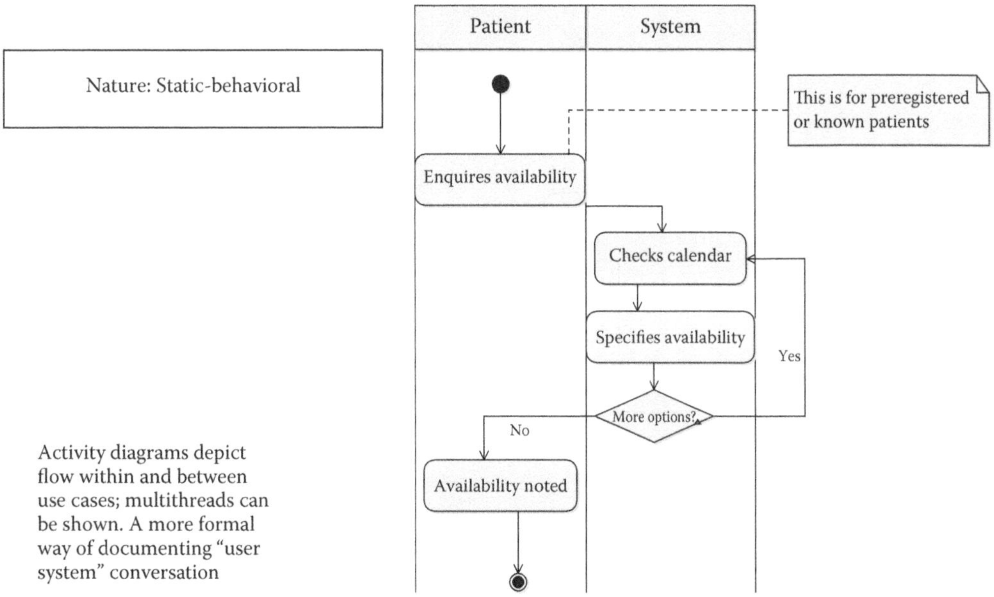

Figure 7.11 Activity diagram in requirements model.

use case diagrams (shown in Figure 7.10), activity diagrams (Figure 7.11), and state diagrams (Figure 7.12) are recorded in this requirements specification document. These UML diagrams are welcomed in CAMS as adding formality to the modeling of requirements. Bossavit (2009) ratifies the use of UML diagrams in the context of Agile: "An Agile approach consists not of dismissing notations such as UML…, but of putting them in their appropriate place." Thus, additional UML-based diagrams can also be used here depending on the needs of the project. Furthermore, the nonfunctional requirements, for example, performance, security, and reliability, can also be documented in this requirements specification.

Product backlog: This contains the high-level requirements that are ordered according to the priorities determined by the customer and the team. They can be changed during the project execution to meet the changes in the environment and user needs.

Business analysts undertaking requirements modeling explore the business domain together with the users and domain experts. This results in the identification of key business entities that can be put together in a business-level class diagram as shown in Figure 7.9. This figure shows

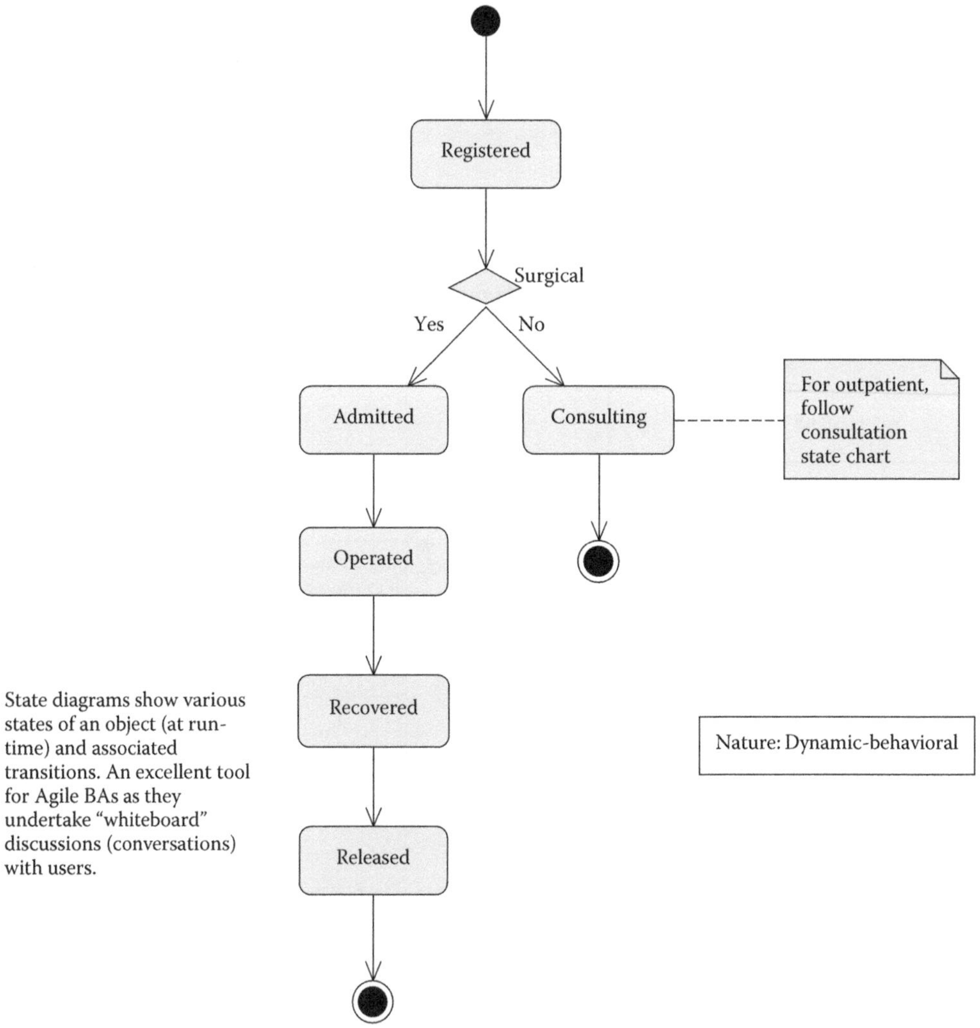

Registered
Surgical
Yes
No
Admitted
Consulting
For outpatient, follow consultation state chart
Operated
Recovered
Released
Nature: Dynamic-behavioral
State diagrams show various states of an object (at run-time) and associated transitions. An excellent tool for Agile BAs as they undertake "whiteboard" discussions (conversations) with users.

Figure 7.12 Dynamic modeling with state diagram.

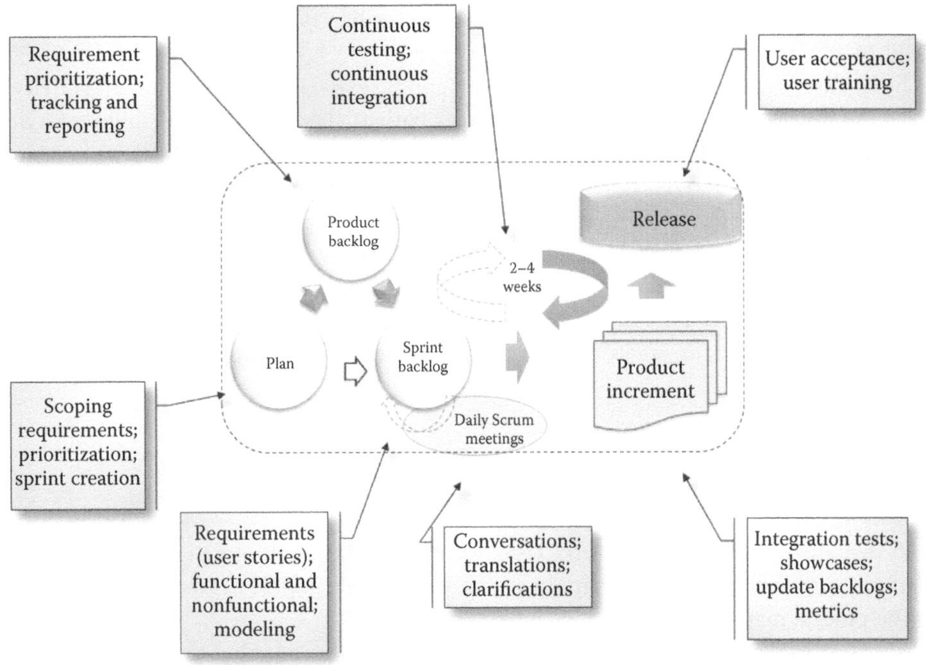

Figure 7.13 Business analysis touch points in Scrum.

classes such as hospital, department, and doctor. There are three types of departments, namely, surgical, consultation, and dentistry. The surgical department is associated with the operating theatre. This is a static structural diagram with these key entities and their relationships. The two basic relationships between classes are inheritance and association, with a specialized form of association called *aggregation*. Multiplicities, shown in circles on Figure 7.9, indicate the number of instances (or objects) of a class associated with another class. Requirement models can depict these static structural classes derived from the business domain. Developers, especially in an Agile project, can take these classes from the problem domain and develop them rapidly using Agile practices. However, the existence of these classes on a business-level class diagram (or business domain model) provides good opportunity to trace the requirements and enhance the quality with walk-throughs and inspections of these class diagrams.

Figure 7.10 shows a typical use case diagram created by a business analyst working closely with the SME. In this example use case diagram, depicting the scheduling of a consultation in a typical hospital management system, the two key actors are actor patient and actor staff. These actors are associated with the books "Checks Doctor Availability" and "Schedules Consultation" use cases. Documenting the details of each of these use cases is a formal exercise undertaken by the business analyst in an iterative and incremental manner. Thus, even if user stories (or features) are considered as a unit of requirements in a pure Agile approach, still in CAMS, we embed stories within use cases, which form the basic unit of requirements. Since stories do not have a formal place within use cases, the latter is treated as a theme or a subject area for multiple stories. Grouping of stories, as occurs within a product backlog (and later in sprint backlog), can be easily carried out with the help of use case diagrams. As compared with stories, which are written on cards and stuck on walls, with well-organized use case diagrams, it is possible to apply formal quality techniques of walk-throughs and inspections.

Each use case, drawn in the previous diagram, can be expanded visually into an activity diagram. An example of such an activity diagram for a patient checking the availability of a doctor is shown in Figure 7.11. This diagram is static behavioral in nature. Flowing top to bottom, the activity diagram lists the activities corresponding to each of the partitions. Notes are added by way of explanations and clarifications.

Figure 7.12 is a dynamic behavioral model, also created by business analysts during the creation of the requirements modeling process map. This is the state diagram that depicts the various states of an object (or instance). In the example shown in Figure 7.12, a typical patient object is shown as going through the states of registered, admitted, operated, recovered, released, and, alternatively, consulting.

Activities and Tasks in Requirements Modeling

Table 7.5 demonstrates the activities and tasks with the corresponding deliverables and roles for the requirements modeling process map. In addition, the Agile practices, which would be utilized during the process map execution, are included.

As is seen through the discussion thus far, BA adds significant value to a project. Therefore, BA remains a vital aspect of a CAMS-based project. Agile practices have been embedded in the core BA process map, namely, that of requirements modeling. This value of BA in a CAMS project is further visible in Figure 7.13. This figure is a pictorial representation of the touch points of BA activities corresponding to a pure Agile method (such as Scrum). These touch points are an indication of how well BA activities can fit in even a pure Agile project. These touch points of BA and Scrum open up the doors for CAMS use in practice. Within the boundary in Figure 7.13 are the activities of plan, product backlog, and sprint backlog. These Agile activities can benefit by the many opportunities for formal BA to make a positive contribution to the project. For example, the plan can benefit by undertaking the scoping of requirements, which will provide input into sprint creation. The requirements prioritization and tracking undertaken in BA positively influences the product backlog. Similarly, user acceptance testing activities (in which business analysts participate) help in the Agile activity of releasing a product. Understanding and expanding on this figure can provide BA value even if a project does not follow the CAMS-based process map. Projects that are based on CAMS will find these touch points naturally occurring as they step through the activities and tasks of the process maps.

Conclusions

This chapter discussed the relationship between business analysis and Agility. The composition of BA as a profession together with the Agile principles and practices is an important cornerstone of CAMS. The discussion here, however, covered all areas of work that span needs analysis at the highest level and requirements modeling and testing at a detailed project level. The importance of BA frameworks in organizations was highlighted together with their relevance in composite Agile. The discussion in this chapter extends into project management. CAMS and project management is discussed in Chapter 8.

Table 7.5 Requirements Modeling Process Map

Activities	*Tasks*	*Deliverables*	*Roles*
A5-1: Domain analysis	Create project scope Conduct research Identify critical performance area Create package diagram Agile practices: AMP10: Brainstorming AOP3: Continuous documentation AMP11: Active stakeholders participation	D50: Domain analysis report D90: Glossary of business terms (MOPS)	R50: Business analyst R70: Subject matter expert/ domain expert R10: User
A5-2: Requirements envisioning	Determine the high-level scope Determine initial "requirements stack" Divide requirements into backlogs/executable specifications Agile practices: ARP4: Negotiate requirements ARP9: Requirement prioritization AOP3: Continuous documentation AMP10: Brainstorming ARP12: Active listening ARP1: Close liaison with user	D80: Software requirements specification D70: Product backlog (initial)	R50: Business analyst R80: Requirements engineer R10: User R70: Subject Matter expert/ domain expert
A5-3: Storyboarding	Organise user stories workshop Provide operational description Provide interface descriptions Agile practices: AMP6: Workshops ARP11: User interviews ARP1: Close liaison with user ARP4: Negotiate requirements ARP9: Requirements prioritization ARP2: Describe outcome during discussions AQP10: Story testing	D80: Software requirements specification	R50: Business analyst R80: Requirements engineer R10: User

continued

Table 7.5 (*Continued*)

Activities	*Tasks*	*Deliverables*	*Roles*
A5-4: Use case modeling	Use case workshop Identify actors, use cases Refactoring use cases Document use cases Additional use case diagrams Activity diagram Draw use case diagrams Develop Class-Responsibility-Collaborator (CRC) cards Agile practices: ARP11: User interviews AAP9: Whiteboard sketching AAP6: Paper modeling AMP10: Brainstorming ARP12: Active listening	D80: Software requirements specification	R50: Business analyst R80: Requirements engineer R10: User
A5-5: Context modeling	Create use case diagram Create activity diagrams (or alternatives, such as BPMN-based process diagrams) Agile practices: AAP9: Whiteboard sketching AAP6: Paper modeling AOP3: Continuous documentation	D80: Software requirements specification	R50: Business analyst R80: Requirements engineer R10: User
A5-6: Business class modeling	Apply multiplicities Add class details Create business class diagram Create business sequence diagrams (based on instances of use cases) Agile practices: AAP7: Model storming AAP9: Whiteboard sketching AAP6: Paper modeling AOP3: Continuous documentation	D90: Glossary of business terms (MOPS) D80: Software requirements specification	R50: Business analyst R80: Requirements engineer R10: User

Table 7.5 (*Continued*)

Activities	*Tasks*	*Deliverables*	*Roles*
A5-7: Requirements analysis	Review critical performance areas and prioritize them Analyze use cases to identify business entities Document business entity Creation (optionally) data flow diagram (or collaboration diagram) Agile practices: AAP8: UI throwaway prototypes ARP9: Requirement prioritization AAP7: Model storming AAP9: Whiteboard sketching AAP6: Paper modeling AOP3: Continuous documentation	D70: Product backlog D80: Software requirements specification D90: Glossary of business terms (MOPS)	R50: Business analyst R80: Requirements engineer R10: User
A5-8: Instance modeling	Create sequence diagrams Undertake quality checks of sequence diagrams Create state diagrams Undertake quality checks of state diagrams Agile practices: AAP9: Whiteboard sketching AAP6: Paper modeling AOP3: Continuous documentation	D80: Software requirements specification	R50: Business analyst R80: Requirements engineer R10: User
A5-9: Operational analysis	Investigate and document: Operating system needs Security needs Performance needs Technical prototype Bandwidth needs Agile practices: ARP13: Develop trade-off matrix AAP9: Whiteboard sketching AOP3: Continuous documentation	D80: Software requirements specification (operational specifications)	R50: Business analyst R80: Requirements engineer R10: User

Agile in Practice: Road Map 7

- Organize a workshop/discussion session with the lead business analysts in your organization.
- Present an outline of Agile principles and practices to the business analyst community in your organization.
- Discuss the current BA framework (if available and used) in the organization. This can be a formal framework (such as the IIBA's BABOK, or SFIA or AIBA) or it can be an informal one providing the basis for BA work within your organization.
- Explore with the business analyst community in your organization the importance and relevance of BA work within the BA framework. Especially note the issues associated with the use of the framework. Note especially the pressure points for BA work currently in the organization.
- Reconvene the discussion on BA framework in the context of Agile practices. Note whether business analysts and other stakeholders believe Agile practices will add value to their work.
- Step through the requirements modeling process map with particular emphasis on the Agile practices. Are there any additional Agile practices that are of interest/in use? These need to be embedded in the requirements modeling process map as well.
- Modify the requirements modeling process map to suit the way in which requirements are gathered in your organization.
- Review the deliverable templates and the diagrams used within those templates for the modeling of functional requirements. This will also include a review of the tools and techniques used for the modeling of functional requirements.
- Review the deliverable templates for nonfunctional and interface requirements. As per discussions in this chapter, the nonfunctional requirements, in particular, will require the creation of prototypes. How does your organization currently capture and model nonfunctional requirements? Review that process in the context of this discussion on CAMS.
- Modify/embed Agile practices within the requirements modeling process in order to carry out requirements modeling within your projects. Undertake a collaborative walk-through of the process map in order to have a "buy-in" of all parties involved.
- Consider a pilot project to experiment with composite Agile in the context of BA.
- Discuss the important issues of quality and user acceptance testing that will appear in a CAMS-based project.

Discussion Questions

- What is the importance of BA in an organization? What would happen if no BA is undertaken at all and projects directly produce code? (Discuss not only in the context of new development but also in terms of maintenance.)
- What are the core areas of work of a business analyst? How do they add value in projects?
- How does BA work differ in requirements modeling as compared with needs analysis? Why are both important?
- Identify three key roles with which you would interact as a business analyst. What challenges do you envisage in your interaction with these roles? How would you overcome them?
- Discuss two important points of comparison between the IIBA's BABOK and SFIA's subset of BA skills.

- Discuss and modify two Agile practices within the activities of the requirements modeling process map.
- Create a suite of simple diagrams based on Figures 7.10 (use case), 7.11 (activity), 7.9 (class), and 7.12 (state) of the UML. Which Agile practices come in handy while drawing these diagrams?
- Discuss the advantage and challenges in the Agile touch points in Scrum (Figure 7.13).

References

Ambler, S.W., Rethinking the role of business analysts: Towards Agile business analysts? *Agile Modeling*, http://www.agilemodeling.com/essays/businessAnalysts.htm.

Beal, A., Why skilled business analysts will not go away in an Agile world, *Modern Analyst*, July 11, 2011.

Bossavit, L., Making sense of Agile design practices, *Cutter Executive Update*, 10 (12), 2009.

Brennan, K., Move to Agile requirements, avoid analysis paralysis, Cutter e-mail advisory, 28 July 2010.

Davenport, T. H. and J. E. Short, The new industrial engineering: Information technology and business process redesign, *Sloan Management Review*, 11–27, 1990.

Fischer, B., The role of the Agile evangelist: Part I, *Cutter Executive Update*, 10 (15), 2009.

Hammer, M. and J. Champy, *Reengineering the Corporation: A Manifesto for Business Revolution*, Harper Collins, New York, 2003.

IIBA (International Institute of Business Analysts), *A Guide to the Business Analysis Body of Knowledge*, http://www.iiba.org, 2009.

IIBA, The Agile extension to the BABOK Guide.

International Software Testing Qualifications Board, http://istqb.org/, viewed 16 March 2012.

Lindley, D., Computer professional education program of the ACS, *CPeP Academic Conference, April 2010*, Adelaide, 2010, www.acs.edu.au.

Nott, D., 2010, Sustainability & agility, http://www.alinement.net/component/content/article/8-styles/41-sustainability-a-agility-with-bpm?format=pdf.

Orr, K., Business process modeling fundamentals, *Cutter Executive Report*, 10 (7), 2007.

Sherringham, K. and B. Unhelkar, Strategic business trends in the context of green ICT, *Handbook of Research in Green ICT: Technical, Business and Social Perspectives*, ed., Unhelkar, B., IGI Global, Hershey, PA, p. 65, 2010.

Silver, B., The ABCs of BPM, *Information Age*, 2006, http://www.infoworld.com/d/applications/abcs-bpm-807.

Unhelkar, B., *Verification and Validation for Quality of UML Models*, John Wiley and Sons (Wiley Interscience), pp. 290+, July 2005.

Unhelkar, B., Business analysis in the information age: Mapping to an SFIA skill set, *Cutter Executive Update*, 13 (7), 2010a.

Unhelkar, B., Business analysis in information age: Part—I; Relating business analysis to enterprise architecture, *Cutter Executive Update*, 13 (4), 2010b.

Unhelkar, B., Business analysis in agility, *Cutter Executive Update*, 11 (18), 2010c.

Unhelkar, B., Relating business analysis to enterprise architecture, *Cutter Executive Update*, 13 (4), 2010d.

Unhelkar, B., *Green ICT Strategies & Applications*, Auerbach, New York, NY/Boca Raton, FL, 2011.

Unhelkar, B., *Process QA for UML-based Projects*, Addison-Wesley, Reading, MA, 2003.

Unhelkar, B. and A. Ginige, A framework to derive holistic business transformation processes, *Proceedings of International Conference on E-Business, 2010*, Paper 44, 2010.

Wiegers, K., When telepathy won't do: Requirements engineering key practices, *Cutter IT Journal*, 13 (5), 2000.

Chapter 8

CAMS Project Management and ICT Governance

Objectives

- Combine the proven project management frameworks with Agile to arrive at a composite Agile project management approach
- Enable organization of composite Agile projects based on project characteristics such as project type, size, and budgets
- Combine the project management process map with Composite Agile Method and Strategy (CAMS)
- Show the approach to prioritization of work based on critical performance areas (CPAs) and the popular Agile technique of Must-Should-Could-Won't (MoSCoW)
- Outline the importance of information and communications technologies (ICT) governance (such as Information Technology Infrastructure Library [ITIL] and Control Objectives for Information and related Technology [CoBIT]) within composite Agile at an organizational level
- Note the significance of Agile risk management in composite Agile projects and across a Lean-Agile organization
- Present a composite view on leadership and management in Agile projects—balancing the value-based and task-based approaches, respectively
- Present a combined team structure in CAMS-based projects that takes the best from Agile and planned team formations, including a flattened team structure by encouraging a "top view" rather than a "side view" in terms of organizing Agile teams
- Present the importance and relevance of individual subjectivity in composite Agile and balance it with the need for homogeneity in Agile teams

Introduction

This chapter discusses two important areas in an organization that are interrelated—project management and information and communications technologies (ICT) governance in the context of the Composite Agile Method and Strategy (CAMS). Projects can be understood as formal, planned initiatives in an organization with specific start and end points. Agility has had its maximum impact within software development projects. Conversely, a program of work is often an ongoing initiative within an organization that undertakes continuous improvement within and across an organization. A program is made up of multiple projects, requiring Agility to have corresponding formality as a business organization deals with multiple projects in a program. The complexity of multiple projects within a program can quickly escalate beyond control, especially if the project relies entirely on pure Agile practices. The Agile practices can be called *subjective* as their effectiveness is reliant on an individual. This subjective nature of Agile practices needs careful consideration in order to successfully integrate them in formal project management. For example, psychosocial frameworks such as Myers–Briggs and transactional analysis (TA) start assuming more importance than ever before in Agile projects. CAMS attempts to integrate the subjective elements of Agile with the planned aspects of standard project management.

Most projects deal with development and change. Therefore, the focus of most methodologies is on how to produce a high-quality product within the given project parameters. However, a key consideration in development should be what happens to the product *after* it has been developed and released in production. A vital consideration of methodologies should be the maintenance cycle of a solution (such as a software system or package that has been released in an organization). Maintenance considerations, however, cannot be handled after the system or product has been released—it is too late at that stage to do anything substantial about maintenance. This is because once a development is completed, there is minimal opportunity (and minimal motivation to provide time and budget) to undertake modeling of requirements or the creation of detailed system architecture. Maintenance of such a system requires the ability to trace the requirements to the source, change the processes and code, test the changes as well as undertake regression tests, deploy the changed system, and accept further inevitable changes. Significant documentation, modeling, and control are required in this maintenance life of a system—for which there appears to be no life cycle. CAMS pays attention to the creation of requirement models and system architecture to not only enhance the quality of a product but also enhance and optimize its maintenance. Once a composite process for development is in place, it also starts catering to the anticipated issues in the maintenance and operations phases of a product. This is where the maturity of processes and governance standards can also play a vital role. Information technology (IT) governance is an ongoing control and reporting of activities related to IT, which can enhance the operational performance of a system. IT governance provides a mechanism to control services and systems together with its underlying hardware and support structure for business as usual (BAU). Therefore, when an organization adopts a composite strategy together with Agile methods, it becomes imperative for that organization to consider IT governance within Agile, and this is addressed in this chapter.

Planning and Agility in CAMS

"Responding to change over following a plan" says the Agile Manifesto. Practical experience suggests that the best response to change is possible only when there is a plan. Thinking outside the box is made possible only by a clear understanding of the box itself and its perimeter. Therefore, in

CAMS, planning is given utmost importance. When there is a need to handle change, it is undertaken *together with* respect to the plan (Maharmeh and Unhelkar, 2008). Planning is associated with a certain *wastage*. This so-called wastage is the effort spent in preparing the plan and then shelving it in practice. CAMS considers the entire effort to draw a plan as an exercise in setting the parameters "of the box." Subsequently, even if the plan is shelved (and there is no reason to believe that every plan is shelved), there is still tremendous value gleaned in the very exercise of chalking out a plan. Eventually, the plan itself may not be put to full use, but the exercise of arriving at a plan is its use in practice.

Figure 8.1 elucidates the synergy between the key characteristics of planned and Agile approaches in CAMS-based projects in practice. The well-known quartet of time–budget–scope–quality is of primary consideration in planned methods. Agile approaches, on the other hand, give primary consideration to the values of trust, honesty, simplicity, and courage. Planned methods optimize the four factors using task-based work that is partitioned, planned, controlled, and standardized. Agile values downplay formality in planning and, instead, focus on team-based sharing of tasks, welcome subjectivity, and change the working style and priorities depending on the situation and context. Figure 8.1 indicates that a practical project will need both planned and Agile characteristics. That is what CAMS is meant to be—a combination of factors.

Thus, the planned characteristics are more management focused, whereas the Agile ones are best served through leadership and facilitation. Therefore, planning in CAMS will be based on using lightweight artifacts to capture the essential aspects of requirements quickly; these requirements are then modeled in a prototype and the output used in further formalizing the plans.

Agile values lead to Agile development, which, if successful, leads to Agile management across the firm, finally creating the Agile organization (Dooley, 2009).

Iterative and incremental composite Agile plans have two aspects to them. First, these plans aim to deliver the product in an iterative and incremental manner. Second, the plans themselves are updated incrementally—based on the development and delivery of an iteration. Miller (2001), also referenced by Ghanbary and Day (2010), discusses the risks associated with pure Agile

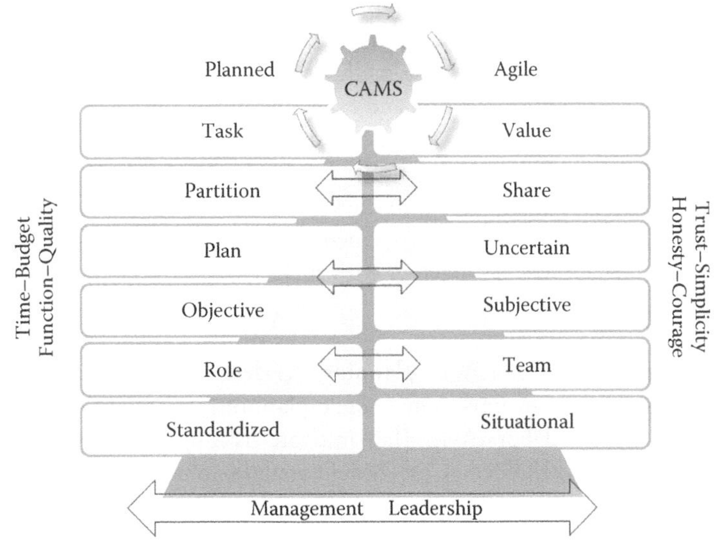

Figure 8.1 Combining planned and Agile factors in CAMS-based projects.

approaches. The following is a brief list of those Agile characteristics, their associated risks, and the way in which a composite approach to Agility helps in handling them:

- Iterative and incremental: Small software releases with rapid development cycles lasting 1–4 weeks. The potential risk here is the impact of each software release on the other parts of the system. Planning and modeling enable detailed considerations of impacts of releases on previous functionalities that have been delivered iteratively. Objective planning supports initial iteration but more like an exploration of requirements to enable formal planning rather than launching of actual development.
- Collaborative: The customer and developers, collaboration with each other constantly through face-to-face and close communication. While this works well for development where the stakeholders can get together physically, it can still be a challenge for outsourced development. Formal models of requirements within computer-aided software engineering (CASE) tools not only enable off-site collaboration but also provide the vital traceability required when the system moves to maintenance. Formality in collaboration works to enhance the overall output of collaboration rather than hindering it.
- Ease of learning: The practices associated with Agile methods are relatively straightforward and easy to learn. The challenge, of course, is the dissipation of the principles and values across the entire project. Furthermore, ease of learning does not always translate into ease of practice. Finally, while some practices work well during high-level understanding of business requirements, when it comes to undertaking detailed analyses, formal modeling techniques such as the Unified Modeling Language (UML) can play a major role. This usage of standardized and formal modeling techniques requires careful training and coaching including the training needed for an associated CASE tool.
- Adaptive: The Agile method should facilitate changes anytime during the development cycle. This factor works well in straightforward development when the teams are synchronized well, although, as discussed later in this chapter, such ideal Agile team models are rare. In such cases, the adaptability of a method needs to be carefully balanced with the rigors of its activities and deliverables. Formal and proper modeling is also required to evaluate the change in business requirements and business rules and to enable controlled adaptation.
- Development centric: Indeed, all Agile methods are development centric. This means that the Agile values of sharing, team work, and expecting uncertainties all work well together in undertaking development projects. The risk in such understanding is that the development-centric nature of Agile approaches may not always work well in large-scale multidimensional and global projects. Nor will such approaches provide value during the maintenance phase of a product. Combining project management, business analysis, and governance-related activities of planned approaches together with subjectivity of Agile practices is the best way to ameliorate this risk.

Collaboration is at the center of Agile planning. As described by Coplien, the Lean secret is, "Everyone All Together, From Early On."* Agile planning techniques provide the basis for identifying risks and issues collaboratively. They mitigate risks by having frequent, high-quality communication among all stakeholders. Cost–benefit analyse, in particular, help provide insights into risks and trade-offs.

* Discussed by Steve Berczuk in Cutter Exec Report: Starting Agile Adoption: Part II—Avoiding Common Pitfalls of Planning.

Declaration of Interdependence and Agile Project Management

Closely accompanying the Agile Manifesto and influencing project management in the Agile era is the "Declaration of Interdependence"* (Cockburn et al., 2011). This declaration was put together by the founding members of the APLN (Agile Project Leadership Network, first headed by Alistair Cockburn now simply Agile Leadership Network; see http://www.agileleadershipnetwork.org/) and is focused on "making people great project leaders." This focus on leadership is important in CAMS-based projects in that it combines traditional management with Agile leadership. There are six value statements based on the APLN view that reflect the most important aspects of modern project management in the context of Agile. The following discussion expands on these value statements (which start with a "We") in terms of their impact in CAMS-based projects.

1. *Increase return on investment by* making a continuous flow of value our focus. Instead of considering tasks to achieve, Agile project management aspires for a continuous flow of value to the stakeholders and business. As the business ecosystem is dynamic, it is imperative that the return on investment (ROI) made by the organization is measured in terms of ongoing value. CAMS, through the application of formal metrics and measurements, can provide justification for the investments made in undertaking Agile business transformations. While the Agile principles provide value focus, the formal planning and execution of project planning and management provides the metrics for ROI.
2. *Deliver reliable results by* engaging customers in frequent interactions and shared ownership. Reliability of results within projects can be varying and subjective. Instead of partitioning work and assigning it to individuals, this statement focuses on sharing between customers and developers to deliver results. Project management moves, through this value, from being an individual, task-driven exercise to an interactive exercise with task sharing. CAMS, through its combination of leadership and management, provides a mechanism for task sharing. Leadership, in CAMS, is a facilitation exercise. However, this leadership is also combined with the creation and assignment of tasks, tracking their progress, formal reporting, and incorporating feedback. This combination of leadership and management leads to reliability in project output.
3. *Expect uncertainty and manage it through* iterations, anticipation, and adaptation, which are parts of a strategy to manage uncertainty. The overall iterative approach in CAMS dissuades the notion of a product as a deliverable at the end of a project. Products are not verified only at the end but throughout the development process. However, CAMS also does not rely entirely on Agility; instead, appropriate controls are applied during the development to prevent uncertainty. In CAMS, change is accepted as much as it is also discussed and prevented from impacting the development schedule. Iterative approaches are the key to modern project management and, in particular, Agile projects that have a significant subjective element in them. Uncertainty cannot be managed without anticipation, adaptation, understanding, and control. CAMS-based projects exhibit these dual characteristics of iteration and control.
4. *Unleash creativity and innovation by* recognizing that individuals are the ultimate source of value and creating an environment where they can make a difference. Subjectivity in terms of the skills and motivation of individuals has long been the bane of planned processes. Planned processes for developing software (in particular) strive to modularize the subjectivity of individuals.

* The project/product management, http://pmdoi.org. Declaration of interdependence was written in 2005 as an adjunct to the "http://agilemanifesto.org. Agile Manifesto.

Such a value statement encourages and embraces individualistic, subjective characteristics of people working on projects. Once the right individuals are put together in a project, managing such a project becomes more of a facilitation and removal of any road blocks than keeping track of tasks and deliverables. CAMS, however, also considers the need for structure within a project. Therefore, CAMS-based projects have a formal team structure and well-defined roles and responsibilities. Controlled and managed creativity is the way of CAMS.

5. *Boost performance through* group accountability for results and shared responsibility for team effectiveness. This value statement also ties in neatly with the second point—encouraging sharing of responsibilities not only between customers and developers but also between team members in various roles. Leadership plays a vital role in fostering group accountability and sharing of tasks. Personal relationships, communication, and collaboration play an important role in boosting performance as they facilitate synchronous, team-based work with opportunities for individuals to express their creativity.
6. *Improve effectiveness and reliability through* situational specific strategies, processes, and practices. This important value statement enables project leadership to be effective by being fully aware of the dynamically changing situations, both within and outside projects and organizations. While the organizational strategies influence the processes and practices at the project level, CAMS also encourages this influence to vary depending on the situation. Thus, project type, size, and risks associated with the project will dictate the strategies, processes, and practices employed in the project.

Agile challenges at project and organizational levels were discussed in detail in Chapter 3. In particular, Figures 3.3 and 3.6 focused on the challenges emanating from the type and size of projects. Figure 8.2 highlights the factors that influence the formation and use of CAMS within projects. Although, typically, they are IT projects, these factors equally apply to any other type of project. The following are the factors and the way they influence the activities, roles, deliverables, and practices in CAMS:

- Project type and size: Ascertain whether the project is product development, service related or, an infrastructure project. For example, an infrastructure project such as setting up of a data center will require a greater use of formality in planning, execution, control, and

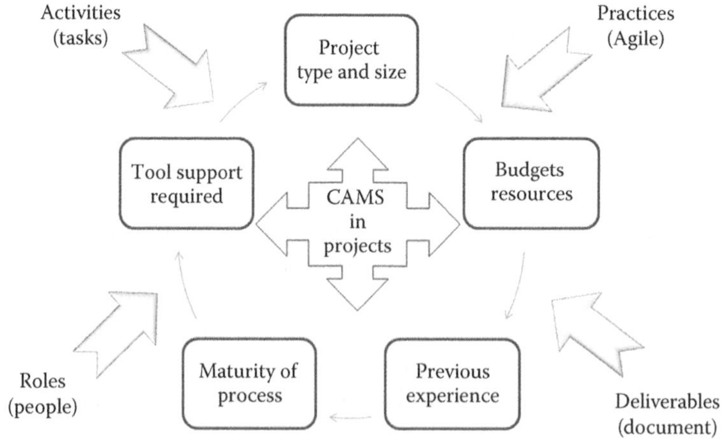

Figure 8.2 Factors influencing CAMS in projects.

tracking. CAMS, in such projects, will encourage use of formal deliverables and templates and application of quality assurance techniques to models of architectures and designs. On the other hand, a small mobile application implementation project can afford a much greater agility within its execution.

- Budgets and resources: What is the budget for the project (based on cost–benefit analysis of the initiative) and what resources are available for the same? Answers to these questions will dictate the extent to which formality and Agility will be balanced in CAMS. For example, higher budget and resources than a traditional project will enable the creation of a detailed CAMS instance with due consideration to methods friction. A smaller than usual budget will rely on Agile principles and practices—even though such practices may have risks associated with the development output.
- Previous experience: How well experienced is the project team with the use of both formal and informal approaches to its project? For example, a team well versed in formal project management approach will find it easier to create relevant deliverables and models based on templates. This kind of a team should focus on learning the Agile values and practices and embed them within their formal approaches (as has been done in this chapter for the project management process map). Alternatively, a team experienced in pure Agile methods should expand its view and encompass the formality of deliverables, tasks, and roles within its development approach. Thus, the previous experience of a team and its members needs to be considered in putting together a CAMS instance for a project.
- Maturity of process: The need for process maturity has a significant bearing on the freedom a team has to practice Agile methods. For example, a legally binding contract that requires the development to proceed only based on sign-offs will require a highly mature process with its deliverables following precise templates and activities dictating the sign-offs. Not only does maturity of a process dictate the formality of deliverables, but it also implies that the activities carried out in producing those deliverables are repeatable. The need for a higher process maturity enforces greater formality and planning as compared with Agile practices.
- Tool support required: The extent of CASE tool usage as required by a method for development and maintenance of the many artifacts of a project is an important factor in deciding the balance for a CAMS instance. For example, if a globally dispersed project requires extensive CASE tool support for modeling, designing, and architecting its software system, then the extent to which Agility can be practiced in such a project will be limited. CAMS will then encourage Agile practices only at individual, personal levels rather than across a dispersed team.

Organizing Composite Agile Projects

Organizing a composite Agile project is a part of management responsibility. Organizational leadership and business stakeholders are much less concerned with the type of method (process) being used in IT projects. Words such as "Scrum" and "Sprint" are of mild interest from a development perspective; they assume importance only in the context of *what* they deliver. The *how* of IT delivery is not a primary issue with the organizational leadership unless it disrupts business planning. Composite Agile tries to bring together the interests of business stakeholders not only in what is being delivered but also in "how" it is being delivered. This is done particularly with respect to Agile to disperse the myth that methods are all about software development. Instead, CAMS attempts to draw a linkage between the "what and how" of business together with that of software.

This expansion of Agility across the organization and its projects is also crucial in avoiding "methods friction" (discussed in detail in Chapter 4). Methods, standards, and processes used by business stakeholders cannot be completely oblivious to those used in software development and service maintenance. Pure Agile approaches, focused heavily on development, also tend not to worry too much about the "other" methods used by business. That is why there appears methods friction, particularly at an organizational level, when only a pure Agile approach to software development is used. CAMS provides consideration to both planned and Agile factors and that too at both projects and organizational levels. This line of thinking has been explored by some "Agilists." Notably, the work by Highsmith (2009), Ambler,* and Beck (1999) reflects this thinking.

Highsmith's five major phases in his Agile project management can be understood as follows:

1. Envision: This phase is focused on understanding the vision of the product and the objectives to be achieved at the end of a project. Envisioning needs to happen within the constraints and limitations of the project parameters. Therefore, seeking and incorporating input from the project community is important in achieving a common vision of the product. Envisioning can also help in getting the team members to understand each other and to start working together.
2. Speculate: Involves development of a capability and release plan that will respond to the vision. Depending on the techniques used in gathering requirements, the releases can be based on a group of stories (or, alternatively, based on use cases and packages). Previous experience of project work with an organization can provide additional input to improve the accuracy of speculation. The use of metrics can bring in the necessary formality in this phase.
3. Explore: Here, the project team delivers stories in short and sharp iterations. These are the "done" stories that enable a project team to further explore the requirements, thereby creating an internal feedback loop. Exploratory delivery offers opportunities to reduce risks. This is so because each release of the product provides the users and the developers with information and insights on its usage. This, in turn, reduces the uncertainty in terms of what to expect at the end of the project.
4. Adapt: This is a phase that continuously incorporates feedback based on the results delivered. Multiple factors such as the discovery of new risks, synchronicity of the team, expectation of business stakeholders, and growing understanding of team leadership—all enable and encourage adaptation within the development project.
5. Close: This is an important concluding phase of a project. Every project is a learning opportunity. This opportunity needs to be used to ascertain what went right and to identify the areas for improvement in the project. Formal conclusion of a project captures its essence, especially its tacit learning. Documenting of that tacit learning results in data and information about projects within an organization that can be used in subsequent projects. The closing of a project can be considered as a part of knowledge management within an Agile project environment.

Ambler too has discussed what he calls an *Agile software development life cycle* (SDLC) at a very high level. This Agile SDLC is highly collaborative, iterative, and incremental. The "phases" in this life cycle are called *iterations*. These iterations can be understood as follows:

- Iteration 1: This is the work that occurs before a project becomes a project. This is where business needs exploration and pre-project planning that primarily deals with the viability of a project are carried out.

* Ambler, S., http://www.ambysoft.com/.

- Iteration 0: This is the project initiation iteration. The work in this iteration deals with project-specific factors such as time, budget, costs, and stakeholder management. Additionally, creation of the project environment and modeling of the initial, high-level solution architecture may also occur here.
- Construction iterations: This is the popular, fundamental software development iteration—"analysis–design–coding–testing." This iteration is repeated multiple times as required.
- Release iteration: This is the iteration wherein a fully tested system is released and deployed to the users. This area of work in an Agile project needs to be accompanied by user training and support for its usage.
- Production: This is the ongoing phase of a system in which it becomes part of the operations in an organization. This is a phase that continuously integrates new releases, upgrades new versions of the product, reports on errors, and undertakes overall maintenance of the system.
- Retirement: This is where a system is removed from production. Multiple interfaces of a system and its dependencies on other systems and databases need to be considered in this retirement. Furthermore, care has to be exercised to ensure successful transition of current users along with their relevant data to a new system.

Finally, Beck (1999), in discussing the Extreme programming (XP) process life cycle, also comes close to the aforementioned life cycles. XP's life cycle consists of five phases. These phases can be interpreted and understood as follows:

1. Exploration phase: This phase starts with the writing of story cards by customers. The team socializes with the customer in terms of what is expected in the first release. The team also becomes familiar with the tools, technology, and practices to be used in the project.
2. Planning phase: In this phase, the project team sets the priority order for the stories and an agreement on the contents of the first small release. They also estimate how much effort each story requires and agree on a schedule. Focusing on an initial, small release helps in creating realistic schedules.
3. Iterations to release phase: This phase includes several iterations of the module being developed before it is released for the first time. The schedule from the planning phase is broken down into a number of iterations. The first iteration produces a working part of the system. This iteration also produces a high-level architecture of the system. User acceptance tests, created by the customer, are applied to the first iteration. Subsequently, as more iterations are produced, user acceptance tests are applied to all of them. At the end of the last iteration, the system is ready for production.
4. Production phase: This is the phase where the system is released to the customer. Additional and ongoing testing of the system is carried out here to ensure that its functional as well as nonfunctional requirements (NFRs) are being met.
5. Maintenance phase: This phase requires production support efforts for customer support tasks. Therefore, the development activities decelerate as the system moves into this phase. If the development is accompanied by requirements models and architecture documents, then such documents become handy in tracing the requirements and investigating the changes that are invariably required in this maintenance phase.
6. Death phase: This phase is reached when the customer no longer has any stories to be implemented. This can be the phase where there are no more changes to the code from a development viewpoint and the system is assumed to be fully operational. This is considered the end of the project itself.

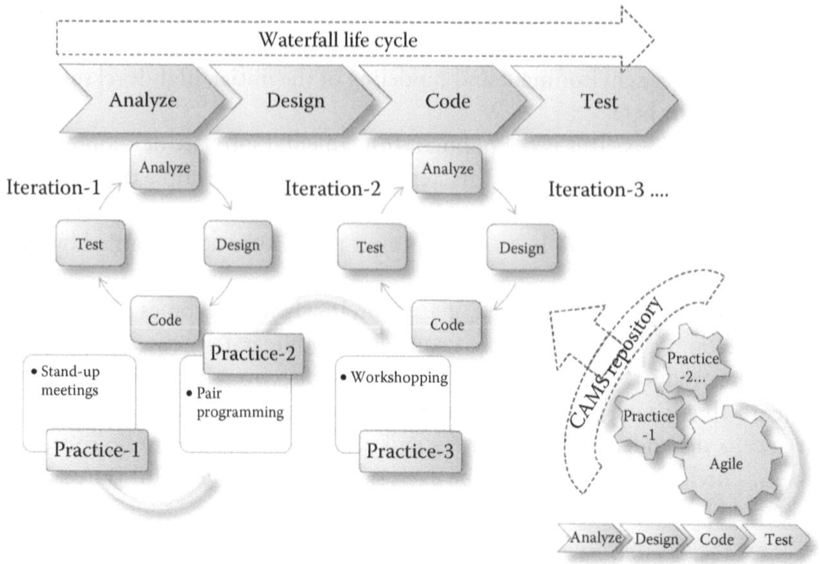

Figure 8.3 Development of a project-level instance of CAMS.

Figure 8.3 shows how an instance of CAMS can be created for use at a project level (as against an organizational level). This building of a CAMS instance is based on the fundamentals of CAMS discussed in Chapter 4 (especially Figure 4.9). The top layer in Figure 8.3 reflects the waterfall life cycle. This sequential life cycle provides a linear control for the project. This linearity of phases is also important in figuring out their dependencies. For example, the well-known analysis–design–code–test cycle has each phase dependent on the completion of the previous phase. This layer of a project proceeds in a planned, unilateral way.

The next layer of a CAMS-based project is immediately influenced by the iterative approach of Agile. Iterative development, which repeats the activities and tasks in order to increment the deliverable, is an important part of Agile approaches. Accordingly, the iterations (1, 2, 3, and so on) shown underneath the top layer in Figure 8.3 repeat the analysis–design–code–test cycle for a smaller part of the overall solution—perhaps a package or a subsystem. Agile practices specific and relevant to a project are embedded within each of these iterations. The Agile practices and software development techniques are sourced from the CAMS repository represented at the bottom right of Figure 8.3. This CAMS repository belongs to the documentation and knowledge repository of processes within the organization. For example, this repository can belong to a method's database or an intranet site managed by a Center of Excellence (CoE) in the organization (CoE is discussed in Chapter 10).

While Figure 8.3 shows a project-level CAMS, projects are hardly ever undertaken in isolation. Multiple projects make up a program of work for, say, a large-scale business transformation. CAMS encourages continuous focus on understanding and synergizing the interplay between multiple projects as well as the many methods that are used in these projects. Figure 8.4 shows the unfurling of a CAMS iteration that would apply to such a program of work. Thus, this figure is an expansion of the concept presented in Figure 8.3. When applied in practice, this CAMS iteration expands into multiple iterations. Furthermore, depending on the type and size of project, each iteration can have increments within it.

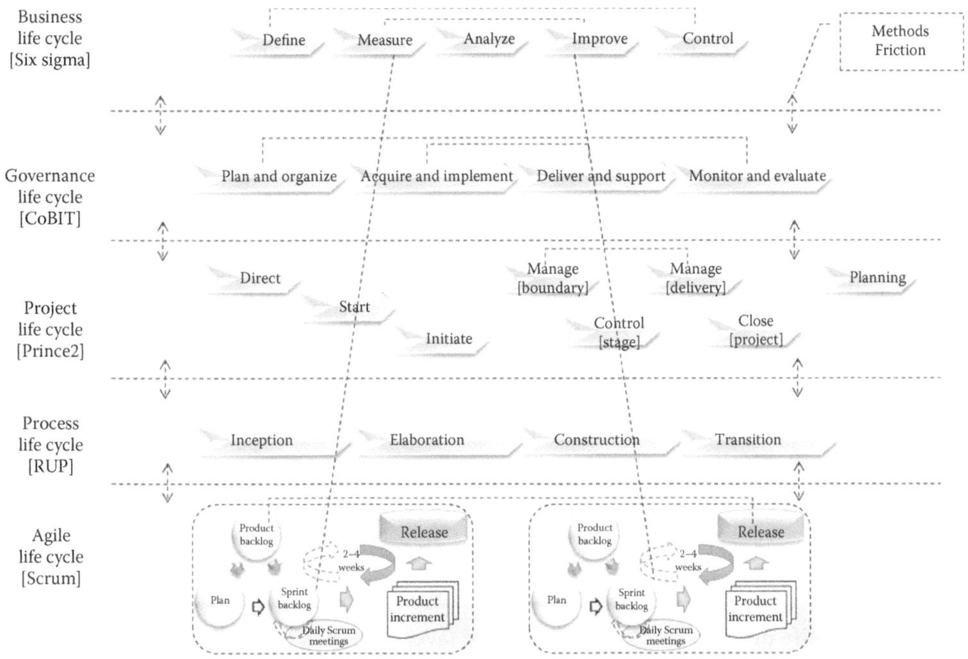

Figure 8.4 Unfurling a full CAMS iteration and increment for a program of work.

A crucial point to note in Figure 8.4 is the way it shows the combination of the various processes that are being used across the entire organization. Life cycles belonging to business, governance, project, development process, and Agile are listed on the left in Figure 8.4. Examples of these life cycles are shown underneath in brackets. Other example processes and frameworks corresponding to these life cycles will also hold true in this CAMS structure. Considering the many processes, their life cycles, and their application across multiple projects is crucial in the way CAMS attempts to avoid methods friction.

Figure 8.5 shows an alternate, practical view of a real-life project with multiple layers of work. This project view combines the fundamentals of the CAMS life cycle expressed in Figure 8.3 and the layers of work shown in Figure 8.4. The top-level area of work shown in this figure is based on the waterfall life cycle. The next layer shows the methodological approach used in exploring the needs of a business in undertaking an initiative (project). Formal business analysis skills and competencies (discussed in detail in Chapter 7) come into play here. Business analysis provides the opportunity for business to explore its core needs and, subsequently, decide whether an initiative should be undertaken in the first place. This decision is followed by scoping and estimation of the work, which becomes part of project planning. The analytical work itself leads to the identification and modeling of the functionality of the system. A composite approach uses Agile principles and practices together with formal requirements modeling to create a functional model of the system. Such a functional model is also accompanied by an initial solution design (akin to a prototype). These models assist in identification of gaps in key business entities and the corresponding data. The data gap between existing data formats and newly anticipated data requires careful transition. This identification and modeling of the gap occurs much earlier in a composite approach than in pure Agile approaches. Implementation as the last formal layer of a real-life CAMS project starts with that gap definition followed by planning, implementation (coding), testing, and deployment.

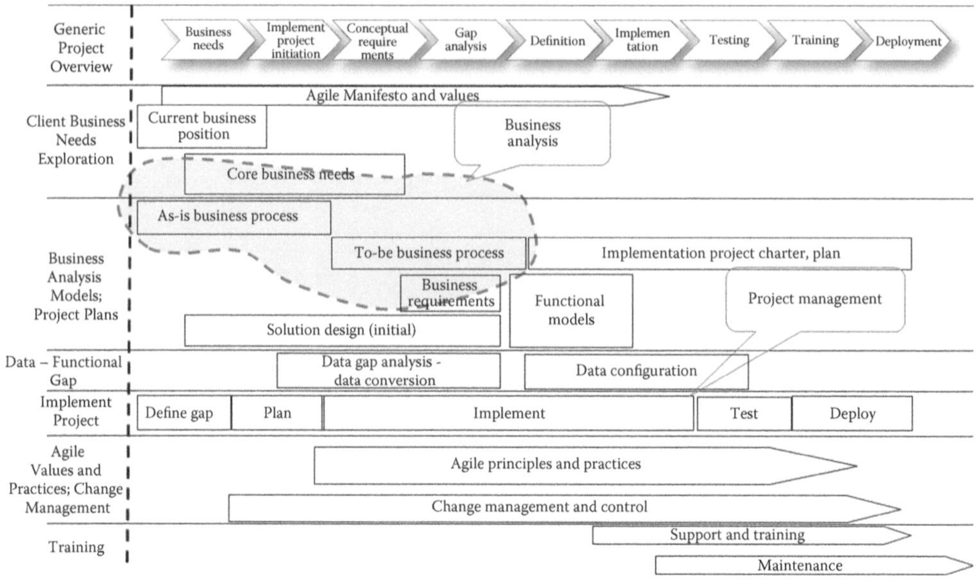

Figure 8.5 Real-life projects made up of multiple layers of areas of work.

The last but one layer shows the positioning of Agile practices with CAMS as well as the formality of change management. The final layer is a reminder of formal support and training during deployment as well as the maintenance cycle.

Project Management Process Map

Project management with CAMS is a combination of the formality of project planning and the subjectivity derived from Agility. The concepts of a composite approach, including its multiple layers and methods friction (as shown in Figures 8.3 through 8.5), need to be planned and organized within a process map. Figure 8.6 depicts such a project management process map. This process map, as part of CAMS, comprises formal activities of project planning, team formation, project launching, project scoping, environment creation, and risk minimization. These are examples of activities and tasks carried out in formal project management. This project management process map is used in organizing and tracking a project. Accurate tracking of a project also involves the understanding and management of risks. Therefore, project management also includes ongoing identification of risks, their prioritization, tracking, and control. These project management activities culminate in formal reporting and feedback on project status. Various stakeholders including the user, the steering committee, and the project sponsor are updated through reporting by the project management. The formal activities, tasks, and deliverables of the project management process map are interspersed with Agile practices. Examples of these Agile practices are also shown in Figure 8.6.

Roles in Project Management Process Map

The following are the roles in a project management process map.

- Project manager: This role is responsible for managing the project. This role undertakes project planning, launching of the project, its continuous monitoring, and reporting.

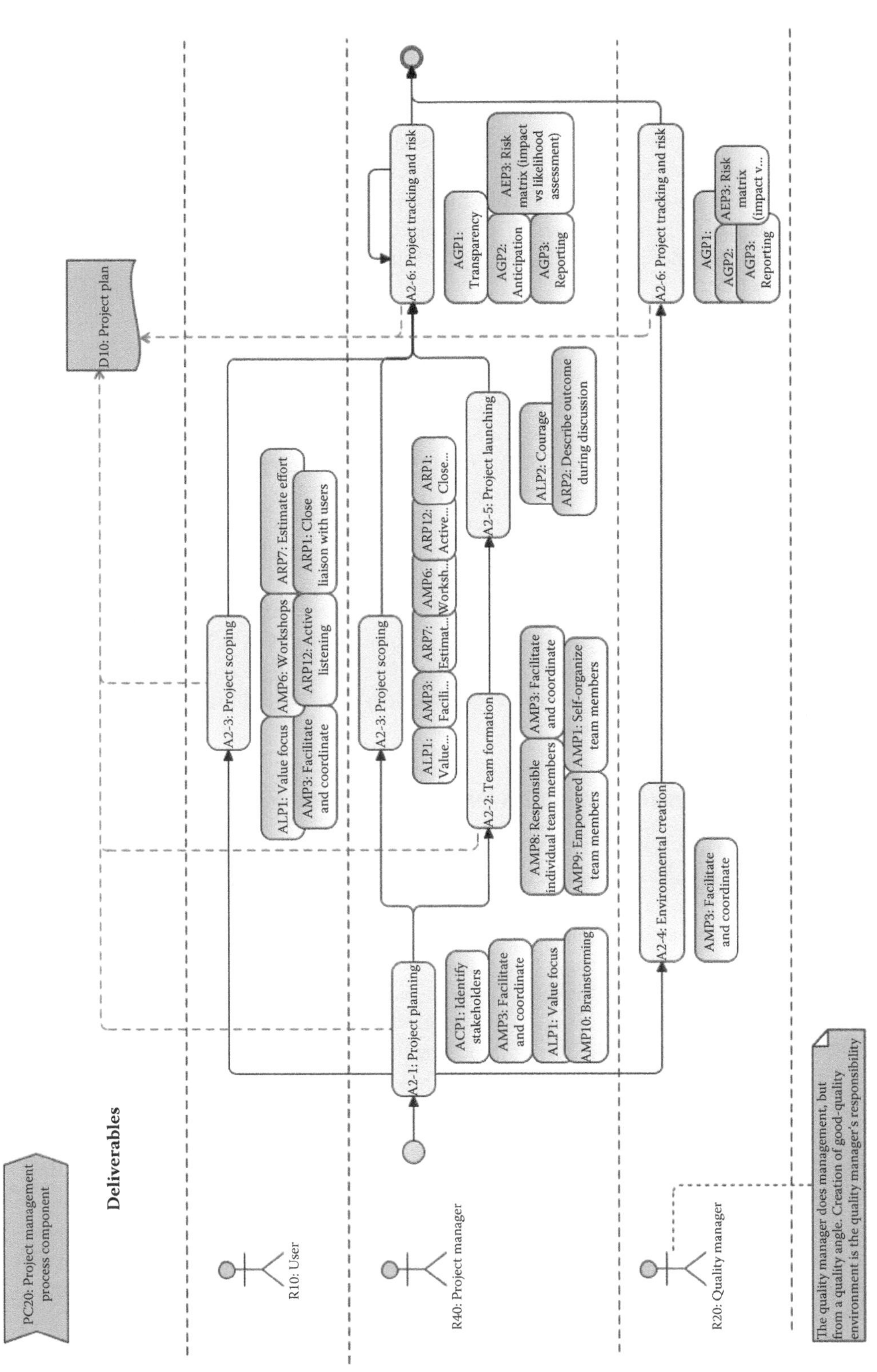

Figure 8.6 Project management process map in CAMS.

The project manager is also involved in team formation and its operational structure. Application of Agility allows the project manager to work toward facilitation and leadership rather than task management.

- Quality manager: This is the role that leads the quality initiative and supports the project manager. Thus, the quality manager undertakes quality activities such as walk-throughs, inspections, and audits. Quality roles are further described in detail in Chapter 9.
- User: This is an important role throughout the project. In the project management process map, this role participates, along with the project manager, in scoping the project and prioritizing the risk and helps in ascertaining their impact on schedules.

Deliverables in the Project Management Process Map

Pure Agile approaches give phenomenal precedence to working software before documentation. Therefore, the overbearing focus is on development itself as compared with any associated documentation. As Schwaber (2001) says, "The working software itself is the only deliverable on which we base a serious evaluation of progress." CAMS, on the other hand, gives equal credence to documentation. The project plan thus becomes an important deliverable.

The project plan is the key planning instrument within CAMS-based projects. Such a project plan can comprise of many subdeliverables. For example, the project plan can contain the organizational aspect of the project. This includes the project brief and details such as the type and category of project, its approach to quality, and the resources required. In addition, the project plan can also comprise the project schedule, budget, and timeline. A CAMS-based project plan is a living document. That means the plan will continue to evolve and be updated as the project progresses. Besides, the project plan will balance management with leadership and will not prevent the use of subjective leadership in a project.

Activities and Tasks in the Project Management Process Map

Table 8.1 lists the activities, tasks, and the corresponding deliverables and roles for the project management process map. Moreover, the Agile practices, which would be utilized during the process map execution, are also briefly mentioned in this table.

The project management process map described in Table 8.1 is a CAMS-based approach that brings together formal project management activities with Agility. While this process map is a generically applicable unit of a process, Agile principles and practices can also be built into project management methods, for example, Projects in Controlled Environments (Prince2) or Project Management Body of Knowledge (PMBOK) (Unhelkar, 2010). Table 8.2 shows the major activities (phases) of Prince2 and provides a description of how these activities are affected by Agility.

Business needs explored through business analysis can result in a large area of work within an organization. An area of work resulting from an overall business transformation program will comprise changes to multiple organizational functions. These organizational functions include, for example, human resources (HR) and organizational structures, software systems–applications–packages–networks and security, and data conversions. Therefore, a large area of work has to be divided into multiple smaller and manageable areas of work. Scoping smaller areas of work will provide the basis for one or more projects. This is what is shown in Figure 8.7. Prioritization of these many projects (as also shown in Figure 8.7) will depend on the time–cost–quality–functionality required. Stakeholders, especially domain experts, provide an increasingly improving understanding of the requirements as the initial iteration evolves. This increased understanding

Table 8.1 Activities and Tasks in Project Management Process Map

Activities	*Tasks*	*Deliverable*	*Roles*
A2-1: Project planning	Understand and categorize project Create a high-level project plan that extends the project brief Create project organizational plan Create project task plan Assign resources to tasks Organize and undertake quality checks Agile practices: ACP1: Identify and collaborate with stakeholders AMP3: Facilitate and coordinate discussions and negotiations ALP1: Maintain value focus throughout the project AMP10: Facilitate brainstorming among key stakeholders in terms of project goals and outcomes	D10: Project plan	R40: Project manager
A2-2: Team formation	Identify resources (team members) for the project Undertake recruitment and organization of the project team Manage and direct the team in the project Identify and obtain development technologies and related resources for the team Agile practices: AMP8: Develop responsible individuals as team members AMP9: Empower team members by enabling them to take decisions AMP1: Enable team members to self-organize themselves AMP3: Facilitate and coordinate team activities	D10: Project plan	R40: Project manager

continued

Table 8.1 (*Continued*)

Activities	*Tasks*	*Deliverable*	*Roles*
A2-3: Project scoping	Identify project scope, time, budget, and functionality of the project Develop high-level timeline (schedule) for the project Identify and agree on out-of-scope objectives with the users Prioritize functional and nonfunctional requirements for the project Identify, agree on, and record key in-scope objectives of the project Identify and record gaps in requirements by the users and existing, available functionalities Prioritize required features and their functionalities Agile practices: ARP7: Estimate effort for the project upfront AMP6: Workshops AMP3: Facilitate and coordinate ALP1: Value focus ARP12: Active listening ARP1: Close liaison with users	D10: Project plan	R40: Project manager R10: User
A2-4: Environmental creation	Organize hardware for the project Organize networks, systems for development (e.g., compilers) Install database for development and unit testing Create the overall working environment for the project Organize and install necessary CASE tools to be used in the project Agile practices: AMP3: Facilitate and coordinate		R20: Quality manager

Table 8.1 (*Continued*)

Activities	*Tasks*	*Deliverable*	*Roles*
A2-5: Project launching	Launch the project Set and manage project expectations on an ongoing basis Agile practices: ALP2: Courage ARP2: Present outcomes and goals in a transparent manner		R40: Project manager
A2-6: Project tracking and risk	Monitor risks Monitor iterations Monitor resources Monitor expectations Agile practices: AGP1: Transparency AGP2: Anticipation AGP3: Reporting AEP3: Risk matrix (impact vs likelihood assessment)	D10: Project plan (task)	R40: Project manager R20: Quality manager

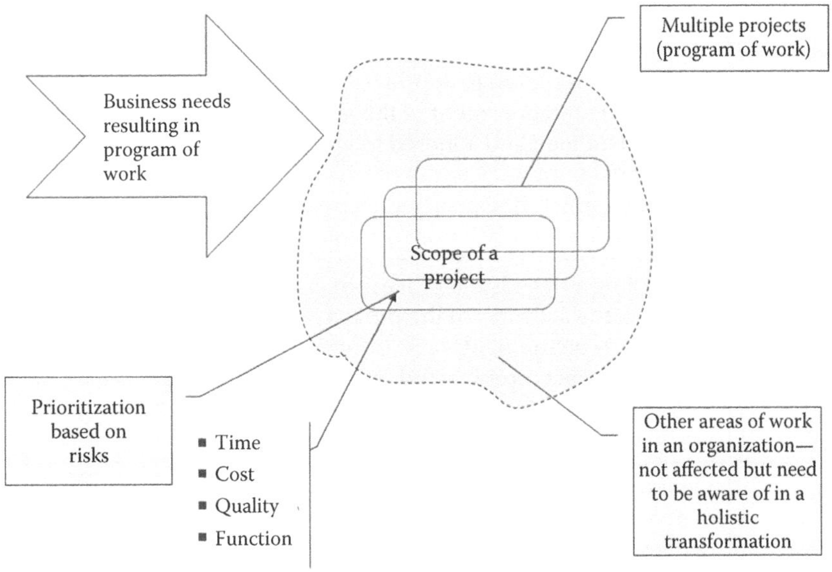

Figure 8.7 Scoping a program of work.

Table 8.2 Prince2 Major Activities and CAMS

Activities	*Description*
Directing a project (DP)	CAMS directs a project with slight variance from Prince2. The project features are listed and prioritized on an ongoing basis (as discussed earlier). The direction of a project is restricted to goals and the prioritization of high-level packages. The detailed execution of the project is hands off. The monitoring of progress of the deliverables, regular guidance, and advice to the team is similar to that in Prince2
Starting up a project (SU)	Composite Agile starts a project semiformally as compared to the formality of Prince2. However, the Agile approach focuses on managing four variables, namely, cost, time, quality, and scope for each iteration (release), which is similar to the formal project management approach. What is different is the minimal formality in letting the customers, together with the managers, choose the values of these variables. For large and complex projects with multiple subfactors within these factors, Prince2 provides the required formality and control in starting a project
Initiating a project (IP)	Initiating a project is the process of documenting the business case and making sure the time and effort considered for the project are proper and include the risks involved. This practice is applied in some Agile methods. The launch of a project provides the formality of its starting point, thereby enabling the monitoring as well as measuring processes to kick in. Thus, the time, costs, and resources that are planned for a project start getting utilized and monitored from the project initiation point. A subset of the initiation formality of a project can recur at the beginning of each iteration
Managing stage boundaries (MSB)	Managing stage boundaries is about providing the project team the information required to approve the completion of the existing stages and allow commencement of the next stage. These boundaries are not very well defined and adhered to in pure Agile approaches. CAMS gives significant importance to the completion of a stage (or iteration in most cases) by formal showcasing, documentation of the metrics, and incorporating feedback from the completion stage
Controlling a stage (CS)	Controlling a stage is the process of monitoring, controlling, and suitably changing the activities of the project manager to ensure a stage (or iteration) is on the right track. Control also involves responding to unpredicted occurrences and risks. CAMS encourages Agile practices within a stage but uses the control activities of Prince2 in a more formal way than Agile
Managing product delivery (MP)	On the basis of Agile practices, managing product delivery is a continuous activity in CAMS. Commonly agreed features are developed and tested in each release. The success of final product delivery is based on meeting the expectations of the customer. Participation of the customer throughout the development is encouraged in order to ensure that there are no last minute surprises from the customer

Table 8.2 (*Continued*)

Activities	*Description*
Closing a project (CP)	This Agile practice appears in most Agile approaches, as was mentioned earlier. Prince2 closes a project in a formal manner with participation from the user and developer. CAMS recognizes that there is a difference in closing a project in terms of achieving its output (or deliverables) versus achievement of its business goals. Although the two are separate, they are still interrelated. Therefore, closure of a project after it has produced its outputs still needs to leave space for comments on whether it has actually achieved its business goals. These are two separate lessons to be learnt from a project. Metrics that capture project data in terms of the planned elements of the project (Figure 8.1) also need to be stored at this stage, with opportunities for their potential use in subsequent projects
Planning (PL)	Planning a project in CAMS is not considered as an isolated starting stage of a project. Instead, planning incorporates, right at the beginning, the use of lessons learned from the previous project/s. As shown later in Figure 8.10 (document flow in CAMS), the "post-project reviews" is an important element right at the start of a project or program of work. This planning is also a more intense and formal activity than the planning in pure Agile methods, which is mostly carried in the heads of people rather than in documents

of the requirements will also change the scope, time, and budget of the projects and needs to be incorporated in the prioritization process (based on Ghanbary and Day, 2010).

Note how the Agile values shown earlier in Figure 8.1 can only indirectly influence this scoping of a project. The planned elements from that figure have a more direct influence in scoping one or more projects. Agile values and practices start assuming importance later, once the project has been initiated. CAMS also encourages awareness of any other areas of work that may be part of BAU and not directly be affected by the in-scope projects.

Business objectives in CAMS can be ascertained at two levels—there are the organizational-level objectives that are based entirely in the business space and the project level objectives. The organizational objectives—part of an overall program—are broken down in detail in terms of project-level objectives. In either case, prioritization of objectives is required. Figure 8.8a shows a way in which a business objective can be divided into smaller parts and prioritized within CAMS.

An example business objective in Figure 8.8a is stated in terms of the "what," "why," and "how" of the system. A critical requirements analysis (CRA) is undertaken as a part of evaluating alternatives and the order of importance of the objectives. The breaking down of a major program-level objective into smaller scoped objectives is undertaken here. Such decomposition of objectives into performance areas helps the users, project managers, and team members in understanding the priorities of work. Formal representation of these performance areas in CAMS is accomplished through UML packages in projects (Unhelkar, 2005a).

Ambler (2009), in discussing Agile portfolio management, also discussed the importance of prioritizing multiple projects within a program of work. As Agile developers implement requirements in priority order, Agile portfolio managers should initiate projects in priority order.

The CRA starts by a clear formulation of the business objective of the software project. This is akin to the mission statement of the project. A clear understanding of the objectives helps all

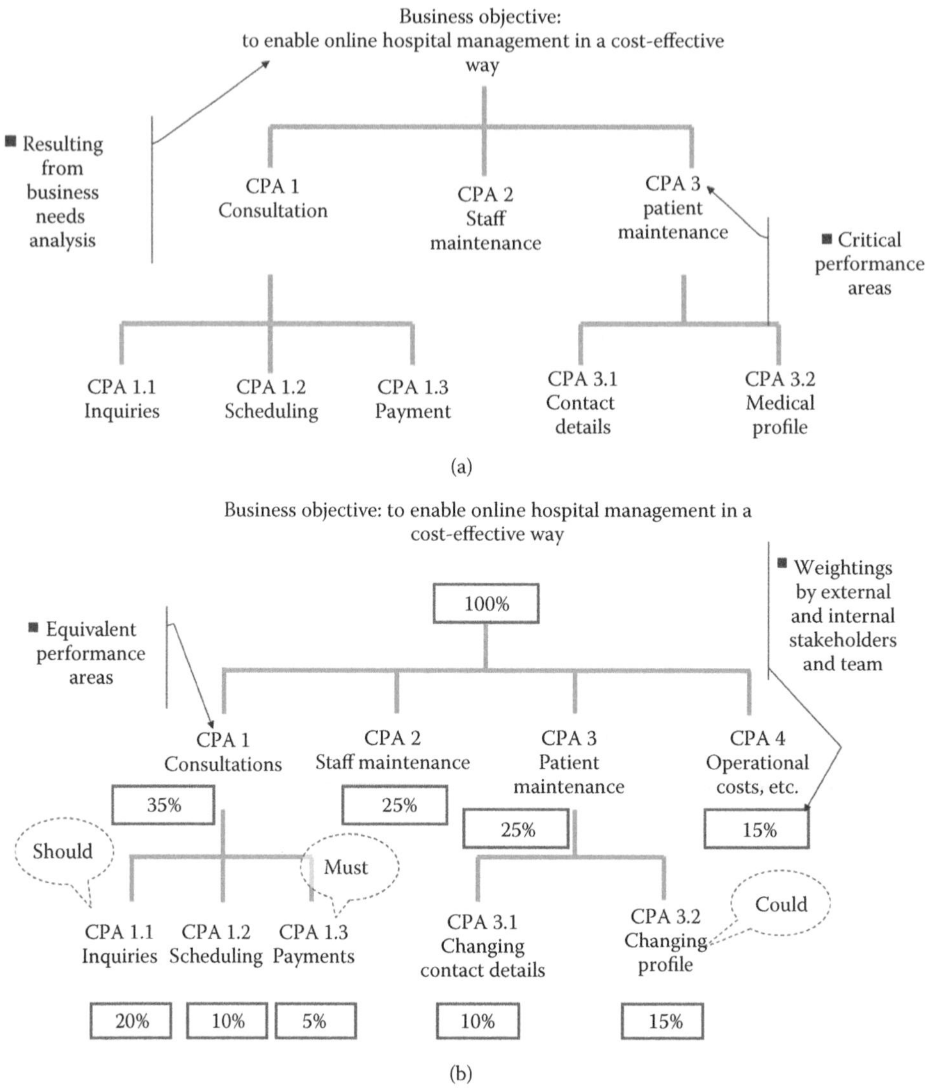

Figure 8.8 (a) Dividing the business objective into performance areas (prioritization: step 1); (b) providing weightings to performance areas (prioritization: step 2).

stakeholders in the project understand what the project is all about. Although business objectives can be drafted in different ways, one suggested way is shown in Figure 8.8a for a Hospital Management System (HMS) project, which can be described as follows:

Business objective:
To enable online hospital management in a cost-effective way (What)
By implementing a comprehensive E-hospital strategy through an HMS (How)
Resulting in excellent patient service anytime anyplace (Why)

While the above statements are enough in themselves for a detailed project scoping to occur, they are still an important indication of the direction toward which the organization is moving.

Table 8.3 Determine Performance Criteria for Prioritizing Projects

Business Objective/CPA	*Performance Criteria (Examples)*
BO: To provide a cost-effective response to a patient's basic hospital interactions	Transaction time Transaction accuracy Transaction cost
CPA 1: Consultations CPA 1.1: Enquiries CPA 1.2: Scheduling CPA 1.3: Payments	Time taken for basic hospital interactions should not exceed 2.5 s; 99.9% of all transactions should be accurate; inaccuracies should be reported
CPA 2: Staff maintenance	Creation, management, and closing of hospital staff details. Changing of details will involve administrative staff of the hospital
CPA 3: Patient maintenance CPA 3.1: Changing address and phone details, etc. CPA 3.2: Changing medical profiles	Errors in address changes/updates (%) Errors in profile changes/updates (%)

BO, business objective; CPA, critical performance area.

The "*what*" in the above statement shows what the initiative is all about; the "*how*" describes the approach that is taken to achieve the objective; and the "*why*" gives the argument or reason for the project initiative in the first place. This business objective will be entered in the business case document mentioned in the business evaluation process map (Chapter 6).

Figure 8.8a shows how the business objective is further divided into the corresponding critical performance areas (CPAs). These divisions are undertaken in workshop settings, with considerable input from domain experts and users of the system. It should be noted that practical CRA requires good analytical skills, including the ability to conduct interviews and workshops. Technical skills are less important in CRA than the facilitation and negotiation skills of business analysis.

The CPAs listed in Table 8.3, resulting from the CRA exercise, provide excellent potential subsystems. These subsystems, represented as packages in the UML, are further decomposed into lower level CPAs and packages. Once these packages have been identified, they can be prioritized. This prioritization exercise is carried out in a workshop environment through collaboration and communication with the users. The resultant percentage priorities are as shown in Figure 8.8b. Alternatively, a popular prioritization technique called Must-Should-Could-Won't (MoSCoW, briefly outlined in the sidebar) can also be applied to the detailed (lower level) CPAs of a system.

SIDEBAR Must–Should–Could–Won't (MoSCoW)

Must: This is a feature that has to be developed and provided by the solution irrespective of the cost and effort. These are the core requirements of the system, and the product owner together with the domain experts can finalize the "M" priority. For example, creation of a patient entity in an HMS is an "M" priority because without the basic patient record, the rest of the system will have no meaning.

Should: This feature is also a necessary part of the solution but has a potential workaround. "S" requirements are of high priority but cost, time, and effort can have an impact on these requirements. Hence, these are requirements for which alternatives should be explored. For example, in an HMS, the "enquiry" function is necessary; however, if it cannot be provided through a Web Service on the Internet, perhaps the support of a call center could be enlisted.

Could: These are the features that can fall under the category of a "wish list." A "C" requirement will be nice if satisfied but is not a mandatory part of the solution. For example, enabling a patient to change his or her profile using the online HMS is a "C" priority requirement. This feature can be implemented if time and budget are available to do so.

Won't: These are features that are good enough (important enough) to be listed as an output of early analytical work. Although the stakeholders and the development team agree to make a note of the feature, there is no pressure to consider that feature in the immediate release. For example, in an HMS, requirements relating to detailed calculations of outpatient operational costs may be noted but may not be prioritized beyond a "W."

Irrespective of the prioritization approach used with CAMS, it is vital to keep in mind that early priorities invariably change. This change is a result of multiple factors such as changing external circumstances of the business, movements by the competitor, or the impact of new legislations. Even more important to keep in mind is the impact of development on the priorities. Agile approaches are known for their anticipation of changes in requirements. The same anticipation is required in terms of changes to the priorities of those requirements. As the development progresses, the team members learn better ways of doing things. This growing knowledge and experience of the team also influences priorities. The steps undertaken in prioritizing requirements can be summarized as follows:

- Break down the key business objectives into detailed CPAs.
- Collaborate with the key business stakeholders, domain experts (subject matter experts), business analysts, and developers to identify key performance areas. (Note: these will include not only the really important areas but also those that are perceived as important.)
- Ensure that all performance areas (or features or packages) that are being considered for prioritization roughly have equal weighting. Such equality of features is important for prioritization to ensure the priorities are not skewed by the size of the features; however, in almost all practical exercises it is impossible to arrive at exact equality of size. For example, in Figure 8.8b, it is very difficult to compare the priority of staff maintenance (CPA2) with patient maintenance (CPA3) unless the two are roughly equal in terms of their size and effort.
- The product owner, together with the Agile coach, should get the team involved in identifying the business and project risks and discuss prioritization in the context of that risk.
- Use MoSCoW prioritization techniques or the percentage prioritization—shown by way of examples in Figure 8.8b. This can be done by asking the workshop participants to assign a percentage priority to the CPAs (this percentage is based on which performance areas are critical to the success of the project, as listed briefly in Table 8.3).
- Consider the CPAs as packages with the highest priority in the first iteration of the project. However, still discuss with the domain experts the dependencies of the CPAs on each other (mainly because even if a CPA is perceived to be of low priority, if there are dependencies on it, then it will have to be developed first). Cost of development is important only at a higher level—when it comes to lower level prioritization, dependencies and risks assume greater importance.

- Lower level CPAs are candidates for use case diagrams, or alternatively, in large systems they become lower level packages.
- Prioritization can be an iterative process in itself—with the product owner undertaking an approximate prioritization exercise followed by a joint workshop of key stakeholders and all team members wherein the prioritization of features is reevaluated and refined.
- Reflect on the lessons learnt in the initial iteration (or release). Bring this added knowledge and experience in the mix when priorities are assigned (e.g., an improved way of modeling or development will imply increasing the priority of a CPA that was earlier on lower priority).
- All prioritized CPAs and features that have been prioritized will have to be re-prioritized on an ongoing basis as the project progresses through iterations and increments.

Figure 8.9 provides a simplistic view of the iterations and prioritization occurring in an Agile project. CAMS pays greater attention to formally creating iterations and prioritizing them. Agile, on its own, encourages the documenting of features through story cards. These Agile user stories, written on story cards, are put on physical walls on big display areas of an Agile project (stories were discussed in Chapter 5). The iterations shown on the wall charts in Figure 8.9 can only be shown in retrospect—as it is not possible to ascertain which feature will be actually delivered within an iteration. Keeping the iterations themselves *dynamic* is an important part of ongoing prioritization. Just as the dynamic changes to the requirements within projects can be a challenge, similarly prioritization of features on an ongoing basis can also be a challenge. Depending on the changing needs, varying criticality, increasing demand for security and reliability, and the insights gained by the product owner as the iteration progresses, stories that were an "M" can shift to a "C" as they progress in their development from "To do" to "Doing." This is being shown, by way of example only, in Figure 8.9. Needless to say, the time, budget, and size of a project will impact on these changing priorities. For example, story-4, which may be developed in iteration-3, may move from "W" to "C." As also shown in Figure 8.9, story-2 moves from "M" to "S" soon as its development starts, whereas story-3 reverses from "S" to "M." The critical requirement analysis and its percentage weighting discussed earlier can also play a part in shifting the priorities of stories—if applied at this level.

Deliverables (primarily documents) are an important element of CAMS. All process maps outlining the various ways in which work can be carried out in a project and in an organization

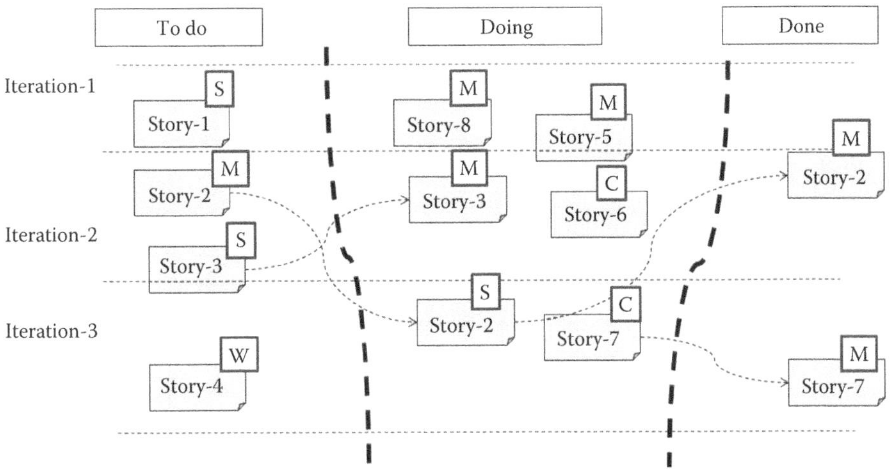

Figure 8.9 Priorities and iterations on Agile project charts.

contain deliverables. The formal, planned aspect of CAMS requires careful consideration of all the deliverables that are produced through the process maps. Project management assumes the responsibility of formalizing these deliverables, standardizing them through templates, storing them as they incrementally get updated, and making them available for use in current and future projects. Thus, management of documents is an important part of overall knowledge management within a CoE for an organization. Having a very basic flow of the deliverables themselves in mind is an important part of formal project management.

Figure 8.10 shows an example of such a document flow. This document flow enables visualization of the overall work happening in a project. Figure 8.10 shows the key documents as examples with their dependencies. The numbers as prefixes to the document name can help in their organization, storage, and retrieval. (The numbers in Figure 8.10 are examples only, and they can be changed based on the needs and protocols of the project.) Figure 8.10 also shows four basic groupings of these documents for easier control and reporting. The following is a brief description of these documents:

- 10—Business need statement (problem statement): This document describes the highest level need of the business. This can be a two- or three-page document describing the challenge perceived by the leadership/board to the business. This can also be the key statement (business objective described earlier) of the project.
- 15—Post-project reviews (metrics; patterns): This is a document or suite of documents that have captured the essence of previous initiatives/projects in the organization. This document/s will also contain details of metrics and measurements of time, budget, efforts, project velocity, and so on, recording from the post-project reviews (closures) of previous projects.

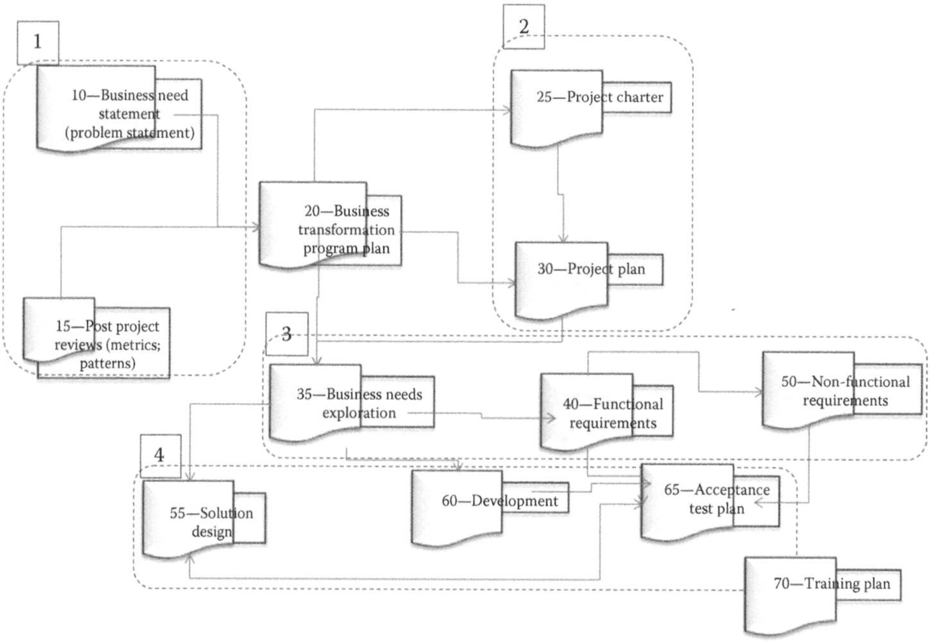

Figure 8.10 Document flow in CAMS.

- 20—Business transformation program plan: This plan provides an overview of the overall transformation and change management required in the organization. This is not a detailed document but a high-level document that outlines the various initiatives (projects) being undertaken in the organization as a part of transformation.
- 25—Project charter: This is a brief description of the project (about two pages), which provides the key details of the project including its title, number, budget, manager responsible, and so on.
- 30—Project plan: This is the detailed plan comprising the details of the time, budget, and resources of the parties responsible and interested in the project, and a detailed time line (task plan) that is usually created and monitored separately from the organizational plan for the project.
- 35—Business needs exploration: This is a business analysis activity that explores the business interest in the project in detail. In fact, this is where the process of deciding whether a program of work should be undertaken at all is documented.
- 40—Functional requirements: These are the results of discussions between the requirements modelers and the users in terms of the functionality expected. These requirements are documented using use cases, activity graphs, and other relevant UML diagrams.
- 50—Nonfunctional requirements (NFRs): NFRs are documented separately because of their importance as well as their sequence in the requirements modeling process. NFRs appear early in the project and apply to multiple modules and the system simultaneously.
- 55—Solution design: The solution design expands on the functional and nonfunctional requirements to produce a model of the solution. This deliverable is usually produced within a CASE tool used in the project.
- 60—Development: Development is the main output of the project and comprises the actual code that is being developed. This is the deliverable of maximum interest in pure Agile approaches. CAMS considers this as not the only deliverable of interest as the gathering and modeling of functional and nonfunctional requirements as well as the solution design all feed into development.
- 65—Acceptance test plan: Put together with the users, this deliverable enables management of expectations as well as testing of the quality of the product. The results from the tests, feedback to the developers, and regression testing are all a part of this deliverable.
- 70—Training plan: This plan is also undertaken with help and input from the users and other business stakeholders. This training plan is part of the overall change management required when a solution is delivered to business.

The discussion thus far focused on the process and techniques of project management. This project management and its corresponding process map provide the formal view of how a project needs to be organized. CAMS continues to explore the opportunity to bring together the formality of project management (e.g., provided by Prince2) with the practices of pure Agile. CAMS, however, provides ample opportunity for subjectivity and leadership skills to emerge in a project. These leadership skills, however, need their own basis and a framework to enable their safe usage in a project. These skills, roughly clubbed under “soft factors” in a CAMS-based project, are now considered in detail.

Leadership and People Management in Agile Projects

The Agile Manifesto says, “individuals and interactions over processes and tools.” In practice, and especially in large and complex projects, processes and tools provide excellent background support to enable those individuals to interact and collaborate. Therefore, individuals and their interactions need to be promoted "together with" processes and tools. For example, some individuals find it challenging to work in an iterative and Agile manner. These individuals are used to the formality of planning, modeling, and documentation. When the work of a team of individuals made up of those who can and cannot work iteratively has to be coordinated and merged to produce a release, the project leader has to use competencies and frameworks that are different from the software development frameworks and life cycles.

An understanding of the human aspect in project leadership will provide engagement and involvement of team members with each other as well as parties external to the project. The precedence given to individuals in Agile projects can be brought to fruition much more easily if it is couched within a framework.

Thus, psychology, sociology, and culture—the words that were more or less a taboo in erstwhile software engineering literature—are now gaining importance. Agility with its importance to individuals at all levels within a project and even across an organization demands attention to the "soft" factors at work. While these factors are applied within software projects by Agile, within an overall CAMS, the soft factors are applicable across multiple projects and, even more importantly, across the entire business. This consideration of soft factors across the operational aspect of an organization is a crucial CAMS differentiator as compared with pure Agile or fully planned methods.

Soft Issues and Subjective Skills

Investigations into the comparative successes of some projects over others have led to a gradual understanding of the importance of sociological dimensions of IT project management (Unhelkar, 2003). For example, when the technical dimension of two projects is similar (say, they both use Java and the SQL Server) and still the projects end up differently, then the way in which the development method was used can be a determining factor. What can be intriguing, however, is how two projects with similar technologies *and* methodologies end up at different ends of the success spectrum. Obviously, the answer lies beyond technology *and* methodology. Increasingly, practical IT experience, including, in particular, Agile approaches to development, suggests that while excellence in technology and methodology is a necessary condition for the success of IT projects, it is not sufficient. Leadership, motivation, experience, communication, and politics have started assuming importance. This brings into focus the principles and practices of sociology that have a major role to play in the composite Agile way of undertaking projects.

SIDEBAR

The subjectivity arising from people issues was aptly stated by Lanier (1997) in the commemorative issue of *Communications of the ACM* on the first 50 years of computing: "The easiest predictions to make about the next 50 years of computer science are those centering on the computers, not the people. It is when people are brought into the equation, however, that the business of prediction becomes difficult. The biggest surprise from the first 50 years of computers is that computation turns out to be a cultural object in its own right, with all its warts and semicolons." The phenomenal importance of "human issues" in information technology (IT) project management has also been discussed by DeMarco and Lister (1987) and Constantine (1989, 1995, 1996). The latter states, "Good software does not come from CASE tools, visual programming, rapid prototyping, or object technology. Good software comes from people. So does bad software." The conclusion is inescapable—we must address sociopsychological factors as well as the traditionally discussed IT management functions.

The application of these software factors in practice, however, may not be easy. That is perhaps the reason why they have not been accepted in formal approaches to software development. One of the reasons for the popularity of the Agile Manifesto is that it gives respectability to these soft factors in project work. An opportunity is created to incorporate soft factors in project life cycles even if they cannot be put in a model or a formula. The role of human aspect in the success or otherwise of any initiative is vital. This is particularly so in Agile projects where Agile values such as trust, honesty, and courage are all based on the subjectivity of human behavior.

Thomsett, under the banner of "even more extreme project management" highlights the crucial importance of person-to-person relationship in the success of an Agile project. In advocating the partnership between the project sponsor and the project manager, he says, "The project manager (should have) the right to see their sponsor within one minute and have a decision in one minute..." (Thomsett, 2003). While such collaboration may not be practical in all cases, still the need to facilitate Agile decision making in projects cannot be overemphasized.

CAMS gives due respect to personality traits in projects. It extends and builds on traces of past psychological considerations in IT. For example, Weinberg (1971) alludes to the complexity of software projects coupled with their fuzzy nature. The fuzziness of these factors has been misconstrued by IT project management as either inconsequential or too difficult. Most formal project management methods make scant reference to the psychology or sociology of projects. Also, IT managers are not trained as psychologists. CAMS suggests some simple, usable psychosociological frameworks that can provide significant impetus to work in IT projects. These usable frameworks promise major value in Agile approaches and, in CAMS, compliment the rigors and maturity of processes (as ascertained, for example, by the Capability Maturity Model, CMMI). The following discussion presents a brief outline of such a framework and creates and demonstrates the applicability of the framework in CAMS.

While the traditional, planned projects are driven by management principles and practices, Agile projects are facilitated by leadership. CAMS brings together both—*management* by maintaining schedules, tracking progress, assigning, and reviewing work; and *leadership* through facilitation, removal of roadblocks, communication of goals, and provisioning of value. Leadership, particularly using composite Agile, is in itself a fine balance between the rigors of planned processes and handling of the inevitable human capriciousness, irrespective of planning. Figure 8.11 shows the two styles of managing a project.

- *Leadership*—subjective approach that is driven by values; relatively fuzzy as compared with "management"; risky; Agile (synchronous team). As the focus of leadership is on values, it has to accept greater risks than planned approaches.
- *Management*—task-based; measurable; planned (closed team). Management is more amenable to "standard" project management that is based on concrete parameters such as time and budget.

Leadership in Agile projects has to facilitate interaction, dialogue, collaboration, prototyping, and feedback. The questioning and listening competencies (mentioned as the basis for the conversational paradigm of software development in Chapter 1, and as part of explorations by business analysts—Chapter 7) have to be nurtured by project leaders. Agile requires organizational changes such as dedicated team members, and, often, money for training, coaching, and tools (Fischer, 2009). This, in turn, provides value and meets expectations of users and stakeholders. Social interaction and cognitive skills play an important part in leading Agile projects.

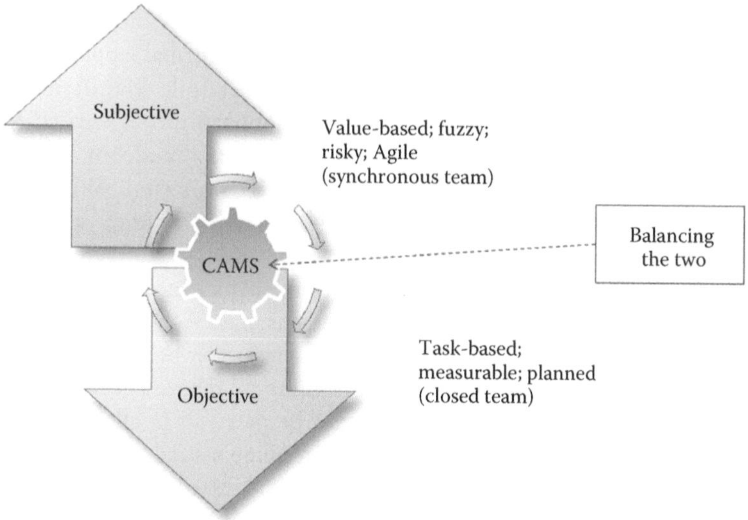

Figure 8.11 Leadership versus management.

SIDEBAR

Agile's emphasis on people and their frequent interaction sidesteps the formalities involved in requirement engineering, designing, and documentation. This enables the developers to focus on software technologies and the working solution. This approach also works well in development. The challenge seems to arise when successfully developed solutions transition into production. That is where the need to trace the changes back to the requirements and balance the designs arises. To add further to the complications, successful developers who developed the solution collaboratively have "moved on."

Agile projects need "leadership over management." That, of course, implies accepting and capitalizing on "subjectivity and the individual." One person is not treated the same as another in terms of his or her competencies, capacity to deliver, and motivation to be part of the team. For example, the role of a developer will change in terms of throughput and quality depending on "who" is fulfilling that role. So, if one Agile project delivered with five developers, there is no guarantee that another Agile project with similar features will deliver with five developers. This uncertainty of estimations holds true even if the five developers are the same. This is so because the same person will behave differently when he or she is placed in different settings—made to interact with different people. The need to match requirements to people, and to match people to people is a great project leadership skill that will create collaborative working relationships. Having said that, in practice, most project managers are highly restricted in their ability to select the type of people they would like to have. Hence, the matching of people to people may become more important in facilitation than even that of people to skills.

Agile Team Formation

While pure Agile methods radically disturb the traditional team structures, CAMS synergizes the formal reporting hierarchy with the freedom and responsibility for individual developers.

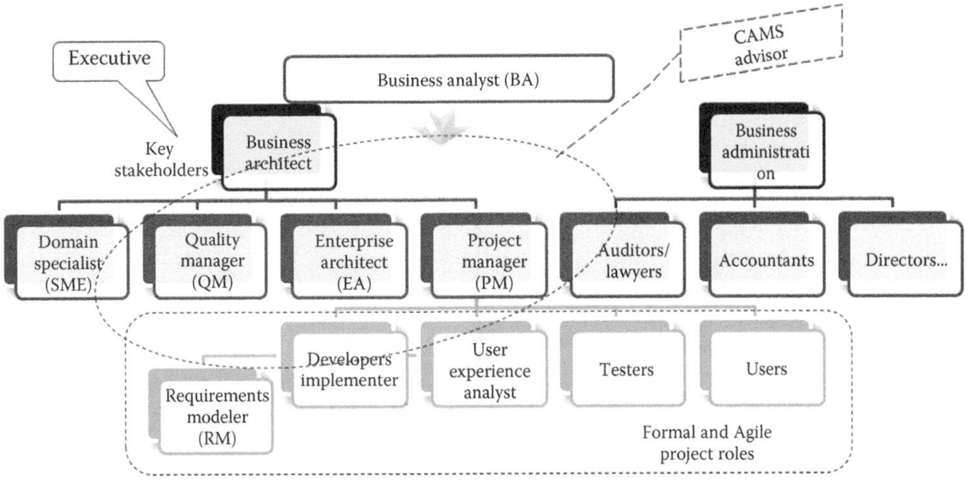

Figure 8.12 Project team structures—CAMS.

Figure 8.12 shows such a composite project team structure used in CAMS. There are Agile project roles such as developers, testers, and users. There are also roles that would otherwise not exist in a pure Agile approach—requirements modelers, project managers, and user experience analysts. The architectural, management, and administrative roles in these projects need not always be project specific; they are increasingly on the boundary between projects and organization and may reside within the CoE of the organization. The business administrative side, although by no means complete, shows the involvement of nonproject roles in projects (software and nonsoftware). The business analysis role is shown apropos the discussion in Chapter 7—providing a high-level analytical skill set that appears much before a project becomes a project.

The project manager in such teams works alongside the domain specialist, quality manager, and the architects to ensure ongoing prioritization and sustainable feeding of work to the development team. Development teams are beset with overloading of work as well as diversion of attention because of the need to handle multiple tasks simultaneously. A semiformal team structure, such as the one shown in Figure 8.12, can understand the work given and attempt to complete it in time. Agile principles can further ensure that a team falling behind is not further loaded with demands to complete in ever-shortening time frames. CAMS is aimed at helping teams formalize their structure and overcome the aforementioned chronic challenges of overloading and dispersal of attention.

Real project teams are made up of real people. Therefore, like people, teams are difficult to generalize. Having an understanding of the purpose for which a team is formed, its background structure, and its dynamics can be very helpful in creating a successful team, and keeping it motivated right through the project. Figure 8.13 provides a simple basis for understanding team models. Thomsett (1994) has further developed on Constantine's (1989) excellent description of the various ways in which teams can be organized. These four possible team structures are as follows:

1. Closed: These teams follow the traditional hierarchical structure and are good for traditional development and maintenance of legacy applications such as payroll and accounting systems. These closed teams are structurally strong as they resist subjectivity of individuals. The strength of the team structure can be used in forming a composite team.

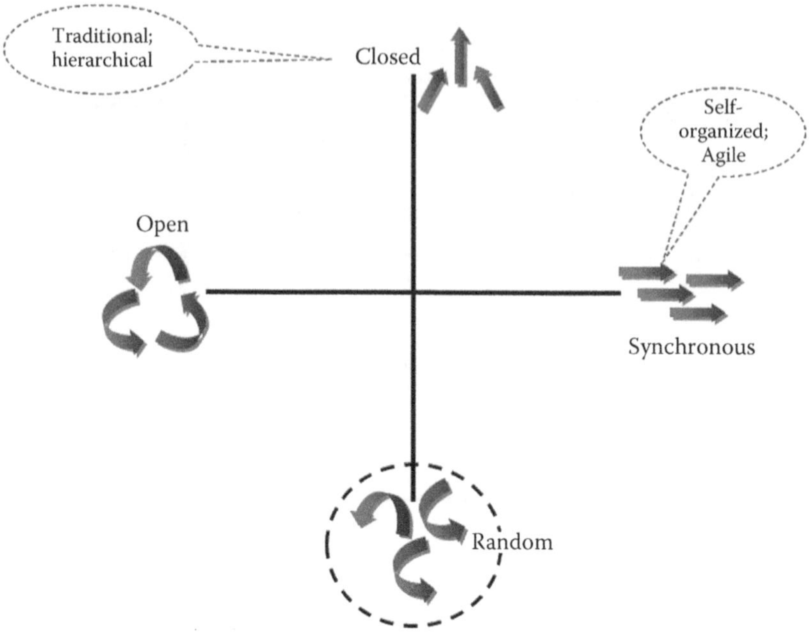

Figure 8.13 CAMS team organizational models. (Based on Constantine, L.L., Teamwork paradigms and the structured open team, *Proceedings of the Embedded Systems Conference*, Miller Freeman, San Francisco, CA, 1989.)

2. Open: These teams perform as collaborators. There is very little hierarchy and no tradition. The lack of hierarchy is particularly appealing to new programmers. Most Agile methods promote an open team structure.
3. Random: These teams are innovative and task based. These teams comprise three or four experts who are put together to achieve a short-term breakthrough goal. They do not have a hierarchical management, neither do they need open collaboration; it is the goal or objective provided to the team that drives its functioning. Such teams cannot be expected to perform in a cohesive manner for an extended period of time.
4. Synchronous: These are, as Constantine calls them, *Utopian** (out of the world) teams. They perform on total understanding and harmonious alignment. This is the team structure that every project manager hopes to achieve.

CAMS aspires to produce such a well-aligned and synchronous team. Such a team will have structural rigor and yet it will be able to function coherently and with minimum control. A composite team will correlate personality traits with the paradigm of software development. Project leadership in CAMS will focus on creating and aligning a synchronous team rather than on its operation. A couple of important psychosociological frameworks that can be used by project leaders in order to facilitate such synchronous teams are the Myers–Brigg personality framework and the TA framework that deals with structure and dynamics of organizations and groups.

To start with, consider the Myers–Briggs Type Indicator (MBTI). MBTI is made up of four pairs of personality traits. These personalities are E, extroversion; I, introversion; S, sensing; N, intuition; T, thinking; F, feeling; J, judging; and P, perceiving.

* Meaning "out of the world" for such teams are indeed out of the world.

These are described below in the context of composite Agile:

- Extroversion (E) and introversion (I): The E individuals are outward going, whereas the I personalities prefer to look inward. The strengths of the E personalities such as being talkative, outgoing, conversation initiators can be used by astute project leaders in placing these individuals in contact with business stakeholders, users, and domain experts. The introverts, who are quiet and reserved, can perform better in a CAMS-based project when they deal with enterprise architects and business architects where issues are discussed more from a stability than change viewpoint.
- Sensing (S) and intuition (N): S individuals understand and absorb requirements and features in a linear fashion. The N person works through abstraction—taking in information as an insight rather than a logical conclusion. Project leaders in CAMS can use the S individuals much better in the second and third iterations—where the approach to developing features is well established; the N individuals (or individuals exhibiting more of N rather than S characteristics) can be included up front to develop the features and stories of the very first iteration as these are the people who relish new and exciting tasks that seem to defy logic.
- Thinking (T) and feeling (F): Thinking is focused on the logical, step-by-step way of understanding and solving problems. Feeling in MBTI gives deference to the emotional aspects of decision making. Therefore, the F people are given significant opportunity to contribute to Agile projects where the emphasis is on the individual's subjectivity and motivation. Thinking, of course, brings in rigor and firmness in decision making with due input from past project data including metrics and measurements. T people are likely to be comfortable with the planned process aspects of CAMS, whereas the F people will accept the fuzziness of the Agile principles and practices in CAMS.
- Judging (J) and perceiving (P): Judging indicates organizational tendencies that can be put to excellent use in planning a project, assigning roles and responsibilities, and eventually tracking and controlling the project. These characteristics can be used in the formal, planned aspect of CAMS. Processes and their maturity are also well understood and accepted by the J individuals. P persons, on the other hand, may even appear to be disorganized and seem to be distracted in completing their tasks. However, P individuals are adaptable, spontaneous, and open-minded and, thereby, quite Agile. CAMS suggests that project leaders spot these perceiving characteristics and make provisions for them in the project. The adherence to timeliness and deadlines are part of the characteristics of J individuals, who find it easier to work with the planned aspect of a CAMS project.

These aforementioned MBTIs need to first be understood by a project leader with respect to themselves, the organization, their team, and members of the team. The four pairs of characteristics described here are not watertight compartments. These personality types are really tendencies exhibited by individuals. Understanding their own personality type helps the project leader to see where they will be demanding rigor from the team or where they will allow greater freedom for individual team members to undertake their tasks without supervision. Second, understanding these characteristics as tendencies tells a project leader that individuals occasionally exhibit characteristics that differ from what their personality types indicate. Finally, an astute project leader will also realize that these are not just traits of an individual but can also be considered as team traits. At times, a team might exhibit an I–S–T–J personality whereas, at other times, it may exhibit an E–N–F–P personality.

The TA framework has been one of the simplest mechanisms for project leaders to understand personality traits. TA was put together by Berne (1972) and is based on the interactions (transactions) between two or more individuals. The fundamentals of TA comprise the ego states (parent–adult–child) and life positions. Life positions have been described by Berne as the world view of an individual that seems to persist irrespective of the changes in situations and emotions. Not only do individuals behave as per their life positions but even teams, organizations, and nations can be said to have personality traits based on their life positions (Harris, 1981). There are four life positions appearing in the TA framework:

I am OK—you are not OK: This is mostly didactic, and the person tends to respond from a position of superiority. The active ego state is the parent most of the time.

I am not OK—you are OK: This is a team member who always feels inferior. The active ego state is the adaptive child.

I am not OK—you are not OK: This team member shuts himself out from the group, and in the extreme case withdraws completely.

I am OK—you are OK: This is the position of good leaders and motivators. These are the people who maintain universal respect for themselves and others, even in utmost adversity. The active ego state is adult most of the time, but parent and child are allowed uncontaminated display.

Creating software teams and assembling people within the teams is best accomplished if the life position of the people is "I am OK—you are OK" (Unhelkar, 2005b). Not only do people exhibit life positions, but teams, projects, organizations, and nations also exhibit these positions. Needless to say, people (and the project teams that comprise people) cannot always be categorized into one or the other life position, but awareness of this view of the world that a person or team exhibits can play a crucial role in the success of the team. This also enables us to map the software team models (based on Constantine [1989]) discussed to corresponding life positions.

As shown in Figure 8.14, the synchronous team (the one that Agilists have been advocating) exhibits the most ideal life position of I am OK—you are OK. This is the team with good leadership (as against management). Good project leadership in CAMS strives for an "I am OK—you

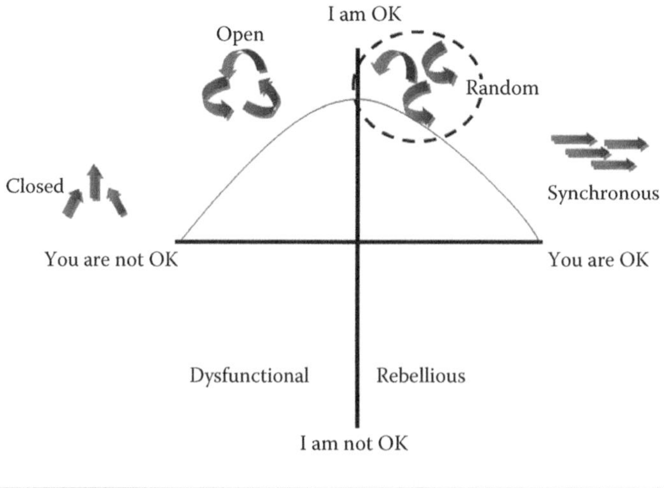

Figure 8.14 TA life positions and corresponding team structures.

are OK" life position for all individuals. This collaborative functioning with deep respect for individuals, their capabilities, and their limitations, provides excellence in CAMS-based team performance. An associated aspect of such collaborative functioning is the understanding of the TA ego states. While detailed discussion of the ego states is out of scope for CAMS, it is worth mentioning them in the context of team dynamics. Berne has identified three ego states: parent (controlling), child (emotional), and adult (factual). In a daily stand-up meeting, for example, team members can be encouraged to suspend their "child" tendencies and, instead, focus on aligning with the team goals through their functioning "adult" personality part. Good project leadership also works to create situations, such as social events and "after hour drinks," where the "child" personality of an individual has an opportunity to express itself. A composite Agile project has to be a relaxed place to work; and that appears to be the best way to produce quality outcomes.

The closed team, on the other hand, has the rigor and formality associated with its hierarchy. This is where formal project management plays a major part. The project manager here would be playing the instructional role—telling team members what to do and what not to do. Management (as against leadership) usually exhibits the "I am OK—you are not OK" life position. The other two team models are still constructive team models and they fall somewhere in between. The other extreme of these life positions is the totally negative "I am not OK—you are not OK" position, which means there is no team at all and people are unable to work together in any sensible form. This situation may provide some opportunities to study dysfunctional teams. In the context of the current discussion on CAMS-based leadership, where it is assumed that individuals have got together for work, the discussion of an "I am not OK—you are not OK" situation is out of scope.

The crux of project formation is the identification, recruitment, and organization of team members. Description of job roles, rewards structures, and personal growth all follow on from the most fundamental part of team building—recruitment. While a traditional, planned team has its objectives and roles well-defined, the one that is following an Agile approach will find minimal description of roles and hierarchies.

CAMS encourages up-front effort to get the team right through a combination of formal job description and selection along with ensuring the "best fit" for the individual. All teams have to face the challenge of getting the people to gel together. Team-building exercises can only improve on the people you have—getting the right people is a more basic challenge. The project leader (or an Agile coach) can herself be nominated by the decision makers responsible for the program of work. The steering committee can then delegate the responsibility of team formation to such a person. At times, this "manager" may be put in charge of a preassembled team—which is not a favorable situation.

In assembling a team, it is vital to keep in mind that those people who are effective individually may not necessarily be able to perform well in team environments. The suggestion is the best-fit approach, as shown in Figure 8.15. The aim is to create a team that is likely to function as smoothly as possible. It is possible that such a team is *not necessarily* made up of the best technical people. The project leadership responsible for assembling the team may at times have to let go of a technically superior person if, based on interviews and reference checks, it is apparent that the person does not fit in very well with the existing team members. The end result of this selection process is a team where most members fit well with each other, and the team itself fits well with the rest of the organization. Lack of cohesiveness can cause an untold amount of misery rather than lack of technical talents. Technically brilliant individuals need to learn to work together with others who may not be as brilliant—or, alternatively, project leaders need to isolate the work that can be carried out by an individual and allocate that work almost like a "contract." While this

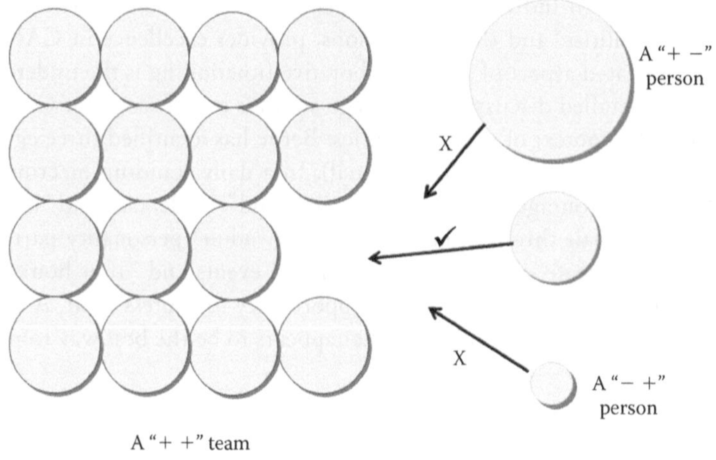

Figure 8.15 A homogeneous smoothly functioning synchronous team is based on the best-fit approach.

may not be a formal contract, it still amounts to an extremely defined work that is not encouraged in pure Agile approaches. Homogeneity of the team, as suggested by the best-fit recruitment approach, is vital for quality. A highly technically competent programmer who does not fit well will negatively influence the agility of the team. Negative attitude results in decreased productivity and quality far more than the ability (or lack of) of a single programmer to produce complex code. It is therefore imperative that the recruitment procedure within the organization is focused toward considering people who have a strong "adult" personality trait and who operate from the OK life positions.

Using formal questionnaires to ascertain personality types, coupled with subjective interview techniques, is a common way to ensure team homogeneity. In cases where technical competence is the overriding factor in a project, special short-term roles should be created with specific objectives in mind. Once those objectives (for example, creation of a distributed architecture) are achieved, that role can be disbanded. This will obviate the possible mediocrity that may result from overzealous application of the principle of homogeneity of the team, as discussed here.

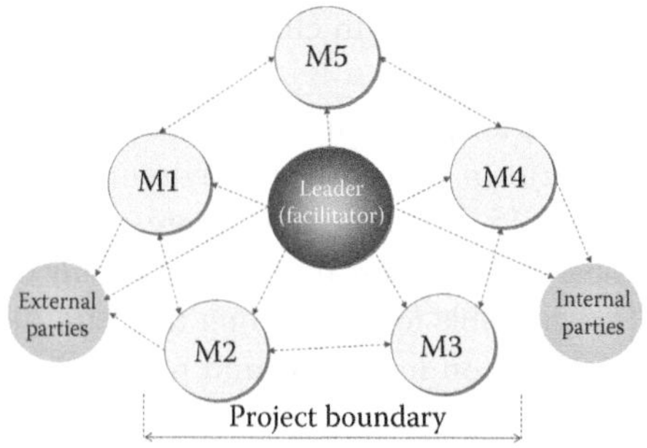

Figure 8.16 Flattening the pyramid (top view of a "+ +" team organization). (From Unhelkar, B., *Proceedings of IT Project Management by AIC Conferences*, Auckland, New Zealand, 15-17 April 1996; Unhelkar, B., *Process Quality Assurance for UML-Based Projects*, Addison-Wesley, Boston, 2003.)

Figure 8.16 shows the flattening of the pyramid of project team organization (top view) (Unhelkar, 1996, 2003).

Organizing the team structure follows assembling the right people. While the four possible team structures discussed earlier can be very helpful in achieving this goal, and while the synchronous team remains the goal of every project manager, CAMS also encourages a team structure that is as nonhierarchical as possible. This is essential not only for the project team members onboard for the long term, but also for the specialist staff that might be added to the project from time to time, and who may not be interested in the actual reporting structure.

Hammer and Champy (1994) have discussed "flattening the pyramid of the organizational structure" in their reengineering approach to business. The same idea can be applied in project teams dealing with software. A synchronous CAMS team is not organized in a hierarchical pyramidal manner, but is rather flat. In order to understand this flatter, nonhierarchical structure, it is best viewed from the top as a flatter team (Figure 8.16). Such a structure implies a less rigorous reporting structure and the project leader playing a hands-off role. This leadership is a facilitator role, organizing and coordinating activities, and creating and managing the environment rather than enforcing tasks. In a CAMS project, leadership also facilitates the processes and tools that ensure quality within the project.

A typical team with a leader (project manager) and five team members, when viewed from above, is illustrated in Figure 8.16. This composite Agile project structure is a flat *circular* arrangement with many advantages in terms of organization and communication. For example, communication is now facilitated not only between the leader and members (L–M1, L–M2, and so on) but also among members (M1–M2, M2–M3, M4–M5, and so on). The position of the leader is not viewed as superior (as it would be for a front view), but is seen at the same level as the other members of the team. The leader is the facilitator in this case. This facilitation occurs internal to the project, outside the project boundary, as well as external to the organization. Figure 8.16 also highlights the "Agile coach" role of a leader in terms of protecting the team from disrupting influence (both external and internal) and removing road blocks. This composite team structure caters to both the structural and the dynamic aspects of its functioning.

SIDEBAR

Capretz and Ahmed (2010) discuss the crucial importance of personality traits and their interrelationship with software engineering. Murugesan also highlights the need to study the intricate dynamics of individuals and their personalities and the corresponding effect on software development—especially in this Agile era. Are there any specific personality traits of individual software developers that can make them work well in an Agile project? Are there other personalities that would be more comfortable with a planned and up-front organized project? The Myers–Briggs Type Indicator (MBTI) and transactional analysis (TA) promise to provide the basis for further investigations into the correlation between human traits and software development life cycles (SDLCs). With the advent of Agility, though, this correlation has to be also extended and applied to the way in which individuals and teams work across an organization. These frameworks can provide valuable support to project leaders and also organizational leaders in terms of what they need to do to encourage and support individual workers. The motivation, throughput, retention, and growth of an individual can depend substantially on the understanding his leader has of these personality types. CAMS encourages project leadership to understand and apply personality types to various iterations of the life cycle and also to the various roles within a project. The very basic phases such as analysis and design, or coding and testing can each benefit by an appropriate personality type assigned to take up corresponding roles within the process maps.

IT Governance and Business Agility

While project management is responsible for the delivery of outcome from a project, the role of IT governance is to ensure uninterrupted and ongoing systems and services. These services are based on service-level contracts derived from negotiations among internal as well as external parties. IT governance, thus, has a significant role to play in the operational success of an organization as compared with the one-off success of a project.

Business architecture, as per The Open Group Architecture Framework (TOGAF) version 9, (Open Group, 2009, p. 10), is made up of business strategy, governance, and key business processes for the organization. The business strategy focuses on two key strategic elements, "accelerate profitable growth" and "enhance operational excellence." Growth depends on leadership, improvement in customer satisfaction, and innovation. Operational excellence eventuates through margin leadership (i.e., lower costs as a proportion of selling price), efficiency in supply chain management, lowering of costs, and optimizing working capital. IT governance plays a crucial role in enabling operational excellence through management control, reporting, and continuous improvement.

Furthermore, the compliance requirements emanating from the Sarbanes–Oxley legislation has changed the way in which an organization's IT systems operate. Since the requirements of the legislations pin the responsibility of financial control and reporting through IT systems on the organization's directors, the need to impose strong systems control is on the rise.

Governance provides that overarching control of operational processes and services within and across organizations. Business processes, function, information requirements, IT assets, and even people can be covered by IT governance frameworks. According to Broadbent and Kitzis (2005), good governance enables faster, better decision making. This enhanced decision making is based on clarity of goals and conversion of IT maxims into strategic actions. In CAMS, strong IT governance tied together IT and business strategies, and then applied this to the operational aspects of the organization.

Owing to the inherently controlling nature of IT governance, every discussion on business Agility has to ask the big question—will IT governance hinder Agility? Conversely, will Agile values and principles, based on trust, honesty, and courage, support IT governance? At times it appears as if Agility and governance are vying with each other for attention. Bringing a synergy between the two, however, is crucial for the success of composite Agile in business. CAMS aspires to add Agile values to IT governance frameworks such as Control Objectives for Information and related Technology (CoBIT) or Information Technology Infrastructure Library (ITIL). Improvement in IT services can be made through interactive gathering of requirements for improvements, demonstration of changes, and use of learning cycles.

In IT environments where organizations have grown by acquisition, IT project management, and governance have a lot more to handle in terms of integration of processes and methods—integration of systems and data. Considering IT governance in detail in CAMS goes a long way in reducing the potential methods friction that a governance framework can impose. The following are the specific advantages (especially in reducing methods friction) in considering an IT governance framework in the context of CAMS:

- Enhance trust between the IT department and the business by enabling business to understand the decision-making processes in IT through transparency and accountability in those decisions.
- Provide input into the business risk management. IT governance clarifies the contribution of IT in business and, thereby increases the ability of the business to manage risks.

- Map governance and control functions with those of project management—while projects can be managed through processes and standards, issues in project management can be better handled when they relate to existing IT governance standards and processes.
- Relate IT governance to enterprise architecture frameworks. This relating enables the architects to work within the controls and bounds of governance frameworks. Documentation of governance and the corresponding documentation of enterprise architecture models help in bringing about this productive relationship.
- Provide input into change management. IT governance helps change management, especially the one brought about by application of Agility, through its well-documented procedures. Once the existing processes are known through their documentation, it is easier to change them.
- Involvement of IT operational staff in business functions. It is important for the staff to know where and how they add value to business functions. Similarly, it helps business understand the contribution of operations staff. Agility in operational functions may not directly deal with delivery of software, yet it is crucial in helping continuous improvement.
- Bring about stability in infrastructure and systems applications that is critical to business. Implementation of governance standard can benefit the IT department by improving their quality of service (QoS), including increased system uptime, faster problem resolution, and better security. This is more so when Agile values are practiced together with the governance standard.
- Improve systems delivery mechanism through trust and collaboration with business.
- Encourage business to understand and make desirable use of IT.

SIDEBAR

Practitioners of methods are comfortable in bringing together the concepts from tried and trusted planned methods with the principles and practices of Agile. Yet, development effort is only a fraction of the overall time, money, and efforts spent in maintaining a system. As Ambler (2011) correctly asserts "... we've come to recognize that the majority of IT spending is devoted to the operations, support, and maintenance of systems, and only a very small portion to actual development of new functionality." Maintenance of a system or a suite of systems and its associated processes leads the discussion of CAMS into the realm of governance. IT governance standards such as Information Technology Infrastructure Library (ITIL) and Control Objectives for Information and related Technology (CoBIT) provide a commonly accepted basis for maintenance of systems and services. Therefore, these governance standards are readily embraced in CAMS. What is even more important than embracing these standards is the interplay between a chosen governance standard and the rest of the methods used in the organization. By considering IT governance in the context of development, project management, and business, CAMS works to reduce the potential methods friction in an organization.

The IT Governance Frameworks

There are two popular IT governance frameworks that were referred to in the original discussion on CAMS in Chapter 4. These frameworks are CoBIT and ITIL. The IT Governance Institute (ITGI, http://www.itgi.org/) highlights the increasing importance of service standards and service quality improvement. The following is a discussion of these two frameworks from a composite Agile perspective.

Control Objectives for Information and Related Technology (CoBIT)

CoBIT, as its full form "Control Objectives for Information and related Technology" suggests, is a framework for IT governance and control. With its origins in the US-based Auditors Association around 1996, CoBIT establishes clear links between business and IT goals. CoBIT enables managers to bridge the gap between control requirements, technical issues, and business risks. Development of IT policy and good practices is supported by CoBIT through its process model. The CoBIT process model is made up of 34 processes that include planning and organizing; acquiring and implementing; delivery and support; and monitoring and evaluation for IT control throughout organizations. The practices of CoBIT enable organizations to align IT with business goals, enhance value delivery of services and new projects, manage risks and resources, and measure performance.

SIDEBAR

Control Objectives for Information and related Technology (CoBIT) is an IT control and governance framework and supporting tool set developed by the Information Systems Audit and Control (ISACA) (www.isaca.org), and the IT Governance Institute (ITGI) (www.itgi.org). CoBIT facilitates optimal management of IT assets. CoBIT also documents the critical success factors that determine the effectiveness of the IT security and risk management controls. This enables organizations to align their business and IT goals and enables them to comply with Sarbanes–Oxley. Organizations also use the CoBIT framework to operate efficient and effective IT teams. These teams are controlled through governance practices that improve the management's understanding of the IT function within the organization (Ezcobit, 2009).

Table 8.4 describes four CoBIT activities in the context of Agile.

Information Technology Infrastructure Library (ITIL)

The Information Technology Infrastructure Library (or ITIL) comprises a set of guidelines that help IT departments in improving their QoS. Examples of issues associated with QoS include quicker resolution of problems, improved system uptime, and better security. Although its focus is the IT department, the influence of ITIL is felt across the entire organization. For example, by enabling improved capacity estimation at run time, ITIL can help alleviate problems such as server overload and time-outs. The ensuing improvement is felt in the business space of the organization. Similarly, through robust technical guidelines and policies, ITIL can prevent breaches of security. Since a significant part of the organization is exposed to the outer world through Web Services and even social media, this electronic security becomes paramount. ITIL thus helps in both business and IT governance and operations.

ITIL comprises disciplines that impact the business through IT services. These disciplines include services delivery and support, planning and implementing service management and security management, managing IT infrastructure and applications, and managing overall software assets of the organization.

SIDEBAR

Information Technology Infrastructure Library (ITIL) is a British government initiative. ITIL comprises key activities and a description of how they fit together. Also known as Infrastructure Management Service (IMS), ITIL is embraced by both IT and business areas of organization to provide a best practice framework for service management. Service management provides a

Table 8.4 Major CoBIT Activities and Agile

Activities	*Description (Agile Touch Points)*
Plan and organize	This activity defines the strategic IT plan, IT processes and organization, and management of IT human resources. This activity is also associated with quality, risks, and prioritization in projects. CAMS emphasizes early IT planning and quality management of CoBIT. While quality in pure Agile projects is based on user/customer feedback and nondocumented agreement, the formal documentation of CoBIT is most welcome in CAMS especially in large and/or outsourced projects
Acquire and implement	This activity focuses on identifying, acquiring, and maintaining IT resources, automated solutions, software, and technology infrastructure. Bayer (2008) discusses Agile's association with vendor and package selection wherein the values and principles of Agile (especially collaboration) can be applied not only within the organization but also with the vendor. CAMS recommends involvement of the users of the IT resources up front in the decision-making process for acquisition and implementation
Deliver and support	This activity deals with defining and managing service levels, third-party contracts, performance measures and issues, operation of physical environment, and user training. Agile touch points include identification and prioritization of development elements. The main focus of Agile delivery is the provision of a working software with continuous user involvement as well as related training
Monitor and evaluate	This activity deals with ongoing monitoring of delivered processes and software. This activity is based on internal controls that also enable compliance with laws, regulations, and contracts. Seemingly, this activity may have little to do with Agile. However, Agile values across an organization also imply their use in monitoring of services, their levels, and issues within them. Agile principles enable anticipation of issues as the operations are monitored; CAMS takes this subjective anticipation and applies metrics to evaluate performance. Thus, CAMS makes best use of this activity together with Agile principles

coherent mechanism to model an IT department that will enable efficient and effective service deployment. This modeling and coherence is facilitated by the set of policies and practices on planning, delivering, and supporting "IT service features," and managing IT and IT infrastructure (based on Long, 2008).

Since ITIL focuses on mapping of IT strategies with business strategies, it has substantial relevance to our discussion of Agile in practice. The core activities of ITIL (2009) are discussed below in Table 8.5 in the context of Agile.

Conclusions

This chapter described project management within CAMS. It also described in detail the importance of leadership and management in the context of Agile projects. The psychosociological issues

Table 8.5 Major ITIL Activities and Agile

Activities	*Description*
Service strategy	This activity provides guidance on the explanation and prioritization of service providers and their customers' investments in services (Addy, 2007). The service strategy can be influenced by high-level Agile requirements that are identified through user stories and result in iterations. A collection of user stories at a higher level of granularity can be used as a strategic approach to overall requirements. Most importantly, business priorities and technical estimations can be combined to ascertain the level and scope of services. Service strategy can also be based on service-oriented architecture (SOA) and incorporate Web Services—with subsequent opportunities for collaboration (Unhelkar et al., 2009)
Service design	Provides guidance on design of new or modified IT services through a catalog. Agile can make use of this catalog to develop and store services (typically these would be technical components using Web Services). Agile methods include the practice of validating the correctness of requirement to the customer through continuous customer involvement and feedback. This can be employed in service design in ITIL. For example, the list of requirements in Scrum can be mapped to this practice of ITIL. Agile can also be used to specify a level of service expected, and align the security needs of services to the business needs. At Web Services level, Agile requires the developer to test the code that has been implemented for its functional correctness. However, a greater challenge in Agile arises in testing the nonfunctional (or operational) area of business such as security and volume
Service transition	Facilitates transition of a service to the operational area of the business. This requires proper planning and controlled changes to the services. However, such planning and control management are much less emphasized in Agile methods. Therefore, the use of formal service transition of ITIL will improve the development of Web-Services-based components using Agile. There could be additional advantages in the future of tracking and maintaining services
Service operation	This is when the service has become operational. Agile approach will have an impact on service operation only at a technical level, wherein Web Services have been developed and deployed in operation. ITIL can be used in providing guidance in monitoring the service during operation including recording faults during operation. Identifying and fixing service failures during operation and quickly restoring service operation to a user are part of ITIL. Later, the events that caused the failures are identified and analyzed to ensure their occurrences are lowered. This is similar to the concepts of continuous testing and test-driven coding in Agile methods. Agile methods handle problems in a just-in-time (JIT) manner (Cottmeyer and Henson, 2008)

Table 8.5 (*Continued*)

Activities	*Description*
Continual service improvement	Provides guidance on the things that need to be controlled and measured for improving the business perspective of service quality (Long, 2008). Continual service improvement in ITIL deals with engaging IT and business management in an ongoing dialogue. Such dialogue would also provide measurements for service availability, reliability, as well as performance and reporting. The Agile approach of user participation during development also needs to be extended during the maintenance of services. Service orientation should enable developers to produce ongoing improvements by isolating and updating services on a "need" basis

associated with IT projects were presented through the TA and MBTI frameworks. IT governance was presented through CoBIT and ITIL together with its importance in CAMS. The controls and measures of governance frameworks together with leadership and mentoring through Agile principles are the best way to achieve quality. Chapter 9 deals with the issues of quality management, assurance, and testing in composite Agile.

Agile in Practice: Road Map 8

- Discuss the current project management method in use in your organization (Prince2, PMBOK, or any other) with your project management office (PMO) and/or Center of Excellence (CoE). Check with the CoE if there is an understanding of the declaration of interdependence there. If not, identify opportunities in your organization where that declaration of interdependence can be used.
- What are the key strengths and limitations of your current use of project management? List the main issues in managing current projects (you have the opportunity to bring together the right mix of Agility and control).
- List the portfolio of projects with their demographics as discussed in this chapter (type, size, budgets, number of people etc.). This list will provide you with potential projects that can benefit by the application of CAMS.
- Relate the projects to an existing IT governance framework (or, in the absence of such a framework, with any existing mechanism to control projects as well as systems in operation).
- Take a pilot project and discuss the creation of a real-life composite project instance (this will be based on an existing PM process such as Prince2, but will also have a business layer as well as a technical development layer; also note the need to consider existing governance standards in such a CAMS instance—Figures 8.3 through 8.5).
- Review the Agile practices embedded in the project management process map shown in Figure 8.6.
- Follow the creation of scope, work areas, and prioritization in the pilot project (you may want to experiment with CPA and its percentages versus MoSCoW approach to prioritization).
- Review and update document templates in use (if not available, create relevant templates) as shown in Figure 8.10.

- Update the project manager of the pilot project with the various team models and psycho-sociological frameworks. Discuss the possibility of use of one or the other to enlist resources for the project.
- Create a small survey "before" start of the project, which will list between 5 and 10 questions on what the team members expect in terms of sociocultural environment in a composite Agile project; follow that later "after" the project is completed with another quick survey to ascertain if "leadership" as described in this chapter works. Fine-tune the leadership process if it is acceptable. Ask detailed reasons if the approach is rejected by the team members (e.g., Did the flattened hierarchical structure make sense? Is viewing the team structure from the top helpful in bringing about a change?).
- Allude to TA and its life positions as an excellent sociocultural technique to be used in CAMS-based projects.
- Discuss the importance and relevance of individual subjectivity in composite Agile and balance it with the need for homogeneity in Agile teams.
- Present a flattened team structure by encouraging a "top view" rather than a "side view" in terms of organizing Agile teams.
- Discuss the potentially vying nature of IT governance and Agility.
- Outline the way in which Agile values and practices can be used in IT governance frameworks (ITIL and CoBIT) under the CAMS umbrella.

Discussion Questions

- Compare the planned and Agile factors in a project in the context of your organization. Discuss how time–budget–function–quality can compete with trust–simplicity–honesty–courage, and advise how you would try to bring these two vying groups of factors together.
- What is the relevance of declaration of interdependence in the context of CAMS-based project management?
- What are the project factors/demographics influencing a CAMS instance? Discuss in detail, with examples, any two factors (shown in Figure 8.2).
- What are the two well-known IT governance frameworks in use? Discuss any one of the two in terms of its phases and the associated challenges.
- Undertake an exercise of creating 15 tasks for a composite Agile project based on various methods being used in your organization corresponding to the layers shown in Figure 8.4.
- Discuss the areas where these 15 tasks create methods friction. Suggest strategies for reducing that methods friction.
- Embed Agile practices in the relevant tasks out of the 15 you have created and map that against the project management process map.
- Which deliverables out of the ones shown in Figure 8.10 are most important in a package implementation (e.g., enterprise resource planning (ERP) implementation) project as against a new development project? Answer with examples.
- What is the difference between leadership and management? Why would you want both in a project rather than one over the other?
- Describe the four team organizational models of Constantine (Figure 8.13) and explain which model best describes an Agile team. Further, explain how the same team model will work in a CAMS-based project.

- Why is it important to have a homogeneous team as compared with a group of brilliant individuals? Explain in the context of TA or the Myers–Briggs personality frameworks.

References

Addy, R., *Effective IT Service Management to ITIL and Beyond!* Springer, Berlin, Heidelberg, p. 89, 2007.

Ambler, S.W., Portfolio management and Agile software development, *Cutter Executive Report*, 2009.

Ambler, S.W., Disciplined Agile delivery and collaborative DevOps, *Cutter IT Journal*, 24 (12), 2011.

APLN Cockburn, A., D. Anderson, S. Augustine, C. Avery, M. Cohn, D. DeCarlo, D. Fitzgerald, J. Highsmith, O. Jepsen, L. Lindstrom, T. Little, K. McDonald, P. Pixton, P. Smith, and R. Wysocki.

Bayer, S., Agile software package implementations, *Cutter Executive Report*, 9 (8), 2008.

Beck, K., *Extreme Programming Explained: Embrace Change*, Addison-Wesley, Reading, MA, 1999.

Berne, E., *What do you say after you say Hello: The Psychology of Human Destiny*, Corgi, 1972.

Dooley, B.J., Implementing organizational change for Agile development, *Cutter Executive Report*, November, 2009.

Capretz, L.F. and F. Ahmed, Making sense of software development and personality types, *IT Professional*, 12 (1), 6–13, January/February 2010, http://doi.ieeecomputersociety.org/10.1109/MITP.2010.33.

Constantine, L.L., Teamwork paradigms and the structured open team, *Proceedings of the Embedded Systems Conference*, Miller Freeman, San Francisco, CA, 1989.

Constantine, L.L., *Constantine on Peopleware, Yourdon Press Computing Series*, Prentice-Hall, New Jersey, 1995.

Constantine, L.L., Panel on Soft issues and other hard problems in software development (Ward Cunningham, Luke Hohmann, Norman Kerth), *Proceedings of OOPSLA'96, 6–10 October 1996*, San Jose, CA, 1996.

Cottmeyer, M. and V.L. Henson, *The Agile Business Analyst*, VersionOne Inc, 2008, viewed 12 March 2009, http://www.versionone.com/whitepapers.asp.

Ezcobit Benefits from using COBiT, 2009, viewed 20 September 2009, http://www.ezcobit.com/UsingCobit/html/00Intro6.html.

Fischer, B., The role of the Agile evangelist: Part I—Why you want one in........, *Cutter Executive Report*, Boston, USA, 2009.

Ghanbary, A. and Day, J. Success of Agile environment in complex projects, *Australian Information Warfare and Security Conference*, Perth, Australia, 2010, http://ro.ecu.edu.au/isw/31/.

Highsmith, J., *Agile Project Management: Creating Innovative Products*, Addison-Wesley, Reading, MA, 2009.

ITIL What is ITIL? APM Group Ltd, 2009, viewed 16 July 2009, http://www.itil-officialsite.com/AboutITIL/WhatisITIL.asp.

Long, J., *ITIL® Version 3 at a Glance*, Springer, New York, NY, 2008.

Maharmeh, M. and B. Unhelkar, Investigation into the creation and application of a composite application software development process framework, *Proceedings of ITNG Conference, ITNG 2008, 7–9 April*, Las Vegas, NV, 1286, 2008.

Miller, G.G., The characteristics of Agile software processes, *The 39th International Conference of Object-Oriented Languages and Systems*, Santa Barbara, CA, 2001.

Schwaber, K., The Agile alliance revolution, 1 May, 2001.

Thomsett, R., When the rubber hits the road: A guide to implementing self-managing teams, *American Programmer*, 37–45, December 1994.

Thomsett, R., Even more extreme project management—Part 2, *Cutter Executive Report*, 2003.

Unhelkar, B., Developing the vital leadership skills required of an IT project manager, *Proceedings of IT Project Management by AIC Conferences, 15–17 April 1996*, Auckland, New Zealand, 1996.

Unhelkar, B., *Process Quality Assurance for UML-based Projects*, Addison-Wesley, Boston, MA, 2003.

Unhelkar, B., *Practical Object Oriented Analysis*, Thomson Publishing, Australia, p. 221, 2005a.

Unhelkar, B., Stop playing games! Transactional analysis and IT Leadership, *Cutter IT Journal*, 18 (4), 2005b.

Unhelkar, B., Agile in practice: A composite approach, *Cutter Executive Report*, 11 (1), 2010.

Unhelkar, B., A. Ghanbary, and H. Younessi, *Collaborative Business Process Engineering and Global Organizations: Frameworks for Service Integration*, IGI Global, Hershey, PA, 323 pp., 2010.

Further Reading

Abrahamsson, P., O. Salo, J. Ronkainen, and J. Warsta, *Agile Software Development Methods. Review and Analysis*, VTT Publications, Espoo, Vol. 478, 2002.

Ambler, S.W., Agile software development, *Agile Modeling*, 2006. (Also see www.ambysoft.com for Scott Ambler's scholarly articles; viewed 9 March, 2012.)

Badr, I., *Rapid Development through Agile Modelling*, Telelogic AB, 2006, viewed 4 June 2006, http://www.telelogic.com.

Beck, K. and M. Fowler, *Planning Extreme Programming* (XP Series), Addison-Wesley, 2001.

Cohen, D., M. Lindvall, and P. Costa, An introduction to Agile methods, *Advances in Computers*, Elsevier Science, New York, pp. 1–66, 2004.

Constantine, L. and L. Lockwood, *Software for Use: A Practical Guide to Models and Methods of Usage-Centered Design*, Addison-Wesley, 1999, www.foruse.com.

DeMarco, T. and T. Lister, *Peopleware: Productive Projects and Teams*, Dorset House Publishing Company, 1987.

Devereaus, M. and R. Johansen, *Global Work: Bridging Distance, Culture and Time*, Jossey-Bass, pp. 38–39, 1994.

Ghanbary, A., Collaborative business process engineering across multiple organisations, *Proceedings of ACIS 2006*, Adelaide, Australia, 2006.

Hammer, M. and J. Champy, *Reengineering the Corporation: A Manifesto for Business Revolution*, Harper Collins, New York, 2003.

Harris, T., *I'm OK, You're OK*, Pan Books, London and Sydney, 1981.

ITGI, COBIT case study: IT risk management in a bank, viewed 20 April 2011, http://www.isaca.org/Knowledge-Center/cobit/Pages/COBIT-Case-Study-IT-Risk-Management-in-a-Bank.aspx.

ITGI, COBIT-transforming enterprise IT, viewed 6 April 2011, http://www.isaca.org/Knowledge-Center/cobit/Documents/COBIT-Overview.ppt.

IEC , ISO38500 (ISO 38500) IT Governance Standard, 2008, viewed 20 April 2011, http://www.itgovernance.co.uk/products/catalog/1863.

James, M. and D. Jongeward, *Born to Win: Transactional Analysis with Gestalt Experiments,* Addison-Wesley, 1971.

James, M., *The OK Boss*, Addison-Wesley, 1975.

Kriendler, J., Cultural change and object-oriented technology, *Journal of Object Oriented Programming*, 5 (9), 6–8, 1993.

Lanier, J., The frontier between us, *Communications of the ACM*, 40 (2), 55–56, 1997.

McWalters, M., Human nature, *Understanding Psychology*, McGraw-Hill, Australia, pp. 18–23, 1990.

Meyer, B., *Object Success*, Prentice Hall, 1995a.

Meyer, B., Object technology: What's in it for management, *Proceedings of Object'95 by AIC Conference,* 1995b.

Moir, S, The Calder-Moir IT governance framework, 2008, revisited on 20 April 2011, http://www.itgovernance.co.uk/presentations/IACONPresentation-AlanCalderonITGovernance-12March08.pdf.

Morrison, J. and J. O'Hearne, *Practical Transactional Analysis in Management*, Addison-Wesley, 1977.

Shanmuganathan, R., IT governance—Is key to business success, 2009, viewed 20 April 2011, http://www.isaca.lk/uploads/20090429-cxoforum/01-ramesh.pdf.

Suzman, N., IT governance, the "enabler" for business agility? 2007, viewed 20 April 2011, http://www.enablevalue.com/itgovernance/itgovernance_agility.html.

Symons, C., IT governance framework, 2005, viewed 20 April 2011, http://www.cba.co.nz/download/Forr051103656300.pdf.

Unhelkar, B., Managing objects, Managing people: A peopleware perspective of object oriented development, *Proceedings of Object Orientation by AIC Conferences 3–5 July, 1995,* Johannesburg, South Africa, 1995.

Unhelkar, B., Transactional analysis (TA) as applied to the human factor in object-oriented projects, *Handbook of Object-Technology*, ed., Zamir Saba, CRC Press, Boca Raton, FL, pp. 42/51–42/12, 1999.

Unhelkar, B., Agile in practice: A composite approach, *Cutter Consortium Executive Report,* 11 (1), 2010.

Weinberg, G., *The Psychology of Computer Programming,* Van Nostrand Reinhold Co., New York, 1971.

Wells, J.D., Extreme programming: What is extreme programming, 1999, viewed 14 June 2006, http://www.extremeprogramming.org/What.html.

Worthen, B., ITIL power, 2005, viewed 20 April 2011, http://www.cio.com.au/article/5833/itil_power/.

Chapter 9

Composite Agile: Quality, Testing, and Metrics

Almost all quality improvement comes via simplification of design, manufacturing... layout, processes, and procedures.

–Tom Peters
(*Author of* In Search of Excellence)

Objectives

- Discuss the three aspects of quality in the context of Agility—quality management, quality assurance, and quality control (testing)
- Describe in detail the three aspects of quality in the corresponding process map within Composite Agile Method and Strategy (CAMS)
- Discuss the application of formal quality techniques (walk-throughs, inspections, reviews, and audits) together with relevant Agile practices (showcases, test harnesses, stand-up meetings) in composite Agile projects
- Outline the syntax, semantics, and aesthetic aspects of quality checks and the corresponding levels at which they are applied (artifacts, diagrams, models)
- Address the use of verification and validation (V&V) in the context of two Agile methods—Extreme programming (XP) and Scrum
- Outline the challenges of testing in an Agile project
- Discuss organization of testing (test plan, test design, and test cases) in projects
- Differentiate between functional (based on user stories) and technical (based on classes) test cases
- Highlight relevant testing standards such as International Software Testing Qualifications Board (ISTQB) in the context of Agile
- Describe Agile metrics and measurements in Agile projects and their relationship to quality
- Highlight approaches to estimation based on metrics in Agile projects
- Present CAMS-based metrics corresponding to areas of work and roles within projects

Introduction

This chapter discusses the quality aspect of composite Agile at both project and organizational levels. Agility, particularly through its values of collaboration and communication, makes a major contribution to the overall quality of a product. Agile values enable the users of the product to closely participate in its development. This, in turn, also results in enhanced expectation management. The quality discussion in this chapter provides a Composite Agile Method and Strategy (CAMS)-based perspective on quality. This CAMS perspective includes management of the quality function across the organization as a whole, application of quality assurance techniques within projects, estimation of effort and output through metrics, and testing the product as it is being developed. Quality is crucial to the success of any initiative—irrespective of the methodology being used. Quality is also not piecemeal—a small part of a product or, for that matter, of an organization cannot claim to be of high quality if the rest is not. Therefore, quality can only be holistic in the way it gets applied in an organization.

Good quality is all about satisfying the needs of the user but "quality," and especially "good," are highly subjective terms (Unhelkar, 2003). The reference point against which quality is judged depends on the needs of the user at a particular time and place, and in a given situation. As all of these situations can change, quality remains vague in its definition. Despite that vagary, however, quality remains dear to everyone's heart. Quality approaches need a combination of "head" or logic together with the "heart" or subjective and emotional nature of quality—quite in line with the composite Agile approach at project and organizational levels. This chapter discusses these dimensions of quality.

Starting with setting the context of quality in an organization, this chapter discusses the way in which quality management encompasses quality assurance and testing. The three CAMS process maps relating to quality management, quality assurance, and quality control are also presented in this chapter. This discussion also includes the way in which known quality techniques, such as walk-throughs and inspections, work with the Agile practices of showcases and stand-up meetings. Quality includes verification and validation (V&V) of not only the product that has been delivered but also of the models and architectures that are used in CAMS to create the product. Therefore, the three dimensions of syntactical, semantics, and aesthetical quality checks are discussed. This chapter then discusses the way testing is organized, its major activities, and its deliverables. For example, there is a discussion in this chapter on the way functional tests can be organized as against technical tests. This chapter also alludes to an increasingly popular testing framework, the (ISTQB, 2012). This discussion is followed by a suite of Agile metrics that can be applied within CAMS.

SIDEBAR

Coplien (1994) references Christopher Alexander in order to come closer to what is meant by quality. Architect and mathematician Alexander is well known in the architectural world, especially for the application of his measures of quality to architecture, or to any creative process for that matter. During his keynote address at OOPSLA'96 (Alexander, 1996), Alexander described quality in broad terms as the ability of a system* to "be alive," that is, to be a part of, and to support, our lives. "Coherence," as well as another subjective term "happiness," was also a part of that address. At a lower level, this quality is utilitarian, aesthetically pleasing, robust, and whole. But Alexander notes that any attempt to name or measure the quality is futile: that

* Not necessarily a software system.

all words confuse more than they explain. Gabriel (1993) also discusses Christopher Alexander's definition of "quality without a name":

> A system has this quality when it is at peace with itself, when there are no internal contradictions, when it is not divided against itself, when it is true to its own inner forces. Alexander's words to define this quality are *alive, whole, comfortable, free, exact, egoless,* and *eternal.*

Thus, it appears that quality cannot be named or pinpointed. Perhaps, quality comes philosophically closer to the definition of Tao, "the Tao which can be named is not the true Tao (Cheng, 1981). The discussion on quality is thus closely associated with Agility. Agile values such as trust, honesty, and courage are subjective, qualitative, and difficult to measure, yet absolutely crucial to a business or technology outcome. Agile practices too have a significant qualitative element within them. For example, the agenda for a daily stand-up meeting, the depth of a user story and planning, and estimating an iteration are all based on a combination of advice from the method and personal knowledge and experience.

Quality Context: Management, Assurance, and Control

Perry (1991) in *Quality Assurance of Information Systems* starts with a dictionary definition of quality:

> The dictionary defines quality as an attribute or characteristic that is associated with something. Thus, Quality cannot be universally defined but rather must be defined for the item in question.

Therefore, quality depends heavily on the "context." Users are interested in how the tools (products) help them in their work. Developers and managers, responsible for the development of products, need to follow a discipline and a set of standards that would facilitate the creation of such products. Such an approach has to cater to the ever-changing "context."

A good starting point to understand quality is establishing the "context" in which the end user of the product operates. As the context changes, there will be changes to requirements. Accommodating vacillation between "may be" and "may be not" for a feature can be very helpful in planning *beyond* simply producing the product. This is where concepts broader than those dealing with mere development, such as domain-level requirements, extensive and varied prototyping, user training, and usability come into play.

Agile methods focus extensively on the context of the user and have the user in the center of the development activity. Accepting the ever-changing nature of the business and, therefore, the inevitable changes that a user is going to demand from the product, makes for a vital ingredient of quality. This changing context of the user and the business has to be also considered in understanding and promoting the quality of products, services, and operation in an organization.

The issue of quality remains vital to every user as it dictates the user experience of a product or service. Thus, even without a precise definition, there remains substantial need for efforts in improving the quality of our products, processes, and communication mechanisms as is feasible (Unhelkar, 2003). This objective effort encompasses usage of detailed checklists for quality verification, following a formal process for development, and attempting to measure and improve quality. Thinking, debating, and formulating quality concepts and standards and then implementing them at the organizational and project (development) level is vital for holistic quality.

Quality requires regular evaluation of overall project performance. Such evaluation ensures that the project team is meeting quality standards. Quality metrics and measures can play an important role in supporting quality evaluations. V&V practices are applied, measured, and fine-tuned to achieve ongoing quality results. As Agile development projects operate on smaller, visible iterations, quality initiatives need to also mirror the same. Hence, there is a need for quality practices in all activities within an Agile approach. CAMS process maps also embed quality activities and practices within them including requirements modeling, system design, and implementation. The CAMS process maps specific to the quality function in this chapter are the ones for quality management, quality assurance, and quality control.

Figure 9.1 shows the three levels or dimensions of quality understood and applied in CAMS: quality management, quality assurance, and quality control. While quality management is the holistic aspect of quality that applies across the organization, quality assurance and control are closely applied in a project.

Quality management is the strategic aspect of quality for the organization that feeds into projects. In this high-level work of quality management, the overall planning of the entire project work is detailed in order to manage the quality of the final product. Quality management involves overall planning of processes and procedures in order to ensure quality of the final outcomes. Creation of organization-wide policies and procedures, creation of a good quality development and testing environment, giving consideration to environmental factors (DeMarco and Lister, 1987), creation and management of teams, and handling the overall sociology within the project are examples of the responsibility of quality management.

Quality assurance (QA) is the process aspect of the project itself. It deals with the configuration and deployment of process. Following a quality process reduces errors and increases the chances of a more satisfactory acceptance test. Quality assurance also provides all necessary techniques to verify and validate the models. These techniques include syntax, semantics, and aesthetic checks (discussed in detail later in this chapter) in the three modeling spaces (Unhelkar, 2005). It provides the templates for deliverables and verifies the compliance of the deliverables to the standards within the project. This results in an overall quality of models and processes, which is reassuring to the stakeholders in terms of the expected and accepted level of quality of the system.

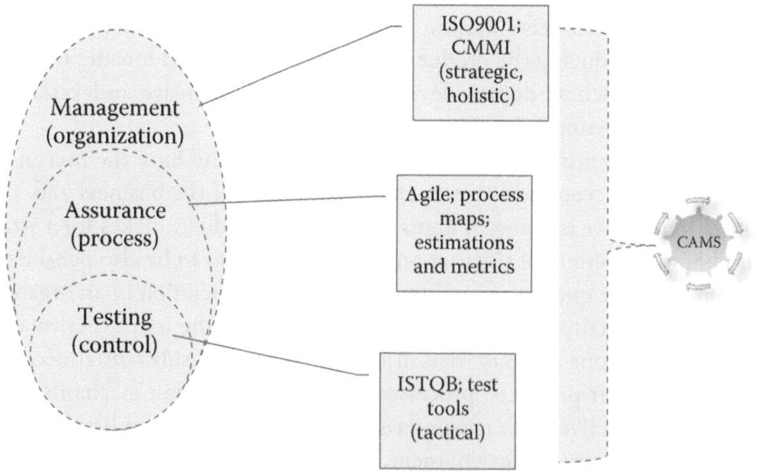

Figure 9.1 Quality and CAMS: management, assurance, and control.

Quality control (QC) deals with the actual testing of the product, requiring tactical skills on the part of the testers. Since testing involves "detection" of errors, it is the "policing" work undertaken on the software system. Testing means, very simply, passing a suite of varied test data through the actual software components that have been developed. Testing work involves detecting as many errors as possible during development before the system is released into production. Testing of software products plays a crucial role in their deployment—this is especially so within large organizations. Testing is important for developers as well as users of software products.

In order to successfully carry out a project, the quality parameters need to be mapped across all activities of an Agile project. Correctness, efficiency, timeliness, accuracy, usability, and effectiveness can be considered as the quality parameters. Table 9.1 further expands that mapping and shows the software quality parameters and corresponding Agile practices related to that quality parameter.

The quality parameters in Figure 9.1 are subjective. As mentioned earlier, the way in which these quality parameters are interpreted can change depending on the context in which a user employs the product. Despite the subjective nature of these parameters, it is still important to continue to apply the Agile practices as well as the formal quality techniques to the products being developed. Verification and validation (V&V) is a term that represents the quality techniques and their application in projects. CAMS-based projects depend substantially on the application of validation and verification to the product being developed. Validation can be considered as a quality process that ensures the right product is produced. Effective validation is crucial to the acceptance of the product within a project (Ghanbary and Day, 2010). Verification is performed to ensure the product is right. Therefore, verification includes techniques of inspections and walkthroughs to ensure the correctness of functionality and code.

Validation, in particular, requires close collaboration with the user and other business stakeholders. One reason for the popularity of Agile approaches is that validation is carried out throughout the development effort. Without validation, the product may not meet the needs of the users. Verification is formally undertaken as part of iteration and can include unit testing, functional testing, and regression testing. Thus, while validation aims to answer the question "Is it the right product?", verification answers the question "Is the product right?" Verification helps in checking correctness of outputs against requirements (Savive, 2006).

Both verification and validation (V&V) benefit by continuous testing, and a quality process that includes users in all its steps is the most ideal way to improve quality. Agility, by its very nature, overcomes the known lack of visibility in testing products. Herschmann (2010) also suggests the many ways in which testing can be carried out in Agile projects. CAMS, through its planned elements, makes visible the business requirements that drive user acceptance testing. The real-time visibility into testing is an important ingredient in enhancing quality and, especially, its perception by the users. The following are the considerations that build on the Agile activities in Table 9.1 in order to promote quality within projects:

- The entire team should be responsible for quality—as much as it is responsible for development in a pure Agile approach.
- Every team member should be fully conversant with the composite process that applies to her or his work from a quality angle (i.e., be aware of the process maps within CAMS).
- Innovation and lateral thinking in the project can be encouraged provided it is rooted in the formality of planned methods (process maps). This will ensure innovation is not left entirely to an individual.

Table 9.1 Quality Parameters and Agile Activities

Quality Parameters	*Agile Activities*
Correctness	Document user stories in the right format in close collaboration with the users to ensure that they reflect what the users exactly want Conduct regular walk-throughs and inspections of requirement models, design, and code Pay careful attention (listen) to and evaluate user feedback on any artifacts Undertake continuous testing of the product (integrated code in software) Conduct regular nonfunctional (operational) tests on integrated code to ensure it is correct Ongoing demonstration of the working code to the user to gauge expectations and correct any errors of misunderstanding
Efficiency	Adhere to design coding standards (e.g., UML) for development and relevant modeling and architectural standards where relevant Encourage task sharing (e.g., pair programming) throughout the life cycle of a product Maintain simplicity of design (e.g., by layering) Ensure visibility of design and development by ongoing demonstration of the product
Timeliness	Create iterations in development and follow the iterative development time frames Create increments of development modules and develop them iteratively Separate releases of a product from its corresponding iterations and pay individual attention to each of them Go slow in order to go fast—as a piece of code written carefully may take more time but eventually will require less testing and rework. Thus, time is saved overall if it is spent earlier in the development Use patterns and frameworks for simplicity and accuracy of designs that will also save time as the starting point for designs will not be from scratch. Patterns will enable designs to be based on tried and tested situations in development
Accuracy	Identify and execute tests corresponding to user stories for functional requirements and other features listed under nonfunctional requirements Undertake verification and validation of the models, architectures, and designs with walk-throughs and inspections—and in close collaboration with all stakeholders Make use of previous metrics if available (through, say, a Center of Excellence) in order to increase the accuracy of estimates

Table 9.1 (*Continued*)

Quality Parameters	*Agile Activities*
Usability	Apply principles and practices of usability to the interfaces and executable system Ensure on-site customer involvement and listen to their feedback Enable the system to transition from a novice user to an expert (through changes in its interfaces and support to cater to the growing expertise of the user)
Effectiveness	Collaborate with stakeholders to understand the real value they are looking for from the system. This is the only way to ensure the system is effective (as it may be accurate but if it does not serve the purpose of the user, it may not be effective in practice) Focus on creating value for every feature that is being developed; eventually, focus on the value stream for a suite of processes and the system Demonstrate every increment of the product to the user to gauge its value addition the work done by the user Continuously test and incorporate feedback from the many stakeholders during development of the product

- Specific quality criteria (Table 9.1) should be addressed through not only the Agile activities described in the table but also through formal documentation of requirement models, architectures, designs, and test cases.
- Iterations and increments should be planned in such as way as to elicit immediate feedback from the user. The feedback should be incorporated in the product and the result demonstrated to the user as soon as possible.
- Users should also be kept aware of the development activities and be updated with the fixes and enhancement that are undertaken by the development team.
- Quality should be part of the overall business strategy of the organization and not independent of it—this will ensure that the interdependencies between quality and other organizational functions is catered to in the quality initiative.
- Sufficient attention should be given up front to the nonfunctional and usability aspects of quality. These are the quality features that are usually left to the last iteration for testing. However, they should be tested early in the development and should be sufficiently tested.
- Testing needs two types of life cycles—one that occurs logically, from start to finish; and the other that starts suddenly, from any point in the system or the business, and can break off at any point in time.
- Quality strategy should include procurement and use of appropriate tools. These tools not only test the product and its quality but also help in estimating testing efforts in a project.

SIDEBAR

Agile projects have test-driven development (TDD) that focuses on test cases and test harnesses as a means to developing code. Tests can be written for the functional, nonfunctional, and interface requirements in an Agile project. These tasks require not only expertise in testing-related activities but also in test planning, test execution, control, and reporting. Thus, as a project, test planning benefits by accuracy and reliability of estimation and measurements to improve and maintain as well as control quality throughout the product life cycle.

Speed is not synonymous with quality. Therefore, particularly in composite Agile, delivering the product quickly is not considered sufficient for quality in a project. In fact, at times, the product may even be "slow" in delivery (as was mentioned in the last Agile value in Table 2.2 "Unhurriedness"), but if it meets or exceeds expectations, it will be considered of high quality. Development and deployment of a product is also not a sufficient criterion for quality in a composite Agile approach—due diligence is required in terms of the strategy and method for maintenance of the product.

The "standards" in the quality domain usually refer to an international set of guidelines for processes that enable effective quality management. These standards are valuable in understanding the quality approach required as also the comparison between organizations and industry.

Examples of known standards in the quality assurance and testing domain include the ISO9001 in terms of overall quality management function, International Software Testing Qualifications Board (ISTQB) for a testing framework and certification, Software Process Improvement and Capability Evaluation (SPICE) for process improvement, and Capability Maturity Model (CMMI) (the latter with particular focus on process maturity). Undertaking organizational-level initiatives in quality requires awareness followed by appropriate use of these standards. Typically, a Center of Excellence (CoE) in an organization would take charge of the standards, their upkeep, and their deployment in the organization. Table 9.2 presents these standards in the context of composite Agile.

Quality Management Process Map

The quality management process map strives to bring together the many planning and organizational aspects of the project with a focus on quality. Planning for the project while keeping quality in mind, identifying the standards (e.g., Unified Modeling Language [UML] for modeling), setting the expectations of the users and, most importantly, getting the right people together for the quality work are some of the responsibilities of this process map. Figure 9.2 depicts the quality management process map and comprises such activities as quality planning, quality expectations, quality environment creation, quality team formation, quality standardization (process, model, and others), and test planning.

Roles in Quality Management

- Quality manager: This is the main role in the quality management area. The quality manager organizes and manages the quality function, which includes the creation of a quality environment and quality planning.
- User: The user highlights the expectation in terms of quality and provides feedback on the project/team's ability to meet those expectations.
- Quality analyst: The quality analyst carries out the quality function alongside the quality manager and mainly performs activities relating to process and model standardization.

Deliverables

- Quality plan: This contains the overall approach to quality across the organization and provides the input to the project.

Table 9.2 Standards in Quality Domain

Standard	*Composite Agile Relevance*
CMMI (currently v 1.2): Capability Maturity Model of the Software Engineering Institute of Carnegie Mellon University	Primarily focuses on the maturity of processes used in developing software systems. This standard provides a measure of formality and repeatability of activities and tasks within a process. CAMS process maps with embedded Agile practices can be subjected to CMMI maturity; this, in turn, can be used for process improvement
ISO9001: 2000: International Organization for Standardization	ISO9000, published by the International Organization for Standardization, provides an overarching framework for quality requirements within projects and across the organization. Agile quality practices and V&V of deliverables can be carried out within the framework of this quality standard
ISTQB: International Software Testing Qualifications Board	Provides an increasingly popular testing certification whose competencies form the basis of a testing framework. The testing competencies in this framework are measured across three levels: foundation, advanced, and expert. The quality control process map of CAMS provides the starting point for application of this framework in projects. The ISTQB has initiated the creation of Test Body of Knowledge (TBOK)
SPICE: Software Process Improvement and Capability Evaluation (also determination)	This is a global initiative to develop an international standard for assessing software processes. Focusing initially on software development processes, this standard now encompasses all processes related to software such as project management and quality assurance. Currently, SPICE covers six major business areas: organizational, management, engineering, acquisition supply, support, and operations. Owing to its wide coverage of organizational processes, an opportunity exists to apply SPICE to CAMS

V&V, verification and validation.

- Standards: This contains the requirements for all levels within the project, which includes documentation, design, testing, and coding.
- Test plan: The test plan contains the organizational and management aspect of testing within the project.
- Quality process: This contains the overall quality process including the quality management assurance and control process maps that can be customized and followed by the project team members.

Activities and Tasks in Quality Planning

Table 9.3 demonstrates the activities and tasks with corresponding deliverables and roles for the quality management process map. In addition, the Agile practices, which would be utilized during the process map execution, are included.

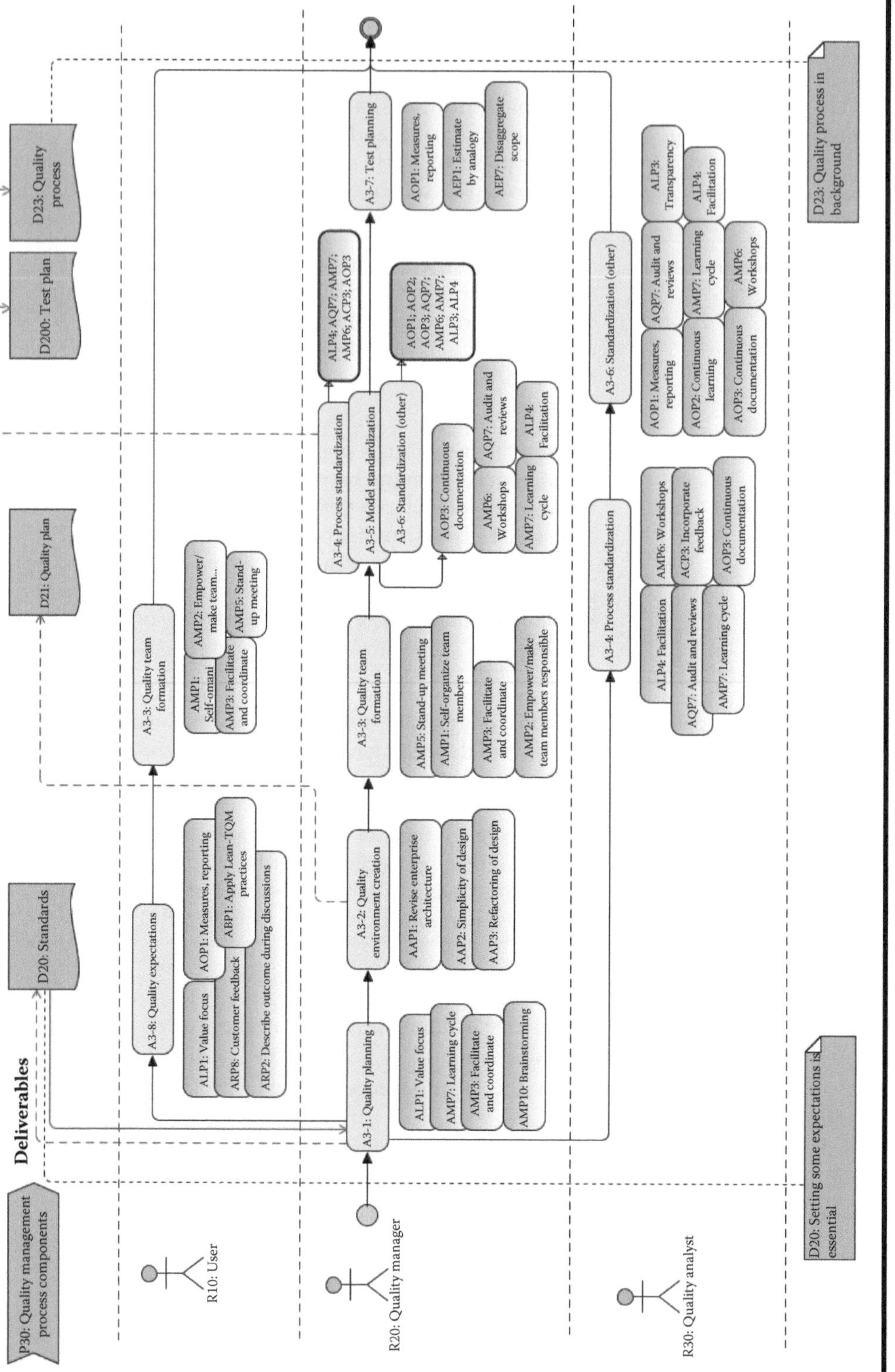

Figure 9.2 Quality management process map in CAMS.

Table 9.3 Quality Management Process Map

Activities	*Tasks*	*Deliverable*	*Roles*
A3-1: Quality planning	Quality criterion Time and budget Standards Agile practices: ALP1: Value focus AMP7: Learning cycle AMP3: Facilitate and coordinate AMP10: Brainstorming	D20: Standards	R20: Quality manager
A3-2: Quality environment creation	Analyze user stories (noun analysis; activity diagram analysis) of packages Document business entities (classes and objects) of packages Create functional prototype of packages Create physical environment Enhance e-factor Support development environment Agile practices: AAP1: Revise enterprise architecture AAP2: Simplicity of design AAP3: Refactoring of design	D21: Quality plan	R20: Quality manager
A3-3: Quality team formation	Identify people Quality roles to project roles People into quality team Agile practices: AMP1: Self-organize team members AMP2: Empower/make team members responsible AMP3: Facilitate and coordinate AMP5: Stand-up meeting		R20: Quality manager R10: User

continued

Table 9.3 (*Continued*)

Activities	*Tasks*	*Deliverable*	*Roles*
A3-4: Process standardization	Quality software process Process standards Software development process Process standards benchmark Process CASE tools Agile practices: AOP3: Continuous documentation AMP6: Workshops ACP3: Incorporate feedback ALP4: Facilitation AQP7: Audit and reviews AMP7: Learning cycle	D200: Test plan D23: Quality process	R20: Quality manager R30: Quality Analyst
A3-5: Model standardization	Identify operating system needs Project-level modeling conventions UML-based modeling Agile practices: AOP3: Continuous documentation AMP6: Workshops ALP4: Facilitation AQP7: Audit and reviews AMP7: Learning cycle	D200: Test plan D23: Quality process	R20: Quality manager
A3-6: Standardization (other)	Language standards Quality standards Documentation standards Middleware and distribution standards Database standards Agile practices: AOP1: Measures, reporting AOP2: Continuous learning ALP3: Transparency AOP3: Continuous documentation AMP6: Workshops ALP4: Facilitation AQP7: Audit and reviews AMP7: Learning cycle	D200: Test plan D23: Quality process	R30: Quality analyst R20: Quality manager

Table 9.3 (*Continued*)

Activities	*Tasks*	*Deliverable*	*Roles*
A3-7: Test planning	Specify details of packages Organize test resources Test time and budget Agile practices: AEP1: Estimate by analogy AEP7: Disaggregate scope AOP1: Measures, reporting		R20: Quality manager
A3-8: Quality expectations	Set user's expectations of quality Provide continuous feedback Quality assurance Agile practices: ALP1: Value focus ARP8: Customer feedback ARP2: Describe outcome during discussions AOP1: Measures, reporting ABP1: Apply Lean–TQM practices		R20: Quality manager R10: User

Quality Assurance Process Map

Figure 9.3 presents the quality assurance process map. Following on from the process of quality management this quality assurance process map undertakes the actual effort of assuring the quality of the output of the project. The quality assurance process map is not an independent process map but interacts with the project manager, and the quality manager plays key supporting roles in the execution of this process map.

Roles in Quality Assurance

- Quality manager and project manager: The quality manager checks the quality function as well as the quality standards compliance including metrics. The project manager focuses on organizing and planning. The project manager facilitates application of Agile principles and practices in the activities carried out here. The project manager is also a leader, exhibiting leadership characteristics (Chapter 8).
- Quality analyst: The quality analyst assures the quality of the models and code.
- Project team: The project team carries out the development functions including specific quality functions.

Deliverables

- Quality software process (QSP): This is the software process that the project team should follow. Such a process would be a combination of formal process maps and Agile practices.

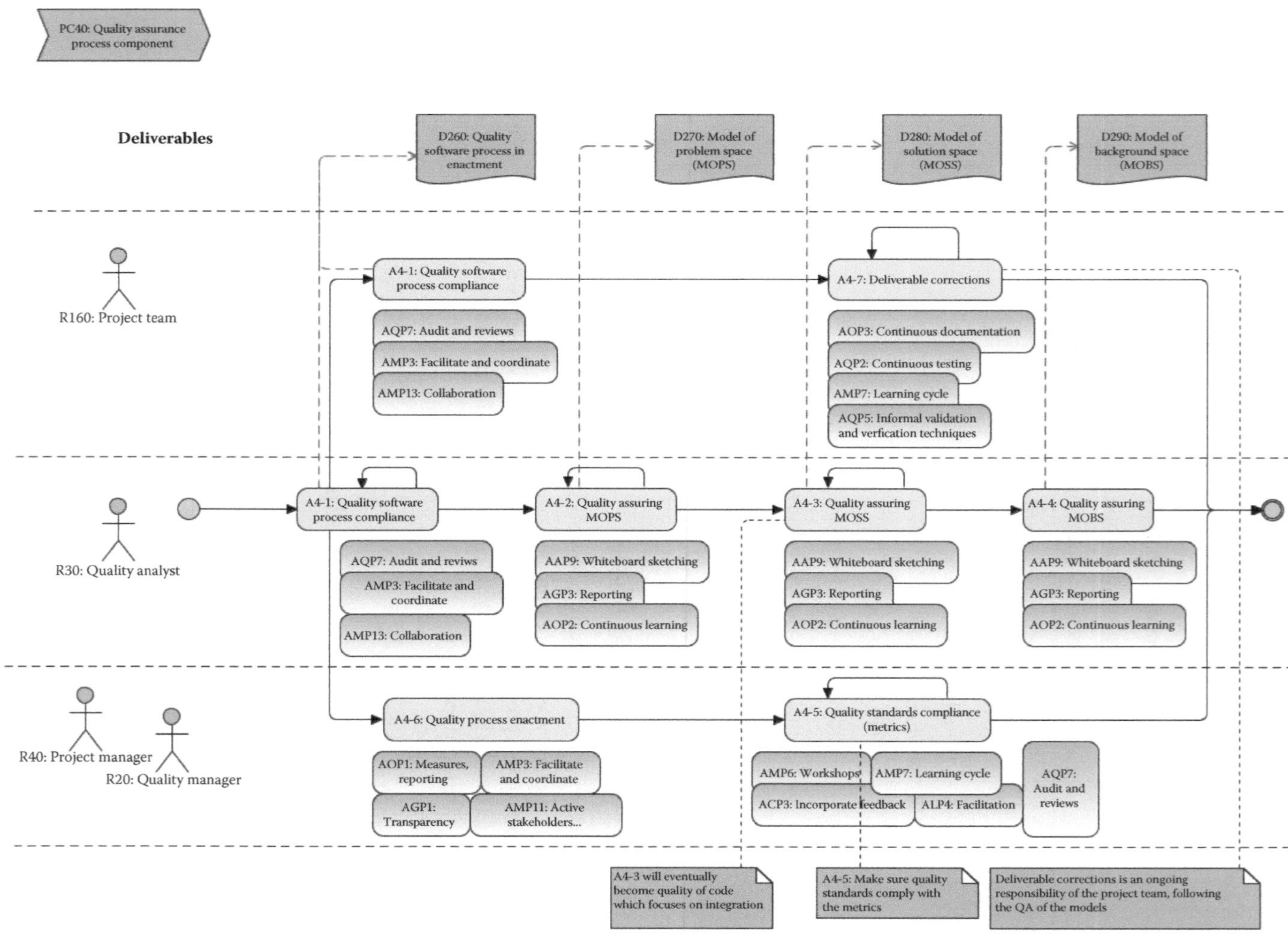

Figure 9.3 Quality assurance process map in CAMS.

Thus, a quality software process is a subset of CAMS focusing only on the quality aspects within a project. The quality of models is further illustrated in Figure 9.6.

- Model of problem space (MOPS): This model primarily contains the functional requirements and nonfunctional requirements (NFRs) of the business problem or need.
- Model of solution space (MOSS): This is made up of the solution design and code that is developed using technologies (specific to software development).
- Model of background space (MOBS): This is made up of architectural constraints, quality issues and deployment models.

Activities and Tasks in Quality Assurance

Table 9.4 shows the activities and tasks with the corresponding deliverables and roles for the quality assurance process map with Agile practices.

Quality Techniques and Agile Practices

Within CAMS, the quality function of an organization makes use of a combination of formal quality techniques and Agile practices. These techniques and practices are shown in Figure 9.4. The focus of these quality techniques is prevention of errors rather than detection of the errors in the final product—which is the focus of quality control. Figure 9.4 shows the three groups of quality techniques:

1. Formal techniques of walk-throughs, inspections, reviews, and audits that can make use of checklists, interviews, and workshops.
2. Examples of Agile practices that can directly add value to quality through stand-up meetings, writing of test harnesses, and showcasing.
3. Supporting techniques of checklists, interviews, and workshops that can be used with the previous two groups of quality techniques. These techniques are briefly discussed below in the context of CAMS.

The following is a brief description of these V&V techniques. Some of these techniques get further expanded within the process maps when used in practice.

- Showcase: Showcases are a formal presentation of a working output to all stakeholders before a release. Showcases are part of pure Agile approaches, but are readily embedded within some CAMS process maps.

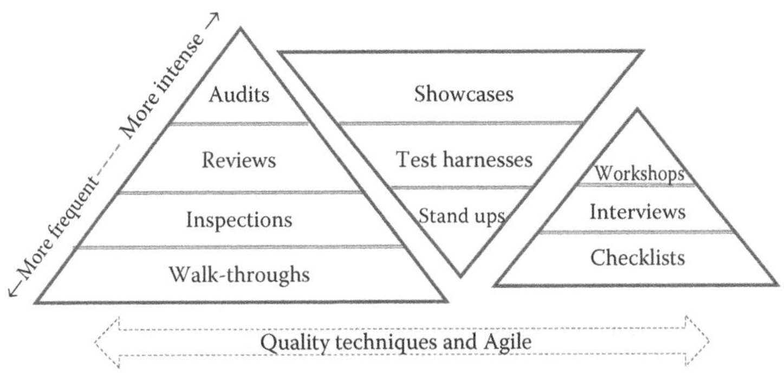

Figure 9.4 Applying quality techniques in Agile projects.

Table 9.4 Quality Assurance Process Map

Activities	*Tasks*	*Deliverable*	*Roles*
A4-1: Quality software process compliance	Identify relevant process elements Apply necessary process quality checks Apply sufficient process quality checks Correct errors in process elements (malleability) Agile practices: AQP7: Audit and reviews AMP3: Facilitate and coordinate AMP13: Collaboration	D260: Quality software process in enactment	R30: Quality analyst
A4-2: Quality assuring MOPS	Identify model and elements for checking Select quality techniques Apply quality checks Mark and report errors Checks after fixed Agile practices: AAP9: Whiteboard sketching AGP3: Reporting AOP2: Continuous learning	D270: Model of problem space (MOPS)	R30: Quality analyst
A4-3: Quality assuring MOSS	Identify model and elements for checking Select quality techniques Mark and report errors Checks after fixed Apply quality checks Agile practices: AAP9: Whiteboard sketching AGP3: Reporting AOP2: Continuous learning	D280: Model of solution space (MOSS)	R30: Quality analyst
A4-4: Quality assuring MOBS	Identify model and elements for checking Select quality techniques Apply quality checks Checks after fixed Mark and report errors Agile practices: AAP9: Whiteboard sketching AGP3: Reporting AOP2: Continuous learning	D290: Model of back-ground space (MOBS)	R30: Quality analyst

Table 9.4 (*Continued*)

Activities	*Tasks*	*Deliverable*	*Roles*
A4-5: Quality standards compliance (metrics)	Project standards Language standards Modeling standards Database standards Industrial standards Management standards Organizational standards Quality standards Process standards Agile practices: AMP6: Workshops ACP3: Incorporate feedback ALP4: Facilitation AQP7: Audit and reviews AMP7: Learning cycle		R160: Project team
A4-6: Quality process enactment	Organize quality process enactment Estimate and measure quality process Refine quality process Agile practices: AOP1: Measures, reporting AGP1: Transparency AMP3: Facilitate and coordinate AMP11: Active stakeholders, participation		R40: Project manager R20: Quality manager
A4-7: Deliverable corrections	Correlate the achieved deliverables to expected Analyze deliverables Correct deliverables Agile practices: AQP5: Informal validation and verification techniques AOP3: Continuous documentation AQP2: Continuous testing AMP7: Learning cycle		R160: Project team

- Prototype: Prototypes are both static (as in the prototype of a user interface) and dynamic (as in the prototype of a test database loaded with dummy records). Prototypes are most helpful in nonfunctional testing.
- Walk-through: A walk-through is a quick check of the artifact by going through its model or functioning step-by-step. The owner of the artifact can do the walk-through. A checklist (also shown in Figure 9.4) can provide guidance on what to check during a walk-through. Walk-throughs, which reflect Agile characteristics, are more frequent and less formal than the other quality techniques. In CAMS, walk-throughs are conducted for the formal modeling elements of a product (e.g., a UML diagram or a database schema). Walk-throughs can be embedded in a quality assurance process map associated with a deliverable. A formal walk-through of an artifact can take half an hour to an hour approximately. Therefore, a walk-through can use the format of a stand-up meeting in Agile without necessarily involving all stakeholders.
- Inspection: An inspection is conducted with the specific aim of finding errors. Thus, an inspection is more formal and more robust in ensuring the quality of a particular artifact than a walk-through. An inspection is most beneficial if it is not led by the producer (owner) of the artifact being inspected. In Extreme programming (XP), for example, where pair programming is popular, an inspection can involve the pairing partner on a regular basis throughout the development. However, within CAMS, it is important that a separate, dedicated activity of inspection is carried out in the presence of two or more stakeholders. Owing to their formality, inspections require preplanning, which is a part of the project management process. Technically, a test harnesses can be written to check out (test or programmatically inspect) the code within software projects.
- Review: A review is a formal quality technique that ensures that a particular deliverable is meeting its syntax, semantics, and aesthetics criteria (these are described in the next section). A review is a formal activity that is carried out on an entire system, a release within a system, and/or a suite of deliverables or models representing the system. Showcases in Agile provide an excellent mechanism to conduct formal reviews of a product before it is released. These showcases include all stakeholders and are conducted in a workshop environment. In CAMS reviews, the owner/producer of the model is discouraged from defending her model. While all stakeholders in a project participate in a review, users particularly make vital contributions through their practical business knowledge and experience. User contribution can change the parameters of the product being reviewed. For example, a piece of code that satisfies all quality checks may still need to be revised if, during a review, the user mentions that the original operational requirement of a certain number of hits per minute is now not valid and needs to be increased. While Agility strives to obviate these situations through collaboration throughout development, CAMS extends it further and formalizes it in reviews.
- Audit: An audit is the most formal of all quality techniques. It requires a preparation, followed by a rigorous inspection and review of the artifacts or products. Thus, in a way, audit supersedes inspections and reviews. An audit can be undertaken without the presence of the producer of an artifact. Thus, an audit may make greater use of checklists and interviews than a workshop. Formal audits can be further divided into internal audits and external audits. Both audits have the capability to bring in not only the technological and sociological elements discussed so far but also the legal issues. This is where the formal documentation of CAMS plays a helpful role. Audits result in a formal report on the status of the project, as well as possible suggestions for risk reduction and risk rescheduling.
- Checklist: Checklists provide the most basic form of quality techniques. They can be used to conduct a walk-through, inspection, formal review, or a detailed audit. Checklists provide

the baseline against which the quality of a model or a product is verified. Checklists can appear in various mediums—paper-based checklists; electronic checklists, which can do some basic analysis on the results of the checks; and checklists deployed on the company intranet. Electronic checklists are particularly helpful in an outsourced project in providing feedback on the status of a release and its contributing models and artifacts.

- Interviews: Interviewing techniques also need to be kept in mind for quality initiatives. Interviews require preparation beforehand, creation of an agenda, preempting the people being interviewed beforehand, and checking to ensure the mechanisms for conducting interviews (such as the communications technologies of phone or Internet) are working. Interviews are ideally conducted face-to-face but that opportunity may not always exist. Recording of interviews can provide an excellent mechanism to review them and get the salient points out of what is being expressed—typical requirements for a project.
- Workshop: Workshops, as a formal quality technique, provide immense benefits of group work. Workshops bring together project participants with varying expertise. Workshops can be organized for the purposes of inspections, reviews, and audits. They are also conducted for requirements capturing and requirements modeling. Workshops require facilitation; playacting during workshops is an important aspect of quality techniques. Finally, it is important to consolidate the workshop at the end, and to report on the progress. At the conclusion of the workshop, it is important to summarize what has been achieved, what should be done next (in terms of action items), and the strategy to handle parking lot issues. A summary of the minutes of the workshop is circulated to all concerned parties, and the next workshop scheduled tentatively, if possible.

Walk-throughs and inspections are examples of quality techniques outlined in Figure 9.4. These techniques can be applied on the basis of the understanding and experience of the team. Figure 9.5 presents the three key types of quality checks that can be applied during walk-throughs

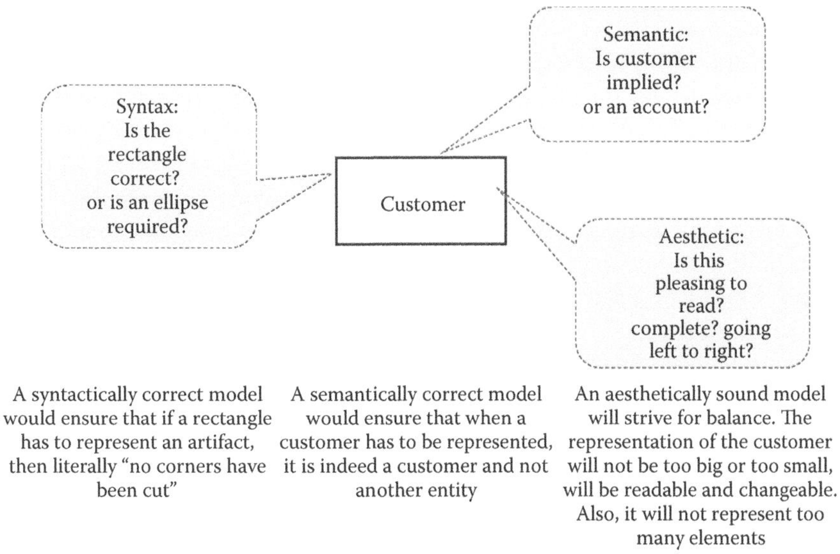

Figure 9.5 Three types of quality checks—syntax, semantics, and aesthetics.

and inspections—especially when the quality of a model or architecture is being ascertained. The syntax, semantics, and aesthetic checks are briefly described next.

- Syntax check is to ensure that the standards for a model are accurately adhered to. For example, in Figure 9.5, the syntax of the modeling language (UML, in this instance) indicates a rectangle to represent a class. Syntax checks ensure that the correct notation is used to represent a class. Syntax checks can also be applied at the code level (based on the programming language or environment in use). Computer-aided software engineering (CASE) tools assist enormously in ensuring syntactical correctness.
- Semantic correctness deals with accuracy of representation of the meaning behind a model or artifact. For example, a user story that is correctly written from its formatting viewpoint may still be wrong from its implied meaning perspective. Figure 9.5 presents another example wherein the class customer should semantically imply a customer and not an account. The semantics aspect of model quality not only ensures that the diagrams produced are correct but also ensures that they faithfully represent the underlying reality.

Once we have the syntax and the semantics correct, we need to worry about the aesthetics of the model (Ambler, 2003). Very simply, aesthetics imply style. Often, while reading a piece of code, one is able to point out the "style" or programming and hence trace it to a programmer or a programming team. Although the code (or, for that matter, any other deliverable) may be accurate (syntactically) and meaningful (semantically), still a difference arises because of their styles. This style of modeling has a bearing on the readability of the models and their comprehensibility. Figure 9.5 reminds us of this aesthetic check by asking an important question, "Is this model pleasing to read?"

Walk-throughs and inspections make use of the levels of checks—syntax, semantics, and aesthetic. Each of these checks applies to a piece of code, a diagram in UML, an entire model of requirements (or design), and to the release of a system. Each type of check plays a role in quality assurance based on the type of artifact being inspected. Therefore, it is not necessary to have all types of checks applying to all artifacts, diagrams, and models produced (see Figure 9.6).

The three levels of checks to artifacts and models apply as follows:

1. The artifacts (or "things") such as code, basic models, user stories, and use cases, specifications and associated documentation of these artifacts: Syntax checks, followed by semantics checks, are most effective on these artifacts. This is the ground-level nitty-gritty checking of the artifacts and deliverables.
2. The diagrams, their interdependencies, and product iterations (releases): This is where continuous focus on semantics checking is invaluable—especially as the product is still being developed. This will be the equivalent of a standing view of the model being verified and validated. User participation is most helpful in checking the semantics as compared with the syntactical checking.
3. The complete models or architectures of a system, and the system (final release) itself: This is where the final check takes place through the syntax, semantics, and aesthetics checks. This will be the bird's-eye view, enabling checks of symmetry and consistency, resulting in enhancing the aesthetic quality of the models and the product.

Figure 9.7 describes the way in which the quality assurance techniques discussed this far can be applied to an XP iteration and life cycle. As seen in Figure 9.7, the requirements in XP are written in the form of story cards. These stories (or features) are prioritized for the development iteration. V&V techniques of interviews and walk-throughs are applied in understanding and prioritizing

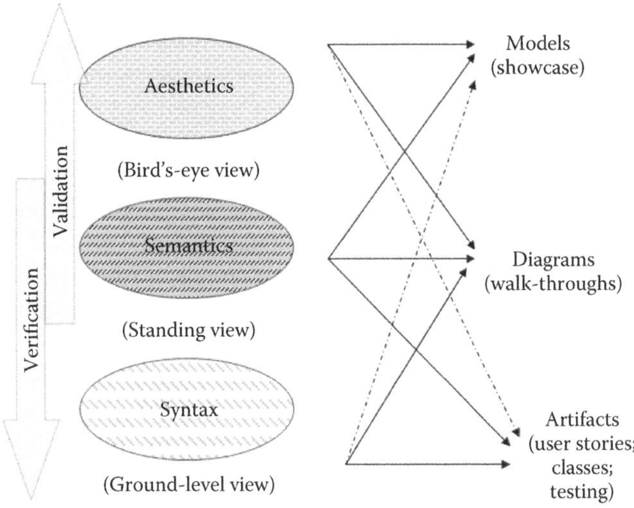

Figure 9.6 Syntax, semantics, and aesthetics verify and validate the artifacts, diagrams, and models. (Based on Unhelkar, B., *Verification and Validation for Quality of UML Models*, Wiley Interscience, New York, [2005].)

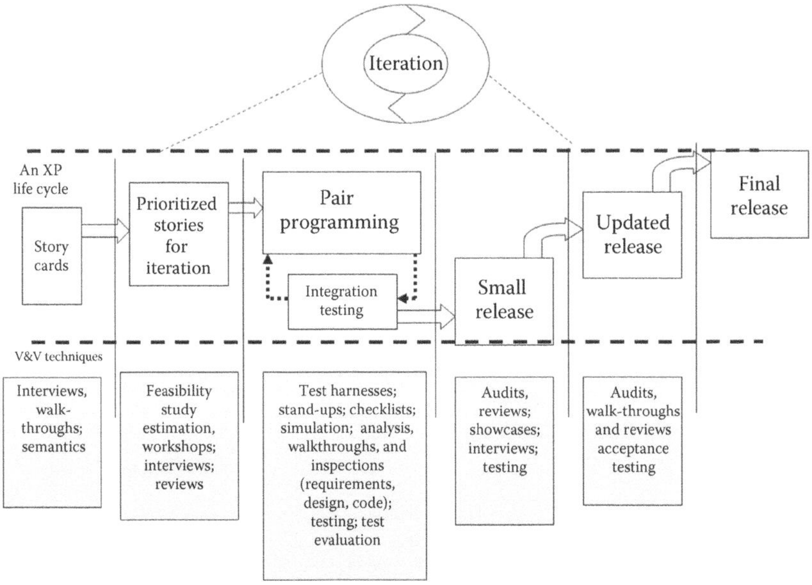

Figure 9.7 Applying V&V in CAMS (XP specific).

the requirements. Any associated user documentation (such as separate requirements statements and business rules) can also be subjected to V&V here. Once the prioritized requirements move into development, the XP-specific Agile practices (e.g., pair programming) kick in. Writing and execution of test harnesses, and walk-throughs and inspections of design and code provide quality value here. The code is then passed through unit and integration testing and a small release of the iteration is carried out. This ongoing integration testing is vital to enhance the quality of the product. Integrating and testing software regularly, often multiple times per day, is critical to the success of an Agile team (Cottmeyer and Stevens, 2009). CAMS, however, further encourages carrying out of formal audits and reviews that also include "nonexecutable" approaches to testing, as shown in Figure 9.7. In the meantime, if there are any changes in the requirements, then these major steps need to be repeated. The product/system is updated and released for full user acceptance test (and for rework, as also a regression test).

Figure 9.8 shows another example of an Agile method, Scrum, together with the areas where quality techniques play a part. Scrum artifacts include the plan, product backlog, and sprint backlog, which can all be subjected to quality walk-throughs and inspections. The semantics behind these documents becomes most important here. For example, a sprint backlog list needs to be checked in close collaboration with the users for its meaning, priority, and associated risks. During development, however, the quality of the product can be improved through walk-throughs in the daily stand-up meetings, prototyping, and simulation (particularly for NFRs). Finally, before the product is released, a showcase can be conducted where syntax and semantics as well as the aesthetics of the product are the focus of quality checks. Close collaboration with users during the development can reduce the "surprise" factor at the showcasing stage. Reviews and audits can also verify and validate that all phases have been completed satisfactorily. Reports of V&V activities can be formal or, alternatively, can also be provided during the daily stand-up meetings.

Quality Control Process Map

Testing is a key component of Agile development. The widespread adoption of Agile methods has brought the need for effective testing into the limelight, and Agile projects have transformed the

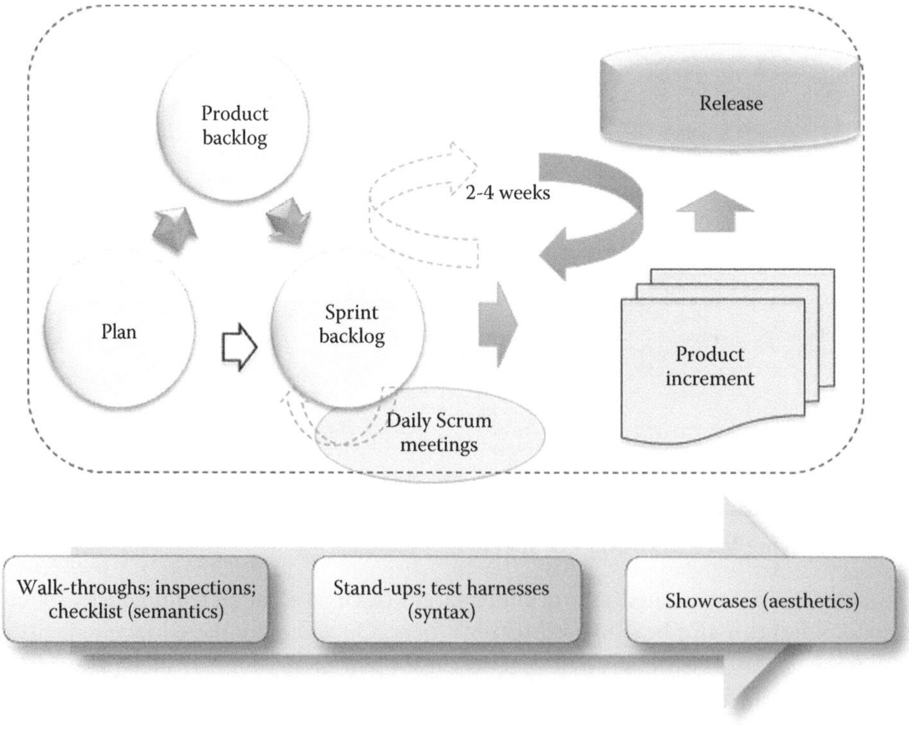

Figure 9.8 Applying V&V to a Scrum life cycle.

role of testers (Crispin and Gregory, 2008). Figure 9.9 presents the quality control process map within CAMS that focuses on testing.

Roles in Quality Control

- Tester: The tester, who executes the testing process is the main role here.
- Quality manager: The quality manager manages the quality function such as quality environment creation.
- User, system designer, development team: These roles participate in providing input in testing, understanding testing themselves, and managing expectation.

Deliverables

- Test plan: A test plan organizes the testing function, including details of resources and schedules of testing.
- Test design: The test design mainly provides strategies for testing, for a specific subsystem or package. NFRs for the package can be tested here.
- Test environment: This is the physical environment such as databases, operating systems, and applications. This environment should be created before testing.
- Test data: These are created on the basis of sampling mechanisms and provided within the test environment.
- Test result: The test result includes the output of the formal testing activity, collated results, and updates on fixes.

These deliverables assist in organizing the overall testing (discussed later in Figure 9.10).

Activities and Tasks in Quality Control

Table 9.5 demonstrates the activities and tasks with corresponding deliverables and roles for the quality control process map with Agile practices.

Organizing Testing

The quality control process map is indicative of how important testing is to a project. In fact, testing assumes the status of a project within a project. Table 9.6 lists the typical and important activities that are undertaken in a large and complex project. These activities are described in the context of Agile.

Testing activities can be based on a combination of testing approaches. The quality manager can choose the right combination of testing approaches when the quality control process map is used. These testing approaches are as follows:

- Black–white box testing deals with the openness or closeness of the code. Pure Agile approaches focus more on white box testing.
- Manual or automated testing indicates the type of people and tools used in testing.
- Vertical or horizontal testing indicates behavioral versus technical slicing of the system for testing.
- Equivalence partitioning and boundary values indicate how the test data are to be sampled for testing.

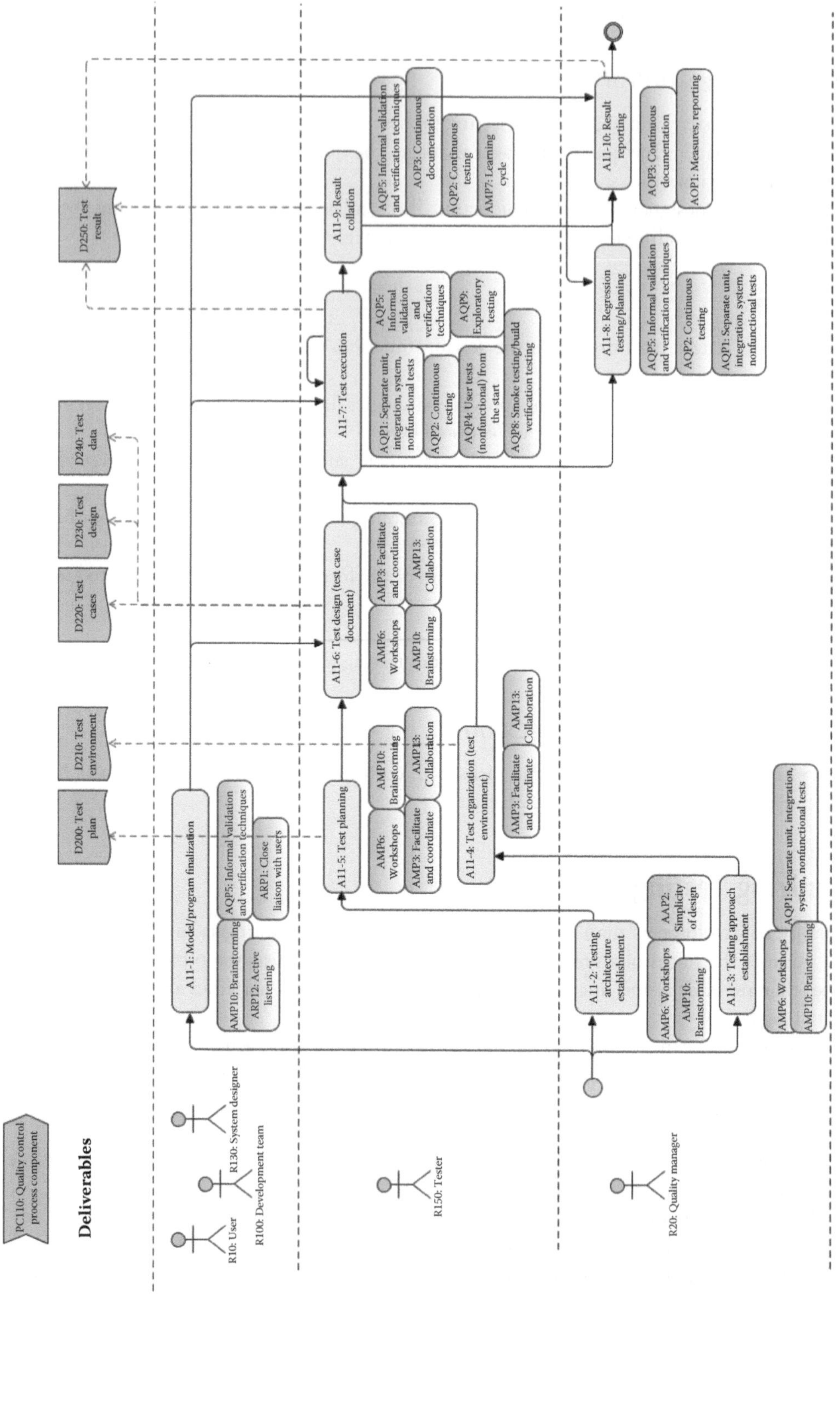

Figure 9.9 Quality control (testing) process map in CAMS.

Table 9.5 Quality Control Process Map

Activities	*Tasks*	*Deliverable*	*Roles*
A11-1: Model/ program finalization	Model/program submission for testing Model/program correction based on testing feedback Model/program finalization with users Agile practices: AQP5: Informal validation and verification techniques AMP10: Brainstorming ARP1: Close liaison with users ARP12:Active listening		R10:User R100: Development team R130: System designer
A11-2: Testing architecture	Identify testing architecture requirements Determine components for testing Agile practices: AMP6: Workshops AMP10: Brainstorming AAP2: Simplicity of design		R20: Quality manager
A11-3: Testing approach establishment	Pre-investigate various testing approaches Determine the most suitable testing approach Agile practices: AMP6: Workshops AMP10: Brainstorming AQP1: Separate unit, integration, system, nonfunctional tests		R20: Quality manager
A11-4: Test organization	Testing resources Physical test environment Technical test environment Test tools Agile practices: AMP3: Facilitate and coordinate AMP13: Collaboration	D210: Test environment	R150: Tester

continued

Table 9.5 (*Continued*)

Activities	*Tasks*	*Deliverable*	*Roles*
A11-5: Test planning	Based on test plan Testing risks Acceptance criteria Test cycles Review test plan Agile practices: AMP6: Workshops AMP10: Brainstorming AMP3: Facilitate and coordinate AMP13: Collaboration	D200: Test plan	R150: Tester
A11-6: Test design	Create and document test designs Architectural needs Reuse existing test designs Create test cases Verify test cases Test cases as development Agile practices: AMP6: Workshops AMP10: Brainstorming AMP3: Facilitate and coordinate AMP13: Collaboration	D220: Test cases D230: Test design D240: Test data	R150: Tester
A11-7: Test execution	Testing Manual test cases Automated test cases Retest after fixes Incidences Software incidences Agile practices: AQP1: Separate unit, integration, system, nonfunctional tests AQP2: Continuous testing AQP4: User test from the start AQP5: Informal validation and verification techniques AQP8: Smoke testing/build verification testing AQP9: Exploratory testing	D250: Test results	R150: Tester

Table 9.5 (*Continued*)

Activities	*Tasks*	*Deliverable*	*Roles*
A11-8: Regression testing/ planning	Run test to identify if changes introduced new errors Document results Agile practices: AQP5: Informal validation and verification techniques AQP2: Continuous testing AQP1: Separate unit, integration, system, nonfunctional tests	D250: Test results	R20: Quality manager
A11-9: Result collation	Correlate the achieved results to expected Analyze result Rerun tests if necessary Agile practices: AQP5: Informal validation and verification techniques AOP3: Continuous documentation AQP2: Continuous testing AMP7: Learning cycle	D250: Test results	R150: Tester
A11-10: Result reporting	Combine and merge all gathered tests data results Analyze and prepare documentation Agile practices: AOP1: Measures, reporting AOP3: Continuous documentation	D250: Test results (finalized report)	R20: Quality manager

Test plans and real-life tests are a combination of the above approaches.

Figure 9.10 shows the way testing is organized in a software development project. The *test plan* is at the highest and strategic level and includes consideration of the testing architecture; the *test designs* are at the package or subsystem level and need to consider use-case-based versus class-based testing; and the *test cases* are at the detailed unit level. These three aspects of test organization are discussed next.

1. *Test planning* is focused on the higher, strategic aspect of testing where the scope of testing, the time and cost of required resources, and other such complexities need to be decided. Thus, although testing itself is tactical in nature, it benefits—by its own careful approach—planning and management. For example, the type and size of projects (as discussed in Chapter 8) will influence the way in which a test plan is created. A test plan for a large integration project will focus on the quality of interfaces between the newly developed system and a background

Table 9.6 Major Testing Activities and Agility

Activities	*Description*
Test planning	Test planning is focused on the higher, strategic aspect of testing where the scope of testing, the time and cost of required resources, and other such complexities need to be decided. Test planning requires the formality of planning but can take input for estimations based on previous project metrics. These metrics, in Agile project management, such as project velocity and burn-down charts, can be valuable sources for estimating testing efforts in a project. Test planning also includes resourcing and their positioning in a project. Some of the composite Agile practices and leadership discussions (undertaken in Chapter 8) also apply to test planning
Test design	Test designs can be created on the basis of the understanding of the system at a subsystem or component level. Packages and subsystems form the unit of test designs. Test designs need to cater to both functional and nonfunctional testing. Agility provides an excellent opportunity to visualize the functional features of the system. However, the nonfunctional features that apply to a package or subsystem cannot be easily put up on a card. Hence, test designs need to go beyond the pure Agile approaches to ascertain the overall testing needs. Each test design has to handle the creation of test beds for that specific test area and also participate in full integration testing across a suite of releases. A test design is made up of number of test cases
Test case	Test case is the primary unit of testing. Good test cases come from and are as important as good use cases, especially in user acceptance testing (UAT). Technically, test cases can be "test harnesses," which are small programs used to pass many variations of test data through the programs being tested. Test cases can be functional, nonfunctional, and interface
Test data	Test data are as important as test cases. Test data can decide the range and depth of coverage of testing because they provide a suite of valid and invalid data. Since not every possible variation of data can be tested, it is important to come up with a good spread of data that covers equivalence of data and boundary values
Test execution	This is the actual execution of the test cases. On the basis of the planning and design, these test cases are executed in an iterative and incremental manner. Test execution will depend on whether functional, nonfunctional, or interface tests are being executed
Test reporting	This is the recording of test results, their collation, and reporting. The reporting can be online, in real time, or a summarized version of the test results. Reporting is vital in deciding the need for and extent of regression tests
Test closure	This is the final activity in testing, undertaken at the completion of the testing phase of the project. Closure is important to help understand the effort spent, the lessons learnt, and how to improve for the next project

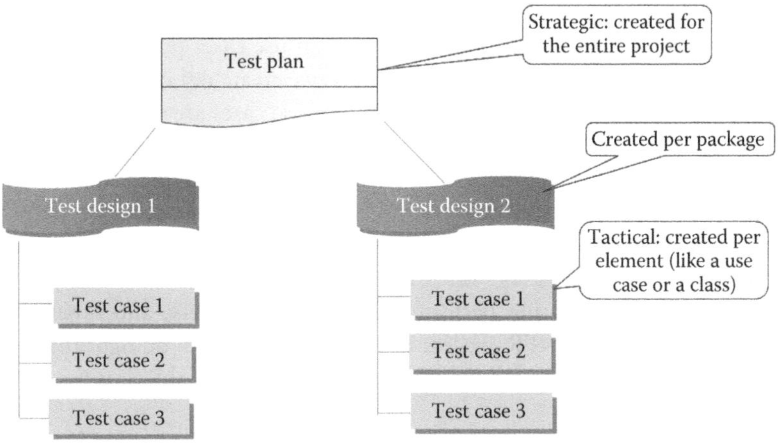

Figure 9.10 Organization of testing. (Based on Unhelkar, B, *After the Y2K Fireworks: Business and Technology Strategies*, CRC Press, Boca Raton, [1999].)

legacy application, while a test plan for a data-warehousing project will focus on the accuracy and relevance of the data being used. Planning for test automation as well as continuous integration provides a foundation for focused attention to quality and frequent delivery of working software. Within CAMS, a large project is also provided with a much larger system testing life cycle and will have to factor in the costs and time for rework resulting from testing. In large projects, test planning has to cater to multiple tiers of testing. For example, the test plan will have to provide for immediate test harness creation and execution by developers, separate dedicated testing with users and, eventually, regression testing based on rework. Small projects, on the other hand, may focus on testing almost the entire product as it becomes available and may have relatively few walk-throughs and inspections as compared with large projects. Typically, the test plan would include a strategy for testing, the resources required for the tests, the risks associated with testing, scheduling of test cases, approach to reporting the errors and retesting them, and the creation and maintenance of the test environment that would be required to conduct the testing. Thus, a good test plan would specify the modules to be tested and the resources available to do so. A good test plan would try and start the testing activity as soon as the first package has been implemented. This would require the test plan to be developed during the initial iteration of the process. It is also important to focus on the customer-oriented external product attributes of functionality, reliability, and usability of software (Younessi, 2002) when creating the overall test plan.

2. *Test designs* can be created on the basis of the understanding of the system at a subsystem or component level. Packages, discussed during the Critical Requirements Analysis (CRA) in Chapter 8, are an excellent starting point for the test designs. Test designs give a broad coverage of the required functionality rather than the lower level test cases for each unit of the system. The test designs resulting from package diagrams as well as from the use case documentations within a model of the problem space will ensure modularity in approaching testing. The user can also contribute to these test designs and may use the same in order to conduct acceptance tests. Test design also forms the basis for NFRs testing. NFRs apply at various levels within an organization. Packages are the optimum level to test them out as they deal with multiple use cases and classes.

3. *Test cases* form the crux of the testing effort. Writing good test cases is as important as writing good user stories or use cases. Well-written use cases provide an excellent starting point for good test cases. This can be seen here, as we create test cases to test the use cases. It should be noted, however, that test cases based on use cases are written for user acceptance testing. There are many other areas of testing that require creation of test cases. For example, technical test cases are the test harnesses that are relatively small programs to test out classes. These test harnesses verify and validate the algorithms by executing as many branches of the logic as possible and by passing a large variety of test data that have been separately created for the purpose of testing. Test cases for NFRs are yet another category of technical test cases that focus on testing performance, volume, security, and other similar NFRs. The test cases focusing on NFR are less interested in the logic, or algorithm, of the classes and more interested in the overall operational performance of the class (or database) that is being tested.

Figure 9.11 shows another important aspect of testing—functional versus technical testing. Functional testing focuses on the way a system is used, whereas technical testing focuses on its actual code. Functionality is documented in Agile approaches using story cards. CAMS creates a combination of stories and use cases. The classes shown from left to right in Figure 9.11 represent the technical code of the system. User stories (and use cases) have a many-to-many relationship with classes. A test design, therefore, will have these two aspects of testing overlapping each other. Classes are the focus of testing in pure Agile approaches with the responsibility of that testing taken by the programmers and designers. User stories and use cases are very well tested by users and business analysts who have initially put them together. Acceptance test cases, therefore, will be focused on user stories and use cases, whereas technical test cases including writing of test harnesses (a set of automated test data against which the actual testing is carried out—test harnesses

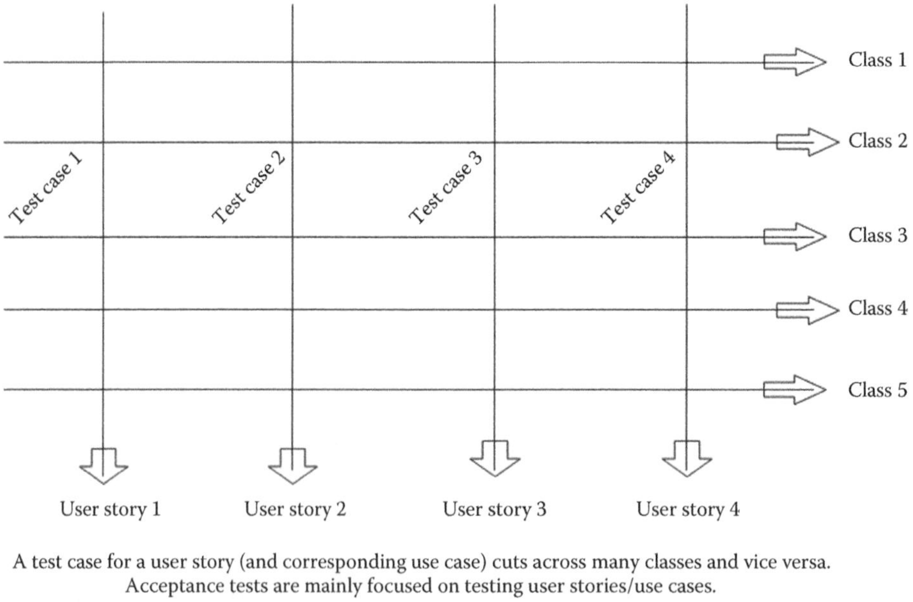

Figure 9.11 Functional versus technical test cases.

generally cover most aspects of functionalities of a software system, covering all the extreme cases as well) will be focused around the classes.

Test Data

Test data requires separate attention during test planning and test execution. A good, properly dispersed suite of test data can enhance the quality of testing itself. Test data has to balance between attempting to over-test the same functionality versus not testing it sufficiently enough. There are two aspects of putting together large-scale test data—boundary values, which are the extreme edge of a suite of anticipated data for a class or a system; and equivalence partitioning, which is creating equal parts from a suite of anticipated data. Then select one or two samples from each part to create a test data suite. Table 9.7 shows examples of valid and invalid test data.

The number of classes that have to be tested and their corresponding complexity also need to be considered in creating test data. Highly complex classes may not always need large amount of data, but their data for testing will be unique to the algorithms being tested. On the other hand, verifying the usability aspect of an interface (screen) may simply require a careful walk-through of the screen and its dependencies with no data at all. Test data, which resides with the test design for a component, should also handle the testing of a class, a package, or an entire release/system. Each of these three test elements will require a different suite of test data. Finally, dependencies between classes also need to be incorporated in test cases that deal with testing the entire component, as against individual classes.

For example, a set of test cases within a test design may test the date class, and another set of test cases may test the account class. A good test design will ensure that there is a third group of test cases that test the working of the two classes together.

When it comes to the testing of NFRs, the quantity of test data becomes far more important than in functional testing. Table 9.8a and b shows examples of NFRs, their levels, and corresponding comments on their test cases.

Table 9.7 Example Test Data

Input for "Date" Field	*Comment*
30 September 2012	Typical valid standard input. If this input data is accepted by the system "Accept," then the corresponding test will be a "Pass"
31 December 2012	Another valid input data that is on the boundary (therefore, this is a boundary value). As with the previous case, if this data is accepted during the test, "Accept," then the test is a "Pass"
29 February 2012	A unique and valid boundary value that should be accepted by the system for the test to be a "Pass"
29 February 2013	An invalid input. If the expected date is for a non-leap year (e.g., 2013), then this date should not be accepted; and if the system accepts this date (29 February) for the year 2013, the test will be a "Fail." If the system rejects the date, the test is a "Pass"
00 00 0000	Another invalid input. System should reject this input for the test to be a "Pass"

Table 9.8(a)

Type	*Level*	*Description*	*Test Cases*
Scalability	System	System should be able to scale from 10,000 to 10 million users in 2 years	Test data will have to be loaded for the range of tests to be conducted. As only data load is being tested, there is no need for spread of test data
Performance	System	All Internet-based queries should be of duration less than 3 seconds	Since performance requires queries to be executed within a specific time, test data will need reasonable spread to test the search capabilities
Operating platform	Organization/ customer	Linux, NT	Testing the working of an operating system does not require test data as such. However, an initial release of the system is needed
Security	Organization	128-Bit encryption	Test data can provide some variation in terms of testing the security of the system. Minimal test data but maximum available modules of the system are required for this NFR test

Table 9.8(b)

Scalability and Load	*Environment*	*Conditions*
10,000 records with entry points within the firewall	Single-system test environment with associated test database	All system functions should work for this load simultaneously
10 million records with multiple sources of entry within and outside the organizational firewall	Dedicated database environment with external interfaces (e.g., cloud computing). A multiple system test environment will be required to test separate aspects of the data including mirroring, backups, and integrity of data	All system functions to operate normally; independent, separate system functions should be able to upload data without conflict

Scalability, together with the load capacity of the system (and database), requires additional attention in terms of creation of test data. Table 9.8b expands on the scalability in Table 9.8a by highlighting additional attention that needs to be paid in test designs for creation of test data for load and scalability testing.

Analyzing Risks in Testing Risks: Analyzing

Test management is derived from project management. This is mainly because within a project, testing can be a major activity that forms a project in its own right. There are risks and advantages in carrying out in-depth and extensive testing of a product. For example, if a test manager decides to test every functional and nonfunctional feature of a product for all its variations, it can take an inordinate amount of time. If, on the other hand, features are not sufficiently tested, the system can go into operation with errors in it. A test manager in CAMS has to balance the Agile values with the planned values in undertaking testing. At some point in time, during most testing exercises, a test manager has to make a judgmental call as to when testing is deemed complete. A product cannot be left forever in testing, and a product cannot be released until it has been sufficiently tested. This decision requires analyzing the risks associated with what has been tested and what has been left out. In addition to the risks associated with choosing the scope of testing, there are also risks associated with the actual testing cycle. This risk includes situations that can hamper the testing effort (like resources, system, or network availability).

Test management within CAMS is a combination of formal testing including test plans, designs, and execution together with the Agile testing that is embedded within the Agile practices for development. Ongoing identification, analysis, and prioritization of risks are vital for successful test management. Analyzing testing risks during the initial iteration of the development process helps avoid issues of time and budget at the later testing stage.

The following are some common examples of testing risks that test managers are required to handle. While these are risks common to any testing, they can also provide valuable reminders with CAMS-based projects:

- Limited experience of staff specific to the technology being tested: For example, object-oriented systems require a special focus on encapsulation of components and inheritance of objects. Without this special focus, the benefits of object orientation may not be fully realized. Alternatively, the technology of cloud computing may require specific experience in both cloud and associated NFR data for testing. Yet another example is distributed and mobile applications that need to be tested in dynamic environment networks. These networks need to be replicated to simulate real-life situations in order to have accurate testing. The risks associated with lack of technical knowledge can be mitigated by exposing the staff involved in testing to those technologies.
- Lack of importance for models: In particular, in Agile projects, there is minimal importance given to models. If models are at all created in an Agile project, they are sketches used as means for discussion. However, in CAMS, models and architectural diagrams play a major part in enhancing the quality of the system. Furthermore, it is the quality of the models themselves that also demands significant attention. The checks for syntax, semantics, and aesthetics, mentioned earlier, apply directly to the quality of models. Testers should also be able to understand software models (e.g., a class diagram or a cloud-based architectural diagram) that gives them an idea as to how testing should be organized.
- Nonavailability of suitable test environment: It is essential to test the system under a separate dedicated test environment during both system and acceptance tests. This includes not only the physical test environment in which the testers sit and execute the tests but also the software environment, including the separate operating system, test database, and latest software release. Creating and maintaining this environment is a testing overhead that needs to be considered during test planning. If a suitable test environment is not created early in the testing cycle, then it poses a significant risk to the project.
- Discovery of major errors in the later cycles of testing: Regression tests ensure that the errors detected in the earlier cycle are fixed, and that those fixes have not created problems elsewhere. Significant risks are associated with the assumption that no major problems

will be discovered during the later cycles of testing. Provision must be made for fixes and regression tests if errors are found.

- Unavailability or insufficient test data: As discussed in detail earlier in the section on test data, if suitable test data are not available for creating the test database, then sufficient and thorough testing will be hampered. Design and creation of data is a vital element of test planning, without which the testing of the system is at considerable risk.
- Inappropriate or irrelevant hardware: This type of hardware, in terms of machines, memory, and communications, should be available for testing. This is a project management risk that has to handle the availability and ongoing maintenance of the test environment.
- Lack of user awareness: Users need to be continuously updated on the availability of releases and encouraged to undertake dedicated testing of their own. Users may also need help in creation of test data, mechanisms to report bugs, and sharing of test results. Agile values of collaboration and face-to-face conversations can help mitigate this risk, but there is still a need to impress upon the users to plan for detailed acceptance testing.
- Insufficient prioritization of testing: Depending on the individual risks and the dynamically changing needs of the users, the test designs and test cases themselves need to be prioritized. It is essential that techniques, such as the MoSCoW or CRA (described in Chapter 8 on project management), are used to prioritize not only the development but also the associated testing. This will ensure that the test manager can assign sufficient resources and sequence them in order to mitigate the risks. Prioritizing testing involves understanding the type of tests (functional vs nonfunctional), availability of resources (dedicated testers, users, or only developers), and the criticality of the project itself.

Composite Agile Metrics and Measurements

This discussion is focused on managing, assuring, and testing. An important yet challenging aspect of quality is its measurement. This challenge emanates from the fact that quality is elusive (not easily definable) and subjective (depends on the context). Despite its elusiveness, attempts to measure and improve quality are important. The very effort of setting the metrics and measuring quality has a positive effect on a project. Closely accompanying quality and testing metrics are other project management metrics associated with time, costs, and resources. Measuring these project parameters is equally important in estimating efforts and improving quality. Metrics provide information to the management on controlling and directing a project. Comparison among projects, within the organization, and across a collaborative cluster is also enabled through metrics and measurements. Metrics and measurements are also required to measure the quality of service (QoS) during the operation of a system. Pure Agile approaches eschew the traditional project management measures of time, budget, and resources. Instead, the focus in Agile is on values and quality. The challenges in measuring and understanding the subjective parameters of an Agile project are similar to those in measuring quality in traditional, planned projects. The Agile measures can change depending on the context; they are subjective. CAMS encourages metrics for the traditional (planned) as well as Agile parameters within a project. Metrics for the planned aspects in a project can use corresponding process maps of CAMS. For example, the measures associated with the planning of a project and modeling of requirements can use the project management and the requirements modeling process maps. Some Agile metrics, such as project velocity, are quite close to the aforementioned project management metrics. Measuring of Agile values, such as simplicity and honesty, and Agile practices, such as pair programming, is difficult in practice. This section discusses the challenges associated with measurements, suggests some CAMS metrics, and outlines the way in which a metrics program can be implemented (typically through a CoE in an organization).

Metrics provide a language for communication within the organization. Metrics can be used in projects and also in measuring the performance of an organization in its business-as-usual state. Metrics enable measurement of current work, estimation of future work, and comparison among work. Each work area in an organization has its own terminologies. Metrics enforce the use of a common terminology to explain that which is being measured. This, in turn, helps in not only the recording and storage of data but also in analyzing it to gain insights. Consider, for example, the terms used by developers as they undertake testing in an Agile project. Technical terms such as defect in data load, bugs in referencing, or garbage in the memory may not have much relevance to a user on the project. Business stakeholders (e.g., executives and customers) have their own interpretations of these words. Furthermore, they also have their own business terminologies usually derived from the business domain. Further ambiguities exist in terms such as maintainability, usability, performance, reliability, and user-friendliness. Putting together a suite of metrics agreed upon at the start of an initiative, and with provision for changing and improving those measures, is crucial for the success of a project.

The composite Agile approach to metrics and measurements is a very organic approach. Initially, the metrics are agreed upon tentatively by all the stakeholders. With the start of the project, these metrics are measured. The resultant primitive data is immediately analyzed in order to gain insights—such as the progress of the project or the number of errors being detected. On the basis of this feedback, metrics are fine-tuned to measure new data.

SIDEBAR

Goodman (1993) defines software metrics as "The continuous application of measurement-based techniques to the software development process and its products to supply meaningful and timely management information, together with the use of those techniques to improve that process and its products." Thus, a software metrics can help us understand, track, control, and predict the output (products) from software projects and their associated processes. However, with the use of Agile values and practices in software development projects, the need to combine traditional project management metrics with Agile ones is obvious. CAMS metrics combine traditional project and software metrics and measurements derived from planned processes and governance standards with Agile metrics. Project management metrics have been based on the iron triangle of costs, schedule, and scope. Agile approaches suggest that the user should choose one of these variables and leave the rest to the project managers and developers. This selection is itself made possible through estimate and measure of cost, time, functionality, and quality in an appropriate way.

Challenges of Agile Projects Metrics

Agile approaches to software development, which are based on the conversational paradigm, present some interesting challenges in applying metrics and measurements. This section further expands on the challenges related to metrics within the context of Agile projects.

- Lack of focus on traditional project parameters: Estimating the key project parameters for a software project is a major challenge of project managers at the start of a software project. Agile methods sidestep this challenge by ascertaining that the cost, time, and scope in an Agile project will be arrived at "iteratively" as the project progresses. Within an Agile approach, these project parameters are not given as much importance as quality and value are.

This approach can work when the Agile team members are closely aligned with each other and are operating within the project boundaries. In practice, however, with contract-based development projects cutting across projects and organizations, Agile methods provide very little opportunity for accurate estimations of these project parameters.

- Difficulty in formalizing requirements: Requirements in Agile development are mainly captured with the help of story cards. These brief descriptions of requirements, collaboratively written and pasted on a wall chart, provide the right information to the developers at the right time. However, these changing requirements present a significant challenge in terms of their measurements. A static story card is itself difficult to quantify in terms of the effort required to take it to a "done" state. Comparing two stories is also difficult as the stories differ in the way they are interpreted and developed. Also, a collection of dynamically changing stories is quite challenging to measure based on their categorization and prioritization. This is especially true within the CoE of an organization, which plans to use that data for estimating future projects. This difficulty arises because of the subjective nature of the stories, their "conversational" interpretation, and insufficient focus on formal measurements in an Agile project. This difficulty is further compounded by the lack of use of CASE tools for modeling of requirements and tracking their development.
- Uncertainty in planning the iterations: The number of iterations in an Agile approach can add uncertainty at the start of the project. This is mainly because Agile, subscribing to the Agile Manifesto, is not keen to decide on the precise number of iterations at the start of a project. This is understandable as the requirements for the project are themselves not clear at the outset. However, as the requirements start getting documented in the form of user stories, they also start giving shape to the iterations. At this stage, though, the project is on its way and the subsequent iterations are decided on the basis of how the initial iteration has progressed. This can be a very challenging situation for both project managers and the business stakeholders. This challenge of iteration planning is further exacerbated by the uncertain length of the iteration. An organization following Agile for the first time is not able to decide the iteration interval easily (Nguyen, 2009). The uncertainty in the length of an iteration is due to the up-front issue of changing requirements. Agile approaches can also give an impression that each iteration may be of approximately the same length. This is not true in practice as some iteration could have excessive story points, which could lead to longer development times. This uncertainty adds to the challenges of planning iterations in Agile.
- Multipurpose daily stand-up meetings: The daily stand-up meeting is a flagship activity within an Agile project. These short, sharp, daily meetings (based on Scrum) provide valuable information on the project status and its progress. The difficulty in terms of metrics is the differing output resulting from the meetings. Each meeting focuses on stating the achievements and identifying the roadblocks. This, in itself, works well in a synchronous team. The measures of the milestones and measures of the roadblocks can quickly become very subjective. Thus, the knowledge gained in terms of development in one project stays within that project and cannot be easily applied across other projects.
- Fuzzy measure of person-days: Estimating development within a project relies substantially on the measure of person-days (resources) for a particular requirement. Execution of sprints and iterations does not provide a concrete measure of the person-days required on a project. This measure is difficult even in traditional projects where the efforts put in by developers within a day and the quality of the output can vary. Traditional software project measures such as person-days spent and lines of code developed are shunned in Agile approaches. Hence, Agile projects end up with nonstandardized estimation of efforts.

- Continuous testing during development: Continuous testing of a product as it gets developed during a sprint/iteration has a positive effect on managing expectations. This continuous testing, however, becomes an integrated part of the development process. Furthermore, continuous integration of releases and products also implies much less separate, dedicated testing of the product. Therefore, there is very little project data that is dedicated to testing, which becomes available. Dedicated testing phases, specific user acceptance testing, non-functional testing, and usability testing (by walk-throughs and inspections) provide test data that can be used in project estimations.
- Subjective interpretation: Metrics are statistical data on a project that can be interpreted differently by different individuals. A person's motivation and his or her alignment with the rest of the team cannot be easily measured. Since Agile methods focus on task sharing and not on task management, the traditional way of measuring a person's performance (tasks completed) is also not used in Agile methods. The project manager, working as a leader, has to somehow arrive at a correlation between the time spent and an individual's actual productivity. This exercise can throw the measures of productivity out of balance.
- Varying development styles: Development can be carried out in many different ways within an Agile development life cycle. As Agile involves iterations, there could be small teams working on different features of the same product. Each team has the freedom to evolve its own style of development. Completion of features, their quality, and the comparison of overall output between the teams is very challenging in an Agile approach. Quality and output cannot be easily measured in a standardized manner in an Agile project.

Fundamentals of CAMS Estimation

Despite its uncertainties, estimation and metrics are an important part of any project. Without some attempt at quantifying objectives, the software development process becomes intangible and untraceable. Ebert (2005) emphasizes that metrics also ensure "the business is successful" and guided with "better decision" by showing the status and progress of developing endeavours. Thus, metrics can assist in estimating and tracking internal development within organizations. Metrics can also help in enhancing communication within an organization. Estimation and metrics in a CAMS-based project are spread over the traditional measures of time, cost, and functionality for a particular iteration; they also attempt to include quality and value, as much as possible, within the traditional metrics. Listed below are some basic estimation principles that need to be kept in mind in practice:

- Recursive estimation: All estimates should be made and reviewed multiple times in order to arrive at the final estimate. Estimation should be a recursive activity that makes use of the past projects' data, current measures, and related risks. Quality increases with appropriate decision of time frames for iteration and release (Layman et al., 2006).
- Collaborative estimates: All measures and ensuing estimates need to be made in close collaboration with customers and users. While customers and users are closely associated with development in an Agile project, in CAMS, the focus is also on the interpretation of past projects' data, collected formally, in estimating new projects. For example, users can provide input in terms of the way the stories were developed by a team in a previous project and its final value to the users. If the previous attempts led to rework, then that information can be used in creating and revising estimates for the current project. A collaborative estimation is a team-based process that would bring forth any concerns from any parties at an early stage in the project (based on Steindl and Krogdahl [2005]).

- Facilitate self-estimations: In addition to carrying out collaborative estimations, it is also important to provide opportunities to individual developers to make estimations for their own work. This self-estimation has a positive effect in increasing the accuracy of the overall measures of the project. Self-estimations are also positive morale boosters. However, it is important to integrate these self-estimates within the overall estimates for a project.
- Basing on real data: CAMS-based projects provide factual data derived from the project parameters. As project numbers grow within an organization, so does the project data. This data and information, stored in a dedicated project metrics database, can be increasingly used for new project measures and estimations. Lessons learnt in applying metrics in previous phases or projects can provide valuable data for new projects.
- Agreeing on a unit of measure: Is a user story a unit of requirement? Is a class a unit of development? Also, is a person-day properly understood within a project? Agreeing on these units is important in order to arrive at time, cost, and scope parameters for a project. Practical experience suggests that arriving at a unit of measure is probably the most important challenge in a metrics and measurement program. Agreeing on what is a unit of measure, how it will be measured, and where it is stored are vital steps for the success of a metrics program in CAMS. For example, defining an "ideal day" (as a workday with no interruptions or blockages) helps in measures and estimations.
- Set estimation rules and guidelines: In order to have a successful metrics program it is important to have a suite of rules and associated guidelines for their use. The previous point, in terms of setting a basic unit of measure, is augmented here through the rules to measure that unit. The differences in individuals, team structures, project dynamics, risks, and expectations, all play a role in estimations and metrics. Rules and guidelines help neutralize some of these subjective elements to enable close to accurate measures. For example, Agile's popular "Planning Poker" game to estimate effort provides opportunities to objectify the effort required. Estimation rules help in formalizing and objectifying the effort estimates.
- Communication of metrics and estimates: It is vital that the metrics themselves and associated data are collected, stored, analyzed, and interpreted across the project and the organization. Expanding the communication of the metrics and measurements improves the project communication itself. For example, making all stakeholders (especially outside the project boundary) regularly aware of the anticipated project velocity can immediately improve expectations. Wider communication of metrics can also help in wider input into the next suite of data—thereby helping trend spotting.
- Accuracy in measurements: Whatever is the agreed suite of metrics in a project, it needs to be measured accurately. Process tools can help in measuring activities and tasks. The number and size of deliverables can also be accurately measured within CAMS-based projects. Simplicity of measure, ease of measurement, and a single point of collection are techniques that help enhance accuracy in measures. Value and quality, however, remain difficult to measure. Measures such as customer satisfaction are also very challenging to measure accurately. Tools, surveys, checklists, and past metrics provide help in improving accuracy of measurements.

SIDEBAR

Estimates are based on a combination of an individual's experience and available data. Repeatability of process is crucial for improved estimates. Therefore, a process higher on a Capability Maturity Model (CMMI) has better opportunity for improved estimates. Project management and quality can improve with having better estimate. A well-known estimation formula is that of Program Evaluation and Review Technique (PERT). When it comes to CAMS estimates, this formula, which applies to planned project management approaches, can still hold.

$$\text{Estimate} = (\text{Optimistic} + \text{Pessimistic} + 4 \times \text{Most likely})/6.$$

CAMS Metrics in Practice

CAMS metrics in practice are a combination of traditional project management data and the suggested Agile metrics. CAMS also identifies Agile metrics that are, in fact, traditional project metrics. For example, a project velocity metric of Agile can be interpreted to figure out the time and cost associated with the project. CAMS-based metrics also provide a statistical view of the current state and the anticipated progress of the project. CAMS metrics and estimations help organizations in creating and managing their initiatives. In addition to planning properly for a project, good metrics also enable spotting of trends that help anticipate and prepare for issues and challenges in the project.

Composite Agile metrics data can be collected in primitive metrics form and then analyzed on the basis of needs and interests. Alternatively, some metrics may be used to undertake analysis prior to occurrence of issues. This analysis is typically undertaken by a CoE, which stores the metrics and measurements across multiple projects. On the basis of the collected data, issues are evaluated for further decision.

SIDEBAR

Every metric that is used in projects needs to answer two important questions: "Why to measure?" followed by "How to measure?" Answers to these questions help understand the purpose of the metrics and the approach to be taken to carry out the actual measurements. A popular approach to formulating metrics is the Goal–Question–Metric (GQM) approach. A metric is formed on the basis of understanding its goal—is it to measure the progress in a project or to identify the errors within a piece of software? Goals can be set (and measured) for products, processes, and related resources. Following the setting of goals, questions are asked in order to figure out how the goal is to be realized.

Thus, a goal gets further clarified through the questioning process. Consensus among the users of the metrics is essential for it to be valuable. Therefore, users, developers, analysts, testers, and managers need to be involved in undertaking GQM. This collaborative setting of metrics helps all parties understand the reasons for collection of data, the place where it will be used, and the assumptions associated with its use. Metrics in software projects can be divided into two categories, primitive metrics and derived metrics.

Primitive metrics are directly extracted from the project, such as lines of code (LOC), person-days, number of defects, and budget. These are single-dimensional basic metrics. Further analysis of these primitive data leads to derived metrics. These derived metrics correlate primitive metrics to provide further insights into the state of a project. For example, the team velocity or stability of requirements are metrics based on analysis of primitive data.

CAMS metrics further extend the available metrics used in an organization. Existing data in the organization can be plugged into CAMS metrics in order to provide uniformity and help estimates. Estimates can be made at the start and end of an iteration, a release, and at the conclusion of a project. CAMS identifies metrics on the basis of the different phases of a development life cycle (Figure 9.12). For example, some metrics are relevant for planning, others in measuring

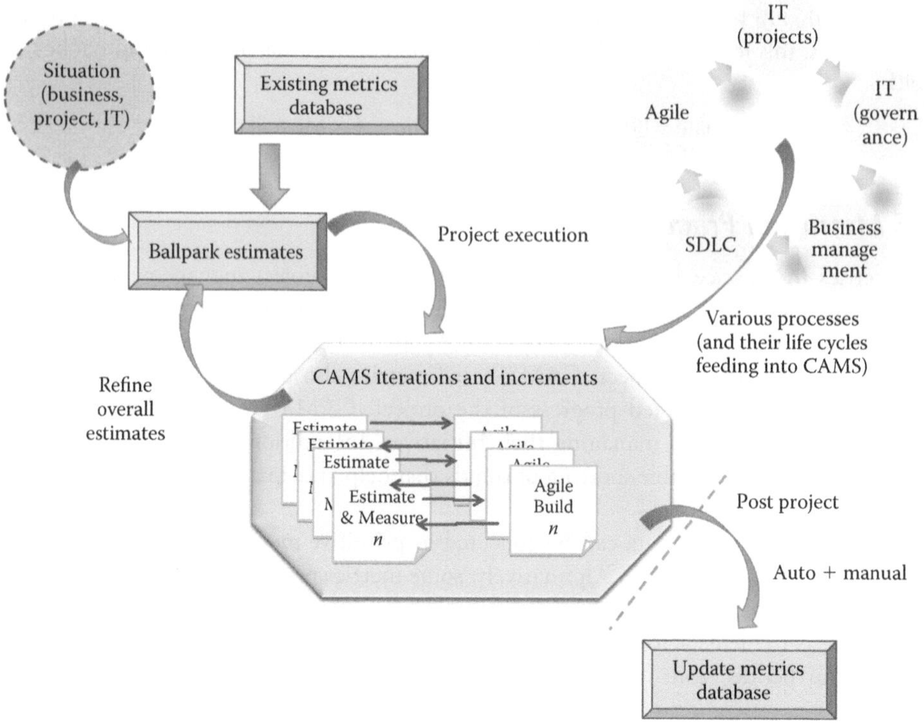

Figure 9.12 CAMS metrics life cycle.

the scope of the requirements, and some others in measuring the development and test efforts. The following is a discussion on these groups of metrics used in CAMS-based projects.

Planning Metrics

Planning includes decomposing the goals of a project, identifying the time, money, and resources required for the project, and assigning activities and tasks to the resources. Plans are made up of basic project plans associated with the creation of the risk management plan, configuration management plan, problem reports, software quality assurance plan, and acceptance criteria. The project management process map of CAMS discussed in Chapter 8 can be used to ascertain the project measures. Also, the earlier described estimate approach—most likely, optimistic and pessimistic—can be combined to arrive at the overall planning data. Table 9.9 suggests some Agile planning metrics.

Requirements Metrics

The requirements phase deals with gathering and analyzing requirements as well as designing the system on the basis of requirements. CAMS-based projects that follow the requirements modeling process map and associated activities are discussed in Chapter 7. Requirements modeling includes gathering, modeling, and managing requirements. These requirements can be made up of the functionality expected, the nonfunctional or operational requirements of the system when it is deployed, and the usability and quality requirements that apply across the entire environment.

Table 9.9 Metrics for the Agile Planning Phase

Example CAMS Metric for Planning	*Description*
Cost (budget) for development	This is based on previous project data, current objectives, and associated risks. It results from a cost–benefit analysis including anticipated ROI
Benefit (monetization)	This metric highlights the costs associated with project milestones and helps monetize business benefits corresponding to milestones (time, quality, functionality)
Risk management	This involves managing risks through its accurate monetization. This metric can clarify the apportioning of risks between the program sponsor and the project execution
Business integration cost	Program budget and costing include estimate of business time spent addressing project issues. Integration also requires an understanding of the business infrastructure and needs to be included in the calculations
Functionality (scope)	This is based on a combination of high-level user stories and initial use cases. Other approaches to functionality, such as a prioritized list, are also helpful in planning the overall scope of the project
Resources (people)	These are a number of developers required on a project. Developers can play different roles in Agile. However, a formal project structure of CAMS assigns specific roles to people. Therefore, this metric has to identify the roles and the number of people required within the role
Person-day	This metric measures an ideal, uninterrupted working day in Agile. This measure is critical in arriving at the total days (and hours) required for a project. Total time worked on a project (or feature), if measured correctly, can help in identifying the development trend in the organization, and thereby make an estimate of the time required for a project
Iterations and lengths	The number of iterations required for a project can be based on decomposition of objectives and past project experience. The higher the risks, the more should be the number of iterations. The initial iteration has to be shorter (15%, see Chapter 8 and discussion on iteration distribution) to enable communication and understanding of measures across the project. The major iteration is the longest in terms of time and requires maximum effort; this is followed by a relatively shorter final iteration, in a project with three iterations
Outstanding work (burn down)	This metric is more important in tracking a project as it progresses. Outstanding work represents the work that is yet to be completed in comparison with that which has already been completed. Unified person-day measures and functionality measures are vital in ascertaining outstanding work

ROI, return on investment.

Table 9.10 Metrics for the Agile Requirements Phase

Example CAMS Metric for Requirements	*Description*
Critical performance areas	These provide the high-level measure of the overall requirements of the project. These CPA become packages representing the subsystems for development
Use cases	These are the lower level functionalities of the system. Each use case can provide a unit of behavior of the user and the system
Features/stories	These are the most popular measures of requirement within an Agile project. It is important to decide the complexity and size of a typical user story within a project in order to use it to estimate the overall requirements (which then dictate the development)
Nonfunctional features	These are a list of nonfunctional requirements (NFRs) and corresponding effort in terms of developing and satisfying them
Interfaces	These are front-end interfaces with the user, their complexity, and their usability; and other system interfaces (e.g., printers) are also listed and measured for their effort
Infrastructure	This is a list of infrastructure requirements that go beyond the project (usually at organizational level). Existing data on organizational infrastructure and specification of new infrastructure (e.g., a new mobile transmission tower or setting up of a new green data center) are listed and measured through this metric

Requirements need to be clearly stated and measured as precisely as possible to provide accurate estimates in planning and tracking work. Table 9.10 describes important metrics from a requirements perspective.

Development Metrics

CAMS-based projects have a detailed development life cycle dictated by the design and implementation process maps discussed in Chapter 5. The development phase includes coding of the solution, assembling together previously coded software components (e.g., code libraries for use), or implementation of packages. Each of these implementation activities has a variation of the standard development metrics. Coding is the lowest level of abstraction for the software development process. Software coding has typical tasks such as source traceability analysis, source code and documentation evaluation, planning for unit/system/integration and acceptance testing, functional test case identification, error evaluation/resolution, and final test report generation. Table 9.11 describes important metrics from the quality perspective for this phase.

Testing and Release Metrics

Testing in CAMS is guided by the process maps associated with quality control, described earlier in this chapter. Testing can cover unit tests, system tests, integration tests, and regression tests. Quality assurance and testing personnel will experience changes in scheduling as testing becomes

Table 9.11 Metrics for the Agile Development Phase

Example CAMS Metric for Development	*Description*
Projectvelocity	This is a popular Agile development metric that is closely associated with project planning. Agile team velocity approaches describe a number of story points that can be delivered by a team in a specific iteration
Outstanding work	Agile teams are regularly encouraged to estimate the overall outstanding work as well as the work remaining on each active task
Features completed	This metric is used to measure the amount of work accomplished by the team of developers. The features or stories completed are listed here. In Agile, this measure becomes interesting as it has at least two criteria for completion—"done" and "done-done." A done measure indicates that a feature or user story is completed in its own right; and "done-done" indicates its completion in the context of all other features and stories
Completion rate	This is a derived metric based on the overall time allocated for a given piece of work and the time taken to actually complete the task. This metric can provide very valuable information in improving the trends in completion rate, and therefore, the overall estimate for an iteration in a project

a part of the development process and is continuous rather than occurring only at the end of the project (Brian, 2009). A systematic approach to testing in CAMS includes the process-map-based activities and tasks and the Agile practices that facilitate iterations and continuous testing. Quality control dictates identification of defects, their logging, and their resolutions (see *Defect Management* by Younessi (2001)). The quality techniques of walk-throughs, inspections, reviews, and audits need to be estimated within a project, and their results documented and used in improving the quality of the product.

Table 9.12 provides examples of some CAMS-based metrics that can be used from a testing and quality perspective.

Role-Based CAMS Metrics

Table 9.13 shows CAMS metrics derived from the focuses that are the main concerns of the roles in the corresponding CAMS tasks. Out of the metrics illustrated in the table, the 18 metrics that are selected to study in this research are marked with an asterisk. Appendix III has further expanded details on these 18 metrics.

Applying Estimation and Metrics in CAMS

CAMS encourages the creation and application of metrics in the form of a quality strategy of the organization. Quality management, assurance, and testing process maps provide the basis for an overall quality approach in an organization. Identification and application of estimation and

Table 9.12 Metrics for the Agile Testing and Release Phase

Example CAMS Metric for Testing	*Description*
Defects	This is a basic measure of bugs or errors (defects) identified through the testing process
Testing frequency	This metric indicates the number of times a particular test has been carried out. This frequency can be for a unit test, an acceptance test, or even a regression test. This metric can be arrived at as a ratio by dividing test suite runs by person-days (Layman et al., 2006). The quality would be higher with a higher ratio of test run frequency
Defect removal efficiency	It is the indicator of the expertise of the developers in fixing the errors discovered during testing. This can be a percentage measure of the defects fixed over the defects reports. Defect removal efficiency can be improved by automation in reporting, accuracy in prioritization (and dependencies of one defect on another), and technical expertise in fixing the defects
Defect density	This metric gives a ratio of defects delivered to and reported by a customer once the product is released (Layman et al., 2006). A higher ratio depicts lower quality

metrics need to be coordinated across multiple teams, projects, and time (i.e., previous project metrics data need to be used in estimating current and future projects). Galorath (2009) has described major steps and related activities in implementing metrics. The following are the steps that can be used in applying metrics in CAMS-based projects:

- Identify the purpose of estimation: Define and document the purpose of estimations and the expectation from the data. A baseline can be created to include planning goals, initial business requirements, and so on, to ascertain what the metrics will achieve. Once the purpose becomes clear, relevant metrics can be created and used.
- Agree on the rules for metrics: Recognize constraints associated with the project and related applications that affect metrics and measurements.
- Decide who will measure and what will be measured: Responsibilities for metrics must be assigned to the roles. For example, the developer can measure the person-days spent on a feature, whereas the project manager focuses on the project velocity. This should include trained and skilled people, proper technology, and tools as well as a documented and repeatable estimation process.
- Evaluate metrics: Subject the metrics themselves to a quality evaluation. Are the metrics still fit for the purpose for which they were created? Organizations should use a metric evaluation checklist in order to confirm the use and purpose of every metric (Hartmann and Dymond, 2006). Ensure that the data associated with a metric is properly collected, applied methods are efficient and verified, identified results are precise, and the quality is properly maintained. Metrics evaluation should make sure that adopted ground rules are consistently applied throughout the estimation process and all the related assumptions are properly assessed beforehand.

Table 9.13 CAMS Metrics Based on Roles

Role	*CAMS Activities (Embedded in Process Maps)*	*Focus of the Metric*	*CAMS Metrics (Examples)*
Project manager	Planning-requirement prioritization (scope)	Size of system	*The number of users in the system (includes the overall users and the number of concurrent users logging in at a given time) *The number of subsystems/components/packages in an overall solution. This provides the overall size of the system *The number of dependencies among subsystems/components/packages (indicating the complexity of the system)
	Planning-requirement prioritization (time)	Length of time	*The time schedule of the project—based on agreement on the scope and functionality of the project, number of iterations required, and the past project velocity number
	Planning-requirement prioritization (budget)	Budget or amount invested	*The sum total of investment in the project. The figure is extended further for returns on investment as well as risks associated with the project
	Monitoring team (performance)	Team Velocity	*The speed of delivery of a feature (user story) or, at a higher granularity, the use cases
			*The average efficiency of response to changes by the user (can also be extended to ascertain the defect removal rate)
	Risk management—collaborative(risk)	Qualitative	*The average potential impact of risks based on changes, user stories, etc.
		Quantitative	*The number of identified risks per user story

continued

Table 9.13 (*Continued*)

Role	*CAMS Activities (Embedded in Process Maps)*	*Focus of the Metric*	*CAMS Metrics (Examples)*
Business analyst	Requirements—collaborative (requirement)	Complexity	*The number of user stories or features to be developed and the way in which they are related to higher granularity (e.g., use cases) *The number of dependencies among user stories
	Change Management—negotiable requirement (change)	Volatility	*The change frequency over unit period—this metric can be applied to many project situations including changes to the requirements (stories), changes to a piece of code (development), changes to designs, and changes in testing
Architect	Design-user feedback (architect)	Reusability	*Tolerance to change— this can be measured as the changes required to design as a result of changes in the requirements
Programmer	Coding/ implementation-pair programming (code)	Complexity	The level of coupling between classes and the extent of dependencies among them. This metric has been popular in the object-oriented development approaches *The number of layers within an architecture/design solution. While a larger number of layers can indicate complexity, this is also an indication of the approach to manage such complexity
		Readability	*The compliance with standards and frameworks being used in a project
		Ownership	*The number of owners/ contributors to a requirement, a feature, a design, a package, or a piece of code

Table 9.13 (*Continued*)

Role	*CAMS Activities (Embedded in Process Maps)*	*Focus of the Metric*	*CAMS Metrics (Examples)*
Tester	Testing—continuous (deliverable)	Defect rate	*The number of defect per test run
		Performance	*The loss or gain in performance comparing the previous integration with the current one
	Quality assurance—user feedback (deliverable)	Acceptance	The level of user satisfaction in user acceptance testing
Customer	Change management—negotiable requirement (change)	Certainty	The number of TBD (to be decided) issues per user story (or use case)
All Roles	Communication—verbal communication	Understandable	The ease of expression and understanding of a feature or a solution
		Granularity	The details of documentation for a deliverable covering requirements, architecture, design, and testing associated with a piece of development
		Collaboration	The frequency of communication among team members and across teams The outcomes from each communication effort The ratio of time for communication to overall working time in a project

- Separate metrics from measurements (data): Ascertain the metrics in a collaborative manner, but then separate the metrics from the process of collecting the data. Data collection can become an important exercise that requires use of automated tools or manual entry of information within a project. A schedule for data collection needs to be determined and defined.
- Create a baseline: This is the starting point of the use of metric. A baseline bounds the metric collection program and thereby facilitates analysis and trend spotting. This provides the time boundary for data collection. This also enables analysis of data based on the timeline in subsequent projects.
- Determine metrics risks: Risks in metrics are not only the project risks but also the risks associated with understanding and applying metrics. For example, an incorrect suite of data

may get inadvertently analyzed and used in estimating new tasks for a team. This risk has to be factored in and avoided through accuracy of measurements. The impact of a risk can be reduced and even avoided through accuracy in data collection.

- Estimate validation and review process: The techniques of V&V can also be applied to the estimates made in a project. This is a collaborative effort to cross-check the accuracy of data used in estimation, potential risks associated with dynamically changing situations, and subjective factors that may not have been easily quantified within the metrics.
- Post project reviews of metrics and documenting lessons learned: Each time a particular metric is used in practice, identify its accuracy and impact. This is usually done at the end of a project during the post-project review. This documentation on how a metric was used provides valuable information on its efficacy. Lessons learnt in the process can be used in further estimates in a project. This documentation also provides validity of the process used in estimation. Actual results versus earlier estimations can be standardized for future estimates.

Conclusions

This chapter discussed two important areas associated with CAMS—quality and metrics. The quality aspect of this work was presented through the three process maps of quality management, assurance, and control. Further details on testing, its various types, and the way it is used in practice were provided. The discussion on metrics was focused on the use of both traditional and Agile metrics for managing projects and assuring quality. This discussion completes the various aspects of CAMS needed by an organization. We now move into the discussion on how CAMS can be adopted by an organization—the topic for Chapter 10.

Agile in Practice: Road Map 9

- List the existing areas of metrics and measurements in your organization. Discuss with key stakeholders in terms of how they use the current metrics.
- Create a short two-page summary document on how metrics and measurements currently help your organization in managing quality.
- Review all quality management documentation, particularly the way it relates to project management.
- Discuss a strategy to implement the three quality-related process maps in your organization. Also discuss the challenges you will face in implementing these process maps.
- List the current tools used in testing. Review their sufficiency. Plan and budget for incorporation of new testing tools, if required in your organization.
- Revisit the creation of test beds and test data. Apply the discussion in this chapter to change the way in which test data is created and used in your organization.

Discussion Questions

- How is quality management different from quality assurance? Explain with examples.
- Argue for a need to give more importance to quality assurance than quality control.

- Identify examples of situations that will benefit by walk-through and inspections. Explain how a checklist can help in a walk-through or inspection.
- An Agile showcase is usually run in a workshop format. Explain how this showcase is different from a requirements-gathering workshop.
- What are the challenges of testing in an Agile project?
- What is the difference between verification and validation? Explain with examples.
- Explain briefly the three types of quality checks and the levels at which they function best.
- What is the difference between test cases for functional tests and the ones for nonfunctional tests? (Explain in terms of when they are created, what they are made up of, and when they are executed.)
- What, according to you, are the two key metrics and measurement challenges in an Agile project?
- Compare a planning metric in CAMS with a corresponding development metric.
- Project estimates often omit the impact of the operational business surrounding a project. This results in higher than estimated costs and efforts. Discuss the use and expansion of metrics to include factors "beyond a project" that will help in wastage in projects, wasteful projects, and even nondelivery from projects.

References

Alexander, C., The origins of pattern theory the future of the theory, and the generation of a living world. Keynote address at *OOPSLA is a Popular Conference on Object Technology and it Stands for Object Oriented Programming, Systems, Languages and Applications*, San Jose, CA, 1996.

Ambler, S., *Quality in an Agile World*, Ambysoft, Inc., 7 (4), 34–39, 2005.

Cheng, M.J., My words are very easy to understand, *Lectures on the Tao The Ching*, translated from the Chinese by ed., Gibbs, T.C., North Atlantic Books, Richmond, CA, 1981.

Coplien, J.O., The column without a name: Setting the stage, *C++ Report*, 6 (8), 8–16, October 1994.

Cottmeyer, M. and D. Stevens, Rethinking the Agile enterprise, *Cutter Executive Report*, 10 (7), 2009.

Crispin, L. and J. Gregory, *Agile Testing: A Practical Guide for Testers and Agile Teams*, Pearson Education (Addison-Wesley), Upper Saddle River, NJ, 2008.

DeMarco, T. and T. Lister, *Peopleware: Productive Projects and Teams*, Dorset House Publishing Co., Inc., New York, 2nd ed., 1999.

Dooley, B.J., Implementing organizational change for Agile development, *Cutter Executive Report*, 10 (11), 2009.

Ebert, C., *Best Practices in Software Measurement: How to Use Metrics to Improve Project and Process Performance*, Springer, Berlin, 2005.

Ebert, C. and D. Reiner, *Software Measurement: Establish, Extract, Evaluate, Execute*, Springer, Berlin; New York, 2007.

Gabriel, R., The quality without a name, *Journal of Object Oriented Programming*, 6 (5), 86–89, 1993.

Galorath, D., Software sizing, estimation, and risk management, 2009.

Ghanbary, A. and J. Day, Success of Agile environment in complex projects, *The Proceedings of the 11th Australian Information Warfare Conference,* 30 November–2 December, 2010, Perth, Australia, 7–12.

Goodman, P., *Practical Implementation of Software Metrics*, McGraw-Hill London, UK, 1993.

Hartmann, D. and R. Dymond, Appropriate agile measurement: Using metrics and diagnostics to deliver business value, *IEEE CNF (Agile Conference)*, pp. 1–6, 2006.

Herschmann, J., Top 6 tips for Agile testing, IT Professionals Developers Solutions eBook Library Webopedia, July 29, 2010, viewed March 2012, http://www.devx.com/architect/Article/45255.

International Software Testing Qualifications Board, ISTQB viewed 16 October, 2012, http://istqb.org.

Layman, L., L. Williams, and L. Cunningham, Motivations and measurements in an agile case study, *Journal of Systems Architecture*, 52 (11), 654–667, 2006.

Nguyen, D., *Automated Regression Testing Challenges in Agile Environment*, Vietnamese Testing Board, viewed 14 October 2009, http://www.vietnamesetestingboard.org/zbxe/?document_srl=160933.
Perry, W., *Quality Assurance for Information Systems*, QED Information Sciences, Wellesley, MA, 1991.
Steindl, C. and P. Krogdahl, Estimation in agile projects, *IBM Academy of Technology Best Practices in Project Estimation Conference,* IBM Corporation, pp. 1–36, 2005.
Unhelkar, B., *Process Quality Assurance for UML-Based Projects*, Pearson Education (Addison-Wesley), Boston, FL, p. 394+, 2003.
Unhelkar, B., *Verification and Validation for Quality of UML Models*, John Wiley and Sons (Wiley Interscience), New York, pp. 290+, 2005.
Unhelkar, B, *After the Y2K Fireworks: Business and Technology Strategies*, CRC Press, Boca Raton, 421, 1999.
Younessi, H., *Object-Oriented Defect Management of Software*, Prentice-Hall, Upper Saddle River, NJ, 2002.

Further Reading

Abrahamsson, P., O. Salo, J. Ronkainen, and J. Warsta, *Agile Software Development Methods: Review and Analysis*, VTT Publications, Espoo, pp. 5–73, 2002.
Ambler, S., The Agile system development life cycle (SDLC), 2005–2009, viewed 30 September 2009, http://www.ambysoft.com/essays/agileLifecycle.html#Development.
Coffin, R. and L. Derek, A practical guide to seven Agile methodologies, Part 1, 2006, viewed 30 September 2009, http://www.devx.com/architect/Article/32761/0/page/1.
Fowler, M., and J. Highsmith, The Agile manifesto, *Software Development*, 9 (8), 1–7, 2001.
Geek Explains 2008, Evolution of Agile methodologies: Engineering vs Agile methodologies, viewed 2 October 2009, http://geekexplains.blogspot.com/2008/10/evolution-of-agile-methodologies.html.
Larman, C., *Agile and Iterative Development: A Manager's Guide*, Addison-Wesley, Reading, MA, 2nd ed, 2003.
Pierce, P., Software verification and validation, *IEEE Conference*, 265–268, 1996.
Savive, Verification and validation, 2006, viewed 1 October 2009, http://www.savive.com/inform/vandv.html.
Shukla, A. and L. Williams, Long term life cycle in Agile methodology, *Software Engineering and Education*, 171, 2002.
Software Engineering Technical Committee of the IEEE Computer Society, IEEE standard for software verification and validation plans, *IEEE Journal*, 1–31, 1986.
Wallace, D. and R. Fujii, Software verification and validation: An overview, *IEEE Journal*, 6 (4), 10–17, 1989.

Chapter 10

Agile Adoption in Organizations

It is not necessary to change. Survival is not mandatory.

–W. Edwards Deming

Objectives

- Outline the process of transforming a business to an Agile business using the Composite Agile Method and Strategy (CAMS)
- Detail the progress in the adoption of Agility across the organization in order to provide business benefits as well as software benefits
- Overview the organizational adoption of CAMS (reasons and value) within the context of business change (business transformation)
- Detail the major phases in Agile business transformation (ABT), (Diagnose–Plan–Enact–Measure–Review), and the major considerations within those phases when adopting CAMS
- Explain the external factors influencing (and being influenced by) organizational adoption of CAMS (with due consideration to the corresponding internal factors)
- Review the eight organizational focus areas and their role in undertaking business transformation from a CAMS perspective
- Focus on upgrading the skills and training required in the people–process–technology–money dimensions of a business adopting CAMS
- Provide sample configuration of CAMS—comprising multiple organizational processes—after it has been fully adopted by an organization
- Describe a Center of Excellence (CoE) in an Agile organization and the role and importance of CoE in assisting and promoting CAMS within the organization
- Outline a perspective on the Capability Maturity Model (CMMI) and its application to composite process maturity in an Agile organization

Introduction

Composite Agile Method and Strategy (CAMS) considers organizational agility as a strategic approach to business management as much as it is a methodology. CAMS is more than a method issue limited to how well a piece of software should be developed. CAMS adoption is not even limited to bringing in a collection of methods across the organization. Rather, CAMS professes a comprehensive and strategic approach to organization-wide agility capacities and capabilities necessary for business. This includes people–process–technology–money aspects of the entire business.

While adopting Agility across an entire organization is more complex than adopting an Agile method in a software project, the rewards are correspondingly greater. This complexity of organizational agility (issues of incumbency, communication, sustaining business, social, psychological, and cultural, to name a few) combined with the dynamic business environment provides challenges to the adoption and management of Agile within a business (Larman and Vodde). Despite these complexities and associated challenges at the organizational level, Agility provides significant value to a business. This value is primarily derived from the enhanced ability of the business to respond to changing external and internal circumstances.

This chapter discusses the many important issues relating to organizational adoption of Agility. As a strategic organizational-level initiative, Agile adoption changes an organization significantly but such success comes from well-managed business transformation programs. The scope of such Agile business transformation (ABT) extends well beyond the boundaries of the organization. For example, organizational agility impacts external entities such as customers, suppliers, and strategic partners. In addition, aspects such as the potential exposure of an organization to external legal and compliance, which may result from a relaxing of rigors of processes and documentation (inherent within Agile), need to be managed.

Some noteworthy issues are discussed in this chapter (Chapters 11 and 12 being case studies). This chapter discusses the adoption of CAMS at both the project and organizational levels, associated issues and challenges in its adoption, and suggestions on overcoming those challenges.

Organizational Adoption of Agility and Business Transformation

Organizations adopt agility in order to respond effectively to internal and external changes. In fact, business leaders cannot make do only with responses to stimuli; they adopt organizational agility in order to initiate rapid changes of their own. For most modern business leaders, the weekly or even daily reporting structure that facilitates decision making appears outdated. Appropriate and timely updates on the status of a business to facilitate decision making are required. Business transformation for Agile is an attempt to enable the business to achieve the agility that enables it to respond rapidly to changes and, at the same time, initiate its own creative changes.

The change to an Agile business brings about a change to the organization's internal operating structure, alters its relationship with external parties, and affects the business ecosystem. This wide-ranging impact of changing to an Agile business is ratified by Brenner (2009) who says "One common error in attempting large-scale adoption of Agile methods is the assumption that the impact of the change in software development methodology will not cross the boundaries of seemingly unrelated entities of the business, such as human resources, facilities, legal, or plant security."

Transforming to an Agile business depends significantly on the type and size of business, the goals of transformation, and the subsequent deliverables. For example, a small transport company would transform only its operational processes, whereas a large auto manufacturer will transform all its business dimensions to Agile simultaneously.

There is further need to segregate processes that relate directly to the operation of the business and the process that handles the business transformation. Successful ABT needs to consider the two aforementioned processes separately. The business transformation process considers the activities and tasks that need to be undertaken for transformation, the people who will undertake the transformation, and the deliverables that will be produced at the end of the exercise. The other suite of processes includes the existing organizational processes that will change as a result of the transformation. Similarly, the roles of those that effect the transformation and of those that get transformed are different and need to be formally recognized. For example, the people involved in transforming the business include the decision makers, business analysts, process experts, and regulators. Examples of roles that undergo transformation include managers, developers, designers, and testers. External parties such as customers and business partners also undergo change when Agile is adopted.

Unhelkar and Ginige (2010) have also presented an approach to deriving strategic and consolidated business transformations that can be applied to adopting Agile across the organization. Such transformation includes changes to the enterprise, its people, and processes, its enterprise architecture (EA), as well as its technologies. In such wide-ranging changes, not all impacts can be identified by organizations adopting agility. However, they can all be brought into consideration by iterating the adoption of Agility through a framework such as CAMS.

The transformation and Agile adoption can change depending on the type and size of the business. For example, in the case of small and medium enterprises (SMEs), not all types of deliverables (such as detailed architecture documents or planned user training) are required. In case of large and global organizations, a significant amount of planning, budgeting, and organization of resources is required for successful adoption of agility across the enterprise. Depending on the demographics of the organization, it can take from 1 to 3 years for a composite Agile approach to be fully adopted and integrated within the organization. This time is required to equip and train the organization (typically its Center of Excellence [CoE] for CAMS) in the organizational methods/processes/standards in use, their "methods friction," and approach to implementing CAMS. CAMS implementation begins with the creation of process elements within a repository. These repositories can be used to select appropriate elements and configure an instance of CAMS. Enabling an organization to configure and instantiate its own CAMS is a part of successful Agile transformation.

Apart from the methods in use, the organization, as an operating entity, can have its own business and technical challenges. Adoption of agility across the organization aims to help the organization abate those challenges. The existing state of the organization, possibly with troubled projects and lumbering organizational functions, presents a separate dimension to the challenges in organizational adoption of agility. These existing organizational challenges, coupled with issues associated with ABT, can become formidable in a short span of time because of their complexity. CAMS brings about changes to the organization, which include its business strategies and methods, its use of standards and practices, its project management methods, and its EA and design standards. Separating the business transformation for Agility and the existing organizational responsibilities is advisable in reducing the overall complexity of Agile adoption.

SIDEBAR

The adoption of CAMS by an organization will involve sociocultural issues, psychological and motivational issues, leadership and political issues, issues relating to establishment of a Center of Excellence (CoE), use of program office (PMO), development and maintenance issues, budgets and costs issues, support and services issues, architecture and infrastructure issues, and legal and environmental issues. Handling these issues requires an integrated, systems-based approach to the organization (this is also the *Systems Thinking* approach, as described by Senge in *Fifth Discipline*). Unhelkar (2010a) in *A Step Apart From Purity: Composite Agile Method and Strategy* has further argued for the need to handle people issues by getting together project sponsors, business stakeholders, customers, and users, along with architects, designers, developers, and testers, to carry out Agile initiatives within organizations. Thomsett (2010) advises the beginning of the Agile business transformation (ABT) with a series of "fierce" conversations around culture, values, and behaviors. Such conversations, he argues, will ensure that the people who will be involved in implementing the various Agile models are fully aware of the potential cultural impacts of the Agile models. The formal planned aspects of transformation to Agile include identifying the goals of transformation, documenting the operational functions/processes that will undergo transformation, and applying verification and validation techniques to the deliverables.

Figure 10.1 shows the overall process of business transformation for Agility. This business transformation is a planned and strategic approach to transitioning an existing business to an Agile business. This Agile business will be collaborative, highly interconnected, communicative, and in sync with the business ecosystem (comprising industry, government, and society) in which it exists. The process of changing the organization from where it is right now (slow-moving, perhaps inefficient, rigid, and disconnected with the environment in which it exists) to a Lean-Agile organization that is well aligned with its customers and the environment in which it functions can be understood as ABT.

Thus, Agile business transformation (ABT) can be defined as "a strategic management initiative that brings about a fundamental change in the people, processes, technologies, and economies of a business that make it Lean, cohesive, and holistic, thereby making it capable of rapid and effective responses to external stimuli and able to initiate its own changes."

A centralized organization that is driven top-down will find it difficult to respond effectively to changes from both outside and inside the organization. The hierarchical structures

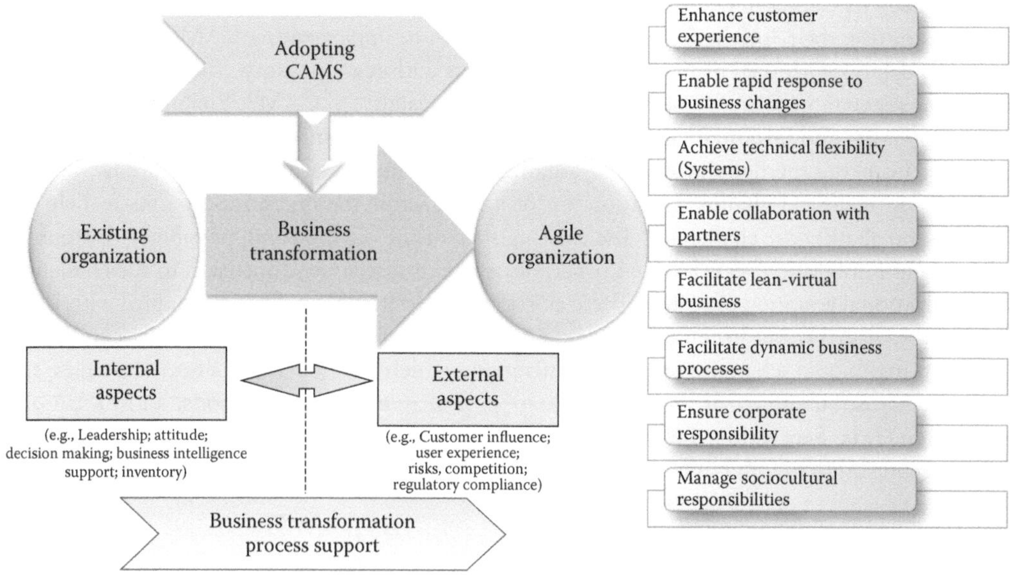

Figure 10.1 Organizational adoption of CAMS—part of the business transformation exercise.

of such an organization will prevent rapidity of response. A transformed organization will be collaborative, Agile, and Lean, with minimal infrastructure overhead (moving toward virtual) and imbued with continuous change. This organization will be customer-driven and capable of providing personalized services to its customers. In fact, the entire organization, including its business strategies and methods, its use of standards and practices, its project management methods, and its EA and design standards, will all undergo transformation to an Agile way of doing things.

The advantages of organizational agility were highlighted in the earlier chapters of this book. An ABT, as shown on the right in Figure 10.1, aims to realize those advantages. On the basis of the discussions thus far, the following are the advantages that an organization aims to achieve by transforming itself to an Agile business:

- Enhance customer experience through personalized and location-specific services, as agility increases the ease with which an organization can reach out to customers (particularly through mobile technologies).
- Provide customers with additional products and services by collaborating with other businesses through horizontal and vertical cluster formation.
- Enable a business to respond rapidly to external changes and pressures that can pose risks—especially if they are time-bound.
- Enable a business to quickly initiate its own changes, which will provide it with strategic advantages and opportunities to capitalize on new technologies, regulatory changes, or market niche.
- Achieve technical flexibility with its information technology (IT) systems, which will enable it to quickly change the systems and also rapidly upgrade the systems.
- Facilitate increased collaboration with partners as well as regulatory entities. This is achieved by extending the organization's global reach, ease of outsourcing, and wide coverage for the organization's products and services with the use of communications technologies and Web Services.
- Facilitate lean-virtual business by reducing internal costs and improving the quality and efficiency of procurement, inventory, and development activities.
- Facilitate dynamicity in business processes—change the business processes of the organization to quickly and effectively respond to the changing needs of the customer in a location- and time-independent manner.
- Ensure corporate responsibility by providing standards and consistency through governance frameworks, improved corporate accountability, and regulatory compliance through timely, accurate, and detailed reporting on the business performance.
- Manage environmental responsibilities with Lean and efficient business processes, efficient data centers, and sustainable human resource (HR) policies.
- Enhance electronic presence through social media by exposing the right areas of the organization to customers, potential customers, and business partners.

Adoption of CAMS: Reasons and Value

Organizational adoption of CAMS is a process in itself. Figure 10.2 shows the major stages through which the organizational adoption of CAMS progresses. It starts with the CAMS business case where cost justifications and risks relating to CAMS adoption in the organization are considered. Once this justification is accepted by the many business and technology stakeholders, the

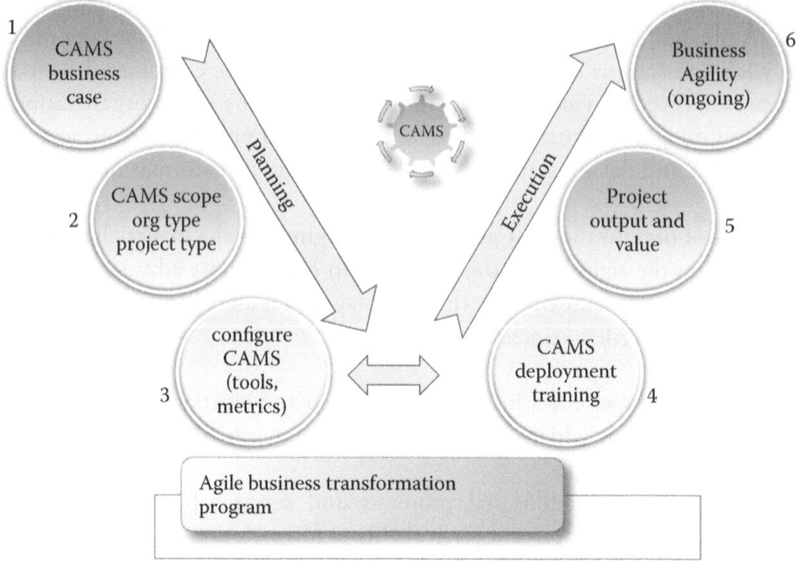

Figure 10.2 CAMS organizational adoption reasons and value.

transition is scoped within the adoption process. The senior management helps decide the extent to which CAMS will be used across the organization. This is an important decision because the adoption of CAMS can occasionally progress from division to division.

CAMS adoption and instantiation will change depending on the type, size, location, and goals of the organization, as well as on the type and size of projects within its program. CAMS will continue to draw relevant elements from planned processes, architectural frameworks, and governance standards, together with Agile values, to suit the organization. This leads to the configuration of CAMS—possibly with the help of tools and technologies that support the processes. Associated metrics (discussed in detail in Chapter 9) are also embedded in the CAMS configuration.

The execution of CAMS starts when it is deployed across the organization. Unlike the deployment of a specific method, CAMS deployment is a combination of the redeployment of existing methods together with Agile values, principles, and practices. As CAMS is deployed, it also mandates training and upskilling for all personnel. Multiple projects can use CAMS, and their output and value are measured and reported at project and organizational levels. Eventually, CAMS disperses through the entire organization, rendering the business collaborative, Lean, and Agile on an ongoing basis. This is what is meant by the self-sustaining capability of an Agile organization. An Agile organization can not only deliver products and services as per expectations but it is also highly responsive to external and internal changes.

CAMS Organizational Adoption—High-Level Road Map

Figure 10.3 shows a high-level road map for Agile adoption. This road map provides an outline of the adoption process as well as provisions for continuous monitoring and change as the organization adopts CAMS. The road map stresses continuous tailoring of CAMS to business needs *during* its adoption. Change management and problem-solving skills on an ongoing basis become very important as this road map is executed.

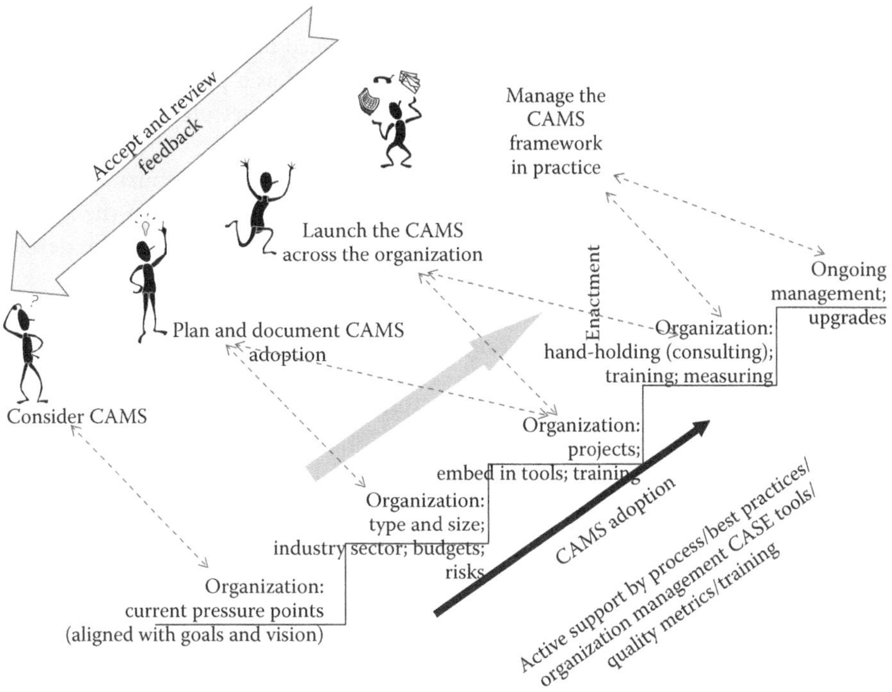

Figure 10.3 CAMS organizational adoption—high-level road map.

In Figure 10.3, the "consider CAMS" phase indicates that the organization is investigating and weighing various options, issues, and factors in terms of Agile adoption. This is the state when the organization realizes that an Agile and Lean collaborative business is integral to its business strategy for survival and growth.

Once the key stakeholders in the organization are convinced of the need to adopt CAMS, the organization moves to the next phase of "Plan and document CAMS adoption" (Figure 10.3). This includes envisioning the framework, technologies, and processes for Agile adoption and usage. The organization may be considered in a strategic mode thus far. Once the strategic aspect of CAMS is consummated, the practical phase of ABT begins.

The third stage is the one in which CAMS is launched across the organization. With the commencement of this practical enactment phase of the ABT, various additional and valuable activities, such as handling the "feedback" from the stakeholders in terms of the efficacy of Agility, mechanisms to manage the process in practice, and approach to measuring the results of the CAMS, all come into play. The organization eventually moves to the ongoing management of the CAMS framework in practice. This ongoing management also includes acceptance of feedback and reviews from various layers of the organization impacted through Agile adoption.

The following are the key considerations in ABT based on CAMS (in addition to using them for organizational adoption of CAMS, they can also be used to verify whether the transformation has indeed provided value to business):

- Organizational adoption of CAMS is an enterprise-wide transformation effort. Therefore, as an organization becomes Agile, every aspect of its operations (including its IT and non-IT

processes) are affected. For example, the interaction between systems, processes, and organizational elements become fuzzier in Agile than in planned processes.
- Organizational adoption of CAMS needs to be managed as a project. Here, planning the change comes into play, especially as the organization is itself getting newly acquainted with the Agile values, principles, and practices.
- Organizational adoption of CAMS requires the discipline of change management. This is particularly important, as, occasionally, the business tends to think that the Agile change is restricted to software development and that changes within the software development processes will not affect them.
- A convincing business case for organizational adoption has to include cost, benefits, and risks. Since the organization is adopting this transformation for the first time, it will not have any data relating to CAMS internally. External data in terms of returns on investment and risks need to be used in creating the business case.
- The organization needs to be a learning organization (Senge, 1990). It is through "learnability" that an organization remains Agile. Agile values and practices are promoted, updated, and optimized on a continuous basis in a learning organization. Conducting regular retrospectives on an ongoing basis is one of the keys for successful enterprise-scale adoption of Agility.
- Agile adoption will require establishing and capitalizing on knowledge management systems and processes within the organization. For example, capturing and reusing experiences in pure Agile and business processes can be undertaken through setting up of a CoE.
- Adopting composite Agile across organization will be disruptive. This is mainly because CAMS ensures balance—particularly by not hurriedly discarding the established formal practices, associated models, and documentation in the organization. CAMS, however, is a combination of Agile and planned approaches to software *and* organizational processes, resulting in a totally new way of work. This can be considered as a "disruptive" adoption of processes working together to realize pragmatic outcomes.
- People, the roles they fulfill, and their hierarchical structures change during organizational adoption of Agility. Leadership plays an important part in understanding and adopting CAMS. Changes to roles may not always be obvious or easily discernible by those affected by them. Therefore, it is important that all such changes are predefined and agreed to by all parties involved in the change. For example, middle management roles are likely to change with the need for higher skills (as the flattening of the hierarchical pyramid takes place—see Chapter 8) in adopting CAMS. In an Agile learning organization, this middle management layer can provide the necessary means to disperse Agile values and practices. Therefore, these roles need to be considered in the context of the entire organization and not of just individual projects.

An important part of planning for CAMS adoption is the creation of an instance of CAMS that is specific to the organization. The following are the steps that an organization can adopt to come up with its own instance of CAMS:

- Review of existing methods at the project, governance, and business levels. This would include identification of existing methods at these levels and/or the discovery of a gap in terms of a method at a particular level within the organization.

- Identify the challenges currently faced by the organization in terms of development and maintenance approaches (this is particularly true if the organization already has an Agile approach in place).
- Communicate across the organization the need to transform to an Agile business.
- Identify the elements from the higher level (business level) processes that map/correlate to the practices of Agile (as described in the CAMS repository).
- Embed the Agile practices within those higher level processes (as described in configuring CAMS).
- Align processes with each other by reducing "methods friction" (Unhelkar, 2012). This is called "process alignment".
- Align the business internally to its existing technologies and systems and externally to its business partners and customers.
- Create or use a CoE.
- Validate the CAMS instance through walk-throughs in a workshop format.
- Execute CAMS on an ongoing basis; continue to modify the CAMS instance depending on the changes to the external environment of business.
- Create and apply metrics and measurements to the entire CAMS life cycle; update the data to provide further benchmarks for the organization in terms of productivity and quality.

Agile Business Transformation—Internal and External Factors

As an organization adopts agility, many internal and external factors come into play. Figure 10.4 shows the external factors that affect business Agility (shown on the outside of the box) and the

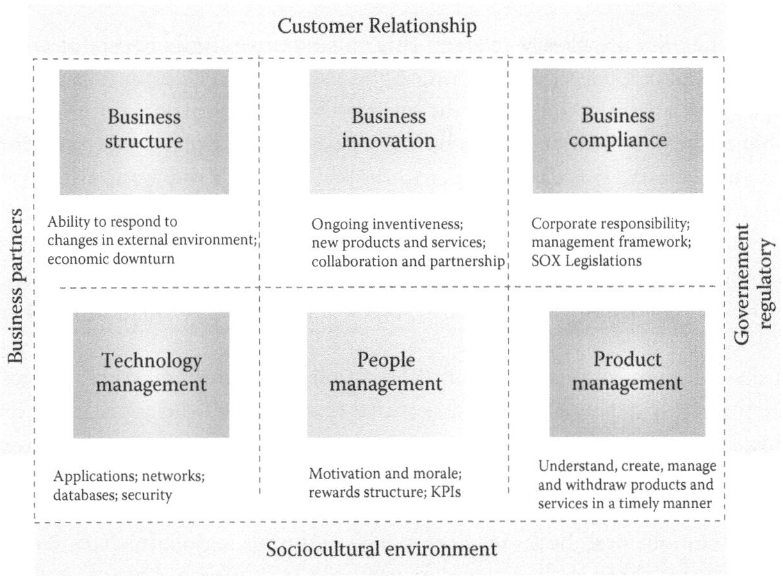

Figure 10.4 External and internal factors to consider in business transformations.

way in which the business responds to these factors internally (shown on the inside of the box). These external and internal factors affecting ABT are discussed in greater detail next.

External Influencing Factors

The external influencing factors an ABT include customer relationship, business partners, government and regulatory requirements, and the sociocultural environment in which the business exists. These factors are discussed next.

Customer Relationship

ABT impacts the customer relationships of the organization. Through agility, the organization becomes more flexible in its offerings (customer centric). This, in turn, enables the customers to configure their own requirements from the organization. With agility, customers can also be invited to participate in business decision making in terms of product design and service expectation. The transforming organization needs to ensure that it aligns its Agile changes with its customers. For example, if an organization changes the way in which it offers a product, the customers need to be made aware of those changes. An Agile bank offering customers the ability to put together their accounts in different formats that suit them will have to educate and align the customers to such offering. The demographics of the customer also need to be considered in adopting Agility. For example, an elderly population of customers who are dealing with their superannuation accounts may not want all the agility and flexibility that a bank is offering. These customers need to be treated differently from the ones who are comfortable in exclusively dealing online with the organization.

Business Partners

Collaboration and agility are closely related. This collaborative–Agile nature of an organization was discussed in detail in Chapter 6. Adopting Agile, especially in its composite format across the organization, implies a definite impact on the business partners of the organization. For example, the relationship of the organization and its business partners will expand on the basis of the Agile values of trust and honesty. This has relevance to the way in which an organization communicates physically and technically. For example, production schedules of an organization can be exposed to a supplier electronically to reduce inventory. An organization adopting Agile can hardly ever do so in isolation. Business partners are affected by the transformation and, therefore, they need to be taken into confidence in the very early stages of Agile transformation (Sherringham and Unhelkar, 2010b).

Through the communications aspect of information and communication technology (ICT), businesses are invariably dependent on and sensitive to changes in the applications and behavior of their business partners. This is because any change in any business process of an organization has immediate ramifications for the processes of the business partners. Starting right from the ubiquitous spreadsheet used by a small business through to the comprehensive enterprise resource planning (ERP) solutions used by large corporations and multinationals, sharing of information with business partners through ICT plays a core role in business decision making. Partners influence every aspect of an organization's marketing, management, growth, and expansion. These business partners demand services, implement new technologies, and upgrade their own business processes as a result of Agile adoption by an organization. Sharing of information with these partners can not only avoid issues relating to process mismatches with them but the partners can themselves provide assistance in enabling a comprehensive Agile transformation (especially if they have adopted the Agile values themselves).

Government Regulatory Factors

Adopting agility at the organizational level requires careful consideration of the legal and regulatory requirements that are usually external to the organization. While Agility promotes collaboration and open communication, there may still be the need to document the interactions from a legal viewpoint. Understanding the regulatory requirements, ongoing changes to legislations across multiple collaborative partners and their regions, and the impact of these legal requirements on the organization are crucial factors in organizational adoption of Agility. Interactions of the organization (especially large and global organizations) with governmental structures may have to be documented in detail—facilitating traceability and audit. Irrespective of the desire of the organization to be Agile, some of these government–business interactions cannot be Agile in the pure sense. A combination of Agile values and corresponding formal documentation is required in dealing with this factor during transformation.

Sociocultural Environment

The sociocultural environment in which the organization exists and operates is immediately affected when Agility is adopted by the organization. Similar to the consideration to the demographics of customers, the social environment of an organization requires due consideration in terms of its acceptability of Agility. For example, a business that deals with selling goods online to a teenage audience will find it relevant to investigate the social media (Albright, 2012) frequented by these potential customers. Agility at the business level will change the way in which goods are sold online. Collaborative Agile, in particular, will expand the reach of the organization to beyond its geographical boundaries. In such cases, a proper study of the sociocultural environment and the way it will be affected by Agility is required as a part of ABT.

Internal Factors and Responses

Business Structure

Structural flexibility of a business is its ability to change internally so as to respond to external pressures. The structural model of the business needs to be flexible enough to allow it to respond to external demands. The global economic downturn came down upon businesses without much warning. A flexible business model and associated Agile corporate culture can become capable of handling such sudden external changes. Accompanying the need for structural flexibility of business is the need for the underpinning systems (e.g., HR; customer relationship management, CRM) to facilitate such nimbleness. Communications technologies remove duplication of activities, eliminate redundant activities, merge manual processes with electronic and mobile processes, and improve the overall process flow within and across the organization (Unhelkar et al., 2009). ABT integrates these technologies and tools with processes and people, thus paving the path for a flexible business structure.

SIDEBAR

The source of Agile movement is the Agile Manifesto. This manifesto predominantly focuses on software development. Agile methods, such as Extreme programming (XP) and Scrum, present interesting challenges as an organization adopts Agility. For example, the structures of projects within Agile organizations change. Cross-functional teams, based on pure software Agility, require people to assume new roles and a new set of practices. The role definitions and guidance in terms of the activities these roles have to perform are minimal in a pure Agile approach. This, in turn, can cause people to resist Agile adoption. CAMS brings together the formality of role definitions in Agile projects at the software development level. CAMS also makes the roles explicit—positioning them in formal team structures. While cross-functional teams are welcome, CAMS approaches it gently and with due respect to the needs of individuals for formality and structure around their work. The way in which product-level output can be improved is to sidestep any dramatic shifts in team structures. A Kanban-like approach of starting where the "team actually is" can provide a smoother transition to Agility than the dramatic shifts envisaged in pure Agile approaches as resources skills and expertise are established. At a project level, a composite Agile adoption can be a series of steps along the journey to an Agile business. The end result is an optimal throughput providing a consistent value stream.

Business Innovation

Business innovation can be considered as the ability of a business to creatively generate new products and services, come up with innovative ways of handling the competition, and prioritize its risks. An Agile business creates many opportunities within itself to be creative and innovative. Enabling innovative approach to business often calls for changes in business practices, business operations, and business culture (Murugesan and Unhelkar, 2004) These changes are facilitated in Agile adoption. Agility understands the type of business, the domain in which it exists, its available resources, and its strengths and weaknesses, as well as a supportive culture. Conversely, the need to foster an innovative culture is also high in ABT, which enables people to experiment with processes and technologies to improve and optimize them.

Business Compliance

Business compliance is the need for the business to develop capabilities to meet regulatory compliances. The external demands for government and regulatory requirements alluded to earlier need to be satisfied by businesses by internally reorganizing itself. An Agile internal business structure is able to respond easily to ever-changing legislation. Consider, for example, the Sarbanes–Oxley (SOX) legislation. This legislation provides protection from fraudulent practices to shareholders and the general public and, at the same time, also pins the responsibility for internal controls and financial reporting on the chief executive officer (CEO) and the chief financial officer (CFO) of the company (Raisinghani and Unhelkar, 2007). Agile transformation aims to enable the business to carry out this accountability and responsibility through changes in the internal processes, updating of ICT-based systems to enable accurate collection and timely reporting of business data, and changes in the attitude and practices of senior management. Another example of the need for the business to comply is the rapid implementation of regulations related to carbon emissions. This legislation requires businesses to update and implement their carbon collection procedures, analysis, control, audit, and internal and external reporting.

Technology Management

Technology management in Agile adoption involves handling the changes to underlying technologies that support the business and its processes. Challenges in managing technologies include changes to the wired and wireless networks, service-oriented applications, distributed data warehouses, and complexities of security as the organization transforms to Agile. Businesses rightfully aim to capitalize on the connectivity accorded by the ubiquitous Internet (Arunatileka and Ginige, 2003a; Ginige, 2002). This ICT-based communication results in an enhanced customer experience and improved internal business efficiency (Deitel et al., 2001). For example, an Agile organization will want to provide services to a customer at his/her location. This change will require the organization to move its customer service processes on mobile networks. Corresponding data relating to the customer has to also change to accommodate mobile contents.

Agile transformation requires the business to be prepared for this technological surge that will put pressure on its architecture, its structure, and its operations. Information *and* communication technologies increase the interdependence of businesses on each other. The need for the management of technologies in a holistic manner is justified because of the extensive intertwining of business with ICT.

People Management

Adopting Agility impacts the people within an organization. Managing the employees and other contract staff within an organization, keeping up their motivation, and keeping them abreast of the changes are crucial ingredients of successful Agile adoption. In adopting Agile across the organization, careful attention needs to be given to the career aspirations of individuals, their personal job satisfaction criteria, and their attitude toward agility. Large global organizations employ people in numerous ways including permanent employment, contract labor, and consulting/advisory roles. The approach to each of these engagements differs when Agile is adopted as an organizational culture. For example, a permanent employee will be interested in finding out what happens to his next promotion if the tasks to be performed are "shared". The contract employee may be happy to share tasks but would like to index his contract rates to quality and time. The HR systems and processes supporting these engagements need to be flexible and capable of handling these differences and the changing scenarios. ABT investigates, updates, and ensures a flexible approach to resourcing people, managing them, motivating them, and enabling them to provide their best to the organization and its customers.

Product Management

Product management refers to the need to produce new products and services and to continue to produce existing products with improved parameters (such as time and cost). Agility changes the way the organization captures data related to products, analyzes them, and incorporates the output into product development and deployment. For example, an Agile organization will eschew long-winded analysis of product feedback, but, instead directly collaborate with the customer to derive an instantaneous update on product feedback. This information is immediately made available to the decision makers through Internet-enabled collaborative systems. The processes leading up to product development change and so also the supporting ICT systems, when Agility is adopted across the organization. While the organization develops consistency across its various product lines and its development and deployment activities, collaborative Agile also offers opportunity for "mass customization" (i.e., the ability to produce customized products for each customer but on a mass-production scale). This occurs in an Agile organization because of reduced touch points during a production process. Disposal of used products and withdrawal of a product line in a timely and coordinated manner are also a part of product management. The new Agile organization has a Lean inventory, reduced paperwork, and continuous change incorporated in its product life cycle management (PLM).

Organizational Focus Areas in Agile Business Transformation

Transforming to an Agile business is an organizational exercise in its own right. This transformation process is interspersed with activities such as detailed planning, project accounting, risk management, and metrics and measurements. These phases are a planned and logical approach to transforming to an Agile business. These phases are themselves not new—they are reflected in various other approaches to business management as well. For example, the Lean Six Sigma approach in the business methods space, or even governance standards, such as the Information Technology Infrastructure Library (ITIL), can be easily customized to carry out ABT. These process frameworks can enable ABT by capitalizing on the people, processes, and technologies of the organization.

Business Transformation Process and Organizational Focus Areas

Figure 10.5 further expands on the ABT road map. This road map encapsulates the steps that an organization has to take for its transformation. Typically, a business has to undertake the following in attempting ABT:

- Identify the current status of the organization. This status includes the way in which methods and frameworks are currently being used in the organization—and the business tiers or levels at which they are being used.
- Ascertain the goals of undertaking ABT. While the goals of transition to Agile are already discussed sufficiently in this book, still it is important for an organization to list them specifically during ABT.

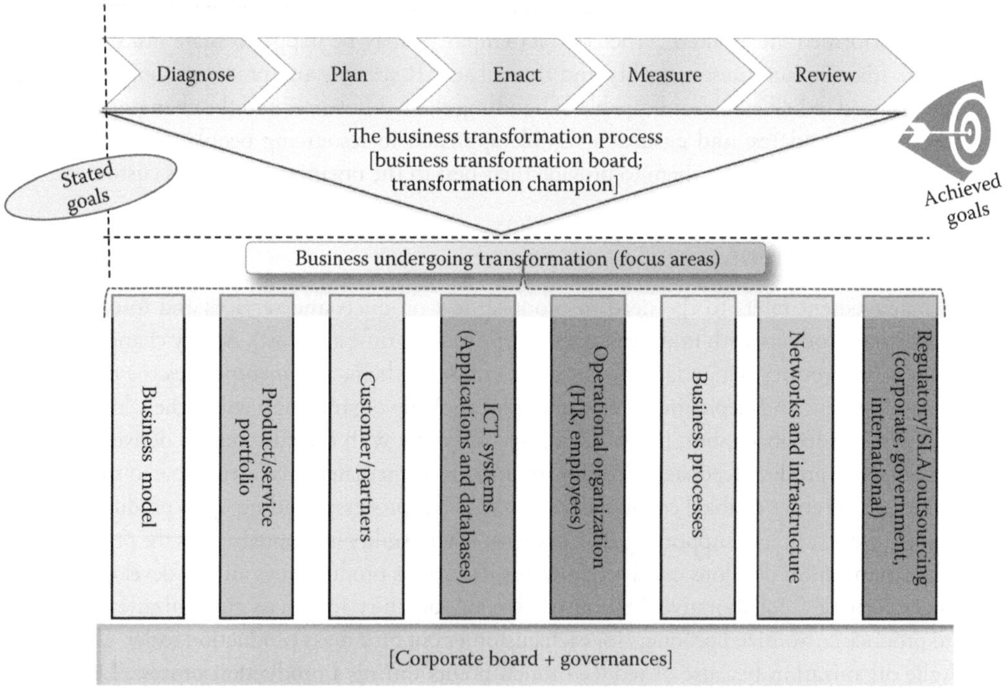

Figure 10.5 Business transformation process and organizational focus areas (CAMS perspective). SLA, service level agreement.

- Care should be taken to ensure that the goals are not set in concrete. This is because the transformation itself is an iterative process and the organization will discover new insights as soon as it starts changing. Therefore, the goals of transforming to an Agile organization can change and may need to be fine-tuned through diagnosis work.
- Add justification for the transformation project using return on investment (ROI) calculations within a business case. This justification can be made more robust through the use of a pilot project and also through information gained from external ABT experiences.
- Organize the ABT including its resourcing, timelines, and acceptance criteria by the sponsor.
- Undertake a review of the "methods" in the organization and develop an understanding of the project portfolio where methods and frameworks are being used in the organization.
- Create a pathway/road map for the transformation.
- Physically execute an ABT that will change the way in which the organization operates. This is basically an organizational redesign.
- At the end of the ABT, review whether the goals and expectations of this transformation project have been achieved or not.

These are steps or phases that control and direct the ABT as a project. These phases can be listed, as shown in Figure 10.5, as diagnose, plan, enact, measure, and review. They are described in detail in order to carry out an ABT.

Diagnose

ABT starts with the diagnostic phase. Diagnosis provides a good understanding of the current state of the organization. The work areas of the business, shown in the bottom half of Figure 10.5, are investigated in this diagnosis phase from the point of view of the transformation. This investigation results in an understanding of the structure and dynamics of the organization, its business goals, and its ability to manage risks. Diagnosis helps an organization take control of its transformation project and focus on its ROI. Diagnosis also identifies opportunities for a program-level value proposition that is aligned to the transformation goals. The influence of the organization's demographics, motivators, goals, size, and type are all included in this diagnosis. The diagnostic phase refines its business case with details of the effort required and a timeline for the transformation.

Plan

The planning and scoping phase of ABT uses the output of the diagnosis phase to create a program for the transformation. Once the significant aspects of the business—especially the work areas—are identified, this planning phase outlines the task plan for transforming each work area. Thus, the outputs of the planning phase are a precise list of tasks, associated resource requirements, and outline of the deliverables to be produced, as well as the corresponding time estimates for the transformation project.

The planning phase also takes inputs from a possible CAMS pilot run in the earlier phase. Alternatively, planning itself can incorporate a pilot CAMS project to test the validity of the plan. A pilot project can identify the many challenges the organization is likely to face in undertaking a full-scale ABT. In the planning phase, the strategic thinking and innovative capability of the organization are put to good use in order to formulate the activities and their sequences in the transformation project. Creative ways of undertaking ABT, including the maximum use of internal and external resources, are explored in this phase.

Similar phases apply with the formation of a CoE for Agile implementation across the organization. Alternatively, the planning phase can include an approach to expand an existing CoE for Agile usage.

The scope of the transformation project, the work areas of the business affected, and the role of the CoE are further discussed and resolved here. The scoping aspect of the ABT project in this planning phase ranks and prioritizes the work areas of transformation and studies the effect of their interdependencies and changes. Once again, the prioritization techniques of Agile (such as MoSCoW) can be used even at this high level to identify the first work area to be transformed within the organization. While the risks are managed in practice during enactment, the planning phase identifies and ranks these risks. CAMS promotes the balancing act required in planning—balancing between costs and benefits, balancing technology with business, and balancing risks with outcome.

Enact

Enactment is the execution of the ABT project. This is the physical stepping-through of the plan created in the previous phase. Enactment of ABT requires the full gamut of project management skills. An ABT project has to undertake risk management and monitoring of progress, measurements, and reporting. Enactment can be led by any work stream or a combination of streams. The following are the issues to be considered during an ABT enactment phase:

- Ongoing identification and classification of risks, their priorities, and ways to ameliorate them.
- Interrelationship among work areas, their dependencies, and management of the lead work area as first priority.
- Delivering intensive Agile-specific training, mentoring, and coaching to staff at all levels in an organization. This training will have to be customized to suit the staff requirements (e.g., business decision makers will have to be coached in terms of the information they use and the uncertainty they can handle through agility; software developers will need a completely different type of training in Agile methods).
- Measurement of the transformation outputs. Use of metrics created during diagnosis and formalized during planning are recommended here to ensure common measures for comparison.
- Reporting to stakeholders and managing their expectations.

Measure and Review

The review phase of an ABT details the outcomes of the project. This phase also facilitates the cross-checking of whether the stated objectives of the Agile transformation are reflected in the outcomes. Furthermore, the outcomes need to be measured and studied not only for the transformed business but also for the new environment in which the business is now operating. The actual outcomes of Agile adoption will be slightly different from the stated goals even in cases of successful ABTs. The difference between the outcomes and the goals could be due to the shifting of both the business and the environment during the time the ABT project has been implemented.

Evaluation of the outcomes includes reviewing in detail the formation of CoE, changes to the supporting software and systems, changes to organizational structures, business portfolio, and business model, and, eventually, changes to the way in which software is developed and maintained. Evaluation feedback is provided to the stakeholders responsible for ABT.

The review process not only ascertains the achievements of the transition but also opens up the doors to further and potentially ongoing enhancements. Therefore, the review process should make provisions for these enhancements in all work areas of the business. Organizations should incorporate changes in accordance with the experience gained from the transition as well as the issues discovered during the transition.

Metrics are required to identify and measure the criteria for optimization and improvement. Metrics provide a set of measurable criteria rather than an ad hoc understanding of improvement resulting from ABT. Therefore, metrics are used to communicate the success of the ABT project to various stakeholders. Understanding the perceptions of the goals in relation to business transformations provides a good suite of measurable criteria. Changes to business processes, ICT systems, and organizational structures are also measured before and after the ABT. Each work area can have its own set of metrics, and these metrics change depending on the industry sector and business type.

Work Areas for ABT

Figure 10.5 also shows the eight most common focus areas of the business that will be affected by ABT. While these focus areas can change depending on the type and nature of the business, the goal of the business undergoing transformation, and the complexity of the organization, they still provide a good understanding of most business structures to enable their transformation. In practice, these focus areas become the work areas of the business transformation. These eight focus areas, or work areas, for ABT are summarized in Table 10.1.

A work area may map onto one or more departments of the business. Similarly, each work area may have one or more stakeholders with specific objectives. It is important to identify these stakeholders corresponding to each work area as early in the transformation process as possible. These stakeholders need to be involved and managed right through the transformation process. Handling their concerns as well as meeting their expectations is vital for the success of the transformation process. These work areas, summarized in Table 10.1, are discussed in greater detail next.

Business Model

Organizational agility impacts the business model as it changes the priorities and goals of a business. The business model of an organization represents the way the business is organized and operated. Organizational leadership deals with this model based on the *vision* and the *value* of the organization. ABT utilizes available resources in coming up with a sensible, sustainable, and profitable business through the business model. The business value to be derived from agility is the primary concern of the business model. Changes to the business model result in changes to the organization's financial position, its revenue model, the risks and exposures it faces, its strategies for expansion and growth (taking over other businesses or offering itself as a target for takeover), its policies and procedures, and its technological sophistication, among others. Thus, the products and services offered, the corresponding revenue structures, customer and partner relationships, and the inevitable need to have a global presence, all have an influence on, and are influenced by, the business model.

Table 10.1 Agile Business Transformation Work Areas

ABT Work (Focus) Areas	*Description*
Business model	Deals with the way a business is organized. Agile changes the business model as the priorities and goals of business are influenced through agility
Product and service portfolio	Provides an overall summary of the offerings of the business. Analysis of this portfolio of products and services helps in ascertaining the priorities and risks associated with ABT
Customers and partners	Describes the external parties interacting with the business and the way they will change and influence ABT
ICT systems, applications, and databases	Covers the software systems and technologies that support the business and the way they need to be upgraded to support an Agile business
Operational/ organizational	Handles the internal parties such as employees and management and their reporting hierarchies within the business. Agile changes these structures at both the project and organizational levels
Business process	Models and describes the way in which all activities of the business are sequenced and carried out. Reengineering of processes is a major area of work as the business undergoes transformation
Networks and infrastructure	Focuses on the underlying communications technologies used by the business. Especially, mobile networks can dramatically enable location-independent product offerings. Security of networks needs special attention in ABT
Regulatory	Deals with legal, accounting, and financial aspects of the business and requires attention in terms of audits and traceability required across the organization

The following are the significant issues to be considered as a business adopts Agility across all areas of its operations (i.e., adopts composite Agile):

- Core value of the business: The core value of the business dictates what the business is all about. This is the primary reason why the business exists. How will the core value change as a result of ABT? Or, does it need to change at all? A radical business transformation can change the core value of the business, for example, from being a nonprofit charity to a profit-making business. Another example can be a core change from being an entirely physical business to an online or virtual business.
- Offerings of the business: In investigating the business model, the transformation project looks at the overall offerings of the business. Furthermore, the physical versus virtual (Web) aspect of the business also gets investigated here during ABT. While the detailed investigation of the product/service portfolio is discussed in the next section, it is mentioned here because the business offering affects the way in which Agility and collaboration are practiced by the business.

- Management and control: ABT enables easier management and control, as it aims to use technologies, such as a knowledge management system, in order to facilitate Agility at all levels of business decision making. Therefore, ABT revises the business model for integrated decision making by the various stakeholders in the business, leading to a much improved management understanding, structure, operation, and control of business than before.
- Finances: The business model deals with financial aspects of the business (such as profit enhancement and cost reduction). This is a separate work area and is discussed in the regulatory as well as people work areas. However, the cost of operating the business, its marketing and sales initiatives, the services and support provided by the business, its customer service, and its financial growth are all investigated, short-listed, and modeled as the business transforms itself.
- Competition and collaboration: The business model changes as it gears up to handle competition. Agility helps the business become Lean and efficient. This, in turn, enables it to compete better. More importantly, though, Agility enhances an organization's ability to collaborate. Collaboration, in turn, impacts the business model of the organization. Collaboration enhances effectiveness of business but it needs to be incorporated in the business model of the organization.
- Strategies and policies: The business model aims to utilize every resource available to the organization, both internally and externally, in order to provide value. An ABT impacts the strategies and policies of the organization, particularly from its futuristic viewpoint. As an Agile strategy, the policies of a transforming organization need to reflect what its core value will be, how it will achieve that value, and what changes it needs to undertake as it moves toward its goals. Business transformation investigates and deals with the changes to the strategies and policies of the organization. For example, outsourcing the noncore aspect of the organization's work—occasionally referred to as smart sourcing—is a significant part of the organization's strategy for optimizing resource utilization. Availability of online, real-time communication facilities enables businesses to create strategies for globally dispersed resources. These strategies and policies of the organization are a part of its business model and are revised and updated to reflect Agility in business.

Product and Service Portfolio

The work area of the product and service portfolio deals with the offerings of the business to its customers and partners. The portfolio contains a list of all products and services that the company has to offer. This portfolio is investigated during ABT to decide which offerings to keep, which to remove, and what new products/services to bring in.* The following are the significant considerations when a business undergoes ABT from the point of view of the product and service portfolio work area:

- Product life cycle management: This is a detailed investigation into the process of arriving at a product (and also a corresponding service that is offered as a product, e.g., an insurance product or a health cover). The new Agile organization will change its product life cycle to reflect Agile approaches to product development. Composite Agile also encourages formal use of methods (e.g., Stage-Gate) to arrive at improved and relevant products for the business.

* For more practical details, see Plainview's "Enterprise Portfolio Management" (www.planview.com/products/enterprise/enterprise-portfolio-management.aspx) and Resource Management System's "Portfolio Approach" (www.rms.net/portfolio_approach_r_pap.htm).

- Customization of products and services: Each product and service needs to be reviewed in order to enable its customization. Agility impacts the customization of products and services. Factors such as customer location, density, and urgency are factored into product development and customization.
- Packaging of products and services: ABT calls for repackaging of existing products and services. This could mean putting together a combination of the offerings in a creative way to enable greater market penetration. Points calculation, reward systems, and premium services can be used to create innovative packaging for products and services.
- Alignment of products and services: An organization may have numerous products and services; occasionally, these offerings conflict with each other. Unless a formal review and investigation into the overall portfolio of products and services is carried out, these occasionally conflicting products remain on the market, reducing the value the business can offer. Agility and collaboration force a review and check of all existing products and services to enable their alignment with the business values as also among each other.
- Service reach for wider and dispersed audience: How far and wide can the products and services of an organization reach? A collaborative-Agile transforming organization aims to reach potential customers through various mechanisms, including physical, virtual, direct, and indirect, individually and in a group. While mobile technologies can be used to provide services to roaming customers through their mobile gadgets and associated networks, Web Services allow reaching a business partner to collaborate for a wider service.

Customers and Partners

Customers and business partners form the external group of individuals and organizations that interact with the business. Each customer category and each corporate partner (client as well as supplier) needs to be modeled in this work area for potential changes. These changes involve the products and services offered, supplies ordered, and relationships managed.

The following are the significant considerations when a business undergoes transformation from the point of view of the customers and partners work area:

- Identification of customer groups: This deals with the creation and understanding of customers such as individual, corporate, regular, high-value, occasional, global-roaming, techno-savvy, school-going, teen-aged, elderly, and so on.
- Personalization of customer service: Customers are increasingly demanding services that are tailored to their needs. These needs are highly personalized, not only for a customer but also in the context in which the customer is looking for that service. This work area creates opportunities for a business to tailor its offerings that are specific to the needs of a particular customer at a particular location. This personalization significantly improves the overall experience the customer has with the business.
- Value addition to customer services: By using technologies such as cloud computing and Web Services, the organization is able to provide additional value to the customer by combining its own offerings with those of other interested and participating businesses. Thus, an airline, for example, is able to offer a hotel and car-rental service by using collaborative technologies.
- Timely service to customers: Changes to the processes of the organization will mean timely services to the customer. Provision of prompt service to the customer should result from many factors coming together including technology, processes, and service/product representatives. This work area investigates the timeliness of service to customers.

- Accessibility: Customers and partners need direct and accurate access to the organization and its services. Connectivity of the Internet and, further, of the mobile Internet facilitates this access easily. This access transforms the business to an "available" business that enables the customer to obtain personalized services from the business. For example, an airline passenger with access to the flight schedule, times, and check-in facility is able to manage himself or herself much better than with the corresponding manual flying procedures. Similarly, accessibility to multiple sources of information such as weather, road conditions, and news reports can all add up to a pleasurable and safe travel experience.
- Changes to partners: This deals with the inevitable changes to the business partner relationships due to transformation. These changes include revisiting the service-level agreements (SLAs). Partners can join a collaboration or leave it. Possibilities of changes include, for example, outsourcing of development and maintenance, sourcing of different suppliers with, say, better green credentials, and "sell-offs" of noncore business.

ICT Systems, Applications, and Databases

ICT systems, applications, and databases are a significant technological work area in ABT. This work area interfaces with practically every other work area of the business. Furthermore, the impact of emerging technologies such as cloud computing, Web Services, and mobile technologies is palpable in and around the entire Agile business. These technologies change the way products are created, customers are managed, and the organization is administered. Depending on the industry section and the technical maturity of the organization, this work area can take a significant amount of planning, coordination, and investment during the ABT.

The following are the significant considerations when a business undergoes transformation from the point of view of the ICT systems, applications, and databases work area:

- ICT asset stocktaking: The IT assets of an organization need to be understood right at the start of the ABT process. This includes an inventory of the hardware, software, networks, and communications equipment. The ICT stocktaking starts providing a picture of the effort required for transformation as well as the areas that need attention.
- Data center status: Investigate the size and flexibility of the data center. Determine whether it is physical or virtual, its power consumption, and so on.
- Software applications: These applications need to be examined with respect to their value to the business. The modern-day need is for these applications to be instantaneously responsive and functioning in a distributed and collaborative manner. Interoperability of applications needs to be balanced against performance.
- Software architecture: Collaboration, distribution, software as a service (SaaS), and service orientation are the mainstay of this investigation. Software architectures have tried horizontal layering, vertical integration, distributed applications, object-oriented approaches, and, now, service-oriented architecture (SOA). Each new approach to information systems has provided advantages and challenges to the business. Businesses have been transformed with the help of ICT, and businesses have used ICT as a means to undertake their complete reengineering. In discussing the challenges of governance related to SOA, Cutter Consortium Senior Consultant Paul Allen notes: "SOA governance tends to get approached in primarily two ways: as a technology or as a cultural phenomenon. The most fruitful approach lies somewhere in between" (Allen, 2009). Pragmatic approaches to governance blend and balance the two with respect to the needs of a particular organization.

- Content management strategies: This focuses on content management strategies, especially the sourcing of latest and accurate contents, before packing it and providing it to the users. Coupled with the need for real-time responses, there is also the exponentially growing need to sift through myriad data, which is lying not only in the neatly organized rows and columns of the relational and legacy era but also in voice, video, and fuzzy data. This work area considers changes to generations of contents, including their varied sourcing (such as including from the users themselves or regular updates based on Web Service calls or subscriptions from other service providers).
- Eliminating duplication: Technologies can facilitate considerable reduction in the duplication of data entry and reduction in errors in the sourcing of data. For example, the business transformation project can incorporate portable mobile and wireless devices in the business processes to enable critical data to be captured at the time and place of its creation. Another example is a radio frequency identification (RFID)-enabled inventory management system that provides accurate stock levels to users without any translation.
- Usability and related issues: The ICT work area has to consider usability of systems formally, especially when dealing with small-screen mobile devices, as well as when providing services to customers with special needs. Systems cannot be transformed in isolation with the users. Principles of usability, as discussed by Constantine and Lockwood (1999), provide a sound basis for creating usable software and other interfaces.
- Security: This refers to both internal and external security, and also its physical and electronic aspects.
- Social networking: This refers to interfacing with sites, such as *Twitter* and *Facebook*, enabling the organizational systems to interact with external systems.

Operational/Organizational

The way in which the business organizes itself and the way it operates is modeled, inspected, and transformed within this work area. The following are the significant considerations when a business undergoes ABT from the point of view of the operational and organizational work area:

- HR structural changes: This includes reporting hierarchies and changes to the responsibilities for job roles (promotions, performance reviews, and politics). Department-centric views of the organization get replaced by a people-centric view. Organizational and team structures change to a much "flatter" structure, and social and cultural issues related to human resources come into play.
- Operational efficiency: This is improving the efficiency of the business process through the application of technologies and process optimization. For example, systems dealing with HR, inventory management, time management, and supply chain management (SCM) systems are upgraded by procuring new software systems/applications and making it easier for users to access the organizational resources.
- Employee personalization: In addition to the earlier discussed customer personalization, the ABT project also enhances value to employees. For example, introduction of mobile technologies in internal employee-related business processes can mean accurate information to the employees on their working conditions, salary status, leave status, and so on. Employees and workers in the organization need to access various services such as e-mail, personal and corporate calendars, and other groupware enterprise applications

while they are on the move. Mobility can be a significant contributor to internal agility of the organization.

- Organizational structure: It considers the traditional need for a hierarchical organizational structure. Customer requests need to pass through a number of different departmental circles in order to reach the right person. Transformation creates a direct path for customer access to managers and employees responsible for providing the service. Business transformation entails changes to the organizational and team structures to ensure that they are Lean and effective, not rigid and hierarchical. Flexibility in team structures is positively enhanced during transformation. The employees, their roles, their responsibilities, and their reporting hierarchy change as a result of the transformation. Electronic and mobile connectivity plays a major role in flattening the organizational structure. Communication channels overlap and intersect in many often-unforeseen ways in a transformed organization.
- Reducing administration: Employee tasks are modified to enable workers to spend more time with customers rather than carrying out their own administrative tasks.
- Flexibility in the workplace: ABT strives to utilize communications technologies to create opportunities for "teleworking." The concept of work itself is evolving and is not limited by office space and office hours. Use of communications technologies enables people with families to better balance their work and personal life; these technologies also offer benefits to people who are physically challenged because of illness or past injuries. However, additional care needs to be taken to ensure the privacy of employees and to ensure that work does not intrude into employees' personal lives. A carefully implemented "working away from workspace" plan can help alleviate these challenges, improve employee morale, and also potentially reduce staff turnover.
- Virtual and collaborative teams: Creation of virtual teams based on the niche skills of various employees, consultants, and managers can lead to multiple offerings by the business as various players can get together to serve the needs of a particular customer. Such virtual teams enable the business to tap into the skills of consulting professionals outside the business for shorter and specific durations. While the purpose of such reengineering of processes is not staff reduction, they do lead to a much more Lean-Agile team structure.
- Improved disaster recovery: Transformation aims to enhance the ability of the business to resume its operations as quickly and efficiently as possible after a disaster. By eliminating dependence on a single location in terms of carrying out operations, the business is well equipped to handle disasters.

Business Processes

The business process work area is directly derived from the process dimension of ABT. Processes describe how the business is carried out both externally and internally. This was discussed in detail in Chapter 7. Hammer and Champy's (1993) work on reengineering the corporation as well as Kalakota and Robinson's (2002) road map to mobile engineering provide valuable background to the work area. The following are the significant considerations when a business undergoes transformation from the point of view of the business processes work area.

- Streamlining of business processes: Business transformation streamlines and organizes business processes through engineering and reengineering. The new and reengineered processes make use of the technologies, policies, procedures, and practices in order to offer improved services. Both internal and external business processes are studied, modeled, and changed for optimization. Business Process Modeling Notation (BPMN) and Unified Modeling Language (UML) activity diagrams are being used to model and achieve this process optimization (Unhelkar, 2006).

- Modeling processes: Processes are identified and modeled along the function areas of the business. For example, there are customer service processes, marketing and advertisement processes, and inventory management processes. These are not department-based processes.
- Collaboration among partners: Changes to the business model to improve and enhance collaboration among business partners are an inevitable output of business transformation. Electronic collaboration, made easy through the technologies of Web Services and outlined in detail through collaborative global business processes, is a mandatory part of business transformation. Such collaborations open the door to interactions between multiple businesses (Unhelkar et al., 2009).

Networks and Infrastructure

The following are the significant considerations when a business undergoes transformation from the point of view of the networks and infrastructure work area.

- Wired and wireless networks and their complexity: While network complexity is increasing, competitive differentiators due to enhanced networks are reducing. Thus, just upgrading networks is not going to provide the organization with a business edge.
- Internet: The Internet, in all its forms, has evolved from a mere means of communication through to becoming a provider of collaborative facilities and social networking. The information dissemination is ever increasing as bandwidths expand and the costs of communications fall rapidly. For example, Voice over Internet Protocol (VoIP), especially with the expanding broadband networks globally, seems to be bypassing the traditional public switching telephone network (PSTN)—leading to Skype, gTalk, and other applications over the Net. The ever-increasing sophistication of broadband networks and their application in social media provide excellent opportunities in adopting agility across the organization.
- Fixed mobile convergence: This provides a significant challenge during transformation, as it requires greater coordination between fixed and mobile operators while creating greater competition. Therefore, effective channel strategies are required.

Regulatory

The regulatory work area of ABT deals with rules and regulations, accounting and finance, and related legal aspects of the business. The changes range from ICT systems and business processes through to their impact on the business model and operational/organizational aspects of the organization. Legal requirements for audit and traceability also come under this work area. The following are the significant considerations when a business undergoes transformation from the point of view of the regulatory work area.

- Financial aspects: How is the organization financially positioned? This work area delves into the current and predicted position of the business, implementation of financial controls, and reporting and validity of the controls. The cost and benefits of ABT and the associated financial risks are part of this area of work.

- Regulatory aspects: It is necessary to consider legislations dealing with regulation of financial practices and corporate control. For example, the SOX legislation, under the tutelage of the Public Company Accounting Oversight Board, provides protection to shareholders and the general public from fraudulent practices and aims to restore investors' confidence. This work area deals with changes to the business to enable the CEO/CFO to take the reins of internal controls and financial reporting through technology upgrades and changes to policies and procedures (Unhelkar et al., 2008). Additional legislative requirements can deal with the increasingly important environmental and carbon legislations.
- Contracts and SLAs: Successful transformation underpins the principles and practices of a legal framework that can be used to understand contractual obligations of the organization, particularly related to electronic transactions arising from collaborative commerce. This is particularly important as Internet technologies are becoming increasingly embedded within software applications such as automated supply chain architectures, Web Services, and mobile platforms (Lan and Unhelkar, 2006). These are the areas of emerging technologies that are resulting in new issues related to their corresponding legal framework, as discussed by Neely and Unhelkar (2005).
- Environment and sustainability: Business transformation keeps an eye on sustainability and the green initiatives of the organization. Businesses need to consider the social as well as legal aspects of upcoming legislation, including those related to carbon emissions. Business practices, accounting and controls, measurement and reporting, and the supporting business packages, all undergo change to enable the business to comply with regulations.

Varying Influence of ABT

Figure 10.6 shows the relative influence of the environment and people in ABT. This figure also acknowledges the fact that ABT is a multidimensional affair. The organizational adoption of agility must consider various influencing factors such as the societal value systems (which also constitute the individual employee and customer), governmental rules and regulations, and industrial standards and lobby groups, as well as the business units that comprise the organization. The changes in the business will be influenced by and will have an influence on the products and services offered, the customer base, seasonal fluctuations, the global economic climate, and the senior management's viewpoints on the current and future position of the company.

The organization belongs to an industry that moves at its own pace. For example, a travel and tourism agency will be influenced heavily by the policies and standards set by the travel industry in that region. Therefore, the ABT of that agency has to consider commonly accepted standards of performance, insurance guarantees, and cancellation policies agreed to by the industry body. Usually, the industry moves at a slower pace than the business itself, which belongs to that industry. This is particularly so in the case of collaborative Agile businesses within that industry sector that would need consensus and the involvement of multiple parties with varying interests in the industry forums. Occasionally, though, the industry can speed up the transformation of a business through commonly agreed policies on how tasks are performed and penalties are applied. For example, if the travel industry body of the region agrees on providing Internet-based paperless ticketing, then the travel agencies will have to immediately transform that part of their business.

Government influences the industry through its rules and regulations. One way this can happen is when the interests of the industry conflict with the common interests of society. Another reason for government to influence business is with regard to the safety and well-being of consumers.

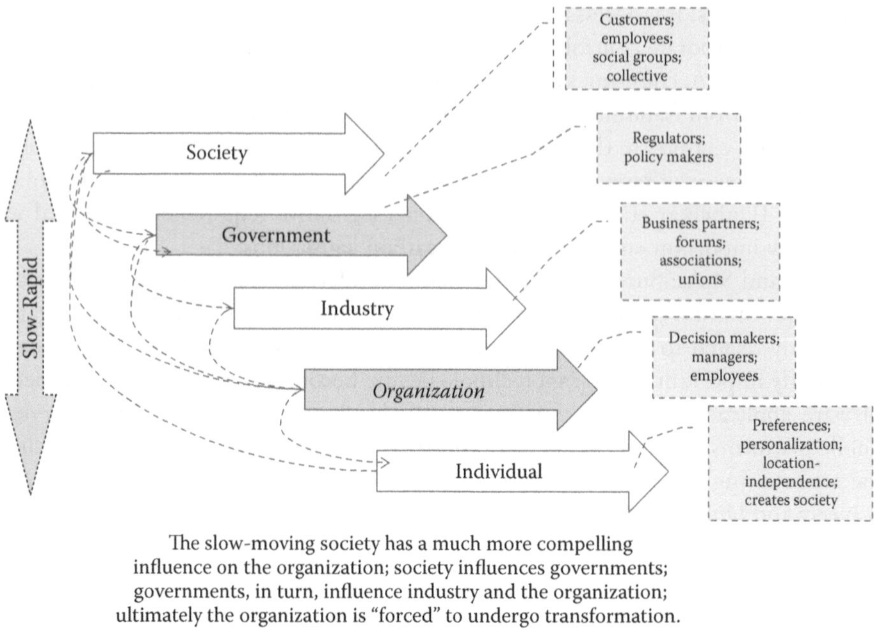

Figure 10.6 Business transformation impacts and influence (CAMS perspective).

SOX, which requires many large businesses to undertake transformation of their audits, controls, and reporting processes, is one such example.

Among all these factors, as shown in Figure 10.6, society is considered to be the slowest to influence business transformation. Even though the individuals that comprise society are able to change quickly and effectively of their own accord, the overall influence of society on the organization takes its own time.

CAMS and Center of Excellence

Figure 10.7 shows CoEs that exist for various functions within a business. A CoE for a particular area in an organization provides strategic advantages to the organization in that area. This is because a CoE exists before a project commences and, later, on completion of a project, the CoE stores information gleaned from the project. A CoE can also be the leadership's response to specific pressure points being felt by the organization.

Figure 10.7 shows CoEs for technology, project management, business analysis, leadership, and process. Each of these areas of an organization can present pressure on the operational and future state of the organization. CAMS can come under the process CoE in order to handle the application of Agile methods across the organization. Even though the process CoE is the starting point for CAMS, the influence of CAMS is not restricted to processes alone. A CoE for CAMS can make use of metrics data from previous projects, resident process expertise, and the business knowledge in the organization to help create a deep understanding of Agility—especially for the leaders and decision makers of the organization. This is extremely helpful in reducing the time taken to achieve complete Agility by business (i.e., from a few years to a year). Organizations implement CoEs in different ways as they deem fit.

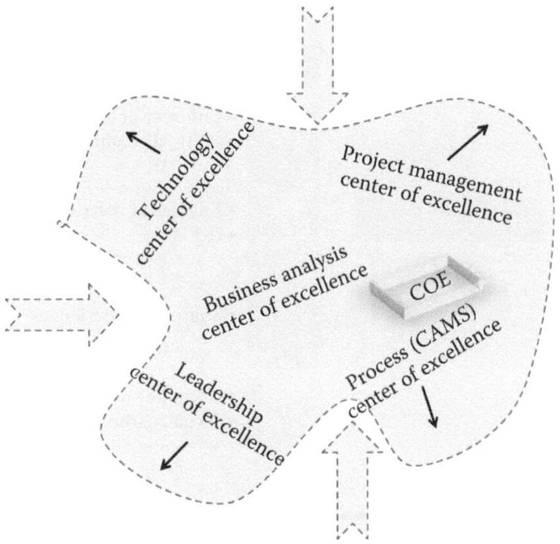

Figure 10.7 Positioning a CAMS Center of Excellence.

The purpose of a CoE is to enable an organization to capture its knowledge base. A CoE is a mechanism to convert the tacit knowledge gained by people during a project (or even during business as usual) into objective, explicit knowledge for the benefit of the business. A CoE for CAMS provides a paradigm for managing the dynamic aspects of an organization's process knowledge. CAMS is itself the result of a continuous dialogue between tacit and explicit knowledge elements within an organization. A CoE can be considered as a body within an organization that provides continuity to the organization.

A CoE is best considered as a part of an organization's daily knowledge management activities. Knowledge management is described as the process of systematically and actively managing and leveraging the stores of knowledge in an organization (Nonaka, 1994). Ideas and innovations are encouraged and fostered as an important component in the dynamics of knowledge management within a CoE. A CoE can be made responsible to identify, create, represent, distribute, and enable adoption of insights and experiences. Such insights and experiences comprise knowledge, either embodied in individuals or embedded in organizational processes or practice. A CoE transforms information and intellectual assets into business value. It is by garnering the collective value of information throughout the organization that a CoE enables organizational agility.

Thus, the knowledge and experience gained by an organization in its use of agility requires a CoE for ongoing refinement. Mentoring and coaching for agility across the organization will also be facilitated by the CoE. A CoE captures data and information, abstracts it into knowledge, and then communicates that knowledge to make it available to users at the point of use. Collaboration of information from various sources including the users, managers, and even the customers is crucial in objectifying knowledge. The CoE for CAMS gathers all the information gained by the organization during its ABT. This information is then abstracted and made available to the users of CAMS.

This would ensure that whenever a new project or initiative is undertaken, all the experience gained from the previous CAMS-based project is made available to the new project. Besides this, the metrics and measurements of the previous projects can also help the new project with its estimations.

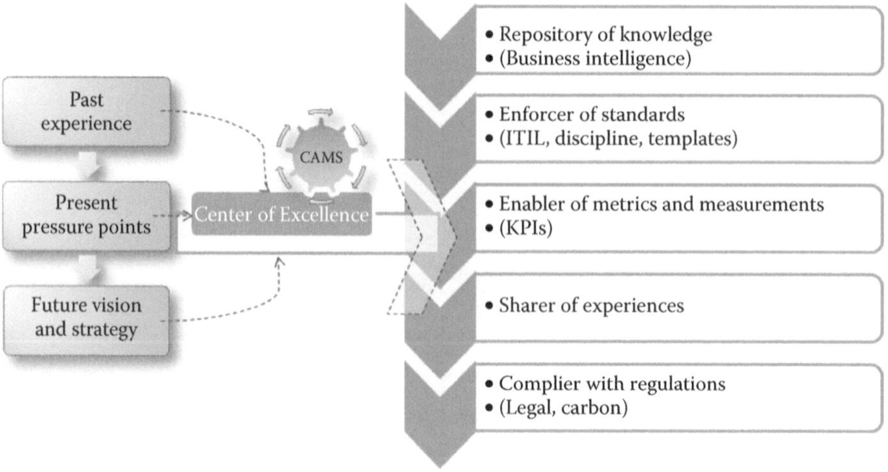

Figure 10.8 Using CAMS Center of Excellence in organizational adoption.

As shown in Figure 10.8, a CoE can handle the following aspects of agility at an organizational level:

What specific aspect(s) of Agility are of interest to the organization? For example, communication and collaboration can be considered as a primary area of interest or, alternatively, technical software development may be of primary interest. A CoE can help connect the function areas with similar interest across the business at both business-related and individual levels. This, in turn, enhances the quality as well as transparency of decision making and knowledge sharing. A CoE can further offer the ability to search and locate subject matter experts who can participate appropriately in projects.

Why is Agile being considered by the organization? Is it a business decision? Or is it driven by technologies? The CoE can help an organization achieve its goal. A CoE can further help the ongoing maintenance of this goal. A CoE can improve employee engagement scores, which, in turn, can help retain talent within the organization.

When is the CoE expected to be operational? This timing of a CoE's operation is dictated by the organization's goals, risks, and urgency. Availability of a CoE before a project commences can provide substantial value to the project in terms of estimation and metrics, use of computer-aided software engineering (CASE) tools, and making expertise available through select people (resources).

How does an organization approach ABT? A CoE can provide estimates, metrics, measurements, and documentation on previous experiences of transformation and change management. This, in turn, can assist in deciding the extent and depth of the CoE. The knowledge body within the CoE can also be dispersed within the organization through differing mechanisms such as organizational intranet, externally accessible Web sites, Wikis, and blogs.

Where are the touch points for the CoE for CAMS? As CAMS can affect multiple layers of the organization, it is important to figure out where exactly will it be used in the organization? The many CoEs shown in Figure 10.7 can themselves have the potential to conflict. The CoE for CAMS should be aware of all other CoEs and the role they are playing in the organization in order to reduce methods friction.

Who are the users of the CoE and who provides the services within the CoE? The experts in the areas of transformation, processes, and business can all be a part of the CoE. The project managers, business analysts, and developers working within a project can tap into the CoE resources.

Configuring, Training, and Upskilling in Agile Business Transformation

An important part of successful adoption of CAMS is the exercise of configuring it for the organization. A typical individual process gets configured for a project. CAMS, however, needs to pay attention to all existing and new processes in the organization. CAMS configuration is a collaborative exercise between business, project management, business analysis, development, and testing. Therefore, CAMS configuration requires collaboration and negotiation across all tiers of the organization.

A pilot project for this purpose can make use of the development and project management elements of CAMS. For CAMS to be effective, other processes from the business methods space and the governance space also need to be included in the configuration. The ever-important issue of methods friction also has to be handled by checking the touch points of the processes that pull in opposing direction. Training and upskilling in the processes included in CAMS, as well as the use of those processes amidst other organization processes, is an important and ongoing part of CAMS adoption. These aspects of the transformation are discussed here.

Figure 10.9 shows the configuration of CAMS that is based on a suite of example methods. This example indicates an organization using Scrum (Agile development), Rational Unified Process (RUP—planned and formal development), Projects in Controlled Environments (Prince2—project management), Control Objectives for Information and related Technology (CoBIT—governance), and Six Sigma (business). A CAMS instance, with this specific suite of methods, is represented in Figure 10.9 by the encircling arrows. In exploring this instance, the process expert (together with the business transformation champion) in the organization has to pay attention to all elements in each of these processes. For example, the roles in RUP, CoBIT, and Six Sigma need to be studied side by side. Similarly the activities (or phases), tasks, practices, and deliverables need to be explored

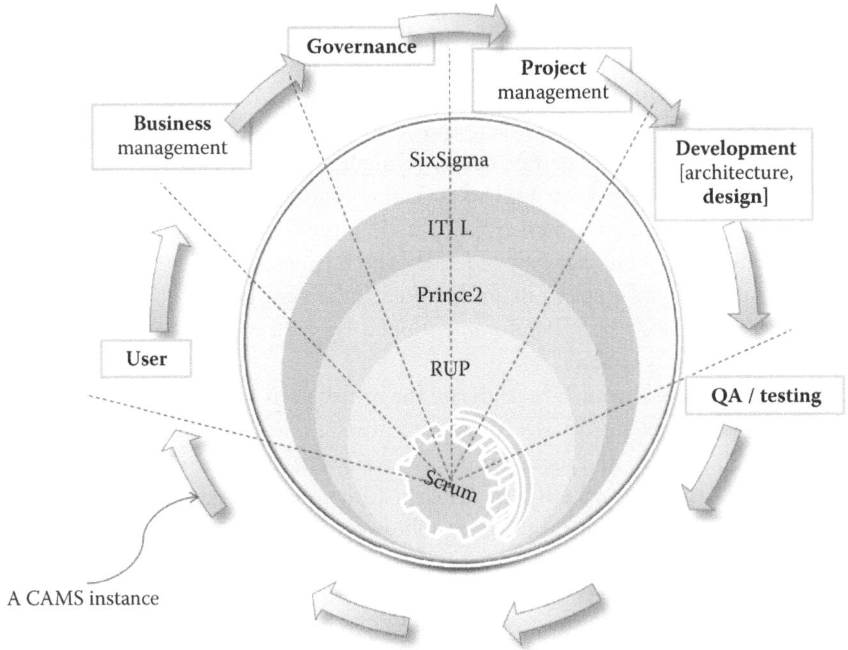

Figure 10.9 Configuring a CAMS instance including multiple organizational processes.

for each of these processes in the context of other processes within the CAMS instance. This exploration will lead to an understanding of how these processes work with each other. For example, the daily stand-up within Agile/Scrum needs to be understood in the context of the formal day-long meeting required to outline the quality of service (QoS) resulting from applying CoBIT.

This CAMS instance is itself likely to be made of iterations—ranging from core technical iterations to business iterations. Thus, not only are the processes studied alongside each other but also the iterative aspects of each process. What is important to note here is that every aspect of the business is involved in each iteration (instance, here). Therefore, the users, business, governance, project management, development, and quality assurance (QA)/testing are involved in *each* iteration of CAMS. However, the emphasis of the process elements from each method will be different depending on what the organization is trying to achieve at that point in time. The "speed" of iterations for each of these processes will also be different. For example, an RUP iteration can last for 2 months, whereas a Scrum iteration can be for 2 weeks. This speed of iterations needs to be considered in overall CAMS iteration—for example, by making provision for iterations within iterations relating to the two processes. Eventually, this CAMS instance has to be mapped to produce releases.

What is shown in Figure 10.9 can be expanded into a multitiered project plan encompassing all levels of processes in an organization. The breadth and extent of this plan will depend on the complexity and size of the project. The basic principle of CAMS in operation holds true irrespective of the size—that is, the composite process maps will span multiple tiers. In this example, CAMS instance Agility (Scrum, in this instance) can provide value to the processes for software projects, business, and governance.

The process of creating a CAMS instance, as expressed in Figure 10.9, can be an important exercise for an organization in its transition efforts. Investigating and configuring CAMS provides the organization with a pathway to upskilling itself during ABT.

Studies have been conducted in modeling and understanding a business in various ways to facilitate transformation. These business models also indicate the multiple dimensions through which a business can transform. For example, one study identified the factors influencing business transformations and the associated risks and advantages (Arunatileka and Ginige, 2003b). These factors were also identified, extended, and separately applied by Arunatileka et al. (2008) particularly for transforming mobile businesses (Unhelkar, 2009). A conceptual framework for business transformation has also been applied by Unhelkar (2008) in mobile business transformation. These studies indicate that business transformation itself has to be considered a process. ABT is therefore treated as a process that helps identify the business goals, the current structure and maturity of the business, and steps to be undertaken to become a new, cohesive, Agile, efficient, and collaborative global business. The aforementioned transformation studies can be abstracted and applied in a generic way to ABT.

Such an ABT framework would also indicate the dimensions or organizational areas for training and upskilling. In adopting CAMS, these four areas are as shown in Figure 10.10 and they are money, technical, process, and social. These areas are specific in terms of upskilling effort but they are not exclusive to each other. Instead, each dimension influences all other dimensions, sometimes leading the way and at other times following up and consolidating the changes. We look at each of these business dimensions in greater detail in the context of CAMS adoption next.

Money

The money (or economic) dimension of ABT deals with changes to the strategic direction of the organization based on costs, profits, and investments. This dimension answers one of the

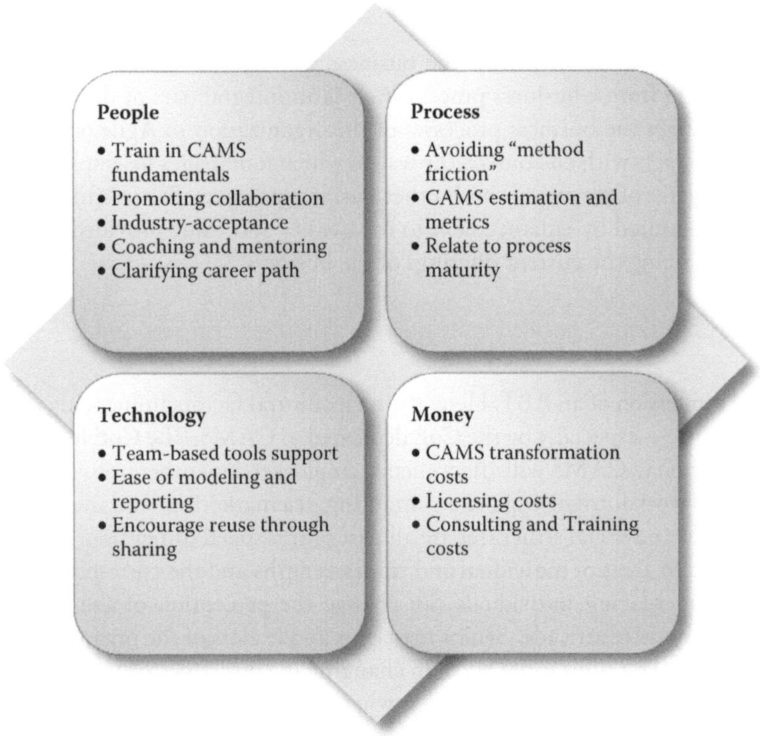

Figure 10.10 Organizational areas for training and upskilling for adopting CAMS.

questions that business leaders ask of themselves: why transform to an Agile business in the first place? The answer includes the financial impact the lack of agility can have on the business. This dimension of transformation concerns itself with the costs and benefits of the transformation exercise in financial terms. The ROI is kept firmly in mind when the business transforms along this dimension. There are then ensuing changes to its model, its investments, its customer relationships, and its partner management. While cost and profit drive the businesses to change, the success criteria of ABT also need to include intangible benefits such as enhanced customer experience.

Technology

The technical dimension is a technologically led conduit for the business to transform into an Agile business. Numerous technologies (both hardware and software) provide tremendous opportunities for businesses to collaborate and becoming Lean and Agile (as discussed in Chapters 5 and 6). These changes include those related to machines and personal devices, computing hardware and software, ICT-based systems that serve the organization, the underlying network infrastructure, and security protocols. For example, incorporation of Web 2.0 and beyond within the organization's system is a technical means of placing the customer/user in the center stage of the business. Technology, such as Internet-based communications protocols, Semantic Web, and mobile and cloud computing, brings about a paradigm shift in the way the business operates. Technology thus provides a creative dimension for changing to an Agile business.

Process

This process dimension deals with how the business conducts its transactions both internally and externally. CAMS from a business process angle is an integral part of this dimension. This is because CAMS changes the business processes of the organization to Agile ones—changing the way the business interacts with customers, the way in which it manages its employees, and the way it sets up and conducts collaborations with other business partners. Successful transformation of this dimension is measured by enhancement to the quality and value provided to the interacting parties without sacrificing the current offerings of the business.

People

This is the social dimension of an ABT. Here, the sociocultural factors influencing the business are given high importance—especially by the CoE dedicated to CAMS. The CoE focuses attention on how the transformation to CAMS will affect clients, employees, and other users of the business. For example, changes to work formats (e.g., telecommuting, telemarketing) and their resultant impact on the organizational and social structures are all part of this social dimension. Due consideration needs to be provided to areas of individual and team strengths and the corresponding weaknesses. For example, customer-facing individuals can change the perception of the organization with basic training and a positive attitude. Senior managers and leaders of the organization, working as individuals, can also have a substantial effect in changing the business to an Agile one. These organizational changes, however, cannot be sudden when people are involved. Training, motivation, and individual aspirations need to be considered, and both performance and functionality need to be kept in balance. Broader social issues such as effects of promoting Agility, balancing risks with advantages, and ethical and legal business practices (including relevant documentation) are also part of the social dimension.

Training and upskilling of people within an organization is a vital part of business transformation—and more so within CAMS. As an organization adopts CAMS, it deals with the challenges of revisiting and upgrading its existing processes, introducing new Agile processes, and, most importantly, permeating the organization's strategic and operational aspects with Agile values. The CoE plays an important part in the upskilling and dispersal of knowledge (in this instance specific to CAMS). Figure 10.11 summarizes this upskilling approach for an organization adopting CAMS.

- Ascertaining current skills and competencies in the organization: This measurement can be based on frameworks such as the Skills Framework for Information Age (SFIA, discussed in Chapter 7 on business analysis). SFIA can be used across the board for multiple processes rather than being limited only to business analysis. This assessment provides an understanding of the knowledge base of the organization in terms of its processes and frameworks.
- Ascertaining current status of all projects/program of work: This assessment indicates the effect of processes within various areas of the organization. For example, if a development project is lagging behind in terms of time–budget–functionality, then the focus of training and upskilling will be on development processes. If, on the other hand, the program of work has produced outputs but the business is still not able to benefit from them, the focus can shift to the business methods space.

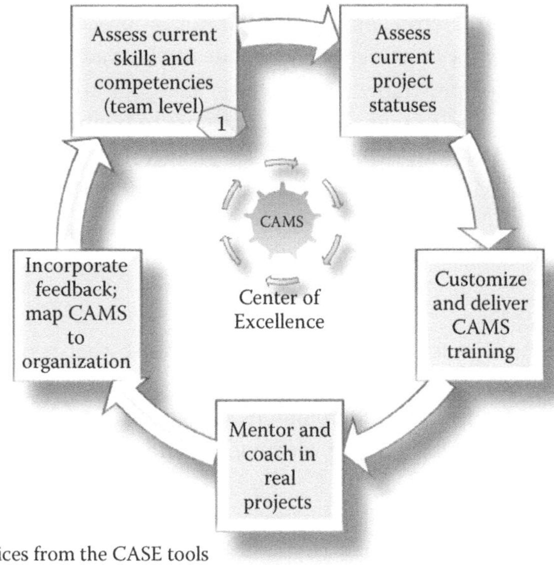

- Separate the Agile practices from the CASE tools
- Train and Mentor process champions in CAMS—especially as part of CoE
- Merge and apply QA techniques to deliverables in all tiers of CAMS
- CAMS will comprise process tools and iterations from individual processes—configure them separately
- Handle methods friction amongst processes
- Demonstrate CAMS through a pilot project
- Involve end users/sponsors in the entire upskilling exercise
- Document the results within the CAMS repository held within the CoE

MethodScience.com, 1998-2012; CAMS

Figure 10.11 CAMS upskilling in organizational adoption using a Center of Excellence.

- Customizing and delivering training: Once the competency level of the teams within the program of work is ascertained and the status of projects understood, customization of training can be undertaken. There are two aspects to training within CAMS: one is the training associated with an individual process or framework (e.g., Scrum or The Open Group Architecture Framework, TOGAF) and the second, even more important part of the training, is with the configuration, instantiation, and usage of CAMS. This is where training relating to process maps, embedding of Agile practices within them, and use of metrics related to CAMS comes in. This is also where the CoE plays a major part in ensuring that the training is suitably customized for the organization (especially with organization-specific projects data).
- On-the-job mentoring: As with the use of any process within an organization, CAMS itself requires mentoring and coaching within the organization. The CoE can draw from the various exiting expertise in the organization, upskill these experts with the principles and practices of CAMS, and then use that expertise in mentoring projects and programs of work. Mere training without associated mentoring can lead to confusion and increased methods friction.
- Feedback and mapping: This is an important task of the CoE for CAMS. The feedback from the business, governance, development, and quality areas of work in an organization needs to be incorporated in CAMS. CAMS is an umbrella name representing multiple

methods in use— therefore, on its own, it is not "a" process to be improved. Instead, CAMS improvement implies ongoing improvement of the way in which individual processes are used, reduction (or preferably avoidance) of methods friction, and strategies for iterations and increments in their usage. Metrics continues to be important in incorporating feedback to improve CAMS—and these metrics are gleaned by the CoE through, say, a pilot implementation of CAMS.

Some important considerations to be noted in practice when CAMS upskilling takes place are as follows:

- Separate the Agile practices from the CASE tools so that people can be trained in each of these areas separately.
- Train and mentor process champions in CAMS by drawing on organizational expertise, inviting these experts for training within CoE, and, eventually, sending them out within the program of work using CAMS.
- Merge the QA techniques within process maps of CAMS to ensure that all deliverables in all tiers of CAMS are subjected to quality checks. Upskilling may separately be required, focusing entirely on QA techniques for the deliverables.
- CAMS will comprise process tools and iterations from individual processes that make up CAMS. In order to effectively upskill people, they need to be trained separately in each of these processes. Each process is also initially configured separately and then merged with the overall CAMS iteration.
- Handle methods friction among processes by investigating their activities, roles, deliverables, and practices. Identify the diverse pull for each of these process elements by the corresponding methods. Then work to reduce the effect of this pull in separate directions. Revisit the speed of each process comprising CAMS. Ensure that the process speeds do not create time-based friction.
- Demonstrate CAMS through a pilot project for that aspect of CAMS which is project-based.
- Involve end users/sponsors in the entire upskilling exercise to ensure that not only are they up to speed in terms of the methods being used within the organization but they also have the right expectation from the changes. This involvement is different from their actual involvement within an Agile project—which is also important to the success of the project.
- Document the results within the CAMS repository held within the CoE. This repository contains the deliverables, practices, and roles that can be used in CAMS. Most importantly, the CAMS repository within the CoE contains the metrics related to CAMS. These metrics (discussed in Chapter 9) provide the basis for estimations, tracking, and control within CAMS-based projects.

CAMS and Process Maturity—The CMM Standards in an Agile Environment

Maturity of a formal software process has been of immense value in formal planned software methods. Understanding the maturity of a process provides an indication of how well the process is executed. Process maturity also provides the basis for improvement and optimization in a process. The Capability Maturity Model Integration (CMMI), also mentioned earlier in this book, provides the most widely accepted guidelines for understanding and improving a process. The CMM

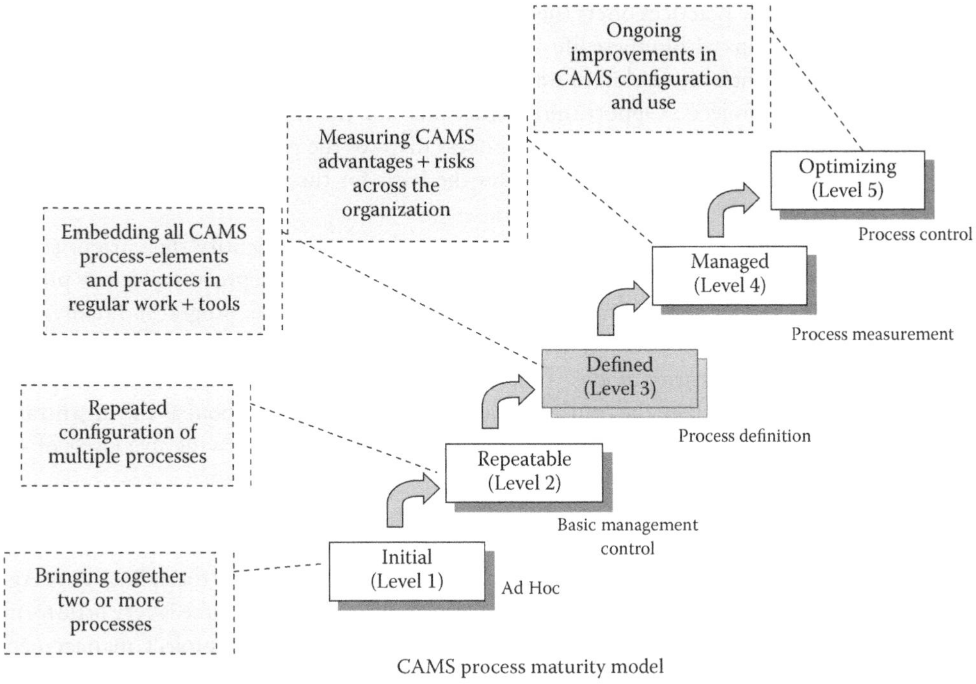

Figure 10.12 Applying Carnegie Mellon University's Software Engineering Institute's Capability Maturity Model (CMMI) to CAMS maturity.

started with measuring the capability of a software process on a scale of 1 to 5. This process maturity scale has also been applied to other non-software-related processes (e.g., green ICT processes [Unhelkar and Philipson, 2009]). CMMI is discussed here from the point of view of the planned aspect of a composite Agile process.

SIDEBAR

The Software Engineering Institute (SEI) continues to work to integrate its various process maturity models (e.g., SW-CMM, SE-CMM, IPD-CMM, and P-CMM) corresponding to software development, systems engineering, integrated product development and personal, resulting in a comprehensive CMM integration production suite, or simply CMMI (Figure 10.12). Once again, the importance of CMMI is its potential to integrate the underlying structure of all process models—resulting in a "framework" against which process maturity can be measured. More importantly, such a maturity model enables measurement and improvement of instances of processes, resulting in substantial savings of time and costs in projects and organizations that adopt these measures.

This discussion explores the opportunity to understand and improve the way in which CAMS puts together an instance of its component processes, the way iterations and increments are created within CAMS, and the use of metrics and measurements within CAMS (Turner and Jain). As Agility is applied beyond software development, so also process maturity can play an important role in optimizing composite processes that go beyond software. As CAMS harmonizes planned and Agile elements, optimization of even the Agile practices can be realized through the rigors defined in the CMMI levels. For example, the merger of life cycles and software engineering process (SEPs) with Agile practices offers the opportunity to repeat the activities, tasks, and deliverables of the process maps within these life cycles—and upskill the developers to efficiently repeat their Agile practices. Efficient creation of iterations and increments can lead to greater Agility in software development projects. Opportunities thus exist for the Agile *practices* to be repeatedly used within the activities and tasks within the process maps of the planned approaches. The measure of the repeatability of process maps provides the basis for the measure of the maturity of a composite approach.

The five levels of maturity of software processes can be used to identify the current state of process discipline within the project. When applied to a suite of projects, process maturity provides information on the efficiency of all processes used within the projects (a program). Finally, when the same process maturity is considered in the context of the organization as a whole, we have a CAMS—CMM process maturity model. Thus, CMM maturity indicates how well an organization is adopting Agility and, also, the transition that needs to be brought about as the organization progresses to higher levels of CMM maturity. The SEI mandates the following five levels of software process maturity:

1. Initial: It is the first level of process maturity. At this level, work progresses in an ad hoc way. Sporadic attempts are made by the organization to implement process discipline. Pure Agile approaches may find themselves at this initial level for the most part. There is very little formal repeatability in an Agile approach. As discussed in Chapter 8 (on project management), Agile practices depend substantially on the individual, his or her motivation, capability of alignment with the team, and working style. The reduction in formality of a process in Agile approaches has its own value, especially as an Agile project is "led" rather than "managed." However, as its name suggests, process maturity is a measure of the maturity of the process. This is where composite Agile, with its formal process discipline steps in. Composite Agile will allow the practices of Agile but within the process maps. This will provide the basis for process maturity measure in a project or an organization. For example, two projects using the same Agile method can still work differently. The process within these projects is at the initial CMM level 1. Therefore, the timings of its delivery and the quality of the deliverables from these projects can differ depending on the individuals within the projects.
2. Repeatable: It is the second level of maturity. This maturity level of a process indicates that the steps within the process can be repeated with confidence within the organization. Therefore, this level indicates greater formality in the use of a process. At this level, the organization establishes the policies and procedures to be used in its various initiatives. Through a CoE, an organization can capitalize on its past experiences of similar projects. Repeatability of activities, tasks, and deliverables provides the advantage of improved metrics and estimations in tracking costs, schedules, and functionality. Process maps within CAMS are the starting point for repeatability of a process within the organization. Agile practices that are embedded with the process maps can be formally repeated. That repeatability produces increased consistency in the output and also forms the basis for comparison among projects. CAMS metrics are easier to apply at level 2 of CMM than at the ad hoc level 1.
3. Defined: This third level of maturity provides the maximum cost benefits to businesses. This is so because this fully defined level provides the necessary control expected of planned methods. Every element of the process is defined in detail at this level. This means the "what," the "how," and the "who" as well as the supporting guidelines of "when" are all defined and formally documented. Thus, in addition to Agile practices, projects at this CMM level will also need fully defined activities and deliverables (as will be provided

by the earlier described process maps in a composite Agile approach). Many nonsoftware development areas of work in an organization such as macro business functions, business architectures, and governance are based on detailed definitions of their activities, roles, and deliverables. These processes and framework of CAMS provide the basis for achieving level 3 maturity easily.

4. Measured: When all the defined areas of both software and nonsoftware processes, mentioned in the previous level 3, can be measured within the organization, then the process reaches level 4 in process maturity. Metrics and measurements help ascertain the quality and contribution of the process in enhancing the quality and value of the output. At level 4, CAMS-based projects can create and refine their metrics and measurements (e.g., project velocity, efforts per story, and so on) together with the process maps of a formal project. Level 4 process maturity provides immense benefits in the way CoEs operate within an organization. Through this level, CoEs can help in project estimations (based on previous measures), comparison among projects, and, most importantly, making changes to the process as a program of work progresses.
5. Optimizing: Once we can measure something, the opportunity to improve on it becomes apparent. When the organization starts to fine-tune process elements, resulting in an optimization of activities and tasks, then the process discipline in the organization can be said to be fully matured. This is level 5 of maturity. Each process map has an opportunity to be optimized during the development of a product. However, other processes within CAMS that are in the business methods space can also be optimized provided they have come through the previous four levels of CMM. While pure Agile approaches advocate continuous improvement of their output, level 5 of CMM draws the attention of the organization to continuously improving the process of producing the output. An optimized process maturity is also immensely valuable as a product or system moves into the maintenance cycle. This is so because matured execution of activities, tasks, and practices produces formal deliverables that enable traceability, communication beyond development, and systematic documentation to refer to in fixing inevitable errors or implementing enhancements.

Conclusions

This chapter discussed the way in which an organization adopts Agility—more specifically, a composite Agile approach to development as well as to the overall business. This Agile adoption was described as an ABT that was based on various high-level steps and phases. This couching of the transformation in formal phases and focus areas within an organization highlights the importance and the impact of CAMS adoption—it is a strategic business transformation exercise that is well beyond the adoption of Agile practices at the software projects level. When an organization gives due credence to both external and internal factors as it adopts agility, it places itself in an excellent position to reduce the risks and maximize value from such adoption. This chapter further discussed the importance of upskilling staff at all tiers within an organization as Agility is adopted across the board. This training, upskilling, and management of CAMS-specific knowledge was described as a function of the CoE for CAMS. Finally, the CMMI and its relevance in CAMS were discussed.

This chapter concludes the informative discussion in this book. Chapters 11 and 12 describe case studies in CAMS.

Agile in Practice: Road Map 10

- Does your organization have a CoE? Identify the work that the current CoE does in terms of processes and methods. Discuss with the business decision makers (strategists who are supporting CAMS) the creation of a CoE and/or its use in transforming to an Agile business.
- Who will decide to transform the business? The decision makers and leaders are brought into play here to take responsibility and provide direction for the strategic change.
- Who will be responsible for the transformation? This is one of the last strategic questions to be answered. Once the responsibility is assigned for transformation, the process can be followed and monitored like a project. Therefore, ABT starts with the CEO and the Board of Directors. These most senior leaders of the organization undertake business transformation to come up with a complete and radical change in the way the business is internally organized and externally perceived. Appointment of a process expert who understands multiple methods within the organization is important here.

Plan and undertake a skills competency assessment of the organization. This is an involved exercise that isolates each of the processes and frameworks in use in the organization and ascertains the competencies of teams in each of these processes. Alternatively, evaluate SFIA competencies in the organization with respect to each process area.

Discuss the state of the business, the way in which its external environment is changing, and the urgency and risks associated with transforming to an Agile business.

Note down the expectations of various stakeholders in terms of an Agile business. These expectations include what the stakeholders want from an Agile business and what they are prepared to give to achieve that Agility. These expectations are crucial criteria for the success of Agile adoption.

Include the customers, business partners, and (if relevant) any government or regulatory authority in outlining CAMS usage. This involvement will ensure that there are no surprises in terms of interacting with business partners or dealing with legislations.

Identify CAMS process champions and bring them in the CoE. Upskill them and then disperse them within various projects in the organization.

Investigate and implement technologies relevant to composite Agile—this can comprise process tools, metrics and measurement tools, modeling and architectural tools, and systems supporting business functions (e.g., ERP system).

Discussion Questions

- Why is organizational adoption of Agility a business transformation program? Explain why ABT is an ongoing continuous program as against a one-off activity.
- How would you go about creating a business case for CAMS adoption? What are the key ROIs for CAMS adoption?
- Provide an example of activity that you would undertake during each of the five major phases of ABT: Diagnose–Plan–Enact–Measure–Review.
- How does the flexibility of a business structure impact its people management? Where do these two internal areas within an organization complement each other and where do they compete?
- How can CAMS adoption in an organization impact the industry in which the organization exists? Why is such industry-level adoption of CAMS slower than its impact on government and society?

- What kind of training is required in CAMS adoption? Discuss in the context of the people–process–technology–money dimensions of a business adopting CAMS.
- Discuss the importance of CoE in an Agile organization. Explain how a CoE can assist in organizational adoption of CAMS.
- Can CMMI be applied to an Agile organization? Discuss the advantages and challenges in applying CMMI to a composite process maturity.

References

Albright, P., Social networking is creating new roles: opportunities in integration, analytics, and UI/UE design, IEEE Computer Society, 2012, viewed 21 February 2012, available at http://www.computer.org/portal/web/buildyourcareer/HS27.

Allen, P., The challenges of SOA governance, *Cutter IT E-Mail Advisor*, 2009.

Arunatileka, S., and A. Ginige, The seven E's in eTransformation—A strategic eTransformation model, presented at IADIS International Conference—e-Society, Lisbon, Portugal, 2003a.

Arunatileka, S., and A. Ginige, Applying seven E's in eTransformation to the manufacturing sector, presented at eChallenges, Bologna, Italy, 2003b.

Arunatileka, D., A. Ghanbary, and B. Unhelkar, Influence of mobile technologies on global business processes in global organizations, *Handbook of Research on Global Information Technology Management in the Digital Economy*, ed., Raisinghani, M., Information Science Reference, 2008.

Based on Lan, Y., A. Ginige, Y.-C., Lan, and B. Unhelkar, *Global Enterprise Transitions: Managing the Process*, IGI Global, 2005.

Brenner, R., A systems view of Agile methodology adoption: Part II—Guiding principles, *Cutter Executive Update*, 10 (7), 2009.

Constantine, L.L. and L.A.D. Lockwood, *Software for Use: A Practical Guide to the Essential Models and Methods of Usage-Centered Design*, Addison-Wesley, Reading, MA, 1999.

Deitel, H., P.J. Deitel, and K. Steinbuhler, *e-Business and e-Commerce for Managers*, Prentice Hall, Upper Saddle River, NJ, 2001.

Ginige, A., A new paradigm for developing evolutionary software to support e-business, *Handbook of Software Engineering and Knowledge Engineering*, Vol. 2, ed., Chang, S.K., World Scientific, pp. 711–725, 2002.

Hammer, M. and J.A. Champy, *Reengineering the Corporation: A Manifesto for Business Revolution*, HarperCollins, New York, NY, 1993.

Kalakota, R. and M. Robinson, *M-Business: The Race to Mobility*, McGraw-Hill, 2002.

Lan, Y.-C. and B. Unhelkar, *Global Integrated Supply Chain Systems*, IGI Global, 2006.

Larman, C. and Vodde, B., *Practices for Scaling Lean and Agile Development: Large, Multisite, and Offshore Product Development with Large-Scale Scrum*, Addison-Wesley, 2010.

Murugesan, S. and B. Unhelkar, A roadmap for successful ICT innovation: Turning great ideas into successful implementations, *Cutter IT Journal*, 17 (11), 2004.

Neely, M. and B. Unhelkar, The role of a collaborative commerce legal framework in IT-related litigation, *Cutter IT Journal*, 18 (11), 2005.

Nonaka, I., *A Dynamic Theory of Organizational Knowledge Creation*, Hitotsubashi University, 1994.

Raisinghani, M. and B. Unhelkar, Complying with Sarbanes–Oxley: Addressing the IT issues and risks, *Cutter IT Journal*, 20 (1), 2007.

Senge, P.M., *The Fifth Discipline: The Art & Practice of the Learning Organization*, Doubleday, 1990.

Sherringham, K. and B. Unhelkar, Customer-centric business strategy: Aligning business and IT, *Cutter Executive Report*, 2010.

Thomsett, R., Agile business: The final frontier, *Cutter Executive Report*, 11 (7), 2010.

Turner, R. and A. Jain, 2002, Where does CMMI come in? Agile meets CMMI: Culture clash or common cause? 2002, viewed 20 February 2012, www.agilecmmi.com, http://www.springerlink.com/content/xxjjnf50twv46x92/.

Unhelkar, B., Mobile enterprise architecture: Model and application, *Cutter Executive Report*, 11 (3), 2008.
Unhelkar, B., *Mobile Enterprise Transition and Management*, Taylor and Francis, 2009.
Unhelkar, B., *Practical Object Oriented Analysis*, Thomson Publishing, 2006.
Unhelkar, B., Avoiding Method Friction: A CAMS-Based Perspective. *Cutter Executive Report*, 13 (6), 2012.
Unhelkar, B. and G. Philipson, Development and application of a green IT maturity index, *ACOSM2009—The Australian Conference on Software Measurement (ACOSM), November*, 2009, Sydney, Australia.
Unhelkar, B., A. Ghanbary, and H. Younessi, *Collaborative Business Process Engineering and Global Organizations: Frameworks for Service Integration,* Business Science Reference, 2009.
Unhelkar, B., A step apart from purity: composite Agile method and strategy, *Cutter Email Advisor*, 2010a.
Unhelkar, B. and A. Ginige, A framework to derive holistic business transformation processes, *Proceedings of International Conference on E-Business (ICE-B)*, Paper 44, 2010b, viewed March 2012, http://www.ice-b.icete.org/Abstracts/2010/ICE-B_2010_Abstracts.htm.
Unhelkar, B., M. Wu, and A. Ghanbary, Integrating mobile technologies in enterprise architecture with a focus on global supply chain management systems, *HandBook of Research in Global Information Technology Management in the Digital Economy*, ed., Raisinghani, M., IDEAS Group Publication, Hershey, PA, 2008.

CASE STUDIES IN CAMS

III

Chapter 11

Case Study: Outsourced Project

Objectives

- Undertake a discussion on how the concepts of Composite Agile Method and Strategy (CAMS) are used in a real-life scenario
- Describe the case study in the context of an outsourced project (Western Australia Mining [WAM] outsourcing its entire enterprise resource planning [ERP] development, customized to its needs, to Mumbai Information Technology Services [MITS]) (both are tentative, hypothetical names, and any resemblance, if at all, with a real organization is coincidental)
- Describe the way in which CAMS is configured and used in practice and the issues associated with such a configuration
- Highlight the lessons learned in the use of CAMS (these include issues and challenges; advantages and value)

Introduction

This chapter describes a case study in the application of the Composite Agile Method and Strategy (CAMS) in practice. The scenario depicted in this case study is of an outsourced project. One of the key reasons for selecting an outsourced project in this case study is the difficulties in applying Agile practices to such projects because of the need to agree on and formalize commercial relationships. All Agile methods work on an implicit assumption of the availability of all stakeholders in the vicinity of the work. In Agile approaches, the business specifying the problem and the developers of information technology (IT) solutions collaborate as closely as they can. This collaboration may not be as readily achieved in outsourced projects. From commercial agreements to outsourced staff not being seen as part of the company, outsourced (and especially offshored) projects face challenges of distance, time zones, and cross-cultural value systems.

Agile practices have a role to play in any development project, and outsourced projects are no different. However, some Agile practices are impossible to carry out (e.g., a daily stand-up meeting with the user and the developers located physically in different countries and time zones). The manner in which Agile practices are carried out changes in outsourced projects.

Through its balanced approach, CAMS increases the chances of success in outsourced projects. The formal, planned elements of CAMS provide the documentation, contract negotiation, and validation required. The core development activities of an outsourced project, however, have much greater opportunity to apply development-centric Agile practices. Later, in this chapter, Figure 11.9 also highlights how planned elements take precedence in the first iteration, and Agile elements are more extensively applied in the subsequent iterations.

The mixing and matching of Agile and planned method elements in CAMS and the caveats and lessons learnt in applying CAMS are highlighted in this short chapter. Earlier, in Chapters 1 through 3, Agile, its challenges, and CAMS as a composite approach to handle those challenges were discussed. Discussions from Chapters 4 through 10 may be considered akin to a road map of CAMS. The discussions in this and the next chapter are more like *actual driving* on the road. The need for continuous feedback and subsequent corrective actions are as important in enacting CAMS as in driving a vehicle.

Outline of the Case Study "MITS"—An Outsourced Project

Mumbai Information Technology Services (MITS) has been in the business of providing software development life cycle services worldwide. Since the advent of the Y2K situation, MITS has grown in reputation and experience in providing a variety of IT-related services including software development, requirements modeling, testing, software integration, and related services. As a result, MITS is comfortable with the use of methods, standards, and the corresponding computer-aided software engineering (CASE) tools. MITS has grown globally and is now "insourcing" software development and maintenance work from organizations around the globe.

One of the recent contracts signed by MITS is for developing, integrating, and implementing a complete software solution for a large mining company in Western Australia—tentatively called WAM (Western Australia Mining) for the sake of this case study. WAM, a mining giant, went through a detailed due diligence study and identified MITS as its "outsourcing" partner for all of its software development and implementation needs. The decision makers of WAM are not interested in "buying" an enterprise resource planning (ERP) package. Instead, they are keen on a ground-up software solution that will cater to their current and future technical and business needs. For example, there is substantial need for the new solution to integrate with the existing applications whose contents are unique to the mining domain. Another example is the extensive need for location-independent mining business processes that will be based on mobile technologies.*

After signing the contract and agreement on the statement of work, MITS has now progressed to a stage where it is required to provide a detailed process that will guide its development, integration, and implementation effort. WAM decision makers have heard of the success of Agile elsewhere. The IT division of WAM is familiar with the Agile Manifesto and the "Declaration of Interdependence." They are keen collaborate with MITS in the use of Agile values and principles.

---

* Location-independent mobile-enabled business processes have been discussed by Unhelkar in *Mobile Enterprise Transition and Management.*

However, their expectations from the overall Agile method are not clearly defined. The insistence on the use of Agile is based on a belief that an Agile approach will make the development visible to them. Conversely, MITS has had experience of Agile and its limitations. MITS started to add more rigor around Agile within development projects and then migrated to CAMS. CAMS was successfully used in two previous projects by MITS—one of which was an offshored IT system development, whereas the other one was for a content management system for a client in the local region.

The overall project time frame is anticipated to be 2 years. The estimated billing by MITS is expected to be $38.5 million over those 2 years. Subsequent maintenance contract for the solution is being negotiated but is likely to be in the range of $4–$6 million per year. This maintenance will include handling of errors, changes to systems based on changes to business processes, ongoing handling of integration with back-end databases, and an assured quality of service (QoS) relating to turnaround time and work. MITS is, however, not contracted to handle the actual deployment of the solution within WAM and its day-to-day operations.

Composite Agile Road Map for an Outsourced Project

WAM is comfortable in the concepts of process maps and the way they will be used in the project. WAM has also agreed to follow some of the early life cycle process maps such as business evaluation and requirements modeling to enable a smooth interaction during development with the vendor.

Since the WAM decision makers and IT division are aware of Agile methods and have come across the Agile Manifesto, MITS has explained the concept of a revised manifesto that balances formality with visibility. The business stakeholders in WAM are made aware of the possibility of not seeing, say, the working code, on a daily basis. Instead, a formal project plan with iterations will indicate the times when a working code will be visible to the client for testing and feedback.

While WAM has used some formal software development processes in the past, there is no desire to follow the maturity of the processes when it comes to software development. Therefore, there is no interest in the maturity of processes based on the Capability Maturity Model (CMM) scale.

Understanding the Project

As MITS has to provide the process to be used in this substantial engagement, it needs to understand and categorize the project. Figure 11.1 shows the first, diagnostic activity that MITS undertakes in terms of understanding the type and size of the project. This activity is undertaken by the project manager from MITS with close interaction with a senior business analyst from WAM. Together, they agree that it is a large, outsourced project with a budget close to $40 million and a 2-year time frame. This large size of the project will mean greater planned elements (derived from the process maps) than the Agile ones (Figure 4.7 in Chapter 4 had depicted this mixing or merging of planned and Agile elements in a composite method configuration depending on the organizational and project characteristics).

An important decision that the client makes in an outsourced project is the areas of work that will be outsourced. In the discussions on business management in Chapter 6, technologies of cloud computing and mobile were seen as providing opportunities to collaborate and share work. Outsourced projects can make use of these technologies to undertake formally scoped areas

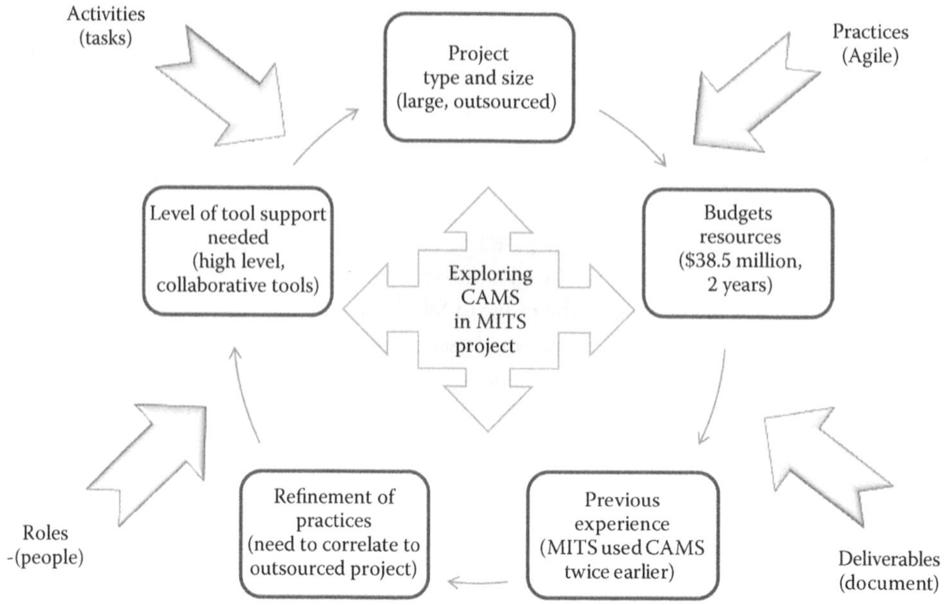

Figure 11.1 Understanding the CAMS project factors in the context of MITS.

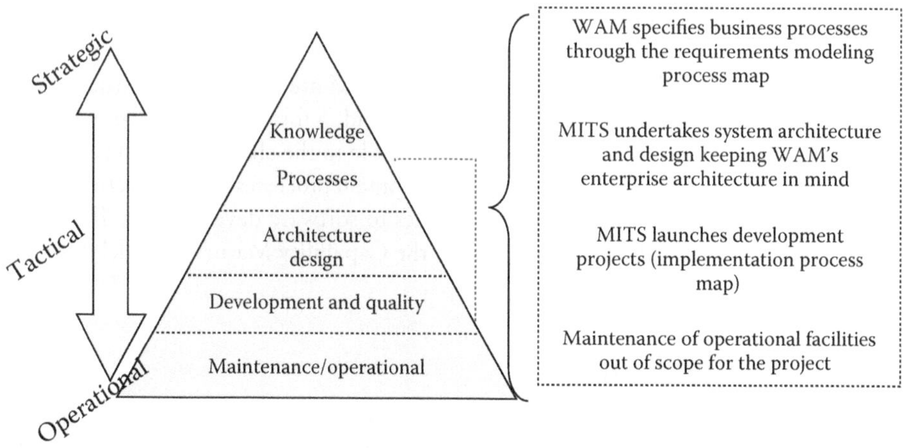

Figure 11.2 WAM and mining business: areas for outsourcing to MITS.

of work. Figure 11.2 shows the philosophy being used by WAM in outsourcing work to MITS. While the high-level functions will be specified by the client, detailed modeling of processes will be undertaken by the outsourcing vendor, MITS, using the requirements modeling process map. Similarly, the system architecture, system design, and development (implementation) of the system are outsourced, and will be undertaken by MITS.

Note that the knowledge management aspect of WAM's business, as also the operational aspect of the solution, have not been outsourced. WAM decision makers believe knowledge management to be strategic to their business and have decided to keep it in-house. The operational aspect of the system is also considered too sensitive to be outsourced to another region. This is also kept in-house.

Extent of Agility in Configuring CAMS

Initial joint investigation of processes used in WAM indicates an overbearing emphasis on Projects in Controlled Environments (Prince2) for managing projects. This is understandable from a mining company's viewpoint. The "visible" project parameters of time, budget, functionality, and quality are always at the fore for a mining company. Project management in WAM is rightly applied at both IT and non-IT project levels. In a mining company, the non-IT projects come from the core business side of the company rather than the IT projects. WAM also has some aspects of Information Technology Infrastructure Library (ITIL) to govern its IT-related services. This is why the company does not wish to outsource the operational aspect of the solution.

The existence of Prince2 and ITIL, together with some development processes can result in "method friction" (Unhelkar, 2012). Greater risks from methods friction are likely to arise when the processes used by WAM intersect with those used by the outsourcing vendor, MITS. Having highlighted this risk, MITS has been invited by the client to carry out a brief survey of the processes and their use within WAM. Two detailed workshops, each lasting half a day, are organized in the physical offices of WAM. These workshops, focused on improving the understanding of the demands from the formal use of Prince2 and ITIL in WAM, are very fruitful. Both parties are able to understand the need for formality and the corresponding practices of Agile that border on informality.

Previous implementations carried out by MITS using CAMS are also highlighted. An agreement is reached and documented in terms of visibility of work. Thus, areas of development work that are internal to the development effort and belonging to MITS are not always made visible to the client; and the client does not impose the stringent deliverables on the vendor. The potential "touch points" for Agile practices by MITS within the bounds of governance and project management processes need to be kept in mind during the project. For example, the ITIL service delivery requirement may not be able to employ any of the Agile practices that are used in the development side of the project.

Figure 11.3 expands on the work that is being outsourced in this project. In order to successfully participate in this outsourced project, the client, WAM, is required to undertake work by

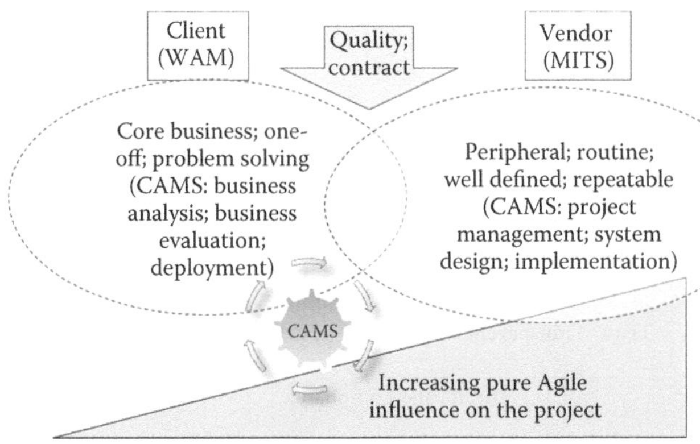

Figure 11.3 A CAMS-based outsourcing project has greater Agility on the vendor side.

following some of the CAMS process maps. The process maps of use to WAM are business evaluation (that will help formalize the understanding of the problem space at a high level for both WAM and MITS; this process map was described in detail in Chapter 6), requirements modeling (as part of business analysis, enabling modeling of requirements through use cases, user stories, and related features for nonfunctional requirements (NFRs); this process map was described in detail in Chapter 7), and deployment (this process map, as described in Chapter 5, is usually carried out by the developers; in the context of this case study, the outsourcing vendor, MITS, completes the implementation work and then hands the solution over to WAM for deployment). The IT division of WAM is keen to deploy the solution itself as this will make it easier for it to operate the solution (i.e., keep the solution system operational).

From the MITS perspective, the process maps of relevance are project management (discussed in detail in Chapter 8), system design, and implementation (both process maps discussed in detail in Chapter 5). Project management, in this particular use of CAMS, starts *after* the scope of the project has been finalized. Therefore, project management here is a task-driven activity (which is not advocated within pure Agile approaches). The process maps of system design and implementation, together with some of the Agile practices embedded in them, will be used by MITS in carrying out the development work. As Spann writes, "there is no single definition for Agile, and there is no agreed-upon methodology." Yet, generic Agile practices are used by MITS depending on the needs and interests of the client.

Figure 11.4 shows the various factors influencing the configuration of CAMS from the outsourcing vendor's perspective. CAMS, as a method, will be used in MITS to deal with the client, the associated technology partners (providing, say, network communications or database expertise that MITS may not have in-house), development team (employing Agile aspects of CAMS), and audits and compliance requirements for the mining sector being ensured by yet another "third party."

The "values" of Agile in this project are interspersed with those of planned methods. As shown in Figure 11.4, this development project has planning, measuring, recording, reporting, and controlling as its major phases. These phases of a planned method, formalized in CAMS through the process maps (especially its deliverables), will be used whenever the two organizations, WAM

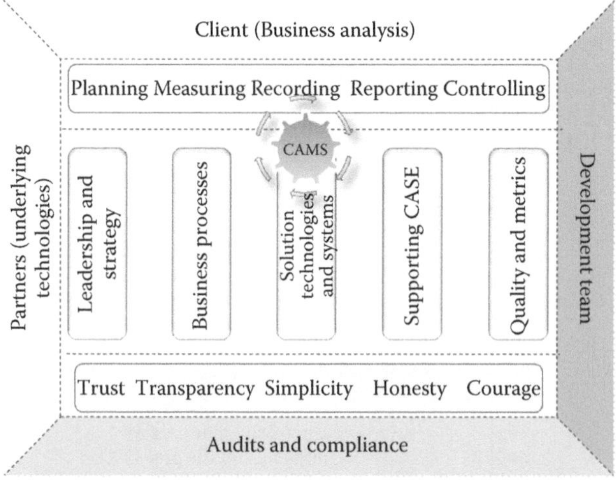

Figure 11.4 MITS—various factors influencing the configuration and use of CAMS.

as the client and MITS as the vendor, are interacting. The Agile values of trust, transparency, simplicity, honesty, and courage have greater opportunity for application within the development environment of MITS.

However, as the development progresses and as the client sees the results from these values, there will be increased opportunities to see these values reflected in the interaction between the two organizations. Initial interactions are usually based on formal, planned contracts and their documentation.

Figure 11.4 also provides a reminder in terms of the tools and techniques to be used during the development. For example, leadership and strategies deal with the project management aspect, whereas supporting CASE tools remind the team members of the use of Unified Modeling Language (UML) tools (e.g., Visual Paradigm, Visio, StarUML, and TopTeam Analyst). While the solutions technologies (e.g., Java–Oracle combination) are dictated by the client, they still need to be discussed for their pros and cons before being finalized.

Table 11.1 provides a summary of the tools, technologies, and management of the project and the corresponding responsibilities of the client and the vendor.

Figure 11.5 shows the major activities (or steps) of comprehensive best practices for smart-sourced projects. These major activities, outlined in a process flow diagram in Figure 11.5, provide support and guidelines in managing smart-sourced projects. CAMS is a combination of a smart outsourcing process and a software development process in the context of this project. The steps shown in Figure 11.5 can help the involved parties understand the requirements, help them adhere to good standards, produce good quality, and reduce risks. Effective procedures for specifying requirements, managing change, and providing effective communication are all required in carrying out these steps. The assumption in this process discussion is that suitable partners (client

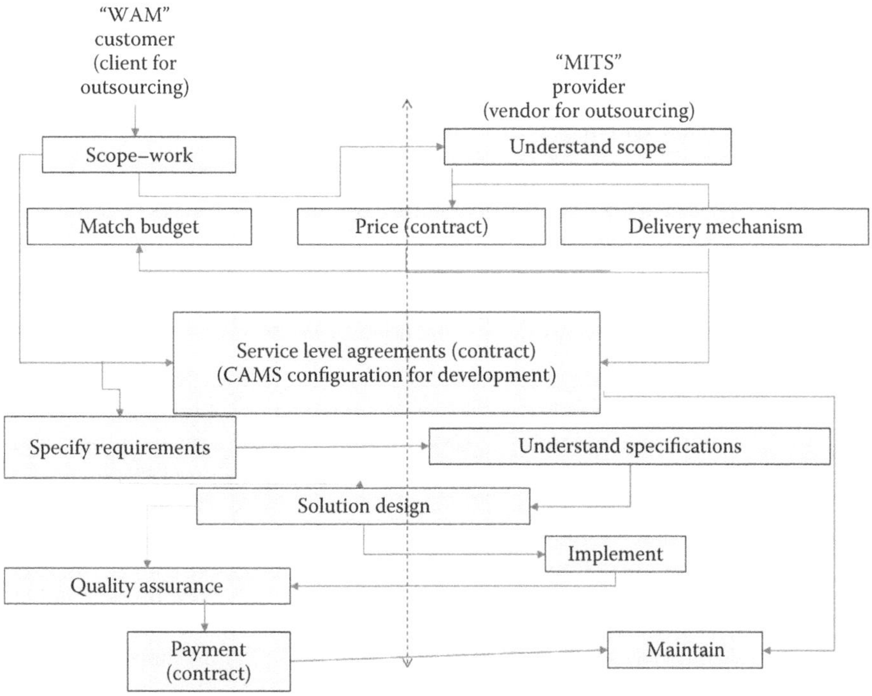

Figure 11.5 Contractual agreement on major activities within the outsourced project.

Table 11.1 Organizational Characteristics with Respect to the Client and Vendor in an Outsourced Project—with Corresponding CAMS Comments

Characteristics/ Features/Traits	*Client Organization "WAM"*	*Vendor Organization "MITS"*	*CAMS Usage*
Geographical region	Perth, Western Australia	Mumbai, India	Vendor is CAMS experienced but client only knows "Agile." Coaching in CAMS required
Leadership, strategy, and management	Keen to embrace Agile values of trust and honesty	Comfortable in applying management to implementation tasks and leadership to the team and its relationship with the client	Need to incorporate Agile values in the implementation process map that will satisfy the client; face-to-face discussion on business strategies
Business processes	Expertise in high-level mining business function. Ease of modeling requirements at detailed level. Business analysts and subject matter experts working together to specify requirements	Expertise in understanding requirement models (use cases and activity graphs) and implementing them. Continuous collaboration with business analysts in WAM. Managing customer expectations	Presentation of the requirements modeling and system design process maps to all stakeholders; embedding agreed Agile practices in them. Finalizing deliverable templates. Undertaking value-stream mappings of business processes
Solutions technologies and systems	Has legacy applications to manage both internal and external business processes	Comfortable in proceeding with the Java–Oracle solutions strategy demanded by WAM	CAMS encourages prototyping in ascertaining technologies and NFRs
Supporting CASE tools and technologies	Tools usage only limited to multiple communications channels; documentation of communication; already using tools supporting Prince2 and ITIL	Extensive user of UML-based tools	Create a project instance based on the relevant process maps of CAMS. This will provide the iterations for the many releases of the product. New project metrics can also be collected based on simple project management tools

Table 11.1 (*Continued*)

Characteristics/ Features/Traits	*Client Organization "WAM"*	*Vendor Organization "MITS"*	*CAMS Usage*
Quality and metrics	Interested in only user acceptance testing and quality control. Agreeable to CAMS-based metrics as suggested by MITS	Extensive modeling, prototyping, and testing of Web Services and security features; walk-through of designs	WAM and MITS to agree on Agile Project metrics—for example, person-day, project velocity, and errors per user story

for and vendor of the sourcing work) have been found. Management attention to extending, modifying, and implementing these steps is highly recommended.

For example, Figure 11.5 shows some of the deliverables that are based on these contract negotiations and formal documentation. The scope of work, pricing, service level agreements (SLAs), requirement specifications, quality assurance (from the client side), and payments are all activities that require formal documentation based on legally binding contracts. These mandatory, contractual activities are undertaken by WAM and MITS to ensure that both parties fully understand their responsibilities. Within these contracts are also specifications of actions in case a party fails to meet its obligations. The repercussions on the project parameters (such as budgets and time) are also documented. These are examples of activities in this outsourced project that are far removed from the pure Agile project based on the Agile Manifesto.

CAMS Process-Map-Based Activities in an Outsourced Project

Organizational challenges emanating from the use of Prince2 and ITIL include the different ownership of the processes (Prince2 belongs to the projects initiatives, whereas ITIL is owned by the operations department). Projects are focused on outcomes and deliverables in WAM; ITIL is, however, used to keep the internal services at an acceptable level across the organization.

WAM decision makers and business stakeholders are fascinated by the successes they have read about elsewhere on the adoption of Agile values and principles. They are keen to use the Agile values at an organizational level. MITS clarifies to them that their interest in Agile values is limited to the project deliverables.

Risks associated with the use of pure Agile in this outsourced project are highlighted by MITS. After understanding the risks, the WAM stakeholders agree on the CAMS approach, which allows them some of the advantages of Agile, and at the same time, enables control, tracking, and reporting of progress. This CAMS usage is restricted to the project and is not considered across WAM as an organization.

On the basis of discussions with WAM, a CAMS instance made up of relevant process maps is created. These process maps are shown in Figure 11.6. Agile practices relevant to these process maps are discussed as a part of the CAMS configuration. These Agile practices are embedded within the process maps. An agreement is reached by both parties to use a CAMS-based approach to projects. As a result, the configuration and instantiation of CAMS is going to proceed directly in practice—without any need to organize a pilot run of CAMS.

MITS has experience in the use of UML in all modeling spaces. Therefore, this project makes use of use case and activity diagrams for modeling the functional requirements; class, sequence, and state diagrams for designing and implementing the solution; and component and deployment diagrams for system architecture and design, keeping the enterprise architecture in mind.

Figure 11.6 shows the details of CAMS-based activities in this outsourced project. This figure can be viewed as a practical version for the MITS project of the core CAMS architecture presented earlier in Figure 4.9. The process maps of CAMS are represented at the top in this figure. These process maps and the corresponding detailed activities undertaken within them are as follows:

- Business analysis (requirements modeling): This is where the high-level mining functions are explored and documented in models. This work is initiated by WAM business stakeholders and supported by MITS. MITS will have to increase its domain specific "mining" knowledge to carry out the requirement modeling. NFRs will apply at various levels—for the system, for modules within the system, and for the entire organization (WAM). Initial iteration and prototyping can be employed to finalize the detailed NFRs.
- Project management: This is the primary responsibility of MITS. The vendor, however, has to work within the project parameters (budget and time) provided by the client. Therefore, activities and deliverables within the project management process map will be sensitive to changes in the requirements and prioritization by WAM. Project management in this CAMS-based project will have Agile project elements. For example, a "product owner" is named from the client side to participate in the project. This product owner will help MITS understand priorities and apply estimations and metrics. As a large project, with multiple project modules, the product owner will change for each module. The "Agile coach" from MITS leads and facilitates the project internally and manages external relationships. This work of the coach includes provision of leadership; but in the role of a project manager, it also includes management of tasks. Thus, this is a dual role within a CAMS-based project.
- System design: System design is carried out by experienced designers in MITS who are also senior developers. This design needs to cater to the constraints of the WAM enterprise architecture. Therefore, the designers in MITS need to establish and maintain close contact with the enterprise architects of WAM who are physically located in a different country/region. The technologies for implementation are dictated by the enterprise architecture and so also the operational aspects of the solution. Therefore, system design in this project is restricted to application and database aspects of the solution (as compared with networks, security, and other infrastructures, which are all provided by WAM). The designs are, however, subjected to the techniques of verification and validation (discussed in Chapter 9).
- Implementation: This is the process map used in carrying out the actual development of the solution at the MITS location. This process map has opportunities to use the core Agile practices such as iterative development, daily stand-up meetings, and even pair programming. MITS, however, uses only some of these Agile practices. Close contact is maintained with the product owner through communications technologies. The progress of development is visible to the client through sharing of technologies and services.
- Quality control: Quality control includes test planning, test designs, actual testing, and reporting. WAM is not interested in technical testing. Technical testing is carried out by the developers accompanied by specialist technical testers who also hold the International Software Testing Qualifications Board (ISTQB) certification in testing. This enables them to streamline the technical testing process right at the start of the project. In the case of

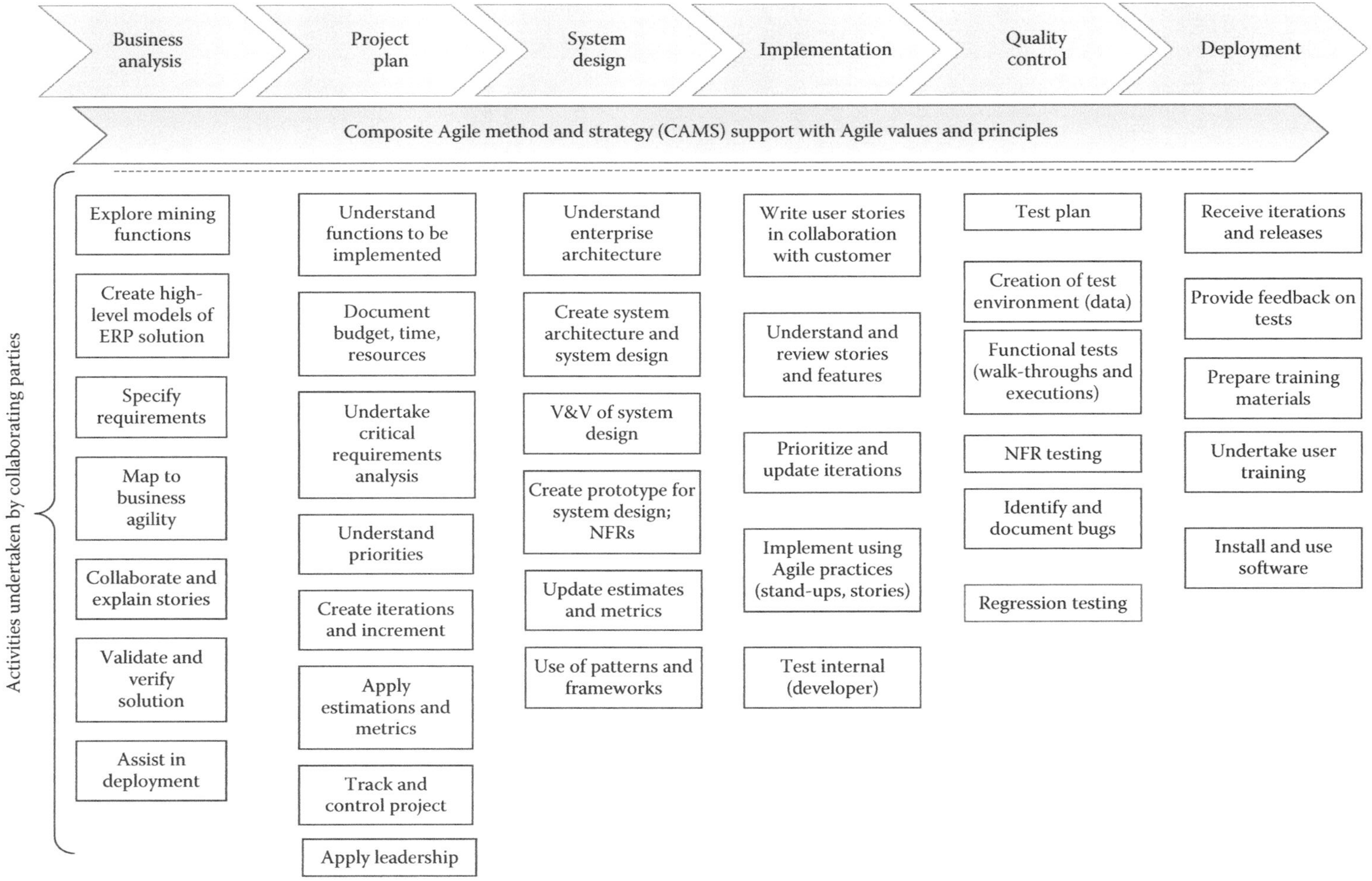
Business analysis
Project plan
System design
Implementation
Quality control
Deployment
Composite Agile method and strategy (CAMS) support with Agile values and principles
Activities undertaken by collaborating parties
Explore mining functions
Create high-level models of ERP solution
Specify requirements
Map to business agility
Collaborate and explain stories
Validate and verify solution
Assist in deployment
Understand functions to be implemented
Document budget, time, resources
Undertake critical requirements analysis
Understand priorities
Create iterations and increment
Apply estimations and metrics
Track and control project
Apply leadership
Understand enterprise architecture
Create system architecture and system design
V&V of system design
Create prototype for system design; NFRs
Update estimates and metrics
Use of patterns and frameworks
Write user stories in collaboration with customer
Understand and review stories and features
Prioritize and update iterations
Implement using Agile practices (stand-ups, stories)
Test internal (developer)
Test plan
Creation of test environment (data)
Functional tests (walk-throughs and executions)
NFR testing
Identify and document bugs
Regression testing
Receive iterations and releases
Provide feedback on tests
Prepare training materials
Undertake user training
Install and use software

Figure 11.6 Details of CAMS-based activities in an outsourced project.

this project, the specialist testers have set up a full test environment. This test environment is capable of handling both functional and nonfunctional testing. The NFR testing commences at the start of the project as the NFRs covering the entire project/system are specified up front. These include the performance, security, and volume requirements. Functional testing will be based on the progress of the development (based on iterations).

- Deployment: This process map, described in detail in Chapter 5, is handled by the technical staff of WAM. This is because the client, in this outsourced project, wants to deploy the system themselves. The operational maintenance of the system has not been outsourced (although the fixing of bugs and errors and incorporation of enhancement of the system are still part of the maintenance contract with MITS).

Creating CAMS-Based Project Iterations

Figure 11.7 shows groups of business processes for the mining business WAM. The three iterations shown in Figure 11.7 are at the highest organizational level. Therefore, the business processes shown in the figure represent major business functions. The development of the solution for the entire organization's operation needs to be divided into many iterations. Examples of three iterations are shown in Figure 11.7. Iteration-1 includes the development of human resources (HR), inventory, and supply chain management for the mining business. Iteration-2 focuses on external business functions such as marketing, customer relationship management, and partner management. Iteration-3 deals with finance, portfolio management, and compliance requirements (associated with mining business). These high-level iterations are based on priorities dictated by the business, interdependencies of modules, and risks associated with their development. When it comes to the

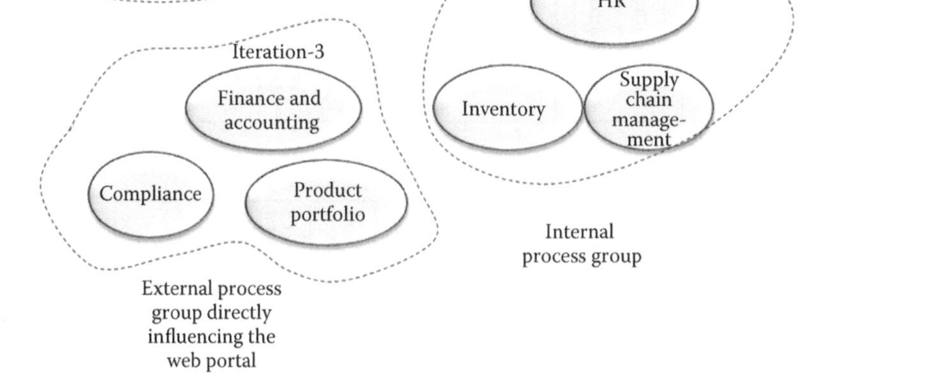

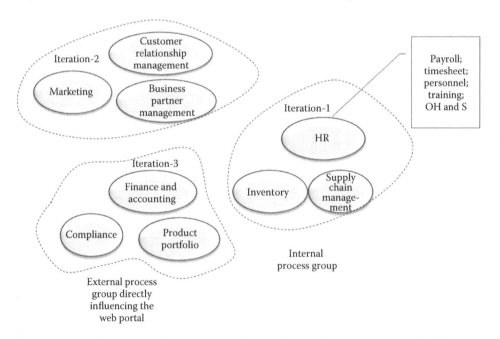

Figure 11.7 Carving out mining business processes to create major iterations for implementation.

actual execution of the project, iteration-1 will be undertaken first in terms of scoping, requirements modeling, development, testing, and deployment. However, this iteration will have increments within it; each module, such as HR and inventory, will have its prioritization and sequencing.

Within the HR module, Figure 11.8 shows an example of a "timesheet" process. This is a typical activity diagram of the UML; it is drawn by a requirements modeler who is familiar with the current and expected timesheet process in the mining domain. The activity diagram shows multiple activities undertaken in the timesheet process. Among those activities, however, there are three specific activities that can be implemented in a system. Hence, these are the 3 activities that are taken over by MITS for outsourced development.

Figure 11.9 shows an example of a development chart for an iteration that includes *timesheet* user stories. This is a practical variation, for this case study, of the discussions undertaken in Figure 4.8 (Chapter 4, discussing user stories) and Figure 8.9 (Chapter 8, priorities and iterations). Consider, for example, the user story-1 "head office enters timesheet data." When this story is in the "To do" chart, there is a higher element of planning that is associated with it by MITS. Therefore, MITS collaborates with WAM in order to ascertain estimations and metrics, prioritization and risks, and other such project management elements. When the same story-1 moves to "Doing" where it is being developed, MITS does not need the details of planning. Instead, the Agile elements take precedence over the planned project management ones. Other stories within the project (for example, story-2) may directly start with a high level of Agile elements in it. This can happen with MITS when the initial stories have been properly understood by the developers, and subsequent stories do not need the same amount of precise time and cost estimation; the risks with subsequent stories is also better understood after the initial stories have been developed. Thus, another way of viewing Figure 11.9 in practice is that the initial iteration in any project (such as the MITS one) will usually benefit from a higher degree of planned elements, control, and reporting. It is also in this first iteration that NFRs are implemented and tested. Subsequent iterations will have fewer planning elements and more of Agile elements in them.

Use of CAMS Metrics in Outsourced Projects

Figure 11.10 shows the way in which CAMS metrics (described in Chapter 10 and listed in greater detail in Appendix III) are applied in this outsourced project. Four roles are shown in this figure, who will be interested in these CAMS metrics—project manager, business analyst, programmers, and tester. There can be other roles (such as an architect) who could be interested in additional metrics that specify, for example, the stability of the system. In this discussion, though, these four roles are shown to be of interest. The areas of work that can be measured include the following:

- Scope of the project with its high-level business functions
- Detailed requirements of the project derived from the high-level functions (and non-functional or operational requirements)
- Prioritization of requirements (using, for example, MoSCoW technique referred to in previous chapter)
- Design-level metrics highlighting complexity and interfaces, actual development (or coding) of the application and associated databases, testing at technical and user acceptance level, verification and validation of artifacts, and eventual deployment (if of interest to the client in this case).

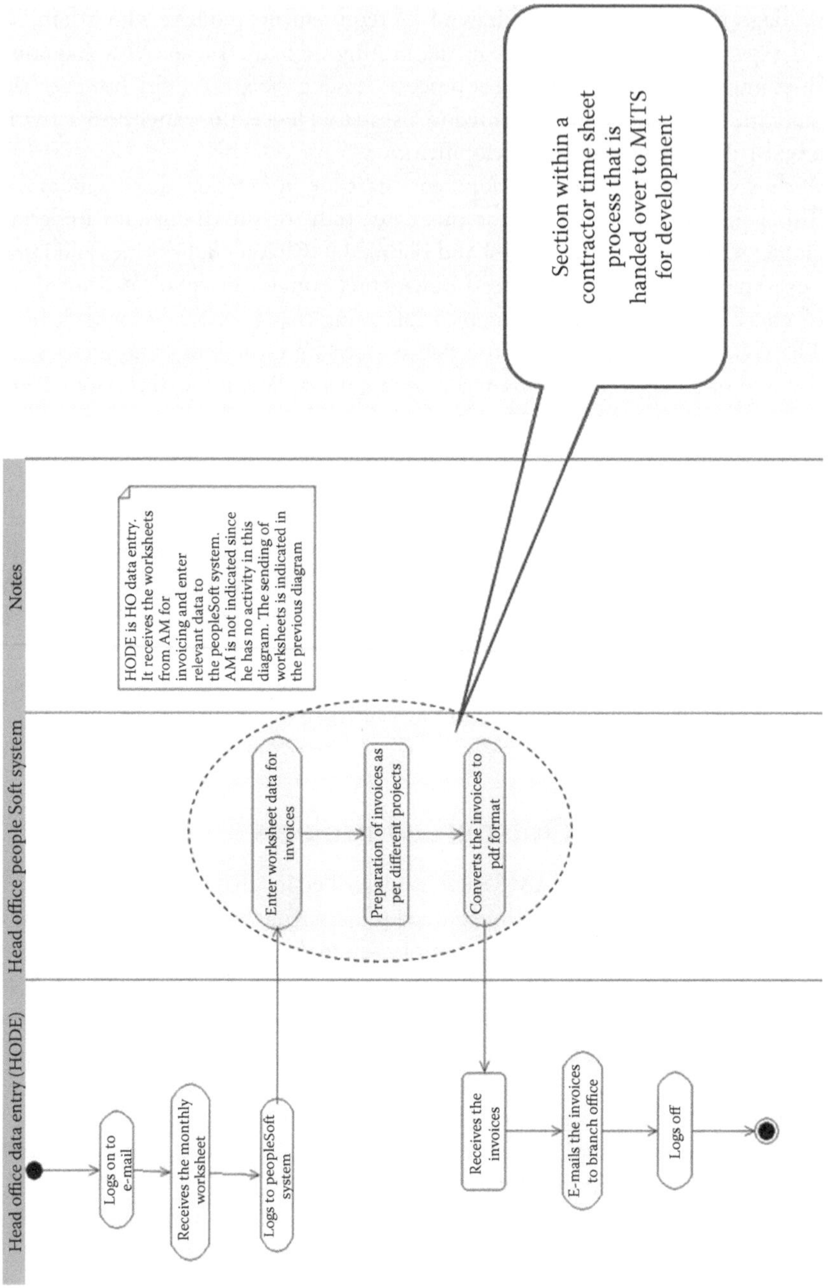

Figure 11.8 Part of timesheet organizing outsourcing: example of a timesheet.

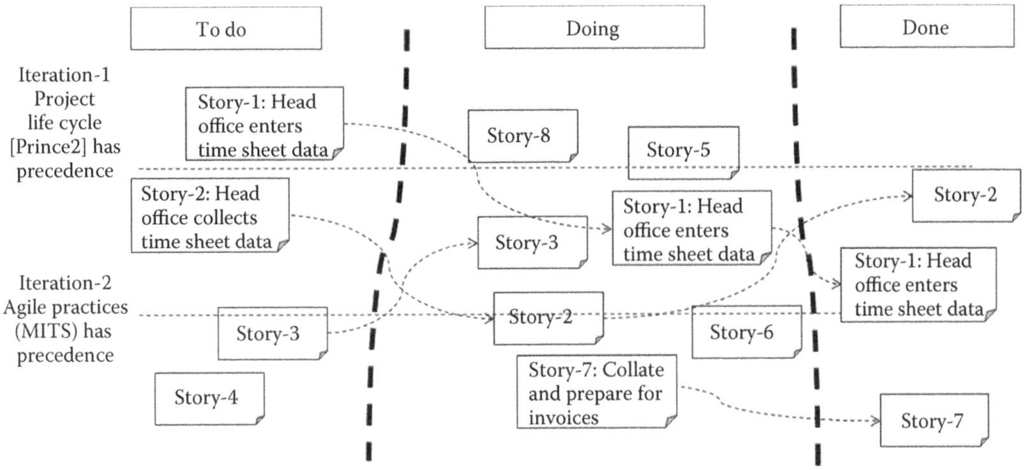

Figure 11.9 Implementing "timesheet" stories developed in collaboration with the client.

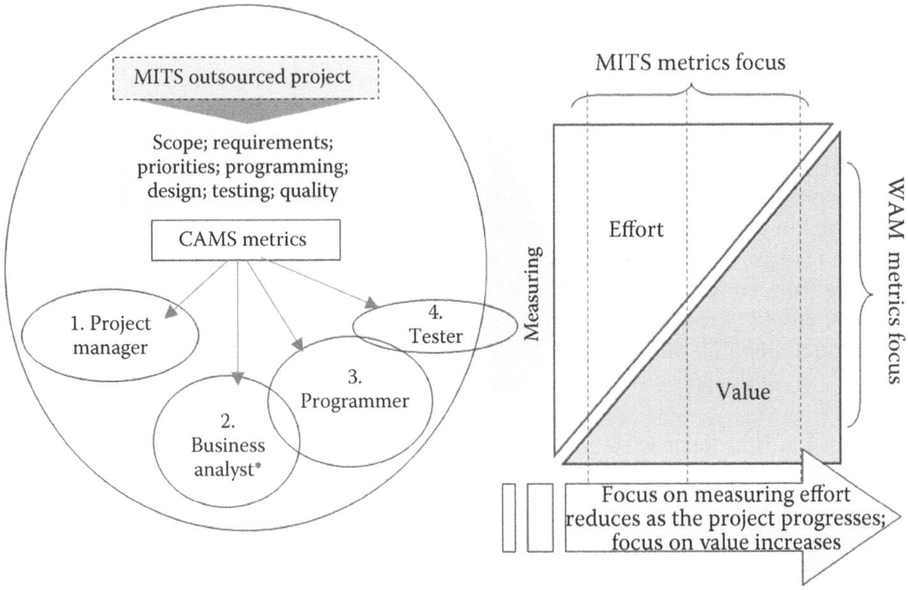

Figure 11.10 Role of CAMS metrics in an outsourced project.

Figure 11.10 also highlights the fact that the focus of these metrics at the start of the project will be on the effort required to carry out a certain task or create an artifact. For example, MITS is able to cost the project based on early scope and requirements documentation. This costing requires metrics that highlight the effort required and associated number of resources, their timings, and their working style (to ascertain the number of person-days required to develop and test the requirements fully). See Table 11.2 for the key groups of metrics in CAMS. Eventually, as the requirements get delivered, the focus of the metrics shifts to the value the functionality provides to the end user. The value-based metrics are of particular interest to the business analyst (* in Figure) who participates in this project from the WAM side.

SIDEBAR

Sherringham reports on how a composite Agile approach to Valued Communities social investment and interaction network Valued Communities – *AHHA* project impacted application development. The pragmatic approach was the use of *Google Adsense* for initial advertising revenues. To have specified its own advertising play at the start of the project was unrealistic as the requirements were not known and the business lacked the necessary maturity. To delay business operations until advertising was complete was not sustainable. The business and the developers had to move forward to get the experience to do their own advertising play. Now that the business has advertising experience using *Google Adsense* and revenues derived, both the business and development team are developing the next suite of changes. (From Keith Sherringham, Director, Valued Communities.)

Overcoming the Challenges of Outsourced Projects with CAMS

SIDEBAR: Outsourcing and Processes

A good-quality sourcing process has been discussed by Unhelkar (2008) as part of a *smart* business strategy. The focus of this sourcing process is not to limit outsourcing to an activity or a task but to make it a strategic approach to business. As has also been discussed by Hazra (2006), a good outsourcing process is considered as a path for smooth delivery of global services. Further, as organizations attempt global delivery of services, they invariably move toward collaborative Agile. Instead of simply looking at the outsourcing vendor as a provider of service, a proper collaborative-Agile approach encourages both vendor and client organizations to consider the relationship as a strategic one. This is the leading direction of Composite Agile Method and Strategy (CAMS) in an outsourced project. CAMS further encourages the use of project metrics and measurements (such as described by Hazra [2007]) in ascertaining benefits as well as understanding risks. For example, formal cost metrics, based on the deliverables of the CAMS process maps, provide a much better estimate of expenses than in a pure Agile approach. The CAMS configuration for an outsourced project provides a sequence of best practices that ensure the sharing of responsibilities and risks by the partnering organizations.

The discussion thus dealt with creation of process maps and embedding them with relevant Agile practices for use in an outsourced software development project. This discussion also delved into the extent of Agility in CAMS and also the practical aspects of dividing areas of work to be "outsourced." CAMS, however, encourages outsourcing partners to extend the relationship further (even if it is contract driven) into a strategic, partnering relationship. WAM is encouraged to outsource its noncore processes to MITS even beyond development and when the system moves into maintenance and support phases. This can happen between WAM and MITS when the two organizations work out a more strategic relationship. In the meantime, both organizations need to be aware of the challenges in their outsourced project and work to ameliorate them through the use of CAMS-based processes. The following are some of the issues that need to be handled by MITS with support from WAM in this project.

Uncertainty in the Scope of Work

Outsourced projects add further uncertainty to the already uncertain status of scope of work. While Agile insists on developing requirements as the project progresses, that does not hold true

Table 11.2 CAMS Metrics in MITS Planning

Applying CAMS Metrics in MITS Planning	*Explanations*
Cost (budget) for development of the solution and its implementation (including integration)	Budget for the comprehensive Agile business transformation is \$40 million. Corresponding time is 2 years. This budget is based on previous projects data and associated risks. Costs to business where milestones are missed (time, quality, functionality) include loss of revenue due to lost business opportunity and reduced customer experience; once system moves to production, though, there are only operational costs (anticipated to be less than \$2 million)
Benefit—corresponding to deliverables	Benefits are made up of two parts—tangible and intangible. Tangible benefits will take more than 3 years to realize. The iterations and process maps of CAMS provide formal deliverables. Benefits are calculated on the basis of (a) deliverables and (b) their application in practice in business
Functional and nonfunctional requirements	These are based on a combination of high-level user stories and initial use cases. Initial estimate, based on the writing of 3 use cases and 12 user stories based on those use cases is that of 35 use cases divided into four packages. A specific number of user stories will depend on the complexity of the use cases, from which user stories are created in CAMS. Priority metrics (e.g., those based on application of MoSCoW) reveal 25 (M = Must) use cases that form the crux of the system. There are 10 specific "features" written on story cards that represent nonfunctional features
Resources (people)	These are the number of developers required on a project. Developers can play different roles in Agile. However, a formal project structure of CAMS assigns specific roles to people. Therefore, this metric has to identify the roles and the number of people required within the role
Defining a person-day	This metric measures an ideal, uninterrupted working day in Agile. This measure is critical in arriving at the total days (and hours) required for a project. Total time worked on a project (or feature), if measured correctly, can help in identifying the development trend in the organization, and thereby make an estimate of the time required in a project
Iterations and lengths	The number of iterations required for a project can be based on decomposition of objectives and past project experience. The higher the risks, the more should be the number of iterations. The initial iteration has to be shorter (15%; see Chapter 8 and discussion on iteration distribution) to enable communication and understanding of measures across the project. The major iteration is the longest in terms of time and requires maximum effort, followed by a relatively shorter final iteration—in a project with three iterations

MoSCoW, Must–Should–Could–Won't.

in the given scenario. WAM key business stakeholders quickly discover that the scope of the project is changing even before it has begun. For example, the NFRs in terms of performance and volume were both underestimated by WAM. MITS technical architects highlighted these underestimations on the basis of their experience of working with the solutions technologies. The changes in database capacities and related hardware and network infrastructure had an immediate impact on the scope of delivery. For example, both parties had to get together face to face to discuss reducing the scope of the very first iteration-1 (Figure 11.7). This was done to enable focus on the prototyping of the NFRs.

MITS is also creating requirement models of the three modules to be developed in iteration-1. Clear definitions of the scope of what is included in the development and, then, what functionalities and nonfunctionalities are to be developed in each iteration are a vital part of reducing uncertainty. Creation of a sample code and getting the users to test the code even before the first iteration can immensely reduce uncertainty. Furthermore, CAMS also emphasizes the creation of nonexecutable models and using them for walk-throughs and reviews to ensure improved agreement on the scope of the development.

A clear definition of the scope of services required, together with the expected performance from the solution, is crucial in such a project. This scoping can also help control costs, as it can eliminate unnecessary and out-of-scope services from being provided and consumed unnecessarily.

While MITS makes all attempts to understand the scope up front, it is still an iterative process itself. Therefore, development of the scope is an iterative process and requires good communication and personal involvement of senior management of both organizations to ensure that the work is properly understood at all levels. As mentioned earlier, a good outsourcing business case for IT projects requires it to be aligned with the overall corporate strategy of the organization. It is this alignment that can come in handy in understanding what the client organization wants from the project and in resolving issues. Hughes and Cotterell (2002) have highlighted the problem of "scope creep" due to unclear business requirements, and how understanding of the scope can help prevent this scope creep in sourced projects.

Leadership and Direction

Leadership can become confusing in an outsourced project. This is mainly because each party to the outsourced contract may be capable of and want to lead the project. The sooner the two organizations develop a strategic partnering relationship, the better it is in terms of leadership and direction.

MITS has appointed a senior development manager to maintain the operational relationship between MITS and the client. WAM has the key business stakeholders from three different departments involved in maintaining the liaison with MITS. The three business people created a small intranet-based survey to understand the comfort level of WAM in using a mixed methods approach. The results indicated that employees were keen to use an approach that will reduce the burden imposed by methods friction.

On the MITS side, the experienced senior manager is more of a leader than a manager. She is, in fact, playing the dual role of a manager in dealing with the client and a leader internal to the development team. As a good project leader for the development project, her style is based on ascertaining dynamically changing situations and fine-tuning the leadership to those situations. (Recollect the flattened hierarchical structure discussed in Chapter 8.)

Payment Contracts Based on Delivery

While the overall pricing for this development was agreed upon before the project started, a key ingredient of the contract was payment based, on delivery. Therefore, MITS had to carefully create the iterations and assign deliverables (derived from process maps) to the iterations. As the two parties discover in this project, the second iteration is usually better estimated and delivered than the first one. This is so because the scope of work becomes better understood and the personalities as well as leadership qualities start playing a positive role. MITS and WAM have agreed on progressive payments on completion of deliverables. Later, during the maintenance phase, payments are based on "quality of services." An important aside in this project is its offshore nature—it is important to consider the various international currency fluctuations and related factors in payments based on contracts.

Once the solution has been tested and accepted by the client, the financial and legal aspects of the outsourcing contract again become important. For example, once a deliverable is produced and accepted at the agreed level during testing, payment of the agreed monies needs to take place from the client to the vendor. Use of formal modeling techniques (e.g., with the UML) can help even in this stage, wherein according to their terms of contracts, payments can be tied to the delivery of software modules that would satisfy a complete use case or a suite of use cases within a diagram.

The pricing information of the project can be used to match it with the budget for the project. The budget is the internal figures of the client organization and they need to match the pricing arrived at by the vending organization. A comparison of the pricing quotations with the internal budget leads to achievement of a sourcing strategy that, according to Scardino and Campbell (2002) provides "an optimal balance among internal and external capabilities, activities, processes, and services to ensure the achievement of business objectives at the lowest risk".

Determining Correct Iterations and Releases to Deliver the Product

As is evident here, the formation of iterations and increments is an important part of this outsourced project. Determining correct iterations, however, is easier in a local project than in an outsourced one. Figure 11.9 and the related discussion show that the second iteration is usually better executed than the first one. Therefore, at the end of the first iteration, all subsequent iterations and the remaining scope need to be revised. The delivery mechanism of the product can also play an important part in the pricing and service-level contract for the project. For example, a part of the solution developed by MITS need not have a physical delivery associated with it. Installing the components on the production server and providing the links to the end users is good enough for delivery of some software components. This delivery mechanism enables organizations to work out numerous mechanisms to provide delivery of their solutions—these can be downloading solutions from the Internet to physical delivery of solutions to the clients' offices.

The scope of the project can also impact the delivery mechanisms. For example, a small project with well-defined scope can easily be delivered across the organizational intranet. A large-scoped project will require additional user and nonfunctional testing before deployment. Similarly a web-service-based project will result in a product with interfaces that can be used by other services which may themselves not be ready for deployment. This can affect the sequencing of delivery and needs to be handled through the creation of a detailed project plan with dependencies (part of the planned aspect of CAMS).

Service Level Agreements after Delivery

Service level agreements (SLAs) enforce the scope and delivery mechanisms of an outsourced project. Thus, WAM and MITS enter into an SLA for both development and maintenance. Development SLAs include meeting the scope and delivery of requirements as also fixing the errors associated with the delivery. Maintenance SLAs deal with keeping the modules and systems operational. Since WAM wants to internally manage the deployment, the SLA related to maintenance will have much less to do with the operational and performance aspects of the system. Instead, maintenance will deal with fixing errors discovered during operation that include data, code, and analytical upgrades.

The SLA between WAM and MITS incorporates the principle of "give and take." If WAM demands higher turnaround time, it is provided with an understanding that this will include higher payments. Increasing the demands for higher quality of service also makes it more expensive, requiring a mutually agreeable level of service quality to be arrived at by WAM and MITS.

The SLA itself also requires regular maintenance based on changes to the internal and external environment. Provisions to create those changes are important and have been made in the SLA. The process of defining, agreeing, documenting, and managing the levels of certain IT services is involved in managing the SLAs (Hiles, 1994). The responsibility of the person in charge of managing the agreement includes continuous monitoring of the performance in the project, providing periodical reviews and reports to the management, and ongoing review of the agreements.

Formal Requirements Modeling

Modeling of requirements was discussed in detail in Chapter 7. MITS, with its UML experience and expertise, is able to model requirements by utilizing the techniques of use cases, activity graphs, and user stories. A challenge in modeling formal requirements in outsourced projects is that of communication. When requirements are modeled in the presence of the developer and the user, those requirements are clearly understood by all parties concerned. Any clarifications required can be provided immediately. However, for outsourced projects, requirements are usually created and modeled in a location different to where they are eventually developed. Thus, outsourced projects add another degree of challenge to that of modeling requirements in Agile projects.

The manner in which MITS approaches requirements is to base them on the scope of the project described earlier. With the formal documentation within CAMS, requirements have traceability: from scope to functionality to code to test and back! NFRs are similarly traced—except that they are not specified with the help of use cases. The NFRs are separately documented in text and also listed as features on story cards.

Typically, in outsourced projects, two parties are involved—the one that specifies what has to be produced (developed) and the other that understands the needs of the client through those specifications (Unhelkar, 2008). The client party that develops the specifications can be said to be in the problem space. The party that provides the solution is in the solution space.

As mentioned earlier, use cases and activity diagrams of the UML provide an excellent mechanism for scoping and specifying the requirements of an IT smart-sourced project. With the help of these modeling constructs of use cases and activity diagrams, MITS creates specifications in close collaboration with WAM. Use of standardized notations and diagrams is a much faster and efficient way of dealing with WAM located in Perth, Australia, than trying to describe the requirements in a few hundred pages of descriptive language. Such formal visual specifications also enable easier tracking of the solution later, and that tracking can also be matched with the payments for the delivery of those services.

Communication between WAM and MITS has to be kept open and lucid, providing opportunities to read, understand, and query on the specifications. The modeling techniques of the UML and the use of corresponding CASE tools are the right techniques to minimize these misunderstandings and improve communications between WAM and MITS.

Iterative and Incremental Implementation of Solution Design

Designing the solution is the technical step in an outsourced project. This is almost exclusively undertaken by MITS by following the solution design process map. While WAM technical staff takes interest in the design of the solution, the design itself is technically owned by MITS. This is an ideal way to approach design in outsourced projects. The vendor, MITS, designs the solution iteratively and continues to present it to the client for verification.

Communication between WAM and MITS is continuously encouraged in CAMS. Agreements on iterations and increments need to be reflected in the SLA, in the payment approach, and in the delivery mechanism for the project.

The modeling and documentation based on UML provide information to both parties and provide the staff of the MITS project with valuable information on how to develop and deploy the solution. All participants in this project, especially the senior development manager of MITS, need to understand and agree on the scope and the preliminary approach to the solution.

The solution is developed from the understanding of the specification as well as creation and acceptance of the design. The step of actually producing the solution is the domain of MITS but, using CAMS, it is undertaken in close collaboration with WAM. MITS has the freedom to develop the solution, but the WAM management has a say in the solution.

Quality Control and User Acceptance Testing

Quality assurance and quality control are both brought into play in MITS development. Quality assurance provides the necessary process to prevent occurrence of errors. Thus, some of the steps described in this section on best practices are part of quality assurance as they prevent misunderstandings early in the project and also prevent occurrence of errors. However, when the solution has been developed it is important to test it out, and that is a part of quality control. Quality control or testing occurs at both vendor and client side of the outsourced project—and there should be provisions for feedback and rectification of errors during this testing phase.

Ongoing Maintenance of the Solution

The solution developed by MITS is well known and understood by the developers. WAM insists on deploying the solution themselves. However, there is a specific service-level requirement that deals with reporting, fixing, testing, and redeployment of errors associated with the solution. MITS, as an outsourcing vendor, takes responsibility for that maintenance aspect—with the SLA being updated every year. WAM management is aware that maintenance, in an IT solution, can cost more than the development of the product over its lifetime. Therefore, this maintenance aspect is included in the SLAs, wherein the vendor is held responsible for keeping the systems up and running and within certain parameters that are all clearly spelled out in the SLA.

Conclusions and Lessons Learned

This chapter presented a short case study on the application of CAMS in an outsourced project. The key lessons in this case study are as follows:

- The type and size of the project dictates the extent to which CAMS will have formal and Agile elements.
- Physical distance in offshored projects has to be provided for in CAMS implementation.
- The process maps of CAMS provide visibility to the formal aspect of a process, with corresponding opportunities to practice Agile.
- Organizational level Agility (business Agility) had no role to play in this outsourced project.
- Contract negotiations and payments based on delivery are crucial in an outsourced project, irrespective of the use of Agility in the implementation aspect of it.
- Clients are extremely selective in areas for outsourcing—in case of WAM, the key knowledge elements of a process as well as the routine or operational aspect of the solution were not outsourced. These are also the areas where Agile development methods have very little role to play.
- CAMS metrics, covering both Agile and planned aspects, provide guidance in terms of estimation (based on previous projects) as well as tracking and control in new projects.

Discussion Questions

- Compare the WAM–MITS outsourcing project with any project within your organization. What are the similarities/differences between the two?
- Why should a CAMS-based outsourced project have more agility on the vendor (MITS) side than on the WAM side?
- What, according to you, are the factors that influence the way in which CAMS is configured for development projects?
- What are the important issues in creating iterations and increments in a CAMS-based outsourced project?
- Discuss a couple of challenges based on the discussion in this chapter (or in your own experience) relating to outsourced projects—and your suggestions for overcoming them.

References

Hazra, T.K., Creating a global delivery model for your sourcing initiatives, *Cutter Executive Report*, 7 (1), 2006.

Hazra, T.K., Smart sourcing: Metrics to manage initiatives, *E-Mail Advisor*, 23 May 2007 (Cutter Consortium Sourcing & Vendor Relationships).
Hiles, A.N., Service level agreements: Panacea or pain? *The TQM Magazine,* 6 (2), 14–16, 1994.
Hughes, B. and M. Cotterell, *Software Project Management,* 3rd ed, McGraw-Hill, p. 190, 2002.
Scardino, L. and C. Christopher, Rush to outsource and trouble will follow, ZD Tech Update, 2002, viewed July 30, 2002, http://techupdate.zdnet.com/techupdate/stories/main/0,14179,2875857-1,00.html.
Sherringham, K., Valued Communities—Ahha, viewed 23 August 2012, http://www.vcahha.com/.
Spann, D., Breaking the facade of truth: An introspective view into and a case study about the "Apparent Truths" of Agile, *Cutter Executive Report*, 9 (12), 2008.
Unhelkar, B., Sourcing methods: Philosophy and practice, *Cutter Executive Report*, 9 (3), 2008.
Unhelkar, B., Avoiding method friction: A CAMS-based perspective, *Cutter Executive Report*, 13 (6), 2012.

Chapter 12

Case Study: Organizational CAMS in an Insurance Business

Objectives

- Present a case study in Composite Agile Method and Strategy (CAMS) that applies at the organizational level (as against only at software development level) based on a real-life scenario
- Describe the scenario in the context of an insurance organization (hypothetically called Hartford Insurance Company, "HIC"), which has contracted a consulting company MethodScience to help it transform into one based on CAMS-based operations
- Present a typical Agile business transformation timeline spanning 18 months through the HIC case study
- Discuss the important issues of "methods friction" in the context of a large organization like HIC and the approach to handle them
- Present the embedding of Agile practices within the methods at business, project management, governance, and software development levels
- Highlight the evolution of collaborative-Agile processes (from informative to collaborative processes) in the context of the HIC case study
- Understand the balance required between the planned and Agile aspects of CAMS and its use through the Center of Excellence (CoE) during the Agile business transformation

Introduction

This chapter discusses an example of the practice of Composite Agile Method and Strategy (CAMS) in a real-life situation related to business operations (as compared with the outsourced project case study in the previous chapter). For the sake of this case study, a hypothetical organization, Hartford Insurance Company (HIC), is described. HIC is the representative of a company that operates in the insurance sector. Insurance uses multiple and varying standards and processes, with compliance in multiple jurisdictions to multiple authorities and is illustrative of CAMS within such an environment.

By nature, insurance is a service industry that prospers and grows on the basis of the timeliness and quality of service to the customer. Insurance is also an industry that heavily relies on risk management practices—assessment and management of risks at every step of the business. Processes play a major role in the accuracy of risk assessments, offering of insurance cover, and management of policies and claims. Although similar factors apply in banking and financial markets sectors, a risk-based approach is part of insurance and is often missing within Agile practices. This case study is also applicable to other financial-services-related industries.

This case study brings in a consulting company in the picture, called MethodScience. MethodScience has the brief to advice HIC in terms of its business transformation initiative. MethodScience is required to go beyond merely dealing with software processes and Agile methods. Instead, the brief requires MethodScience to bring about Agile business transformation (ABT) in a comprehensive and holistic manner while sustaining business operations. MethodScience is expected to work with HIC to develop the latter's capacities and capabilities, and to transfer expertise so that HIC becomes empowered to resolve their issues.

The way in which CAMS is configured and instantiated in this case study demonstrates the value of a CAMS-based approach to the entire organization (as against software development). The importance of the two crucial elements of CAMS, namely, method *and* strategy, are highlighted.

Hartford Insurance Company (HIC) Case Study Outline

HIC has a proud history of providing insurance to a large customer base globally over half a decade. Starting with the face-to-face insurance "salesman" selling insurance policies covering home contents and health, the company has now moved to comprehensive personal as well as corporate insurance business. HIC has also kept abreast with the market by offering new insurance products and their combinations (e.g., home and vehicle, or travel and life). Further examples of HIC's expanding business include underwriting large events (such as entertainment and sports), policies relating to work injuries, and superannuation-related products. As the insurance industry moves forward, HIC has also kept pace in terms of using different media to offer its products. For example, customers can buy on-the-spot insurances using the Internet or through mobile applications.

Internally, though, the company is facing major challenges in terms of systems and technologies. Being in business for a long time has led to a mushrooming growth in its software and support systems. Each major function of the business has its own system, and each layer of the organization has its method, standard, or framework. For example, the commonly offered home and contents policy is based on a legacy application that does not talk with the life insurance system. A "batch" processing is required, overnight, to pass details of one system to another. This leads to challenges in opportunity realization, for example, cross-promotion opportunities and multiple sales staff trying to sell the same products to the same customer.

Enabling system interfaces on mobile gadgets is another important demand from the sales and support staff, for example, the opportunity for sales to expand into rural and farming markets where mobile connectivity is essential for effective business operations. While some basic connectivity to the back-end systems has been achieved, there are substantial performance overheads and time delays in using the systems in remote country areas.

Finally, the senior decision makers are acutely aware of the hierarchical nature of the organization. Each decision goes through multiple tiers of the organization. This leaves the company behind its competitors in terms of crucial decision making.

As a medium-to-large company with close to 7000 employees and contract staff, HIC has a substantial presence on major stock exchanges around the country and beyond. The directors and decision makers of HIC are keen to make a strategic move that will enhance their capabilities for the future. The board has agreed to a strategic decision on undertaking business transformation. The strategic aspect of this decision implies that the board is looking beyond the integration of software systems. The decision includes proceeding with a comprehensive and fully integrated business intelligence (BI) solution. This, the board believes, will bring together the highly dispersed sets of data, information, and business processes. More importantly, though, the board wants the organization itself to be a fully Agile organization. Some of the key concepts of agility in business are considered precious by the chief executive officer (CEO) of the company. The corporate board of HIC concurs with this view.

The urgency of the CEO to undertake ABT is very high. This urgency is based not only on the inability of the systems to integrate but also on the disparity in roles and responsibilities within the organization. For example, not only do the systems serving customers, employees, internal administration, management, marketing, accounting, and legal disciplines not "talk" with each other, even the roles responsible for these disciplines are not in close collaboration. Each user in each role believes he or she is following the most recognized standard or method in the domain. Stringent implementation of Six Sigma, Prince2, and, to a degree, Information Technology Infrastructure Library (ITIL), has complicated the situation further—although these processes were brought into the organization by well-meaning senior decision makers. The CEO is quite keen to ensure that the transformation she envisions reduces this internal bureaucracy. The methods and a plethora of their activities and deliverables are all jumbled up into what CAMS calls "methods friction." This methods friction is adversely impacting HIC's ability to respond to its many challenges.

The current chief information officer (CIO) of the organization has been in the job for about 2 years. Aware of the previous major attempts at HIC to integrate the many dispersed systems, the CIO is also conscious of the business aspects around the planned change. Previous unsuccessful attempts were based on service-oriented architecture (SOA), which resulted in significant performance overheads. While some business functions were able to communicate with each other through the services interfaces, these functions were clogging the entire systems network. There are many operational (nonfunctional) requirements that remain unfulfilled after previous integrations. A badly integrated back-end suite of systems also means that HIC business is unable to put forth new products or modify existing ones quickly. Increasingly complex insurance legislation in multiple geographical regions adds to the challenge. HIC's decision makers (board) are keen to rectify this situation. "Agile" and its values, principles, and practices are desperately needed within HIC.

The challenge for the CIO, who is in charge of this program, is how to go about it. The entire management is convinced of the need to transform, but is not sure how exactly to undertake the transformation. However, the CIO is clear that simply integrating the silos of data and information or implementing a BI system in itself will not suffice and that a large-scale business transformation program that will integrate the entire business, reduce methods friction, and provide agility is required. Knowing that the entire HIC business has to become Agile, it is the risk management of the change that is of major concern.

After detailed investigations and reference checks, the CIO and a couple of senior members of the transformation board (a subset of the overall corporate board) discovered MethodScience. MethodScience is a consulting company located on the West Coast (of the United States) that specializes in the science (and art) of methodologies and their implementations. This company has also a presence in Sydney, Australia, and has undertaken business transformations in many different regions around the world. After due diligence, MethodScience is invited to undertake the transformation of HIC. Very quickly, HIC is made aware of CAMS by MethodScience. The CIO and the CEO of HIC see the application of CAMS across the organization as a strategic move that will integrate technical, process, and people dimensions of their organization. They are able to convince the transformation board of this as well.

MethodScience outlines a practical and usable approach to transform HIC to an Agile business. This outline is also based on CAMS. The CIO and two senior colleagues have dedicated resources to participate in the ABT program. Close to 50 developers together with key users, business analysts, subject matter experts, and two senior project managers are made available for this exercise. The developers are themselves dispersed over two major locations (New Jersey and Boston), whereas the key users are mostly based outside Hartford. Users include franchisees and agents who are part of the HIC "family" but not necessarily employed by HIC.

Thus, many of these end users are continuously on the move and require remote location- and time-independent support from HIC's systems. The initial budget for the project is approximately $20 million over the coming 18 months. A further $3.5 million is put aside for post-project deployment and training. A risk contingency of $8 million is provisioned by the board (MethodScience is helping with the Risk Management plan) for risks associated with the transformation. On the advice of MethodScience, the cost of risk is to be borne by the program of work as endorsed by the transformation board.

Goals of Agile Business Transformation

MethodScience Consulting outlined the scope of business transformation. The objective of the transformation program is to achieve an Agile HIC. This objective has been defined by date and success criteria. This Agility is to be based on a comprehensive software solution (BI) and an integrated approach to the methods and frameworks. The goals of the transformation include effective and integrated use of BI technologies and systems together with a business capable of sustainable change.

The CIO is now increasingly convinced of the existence of methods friction. The CEO agrees and stresses the need to diagnose and investigate the use of the dispersed processes at the business (Six Sigma), IT governance (ITIL), and project management (Prince2) levels, that is, the governance processes themselves need to be governed. Indeed, many directors of the organization know that ITIL only exists for namesake, and perhaps for legal compliance, rather than providing actual governance and a culture of governance.

MethodScience's consulting team has spent time up front to collaboratively define the statement of work (SOW). This end result is a list of quantified goals and objectives of HIC's ABT, with a mechanism for controlled change. High-level estimates of scope and effort are also made in the SOW. Initial discussions in the workshop revolve around people, processes, and technology-related changes. Technology changes are further divided into data and systems. These four areas for transformation relate to the Zachman enterprise architecture model mentioned separately in this chapter.

A high-level gap analysis based on the four factors of people, process, data, and systems is undertaken in the workshops conducted in the first week (Table 12.1). Both parties have agreed that a detailed gap analysis can be conducted later, if deemed necessary. This is mainly based on the understanding that gaps can only be identified once the anticipated Agile organization is clear. A detailed gap is difficult to ascertain in this early stage of the transformation program.

HIC and MethodScience have also agreed not to undertake a pilot study or spend time and effort in a detailed feasibility study. The initial iteration of the transformation itself is meant to provide all information that a pilot (or a feasibility study) would provide. This decision is made possible because both parties are aligned in outcomes and behaviors and are working in an Agile way to achieve the best business result. It is the efforts of both HIC and MethodScience together that have allowed this to occur.

SIDEBAR

Agility of Hartford Insurance Company (HIC) is understood as a time measure between a change in the organization's business environment and the organization's response to that change. HIC has increasingly found it difficult to respond to change in a timely manner. This lack of agility is further exacerbated by the increasing rate of environmental changes. HIC not only needs organizational Agility but also needs to keep up its responses to changing business environment. Business Agility in HIC is meant to be a continuous process.

An overall objective has been defined and quantified. A strategy for achieving the goal has been agreed upon and quantified. From this, goals and objectives for HIC in undertaking an ABT are determined. While all these aspirations provide a basis for the SOW (see following list), both HIC and MethodScience are aware of the priorities and the alignment with strategic intent:

- Enhance customer experience by providing a unified and holistic view of the organization, its products, and services.
- Provide increased options to customers for insurance products on the basis of personalization of services and provide additional location-specific services.
- Enhance customer experience with the purpose of retaining and growing insurance business.
- Improve the system to respond rapidly to changing external and internal circumstances. This rapidity of response will be based on an integrated system that will utilize BI technologies and systems, existing resources, and reengineered business processes.
- Reengineer both external (customer facing) and internal (management and employee facing) processes in order to provide a single "point of contact" for the user.
- Ensure a high quality of service (as specified in the service-level agreement).
- Enable Agile decision making for end users (staff and customers) through the design and implementation of a sophisticated Web portal. This will require detailed consideration of integration between the electronic front-end and the back-end BI system and support. Integrate data and systems at the technical level—using Web Services/SOA.
- Ensure an integrated systems solution that will cover a wide range of insurance services that can be used directly by the customer—for example, creation of a customer profile, provision of tentative quotes, and, once validated, creation of policies expected to be undertaken online through the sophistication of the front-end and the corresponding integrated back-end system. Additional insurance-related functions such as payments for premiums, making of claims, and payment for settlements are required to be undertaken as a combination of online and physical interactions.

Table 12.1 Elements of Agile Business Transformation for HIC—Gaps and Improvements

Elements of Transformation	*Existing Organization*	*Transformed (Agile) Organization*	*Expected Improved Outcomes and Comments*
People Customers Senior management Sales staff Other users	Multiple employees, repeating tasks. Customers end up with multiple touch points for one function. Dissatisfied customers	Single touch point for a function for customers Streamlining tasks, enabling sharing of tasks by promotion of Agile values	Providing greater value to the customer, enhanced customer experience, reduced workload for employees, need for training/upskilling/ mentoring
Process Internal (HR) External (customers, partners, regulatory)	Hierarchical, dispersed across many small departments. Unacceptable response time to customer issues. Inability of staff to reach remote customers	Customer-centric processes. Reduced response time to queries, applications, and processing of insurance services. Mobile-enabled processes	Streamlining of processes through reengineering. Use of comprehensive Web portal for single point of service. Efficiency in processes. Reduced wastage. Modeling and optimization required
Data Existing (needing conversion) New multimedia data	Currently dispersed, siloed, and in multiple storage mechanisms such as Excel and Access spreadsheets	Converted into a single database. Able to store multimedia contents sourced from external databases, third-party content providers and even customers. Accessible on the Internet and mobile devices	Reduced duplication of data and hence fewer errors. Improved control for the management. QA and testing of performance and security required
System Analytics Interfaces Intelligence	Mushrooming growth of multiple systems developed on "as needed" basis	Merging/integration of systems by recasting their functionality into a cohesive business intelligence system. Dynamicity in systems and ability to support goals such as single touch point	Efficiency in IT maintenance; hence less costs. Reduction in methods friction due to streamlined systems. Energy QA and testing required

- Make provisions for insurance products and the corresponding services to be made available through various electronic and mobile media.
- Enable the HIC business people to create new insurance products in response to dynamically changing business situations.

- Ensure that the current and upcoming insurance products are in compliance with the many insurance and environmental legislations.
- Make provision to change the human resources (HR) and organizational structures in response to changing business and technology situations. This changing structure is anticipated to occur across the organization rather than only in projects.
- Update and integrate the HR system to enable practice of Agile values across the organization.
- Enable opportunities to create new markets through business collaborations. These collaborations can be set up physically and executed electronically through Web Services.
- Create the ability to change insurance products and services according to changing government rules and regulations. The rapidity of changes in legislations requires HIC to change the business rules associated with its products electronically, and the BI system is expected to facilitate that change.
- Develop an overall collaborative-Agile organization that will be effective externally (e.g., through wider market coverage and business partnership) and efficient internally (e.g., through optimized and frictionless processes, use of mobile/wireless technologies to improve internal processes).
- Improve corporate accountability and regulatory compliance through timely, accurate, and detailed reporting on business performance.
- Manage environmental and sociocultural responsibilities with efficient business processes.
- Provide an integrated and holistic view of all methods and frameworks in HIC resulting in CAMS being positioned for use across the organization. The integration of methods will include identification and review of *all* existing methods and frameworks in the organization. Ensuing issues associated with "methods friction" are to be documented and handled by MethodScience's process consultants through CAMS.
- Identify and manage risks; track and report transformation and training and mentoring of stakeholders.

Composite Agile Road Map

The details of CAMS adoption and business transformation of an organization were discussed in Chapter 10. MethodScience works together with HIC staff dedicated to the transformation exercise in order to create a CAMS adoption road map. HIC provides the output of a strengths–weaknesses–opportunities–threats (SWOT) analysis they had done in order to decide on the Agile business transformation exercise. MethodScience extends that analysis in order to fully understand the current organization and outline the road map for transformation. Key outputs from this analysis are as follows:

Strengths: Long-time presence in the market; well known in the region; fully understands the insurance market; considered innovator in the domain; has a forward-thinking senior management team. Staff is well versed with methods and frameworks and can see the value of the methods.

Weaknesses: Burdened with siloed data and processes and, therefore, unable to correlate information to create intelligence/insights; unable to expand technologies to support potential business; unable to innovate without supporting technology; has extensive "methods friction" because of multiple methods being following rigidly at the development, project, business, and governance levels.

Opportunities: Market needs for dynamicity in insurance products; needs for personalized and location-independent products; not too far behind at this stage from other local/regional competitors; availability of global collaborators who are interested in partnering. Staff highly supportive of changes to an Agile business.

Threats: Globalized market, and therefore globally offered insurance products and services; stringent and changing legislation that demands higher compliance from insurance providers; changing global financial scenario.

Further to the SWOT analysis, the following are some of the key points noted by MethodScience in terms of HIC's transformation:

- As a large organization, the transformation of HIC will be based on major phases supported by activities and tasks within the phases.
- The current state of the systems in the organization has much less bearing on the new BI system; however, data conversion will be a major exercise.
- The current state and maturity of the organization in terms of the use of development, management, and governance processes indicates that the processes can work on their own, but create "method friction." This understanding of the processes also gives an idea of the metrics to be used to measure the current maturity and, later, during review, to measure the new maturity of the processes.
- Insurance processes are reliant on systems support and require extensive modeling and engineering. Therefore, transformation to an Agile business for HIC will be transforming it to collaborative business processes.
- The demographics and maturity level of HIC indicate that the work areas for transformation will focus on business processes, systems and databases, organizational HR, business model, and customers. The underlying networks and related infrastructure will not change substantially. Interdependencies between work areas are also investigated. For example, personalization and location independence of business processes will require to be integrated with mobile technology support.
- Extensive visibility of the ABT process to the organization is required by creating an internal Web site with regular updates and by undertaking regular briefings and updates through newsletters.
- Draft, discussion, and finalization of service-level agreements (SLAs) and other contracts will be necessary to drive the transformation.
- Formal reviews and use of metrics should be planned before, during, and after the completion of the transformation.

Figure 12.1 shows the major phases in undertaking CAMS adoption across HIC. This transformation of HIC has four major phases to it—diagnose, plan, enact, and review. While these phases also benefit from the use of Agile principles, such early use of Agility in this environment is limited to MethodScience. MethodScience consultants, working closely with the HIC transformation board, work through these four phases of diagnosis, identification of transformation work areas, enactment of the transition, and its review as follows:

1. Diagnosing and understanding the current status of HIC is the crucial first step in undertaking ABT. These goals include dynamic customization of the products and services, cost reduction, profit enhancement, flexibility in organizational structure, and value addition to customer

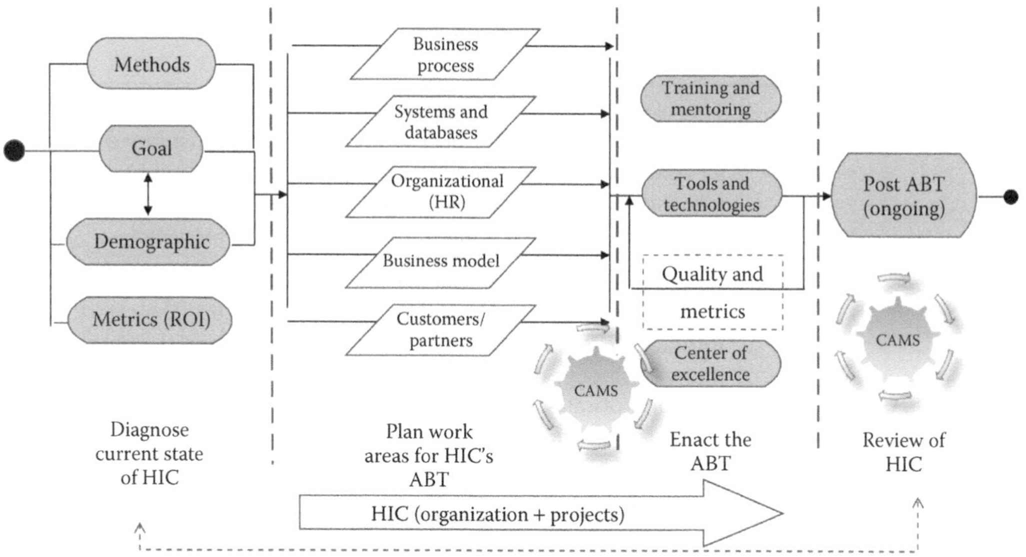

Figure 12.1 Major phases in adopting CAMS across HIC organization.

services provided with a personalized angle and timeliness of services. In addition, HIC is also indicating a need to consider sustainability factors together with environmental intelligence in this transformation exercise. MethodScience consultants together with HIC staff list the major methods in use—Six Sigma, Prince2, some part of ITIL, and a software development and maintenance process that is more or less sequential. Because of the large size of the organization, the scope of ABT is also large (made up of all organizational functions). The location of the organization, in an industrially developed country, indicates minimal challenges in terms of available physical infrastructure (such as office space and communication). The two parties also get together to decide on the metrics that they will use to ascertain the success of the ABT. These return on investment (ROI) metrics are suggested by MethodScience on the basis of their previous CAMS implementation experiences and refined by HIC. Some example metrics are similar to the ones discussed in Chapter 11 (see Table 11.2).

2. Work areas of HIC that are used in ABT are derived from the current organizational structure and operations. In Chapter 10 (Figure 10.5 in particular), we discussed these work areas in an organization in adopting CAMS. Out of the eight most important areas (or major functions) of a business, the ones selected for HIC are shown in Figure 12.1. These areas are selected and described on the basis of the type and nature of the insurance business, the goals described by HIC, and the demographics of the organization. The selected work areas are summarized in Table 12.2.

Enactment of transformation is also carried out through each of these work areas. Each work area has a key stakeholder with whom MethodScience liaises during the transformation. During enactment of the ABT, each key stakeholder is involved in corroborating and refining the goals, identifying the risks within the specific area of work, agreeing on metrics and measurements, and organizing the validation and deployment of the systems and processes. Collaborating with these stakeholders, handling their concerns, and meeting their expectations are vital for the success of HIC's transformation program. Each element of transformation (described in the rows in

Table 12.2 ABT Work Areas in HIC

ABT Work (Focus) Areas	*Description*
Business model	This work area describes the way in which HIC's business is organized. This organization includes the direct insurance sales structure, as well as selling of products and services through franchisees and agents. ABT will require this model to change and be updated with the collaborative-Agile business model
Customers and partners	This describes the external parties interacting with HIC. Customers, in particular, will experience change as they start interacting with the business through the Web portal. Therefore, many business processes (such as claims submission) will change and incorporate a substantial amount of direct, electronic, or mobile interactions
ICT systems, applications, and databases	This is a major technological change resulting from ABT in the case of HIC. This work area includes the entire CAMS life cycle at the technical and development levels. Requirements, architecture, design, development, and deployment of the BI comprehensive solution will be undertaken here. Corresponding changes are also envisaged in this work area relating to databases. These databases are not just internal to the organization but also include interfacing and relating to external regulatory insurance databases through service calls
Business processes	This is another significant work area in HIC's transformation. The discussions in Chapter 7 on business processes will be applied here in practice. Modeling of processes, mapping values, and value streams to the processes, their optimization, and their compliance are some of the activities carried out here. Reengineering of processes will be undertaken for existing processes (in terms of changing them on the basis of BI technologies). New processes will be introduced and redundant processes dropped
Operational/ organizational (HR)	In this work area, the transformation program will handle changes in the way employees and other staff are organized, trained, and coached in the use of CAMS. The inevitable structural changes in terms of reporting hierarchies within the business will also be designed here. Agility will change the HR structure at both the project and organizational levels

Table 12.1) is led by specialist consultants who have the knowledge and experience in dealing with that area. Following are the specific activities undertaken during enactment:

- Training and mentoring: This is a vital aspect of HR. Large-scale business transformations (and especially the ones that move an organization to an Agile one) are unsettling to people (staff) unless they are carefully managed from an HR perspective. People require regular training, updating on the changes, coaching, and mentoring in terms of their career paths and an improved understanding of the HR structure.

- Tools and technologies: Those associated with processes, systems, and even business modeling come into play during enactment. For example, tools and standards for business process management (BPM) (engineering and reengineering of processes, their modeling with standards such as Business Process Modeling Notation/Unified Modeling Language [BPMN/UML] and corresponding computer-aided software engineering [CASE] tools) will be used. Data cleansing, data conversion, and timing and accuracy of conversion to ensure minimal disruption to existing ongoing business are undertaken. New multiformats of data/contents and innovative ways of sourcing contents and interfacing with content management systems—especially dealing with rapidly changing multimedia contents—are modeled during enactment (execution).
- Implementation: The implementation of BI systems, ensuring their integration with existing and new data, cohesive display of location-specific contents to users, and the operation of the system on existing infrastructure such as networks and hardware are part of the enactment. The organization continues to function while it undergoes transformation. Therefore, there is a need to support the organization while it operates and, at the same time, transform its applications.
- Quality and metrics: These start before the enactment and continue throughout the process. Metrics are also used in post-transformation reviews. Formal reviews of the transformation project ascertain the "rights and wrongs" and measure the results. MethodScience helps HIC in deciding on the metrics but HIC owns the metrics. The data from the metrics provide valuable lessons in the management of the transformed business. Comparison of the results will be based on the same metrics used to measure the parameters at the start of the project. For example, in the case of HIC's transformation, customer experience is measured on the basis of a quick survey of selected customers at the start of the project and then again after the transformation. This survey includes questions such as the ease of use of the organization's Web portal, time taken to get answers to queries, accuracy of the process, and provision of customer support. Similarly, the staff is provided with a suite of questions (before and after the ABT) relating to the use of development and project management processes, corresponding business processes, and the control and reporting hierarchy.
- Center of Excellence (CoE): HIC has two Centers of Excellence (CoEs) in its current operations, one dealing with project management and the other dedicated to quality. Enactment of the transformation makes use of the knowledge resident in both these CoEs and merges them with the new CAMS concepts and knowledge. Knowledge is also gained as the organization transforms, which is stored within the CoE. Creating a new combined body of knowledge and data (metrics) and facilitating its use across the organization are part of the CoE.

On completion of enactment, a post-transformation review (as described above) takes place. This review is not only to ascertain the achievement of goals and ROI, but is also a part of the process of deploying CAMS across HIC.

Figure 12.2 shows a typical ABT plan in action. Each organization is unique in its transition. The timeline of about 18 months for HIC's transition and adoption of CAMS is a good indicator of the way in which most medium- to large-scale transitions occur. HIC follows its own unique path in transition, which depends on its current business state as well as its process maturity state. Although there have been no measures of its processes on its Capability Maturity Model (CMMI), still the indication is that each process is used on its own in an independent and ad hoc manner. Transformation of the organization to CAMS involves identification of methods friction and its reduction if not elimination.

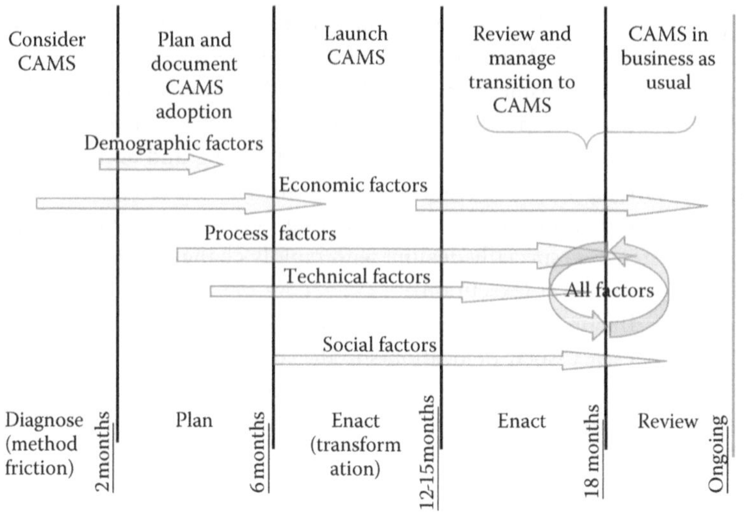

Figure 12.2 Mapping the CAMS adoption phases with timelines for HIC.

In HIC's case, the first 3 months are used in diagnosing and analyzing the current state and methods friction. The next 3 months focus on in-depth planning, which is an extension of the diagnosing phase. Detailed documentation and modeling takes place here. Enactment is the actual execution of the transition plan. This is where the work areas described in Figure 12.2 undergo changes. Processes, systems, business models, and customers will all undergo change. Eventually, the transition will be reviewed and measured. This is also the process of deployment, and takes approximately 3 months.

Diagnose (0–3 Months)

- Identify and document time, budget, functionality, and quality of the BI system implementation.
- Identify the phases in Six Sigma, ITIL, and Prince2. Identify and list the "methods friction" elements, which also include the potential use of Agile methods. This is done by identifying and listing the areas of work where one method (e.g., an IT governance framework) demands formal and in-depth documentation, whereas another method (e.g., Extreme programming, XP) permits minimal documentation. This exercise also includes identification of key roles within these projects and the issues faced by them in using the methods.
- The key stakeholders from each work area are included in the decisions on use of methods and modeling of the processes. MethodScience organizes a series of workshops—on a weekly basis—to discuss the issues faced within each work area and the corresponding challenges of methods friction. This is done by asking a suite of questions to these key roles in terms of how they use the methods, to what extent they need to use the method, and which elements of the "other" methods prevent them from carrying out their tasks.
- A crucial area of work here is the involvement of the HR department in order to understand the current and anticipated organizational hierarchy. This understanding helps in creating the new "flattened" hierarchical structure and the corresponding guidelines for behavior.

Plan (4–6 Months)

The planning and scoping phase of ABT uses the output of the diagnosis phase to create a program for the transformation. Once the significant aspects of the business—especially the work areas—are identified, this planning phase outlines the task plan for transforming each work area. Thus, the outputs of the planning phase area include a precise list of tasks, the associated resource requirements, and an outline of the deliverables to be produced, as well as the corresponding time estimates for the transformation project.

MethodScience also provides input in terms of estimations based on previous experiences. Since there is no pilot project or iteration in this transformation, the first iteration of BI implementation is itself used in lieu of a pilot project. HIC and MethodScience explore creative ways of undertaking ABT during this phase, including the maximum use of internal and external resources.

This phase is also where a CoE for composite agile usage across HIC is established. The scope of the transformation project is refined, and the relationship between the work areas of the business affected and the CoE are further discussed and resolved here. The scoping aspect of the ABT project in this planning phase ranks and prioritizes work areas of transformation and studies the effect of their interdependencies and changes. Once again, the prioritization techniques of Agile (such as MoSCoW) can be used even at this high level to identify the details within the work area to be transformed. While the risks are managed in practice during enactment, the planning phase identifies and ranks these risks. CAMS promotes the balances act required in planning—balancing between costs and benefits, balancing technology with business, and balancing risks with outcome.

Enact (7–12/15 Months)

Enactment is the execution of the Agile business transformation project. This is where MethodScience helps HIC physically step through the plan created in the previous phase. Enactment of ABT requires the full gamut of project management skills. An ABT project has to undertake risk management, progress monitoring, measurements, and reporting. The following are the issues to be considered during an ABT enactment phase:

- Ongoing identification and classification of risks and their priorities, and how to ameliorate them
- Interrelationship among work areas, their dependencies, and management of the lead work area as first priority
- Delivering intensive Agile-specific training, mentoring, and coaching to staff at all levels in an organization. This training will have to be customized to suit the staff requirements (e.g., business decision makers will have to be coached in terms of the information they use and the uncertainty they can handle through Agility; software developers will need a completely different type of training in Agile methods)
- Measurement of the transformation outputs. Use of metrics created during diagnosis and formalized during planning is recommended here to ensure common measures for comparison
- Reporting to stakeholders and managing their expectations

Review and Manage (15–18 Months)

The review phase of an ABT details the outcomes of the project. This phase also facilitates cross-checking whether the stated objectives of the Agile transformation are reflected in the outcomes.

Furthermore, the outcomes need to be measured and studied not only for the transformed business but also for the new environment in which the business is now operating. The actual outcomes of an Agile adoption will be slightly different from the stated goals even in cases of successful ABTs. The difference between the outcomes and the goals could be due to the shifting of both the business and the environment during the time the ABT project has been implemented.

Evaluation of the outcomes includes reviewing in detail the operation of the CoE; changes to the supporting software and systems; changes to organizational structures, business portfolio, and business model; and, eventually, changes to the way in which software is developed and maintained. The evaluation feedback is provided to the stakeholders responsible for ABT.

The review process not only ascertains the achievements of the transition but also opens the door to further enhancements. Hence the review process should make provisions for these enhancements in all work areas of the business. Organizations should incorporate changes on the basis of the experience gained from the transition as well as the issues discovered during transition.

Metrics are required to identify and measure the criteria for optimization and improvement. Metrics provide a set of measurable criteria rather than an ad hoc understanding of improvement resulting from ABT. Therefore, metrics are used to communicate the success of the BT project to various stakeholders. Understanding the perceptions of the goals in relation to business transformations provides a good suite of measurable criteria. Changes to the business processes, information and communications technologies (ICT) systems, and organizational structures are also measured before and after the ABT. Each work area can have its own set of metrics, and these metrics change depending on the industry sector and business type.

Configuring Composite Agile

ABT is set to accrue numerous business benefits to HIC. These include enhanced customer experience and improved internal business efficiency. Transforming to an Agile business requires an ever-evolving understanding of the business goals, the current structure of the business, and the steps in undertaking the necessary change to become an Agile business. At a technical level, this transformation leads to configuration and instantiation of CAMS.

SIDEBAR

Enterprise architecture (EA) frameworks (such as Zachman and The Open Group Architecture Framework, TOGAF) (The_Open_Group, 2010; Zachman and Holcman, 2010) have been used to provide the basis for business transformations. These frameworks can also be used for Agile business transformations. An EA framework can be easily applied to model the future state of the Agile business. For example, the 6 × 6 model of a business as presented in the Zachman framework can be abstracted to create the building blocks for an Agile business. These building blocks will be based on technology, networks, data, functions/processes, and people. Each of these elements can be made up of many subelements, depending on the type and size of business and its transformation goals. Modeling of these elements iteratively and incrementally at the business level helps in breaking down, understanding, and controlling the Agile business transformation. This, in turn, reduces the risks of such transformation and increases the chances of its success.

CAMS would enable reduction in methods friction and improved usage of semantic Web. Implementation of a comprehensive BI solution will include an electronic Web portal that will provide the desired single point of contact for the user (customer and staff alike). HIC's strategy to move away from information silos into collaborative business processes is another complementary activity during this transformation. Overall, though, CAMS provides the basis for integrating business processes as well as internal methods and frameworks.

In order to achieve this, CAMS is configured in HIC to occur at various levels—business, project management, and software development. Configuration of CAMS in HIC involves embedding of Agile principles and practices in HIC's planned processes and governance frameworks. Figure 12.3 shows how the Agile practices are embedded in the formal methods of HIC. At the base of the figure are examples of popular Agile practices. These examples of Agile practices are shown as representative samples (i.e., they are not the actual, comprehensive lists to be used in HIC). MethodScience is working to create a repository of Agile practices that can be maintained by HIC's CoE for processes in an ongoing basis. That repository will contain the entire list of changing Agile practices.

Figure 12.3 indicates how the embedding of Agile elements in the formal HIC processes will work. Consider, for example, the *Define* phase of Six Sigma (these phases were discussed in the context of CAMS in Chapter 6, Table 6.1). Whenever this phase is executed in HIC, it will include Agile principles of collaboration and face-to-face conversation. As a result, an on-site customer will become part of the requirements for any business project within HIC. The presence of an onsite customer provides input to the BI system's implementation activities, as the customer explains the requirements directly.

Another example is the embedding of continuous testing and iterative approaches within the development and implementation of the BI solution. The practice of continuous testing can be applied within a formal process by ensuring that each individual piece of requirement is tested as soon as it is developed (this could be based on individual use cases or user stories, but within the

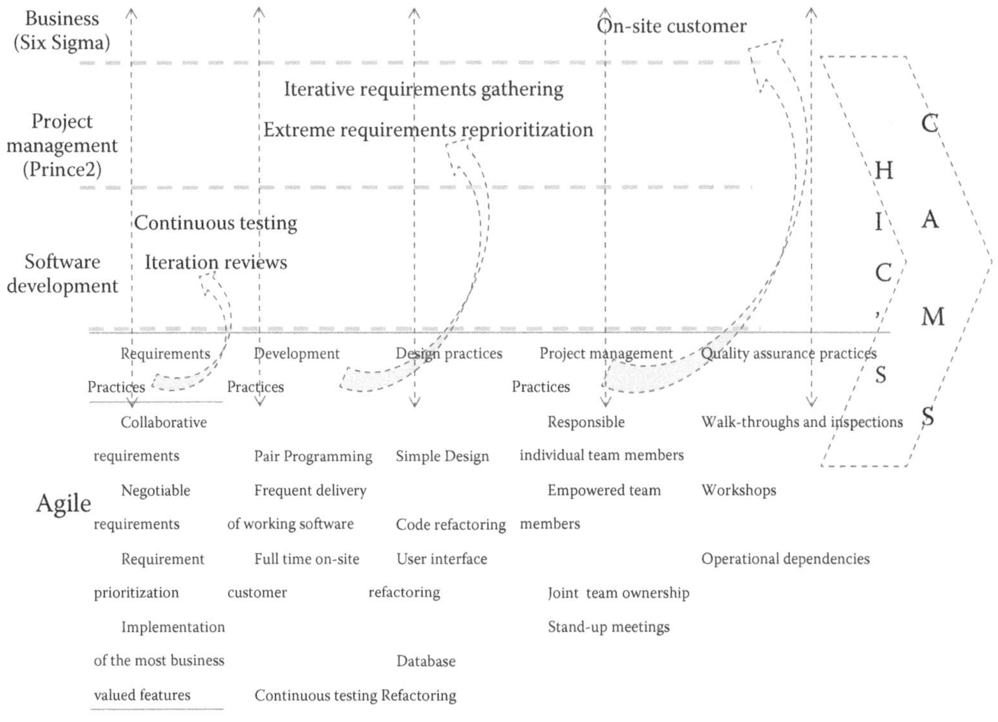

Figure 12.3 Embedding Agile practices in formal methods in HIC.

phase of a formal process). The Agile iterative and incremental approach is inserted in the project plans created within Prince2.

Furthermore, this configuration of CAMS in HIC will happen on a dynamic basis—not prefabricated for all projects but configured afresh for each project and situation. In practice, the phases within each method—operating at business, IT, and project levels—are reviewed against the situation in which they are to be applied. The concept of situational method engineering (SME) discussed by Brinkkemper et al. (2007) and colleagues is a good indication of how HIC can undertake situation-based configuration of processes.

Note that keeping the *instance* of CAMS flexible to incorporate changes in time is vital. Therefore, a CAMS instance is a combination of a project plan as well as practices and guidelines that go along with the plan. Flexibility of methods is required at two levels: first, the flexibility of configuring the method in different ways, and, second, the flexibility accorded by the method in the middle of development/maintenance. CAMS subscribes to both flexibility by ensuring that the project plan remains a dynamic document that is changeable.

The following are the specific steps jointly undertaken by HIC and MethodScience in arriving at a CAMS configuration.

- Two workshops are organized to extend the discussion on methods friction. They consider the process maps of the enterprise architecture; system architecture; and design, implementation, and deployment in these workshops. The area of CAMS instance dealing with software development and maintenance will be made up of process maps and Agile practices.
- Invite the key roles that use these process maps to provide input in terms of associated roles, activities, tasks, and deliverables. Identify areas of the process maps that need to be modified to show where formal techniques and use of the UML can be embedded with Agile practices.
- Start the creation of a CAMS repository in a simple database or spreadsheet (activities and tasks, roles, and deliverables). This repository is moved to a sophisticated CASE tool for processes.
- Agile practices are embedded within the relevant process maps. In the case of business processes, Agile practices are inserted in the relevant phases of the process.

Together, MethodScience and HIC conduct a walk-through of the process maps. This walk-through ensures that the Agile practices are workable. For example, availability of customers (and key users) onsite is easily achievable for HIC. This is because the organization operates in the same regional environment as its customers. Each process map, embedded with its Agile practices, is fine-tuned for a project. The CoE for HIC deploys the process maps through its internal intranet site.

Training and coaching for users and developers of CAMS is organized by MethodScience on a rolling basis. The skills–aptitude–experience–influence matrix is used by MethodScience corresponding to each role in HIC. A brief summary of the matrix used for training and upskilling of HIC staff in using CAMS is shown in Table 12.3.

HIC and Collaborative-Agile Business

Figure 12.4 shows another important output of organizational Agile—a collaborative-Agile HIC that synchronizes with the entire business ecosystem in which it exists. A Political, Economic, Social, and Technological, Legal and Environmental (PESTLE) analysis is conducted to help

Table 12.3 HIC Roles and Examples of Training Upskilling in CAMS

Agile Practice Elements Roles	*Developer*	*Business Analyst*	*Project Manager/ Agile Coach*	*Architect/ Designer*	*Tester*	*User (Super)*
Skills	Java; content management	Stories; rules; use cases	Plan; facilitate	Component diagram	Test harnesses	Usability; rules
Aptitude	Technical; solution-oriented	analytical; strategic	Task-based; operational	Technical; strategic	Analytical	Analytical; strategic
Experience	In development environments	Business domain (insurance)	Managing multiple projects with CAMS	Multiple projects and systems	Testing code, functionality, NFR, and usability	Business domain (insurance)
Influence	Class and component levels	Business process level	Project level	Enterprise level	Class level; for NFRs at system level	Enterprise level

NFR, nonfunctional requirement.

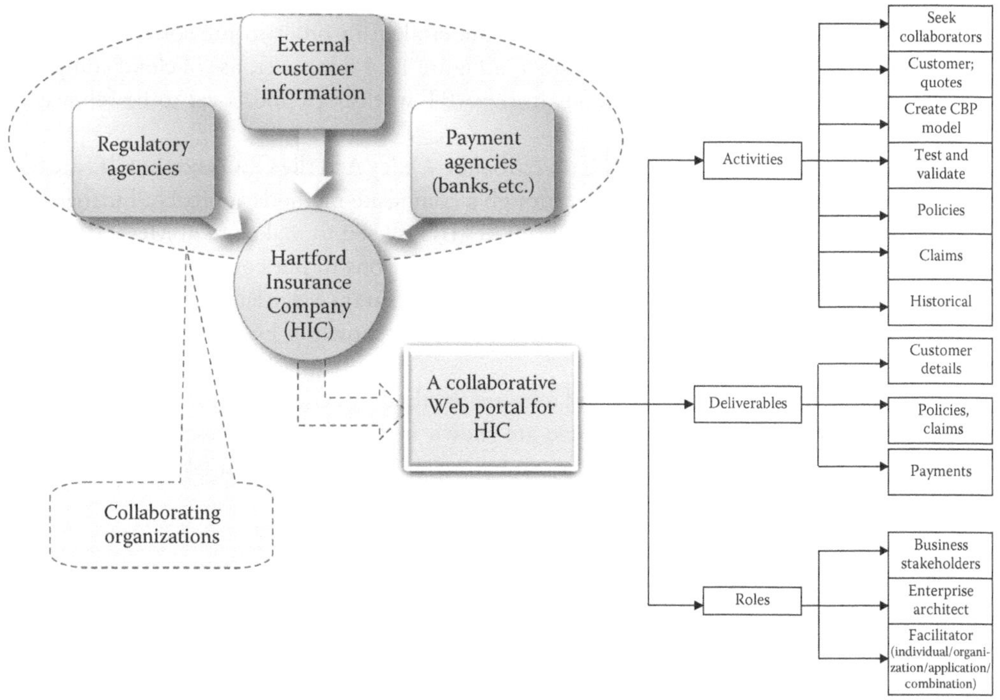

Figure 12.4 HIC collaborations with partners.

understand this business ecosystem of HIC. This analysis also helps understand the clusters that can be part of HIC. Creation of the collaborative business process is then undertaken in an incremental manner. HIC's analysis of the business situation is as follows:

- Political: Internally, luckily, the entire senior management team is in agreement for Agile business transformation. The CEO has nominated and is supporting the CIO in terms of the change. Externally, the business partners also need to undertake the change, and are totally supportive. Figure 12.4 shows the external customers coming into HIC through its collaborative platform in order to facilitate electronic collaboration.
- Economic: The global financial crises and ensuing fallouts have had a major negative impact on the insurance industry. However, HIC's financial position is strong, and budgets have been set aside for transformation as well as the operation of a CoE to support CAMS usage in the organization. In terms of economic transactions (financial) relating to the insurance processes, these will be conducted almost entirely through the electronic/mobile Web portal of HIC.
- Social: HIC has an excellent opportunity to interact with the "new generations" of customer through social media. HIC has a mix of users (staff and customers) with different backgrounds and interest in the use of social media. However, initial surveys conducted internally during the diagnosis phase of the transformation indicate positive attitude toward the use of social media to promote as well as serve HIC's user communities.
- Technological: The legacy burden of HIC is known internally. The budget for the transformation includes a specific amount for procurement and implementation of a BI solution. Data, systems, and process integration are undertaken in order to provide a single-point-of-contact Web portal for HIC, as shown in Figure 12.4. However, use of cloud computing figured only in the initial discussions in the ABT workshops and is yet to be followed in detail.
- Legal: While HIC is compliant with the Sarbanes–Oxley Act, the CEO and the CIO are both keen to make this a real compliance through a composite methods approach. Furthermore, the forward-thinking transformation team of HIC is keen to make use of MethodScience's knowledge of the upcoming green computing legislations to put compliance measures and reporting in place in the BI system. In terms of the insurance legislations, though, the interaction is set up electronically through Web services as shown in Figure 12.4.

A number of activities, deliverables, and roles are required by HIC to carry its business through the Web portal. Examples of some of these are shown in Figure 12.4. These examples will be expanded in practice by HIC to include roles and deliverables from the business itself (rather than technical collaborations).

SIDEBAR

Examples of business transformation and globalization have been presented by Lan and Unhelkar (2005). The discussion in *Global Enterprise Transitions* suggests that transformation of business requires careful handling of all business processes. Business transformation as a process has been highlighted by Unhelkar and Ginige. Arunatileka (2006) further stresses the importance of operational business processes in transformations. In a global survey of practitioners, Unhelkar (2009) also discovered that businesses perceive "business processes" as a major area of value as well as risk. Hence, a transformation process needs to pay particular attention to the operational business processes.

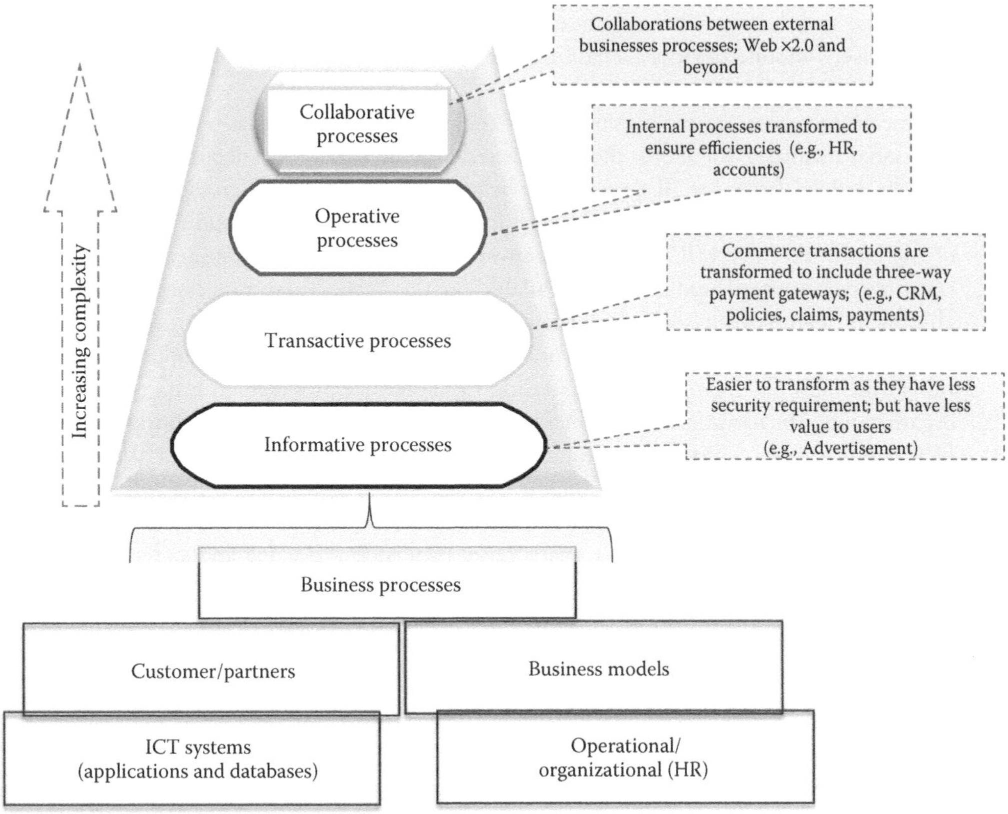

Figure 12.5 Transforming HIC's business processes to collaborative processes.

Figure 12.5 shows the growing importance and complexities of processes in HIC as it moves toward a collaborative-Agile organization. (This figure is a subset of the detailed Figure 6.6 highlighting the use of BI at various levels within the organization.) ABT is concentrating on only four process categories: informative, transactive, operative, and collaborative. In addition to the business process work area for transformation, other work areas such as customers/partners, business model, systems, and operations (HR) also impact the modeling, reengineering, and deployment of actual business processes. These four process categories within HIC are described next:

- The *informative* aspect of HIC's business deals with the provision of timely information to customers and staff. Example of this information includes the company's contact details and relevant details of the users that can be safely provided within the secure walls of the company. Information can be "pulled" by registered users depending on the level permitted. For example, provision of a quote for an insurance policy for a potential customer is undertaken as part of informative business. Informative processes have minimal maintenance and security requirements.
- *Transactive* insurance business is where HIC conducts internet-based financial transactions involving multiple parties. Examples of these business processes include payment of premiums for insurance policies using BPAY or directly through credit cards, submission

of claims, and dealing with associated queries. HIC is able to send and receive messages on the user's mobile devices—enabling the conduct of business independent of location and time.

- *Operation* processes are more complex, as they support the staff in conducting the organizational business. Therefore, these processes provide timely and accurate information—mainly derived from the BI system—to help the staff upsell and cross-sell products and services. These processes also support staff in undertaking administration of the operations of the business. Thus, HIC staff find their HR functions such as timesheets, payrolls, and training pathways all updated and available on the Web. These processes facilitate close alignment of employees (staff) with their customers and the management.
- *Collaborative* business processes expand the previous three processes to include interactions with multiple organizations. Thus, additional service providers to HIC, such as police organizations (in investigating an incidence), insurance underwriters (who associate with HIC), and new franchisees (who want to interact with HIC only through Web services), make use of these collaborative business processes. Use of cloud computing will enable HIC to outsource some of its operational infrastructure and thereby become more Agile in its responsiveness. This operational infrastructure is outside the scope and statement of work for MethodScience; however, the transformation has to handle the need to collaborate with external parties electronically to outsource the infrastructure work.

Balancing HIC's ABT Enactment

As the HIC transformation is launched, MethodScience prepares to handle the variations occurring in the transformation. These variations from the original plan are expected in any transformation

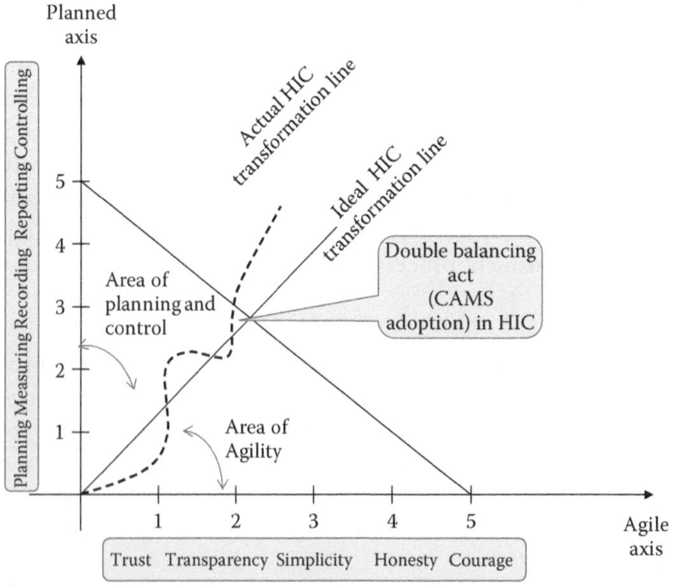

Figure 12.6 Balancing the CAMS adoption plan in practice in HIC.

and MethodScience is prepared for it. There are a number of factors that change the original plans for transformation. Thus, CAMS and its combination of Agile values and planned values come into play even in the ABT. Figure 12.6 shows this variation in the plan and the actual transformation.

The areas of planning and control are represented on the vertical axis and the Agile elements on the horizontal axis. Use of metrics and measurements during the enactment provides data on how much variation occurs in the transformation. The following are examples of the variations that MethodScience has to handle during the transformation:

- Existing Prince2 phases and deliverables are changed to suit the CAMS requirements. However, some project managers refuse to work entirely on "trust." They demand the creation of formal deliverables. The ABT has to provide for this need by creating new deliverable templates that combine existing deliverables into an agreeable deliverable.
- The CoE needs to be further expanded than originally planned—as it now has to include business analysis as well as Agile capabilities. The project management aspect of the CoE has to also understand and include the Agile declaration of interdependence, which was not originally planned for.
- A formal IT governance framework (ITIL) is required by the CEO/CIO. Current ITIL implementation does not provide the necessary control. The HIC decision makers are keen to improve their control even if it means sacrificing some levels of the Agile values (e.g., trust). The extent of control required for legal purposes was also revealed later in the transformation project and had to be handled by MethodScience.
- The project managers/Agile coach demanded extensive training in team models and psycho-sociological frameworks. This was a positive move, as the managers were keen to adopt the "flattened hierarchy" in order to manage their teams. The senior decision makers dealing with ABT had convinced the managers that their jobs were not on the line—hence there was support for a CAMS-based approach to projects. However, there was a significantly high demand for associated "leadership" and facilitation training as compared with, say, Prince2 training.
- Results from the skills and competency assessment of the organization came in much later than planned. This exercise revealed a need for training in Agile values for the nontechnical staff of HIC. This was an important revelation: MethodScience realized that the organizational Agile transformation was demanding more in terms of attitude and experience rather than only skills. A Skills Framework for Information Age (SFIA)-based framework is to be implemented for business analysis work—another area that turned out to be much bigger and involved than originally planned.

SIDEBAR: From the Trenches

View of a practitioner (Bharat Bhambhaney's personal communication, 2012) (Italics mine; Composite Agile Method and Strategy [CAMS] indicates areas of the project that represented CAMS-based thinking.)

The following are excerpts from an e-mail from a practitioner on the use of an Agile method—Scrum—in a project that also benefited by the use of formal planning elements (as presented in CAMS) and using Agile across the organization.

The use of Agile appears to be more relevant as a culture than a methodology (*Organizational Agile*). We were fortunate enough to get a client who understands the value of Agility at the organization level. Our client is Scrum-savvy. However, the need to combine Agile with the many advantages of formal project management, documentation, and quality processes is obvious (*CAMS*). Agile changes everything within an organization—right from the working style of the individual developer to the style of the decision maker (*organizational Agile far more important than software Agile*).

The work we did was on a fixed bid project (*as are most projects in practice*) where achieving a product backlog within time was very crucial to get the project completed. The client had already got their product backlog defined, and we were given 3 months to complete the task. Given 3 months, we divided the project into 6 sprints (2 weeks sprint cycle). Our client still needed to track the project with tasks and deliverables (CAMS). We used a smaller version of a project management tool to track this project (CAMS). That required us to divide the project into tasks; the project management tool was handy in tracking and reporting important aspects of this project to the client (CAMS).

All the areas such as processes, risk management, people management, client communication, and discipline in working style were improved by implementing Scrum together with planning, control, and associated tools and technologies.

Here are the areas that accrued benefits using an Agile approach with some formality in practice:

CULTURAL CHANGES THAT OCCURRED AT THE ORGANIZATIONAL LEVEL (ORGANIZATIONAL AGILE AND CAMS)

1. Cross-functionally ready teams
2. Appropriate platform to judge the capability of the individual
3. Creation of a culture of ongoing planning
4. Help in identifying shadows (*unclear or undefined major activities*)

PROJECT TEAMS OPERATIONS

Project teams benefited due to our Agile approach because of the following reasons:

1. They plan and manage their day to day based work, as they are supposed to be updated in the daily meeting.
2. They plan their leaves and avoid unplanned leaves, as they are part of the planning meeting for the sprint cycle and they know the load of the work well in advance at least for the upcoming sprint cycle.
3. They estimate the tasks better, as they are the ones who participate in the sizing and planning meetings, and Agile encourages developers themselves to do the sizing and achieve the same although support and advise from the project manager is available.
4. They communicate impediments well in advance, as sprint is the time boxed concept and they have to complete in time.
5. They understand the difference between impediments and blockers and treat the problem accordingly.
6. They become proactive when it comes to client communication, and inform their progress and problems much in advance to avoid sprint failure.

PROACTIVE RISK MANAGEMENT

1. Risk monitoring and mitigation plans are increasingly accurate as we combine Agile (based on its time boxed sprints) and project management experience.
2. Infrastructure-based risks are identified and handled within the time frame, as they can be a reason for the blocking of some of the user stories. Thus, infrastructure and nonfunctional requirements became part of the functional development itself.

3. People related risks and contingencies come to the fore quickly – for example, a team members planning a vacation. Personal (yet relevant) information comes to the fore quickly due to sprint planning meetings.
4. Tool and technology related risks (CAMS) can be identified between preplanning and planning meetings so that it helps to decide on the features in the backlog and enable their adjustment based on team velocity.

ENHANCED CLIENT MANAGEMENT

1. Our expectation management of our client was much better as the initial Sprint cycle succeeded.
2. The client appreciated proactive information sharing about risks and challenges and was at the same time happy with the formal deliverables (CAMS).
3. Our use of "Scrum of Scrums" provided an excellent means to manage the complexities of the project and, thereby, keep the client informed.
4. Client's priorities were always considered integrally in the project as the client was part of the requirements and prioritization process (CAMS).
5. The client had no surprises at the end.

OUR KEY LESSONS

- Client should be involved in the project even before the project has started.
- Client should be helped in understanding priorities and business needs (perhaps even with initial development effort).
- Product backlog should be as well defined as possible—especially as our development was contract-driven (CAMS).
- Road map for the project required proper definition together with its milestones (*CAMS*).
- Quality was a joint effort between us and the clients (rather than the client testing the system out at the end of the project) (CAMS).

Conclusions and Lessons Learned

This chapter presented a short case study on the ABT of an insurance organization—Hartford Insurance Company (HIC). The following are the key lessons of this case study:

- Support from senior management/decision makers was crucial for the success of ABT.
- ABT is a holistic change to the entire organization and not just to its software development approaches.
- ABT is more rewarding but equally more risky than only dealing with Agility at the technical level.
- Identifying the work areas and collaborating with the key stakeholders in each of these areas was vital in transforming the HIC's business.
- MethodScience's previous ABT experiences enabled improved estimations and metrics for the transformation.
- Configuration and instantiation of CAMS was most helpful and well received when the users of the methods were involved in the configuration.
- Methods friction could not be fully avoided with the need for regulatory requirements based on ITIL and Prince2.
- There is always a variation between the plans for transformation and its execution.

Discussion Questions

- Discuss the time frames for adoption of CAMS in HIC (provided in Figure 12.2) with your own understanding of how long it takes for a successful business transformation. Highlight the areas that have not been discussed in that timeline, which you will have to handle in your organization if it were to transform.
- In the configuration and instantiation of CAMS at a project level in HIC (Figure 12.3) only a few example Agile practices are shown. Discuss two additional Agile practices that you would like to see embedded in each of the process layers of HIC.
- What is the importance of informative processes in HIC? Discuss this importance in the context of the work areas relating to systems, HR, and business processes themselves.
- What are the risks associated with an ABT if the enactment does not recognize the variations that are most likely to occur?

References

Brinkkemper, S., B. Henderson-Sellers, and J. Ralyte, eds, Situational method engineering: fundamentals and experiences, *Proceedings of the IFIP Wg 8.1 Working Conference,* 12–14 September, 2007, Geneva, Switzerland, 2007.

Lan, Y. and B. Unhelkar, *Global Enterprise Transitions*, IGI Global, Hershey, PA, 2005.

The_Open_Group, 2010, viewed 23 Aug 2012, http://www.togaf.org/ and http://www.opengroup.org/togaf/.

Unhelkar, B., *Mobile Enterprise Transition and Management*, Taylor & Francis, Boca Raton, 2009.

Appendix I: Agile Interview Summaries

Following are excerpts from the detailed interviews that were conducted in order to explore the validity of a composite Agile approach in practice. These interviews were undertaken with the help of a research assistant who investigated the viewpoints of 10 separate practitioner participants. The roles of these participants ranged from developers and architects through to business analysts, project managers, and testers—and included consultants as well as permanent roles. Most interviewees were from the financial/insurance/banking/mortgage sector—which may be a limitation of this study. The primary geographical region for these interviews was Australia, with two participants from India and the United States.

The following is an example interview (all names have been suppressed).

> My name is <<>>. We would like to first thank you for participating in this research project. We highly appreciate it. The purpose of these interview-based case studies is to investigate the nature of Agile approaches. Furthermore, we are exploring the possibility of a composite approach to Agile usage that can be used in other areas of work in an organization—such as business analysis, project management, and information technology (IT) governance. Your answers will be kept confidential and used in a "generic" way to discuss the idea of a composite Agile approach.
>
> Confidential Interviewee Information:
>
> Name: AN
> Company Name: XYZ Consultants
> Company Type (product or service, IT or non-IT, etc.): IT Consulting
> Position/Role: Owner/Senior Consultant
>
> 1. What is the nature of your organization's work (e.g., financial offerings, software development, outsourcing, manufacturing)? What is the nature of your role within the organization?
> 2. What is the current level of acceptance or exposure of Agile methodological approaches in your organization? (The popular Agile approaches include Scrum; Extreme programming, XP; Agile Unified Process, AUP; and so on.)

Are you or your organization considering introducing Agile within your development team? Or does an Agile development team already exist?

If so, for how long and how well have you been trying Agile?

3. What are the advantages of using an Agile methodology in the context of your organization?
4. What are the challenges/problems you face in using your Agile methodology?
5. Agile methods advocate the presence of a user in the development project. Do you use this practice for identifying requirements?
6. Agile methods emphasize on iterative requirements gathering. Do you use this practice in your organization, or do you identify all the requirements at once?
   What impact does this practice have on your organization/development/business analysis?
   Do you use iterative development (small releases)?
   Do you carry out requirements gathering for each iteration?
   What are the challenges of this practice in your organization?
   How do you deal with these issues in practice?
7. Agile methods advocate extreme requirements prioritization, which means that the number of times that you carry out requirement prioritization is equal to the number of project iterations. Do you employ this practice for each iteration, or do you carry it out once?
   Do you interact with the customer for this activity?
   Do the customer's desired features that provide greatest business value drive this prioritization or aspects such as risks, cost, and implementation dependencies?
   What are the impacts of this practice on your organization?
8. Agile methods emphasize on continuous testing, which includes frequent/iteration review meetings for requirements validation, test-driven development (TDD), and acceptance tests. Do you employ any of these practices in your organization? We had set up sessions where test scripts were being built during development sprints. This was done using a testing person being part of every design review or development milestone review.
   In the case of iteration review meetings, who participates in them (developers, customers, quality assurance personnel, management, and other stakeholders)?
   What are the impacts of this practice in your organization? Was more manpower needed because of the amount of parallel processing going on?
   In the case of the TDD approach, what are the impacts of this practice in your organization?
   If your company uses acceptance tests, who participate in this process (developers, customers, quality assurance team)?
   What are the impacts of these tests in your organization?
9. Which methodology does your company use for business management (e.g., Lean, Six Sigma, Kaizen)? What, according to you, would be the impact of Agile methods on these business methodologies?
10. Does your company use Information Technology Infrastructure Library (ITIL) or Control Objectives for Information and related Technology (CoBIT) (or similar standards) for IT service management or IT control and governance? In your opinion, how do Agile methods impact these control standards?

Following are the discussions based on the answers provided by the participants. These answers and the discussions thereon were used to create an instance of Composite Agile Methods and Strategy (CAMS). These answers are discussed from the point of view of major activities within an organization: business analysis, project management, development, testing, architecture, and metrics.

Business Analysis and CAMS

Business analysis in CAMS is an activity spanning both business and technical domains. The business analyst captures the state required by the users through use cases and the corresponding activity graphs. According to one of the participants, the business analyst (BA) must work out what the needs of the business are. The user will say what he or she wants, but the BA has to focus on the needs and not on the wants. The BA should be able to take the subjective value to an objective value.

Pure Agile does not use the BA role in detail; however, most of the interviewees opted for a BA role that could specifically focus on capturing *and* prioritizing requirements. Agile methods go for extreme requirements prioritization for the most valued features. Three of the participants stated that their organization used written requirements specifications and also had frequent requirements prioritization. Prioritization often happens during the planning meetings at the beginning of each development cycle. The highest business value, or the highest risk, drives this prioritization. Three other participants indicated that they identified and prioritized requirements with the customer as an active participant based on business value and risk, whereas the remaining participants were noncommittal on this practice.

Four participants stated that, in their traditional projects, they had a requirement phase but not iterative capture of requirements. In their Agile projects, they would capture high-level requirements iteratively up front, and then the detailed requirements for each iteration. One of the participants stated that his company did not have iterative requirements gathering and analysis, but because they had large quarterly releases and did not have small releases as in Agile, they could not employ this practice for their iterations. They employed this practice only before the development commenced.

One of the participants stated that the challenge of employing this practice was that it suited the projects that were entirely Agile. If the whole project was not Agile, the challenge for the BA was when the whole team was not on board.

The following are the Agile principles that get applied to BA work in CAMS:

- The whole project must be planned around the business priorities (Agile). The BA can play a major role in ascertaining the business priorities, ranking them, and translating them into smaller, manageable chunks.
- The project team must collaborate with the customer all the time through planning, requirements development, and testing. Customers and team members must be available to answer questions as they arise (Agile). The BA can use this principle in his or her regular collaboration with the user on the project.
- Team members must be trusted and empowered, and must be self-motivated (Agile). The project manager, together with the senior business analyst, can use their people management skills to enable a self-motivated team.
- Issues must be solved in a just-in-time (JIT) manner. This is also a joint project management/business analysis function that requires the BA to ensure that the issues are recorded, ranked, and resolved in the shortest possible time.

The following are the Agile practices that get applied to BA work in CAMS:

- Have onsite the customer during the requirement phase for verifying and prioritizing the requirements (XP, Scrum).
- Have the customer onsite during acceptance testing and for writing and executing tests (XP, Scrum).
- Provide a short delivery schedule time for each iteration.
- Allow the customer to experience the system and provide feedback, which will also enhance the planned iterations (XP).
- Respond to change by the onsite customer (such as in XP) or daily meetings with the customer (such as in Scrum) to review the developed or to-be-developed requirements (iterative review).
- Employ iterative and incremental requirement gathering (XP, Scrum).
- Have iteration planning meetings (Scrum).
- Identify and prioritize requirements with the customer as an active participant (Agile) based on business values.
- Prioritize requirements continuously. While in pure agile approaches this may happen multiple times at the technical level, here the approach requires mapping the priorities to the overall business environment, regulations, and governance standards.
- Estimate the time required to develop requirements with developers.
- Have a communication strategy. Encourage/ensure collaboration among the product owner/customer and the technical team members to ensure that the requirements are balanced with feasibility, and the customer will have a better understanding of the effort and cost of the requirements.

Project Management and CAMS

The entire project management in CAMS revolves around iterative requirements gathering and change management. Five of the participants stated that the iterative requirement gathering was crucial in their projects. They also emphasized on gathering high-level requirements at the start of the project before the development proceeds. This is different to the pure Agile approach where the requirements evolve. An up-front attempt at requirements, with relevant development as a prototype or simpler component, helps both the development team and the business representative to gain a high-level understanding of what is required for the project. This assists in improved cost and time estimation for the whole project as compared with pure Agile. These requirements also get validated against a high-level architecture. Whenever a new requirement is introduced, the requirements documentation is updated and given to the developer.

One of the participants emphasized that, irrespective of Agility in development, his company defined the overall project scope very early in the project. The participants also stated that this fits in with the stage game approval process within their organization. Therefore, they can go to a senior executive and get a sign-off at a high level of what the overall scope is.

One of the participants also stated that gathering iterative high-level requirements up front and detailed requirements during the development enables having a component-based architecture before the development starts. Later, if a requirement changes and they need to go and change the architecture, then it is not a huge task because only an existing component needs to be modified.

One of the participants also stated that iterations are not only about management but also about setting user expectations and managing them. Iterative development can help in managing expectations. Another participant stated that sometimes the requirements are too many to gather and document all of them up front. As a result, they need to capture requirements iteratively and validate them with the user.

On the question of defining the scope of the project, one participant was clear in *not* leaving the prioritization to the customer. This was so because if left entirely to the customer, they would want everything. Negotiation of Agile approach is highly beneficial here, even though the requirements may be captured and documented in a traditional manner.

Project planning for an Agile project was also high on the agenda of many participants. Pure Agile was not much helpful in terms of accurate costs and budgets. Therefore, almost all participants suggested the need for up-front requirements capture and prioritization that would feed into the project plan. The participants also stated that they need to make sure that any changes in the priorities can be adopted with the project schedule and plan. They must ensure that the project plan can cope with this new prioritization.

Six of the participants employed the practice of frequent iteration review meetings in managing projects. At the end of each development cycle, they held a meeting with the BA, developers, customers, quality assurance team, and other stakeholders. During these meetings, the developed features were demonstrated, and feedback was provided by the team. CAMS includes these multiple roles in the reviews (as against only the customers and developers).

Scalability in Agile projects in practice was pointed out by one participant through the Scrum of Scrum meetings that are held when the project has more than one Scrum team working on separate but related sprints. The comment was to formalize these sprints within project plans to enable them to be scalable.

Four of the participants stated that frequent review meetings were helpful in ascertaining the project status and progress. This practice also increases customer trust and confidence.

Five of the participants stated that this practice enables validation of the developed features and getting feedback. They stated that this practice also helps in identifying problems early during development.

Two of the participants also stated that this practice improves the quality and makes sure the delivered product has all the functional and nonfunctional requirements.

Development with CAMS

Development and maintenance cycles in CAMS are directly derived from the pure Agile practices. The basic discipline of software development (shown in Figure 1.6 in Chapter 1) is applied in development with CAMS. Agile itself emphasizes on extensive coding; always there must be a working software available. Then it concentrates on testing, testing of code, integration, or functionality. Listening is the process of requirements identification or even requirements validation by the customer. Finally, Agile does a little amount of design, which is mostly creating a structure for organizing the software. These activities of Agile fit into the coding and testing activities of CAMS, wherein they are generally known as the development phase. Prototypes can be used for extensive clarifications in this development phase.

However, operational prototypes are more important than functional prototypes in using Agile because the user is able to provide immediate feedback on the functionality but not on the operational aspects of the system.

Testing and CAMS

Nine of the studied organizations use formal acceptance testing in their development and maintenance cycles. The test plans and the corresponding test cases are created from the requirements. In two organizations, developers, customers, and the quality assurance team participate in this activity. One of the participants stated that they do not have a quality assurance team but the BA and the customer carry out the acceptance testing. Another participant stated that they usually have the technical team involved in this practice rather than the customer. Yet another stated that they involve the business, the testing team, and the BA.

However, the developer does not participate. Three of the participants stated that acceptance tests improve quality of the product and reduce software defects. One of the participants also stated that this practice improves the quality and makes sure the delivered product has all the functional and nonfunctional requirements. Another stated that because these tests are done from the actual users, perspective and the users are involved in the acceptance testing, they provide quite a good and direct response during testing.

The challenge to user testing is the writing of the test cases themselves. While Agile prides itself on continuous testing, CAMS would expect the users to write separate acceptance tests that will be executed *after* the product is released to the users. Two of the participants stated that when the user is involved in writing the acceptance tests, there are issues with the user's availability and also their understanding. CAMS recommends the use of a dedicated quality assurance person (or team) to assist the users in developing and executing acceptance tests.

One of the participants stated that they practice TDD. This practice results in creating a code with fewer dependencies, but they still have a large chunk of their system with dependencies. This results in difficulties in writing appropriate unit tests. This is perhaps due to the large amount of existing legacy code with numerous dependencies within.

Two of the participants stated that they use test-driven requirements gathering, so with every requirement or every function that a system has to deliver, they basically have to ensure right up front that they are developing a test for it. This is done when the actual requirement is defined. So it is very important to engage the testing team and the business people themselves. However, the internal testers or testing team needs to be aware of the requirements up front.

Architecture and CAMS

CAMS advocates the use of an elaborate architecture—perhaps basing it on enterprise-level frameworks such as Zachman and/or The Open Group Architecture Framework (TOGAF). The interview participants noted that, regardless of Agility, there is a need for architecture. On the basis of the responses, and my own experience, an overall architecture framework seems indispensable—as shown in Figure 5.4 in chapter 5. The architectural space influences both the requirements and the solution design. While pure Agile operates well in the solution space, the problem and pure business space are influenced by Agile in terms of what can and cannot be specified in a requirement.

Eliciting high-level business requirements can help in understanding the big picture of what the business wants. This requirement is influenced by up-front architecture work. Together, the requirements and the architecture dictate the solution design. This is the high-level "design" and "listening" of the basic software discipline. A solution design is something that can be planned and then delivered using pure Agile practices.

Even though the precise nature of every story/requirement is not known, still the development team must see the big picture first and then go through their planning and estimations. While the design may "reveal" itself, it happens only with good up-front requirements relating to the architecture.

"Having an architecture framework is one necessary step toward making Agile scalable" stated one participant. Another mentioned that having an architecture ensures that nonfunctional requirements are also captured and catered to.

Finally, CAMS advocates an architectural framework to enable strategic decisions, such as buying a component library, shifting toward cloud architecture in order to make use of services (especially software as a service (SaaS) agreements), and incorporating a formal reuse strategy that goes beyond just code reuse.

Metrics and Estimates in CAMS

CAMS brings together the rigors of higher maturity of processes with the freedom of Agility. However, it should be noted that higher maturity does not necessarily mean higher performance or throughput. On the other hand, higher throughput (such as with Agile) does not necessarily mean long-term stability of the process. CAMS encourages up-front requirements and iterative project management to enable improved estimates of costs.

However, one of the participants stated that the reason why they do not employ iterative requirements gathering is that it did not help them with overall cost estimation and governance. In fact, their current governance processes do not support situations where a full project cost is not estimated as part of business case planning. Therefore, they are using the pure waterfall life cycle.

Estimations continue to remain a challenge in pure Agile because the main reasons for the success of any Agile adoption effort depend on the individuals, their skills, and their personalities (Elssamadisy, 2009). This jeopardizes the formal calculations of time and budget, as individuals are always difficult to quantify, to put in a box.

CAMS uses performance measurements, such as through CoBIT maturity models, to facilitate benchmarking and discovery of essential capability improvements in addition to performance goals and metrics indicating how IT processes satisfy enterprise and IT goals. The performance goals and metrics also measure internal process performance.

Deriving from Scrum, a properly maintained catalog of the sprint backlog can provide some information on how to estimate the team's ability to deliver functionalities. Sprint, as a time-boxed iteration, provides opportunities for improved estimations. However, it can become challenging when a different team (or team members) is involved. The 2–4 weeks sprint duration can be used as one element in estimating the overall development effort. The sprint burn-down chart shows the remaining work in the sprint backlog.

References

Elssamadisy, A, Scaling up Agile adoption by scaling down: Focusing on individual skills for successful Agile teams and organizations, *Cutter Executive Report*, 10 (1), 2009, Boston, MA.

Appendix II: Business-Analysis-Related Associations and Standards

The list in Table II.1 provides the associations related to the profession of business analysis. One of the key areas for further investigation and composition is that dealing with Agility and business analysis. Each of these associations has a framework that can potentially embed Agile practices. This list is provided with the aim of encouraging practitioners to explore these standards in business analysis and use Agile practices within the elements of these frameworks. An initial attempt with relation to the business analysis subset of Skills Framework for Information Age (SFIA) was shown earlier in this book. (Note: this list extends the original list created by Adriana Beal.*)

* In her interesting discussions on *ModernAnalyst.com* and at various other publications.

Table II.1 Associations Related to Business Analysis

Organization	*Brief Description*	*Relevance to Business Analysis*
ABAA—Australian Business Analysis Association	Seeks to define, promote, and support business analysis as a profession. (Now a part of IIBA)	Primary focus is on upskilling individual business analysts
AIBA—Australian Institute of Business Analysis	Committed to professionalizing business analysis globally	Focus is on a business analysis framework (22 × 3 competencies) and upskilling teams and organizations
ABPMP International—Association of Business Process Management Professionals International	Dedicated to the advancement of business process management concepts and its practices	The Guide to the Business Process Management Common Body of Knowledge 2.0 (BPM CBOK® 2.0); and Certification in Business Process Management; both highly relevant to business analysts
AIM—Australian Institute of Management	Aims to develop better managers and leaders for a better society by providing innovative solutions to customers and members and delivering measurable performance improvement	Allied with the AIBA to offer competency-based assessments to business analysts
ACS—Australian Computer Society	Aims to further the study, science, and application of information technology; promote, develop, and monitor competence in the practice of ICT by people and organizations	Runs the "Computer Professional Education Program" (CPeP) with business analysis subject offerings
AMA—American Management Association	Provides knowledge, skills, and tools to achieve performance and manage change	The AMA provides opportunities for business analysts to up skill themselves in management and leadership competencies
IASA—International Association of Software Architects	Dedicated to the advancement and sharing of issues related to software architecture in the enterprise, product, education, and government sectors	The association is committed to improving the quality of the IT architecture industry by developing and delivering standards and education programs and developing accreditation programs and services that optimize the development of architecture profession

IIBA— International Institute of Business Analysis	Well recognized for its support to the growing profession of business analysis	The IIBA supports requirements management, systems analysis, business analysis, requirements analysis, project management, and consulting roles. They own the BABOK
IFPUG—International Function Point Users' Group	Leader in promoting and encouraging the effective management of application software development and maintenance activities through the use of function point analysis and other software measurement techniques	Provides opportunities for business analysts to measure their requirements models and business needs through standardized mechanisms
OMG—Object Management Group	OMG is popular for its modeling standards, including the Unified Modeling Language™ (UML®) and Model Driven Architecture® (MDA®)	These standards, supported by the corresponding CASE tools, provide powerful visual design, execution, and maintenance of software and other processes, including IT systems modeling and business process management
PMI—Project Management Institute	Focuses on the needs of project management professionals across a wide variety of industries	Business analysts can understand the PMBOK and use it to understand the project and organizational context for analysis activities
SEI—Software Engineering Institute	The Carnegie Mellon University's Software Engineering Institute (SEI) has advanced software engineering principles and practices with specific focus on process improvement	The CMM can be applied to business analysis work to understand the maturity and repeatability of business analyst competencies and processes
SFIA—Skills Framework for Information Age	Provides a common reference model for the identification of the skills needed to develop effective information systems (IS)	The framework consists of areas of work versus levels of responsibility—easily adaptable to business analysis work
UPA—Usability Professionals' Association	Promotes the development of usable products that would enhance user experience	Provides business analysts with the perspective of the users—especially when user-centric requirements are to be modeled
ISTQB—International Software Testing Qualifications Board	Provides definitions and guidelines for accreditation and certification of testers	Enables business analysts to participate in formulating test strategies and plans; participate in testing

BABOK, Business Analysis Body of Knowledge; CASE, computer-aided software engineering; PMBOK, Project Management Body of Knowledge; CMM, Capability Maturity Model.

Appendix III: Role-Based CAMS Metrics

The following are the descriptions of some selected CAMS metrics. They are categorized by roles and CAMS tasks.

Project Manager

CAMS Task: Planning—Requirement Prioritization

Planning is one of the major tasks of a project manager. During planning, tasks are scheduled according to business needs and the resources available. From the composite perspective, prioritized requirement is the baseline for a plan of iterations and increments. With a coarse prioritized requirement, the project manager can plan an agenda corresponding to milestones. CAMS maintains the necessary high-level planning up front before implementation.

In this CAMS task, the project manager may focus on the size of the system, duration of the project time, and the allocated budget. These factors that show the overview of expected systems and projects are critical to the overall schedule, and are reflected by the prioritization of requirement. In addition, the plan will be monitored and reviewed against the result in order to evaluate the accuracy of the estimate by the project manager.

The Number of Packages (Subsystems/Components) in the System

The project manager can ascertain the scope of the system through these subsystems or packages. The packages provide the high-level view of the required system. The project manager, the business analyst, and the subject matter expert can enter into discussions to arrive at the number of packages. This CAMS metric measures the number of subsystems, components, or packages. The complexity of the system can also be analyzed with a package diagram as it indicates dependencies. The project manager envisions the system, creates the plans and schedules, allocates time and budget, and assigns resources based on these packages in a CAMS-based project.

The components and packages are not based on a specific coding language. Instead, they simply represent the components from a modeling viewpoint. A high-level understanding of the expected system is produced in the planning–requirement prioritization in CAMS. This high-level metrics is enough to provide a prioritized baseline, and the packages themselves need not change much during the project—for example, five business packages (customer, policy, payment, claim, and settlement—in an insurance domain) and two technical packages (centralized database and Web front end).

The Number of Dependencies between Subsystems/ Components/Packages in the System

Apart from an understanding of the size of the system by earlier metrics, the complexity of the system is an important metric in CAMS for project managers. The level of complexity directly determines requirement prioritization and resource allocation. Dependency between subcomponents needs to be considered in implementation. When planning and prioritizing the requirement, the project manager has to consider these dependencies between packages.

This metric measures the number of connections between subsystems, components, or packages. With this data, the complexity of the system can be analyzed in the aspect of internal relationship.

The connections include internal software dependency, network connection, and other technical communication methods, such as Bluetooth and USB cable.

For example:

Ten wireless connections are required to a switcher.
The web application cannot be implemented before database tables are ready.
The PayPal function depends on the connection to the Internet banking system.

Project Schedule and Rhythm

All the tasks under CAMS are processed iteratively. Therefore, every iteration of a particular CAMS task should be of equal length in time. Iterations are beats of rhythm in which the composite-Agile team undertakes the corresponding tasks regularly. They can provide better control on working deliverables and response to changes. Therefore, maintenance of equal time of iterations is important to CAMS. In addition, milestone and increment constituted of various iterative CAMS tasks are worth a scalable timeline for necessary changes.

On the basis of the prioritized requirement, tasks are initially planned within a time frame for each milestone. The milestones include project kickoff, requirement validation, major releases, and completion of each change requested from customers.

This CAMS metric measures the time allocated for each iteration, as well as the milestone depending on an agreement between the developers and customers. With this data, the complexity of a system can be analyzed in the aspect of time.

For example:

Four weeks per iteration
Six months per release as a milestone

Total Budget and Investment

This CAMS metric measures the budget allocated for each milestone (or iteration). In CAMS, planning is not detailed in the beginning. However, by knowing the budget for iterations, the project manager can easily build up his/her composite-Agile team by gathering staff and resources.

In addition, with this data, the complexity of the system can be analyzed with respect to finance. Requirement prioritization should reflect budget rationally.

For example:

$ 10,000 per iteration
$ 1000 before kicking off project
$ 1000 for implementation of the changes
$ 1000 for the first release
$ 1000 for the second release and the new requirement.

User Load (Peak and Off-Peak)

This CAMS metric measures the number of concurrent users logging onto the system during any given period. During the planning, the expected number of users will be analyzed or directly given.

After the systems are implemented, this CAMS metric can be applied to examine the actual number of concurrent users on the systems compared to the original requirement. During different time periods, the figures vary. With this collection of data, the size of the system can be analyzed with respect to work load.

Systems allowing networking access can apply the metric to calculate the number of users in a time period. It is suggested that the time periods are selected evenly to cover different business hours and nonbusiness hours. To avoid bias, the measurement should be undertaken periodically—weekly or monthly.

For example:

Average 300 users per hour from 9 AM to mid-noon (peak time in business hours)
Average 10 users per hour from mid-night to 6 AM (off-peak time)

CAMS Activity: Monitoring Team Members

CAMS allows the leading roles to take charge of their work and take decisions based on discussion with other composite team members. Meanwhile, the project manager needs to monitor their performance and evaluate their qualification with their product.

During the progress of the project, project managers take the decision to organize all the activities within the teams based on the result of the monitoring. Since team members are empowered to make decisions and respond to changes, the performance of the team may or may not be impaired. Therefore, it is important to compare the result with the schedule. Two aspects of monitoring are the speed of the team and the efficiency of change response.

The Speed of Implementation of a User Story

This CAMS metric indicates the productivity of the composite-Agile team to implement a user story as value. User stories in the list of requirement prioritization should be evenly divided by an estimate of the effort.

To implement a user story, the composite-Agile team should iteratively go through a chain of tasks, such as detailed requirement analysis, detailed software modeling, programming, testing, continuous integrating, and user acceptance testing.

The metric records the time spent on these tasks to measure the performance of a project team.

As a composite-Agile team is regarded as an atomic unit, the time recorded need not necessarily be divided by the number of team members. In addition, it is recommended that the time for each delivery of user stories should be averaged and moderated to evaluate the speed of the team accurately.

For example:

Ten weeks to deliver the user story
Average 10 weeks to deliver a user story

Efficiency of Response to Changes

In order to enhance business agility, CAMS empowers the composite-Agile team members to actively respond to changes and make decisions within the scope of their leading tasks. Therefore, the efficiency of handling changes, which indicates the performance of the team, is critical to CAMS. The project manager needs to pay significant attention to this indicator in order to steer the various members within the team for agreement and collaboration.

This CAMS metric measures the time spent on response to any changes. Change response includes requesting changes, analyzing, approving or rejecting, implementing, and validating them. Therefore, a composite-Agile team should go through these tasks to respond to the changes.

It is noticed that the changes rejected are not counted in this metric, since these changes do not reproduce any substantial value relating to the efficiency of the team. Instead, this CAMS metric only counts the time spent for the accepted changes.

As in the previous CAMS metrics, a team is regarded as an atomic unit.

In addition, the changes vary so that the counting should consider the scale of change. It is suggested that the change be classified by their scope as code level, design level, requirement level, and business level.

For example:

Two weeks to respond to a code-level change
Ten weeks to respond to a design-level change

CAMS Activity: Risk Management—Collaborative

Risk is an important factor that needs to be measured and controlled by project managers. Risk management includes identifying, analyzing, monitoring, controlling, and mitigating risks. CAMS project team members and users collaborate to identify, analyze, and propose the risk relating to their concerns. Project managers identify how large the risks and their impact on the project are.

Metric: The Potential Impact of Risks

This CAMS metric measures the average impact of risks. The impacts of risks vary, resulting in changes to the requirements, changes/reduction of scopes, blowout of budgets, and uncertainty in human resources. It is recommended that the impact of the risks be classified into several levels according to their consequences and their probability. This metric also specifies the likelihood (low/median/high) of its occurrence.

Table A3.1 gives some examples of risks and their classification.

Table A3.1 Risks and Their Classification

Risk Name	*(Probability-Classification) Result*
Risk of requirement defects	(Low change) changes to the requirement (functional, nonfunctional, interface, infrastructure)
Risk in terms of technical specialist requirements	(Low time) more time or budgets
Risk of change in business needs	(Low cancellation) reduction in the scope of projects or, at worst, cancellation of project
Risk of incompatible technology	(High change) change in the design

Average Risks per User Story

This CAMS metric measures the number of risks that are identified and analyzed on the basis of a user story. During implementation, user stories are associated with risks that need to be continuously discovered, analyzed, and monitored. This metric alerts the project manager to the risks. New risks are identified and data associated with them are collected on a continuous basis.

For example:

Ten (low-impact/high-probability) risks identified when doing detail requirement analysis
Three (high impact/medium probability) risks identified when doing integration

Business Analyst

This section discusses some CAMS metrics that relate to the business analyst role.

CAMS Activity: Requirement—Collaborative

In the composite approach, requirement engineering requires collaboration with various team members and customers. This collaboration is for clarifying and communicating the requirements. It is essential to understand the requirements by interacting with the customers and providing suggestions to them. These metrics enable measurement of requirements throughout the project (as against finalizing them before implementation). Building on both traditional and Agile methods, CAMS requirement gains conceptual information, such as coarse prioritization, to guide the composite-Agile team. The details of requirement will be searched and refined just before design and implementation. This approach avoids the potential wastage on detail specification up front, since the fine plan is frequently changed or even discarded during design or even during implementation.

Therefore, in this stage, the business analyst will only examine the size and complexity of the required system at an abstract level.

Total User Stories

The CAMS metric is an Agile metric that measures the number of user stories. These user stories are a combination of the stories themselves, as well as features documented as stories. This metric shows the complexity of the requirement from external perspectives. In addition, the figure can be measured continuously throughout the project so that the size and complexity of requirement can be tracked. For this metric to be of value, the user stories need to be at a similar level and of a similar complexity; otherwise, this metric has little value to indicate the complexity in requirement.

For example:

Three user stories in the requirement

User Story Dependencies

Complexity of requirements is an essential information for business analysts. When writing the requirement, business analysts will collaborate with other composite-Agile team members, as well as customers for clarification of the relationship between user stories. After that, the business analyst will analyze the dependencies—usually through a use case diagram wherein a use case represents a theme or a collection of user stories.

This CAMS metric measures the total number of connections among user stories. By counting the connections or dependencies among the user stories, the complexity of requirement can be understood from external perspectives.

For example:

Three total dependencies among user stories per theme.

CAMS Activity: Change Management—Negotiable Requirement

In CAMS, requirements are negotiable during the project. Users can request changes, and these changes are analyzed and modeled by the business analyst. Customers and the business analyst can negotiate the changes and modify the requirements to confirm the decisions.

From the perspective of the business analysts, the frequency of changes is important because each change will result in requirement prioritization and reallocating the resource.

A stable requirement can not only reduce risks during implementation but also enable the related tasks (design, coding, and testing) manageable and predictable.

Iteration Changes

This CAMS metric measures the number of changes requested and approved per iteration. In iteration, CAMS tasks will be worked through in the order that the change requests will be handled. Thus, iteration is regarded as a unit of time for counting the amount of changes. Continuous collection of this data shows the trends in changes, which can be used for further analyses and process improvement.

A comparison of the number of changes requested with the number of changes approved indicates the rate of acceptable changes. This metric can also demonstrate the quality of requirement and constraints. A well-understood suite of requirements will not change as much as inaccurately documented or incomplete requirements.

In addition, the period for collecting the figures should be equal from time to time. Therefore, it means that iterations should be equally long in time.

For example:

Twelve changes requested per iteration
Five out of 12 changes approved per iteration.

Architect

CAMS Activity: Design—User Feedback

In traditional approaches to development, the system architecture is built once for a particular requirement specification. Although the architecture can scale to large projects, it also takes up a significant proportion of time and resources. The response to change can also be passive in traditional approaches. In contrast, Agile methods pay less attention to static architecture and design. Therefore, user feedback is readily incorporated in the design and the architecture is kept dynamically updated. CAMS adequately considers the gap between response to change and maintenance of a static and structurally sound architecture. A stable architecture in CAMS is not meant to specify all the features of a system up front. Instead, architecture in CAMS is a dynamic document that is valued for its tolerance to change. Architecture in CAMS is expecting changes rather than eliminating them.

Tolerance to Change

The metric indicates the reusability and maintenance of the architecture. When changes occur, the initial architectures are adapted. By avoiding reconstruction, the architectures can modify and reuse the existing module for new changes. However, as the number of changes increases, architectures may be inevitably changed in the structure.

Therefore, this metric marks down the average number of changes resulting in architectural change in each iteration. It simply counts down the number of significant changes in architecture throughout an incremental process, which will be divided by the number of changes approved as shown below.

Tolerance = number of structural changes in architecture/number of changes approved
A smaller figure shows better tolerance of the architecture.
It is noticed that this figure will change along with the project. Continuous counting by iterations is recommended for the project's final review.

For example:

Five structural changes in architecture and 10 changes approved
Then the tolerance indicator is 0.5.

Programmer

CAMS Activity: Coding/Implementation—Pair Programming

Pair programming is frequently used to enhance the quality of the code and clarify the requirements. However, it has its own challenges in terms of resource utilization, cost, and practicality. Therefore,

CAMS suggests an immediate review of the code instead of pair programming. Rather than sharing the same computer to program, one programmer shares his/her code with another team member as a reviewer who edits and debugs the code. Other team members can also make contributions by reviewing and reporting errors.

From the perspective of programmers, the is metric measures complexity, readability, and ownership.

System Layers

This CAMS metric shows the complexity of architecture by counting the layers of the system. To manage implementation and maintain complexity of functionalities, current information systems tend to be tied down to three or more layers. Three-layer systems are typically MVC (model, view, and control). Each layer communicates with the others.

It is suggested that this figure be analyzed with coupling, since a multitier system typically has these two indicators describing the complexity.

For example:

Three layers in the system suggested by architect

Standards Compliance

In a composite-Agile team, documentation is used to record minimal information. Collaboration, based on standards, enables communication and interpretation without excessive documentation.

This metric indicates the state of compliance with standards. Standards are applied at four levels, including pair-wide, team-wide, department-wide, and enterprise-wide. Pair-wide standard is the agreement between a small group of team members, while the team-wide standard applies to all team members. Department-wide and enterprise-wide standards apply across projects and organization. The metric gives a percentage for each level to indicate the uptake of standards at that level (see example). Teams are encouraged to examine the culture and level of communication in order to balance between standardization and informality.

For example, in an Agile team, 6 out of 10 standards are for group, 2 out of 10 standards are for team, and 1 out of 10 standards is applied on department-wide and enterprise-wide, respectively.

The Number of Owners/Contributors

This CAMS metric counts the number of owners by a given collection of source code. Composite Agile promotes sharing ownership of and responsibility to the same segment of the code. Different programmers can create and edit the same source code as owners or contributors. More than one owner or contributor may increase the quality of the source code. However, it does not mean that the code can be completely opened to all the team members for editing, since undesired conflicts on trivial issues will be raised with increasing viewers and editors. This metric provides the information to insist the composite-Agile team to find out the best numbers of pair programming.

For example:

The Java source code file *Submit.java* is owned by two persons and contributed by three other persons.

Tester

CAMS Activity: Testing—Continuous

In CAMS, testing is continuously performed by a tester throughout projects. Continuous testing is an essential Agile task in each iteration. This testing provides feedback on the quality of a system and the defects in the working deliverables. Continuous testing discovers and even avoids errors early in the project implementation. CAMS-based projects not only test continuously but also formally document, control, and report test results. This can ensure the working deliverable not only to fulfill the functional requirements but also to maintain satisfactory nonfunctional performance.

In addition, continuous testing rapidly verifies the change once it is implemented.

Defects per Iteration

This CAMS metric counts the number of defects reported by the tester in each iteration (increment or release). It shows the quality of the working deliverable. However, this metric should be examined with the velocity of team, change frequency, and other related factors. This is because these factors influence the quality.

For example:

Three out of nine detected defects are closed in this increment.
The other six are differed to latter development.

Performance Comparison with Previous Iterations

Apart from defects related to functionality of the software product, nonfunctional requirement should be measured. When a composite-Agile team rapidly responds to changes, the architecture built initially is adapted to the new requirements. Therefore, the performance of the working deliverable will be affected.

For example:

The processing time in the previous integration is 0.3 seconds, whereas while the processing time in the current integration is 0.5 seconds. It is obvious that the performance has degraded.
Thus, the performance loss = 0.2 (i.e., 0.5 – 0.3) seconds.
Therefore, the percentage of loss in performance = performance loss/processing time in pervious integration = 0.2 seconds/0.3 seconds = 66.7%.

Appendix IV: Telecom User Stories

The following table consists of user stories from a telecom transformation project. These user stories are set up in tabular form rather than the standard entries written on 3 in. × 5 in. cards, as discussed in Chapter 5, pages 174–175. The column heads follow the formal approach:

As a (*role*) I want (*something*) so that (*benefit*).

Table IV.1 Examples of Telecom User Stories

Ref.	*Function*	*Title*	*As a*	*I want*	*so that*	*Acceptance criteria*	*Author*	*Priority*
1	Service	Workforce management of field staff	Manager Field staff manager	A work force management system To be able to monitor group movements of field staff	The group movements of the field staff can be monitored by the manager and rescheduled the work when necessary I can improve group output, measure performance, and manage material usage in faults and services	To improve the group output To measure their performance To have management measures in material usage and faults and services It must be possible to view the activities of field staff. It must be possible for a manager to reschedule work		
2	Service provision	Provide contractors with appropriate provision information	Technical officer, New connection	To inform contractors about their service orders	Send efficient service orders I can reduce the time taken between receiving a service and acting it	Service provisioning time will be reduced. To be defined		
3	Service	Customer request logging system	Regional telecom office manager	To record and follow up each and every customer request at the regional telecom office	To improve productivity and achieve maximum customer satisfaction	New service request Fault management under different category (e.g., ADSLm Internet, IPTV, PSTN, CDMA, etc.)		

4	Service assurance	GUI for system failure monitoring	Section head	To look: 1. Outage SW/TX systems 2. Outstanding customer services (ADSL, PSTN, CDMA, etc.) To be able to see outages on the SW/TX systems and outstanding customer services.	To get a clear idea about network availability at any time I can minimize revenue leakage as a result of failures	Alarm information of preset systems (SW/TX) No. of outstanding customers due to failures at same time Revenue leakage due to these failures		
5	Reporting	Generating management report	Line manager as well as their heads Senior manager	Prepare system front-end report (at finger tips) to manage the system	To improve the productivity and efficiency	Fault management report Analysis of customer's revenue pattern Detail of churn customers High revenue, VIP, and priority customer segmentation		

continued

Table IV.1 (*Continued*)

Ref.	*Function*	*Title*	*As a*	*I want*	*so that*	*Acceptance criteria*	*Author*	*Priority*
6	Service fulfillment	Service provisioning delay escalating matrix with managing report	Head of section customer care center	Manage service orders and reduce provisioning delays	To achieve maximum customer satisfaction and reducing unnecessary overhead	Service Order? Pending cases with delay time and responsible persons SLA violation Financial rebate to be paid to affected customer to ensure the trust between SLT and the customer		
7	Materials provision	Materials management system	Operational staff	Material management system	Just-in-time material management Unnecessary material shortages will be minimized. Plan ahead the requirements	Time will not be wasted because of material shortages Customer satisfaction Effective service delivery		
8	Portal	Customer portal	Existing customer Potential customer or third party	Web portal	Chatting with other logged in users or call center Online complaints Online tracking for fault clearance or delivery and other services other news	Online population is increasing. The Web portal can be popularized for many users to log in or just use. Third-party advertisement can be posted		

9	Marketing	Market intelligence on unavailable products	Marketeer Product developers	Waiters for each product by the area, DP, or switch area	So when the development is done in the particular area we can start marketing campaigns We can plan developments to priority area	Waiters or customers who tried for the service should be available in the system database		
10	Portal	Give customer visibility of call details	consumer customer	Customer can view his call details through the GUI	Customer can manage his bill without going up No need for dispute at the end of the month. Can trace who has originated (sometimes servants only at day time)	These fields should be viewed: Date Call originate time Call end time Duration CLI		
11	Call center	Customer identification	Customer care officer	To identify the customer by asking a few questions like "Mother's maiden name," "date of birth" Customer authentication	Will be able to activate any additional service or request to transfer the facilities to another location, over the phone	Customer information (Bus reg. no., N/C no., name, account No.) Customer identification questions and answers		

continued

Table IV.1 (*Continued*)

Ref.	*Function*	*Title*	*As a*	*I want*	*so that*	*Acceptance criteria*	*Author*	*Priority*
12	Service	SLA monitoring	Manager	As system which supports and provides all customer and technical information on SLA and fault alarm log in a single view	Quick SLA service delivery can be given to SLA customers within stipulated time frame	Customer info and contact details Technical Data Online fault log and fault status Fault history		
13	Service	Reconnection Customer reconnection checklist	Reconnection Reconnection officer?	Bundle all products for a particular customer To be able to see a list of all the customer's products	Once I reconnect can I make sure all the disconnected products have been activated? Can I ensure that all relevant products are reconnected appropriately?	1 minute or less 1 minute or less		
14	Sales	Proactive sales/ marketing Advise customer on potential upgrades	Sales/ marketing Person	Pops up possible service upgrades to existing services To inform a customer of potential upgrades available to them	customers can be reminded about the possible service upgrades For example, depending on the bandwidth consumption SLT can benefit from upselling by increasing revenues	Improves revenue, customer relationship, sales, etc. Acceptance criteria to be defined		

15	All	High-revenue customer Associating a tier with a customer	High-revenue customers to be highlighted in the faults ticket Marketing user Sales user Service user	Our maintenance team can attend to those high-revenue customers in shortest possible time To be able to identify which customers are of a particular "tier"	Customer billing details or customer category (as for the revenue) shall be indicated in the faults sheet received by the maintenance team Different service level agreements can be identified and applied to a specific customer	—		
16	Call center	Recording reasons for suspension of service	customer Call Center officer	Details of the disconnections due to credit control system to be displayed for call center officer to be able to see the reason for a disconnection	Call center officer can inform the customer that his/her line is disconnected due to nonpayment I can inform the customer when the disconnection is due to nonpayment	Shall be displayed in the screen of the call center officer		

continued

Table IV.1 (Continued)

Ref.	*Function*	*Title*	*As a*	*I want*	*so that*	*Acceptance criteria*	*Author*	*Priority*
17	Service fulfillment Sales	Product feasibility	Engineer who prepares future development of the OSP network OSP network engineer Call center Agent Salesman	A detailed report on the areas where customers request new telephone facilities but we cannot provide due to limitations of the network	New customer requirements received by sales teams, which cannot be served due to network limitations. Shall be received by the maintenance/ development engineers	A report listing the area, number at customers waiting to get a new telephone service		
18	Service assurance	Escalation on SLA failure	Customer	To escalate the fault tickets automatically when the specified time to clear a fault is not met	An escalation system to be implemented until the delayed fault/ works order is escalated up to management	Escalated e-mail or an SMS to be received by the manager/ engineer		

Index

A

Activities and tasks in a process, 119
- business evaluation process map, 212–214
- deployment process maps, 178
- enterprise architecture (EA), 152
- implementation process maps, 170
- quality assurance process map, 329
- quality control process map, 337
- quality planning, 323
- in requirement modeling of process maps, 262
- system architecture (SA), 154–159
- system design process maps, 166

Adaptive software development (ASD), 24, 54–55
Aggregation, 261
Agile business transformation (ABT); *see also* Hartford Insurance Company (HIC); case study
- adoption of CAMS, 369–373
- Capability Maturity Model Integration (CMMI), 398–401
- CMM standards, 398–401
- CoEs, 390–392
- configuring, training, and upskilling in, 393–398
- external influencing factors, 374–375
- influencing factors, 389–390
- internal influencing factors, 375–377
- money (or economic) dimension, 394–395
- organizational adoption of, 366–369
- organizational focus areas, 378–389
- and organizational focus areas, 378–381
- people dimension, 396–398
- process dimension, 396
- social dimension, 396
- technical dimension, 395
- work areas, 381–389

Agile enablers
- business intelligence, 143
- cloud computing, 142
- integrating applications, 144
- mobile technologies (MT), 142–143
- role of ICT, 141–142
- service-oriented architecture (SOA), 143–144
- social media networks, 144
- Web Services (WS), 143–144

Agile Manifesto, 35, 120, 201, 273, 293
- comprehensive documentation, 61
- customer collaboration, 61
- individual interactions with processes and tools, 59–61
- response to change needs, 61–62
- soft factors, 295
- value statements, 35

Agile methods, 24–25, 34
- artifacts, 174
- ceremonies, 174
- charts, 176
- features, 174–175
- landscape, 40–44
- product backlog artifact, 175–176
- roles, 174
- stories, 174, 478–484

Agile organizational methods spaces
- business, 21
- governance, 22–23
- manifesto, principles and practices, 23, 31
- planned, 21–22
- pure Agile (solution), 22

Agile portfolio management, 287
Agile practices
- analytical, 63
- design, 65
- development, 64–65
- operational, 66
- project management, 65–66
- quality assurance, 66
- requirements, 63–64
- subjective nature, 270
- testing, 67

Agile principles, 36–42
Agile Project Leadership Network (APLN), 273
Agile project management (APM), 54–55

Agile software development
business analysis, 109
Business Process Modeling Notation (BPMN), 109
modeling and architecture, 110–112
Object-Oriented Process, Environment, and Notation (OPEN), 113
process mentor, 113
Rational Unified Process (RUP), 112–113
software processes, 112–113
SWOT analysis, 109
testing, 109–110
Agile touch points, organizational, 104–108, 261
Agile Unified Process (AUP), 49–50
Agile values, 35–36
in business organization, 35–36
Agility
as balance, 25
basis of, 5
budget and, 8–9
business analysis and, 20
business architecture and, 19
business intelligence and, 20
business process management (BPM) and, 248–250
collaborative business and, 20, 192–204
composite approach to, 13
concepts of, 34
contemporary Agile methods, 5–6
correlating with planned processes, 17–19
data warehouse and, 19
defining, 32–34
dimensions in organizations, 19–20
enterprise, 11–13
enterprise architecture and, 19
leadership and, 20
in learning organizations, 191–192
maintenance and, 19
management and, 20
in practice, 7–11
practices in studied organizations, 26
process maps and, 20
quality and, 11
quality assurance, testing and, 20
requirements and, 10
security architecture and, 19
software code and, 19
in software development, 5, 16–17
software model and, 19
strategic, operational, and project performances, 13–15
strategic role in business, 4
time and, 9–10
Architect, 360, 473
Audit, 332
Australian Institute of Business Analysis (AIBA), 104, 224

B

Bluetooth, 157
Booch, 18
Broadcasting business processes, 208
Brochureware, 208
Business Agility, 4, 12, 33
IT governance and, 304–305
Business analysis (BA), 223–224
Agile challenges with, 87–88
associations related to, 464–465
frameworks, 236–248
handling agile challenges in the context, 228–231
meaning, 225–228
practices in CAMS, 231–236, 457–458
Business Analysis Body of Knowledge (BABOK), 104
Business analyst, 360, 421
Business analyst (BA), 107, 258, 471–473
Business-as-usual (BAU) scenario, 224
Business evaluation process map
activities and tasks, 212–214
cost–benefit analysis, 215–216
deliverables, 210–212
PESTLE analysis, 214–215
roles, 210
SWOT analysis, 212–214
Business intelligence, 143
Business leader, 108
Business management, Agile, 184–185
Kaizen, 115–116
Kanban, 116
Six Sigma, 115
Business manager, 108
Business objectives in CAMS, 287
Business process evaluation steps
listing of processes, 253
modeling process reengineering, 253
optimization, 253–254
ranking of processes, 253
removing redundant/duplicated processes, 254
retaining optimized model, 254
Business process management (BPM)
benefits, 248, 250
process characteristics and Lean-Agile importance, 249
Business Process Modeling Notation (BPMN), 109
Business process reengineering (BPR)
concepts of "Lean" and "Lean IT," 250
customer-driven reengineering, 251
fundamental changes, 250
metrics and measures, use of, 251
reengineering exercise, 251
Total Quality Management (TQM), role of, 251
Business strategy, strategic elements of, 304
Business type, Agile challenges with, 83–84

C

Capability Maturity Model (CMM), 6, 140, 295, 322–323
Catalysis, 18
Challenges of Agility
aspects, 72
business analysis, 87–88
enterprise architecture, 89–90
evaluation/testing, 88–89
matrix of, 79–84
metrics and measurements, 89
at organizational level, 91–95
people management, 86–87
at project level, 74–78, 84–86
related to metrics, 349–351
scalability, 84
at various levels within and across organizations, 73, 78–79
Change management, 216–218
external, 217
internal, 217–218
Checklists, 332–333
Cloud computing, 142, 192
CoBIT, *see* Control Objectives for Information and Related Technology (CoBIT)
Cognos, 143
Collaborative-Agile business, 20, 141, 192–204
broadcasting business processes, 208
business size and, 194
carbon-conscious business, 204
change management, 216–218
characteristics of, 194–196
cloud-based architecture, 192
cluster formation, 193–194
collaboration of processes, 207
collaborative business processes, 209
collaborative intelligence (CI), 206–208
customer experience, 196
data sharing, 206
effect of collaborations, 195
electronic collaboration, 205–206
enterprise risk management (ERM), 201–202
evolving complexities, 204–205
global trade, 202–203
information sharing, 206
informative business processes, 208–209
knowledge management collaborations, 196–201
knowledge sharing, 208
legal compliance and tax management, 204
market expansion, 202
mobile collaboration, 206
operative business processes, 209
organizational leanness and restructuring, 203
outsourcing and offshoring, 203
physical collaboration, 205
risks and challenges, 218
transactive business processes, 209
Collaborative business processes, 209
Collaborative intelligence (CI), 143
Common Business-Oriented Language (COBOL), 80
Composite Agile Method and Strategy (CAMS), 7, 26–27, 100, 116–121, 140, 184, 223
advantages, 135–136
APLN view, 273–274
architecture, 123–128, 460–461
balance and coverage, 100–104, 140
budgets and resources, 275
business Agility and, 185–188
in business management, 115–116
business objectives, 287
CASE tool usage, 275
configuration, 123, 131–135
consideration of soft factors, 294–296
deliverables, 291–292
development and maintenance cycles, 459
document flow, 292–293
enactment, 123
estimation, 351–353
final iteration in a development process, 127–128
flexible/risky/iterative scale, 134–135
fundamental of, 101
initial iteration, 126
IT governance framework, 304–307
Kaizen in, 188–190
Kanban in, 189–191
life cycle, 121–122
limitations, 136
major iterations, 122, 127
management principles and practices, 295–296
measurement with, 123
metrics and measurements, 348–351, 353–362, 461
metrics life cycle, 354
need for and value of, 102
organizing a composite Agile project, 275–280
in planned software processes, 112–113
planning and agility, 270–272
previous experience, significance of, 275
prioritization approach, 290–291
process categories, 252–254
process maps, *see* process maps
process maturity and, 275
project leadership and people management, 293–294, 298–300
project management, 458–459
in project management, 114–115
project team structure, 297–303
project type and size, 274–275
repository of Agile practices, 123, 128–131
role-based execution, 135–136
in setting standards for IT governance, 113–114
Six Sigma in, 188–189
in software development, 109–112

Composite Agile Method and Strategy (CAMS) (*Cont'd*)
  testing approaches, 460
  values in practice, 102
Computer-aided software engineering (CASE) tools, 106
Contemporary Agile methods, 93
Control Objectives for Information and Related Technology (CoBIT), 26, 114, 304, 306–307
Creep factor, 10, 82
Critical performance areas (CPAs), 289–291
Critical requirements analysis (CRA), 287
Crystal, 4, 19, 24, 50–51
Customer-driven reengineering, 251
  considerations in, 254–255
Customer relationship management (CRM), 80
Customer satisfaction, 36

D

"Declaration of Interdependence," 273
Deliverables, 120
  business evaluation process map, 210–212
  deployment process maps, 178
  enterprise architecture (EA), 150
  implementation process maps, 168–170
  quality assurance process map, 327–329
  quality control process map, 337
  quality planning, 322–323
  requirements in process maps, 258–262
  system architecture (SA), 154
  system design process maps, 166
Deployment process maps, 176–180
  activities and tasks, 178
  deliverables, 178
  roles, 178
Developer/designer, 15, 108, 152, 164, 166, 170, 176, 178, 234, 256, 337
Development CAMS metrics, 356
Documentation, Agile challenges with, 90–91
Domain analysis report, 258
Dynamic systems development method, 24

E

Enterprise Agility, 11–13
Enterprise architect, 108, 150, 152, 154, 161, 234, 256
Enterprise architecture (EA)
  activities and tasks in, 152
  Agile challenges with, 89–90
  and Agile practices, 154
  deliverables in, 150
  process map in CAMS, 151, 153
  roles in, 150
Enterprise resource planning (ERP), 80, 84, 114, 176, 374, 408
Evaluation/testing, Agile challenges with, 88–89
eXtensible Markup Language (XML), 80
Extreme programming (XP), 4, 19, 24, 44–47, 334–335

F

Feature-driven development (FDD), 24, 55
Formal/planned organizational processes, 118
Frequent delivery of working software, 36
Fuzziness, 5

G

"Greenfield" development project, Agile approaches, 80

H

Hartford Insurance Company (HIC), case study
  ABT enactment phase, 443
  ABT work areas, 440
  balancing CAMS adoption plan in practice, 450–453
  CAMS adoption phases with timelines, 442
  CAMS adoption road map, 437–442
  collaborative-Agile HIC, 446–450
  configuration and instantiation of CAMS, 444–446
  diagnosis and analysis phase of ABT, 442
  enhanced client management, 453
  goals of Agile business transformation (ABT), 434–437
  lessons learned, 453
  organizational Agility, 452
  outline, 432–434
  planning and scoping phase of ABT, 443
  proactive risk management, 452–453
  process categories, 449–450
  project teams, 452
  review phase of an ABT, 443–444
Hospital Management System (HMS) project, 288
Hybrid Agile, 116

I

Implementation process maps, 166–176
  activities and tasks, 170
  Agile elements, 170–176
  deliverables, 168–170
  roles, 166–168
Industrial research activities, aim of, 26
Informatica, 143
Information Technology Infrastructure Library (ITIL), 26, 114, 152, 304, 306–309, 411, 451
Informative business processes, 208–209
Inspection, 161, 332–334
Integration projects, 80
International Institute of Business Analysts (IIBA), 104, 224
International Software Testing Qualifications Board (ISTQB), 322–323

Interviews, 333
Interview summaries, Agile, 455–457
ISO9001 quality standards, 33, 323
ISTQB, 104
IT areas and Agile
architecture, design, and quality factors, 147–148
configuration and, 145–146
Control Objectives for Information and Related Technology (CoBIT), 114
conversion and cleansing of data, 146
features, 132
functional, nonfunctional, and interface requirements, 148
governance, 26
"greenfield" development, 145
Information Technology Infrastructure Library (ITIL), 114
integration and, 146
maintenance of a system, 147
training and deployment of a system, 146

K

Kaizen principles, 26, 53–54, 115–116
Kanban, 116
Knowledge management collaborations, 196–201
advantages, 196–197, 200
documentation, 201
evolution in, 197–199
knowledge synchronization between users and systems, 199–200

L

Leadership *vs* management in Agile projects, 293–294, 296
Lean–Agile business, 12, 250
Lean–Agile IT systems, 12
Lean development, 51–52
Legal and compliance issues, Agile challenges with, 91
Location-aware mobile connectivity, 143

M

Maintenance, Agile challenges with, 90
Matrix of Agile challenges, 79–84
Mentor, 26
Metrics and measurements, Agile challenges with, 89
Mobile technologies (MT), 142–143
Model-driven architecture (MDA), 110
Model of background space (MOBS), 329
Model of problem space (MOPS), 210, 258, 329
Model of solution space (MOSS), 164, 166, 258, 329
Mumbai Information Technology Services (MITS), case study of implementing software solution
Agile practices in CAMS, 411–415
CAMS process-map-based activities, 415–418
contractual agreement on major activities, 413
creating CAMS iterations, 418–419
determining correct iterations and releases, 425–426
existence of Prince2 and ITIL, 411
formal requirements modeling, 426–427
IT division of WAM, 408
iterative and incremental implementation of solution design, 427
lessons learned, 428
ongoing maintenance of solution, 427–428
organizational characteristics with respect to the client and vendor, 414–415
overall pricing, 425
overcoming of challenges, 422
quality assurance and quality control, 427
road map, 409
service level agreements (SLAs), 426
in terms of leadership and direction, 424
uncertain status of scope of work, 422–424
understanding and categorizing the project, 409–411
use of CAMS metrics, 419–423
Must-Should-Could-Won't (MoSCoW), 289–290
Myers–Briggs Type Indicator (MBTI), 298

N

Nonfunctional (operational) requirements and architecture (enterprise and system), 159–164
"constraints," 159–161
data suite (base) requirements, 164
estimations and assumptions, 161
examples, 162–163
organization-level, 163
process (business, system)-level, 164
project (solution)-level, 164
"qualities" or attributes, 159–161
software system level, 164
types, 162
use case (functional) level, 164
Nonfunctional requirements specifications (NFRS), 146

O

Object Modeling Technique (OMT), 18, 110
Object-Oriented Process, Environment, and Notation (OPEN), 20, 26, 101, 106, 112–113, 117, 140
OO software development, 18
Operative business processes, 209
Oracle BI, 143
Organizational domain, Agile challenges with, 82
operational-business problems, 94–95
at a tactical level, 94
Organizational processes, 105–107
Outsourcing of projects, Agile challenges with, 81

P

Package implementation projects, Agile challenges with, 80
People management, Agile challenges with, 86–87
PeopleSoft™, 80
Planning CAMS metrics, 354
Political, Economic, Social, Technological, Legal and Environmental (PESTLE), 184
Prince2, *see* Projects in Controlled Environments (Prince2)
Process advisor, 108
Processes, optimization of, 250
Process maps, 117
  activities and tasks in requirement modeling, 262
  business evaluation, 210–216
  deliverables in requirements, 258–262
  deployment, 176–178
  dynamic modeling with state diagram, 260
  enterprise architecture (EA), 148–152
  functional requirements, 255–256
  implementation, 166–176
  interface requirements, 256
  nonfunctional (operational) requirements and architecture (enterprise and system), 159–164
  nonfunctional requirements, 256
  project management with CAMS, 280–293
  quality assurance, 327–331
  requirements modeling, 255–256, 263–265
  roles in requirements, 258
  system architecture (SA), 152–159
  system design, 164–166
Process mentor, 113
Program Evaluation and Review Technique (PERT), 85, 353
Programmer, 302, 334, 360, 421, 473–474
Project management, Agile challenges with, 84–86, 114–115
  in CAMS, 458–459
  project size, 81–82
  project type, 79–81
  scalability, 84
  in terms of traditional or planned software methods, 83–84
Project Management Body of Knowledge (PMBOK), 106, 115, 282
Project management process map, 280–293
  activities and tasks, 282–285
  deliverables, 282
  roles, 280–282
  scoping a program of work, 285
Project manager, 107–108, 359, 421, 467–471
Projects in Controlled Environments (Prince2), 26, 106, 115, 282, 286–287, 411
Project team structure in CAMS, 297–298
Prototypes, 76, 83, 112, 126, 145, 150, 160, 162, 332
Pure Agile, 6, 18–19, 22, 25, 33–34, 64, 72, 74, 76–77, 79–81, 84, 88, 90–91, 111–112, 117, 121, 135–136, 144, 146–147, 159, 162, 164, 188, 204, 225, 228–229, 236, 261–262, 276, 279, 282, 293–294, 297, 302, 319, 329, 337, 344, 348, 372, 376, 400

Q

Quality Assurance of Information Systems, 317
Quality control process map, 336–337, 339–341
  activities and tasks, 337
  deliverables, 337
  roles, 337
Quality control (testing) process map, 337–348
  aspects of test organization, 341–344
  functional *vs.* technical testing, 344
  major activities and agility, 342
  quality control (testing) process map, 337
  risk analysis, 346–348
  test data, 345–346
Quality management, 317–322
  Agile activities, 319–321
  application of validation and verification, 319
  process map, 322–327
  quality assurance process map, 327–331
  quality assurance (QA), 318
  quality control process map, 336–337, 339–341
  quality control (QC), 319
  quality metrics and measures, 318
  quality techniques and Agile practices, use of, 329–336
  significance to user, 317
  standards in quality domain, 323
  testing approaches, 337–348
Quality manager, 93, 108, 150, 152, 178, 282, 297, 322, 327, 337
Quality software process (QSP), 327

R

Radio Frequency IDentification (RFID), 157, 386
Rational Unified Process (RUP), 18, 20, 26, 106, 112–113, 117, 393–394
Refactoring, 80
Requirement CAMS metrics, 354
Review, 121, 243–244, 332
  phase of an ABT, 380–381, 443–444
Role-based CAMS metrics, 357, 359–361
Role element in a process, 117
  CAMS metrics, 359–361
  quality control process map, 337
  quality management, 322

S

SAP™, 80, 143
Sarbanes–Oxley (SOX) legislation, 114, 215, 229, 304, 376, 448
SAS, 143
Scalability, Agile challenges with, 84
Scrum, 4, 19, 24, 47–49
  artifacts, 49
  business analysis touch points in, 261
  Daily Scrum meeting, 49
  life cycle, 48–49
  meetings, 49
  Product Owner, 48
  Scrum Master, 48
  Scrum of Scrum meeting, 49
  Scrum Team, 48
  Sprint Planning meeting, 49
  Sprint Retrospective meeting, 49
  Sprint Review meeting, 49
Semantics, 334–335
Service-oriented architecture (SOA), 19, 72, 143–144, 157–158, 184, 248, 385, 433, 435
Siebel™, 80
Six Sigma, 26, 115
Skills Framework for Information Age (SFIA), 104, 224
Social media networks, 144
Software Agile (IT development) process, 104
Software development life cycles (SDLCs), 6, 18, 122, 140
  fountain-based, 58
  iterative, incremental, and parallel (IIP) development approach, 58–59
  spiral-based, 57
  waterfall-based, 56–57
Software Process Improvement and Capability Evaluation (SPICE), 322–323
Software stability, 33
Strategic Agile, 93–95
Subject matter expert (SME)/domain expert, 258
Syntax checks, 334–335
System architecture (SA)
  activities and tasks, 154–159
  analysis and maintenance of the ontological elements, 158–159
  availability of networks and communications, 157
  databases, 157–158
  deliverables, 154
  dissemination of information, 159
  external sources, 158
  internal stakeholders, 159
  operational and architectural constraints, 159
  process maps, 152–159
  project manager, role of, 152
  quality manager, role of, 152
  reuse strategy, 154
  roles, 152
  service-based and service-oriented architectures, 157
  system designer, role of, 152
System design process maps, 164–166
  activities and tasks, 166
  deliverables, 166
  roles, 164–166

T

Tactical Agile, 93–95
Task in a process, 120
Taxonomy of organizational methods, 104–108
Technique of a process, 120
Test-driven development (TDD), 4, 24, 55–56, 104
Tester, 108, 361, 421, 475
Testing, Agile challenges with, 88–89
Testing Body of Knowledge (TBOK), 110
The Open Group Architecture Framework (TOGAF), 106, 150, 152, 304
Transactive business processes, 209
Trust, 33

U

Unified Modeling Language (UML), 18, 81, 110–111, 140
  diagrams in Agile projects, 149
Utopian team, 16

V

Voice-over-Internet Protocol (VoIP), 157

W

Walk-throughs, 66, 93, 163, 233, 261–262, 282, 316, 329, 332–336, 343, 351, 424
Web Services (WS), 143–144
Work products of a process, 120
Workshops, 333